Nahuatl as Written

Nahuatl Studies Series
Number 6

Series Editor
James Lockhart
Associate Series Editor
Rebecca Horn

UCLA Latin American Studies
Volume 88

Nahuatl as Written

Lessons in Older Written Nahuatl,
with Copious Examples and Texts

James Lockhart

Stanford University Press
UCLA Latin American Center Publications

Stanford University Press
Stanford, California

© 2001 by the Board of Trustees of the
Leland Stanford Junior University

Printed in the United States of America
on acid-free, archival-quality paper

A separate set of all the Nahuatl examples and texts in the book,
without any translations or explanations, and spaced so as to leave
room for a student's work, can be purchased while supplies last from:

UCLA Latin American Center Publications
10343 Bunche Hall
Box 951447
Los Angeles, CA 90095-1447
e-mail: lacpubs@isop.ucla.edu
http://www.isop.ucla.edu/lac

Library of Congress Cataloging-in-Publication Data

Lockhart, James.
   Nahuatl as Written : lessons in older written Nahuatl,
with copious examples and texts / James Lockhart.
      p. cm. — (Nahuatl studies series ; no. 6)
   English and Nahuatl.
   Includes index.
   ISBN 0-8047-4282-0 (alk. paper) — ISBN 0-8047-4458-0 (pbk : alk. paper)
   1. Nahuatl language — Writing.   2. Nahuatl language — Grammar.
I. Title.   II. Nahuatl series ; no. 6.
F1219.76.W85 L63   2001
497'.45282421 — dc21   2001032285

Original Printing 2001

nacatl in itlaqual quauhtli

(Florentine Codex, Book 11, Chapter 2, Paragraph 4)

Contents

Contents

Preface

HARDLY HAD I myself learned a bit about older Nahuatl than, in the time around 1975–76, I began trying to teach it to others, mainly my own graduate students in history. Since the 1645 grammar of Horacio Carochi had been so important in my own progress with the language, and it was studded with authentic examples from the time, I immediately attempted to use it as the main text. Very shortly, however, all of us saw that Carochi, at least in the form then available, was not ideal pedagogically. Precisely the first part of the book was the least satisfactory and needed the most explanation; many of the examples were highly complex and left one wishing for more detailed analysis and more literal translations than Carochi supplied; even the lucid chapters at the core of the book required a greater familiarity with seventeenth-century grammatical terminology and Spanish phraseology than many students could muster.

Still, I wanted in some fashion to use phrases, sentences, and texts actually written in the first three postconquest centuries as illustrative material, for it is within those years that the whole tradition of Nahuatl writing falls, and the study of that corpus was the goal. I adopted the method of organizing each week's session or lesson around a pageful of examples I had assembled, some straight from Carochi and some from real texts. I quickly came up, however, against the obstacle anyone in such an enterprise will face, that —especially for the earlier lessons—no existing passage can be found to illustrate the desired point succinctly and simply enough, so I fell to concocting examples, and even small texts, trying to stay as close to real documents as possible.

Some of the first pages of examples were handwritten and had to be redone by the students to be sufficiently legible. Then the examples came to be typed, and later yet were produced quite elegantly, using a computer and printer, but nearly all grammatical explanation was left for oral delivery only. For quite a long time I held out against even providing translations of the examples. Finally I gave in. The translations I made were a large help in a way, but in another way something was lost. I am not sadistic, but I have no doubt that with any language, and more particularly with the written form of a rare and little understood language, you learn best, most permanently, even most quickly, if you are forced to reach conclusions, or at least to reconstruct them, by yourself. Furthermore, as soon as you grasp a few general principles and a little vocabulary, you need to put the new knowledge to the test in work with real texts. There was a time when this set of lessons, now consisting of twenty, went only to number eight, which is virtually a real text itself. From then on we worked on authentic testaments, petitions, and the like, and learned the rest bit by bit through practice.

Only the most assiduous, enthusiastic, gifted, and linguistically inclined flourish under such a regime, however. Gradually I added more and more lessons—that is, pages of examples and miniature texts, each illustrating an important grammatical point or two, so that at a session per week we would spend most of a year on the set of lessons, while a more advanced group, subjected to the lessons in a previous year, worked on texts, then after that branched off to undertake independent research projects.

In 1992 I visited the Chapultepec Institute for History and Anthropology in Mexico City with the intention of leading a select group through the lessons on an intensive basis. The group turned out larger and less select than I had anticipated, though highly enthusiastic. There was nothing for it but to begin to write down the remarks with which I had always tried to elucidate the examples. As before, the addition brought both gain and loss. I could develop my ideas beyond the conversational level (though retaining something of the informal tone and the primacy of the examples as the focus of discussion). But the students now had something concrete by way of analysis to refer to, so that they could better afford to forget. Eleven lessons took shape at this stage, written out in what purported to be Spanish.

Over the years I had not forgotten my original ambition to use Carochi for instructional purposes, because the examples included and explained there are an inestimable, irreplaceable resource. By 1998 a bilingual edition with numerous explanatory notes was nearing completion. I felt I had made Carochi usable to a wider audience, but he still was not for beginners, nor does he enlighten us about the characteristics of the written corpus. Something to fill the gap was needed, and I turned to the task of rounding out these lessons, adding at the end some large-scale, fully authentic texts to represent the move in that direction that anyone who would become an independent reader and analyst of Nahuatl writing must take. I hope, then, that this set of lessons can prepare you to go on to real texts on the one hand, Carochi and other advanced grammars on the other.[1]

From the first, the lessons were not meant to be systematic in themselves, but were shaped by the intention of gradually giving students relevant knowledge and skills in a sequence adapted to their need and their ability to absorb. Even now that the set has been considerably expanded beyond its original chaotic and fragmentary form, it is not like a systematic grammar of the language. Some topics that would be a normal part of such a book are never touched on here. In my experience, people can work with texts without them, learning about them quite easily when it becomes imperative. The order of the materials is simply what experience (including some deliberate experimentation) has shown me to be conducive to students' quickly gaining as great and lasting a mastery as possible. I hope I will be pardoned for some repetitions involved in the process, for here as in the past I have found it useful, even necessary, to anticipate later full treatments by earlier sketchy remarks, refer back to and partially repeat earlier fuller discussions, and even sometimes to tackle the same topic twice in different ways. My only excuse is that it seems to work the best. To repeat is human, especially in learning languages.

Now that I am no longer conducting a Nahuatl course, my thoughts have turned more to the person learning the language alone. It is for such a learner that the present form of the lessons is above all intended. But whether you are alone or in a group, poring over the examples is the most essential part of the process. The examples say the same things as the more formal presentation in a more basic way. I recommend that the solitary student in some way produce or acquire a copy of all the examples and texts in the book, unaccompanied by any translation or analysis, and work over them in that form.[2] Indeed, it would be well to have more than one copy. You will need to make lines to analyze words (*ni/mitz/on/no/ne/pechtequi/li/lia*, etc.), make translation notes between lines, and do a great deal of other scribbling. Once you have done it, the marked passages will be nearly useless for your second, third, and further tries, not only because the marks will keep you from new independent analysis and translation, but because your first attempts will inevitably contain errors—thus an unmarked copy should be held in reserve.

Even for an actual organized course using these materials, I think that the analysis given here would best be read at home, with the class working by recitation and conversation over an unelaborated set of the examples and texts. There would be no need to worry much about the integrity of the individual lesson as such. A lesson after all in most

---

[1] In view of the intended complementary nature of this book and Carochi's grammar, I have removed the great majority of the examples in these lessons that once drew directly on the latter. A few of them, however, were too apropos to sacrifice. Hints of an original modeling on Carochi even in organization remain, especially in the earlier chapters.

[2] Such a set has already been prepared, and it is my hope that it can be made available separately from the distributor of the volume proper.

cases simply goes back to one full page of single-spaced examples, and many of the chapters of the present set are too large and complex for a single sitting. In the old days, we rarely finished a full page in one two-hour session and would start next time with the very next unanalyzed example regardless of page. I recommend the same procedure with the present set. We used to spend the bulk of the academic year on the lessons, perhaps not getting to the end even then—with, it is true, part of the time often spent directly on texts. Once or twice I tried two sessions a week, but at least with people already carrying a full academic load, the absolute passage of time seemed virtually to determine the rate of progress, and two sessions a week accomplished no more than one. More important than finishing the set is to learn how to learn, to get far enough to learn more on your own.

The emphasis here falls unabashedly on the written form of the language, all that is left us—and it is a great deal, with much real speech in it—of the Nahuatl of the sixteenth through eighteenth centuries. Until the last few lessons, the language used is for the most part characteristic of Stage 2 (ca. 1545–1650) and indeed of the high point of Stage 2, about 1580 to 1630 or so.

If you feel the need of some grounding in pronunciation, you might turn first to Lesson 17, on orthographic matters. But you will do just as well knowing that the letters in general are pronounced much as in Spanish (for rare is the person who comes to Nahuatl without knowing some Spanish first), that ç represents [s] as in "soar," *x* stands for [sh] as in "shell," and *tl* represents a single complex consonant, never making a syllable by itself. Stress is on the penultimate syllable of a word.

In the Nahuatl examples and in the sample texts (until I include some with their original spelling in the later part of the book), I use an orthography essentially derived from Carochi's grammar, because all in all it corresponds more closely to what is seen in actual texts than does Molina's system, Sahagún's, or the modernized system used in Mexico and by some scholars in this country. I do deviate from Carochi in that whereas he writes *ia* in all contexts and almost never *iya*, when the *y* is root-initial, I write it, as in *niyauh*, "I go," not *niauh*. I may not always follow him on *io/iyo* either, for he is quite inconsistent on that question. I also do not use Carochi's diacritics, not because I think vowel quantity and the glottal stop without importance, but because they are generally not represented in texts written by Nahuas, and to include them would give students a false impression of what they will face when they come to their goal. For the same reason I include no punctuation in examples.

I dedicate this book in the first instance to Rebecca Horn, Andrea and Rodrigo Martínez, Susan Schroeder, and David Szewczyk, and also on the one hand to Muni Alexander, Diana Balmori, Yuri Batres, James Braun, Sarah Cline, Delia Cosentino, Kimberly Gauderman, Nicole von Germeten, Francisco González Hermosillo, Eulogio Guzmán, Robert Haskett, Carmen Herrera, Robinson Herrera, Travis Barton Kranz, Frances Balding Krug, Dana Leibsohn, Juan López y Magaña, Elisa Mandrell, Doris Namala, Federico Navarrete, Leslie Offutt, Jeanette Favrot Peterson, Caterina Pizzigoni, Stafford Poole, Matthew Restall, Carolyn Sexton Roy, Ethelia Ruiz Medrano, Barry Sell, Peter Sigal, Lisa Sousa, Rafael Tena, Kevin Terraciano, Irene Vásquez, and Stephanie Wood, and on the other to Arthur Anderson, J. Richard Andrews, William Bright, R. Joe Campbell, Una Canger, Horacio Carochi, Angel María Garibay, Fernando Horcasitas, Frances Karttunen, Michel Launey, and fray Alonso de Molina.

J. L.
Frazier Park, California
September, 2000

Nahuatl as Written

1. Nouns, Pronouns, and Subject Prefixes

The subject prefixes, the nature of the noun, and the absolutive. The possessive state of nouns. Independent pronouns. Combining nouns. The reverential of nouns. Dictionary work. Examples.

A. *Subject prefixes.* Although its verb forms are notoriously hard to master, the greatest difficulty Nahuatl presents to speakers of European languages lies in the nature of its nouns. Nahuatl nouns have subjects. Each noun in an utterance is at least potentially a complete equative statement in itself. The word for "house" in its dictionary form, *calli*, has a third person subject and by itself means "it is a house," or since in many cases no distinction exists between singular and plural, "they are houses." When I was engaged in my first struggles with Nahuatl, a decisive moment in my comprehension of the language and fascination with it came when, reading Garibay's *Llave del náhuatl*, I grasped something of the structure of the verbless sentence *nacatl in itlaqual quauhtli* (from the Florentine Codex, Book 11), "flesh the its-food eagle," i.e., "meat is the food of the eagle."

Thus nouns are more like verbs in Nahuatl than they are in English. Perhaps for that very reason, they have obligatory affixes which proclaim them to be nouns. Two of these affix sets exist, possessive and absolutive, introducing another formal property foreign to European languages, the distinction between a possessed noun and one which is absolute or not possessed; hence the term "absolutive." Prefixes and suffixes are both involved in defining the two states. Here are the subject prefixes (which are shared with verbs) and the nominal possessive prefixes. They have essentially the same function and meaning as English pronouns, differing only in that they are attached to another word and cannot receive emphasis.

Subject prefixes

ni- (*n-*)	I	*ti-* (*t-*)	we
ti- (*t-*)	you	*am-* (*an-*)	you (pl.)
—	he, she, it	—	they

Possessive prefixes of nouns

no- (*n-*)	my	*to-* (*t-*)	our
mo- (*m-*)	your	*amo-* (*am-*)	your (pl.)
i-	his, her, its	*im-* (*in-*)	their

Here you can already see that in Nahuatl gender is not a grammatical category. Nouns are not masculine, feminine, or neuter, as they are in many Indoeuropean languages, but that is only the beginning of it. Neither the prefixes nor the independent pronouns distinguish gender. Nahuatl has absolutely no way to say "he" or "she," only third person singular subject, no "his" or "her," only third person singular possessive.

Note that the two sets of prefixes have many similarities, which makes it easier to recognize person and number, but can also lead to confusions between absolutive and possessed forms. An *n* appears in the first person singular in both sets, *t* in the first person plural, and *am* in the second person plural. In past times the similarities may have been even greater. It is likely that the second person singular subject prefix once began with *m* like the possessive, but later "you" was replaced by a polite "we." In the second lesson we will see that the object and reflexive prefixes of verbs share many of these similarities.

It helps in distinguishing the two sets that three of the subject prefixes end in *i* and four of the possessive prefixes in *o*. Alas, we cannot always make use of this neat difference. The prefixes are rendered harder to recognize by a system of vowel elision which often causes the prefix vowel to disappear when another vowel follows. It is also true that

1

the first vowel of the nuclear word can disappear.[1] In general, *i* gives way before any following vowel: *ni-tlacatl*, I am a person, but *n-atlacatl*, I am a bad person, inhumane. The possessive *o* displaces following *i* but gives way to *a* or *e*: *no-cal*, "(it is) my house (root -*cal*)," but *no-cniuh*, "(he/she is) my friend (root -*icniuh*)," and *n-auh*, "(it is) my water (root -*a*-)." In general, the hierarchy of vowels for purposes of elision, from strong to weak, is *a/e, o, i*. The *i* of the third person singular possessive prefix, however, is not lost, first because it is long, and long vowels are not elided, but also perhaps because if it were lost nothing would be left.

ti + amolnamacac, soap seller	*tamolnamacac*, you are a soap seller
to + amolli, soap	*tamol*, (it is) our soap
ni + enamacac, bean seller	*nenamacac*, I am a bean seller
mo + epahuaxtli, cooked beans	*mepahuax*, (they are) your cooked beans
ti + oquichtli, man, male, brave person	*toquichtli*, you are a man
amo + oquichtequitl, man's work	*amoquichtequiuh*, (it is) your (pl.) man's work[2]
ni + ichpochtli, unmarried young woman	*nichpochtli*, I am an unmarried young woman[2]
✳ *ti + no + ichpochtli*	*tinochpoch*, you are my grown daughter
i + acalli, boat	*iacal*, (it is) his/her boat

Various suffixes exist for nouns in the absolutive, in both the singular and the plural (the plural was originally used for animate beings only). The most common absolutive singular suffix, and the only one we will consider for the moment, is -*tli*, which has two variants, -*li* and -*tl*. If the noun stem[3] ends in a consonant, the -*tli* form is used, because the *i* is needed to make the word pronounceable (Nahuatl does not permit a word to end in two consonants). But if the stem ends in *l*, the -*li* form is used, because whenever an *l* is followed by *tl* in Nahuatl, the second element assimilates to the first, giving *ll*. If the stem ends in a vowel, the -*tl* form is used, since the final [i] is not necessary for pronunciation. In written texts -*tli* often seems to follow a root ending in a vowel, but in these cases one can deduce the presence of a glottal stop,[4] which was usually not notated.

toch-tli	(it is) a rabbit
pa-tli (pah-tli)	(it is) medicine
cal-li	(it is) a house
tlaca-tl	(he or she is) a person

The plural absolutive suffixes will be discussed in a later lesson. One of them is the glottal stop, as in this sample paradigm of a noun in the absolutive.

nitlacatl	I am a person	*titlaca (titlacah*, etc.)	we are people
titlacatl	you are a person	*antlaca*	you (pl.) are people
tlacatl	he or she is a person	*tlaca*	they are people

The dictionary form of a Nahuatl noun is usually the absolutive in the third person singular.[5] Note that instead of the *m* of *am-* (second person plural) we see *n* in *antlaca*.

---

[1] Elision here refers to the omission of a vowel when two vowels meet at morpheme boundary. Examples are rare in standard English, but consider Spanish *del* from *de el* or *al* from *a el*.

[2] It is hard to say which vowel is lost in situations like this; at any rate, only one generally remains. Some speakers may have retained both, as implied by a form like *iyichpoch*, "his daughter."

[3] A root is the historically basic form of a word. A stem is the form of the root, either identical to it, shortened, or extended, which is used when the word is combined with various kinds of other elements. With Nahuatl nouns, stem and root are often the same, but shortening does occur, as we will see.

[4] The glottal stop (often *saltillo*, little leap, in older Spanish grammars) is a consonant of Nahuatl. In older writing it sometimes appears as *h*, and it is occasionally so represented (in small print) in these lessons for purposes of illustration. In general, following the practice of older texts, it is not written in the examples here.

[5] Some nouns are in Molina's dictionary in possessed form under *te-, to-, no-*, and *i-*.

Nahuatl [m] delabializes, i.e., becomes [n] whenever it is at the end of a syllable (that is, before a consonant or at the end of a word), unless a labial consonant ([m], [p]) follows.[6] Thus the form *an* is more common than *am* itself, given that the majority of Nahuatl roots begin with a consonant. When the noun stem begins with a vowel, the *i*'s of *ni* and *ti* disappear, and the *m* of *am* is retained, so that things look as follows:

natlacatl (*nahtlacatl*)	I am a bad person	*tatlaca*	we are bad people
tatlacatl	you are a bad person	*amatlaca*	you (pl.) are bad people
atlacatl	he or she is a bad person	*atlaca*	they are bad people

If the noun begins with *i*, normally only one *i* will be written in the first person singular and plural and the second person singular. Thus from *icnotlacatl*, "(he or she is) a poor person, orphan," comes *nicnotlacatl*, "I am an orphan."

It is important to understand that the same series of subject prefixes serves for verbs as well. The present stem of a Nahuatl verb is the unmodified root; the plural adds a glottal stop suffix. The verb *nemi*, "to live," runs as follows in the present tense:

ninemi	I live	*tinemi* (*tinemih*, etc.)	we live
tinemi	you live	*annemi*	you (pl.) live
nemi	he, she, it lives	*nemi*	they live

Here we already face one of the primary difficulties in dealing with older Nahuatl texts. With nouns, suffixes clearly distinguish the singular form from the plural, but with verbs in the present tense, since the unwritten glottal stop is the only difference, it is often only through the context that we can establish whether the subject of a given third person form is singular or plural, or whether a *ti-* means "you (sing.)" or "we."

B. *The possessive state of nouns.* Nouns have a unified set of possessive suffixes, but their use in an apparently inconsistent manner has created a quite varied system. The singular suffix is *-hui*, which is used after stems ending in a consonant as *-tli* is with the absolutive, and is reduced to *-uh* after stems ending in a vowel, as *-tli* is reduced to *-tl* in the absolutive. Thus *oquich-*, "man, male," has the possessed form *-oquichhui*, and *o-* (*oh-*), "road," has the possessed form *-ohui*. For *a-*, "water," a vowel stem, the possessive is *-auh*; for *me-*, "maguey," *-meuh*. In practice, nevertheless, *-hui* has largely disappeared and is hard to find beyond the two examples just given. For consonant stems the normal procedure is now omission of the possessive suffix, leaving only the bare stem; thus *cac-tli*, "footwear," has the possessed form *-cac*. If one thinks of the dictionary form as basic, the most common way to indicate the singular possessed form is the simple omission of the absolutive ending: *calli*, "house, it is a house"; *nocal*, "my house, it is my house." The *-uh* for vowel stems is still quite prevalent, but there are many cases in which the possessed form ends in a vowel belonging to the root (*noyollo*, "my heart"; *noma*, "my hand/arm").

oquich-tli	(he is) a man	*n-oquich-hui*	(he is) my man, husband
me-tl	(it is) maguey	*no-me-uh*	(it is) my maguey
pan-tli	(it is) a banner	*no-pan*	(it is) my banner
axcai-tl	(it is) property	*n-axca*	(it is) my property

In the plural the situation with the possessive suffix is simpler; *-huan* is used in all cases. More clearly than with the absolutive, the plural is related to the singular. Once the singular was *-hua*, later weakened to *-hui* in the exposed final position. The plural consists of the same *-hua* plus an *n* plural ending which has protected it from reduction.

---

[6] In actual texts, including those done under ecclesiastical auspices, *n* is often found even before *m* and *p*. It may be that in speech a devoiced [n] preceded even [m] and [p].

A noun manifesting a possessive prefix and suffix continues to be a complete equative statement and continues to take a subject prefix in addition: *nauh*, from *atl*, means "it is my water." From *calli* we can form:

nocal	it is my house (houses)	*tocal*	it is our house
mocal	it is your house	*amocal*	it is your (pl.) house
ical	it is his or her house	*incal*	it is their house

The possessive prefixes before nouns beginning in a vowel can be illustrated by the example of *axcaitl*, "(it is) property, a possession," and *ichcatl*, "(it is) a sheep."

naxca	it is my property	*taxca*	it is our property
maxca	it is your property	*amaxca*	it is your (pl.) property
iaxca	it is his or her property	*imaxca*	it is their property
nochcauh	it is my sheep	*tochcauh*	it is our sheep
mochcauh	it is your sheep	*amochcauh*	it is your (pl.) sheep
ichcauh	it is his or her sheep	*imichcauh*	it is their sheep

As expected, here the *o* of the prefixes gives way before *a* but prevails before *i*: *no-axca* becomes *naxca*, *no-ichcauh* becomes *nochcauh*.

What follows is a set of possessed plurals with a third person subject, using *macehualli*, "(he/she is) a commoner" (in the possessed form, "subject").

nomacehualhuan	they are my subjects	*tomacehualhuan*	they are our subjects
momacehualhuan	they are your subjects	*amomacehualhuan*	they are your (pl.) subjects
imacehualhuan	they are his/her subjects	*immacehualhuan*	they are their subjects

Possessed nouns by no means always have a third person subject, which leads to utterances of the following type:

tinomacehual	you are my subject	*tamomacehualhuan*	we are your (pl.) subjects
timmacehual	you are their subject	*annomacehualhuan*	you (pl.) are my subjects
nimomacehual	I am your subject	*amimacehualhuan*	you (pl.) are his/her subjects
nimacehual	I am his/her subject	*timmacehualhuan*	we are their subjects

As is seen in several of these examples, *ni-* or *ti-* must often be understood as *n-i-* or *t-i-*, i.e., "I his/her," "you his/her," or "we his/her." If the word has an absolutive ending, *ni-* is "I" only. But if a noun's absolutive is missing, it must be possessed, so that it must have a possessive prefix; thus the *i* after *n* or *t* in these constructions can only be the third person possessive singular suffix. Nothing is commoner for beginners or even fairly advanced students than to get absolutely stuck with an interpretation of *nimacehual* as "I am a commoner," unable to imagine any other possibility, when the meaning is "I am his/her subject," and "I am a commoner" is *nimacehualli*.

C. *Independent pronouns.* As we have seen, the function of the prefixes of which we have been speaking is essentially the same as that of the pronouns in English. The grammarian Carochi called them semipronouns, which is still a very good term. They differ from anything in English in that they are attached to nouns and are obligatory; any possessed noun must bear a possessive prefix, and all nouns and verbs have a subject prefix.[1] As incorporated elements they cannot carry emphasis. In order to indicate emphasis or focus, Nahuatl employs a set of independent pronouns consisting of some elements differing little from the ordinary subject prefixes, attached to a base (*-ehuatl* sing., *-ehuantin* pl.):[2]

---

[1] Remembering that the absence of a prefix is the sign of a third person subject.

[2] The independent pronouns have shorter and reverential forms which are left out of consideration here; they can be found under the individual forms in the vocabulary.

nehuatl (*nehhuatl,* etc.) I	*tehuantin* (*tehhuantin,* etc.)	we
tehuatl you	*amehuantin*	you (pl.)
yehuatl he, she, it, that	*yehuantin*	they, those

The presence of an independent pronoun does not obviate the necessity of a subject prefix, which, to repeat (and it must be repeated endlessly for us speakers of European languages) is obligatory for all nouns and verbs.

nehuatl nimacehualli	as for me, I am a commoner
tehuatl tinemi	you are alive

The independent pronouns also emphasize or focus on the entities referred to in possessive prefixes:

tehuantin tocal	it is *our* house
tehuatl nimomacehual	I am *your* subject

The third person independent pronoun can have the force of a demonstrative.

yehuatl nocal	that is my house
yehuatl Martin	that Martín (with the same flavor as in English)

Because of this function of emphasis and focus, an independent pronoun ordinarily precedes the word containing the prefix whose reference it duplicates.

D. *Combining nouns.* Many Nahuatl nouns are compounds, whether well established, familiar forms or combinations made freely on the spur of the moment. Both types are constructed in the same way. In a compound of two nouns, the modifier comes first, without its absolute suffix; the noun modified comes second, retains its suffix, and inflects as needed. This structure closely resembles that of compound nouns in English. From *acatl,* "reed," and *petlatl,* "mat," comes *acapetlatl,* "reed mat"; from *atl,* "water," and *calli,* "house, structure," comes *acalli,* "boat"; from *calli* and *nacaztli,* "ear," comes *calnacaztli,* "corner of a house." From *macehualli,* "commoner," and *tequitl,* "work, duty, tribute, labor, etc.," comes *macehualtequitl,* "commoner's work." If such a construction is not in the dictionary, the reader of texts must be prepared to take it apart, locate the component parts, and try out corresponding theories about its meaning.

calli, house	*tlalli,* land	*callalli,* (it is) house-land, attached to the house[3]
quauhtli, eagle	*pilli,* nobleman	*quauhpilli,* (he is a) nobleman by merit
cihuatl, woman	*tlatquitl,* gear, property	*cihuatlatquitl,* (they are) woman's things, household gear
tlalli, land	*(tla)cohualli,* something bought	*tlalcohualli,* (it is) a purchase of land, bought land

tocallal	(it is) our house-land
quauhpipiltin	(they are) noblemen by merit
icihuatlatqui	(it is) her household gear
notlalcohual	(it is) my bought land

E. *The reverential of nouns.* In Nahuatl reverential or honorific forms are extremely common. Nouns are made reverential by adding the element *-tzin* to the end of the stem. This *-tzin* precedes the absolute ending when there is one: *cactli,* "footwear, sandal"; *cactzintli,* the same thing in reverential form. Since *-tzin* ends in a consonant, the abso-

---

[3]As already seen, *l* plus *tl* gives *ll.* If the dictionary shows no word of the shape given, put *tl* for the second *l* of any *ll* and see if the parts make dictionary words. *Callalli* is in Molina's dictionary with a reasonable gloss, but even if it weren't we could approximate the meaning by reconstructing *calli* and *tlalli.*

lutive singular suffix is always -*tli*, whatever the absolute of the noun in its simple form: *calli, caltzintli*; *atl, atzintli*. Possessed nouns in the reverential singular end in -*tzin*: *nocactzin*, "my sandals"; *nocaltzin*, "my house"; *natzin*, "my water." The -*uh* ending disappears.

The plural of -*tzin* is -*tzitzin*: *nopiltzitzinhuan*, my children, or sometimes *nopilhuantzitzin*. (-*Tzin* was originally a diminutive and still may retain that flavor, as here.)

Note that a word ending in -*tzin* is virtually always a possessed noun, which is a great help in analysis, especially when forms become more complex.

motetlachihuililiz	he/she will do something for someone (rev.)
motetlachihuililiztzin	your deeds done for people

Reverential elements can refer to the particular word in which they are contained (as in *motetlaçotlaliztzin*, "your [honored and appreciated] charity"), or they can, in the ensemble, show a reverential attitude toward the person addressed (like *usted* in Spanish, *Sie* in German, etc.). Above all they serve to elevate the tone of the whole discourse, not only in relation to a certain word or interlocutor. Hence they are used very flexibly; in a single speech the same words can appear once in reverential form, the next time unadorned. In general it is better not to try to produce a translation that will reflect individual reverentials. But exceptions exist. Adding -*tzin* to some nouns already having a sense of humility or misfortune makes them yet more humble or deserving of pity: *nimacehualtzintli*, "I am a poor commoner."

F. *Dictionary work.* The crucial thing for the reader of Nahuatl texts is to be able to reconstitute from the derived forms seen there the forms that appear in the dictionary, in order to establish what they mean. Nouns in the absolutive singular present few difficulties of identification because the third person of the absolutive singular is the citation form; eliminating the prefix *ni-* of *nitlacatl*, "I am a person," produces the dictionary word.

Possessed and combined forms are more difficult. With possessed forms in -*uh*, one usually just eliminates -*uh* and adds -*tl* (since both suffixes are based on a vowel stem): *nauh*, "my water," dictionary form *atl*.

notequiuh, (it is) my task	dictionary:	*tequitl*
imiuh, (it is) his arrow, dart		*mitl*

Some possessed forms with a final vowel (without -*uh*) need the addition of an *i* to reconstruct the root and absolutive form.

maxca, (it is) your property	*axcaitl*
ima, (it is) his/her hand/arm (or pl.)	*maitl*

In the case of possessed nouns with consonant stems, one expects simply to add -*tli* or -*li* as appropriate.

nohuic, (it is) my digging stick	*huictli*
nomil, (it is) my cultivated field(s)	*milli*

Unfortunately, things with consonant stems are not always so straightforward; sometimes the stem of the possessed form is not identical to the root of the word. Many noun roots have weak final vowels (*i* and sometimes *a*) which are lost in the possessed form. An *n* in the possessed form may become an *m* in the citation form.

ixoch, (it is) his/her flower(s)	*xochitl*
icuic, (it is) his/her song(s)	*cuicatl*
icon, (it is) his/her pot(s)	*comitl*

In some cases of this type, you may actually find two varying dictionary entries.

itenan, (it is) his/her/its wall	*tenamitl* <u>or</u> *tenantli*

The combining form of a noun is usually the same as the possessive stem.

quahuitl	(it is) wood
iquauh	(it is) his/her wood
quauhcalli	(it is a) house of wood, jail

But that is not always so; quite often the possessive stem is further reduced than the combining stem. (In the present case, the final *a* of the root is preserved in the combining form to prevent *tl* from being syllable-final word-internally.)

petlatl	(it is a) mat
ipetl	(it is) his/her mat
petlacalli	(it is a) reed chest

Particularly in the beginning stages, but even for experienced students of Nahuatl, a recurring problem is how to determine where the prefixes end and the stem begins. In most cases the solution is not too hard to find once one is conscious of the potential difficulty, but it is all too easy to take one look at a construct, make a provisional analysis, and forget that another one is possible. Until we look carefully and try out all the possibilities, we are not sure whether a noun complex that begins with *im* followed by a vowel is an *i-* third person singular possessive prefix plus a noun stem in *m*, or an *im-* third person plural possessive prefix plus a noun stem beginning in a vowel. It could even be both, as with *imeuh.*

i-me-uh	his/her maguey, from *metl*	*im-e-uh*	their beans, from *etl*

Much more often, what will happen is that you will meet with a new construct such as *imacal* and analyze it as *i-macal*, then find no noun *macalli* and scratch your head, when the answer is *im-acal*, "their boat," from *acalli*. The same thing happens in reverse. You may analyze *imapil* as *im-apil* from a plausible but nonexistent *apilli*, when the answer is *i-mapil*, "his/her finger(s)," from *mapilli*.

Words beginning in the so often weak *i* also cause endless headaches for neophytes. When the *i* cedes before the *o* of several of the possessive prefixes, at first sight the reader doesn't know whether the *o* belongs to the stem or to the prefix, since if two *o*'s should meet at this juncture they would collapse into one. Relatively few words begin in *o*, so all in all your chances are better with first trying the notion that *o* belongs to the possessive prefix. This will leave you with an implausible stem; most words beginning in *i* have two consonants thereafter, and a Nahuatl word cannot begin with two consonants. So you will have to reconstruct a vowel, which may seem a formidable challenge, but in fact in virtually all cases the vowel is *i*.

tochpoch	*to-chpoch*	*ichpochtli*	(she is) our daughter
amochcahuan	*amo-chca-huan*	*ichcatl*	(they are) your (pl.) sheep

But after all, sometimes the *o* belongs to the stem.

amoctzin	*am-oc-tzin*	*octli*	(it is) your (pl.) pulque
nohui	*n-o-hui*	*otli*	(it is) my road

The same kinds of problems will arise with verbs and their prefixes, so be prepared for more of the same in the future. Soon you will be quite attuned to it.

In the early stages of learning to read Nahuatl, it is all very well to learn vocabulary, grasp points of grammar, and understand utterances, but sometimes such attainments almost seem beside the point. What is really needed is for you to be able to find the items in the dictionary. The ability to do so puts you on the road to further progress.

G. *Additional examples.* Here are some more examples. After studying them, cover everything except the first Nahuatl column; reanalyze, reconstruct the absolute form, and retranslate. Also go back through the whole lesson and do the same, covering any explanatory material and redoing the analysis and translation for yourself.[1]

ticihuauh	t-i-cihua-uh	cihuatl	you are his wife (woman)
tehuantin tayacach	t-ayacach	ayacachtli	they are our rattles
annopilhuan	an-no-pilhuan	pilli	you are my children
nohuauh	no-huauh	huauhtli	it is my amaranth[2]
tehuatl tinotatzin	ti-no-ta-tzin	tatli	you are my father (rev.)
mochpoch	mo-chpoch	ichpochtli	she is your (grown) daughter
imetl	i-metl	metlatl	it is her grinding stone
totlachihual	to-tlachihual	tlachihualli	it is something done by us
amoma	amo-ma	maitl	they are your (pl.) hands, arms
yehuatl namauh	n-ama-uh	amatl	that is my paper, letter, book
amocpauh	amo-cpa-uh	icpatl	it is your yarn, thread
intlatqui	in-tlatqui	tlatquitl	it is their property
aminnamictzitzinhuan	am-in-namic-tzitzin-huan	namictli[3]	you are their spouses (rev.)
nimonan	ni-mo-nan	nantli	I am your mother
tochoquiz	to-choquiz	choquiztli	it is our weeping
petlatzintli	petla-tzin-tli	petlatl	it is a mat (rev.)
yehuatl motlaol	mo-tlaol	tlaolli	that is your shelled maize
noquauh	no-quauh	quahuitl	it is my wood, tree, stick
	or	quauhtli[4]	it is my eagle
toquauhcal	to-quauh-cal	quahuitl, calli	it is our wooden house, jail
namil	n-a-mil	atl, milli	it is my irrigated field
icihuatequitzin	i-cihua-tequi-tzin	cihuatl, tequitl	they are her womanly duties (rev.)
notepecen	no-tepe-cen	tepetl, centli	it is my hill maize (unwatered)
antomachhuan	an-to-mach-huan	machtli	you are our nieces or nephews (male speaking)
tinotextzin	ti-no-tex-tzin	textli	you are my brother-in-law (rev., male speaking)
nimohuezhuatzin	ni-mo-huezhua-tzin	huezhuatli	I am your sister-in-law (rev., female speaking)
noqualnemiliz	no-qualnemiliz	qualnemiliztli[5]	it is my good way of life
moquichtlatqui	m-oquich-tlatqui	oquichtli, tlatquitl	it is your man's gear
notlaçomahuiznantzin	no-tlaço-mahuiz-nan-tzin	tlaçotli, mahuiz-tli, nantli	she is my dear honored mother (rev.)
momatzin mocxitzin	mo-ma-tzin mo-cxi-tzin	maitl, icxitl	they are your hands and feet (rev.)
xocoquauhtzintli	xoco-quauh-tzin-tli	xocotl, quahuitl	it is a fruit tree (rev.)
nimomonta	ni-mo-mon-ta	montli, tatli	I am your father-in-law
netzin	n-e-tzin	etl	(they are) my beans (rev.)

---

[1]Or preferably, work with the set of unaccompanied examples and texts available separately at the time of publication of this volume.

[2]When intended as a free-standing, independent declaration, a word like this will in practice usually be prefaced by the clause-introductory particle *ca*.

[3]Actually in Molina's dictionary under *tenamic*, in the indefinite possessed form, "someone's spouse." Other words referring to relationships may also be found in a possessed form.

[4]There is a difference in the quantity of the *a* in these two forms, but it is undetectable in writing.

[5]The word is in the dictionary, but can be analyzed as *qualli*, "a good thing," and *nemiliztli*, "life or living."

2. Introduction to Verbs and Practical Syntax

Object prefixes of verbs. Reflexive prefixes of verbs. A bit of syntax. Additional examples.

A. *Object prefixes.* We have already seen that all verbs have obligatory subject prefixes, the same ones as those of nouns, so they need no further discussion here. An intransitive verb may have these prefixes alone, but transitive verbs bear another set in addition. Any Nahuatl transitive verb requires an object prefix, which comes after the subject prefix. Since as we know there is no overt subject prefix in the third person, the object prefix will come first in that case. Just as with the subject prefixes, the object prefixes are present even when the object is expressed in the sentence as a noun.

These prefixes have elements of similarity with those we already saw. We continue to see *n* associated with the first person singular, *m* with the second person singular, *t* with the first person plural, and *am* with the second person plural, though unfortunately there are some irregularities concerning *t* and *m*. In half of the cases, the object prefix consists of the familiar letter or letters with the addition of *-ech*.

Subject prefixes		Possessive prefixes of nouns		Object prefixes of verbs			
ni	*ti*	*no*	*to*	*nech*	me	*tech*	us
ti	*am (an)*	*mo*	*amo*	*mitz*	you	*amech*	you (pl.)
—	—	*i*	*im (in)*	*c/qui*	him, her, it	*quim (quin)*	them

Note that the third person singular prefix has two forms, *c* and *qui*. The consonant is identical in both cases except for the spelling, so that the difference consists in the presence of an *i* in one case and its absence in the other. This *i* is present only when there is no vowel on either side, in order to avoid two consecutive consonants at the beginning of a word or three inside it, combinations that cannot be pronounced in Nahuatl.

ni-c-nequi	I want it	but	*qui-nequi*	he/she wants it
			an-qui-nequi	you (pl.) want it

A merely orthographic change takes place when the verb begins with *i* or *e*. Thus with the verb *itta*, "to see," one writes *niquitta*, "I see him/her/it." This may look like *qui* instead of *c* even though there is a vowel on both sides, but in fact it is a disguised *c*; the construct should be analyzed *ni-qu-itta*, in which *qu* represents *c* to avoid pronunciation as [s], exactly as would happen in Spanish orthography.

The third person plural object prefix, following the general rules of Nahuatl phonology, appears as *quim* before a vowel or a labial consonant but as *quin* before other consonants: *niquimitta*, "I see them," and *niquimpia*,[6] "I keep them," but *niquincahua*, "I leave them."

nimitzcahua	I leave you	*namechcahua*	I leave you (pl.)
niccahua	I leave him/her/it	*niquincahua*	I leave them
tinechcahua	you leave me	*titechcahua*	you leave us
ticcahua	you leave him/her/it[7]	*tiquincahua*	you leave them
nechcahua	he/she leaves me	*techcahua*	he/she leaves us
mitzcahua	he/she leaves you	*amechcahua*	he/she leaves you (pl.)
quicahua	he/she leaves him/her/it	*quincahua*	he/she leaves them

The forms in the last three lines could equally well be construed as having a third person plural subject, since the only difference between the two persons is the presence of a final glottal stop which is not written: "they leave me," etc.

---

[6]Nevertheless, *niquinpia* is often seen in many kinds of sources, even in grammars.

[7]The forms on this line could mean "we leave . . ."

timitzcahua(h)	we leave you	*tamechcahua*	we leave you (pl.)
ticcahua	we leave him/her/it	*tiquincahua*	we leave them

Since *ti-* is equally "you" and "we," *ticcahua* and *tiquincahua* are ambiguous, as already seen above. *Timitzcahua* and *tamechcahua* are different; logic prevents the meaning from being "you leave you" or "you (sing.) leave you (pl.)."

It would be worth your while to conjugate some more verbs as was done here with *cahua*, for example *ana*, "to take"; *huitequi*, "to strike, beat"; *cui*, "to take"; or *ehua*, "to raise."

Just as the subject prefixes are retained even when the subject also appears as a noun (as in *tinotatzin ticchihua*, "you, my father, do it"), the object prefixes are present in the verb complex when the object is specified in the sentence as a noun; the two refer to each other or are in apposition.

niccahua in cihuatl	I leave the woman.
ticqua in tamalli	You eat the tamal.
anquitta in tlacatl	You (pl.) see the person.
cana in piltzintli	He/she takes the child.

B. *Reflexive prefixes.* The reflexive prefixes of verbs are:

no (n)	myself	*to (t)*	ourselves
mo (m)	yourself	*mo (m)*	yourselves
mo (m)	himself, herself, itself	*mo (m)*	themselves

These come after the subject prefix and also after the object prefix whenever there is one. (When the reflexive prefix is present, the object prefix can be missing, since the reflexive suffices to indicate transitivity.) One of the greatest difficulties with these elements is that they look like several of the possessive prefixes of nouns. In many cases the only sure way of knowing which type of prefix is involved is to establish whether the root is of a verb or of a noun. Only verbs have reflexive prefixes, only nouns have possessive prefixes. But how are we going to establish the part of speech? Some clues exist. Only verbs have object prefixes. In the present tense, nearly all verbs end in a vowel; many possessed nouns end in a consonant. Almost any word ending in *-tzin* is a possessed noun. But often there is no alternative to searching in the dictionary. For example, *maxca* by its form could be a reflexive verb in the third person. Nevertheless, a dictionary search produces no verb *axca*, but we do find the noun *axcaitl*, "property," which with a second person possessive prefix gives *maxca*, "your property." Here is a complete display of a transitive verb (*itta*, "to see") in the reflexive in the present tense:

ninotta	I see myself	*titotta*	we see ourselves (or each other)
timotta	you see yourself	*ammotta*	you see yourselves (or each other)
motta	he/she sees himself/herself	*motta*	they see themselves (or each other)

The reflexive prefixes allow us to distinguish between the written forms of the second person singular and the first person plural: *timo-* is "you to yourself," and *tito-* is "we to ourselves," as can be seen from the above examples.[1] We also see above that the plurals are sometimes reciprocal rather than strictly reflexive in meaning.

Any transitive verb can be made reflexive at times. In many languages there are also verbs which acquire a special sense when reflexive. *Cocoa* means "to hurt someone, etc." *Ninococoa* would be literally "I hurt myself," but it has the sense "to be sick, ill."

---

[1] Earlier the reflexive prefix had been *mo* in all cases, so that there was no distinction between second person singular and first person plural. That still held true in the documents of many areas outside the Valley of Mexico.

Verbs of this kind are found in Molina's *Vocabulario* with the notation "nino": for example, "Cocoa. nino, estar enfermo."

ninococoa	I am sick	*titococoa*	we are sick
timococoa	you are sick	*ammococoa*	you (pl.) are sick
mococoa	he/she is sick	*mococoa*	they are sick

As in Spanish (*se hace*, etc.), the reflexive acts as an equivalent of the passive and impersonal, usually in the third person.

mochihua	it is done
mocahua	it is left, delivered
motta	he/she/it is seen
mitoa[2]	it is said

The reflexive prefix can represent a second or indirect object rather than the direct object as in the above examples. Some verbs are always set up this way; they appear in Molina with the notation "nicno." A verb of this type is *cuitia*, "to acknowledge someone as superior or to confess a misdeed."

nicnocuitia	I acknowledge him/her	*tictocuitia*	we acknowledge him/her
ticmocuitia	you acknowledge him/her	*anquimocuitia*	you (pl.) acknowledge him/her
quimocuitia	he/she acknowledges him/her	*quimocuitia*	they acknowledge him/her
niquinnocuitia	I acknowledge them	*tiquintocuitia*	we acknowledge them
tiquimmocuitia	you acknowledge them	*anquimmocuitia*	you (pl.) acknowledge them
quimmocuitia	he/she acknowledges them	*quimmocuitia*	they acknowledge them
titechmocuitia	you acknowledge us	*annechmocuitia*	you (pl.) acknowledge me
nechmocuitia	he/she acknowledges me	*nechmocuitia*	they acknowledge me
nimitznocuitia	I acknowledge you	*timitztocuitia*	we acknowledge you
tinechmocuitia	you acknowledge me	*antechmocuitia*	you (pl.) acknowledge us

When an object prefix and a reflexive prefix are both present, the reflexive prefix is not always indirect; it is possible, although somewhat rare, that the reflexive prefix should represent the direct object: *quimomaca*, "he/she gives himself/herself to him/her/it."

C. *A bit of practical syntax.* Here are some typical Nahuatl simple sentences. Note that the Nahuatl way of saying that a thing "is" another thing is the verbless conjunction or reciprocal reference of two nouns of the same person and number.

nacatl in itlaqual quauhtli	Meat is the food of the eagle (the eagle eats meat).
ome itlatol	His languages are two (he speaks two languages).
Juan itatzin Leonardo	Juan is Leonardo's father.
Clara inantzin María	Clara is María's mother.

Although most often the possessor comes after the thing possessed, almost any order can be found in sentences of this type because of differences in emphasis and focus that we cannot judge well in the written form. It is possible, though not probable, that the last two sentences could be translated "Leonardo is Juan's father," and "María is Clara's mother." In the absence of case or a fixed word order, it is often hard to determine the function of third person nouns in Nahuatl, particularly when there are several in a sentence.[3] Object and subject are particularly hard to tell apart:

quitta in Juan in Leonardo[4]	Leonardo sees Juan *or* Juan sees Leonardo.

---

[2] Generally, *i* cedes to *o*, but if a glottal stop follows as in this case (*mihtoa*), *i* often prevails.

[3] Greater certainty is often attained by use of the particle *ca*, which separates major constituents, with the one focused on coming first, the statement proper after. *Itatzin Leonardo ca Juan* is unambiguously "Leonardo's father is Juan."

[4] Nahuatl often puts the "article" *in* in front of names and possessed nouns.

In cases like these we must hope that the context will settle the question for us. In others, the internal logic, especially the change of persons or the conjunction of person and thing, leaves no room for ambiguity.

niquitta ical Apolonia	I see Apolonia's house.
tehuatl tipiltzin Pedro	You are Pedro's child.

In the last example, *tipiltzin* is analyzed *t-i-pil-tzin*. That is to say, the second person subject prefix is reduced from *ti* to *t* because it is followed by another *i*, the third person singular possessive prefix, "his/her/its." It is true that by looking at *ti-* alone one cannot know whether it is "you" or "you (are) his/her" (in speech the long *i* of the possessive suffix would be a sufficient sign). But since the absolutive ending is lacking (the word would end *-tzintli*), the noun must be possessed, so that it must have a possessive prefix, which is always present in such cases even when at first glance it does not seem to be. The same analysis applies in the following example.

nehuatl nichpoch Ana	I am Ana's (grown) daughter.

The verb *maca*, "to give," always governs two objects, i.e., it has an indirect as well as a direct object.

itatzin Leonardo quimaca	Leonardo's father gives his land to
itlal inantzin Maria	Maria's mother.

In Nahuatl there is no difference in external form between direct and indirect objects. When a verb has both kinds of object at the same time, almost always only the prefix representing the indirect object appears; the direct object (usually in the third person) is implicit. In the above example it is hard to tell which object is being represented, but in the following one it is clearly seen:

Leonardo nechmaca itlal	Leonardo gives me his land.

D. *Additional examples.* After reading the translations and explanations here, cover them with a piece of paper and analyze and translate the examples again. Do the same with the examples in the lesson above.

moma	verb with reflexive prefix	mo-ma (from ma)	he/she/it is caught
moma	noun with possessive prefix	mo-ma (from maitl)	your hand(s)/arm(s)
mopia	verb with reflexive prefix	mo-pia (from pia)	it is kept
mopial	noun with possessive prefix	mo-pial (from pialli)	your guarded thing
monemiliz	noun with possessive prefix	mo-nemiliz (from nemiliztli)	your life
mocxi	noun with possessive prefix	mo-cxi (from icxitl)	your foot (feet)
mocxiana	verb with reflexive prefix	mo-cxiana (from icxiana)	he/she hurries
mauh	noun with possessive prefix	m-a-uh (from atl)	your water
mana	verb with reflexive prefix	m-ana (from ana)	he/she/it is taken

nicnomacehuia	I deserve or attain it, i.e., get or acquire it
ticmomacehuia	you acquire it
quimomacehuia	he/she acquires it
tictomacehuia(h)	we acquire it
anquimomacehuia	you (pl.) acquire it
quimomacehuia	they acquire it
nechmaca Domingo itlal ical[1]	Domingo gives me his land(s) and house(s).
nimitzmaca nocaltzin	I give you my house(s).
tehuatl tichpochtzin Clara	You are Clara's (grown) daughter.
icaltzin itatzin quimaca ipiltzin	He/she gives his/her child his/her father's house(s).
quimocuitlahuia in Juan in notlal	Juan takes care of my land.

---

[1] Nahuatl most often forgoes any specific word meaning "and" in a series of two or more nouns.

niquimmaca notlal nopilhuan
Apolonia in icihuauh Francisco
quimmaca impilhuan imichcahuan
nomacehualhuan niquimmaca itlal nonantzin
in nocal in notlal ca amo iaxca notatzin

yehuatl Alonso ca amo totatzin
canin ninotta
quimomaca in qualnemiliztli

quicahua in Ana in ical
quicahua in Ana in ical in ichpoch
atle nechmaca Cristobal
tehuantin techmomaca in calli amehuantin
  amechmomaca in tlalli
ayac quitta

ayac motta
imaxca techmaca totatzin tonantzin

nican mopia maxcatzin
amo mopial in notlal

canin tiquitta nochpochtzin
aquin quiqua in tlaolli in etl
tlaolli etl in notlaqual
ompa tiquimitta topiltzitzinhuan
quimana impilhuan
cana inantzin
quicahua inantzin
quicahua inantzin Antonio

tleica anquicahua in qualnemiliztli
amo ticcahua in qualnemiliztli
tleica mitzcahua in mopiltzin
acan niquitta nopiltzin
acan motta nopiltzin
acan quitta nopiltzin inantzin

aic tiquincahua topilhuan

I give my land to my children.
Apolonia is the wife of Francisco.
They give their children their sheep.
I give my subjects my mother's land.
My house(s) and land(s) are not the
  property of my father.
That Alonso is not our father.
Where do I see myself? (Where am I?)
He/she gives him/herself to a good way
  of life.
Ana leaves her house.
Ana leaves her (grown) daughter's house.
Cristóbal gives me nothing.
The house (houses) is given to us; the land
  is given to you (pl.).
He/she sees no one. (or: No one sees
  him/her/it.)
No one is seen.
Our father and mother give us their
  property.
Your property is kept here.
My land is not your responsibility (yours
  to keep).
Where do you see my (grown) daughter?
Who eats maize and beans?
Maize and beans are my food.
We see our children there.
They take their children.
He/she takes his/her mother.
He/she leaves his/her mother.
He/she leaves Antonio's mother. (or
  Antonio leaves his mother.)
Why do you abandon the good way of life?
We do not abandon the good way of life.
Why does your child abandon you?
Nowhere do I see my child.
Nowhere is my child seen.
Nowhere does my child see his/her
  mother.
We never leave our children.

3. More on the Verbal Complex

The directional prefixes. The applicative. The causative. The reverential of verbs. Texts and examples.

A. *The directional prefixes.* Verbs have two directional prefixes, *on* and *hual*. They come after the object prefix and before the reflexive prefix, when those are present. With the speaker as the point of reference, *on* means away, in an outer direction, and *hual* this way, inward bound. *Quihuica*, "he/she takes it" in a neutral sense; *conhuica*, "he/she takes it away, toward another place"; *quihualhuica*, "he/she brings it." These prefixes have subtle meanings not always reflected in a translation. For the beginner, the most important thing is to identify them, so as to be able to remove them and get at the root.

nonaci	I arrive there	*noconhuica*	I take it away
tonaci	you arrive there	*toconhuica*	you take it away
onaci	he/she arrives there	*conhuica*	he/she takes it away

(This is the first time that we have seen the prefix combinations *nocon* and *tocon*. They are equivalent to *ni-c-on* and *ti-c-on*. The *i* of the subject prefix assimilates to the *o* of the directional prefix. In this case, then, *no-* is neither the possessive prefix—since we are dealing with a verb—nor the reflexive prefix—which has to come after the object prefix.)

nihualaci	I arrive here, get here	*nichualhuica*	I bring it
tihualaci	you arrive here	*tichualhuica*	you bring it
hualaci	he/she arrives here	*quihualhuica*	he/she brings it
nimitzonhuica	I take you there	*tamechhualhuica*	we bring you (pl.) here
nechhualhuica	he/she brings me	*namechonhuica*	I take you (pl.) there
titechonhuica	you take us there	*quinhualhuica*	he/she brings them

(*Ch* is the same in Nahuatl as in English. But note that the combination *chu* must always be analyzed as *c-hu*, as in *ni-c-hual-huica*, I bring it.)

Hual- often has the sense or at least the implication of returning after going, of "back."

conmaca çatepan quihualhuica	He gives it to him; afterward he brings it back.

B. *The applicative.* The applicative suffix of verbs appears most often as *-lia*. It has the characteristic of changing the last vowel of the verbal root, if it is *a*, into *i*. Thus from *huica* comes *huiquilia*, with the additional orthographic change of *c* into *qu* in order to preserve the pronunciation. The vowel change is important because you have to reconstruct the original form of the root if you are going to find it in the dictionary. Verbs in *i* do not change; thus from *caqui*, "to hear," comes *caquilia*.

The applicative adds an object to a verb. If the original is intransitive, the applicative will have one object; if it is transitive, it will have two. The original sense does not change, but now the action is carried out in relation to an additional object; it is applied to this object, whence the name. Generally the new object is something like a dative or indirect object, with a translation "to" or "for."

niquitzoma	I sew it	*niquitzomilia*	I sew it for him/her
nipixca	I harvest	*nicpixquilia*	I harvest for him/her
niccahua	I leave it	*niccahuilia*	I leave it to him/her

The sense of the construction depends, however, on the original sense of the verb. If that sense is positive or neutral, the applicative yields the result we have just seen. But if the original sense involves taking or removing, the second object can lose something instead of receiving something.

14

niccui	I take it	*niccuilia*	I take it from him/her
nicquixtia	I remove it	*nicquixtilia*	I take it away from him/her
niquelehuia	I desire it	*niquelehuilia*	I want it from him/her

Some applicatives are irregular in form. Sometimes *l* is omitted; thus from *cohua*, to "buy," comes *cohuia*, "to buy for oneself."[1] In some cases change goes beyond the final vowel of the root (*a* to *i*) to affect the consonant before that vowel; especially, *c* often becomes *x*, and *t* and *tz* become *ch*. From *aci*, "to arrive," comes *axilia*; from *mati*, "to know," *machilia*; from *notza*, "to call," *nochilia*. The many verbs in *-oa* all have an applicative in *-lhuia* (in which the *l* through metathesis has changed its normal position), but for the rest are extremely irregular, and their form cannot be predicted. From *poloa*, "to lose, spend, etc.," comes *polhuia*; from *itlacoa*, "to spoil, harm," *itlacalhuia*. After all, though, as readers and translators we are not in the business of predicting, and we can with considerable confidence say that any verb ending *-lhuia* is the applicative of an *-oa* verb. With enough work in the dictionary, looking for verbs with the same initial letters, we can with any luck find out what *-oa* verb it is.

C. *The causative.* The causative suffix has two forms, *-tia* and *-ltia*, of which the first is more common; there is no difference of sense or function between them. To form the stem the verbal root may change as with the applicative, and sometimes in the same way: *aci*, applicative *axilia*, causative *axitia*. Often the final vowel of the root is lost: *mati*, "to know," causative *machtia*. The causative varies more than the applicative, and the same verb may have two or more variants. Pay attention above all to the final *-tia* or *-ltia*.

Like the applicative, the causative adds an object to the verb. But in this case there is no indirect object; the new object carries out the action indicated by the original verb. The subject of the causative verb makes someone or something else do something.

nicchihua	I do it	*nicchihualtia*	I make him/her do it, have him do it
nicholoa	I flee	*nicchololtia*	I make him/her flee, put him to flight

Often the causative can or must be translated by a verb different from the one used to translate the original one. Nahuatl uses fewer roots and more combinations and derivations of them than most European languages.

ninemi	I live	*nicnemitia*	I make him/her live, i.e., maintain him
nicmati	I know it	*nicmachtia*	I make him/her know it, I teach it to him
niccahua	I leave him/her/it	*niccahualtia*	I make him/her leave it, which can mean I hinder or stop him in some activity, or I throw him out, etc.

D. *The reverential of verbs.* A large percentage of all verbs in older Nahuatl texts appear in the reverential form. As with its equivalent for nouns (see Chapter 1, section E), the verbal reverential is used very flexibly to adjust the whole tone of a conversation or speech to a certain level, and not automatically, consistently, like polite forms of verbs in European languages.

D1. *The applicative reverential.* The most common apparatus for making a verb reverential consists of adding the combination of a reflexive prefix and an applicative suffix to it. In this case the affixes lack semantic meaning; they serve only to elevate the tone of

---

[1]It is easiest and for neophytes perhaps best to think of what happens here as simple *l*-omission. Actually, this sort of simplification of Nahuatl's bloated affix system always involves the omission of one consonant and one vowel (either one first), each belonging to a different morpheme. *Cohua* also has a regular applicative *cohui-lia*, from which the *i* of the verb stem as well as the *l* of the derivational suffix has been lost in *cohuia*. See also pp. 28, 76.

discourse. The meanings in any case nearly cancel each other out (to do something for one's own benefit). The main task of the student is to remove them in order to arrive at the more basic form.

The system works as follows:

nicnocuilia (where *no* and *lia* cancel each other out, so that the form equals *niccui*, I take it)
ticmocuilia = *ticcui*, you take it
quimocuilia = *quicui*, he/she takes it

tictocuilia = *ticcui*, we take it
anquimocuilia = *anquicui*, you (pl.) take it
quimocuilia = *quicui*, they take it

The applicative is seen so often as part of the reverential that you can easily forget that it has any other use. But by removing only the reflexive from the above forms, we obtain a true applicative: *niccuilia*, "I take it from him/her." It also quite frequently happens that a reverential verb complex contains a second applicative suffix: *nicnocuililia* is the equivalent of *niccuilia*, i.e., again "I take it from him/her." And in rare cases, both affixes in a form identical to the reverential can have their original meaning: *quimocuilia* would ordinarily be "he/she takes it (rev.)," but in some contexts it could be "it is taken from him/her."

Let us analyze an example or two to see how hard it can be to recognize the root and reconstruct the dictionary form. In *nimitznomaquilia*, the stem is *maqui*; since no such verb exists, we must remember that *a* becomes *i* before *lia*. But of course the result of our search is not going to be *maqua*; the *qu* of *maqui* is only there to preserve the sound of an original *c* before *a*. The dictionary form is *maca*, to give. *Nimitznomaquilia* is equivalent to *nimitzmaca*, "I give it to you."

In *toconmanilia*,[1] the *m* represents the reflexive prefix *mo*, since *o* cedes to following *a*. The stem is *ani*. As in the other example, *i* must be changed back into *a* to reconstitute the root, *ana*, "to take." The fact that in Nahuatl the majority of transitive verbs (which require an object prefix) end in *a* and the majority of intransitive verbs in *i* can be useful here (although unfortunately there are many exceptions). That is, if a stem ends in *i* but the verbal complex contains an object prefix, we will be especially quick to replace the *i* with *a*. *Toconmanilia* is equivalent to *toconana*, "you go take it."

In *anquimottilia*, the verb almost disappears. Removing *mo* and *lia*, the reverential equipment, we are left only with *tti*. A Nahuatl word cannot begin with two consonants; we must reconstruct an initial *i*, the weakest vowel, which normally cedes before any other. With the already expected restitution of *a* for the final *i*, we recognize the verb *itta*, "to see." *Anquimottilia* is the equivalent of *anquitta*, "you (pl.) see him/her/it." (In mundane documentation, the identification can be even harder; often only one of the two *t*'s of *itta* is written.)

Changing the final *i* of the stem into *a* is not the only possibility. Nahuatl has many verbs in -*ia* and -*oa* which lose their final vowel in almost any derived form. *Quimotlalilia* is equivalent to *quitlalia*, "he/she puts it down, orders it, etc."

D2. *The causative reverential.* The causative suffix is used in exactly the same way to form reverentials as the applicative. *Tictonequiltia* is the reverential of *ticnequi*, "we want it." As with the applicative, if the reflexive is missing, the sense is truly causative. *Quimopololtia* is the reverential of *quipoloa*, "he/she loses, spends, destroys it." But *quipololtia* is "he/she makes him/her lose it." Intransitive verbs tend to have their reverential in the causative (*timonemiltia* is the equivalent of *tinemi*, you live), but not always. Most verbs in -*oa*, whether intransitive or not, have the causative reverential, as with *poloa* just above.

---

[1] It is not customary in most orthographies to write the *n* of the directional *on* as *m* before labial consonants, even though general prescriptions would seem to indicate that that should be done.

D3. *The reverential of* yauh. The important irregular verb *yauh*, to go, falls entirely outside the normal framework for reverential formation. The reflexive form of another verb, *huica*, to take, carry, replaces the usual apparatus.

tiyauh	you go	*timohuica*	you go, rev. (lit. you take yourself)
yauh	he/she goes	*mohuica*	he/she goes, rev.

Since the verb *huallauh*, to come, is nothing but *yauh* with the prefix *hual*, in this direction (the *y* of *yauh* assimilates to the *l* of *hual*), the reverential of this verb is the reflexive of *huica* plus *hual*.

tihuallauh	you come	*tihualmohuica*	you come, rev.
huallauh	he/she comes	*hualmohuica*	he/she comes, rev.

Of course *huica* is not always the reverential of *yauh*: *quihuica*, "he/she takes or carries it." *Huica* has its own reverential of the usual kind, and possibilities for confusion exist, but the reverential of *huica* is distinguished from that of *yauh* by bearing an object prefix over and above the reflexive prefix and the applicative suffix.

mohuica	he/she goes, rev.
quimohuiquilia	he/she takes it, rev.
hualmohuica	he/she comes, rev.
quihualmohuiquilia	he/she brings it, rev.[2]

E. *Texts and examples.* The following two texts, each followed by additional examples, illustrate some of the things we have spoken of in this lesson and the ones before it.

noconnotlatlauhtilia	*in momahuizçotzin*	*noconnotennamiquilia*
1. no-c-on-no-tlatlauhti-lia	2. in mo-mahuizço-tzin	3. no-c-on-no-tennamiqui-lia
I-it-dir.-refl.-address-appl.	sub.[3] your-honor-rev.	I-it-dir.-refl.-kiss-appl.
I address myself to	your honored person,	I kiss

in momatzin	*in mocxitzin*	*in tinotatzin*	*in tinonantzin*
4. *in mo-ma-tzin*	5. *in mo-cxi-tzin*	6. *in ti-no-ta-tzin*	7. *in ti-no-nan-tzin*
sub. your-hand-rev.	sub. your-foot-rev.	sub. you-my-father-rev.	sub. you-my-mother-rev.
your hands	and feet,	you who are [like] my father and mother.	

nicnocuilia	*nicnanilia*	*in motlatoltzin*	*qualli*	*tlatolli*
8. *ni-c-no-cui-lia*	9. *ni-c-n-ani-lia*	10. *in mo-tlatol-tzin*	11. *qual-li*	*tlatol-li*
I-it-refl.-take-appl.	I-it-refl.-take-appl.	sub. your-statement-rev.	good-thing-abs.	statement-abs.
I understand and profit from		what you say.	Good	words are

in ticmitalhuia	*nimitznomaquilia*	*in ixquich nocal*	*notlal*
12. *in ti-c-m-ita-lhuia*	13. *ni-mitz-no-maqui-lia*	14. *in ixquich no-cal*	15. *no-tlal*
sub. you-it-refl.-say-appl.	I-you-refl.-give-appl.	sub. everything my-house	my-land
those that you say.	I give you	all my houses and	lands.

ixquich nimitznocahuililia	*ixquich ticmocuilia*	*nimomacehual*
16. *ixquich ni-mitz-no-cahui-li-lia*	17. *ixquich ti-c-mo-cui-lia*	18. *ni-mo-macehual*
everything I-you-refl.-leave-appl.-appl.	everything you-it-refl.-take-appl.	I-your-subject
I leave it all to you.	You take it all.	I am your vassal,

nimitznotlayecoltilia	*cenca tinechmopalehuilia*	*no nimitznopalehuilia*
19. *ni-mitz-no-tlayecolti-lia*	20. *cenca ti-nech-mo-palehui-lia*	21. no ni-mitz-no-palehui-lia
I-you-refl.-serve-appl.	very you-me-refl.-help-appl.	also I-you-refl.-help-appl.
I serve you.	You help me greatly,	also I help you .

---

[2] By the seventeenth century the applicative of *huica* acquired the sense of owing money, but in that case one will not see the reflexive prefix: *miec tomin nichuiquilia*, I owe him much money.

[3] Subordinator, "article."

1. Verb *tlatlauhtilia*, to pray, implore, direct oneself to.
2. Noun *mahui(z)çotl*; it contains *mahuiztli*, fear, and the abstract suffix *-yo* in assimilated form.
3. Verb *tennamiqui*. *Tentli*, lips; *namiqui*, meet. Phrases 1 and 2 are parallel to 3 and 4 as so often in Nahuatl. There is no necessity to analyze from scratch the second time.
4. Noun *maitl*, arm, hand. Parts of the body are not pluralized.
5. Noun *icxitl*.
6. Noun *tatli* (with a glottal stop after the *a*).
7. Noun *nantli*.
8. Verb *cui*.
9. Verb *ana*. The two synonyms together constitute an idiom meaning to understand well and take advantage of wisdom that is imparted to one.
10. Noun *tlatolli*. It is derived from the verb *itoa*, to say.
11. *Qualli tlatolli* constitutes an independent utterance, the main clause in a larger construction.
12. Verb *itoa*. The particle *in* makes the clause dependent upon the preceding one.
13. Verb *maca*.
14. Noun *calli*. Since a house is an inanimate object, there is no plural suffix.
15. Noun *tlalli*.
16. Verb *cahua*. There are two applicatives, one applicative in sense and the other part of the reverential equipment.
17. Verb *cui*.
18. Noun *macehualli*.
19. Verb *tlayecoltia*. Although *-ltia* is a causative ending, the whole verb is found in the dictionary, and it is not clear what it is derived from.
20. Verb *palehuia*, to help.
21. Same verb. It would have been more idiomatic to add independent pronouns here.

Here are some additional individual examples. After studying them, cover everything except the example itself; analyze and translate. With the reverentials, reconstruct the non-reverential equivalent.

amonaci	*am-on-aci*	you (pl.)-dir.-reach	you (pl.) get there
anhualaci	*an-hual-aci*	you (pl.)-dir.-reach	you (pl.) get here
tonmaxitia	*t-on-m-axi-tia*	you-dir.-refl.-reach-caus.	you get there
tihualmaxitia	*ti-hual-m-axi-tia*	you-dir.-refl.-reach-caus.	you get here
conana	*c-on-ana*	(he/she)-it-dir.-take	he/she goes to take it
quihualana	*qui-hual-ana*	(he/she)-it-dir.-take	he/she comes to take it
conmanilia	*c-on-m-ani-lia*	(he/she)-it-dir.-refl.-take-appl.	he/she goes to take it
quihualmanilia	*qui-hual-m-ani-lia*	(he/she)-it-dir.-refl.-take-appl.	he/she comes to take it
mohuica	*mo-huica*	(he/she)-refl.-carry	he/she goes
hualmohuica	*hual-mo-huica*	(he/she)-dir.-refl.-carry	he/she comes
ticmocuilia	*ti-c-mo-cui-lia*	you-it-refl.-take-appl.	you take it
ticcuilia	*ti-c-cui-lia*	you-him/her-take-appl.	you take it from him/her
anquimochialia	*an-qui-mo-chia-lia*	you-him/her-refl.-await-appl.	you (pl.) await him/her
quimochihuilia	*qui-mo-chihui-lia*	(he/she)-it-refl.-do-appl.	he/she does it

At this point I always pile it on to the student, before the new gains are lost. Here is another brief text to be fully analyzed, with some language of the kind that can be found in the most common document type in the Nahuatl corpus, the last will and testament:

ye nihuehue	*ye nimiqui*	*in nocal*	*niquinnocahuililia*
1. *ye ni-huehue*	2. *ye ni-miqui*	3. *in no-cal*	4. *ni-quin-no-cahui-li-lia*
already I-old-man	already I-die	sub. my-house	I-them-refl.-leave-appl.-appl.
I am an old man already,	I am about to die.	My houses	I leave to

in nopilhuan	*in huei calli*	*nicnomaquilia*	*in nochpochtzin Luisa*
5. *in no-pil-huan*	6. *in huei cal-li*	7. *ni-c-no-maqui-lia*	8. *in no-chpoch-tzin Luisa*
sub. my-child-pl. poss.	sub. big house-abs.	I-her-refl.-give-appl.	sub. my-daughter-rev. Luisa
my children.	The big house	I leave to	my daughter Luisa.

in caltepiton	nicmaca	in notelpochtzin Juan	auh	in oc ce notelpoch
9. *in cal-tepiton*	10. *ni-c-maca*	11. in *no-telpoch-tzin* Juan	12. *auh*	13. *in oc ce no-telpoch*
sub. house-little thing	I-him-give	sub. my-son-rev. Juan	and/but	sub. still one my-son
The little house	I give to	my son Juan.	But	to my other son

atle nicmaca	niccahualtia	in nocal	amo qualli tlacatl
14. *atle ni-c-maca*	15. *ni-c-cahua-ltia*	16. *in no-cal*	17. *amo qual-li tlaca-tl*
nothing I-him-give	I-him-leave-caus.	sub. my-house	not (he)-good-abs. (he)-person-abs.
I give nothing.	I throw him out of	my house.	He is not a good person;

amo nechpalehuia	in nita
18. amo nech-palehuia	19. in n-i-ta
not (he)-me-help	sub. I-his-father
he does not help me	who am his father.

1. Irregular noun *huehue*. Although *huehue* tends to expand beyond the realm of masculinity in compounds, as an independent word it always seems to refer to an old man; old woman is *ilama*.
2. Verb *miqui*.
3. Noun *calli*.
4. Verb *cahua*; has two applicatives.
5. Noun *pilli*. Always means "child" when possessed.
6. Irregular noun *huei*, a big thing.
7. Verb *maca*.
8. Noun *ichpochtli*. When possessed means daughter with the assumption she has reached puberty.
9. Noun *calli* bound to *tepiton*, an irregular form that bears no absolutive ending.
10. Verb *maca*.
11. Noun *telpochtli*, has the same characteristics for males as *ichpochtli* for females.
12. *Auh* is an introductory particle, very useful because it usually implies that a complete sentence ended immediately before it.
13. *Oc*, still; with numbers and quantities it means "more." Noun *telpochtli*.
14. Verb *maca*. *Atle* corresponds to the *-c-* of *nicmaca*.
15. Verb *cahua*. The construction could be translated as "I make him leave my house."
16. Noun *calli*.
17. Or "He is a bad person." Nahuatl generally says "not good" instead of "bad" and in a sense has no word for bad, though stronger words exist to say evil, wretched, and the like.
18. Verb *palehuia*.
19. Noun *tatli*. Do not analyze *ni-ta*. The *n-* alone is "I," and the *-i-* is the third person possessive prefix, "his." The lack of an absolutive ending tells us that the form is possessed.

Yet more individual examples:

quichihuilia	nechhualmotquililia	monemitia
qui-chihui-lia	*nech-hual-mo-tqui-li-lia*	*mo-nemi-tia*
(he/she)-him/her-make, do-appl.	(he/she)-me-dir.-refl.-carry-appl.-appl.	(he/she)-refl.-live-caus.
he/she makes it for him/her	he/she brings it to me	he/she lives

tictoxelhuia	timitztitlacalhuilia	tictonequiltia
ti-c-to-xel-huia	*ti-mitz-t-itlaca-lhui-lia*	*ti-c-to-nequi-ltia*
we-it-refl.-divide-appl.	we-you-refl.-damage-appl.-appl.	we-it-refl.-want-caus.
we divide it	we ruin it for you	we want it

ticnequiltia	quimitalhuia
ti-c-nequi-ltia	*qui-m-ita-lhuia*
we-him/her-want-caus.	(he/she)-it-refl.-say-appl.
we make him/her want it	he/she says it

Verbs in the above: *chihua, itqui, nemi, xeloa, itlacoa, nequi, itoa*.

4. Relational Words

General discussion (using -pan). Specific relational words.

A. *General discussion (using -pan).* English (like many other European languages) has prepositions, words which are placed in front of nouns and pronouns considered to be their objects or complements, with no other indication of the connection, at least in those languages which no longer have case, in order to designate in the first instance physical relations (on, in, etc.) and secondly more abstract relations (a study on something, confidence in someone, etc.). Nahuatl has words that are very similar in meaning and function, but not in structure. In Nahuatl these words always come after something, either a noun or a possessive prefix. For that reason they are sometimes called postpositions. Others consider them a class of nouns, which fits well in some respects; they can be possessed like nouns, and they can be compounded with them. (Up to this point we have said, in the name of simplification, that only nouns bear possessive prefixes, but these pseudo-nouns must be included too.) In fact, the words of this class probably descend historically from nouns. Centuries ago *-pan*, "on, in, etc.," may have been a noun with the sense "surface." But these words lack the absolute or unpossessed form, and they cannot act as subjects or objects of verbs. I prefer to call them relational words.

The two ways in which relational words are used are not exactly equivalent in meaning. The form bound with a noun has a more generic sense:

tepan (from *tetl* and *-pan*)	on stone
ipan in tetl	on the stones (specific stones already in the mind of the speaker)

For this reason the second form is much more common.

To create a compound of noun and relational word, the absolute singular suffix of the noun is removed and replaced by the relational word. The second, more frequent procedure is more complex. A possessive prefix is added to the relational word, agreeing in person and number with the word to which it refers or crossrefers. In the above example, *tetl*, stone, although its sense can be plural, is grammatically a third person singular noun, so that the prefix must be *i*, third person singular possessive. *Ipan*, literally "its-on," can be translated as "on it." But the translator's task is not complete until it is established what the prefix refers to, here "stone," and that element is integrated into the translation: "on the stones." It is true that in the first and second persons, the referent of the prefix is generally not specified: *nopan*, "on me." There are also plurals: *impan in cahuallos*, "their-on the horses," "on the horses."

The relational word in its possessed form is most commonly seen in front of the word to which it refers: *ipan in tlalli*, "on the ground." But it can also follow: *in tlalli ipan*. In view of the reciprocal reference and the agreement, the two parts of a relational phrase can be placed at some distance from each other. It happens frequently that the relational word as an adverbial element comes before the verb while the noun to which it refers comes later: *ipan tleco cahuallo*, "he/she gets up on a horse."

It was said above that a construction consisting of a noun and a relational word has a generic sense. That changes when the noun is possessed, which is by no means rare: *nopetlapan nicochi*, "I sleep on my mat."

A very useful aspect of relational words is their reverential, *-tzinco*. We already recognize *-tzin* as the reverential suffix of nouns. A little further on we will see that *-co* is a locative, one of the relational words itself, but here it lacks a spatial meaning. The combination *-tzinco*, in addition to being reverential, above all identifies the root preceding it as a relational word. In Nahuatl it is indispensable to know from the beginning what part of speech is involved in order to be able to analyze and understand a word correctly, for the different parts of speech share many characteristics, often misdirecting analysis. The element *-tzin* identifies three kinds of constructions:

If a word ends in	*-tzintli,*	it is an unpossessed normal noun.
	-tzin,	it is a possessed normal noun.
	-tzinco,	it is a relational word.

-Tzinco occurs with both simple and compound relational forms.

ipan in cahuallo	on the horse	*ipantzinco in cahuallo*	the same, rev.
cahuallopan	on a horse, mounted	*cahuallopantzinco*	the same, rev.
icahuallopan	on his/her horse	*icahuallopantzinco*	the same, rev.

Some place names (names of sociopolitical units, actually), are the main exception to the use of *-tzinco* as a diagnostic sign of relational words. In these, *-tzin* still has its original diminutive sense, and the word names a unit thought to have emanated from an older or larger one, as Mexicatzinco (from Mexico) or Tollantzinco (from Tollan, Tula). Even in these cases the name is most often a compound relational word grammatically.

It is a characteristic of relational words that they have many meanings and participate in various idioms; many idioms consist of a verb plus a relational word. At times the thrust can be understood quite readily starting from the basic sense, at times not. The following examples illustrate some of the common idioms involving *-pan* (there are many more).

nopan mochihua missa	A mass is said (lit., made) for me.
amo qualli in nopan mochihua	What is happening to me is bad.
nopan quiça	He/she passes by me, close to me.
ipan tlatoa in tamalchihualiztli	He/she is in charge of the tamal making.

Some expressions require more explanation. *-Pan* can have the sense "in the time of." *Ipan Moteucçoma ninemi,* "I live in the time of Moteucçoma (Montezuma)." Very common is a phrase on the order of *nopan aci,* literally "he/she arrives on me," i.e., arrives with me still there, catches or finds me there on arrival. *Ipan aci in tlaneltoquiliztli,* "he/she arrives in the time of the (Christian) faith," i.e., Christianity has already been established at the time of his/her arrival.

Another sense of *-pan* is, approximately, "as." It occurs mainly with the verb *mati,* to know, but also in other contexts. *Atle ipan nimitzmati* (the *i* of *ipan* refers to *atle,* "nothing"), literally "on nothing I know you," that is, I consider you as nothing, think nothing of you (cf. Spanish "no te tengo en nada"). *Piltzintli ipan nechmati,* literally "on a small child he/she knows me," i.e., thinks of me as a small child, or treats me like one.

B. *Specific relational words.* Here follow explanations of some of the other more common relational words, with a few examples of their use.

1. *-Tech* means literally "next to, adhering to," but it is in addition Nahuatl's most general connector, with an infinite number of special meanings. Fortunately, almost all can be deduced quite easily from the nature of the verb with which *-tech* is associated.

itech çalihui in calli	It is stuck, adheres <u>to</u> the house.
notlal itech onaci in otli	My land reaches <u>up to</u> the road.
itech nictlalia nanima Dios	I place my soul <u>with</u> God.
tonacayo itech quiça in tlalli	Our bodies come <u>from</u> the earth.
notech pohui in metlatl	The metate (grinding stone) belongs <u>to</u> me.
itechtzinco nicpohua nocal in nopiltzin	I assign my house <u>to</u> my child.
cenca notech monequi tomin	<u>For</u> or <u>with</u> me money is greatly needed, i.e., I greatly need money.

Note that *-tech* is written exactly the same as the object prefix *tech,* "us" (although there is an unwritten difference in vowel quantity). No confusion need result, for the relational word always follows a possessive prefix or a noun stem, and the object prefix is always found toward the beginning of a verbal complex. Many very distinct things in Nahuatl are identical except for their position.

2. *-Pampa* is "because of, concerning." In its third person singular form, when referring to a whole clause, it can be either "because" or "for which reason" (that is, it can refer either to the preceding or to the following clause). A dependent clause is always treated as third person singular. This word consists of *-pan*, which we already know, and *-pa*, "toward (and other senses)," and it can share meanings with *-pan*; both often mean "for."

topampa quichihua	He/she does it for us, because of us, on our behalf.
quimaca itlal ipampa quipalehuia	He gives him his land because he helps him (*i* of *ipampa* refers to *quipalehuia*).
nehuatl nichpoch ipampa nicpalehuia	I am her daughter, for which reason I help her (*i* of *ipampa* refers to *nehuatl nichpoch*).
ipampa tlalli nihuallauh	I come about the land.

3. *-Huan* is "in the company of, together with, with."

inhuan quichihua itatzin inantzin	He/she does it together with his/her father and mother.
nohuan yoli	He/she lives with me.
nohuan yolqui	one who lives with me, i.e., my relative

-Huan is seen most frequently in the third person singular form, *ihuan*, with almost the sense of "and," but not quite the same.

niquinhuica Fabian ihuan ipiltzin	I accompany Fabián and his child.
quipia silla ihuan freno	It has saddle and bridle.

Note that here the possessive prefix of *ihuan* refers to the following noun. In many cases, as in the two examples here, something of "together with" remains; the second element complements the first, which is more basic or primary. *Ihuan* can also be "moreover, also, in addition":

nictlaçotla in nonamictzin ihuan niquitoa ca nictlaçotla in nopiltzin	I love my spouse; I say moreover that I love my child.

Ihuan is used far less frequently than "and" in English. A series of nouns will most often not include *ihuan*.

notech monequi in tlaxcalli in nacatl in chilli in atl	I need (or use) bread, meat, chile, and water.

4. *-Ca* is "by means of, through, with." It is Nahuatl's most generalized way of expressing instrumentality. Its manner of combining with nouns is not unique, but different from what we have seen up until now. When some relational words are combined with a noun, a "ligature" *ti* is required between the two elements. *Xal-pan*, on sand, but *cuchillo-ti-ca*, with a knife.[1] *-Ca* has numerous idiomatic uses.

ica atl quipaca	He/she washes it with water.
Jesu Christo techmomaquixtilia ica in itlaçoezçotzin	Jesus Christ redeems us with his precious blood.
mitica quimictia iyaouh	He kills his enemy with arrows.
nocamatica niquitoa	With my mouth I say it.
noca tetlatlania	He/she asks (people) about me.

---

[1]The use of the *ti* ligature varies regionally and even sometimes with the individual writer. Though *-pan* does not generally use *ti* in the Valley of Mexico, for the Tlaxcalan area one can find constructions such as *ama-ti-pan*, "on paper."

toca huetzca	He/she laughs at us.
icatzinco itocatzin totecuiyo Dios	In the name of God our lord
domingotica nipaqui nochan	Sunday (or Sundays) I enjoy myself at home.
ce mediotica niccohua nacatl	I buy meat for, worth, half a real.

5. *-Icampa* is "behind." The *i* is long, so that it is not lost as so often in the possessed form; instead the *o* of the possessive prefixes cedes. Neophytes get so used to thinking that any *i* toward the beginning of a construction is the possessive prefix that they remove it and look for this word under *campa*, which is "where," but in this case the *i* belongs to the root (even when it counts as the third person singular prefix as well).

notlal mani icampatzinco teopan	My land is behind the church.
nicampa notepotzco	behind me, in back of me; i.e., when I am dead

6. *-Nahuac* is "near to, close to, next to," somewhat like *-tech*, but not "adhering to." Nevertheless, they are so similar that in older Nahuatl sources coming from peripheral regions, *-nahuac* acts as the general connector instead of *-tech.*

in calli imilnahuac Dionisio icac	The house stands (is) close to Dionisio's field.
Quauhnahuac	close to the woods, Cuernavaca

7. *-Icpac* is "on top of." When referring to people, it means specifically "on the head of." The *i*, as we would expect, is weak and is lost when it comes into contact with the possessive prefixes in *o* or with *tla-.* *-Icpac* also uses the *ti* ligature.

nocpac nictlalia in sombrero	I put the hat on my head.
icpac[2] tepetl tleco	He/she climbs up on top of the mountain.
tlalticpac tinemi titlaca	We human beings live on earth.

8. *-Tlan* is "next to, below." The phrase *-tlan nemi* (containing words meaning to live next to, under) means to be the domestic dependent of someone and has a nominal form *-tlan nenqui*, dependent. *-Tlan* uses the *ti* ligature.

Domingo itlan nemi in tlatoani	Domingo is a dependent of the ruler.[3]
mocaltitlan niquitta in motex	Next to your house I see your brother-in-law.[4]

9. *-Ixpan* is "facing, in front of, before, in the presence of." Some of the most common relational words consist of a relational word plus a noun. *-Ixpan* contains *-pan*, which we already know, and the noun *ixtli*, "eye, face"; thus it means "in the eyes of." The *i* is long.

imixpantzinco in tlatoque nicnamaca	In the presence of the rulers I sell it.
nixpan mochihua in testamento	Before me [the notary] the testament is made.

10. *-Itic* is "inside, within." It contains the locative relational word *-co/c* (discussed in the following paragraph) and *itetl* or *ititl*, "belly, womb." There is a glottal stop after the first *i*, for which reason it is not weak and does not lose out to the *o* of the possessive prefixes. Nahuatl often says "inside" where English would just use "in."

nocalitic onoc nocihuatlatqui	My woman's gear is inside, in my house.
nitic ninococoa	Inside me I am sick, i.e., I have a stomachache or the like.
itictzinco in cemicac ichpochtzintli	in the womb of the eternal Virgin

---

[2]This form looks like the unmodified, bare root, but in fact the first *i* has to be the third person singular possessive prefix. No relational word ever appears in an utterance as a bare root.

[3]Literally, Domingo lives next to or under the ruler.

[4]Since *-tex* refers to a relationship between two men, we know that the speaker is talking to a man.

11. *-Tzintlan* is "below, underneath." It consists of *-tlan*, already with implications of below, and *tzintli*, bottom, anus, lower part, beginning.

in tlalli itzintlan tepetl mani	The land is below, at the foot of, the mountain.

12. *-Co/c* is "in, at," locative in a very general sense. The relational words that we have seen so far deserve to be called words because when they are possessed they appear independently. Some members of the class cannot be possessed and thus are perhaps more like nominal suffixes than words properly speaking. *-Co/c* is of this type. It has two forms, with and without the vowel, like some other elements we have already seen, the nominal absolute and possessive suffixes, and another that we do not know yet, the preterit agentive suffix. The form with vowel appears when the noun stem ends in a consonant, rendering the compound pronounceable, and the short form is seen otherwise, i.e., when the noun stem ends in a vowel.

atlauh-co	in a ravine	*tepe-c*	at a mountain
toch-tli	rabbit	*tlaca-tl*	person
noquich-hui	my husband	*na-uh*	my water
yol-qui	animal	*tlanamaca-c*	seller, vendor

The following forms are all regular by these principles:

tepanco	at the boundary, wall	*ilhuicac*	in the sky, heaven
notepanco	at my boundary, wall	*tocamac*	in our mouths
ithualco	in the patio	*nomac*	in my hands
Xochimilco	in flower fields (place name)	*nomactzinco*	in my hands, rev.

Note that in *nomactzinco*, *-co/c* appears twice, the first time as a locative, the second time without locative sense, as part of the reverential equipment for words of this class. Small though it may be, the element *-c-* has the effect that this construction is not a normal noun but a complex relational word.

A great many place names in older Nahuatl (and in Spanish in today's Mexico) end in *-co/c*. As we already saw, they are not exactly toponyms; they designate hamlets, districts, whole larger sociopolitical units. Mountains, rivers, actual physical features, appear in the absolute form: Coatepetl would be Snake Mountain, and Coatepec a settlement near that mountain. Although not all names of towns and units have the *-co/c* ending in Nahuatl, they do generally end in a relational word, and all are locative. They cannot serve as the subject or object of a verb. Instead of "he rules Xochimilco," Nahuatl says *Xochimilco tlatocati*, "he rules in or is ruler in Xochimilco." To say that one is in a certain unit, nothing is added: *Xochimilco nica*, "I am in Xochimilco." Nor, in a certain sense, is anything added to say to or from a settlement. Relational words in Nahuatl never indicate the direction of movement; that is done in the verb.

Xochimilco niyauh	I go to Xochimilco
Xochimilco niquiça	I come out of Xochimilco
Xochimilco nonaci	I get to Xochimilco (starting from here)
Xochimilco nihualehua	I come from Xochimilco

Some nouns show the locative form with *-co/c* so frequently that the absolute form hardly appears, as with two words in the examples above, *ilhuicac*, in the sky, and *ithual-co*, in the patio. The same thing happens with *tianquizco*, in the market, and *tlapanco*, on the roof. You will rarely see *ilhuicatl*, *ithualli*, *tianquiztli*, or *tlapantli* in texts.[1]

13. *-Pa* and *-huic* both mean "toward," though in line with what was just said, they can also mean "from." Like *-co/c*, *-pa* is a pure suffix that cannot be possessed. *-Huic*, on the

---

[1] The Nahuatl word for flat roof came into Mexican Spanish as *tapanco*.

other hand, on occasion appears independently: *nohuic,* "in relation to, toward me."

tepecpa nitztiuh	I head toward the mountain.
tepechuic nitztiuh	the same
tepecpahuic nitztiuh	the same
tepechuicpa nitztiuh	the same
tepecpa nihuallauh	I come from the direction of the mountain.

Here we see a prime characteristic of these two word-suffixes, that they are secondary and rarely appear any other way than suffixed to another relational word or locative, in this case *-co/c. -Ixpampa,* from *-ixpan* and *-pa,* means "toward or from the presence of." We have already seen *-pampa,* from *-pan* and *-pa. -Copa,* from *-co/-c* and *-pa,* is "in a certain manner" and is compounded with nouns; it also gives different shadings to other relational words.

ixpampa nehua in miquiztli	I flee from (the presence of) death.
noyollocopa nicchihua	I do it from my heart, voluntarily.
ce amoxtli itechcopa in toltecayotl	a book on, about, artisanry

As implied by these examples, *-pa* is broader and more common than *-huic.* Only *-pa* is used to create new compound relational words. It also has the sense of "a certain number of times," combining directly with number words and quantifiers, as in *nauhpa* or *nappa,* four times, or *mochipa,* always (all times).

14. The word *-chan,* residence, home, place where one was born, etc., is generally considered a noun, and in some ways it functions as one. But it seems to be more than anything a relational word. It is never seen in the absolute, neither in texts nor in Molina's dictionary. Above all, *-chan* is always locative; by itself it means "at one's home." We already saw the example *domingotica nipaqui nochan,* "Sunday I enjoy myself at my home." It also takes a reverential in *-tzinco* like any other relational word: *ichantzinco ca,* "he is at his home." Note that to speak of the buildings and the whole physical aspect of the household one uses *calli,* house, which is in all respects a normal noun.

15. The suffixes *-yan* and *-can* are locative, but they are different than relational words in that they belong to the conjugation of verbs and often form true nouns which can act as the subject or object of another verb. They will be discussed later.

Exercise: Cover the translations of the examples of this lesson, analyze them fully, and retranslate them.

Note: Three words in these lessons often translate as "to take"; *ana, cui,* and *huica. Ana* and *cui* are closely synonymous in that they can both mean "take away, take for oneself," whereas *huica* unless further modified means primarily "to take along, to accompany, go with, be responsible for," so that its applicative *huiquilia* was able to cover the meaning "to owe (money)" as applicatives from the other two could not. *Ana* can have the sense "to get a person in order to go somewhere, pick a person up," and hence it is the only one of the three to mean "to arrest, seize." It also can have the implication of stretching, so that the reflexive *mana* often means "to grow." *Cui* means "to take something to oneself." It very often translates as "to get." *Campa niccuiz nahui pesos,* "Where am I to get four pesos?" *In fiscal quicui ome tomin ic tetoca,* "the fiscal gets two reales for burying people." In tandem with *ana* it can mean to "get" a message. It can also mean to get or harvest crops and to fetch things, notably water.

5. Indefinite Prefixes and Deverbal Nouns

Indefinite object prefixes of verbs. Indefinite possessive prefixes of nouns. Nouns in -liz and -l. An illustrative text.

A. *Indefinite object prefixes of verbs.* With the indefinite object prefixes, we have the last elements of Nahuatl's impressive collection of verbal prefixes. We have previously seen that in Nahuatl transitive verbs always require an object prefix. Those that we are already acquainted with refer to specific objects. If it is not known exactly who or what the object is, it is still necessary to put in a prefix of some kind, and that is what the indefinite prefixes are for. The prefix *te* is for personal objects and can be translated "one," "someone," "people," or even "others" according to the context. The prefix *tla* is for nonhuman objects and can be translated "something" or "things." The distinction made here is not the one mentioned once above between animate and inanimate things that is seen in plural formation. *Te* is only for people, while *tla* includes both inanimate things and animals of all kinds. *Te* can represent either the direct or the indirect object, whereas *tla* because of its semantic properties almost always represents a direct object.

Now we are in a position to appreciate the entire scheme for ordering verbal prefixes. It never varies in the slightest. Many of the elements can be absent in a given case, but those that are present will always follow the order shown here (which for the most part we already know). The indefinite prefixes come after all the rest; both of them can be present, in which case *te* comes first:

subject	specific object	directional	reflexive	indefinite object	
				personal	nonpersonal
ni, etc.	*nech*, etc.	*on*, *hual*	*no*, etc.	*te*	*tla*

Let us analyze some examples:

nichualnotlahuiquililia
ni-c-hual-no-tla-huiqui-li-lia
I-him/her-dir.-refl.-indef.nonpers.-carry-appl.-appl.

The verb *huica* is "to take, carry, accompany," but with the directional *hual* it is usually translated "to bring." *No* and *lia* together constitute the reverential. The other *lia* (*li*) is a true applicative, governing a second object. *Tla* is the direct object, so that *-c-* has to be the indirect object. Translation: "I bring him/her something." However, since by the seventeenth century *huiquilia* had the sense "to owe money," and *hual* can refer to the passage of time from the past into the present, another translation would be: "For some time I have owed him/her money."

noconnotemaquilia
no-c-on-no-te-maqui-lia
I-it-dir.-refl.-indef.pers.-give-appl.

The second *no* and the *lia* are the reverential. The directional *on* here is more than anything ornamental; it can be connected with the outward movement of the action of giving, and also as providing distance and greater complexity, hence adding to the reverential effect, but it is not likely to be reflected in a translation. This time (assuming that this is not some exceptional case involving slaves or the like), *-c-* must be the direct object and *te* the indirect object. Translation: "I give it to someone."

nitetlamaca
ni-te-tla-maca
I-indef.pers.-indef.nonpers.-give

This form can be translated "I give something to someone, or to people." It could have the more specific meanings "I serve at table" or "I dispense communion."

In the above cases the specific objects do not appear as nouns. Most frequently, the noun objects are specified, which helps considerably. From the following examples you can gather how the interaction of indefinite and specified objects functions.

nictemaca in tlalli	I give the land to someone.
nictlamaca	I give him/her something.
tinechmotlamaquilia	You give me something.
quicui in calli	He/she takes the house.
quitecuilia in calli	He/she takes the house from someone.
niccui in tomin	I take the money.
nicnotecuililia in tomin	I take the money from someone.
nitlacui	I take something, fetch something.
quitlacuilia in cihuatl	He/she takes something from the woman.
nitetlacuilia	I take something from someone, take things from people.

The last example almost means "I rob, am a thief."

Te and especially *tla* often serve to form a verb which is in effect intransitive from one that is transitive.

ticqua in tlaxcalli	You eat the tortillas, the bread.
titlaqua	You eat something, i.e., you eat.
timotlaqualtia	the same, rev.
itla anquitoa	You (pl.) say something (some specific words, although I didn't understand them; *qui*, the specific object, refers to *itla*, "something" as an independent word).
antlatoa	You (pl.) say things, i.e., you speak.
quichia	He/she awaits him/her/it.
tlachia	He/she looks. (Sometimes the forms in *tla* have different or additional senses.)

B. *Indefinite prefixes of nouns.* Aside from representing indefinite objects in verbs and words derived from them, *te* and *tla* can act as indefinite possessors. Many nouns in Nahuatl (kinship terms and some others) can appear only in the possessed form and never bear the absolutive endings. Nor do relational words have an absolutive form. With *te* and *tla* these words can in a certain way be absolute after all. *Te* can be prefixed to either nouns or relational words, *tla* only to the latter. One cannot, then, proceed on the assumption that any word with *te* or *tla* is a verb or something derived from a verb.

naxca	my property	*teaxca*	someone's or someone else's property
itatzin	his/her father	*tetatzin*	someone's father, the father
mohuan	with you	*tehuan*	with someone, together
tocal	our house	*tecal*	someone's or someone else's house
nixpan	before me	*teixpan*	in the presence of people, in public
icpac in calli	on top of the house	*tlacpac*	on top (not specifying what)
tixpan	before us	*tlaixpan*	facing
itzintlan in quahuitl	underneath the tree	*tlatzintlan*	below
itic in mocal	inside your house	*tlatic*	inside
icampa in tepetl	behind the mountain	*tlaicampa*	behind

C. *Nouns from verbs.* Like all languages, Nahuatl has ways of deriving nouns from verbs. The unusual thing in Nahuatl is that the derived nouns retain relics of all the object prefixes borne by the original verbs, and the nominalizing elements are very similar to elements in verbs, so that it is often very hard to recognize the derived words as nouns. On the other hand, it is easy to identify and locate the verbs from which they derive, which is very necessary, because Nahuatl forms such constructions constantly, for the momentary purposes of an utterance, and by no means all of them are found in the dictionary.

C1. *Nouns in* -liz. The element -*liz* suffixed to a verb stem forms a noun that means, in the first instance, the action of the verb, like a gerund, although it often acquires additional meanings. Since -*liz* ends in a consonant, all of these words have the singular absolute -*tli* (by the nature of their meaning and inanimacy they are virtually never seen in the plural). From *nemi*, "to live," is derived *nemiliztli*, the action of living, or in effect usually "life." The possessed form is -*nemiliz*: *nonemiliz*, "my life"; *monemiliz*, "your life"; *inemiliz*, "his/her life." Given that -*liz* looks no different from the ending of a singular verb in the future tense with an applicative suffix, students make many errors in cases like this about what part of speech is involved. The -*liz* nominalizer even sometimes has the applicative's characteristic of changing a preceding *a* into *i*: from *choca*, to weep, comes *choquiliztli*, "weeping." In the three examples of -*nemiliz* which we just saw, the prefix *i*- can be recognized as possessive, indicating that we are dealing with a noun. But *no*- and *mo*- are identical to reflexive prefixes of verbs. With *no*-, we soon realize that *ni*-, the necessary subject prefix, is missing, so that the form must be a possessed noun. In the third case, *monemiliz* is identical to a reverential third person singular verb in the future tense. Perhaps that is why so many intransitive verbs use the causative reverential (a more common future reverential for *nemi* would be *monemitiz*). Thus in the majority of cases you can with patience and subtlety find some indication that the form is a noun, and in most of the rest the context will provide the solution. At any rate, the matter calls for constant vigilance.

Verbs in -*ia* and -*oa* lose their final vowel before -*liz*. Thus from *choloa*, "to flee," is formed *chololiztli*, "the action of fleeing, flight." Sometimes the construction becomes more difficult to recognize because of the disappearance of *l* and the vowel before it;[1] we saw *choquiliztli*, weeping, but more common is *choquiztli*. From *miqui*, "to die," is formed *miquiliztli*, "death," but more commonly *miquiztli*.

Many nouns in -*liz* bear *te* or *tla* or both. All the objects shown in the finite verbal complexes are reflected in the derived noun; since in the noun the object cannot be specified, the indefinite prefixes come into play.

niquintlaçotla in notatzin in nonantzin	I love my father and mother.
nitetlaçotla	I love people, am a loving person.
tetlaçotlaliztli	action of loving people, love

The verb here is *tlaçotla*, "to love," which in the examples just given takes a personal object, as in fact it usually does. If the normal object of the verb is not personal, *tla* will appear instead of *te*. Nouns from a single verb can vary the prefix according to the sense. *Tlatlaçotlaliztli* is also love, but of things or animals, not people.

nicqua in etl	I eat the beans.
nitlaqua	I eat.
tlaqualiztli	eating

Although not seen in mundane sources, *tequaliztli* would be the eating of human beings; a *tequani* (-*ni* forms agentives) is a ferocious beast that supposedly eats people.

Thus the indefinite *te* and *tla* represent the specific objects of the original verb. What happens when the verb is reflexive? To cover this possibility Nahuatl has an indefinite reflexive prefix, *ne*-, which appears with passive and impersonal verbs and in derived nouns (as well as sometimes in complex applicative and causative constructions).

---

[1] See the discussion of this matter on p. 15, especially n. 1, and p. 76, n. 1.

ninopohua	I am proud, I brag
nepohualiztli	pride, bragging
ninonamictia	I take a spouse, I marry
nenamictiliztli	marriage

If the original verb has two objects, indefinite object prefixes covering both appear in the derived noun.

nicnocuitlahuia in nopiltzin	I take care of my child.
netecuitlahuiliztli	care of people
niquinnocuitlahuia in nototolhuan	I take care of my turkeys.
netlacuitlahuiliztli	care of things or animals
nimitzcahualtia in tlahuanaliztli	I make you stop drinking.
tetlacahualtiliztli	action of making someone stop something; prohibition, hindrance
ticcuilia in notex in itlaol	You take my brother-in-law's maize from him.
tetlacuililiztli	action of taking something from someone, robbery

In these last two examples it is seen that nouns in -*liz* do not have to be derived directly from the basic form of the verb but according to need can include the causative, the applicative, or any derivational suffix, all of which continue to have their normal function in the noun just as in the finite verbs.

C2. *Patientive nouns.* There are also deverbal nouns of a more passive nature, often called patientive. They mean not the action of the verb but the result of the action, that which has been acted upon. They are less fluid than the nouns in -*liz*, and we stand a better chance of finding them in the dictionary. In the most common construction, -*l* is added to the root of the verb; the new noun, with a root in *l*, will have a singular absolutive in -*li*. Most of these nouns derive from transitive verbs and bear *tla-*.

nitlaqua	I eat.
tlaqualiztli	eating
tlaqualli	that which is eaten, food
niccohua in tlalli	I buy the land.
tlacohualiztli	buying
tlacohualli	something bought, purchase

Nouns in -*l* derived from verbs in -*ia* and -*oa* lose the final vowel of the verb.

nictlatia in tomin	I hide the money.
tlatlatilli	something hidden
nicpoloa nollave	I lose my key.
tlapololli	something lost, destroyed, etc.
niquicuiloa in amatl	I write the letter.
tlacuilolli	something written (or painted)

This set of nouns resembles the passive in more than meaning. The most common suffix forming the passive of verbs, as we will learn later, is *lo*, which shares the *l* of these nouns. Often one can arrive at the noun stem by removing the *o* from the passive, as in *tlaqualo*, it is eaten, and *tlaqual-li*, food. But don't count on it, and after all, we as readers and researchers are not called upon for serious composition. Seeing the parallel can help, though.

Another set of nouns with the same sense is created by using a form of the verbal root looking much like the preterit stem. These words are harder to recognize for what they are, but they do bear the same *tla* at the beginning. Since the stems nearly all end in a consonant other than *l*, this set has the absolutive ending -*tli*. Sometimes there are variants in both -*l-li* and -*tli*.

tiquitlani justicia	We request justice.
tlaitlantli	something requested
nicchihua	I make it.
tlachihualli	something made, creature, product
tlachiuhtli	the same
nicnamaca in calli	I sell the house.
tlanamactli	something sold

In the last example here we see that the noun stem is not always identical to the preterit of the verb: the preterit of *namaca* is *namaca-c.*

D. *A small illustrative text.*

tehuatl amo qualli moyollo amo yectli monemiliz amo titepalehuia atle tictemaca amo titeicnelia aic titetlaqualtia ayac ticniuh çan titeyaouh titeichtequilia titetlacuilia titeiztlacahuia titexiccahua titetlatlacalhuia atle motetlaçotlaliz amo qualli motlachihualiz amo no qualli motlachihual motlatol motlacuilol atle ipatiuh

You have a bad disposition and a bad way of life. You don't help people, you give people nothing, you don't befriend people, you never feed people. You have no friends, but only enemies. You rob people and take things from them, you deceive people, you leave people in the lurch, you ruin things for people. You lack charity [or hospitality]. Your actions are bad and their results are bad too. Your speech and your writings are without value.

From here on a detailed, complete analysis of the texts will no longer be given, but only a translation, with some comment at times. Nevertheless, the student needs to repeat the whole process as before, but independently, using the glossary, knowledge already gained, and reference back to the lessons. Mark off all the constituent elements of each word, identify the affixes and the root, establish the part of speech, and then make your own overall translation of the text, at first literal, following the Nahuatl words and word order, then more pragmatic and fluid, as in the translation above.

Note some expressions in the text here. *Amo qualli moyollo*, "not it-good-thing it-your-heart," "your general disposition is bad," "you have a bad disposition." *Ayac ticniuh (t-i-cniuh)*, "no one you-his/her-friend, "you are the friend of no one," equivalent to "you have no friends." *Çan titeyaouh. Çan*, "only, just," often acts like a conjunction with the sense of "but." *Atle motetlaçotlaliz.* "Nothing it-your-love," "your love is nothing," "you lack love." The noun derived from the verb "to love" can mean love, esteem, charity, hospitality, or good treatment. Many of the phrases in the text with *te* as object could be translated in a less literal way. *Titeiztlacahuia*, "you deceive people," could be "you are a cheat," etc.

As with the other lessons, turn the examples into exercises by covering their translations, then analyzing and retranslating them.

6. Some Other Verb Tenses
The preterit. The future. Examples.

A. *The preterit.* The preterit or past of Nahuatl verbs constitutes a very complex topic. As to sense, it combines the functions of the simple past and the present perfect in English, i.e., it means either "I did it" or "I have done it." Morphologically it is a nightmare. A sign of the preterit, the particle *o*, exists, but in the sixteenth and seventeenth centuries it was optional. The tense is defined basically by suffixes and modifications of the root, and in these respects verbs fall into four classes; within the second there are many subvariants caused by phonology and orthography. The variations are such that even the great grammarian Horacio Carochi never managed to classify them adequately.

A1. *A historical view of the preterit.* Perhaps a bit of historical linguistics can aid in comprehension. In very remote times, the preterit was formed by adding a suffix *-ca* to the verb without any other change; the plural was the same *-ca* plus a final glottal stop (or some other sound that later weakened to a glottal stop). This *-ca*, as we will see in a later chapter, still surfaces when words of verbal origin are compounded with other elements. But any element in Nahuatl that comes at the end of a word undergoes processes of reduction over time. An *a* becomes *e*, then *i*, then disappears. Consonants and whole suffixes can disappear. It is a process much like erosion. Since Nahuatl has so many affixes, it is always trying to get rid of all those not absolutely necessary for the meaning.

This suffix *-ca* had different fates according to the context. In the plural, it was protected up to a point by the fact that a glottal stop followed it. For that reason it got only as far as the first step of weakening, reaching our times in the form *-que(h)*. In the plural the preterit is somewhat uniform; all four classes have the same plural suffix *-que*, which is easy to recognize as preterit and also as plural (in contrast to the present tense, where there is no distinction between singular and plural in the written form).

In the singular, without the protection of the final glottal stop, *-ca* weakened to *-que* and then *-qui*. We still have *-qui* as a suffix with some preterit agentive nouns, but it disappeared in finite verbs (with some exceptions on the periphery). Around the same time, the majority of verbs began to lose their final vowel in the preterit. Once this had happened, the modification of the root was sufficient as a sign of the preterit, and *-qui* was no longer necessary; *-que*, however, was preserved because it marked plurality. The great complexity of the preterit as we know it results primarily from the fact that not all verbal roots could be reduced in the same way. Monosyllabic verbs, those with two consonants before the last vowel, and those with a final long vowel could not lose the final vowel. There were also by this time verbs with two final vowels and some with an *a* that had originated in two *a*'s. By the sixteenth and seventeenth centuries (and in many kinds of Nahuatl until today) the result was four classes of verbs.

The first, continuing the original procedure, lost nothing in the preterit. Since the stem was identical in present and preterit, it kept a vestige of the preterit suffix in the singular, now reduced from *-qui* to *-c* (that being possible because of the immediately preceding vowel of the verb stem). The second class, the most basic of the age, lost its final vowel in the preterit, as well as the preterit singular suffix. Essentially the second class represents the overall tendency, while all the rest are exceptions of some sort. The verbs of the third class, in two vowels (*ia* and *oa*), acted in many respects like those of the second class. They lost both the final vowel and the preterit singular suffix. But their preterit stem adds a final glottal stop. My way of seeing this phenomenon is to think that the glottal stop is the vestige of a consonant existing earlier in the root (the present) between the two vowels (two consecutive vowels are very exceptional in Nahuatl). If that is so, the third class is only a variant of the second. The third class includes a vast number of verbs, but the fourth is very small. It too has the added glottal stop in the preterit. The verbs of the third class end in *ia* and *oa*, earlier *i?a* and *o?a*. Those of the fourth class, in *a*, must have ended in *a?a*; when the sound in the middle was lost, the two *a*'s condensed into one. The result of the whole process can be summarized as follows:

1		2		3		4	
aci (ahci), to arrive		*yoli*, to live		*choloa*, to flee		*qua*, to eat	
naci	taci	niyoli	tiyoli	nicholoa	ticholoa	nitlaqua	titlaqua
I arrive	we arrive	I live	we live	I flee	we flee	I eat	we eat
nacic	tacique	niyol	tiyolque	nicholo(h)	ticholoque	nitlaqua(h)	titlaquaque
I arrived, have arrived	we arrived, have arrived	I lived, have lived	we lived, have lived	I fled, have fled	we fled, have fled	I ate, have eaten	we ate, have eaten

The preterits can equally well run as follows:

onacic   otacique   oniyol   otiyolque   onicholo   oticholoque   onitlaqua   otitlaquaque

Note that in the Class 1 preterit the *-c* is not part of the stem. The plural is not *acicque*, but *acique*. *-Que* is simply the plural of the same element that gave rise to *-c*; the consonant of the two suffixes is identical not only in sound but in origin and so does not repeat.

A2.1. *Class 1*. Let us consider in more detail the kind of roots that we find in the first, residual class of verbs which for various reasons cannot be reduced. First, monosyllabic roots:

cui, to take[1]	*quicui*	he/she takes it	*oquicuic*	he/she took it
i, to drink[2]	*qui*	he/she drinks it	*oquic*	he/she drank it

Second, roots with two consonants before the final vowel (like our example *aci*, with the combination of glottal stop and *c*), because a Nahuatl word cannot end in two consonants:

nelti, to be realized	*nelti*	it is realized	*oneltic*	it was realized
itta, to see	*anquitta*	you (pl.) see it	*oanquittaque*	you (pl.) saw it

Third, roots with a long final *o*; we will not see vowel quantity in written texts, but it appears that all final *o* in verbs is long. This type includes all the passives in *-lo* and *-o*.[3]

temo, to descend	*temo*	he/she descends	*otemoc*	he/she descended
chihualo, to be made	*chihualo*	it is made	*ochihualoc*	it was made

Fourth, roots in *-tla*. In Nahuatl, *tl* never ends a syllable except at the end of a word. A verb in *-tla* belonging to Class 2 would end in *-tlque* in the plural, which is impossible.[4]

motla, to throw stones	*nitlamotla*	I throw stones	*onitlamotlac*	I threw stones
tlaçotla, to love	*nictlaçotla*	I love him/her	*onictlaçotlac*	I loved him/her

Fifth, some verbs which phonologically can belong to Class 2 have split in two and have an intransitive variant in Class 1, a transitive variant in Class 2.

---

[1]The *u* of *cui* is not a vowel but part of the complex consonant *cu* [k^w].

[2]It is true that generally the directional *on* is added to give bulk to the word, but not always, and in any case it does not change the essence of the matter.

[3]The vowel of the verb *i* just above is also long, and there is some evidence that *i* of *cui* had historically been long too. The verbs of Class 4 have final long *a*, but I say that they formed the preterit as we know it before the loss of a medial consonant, at which time the final *a* was not long.

[4]Michel Launey first brought me to the full realization of this fact.

ehua, to depart	*tehua*	you depart	*otehuac*	you departed
ehua, to raise	*timehua*	you get up	*otimeuh*	you got up

Sixth, there is a suffix of impersonal verbs, *-hua*, which does not reduce; perhaps it is considered an independent monosyllabic element.

axihua (from *aci*)	arrival takes place	*axihuac*	arrival took place
nemoa (from *nemi*)[5]	living goes on	*nemoac*	living went on

Seventh, all verbs in *-ca* belong to Class 1. The reason is not understood.

maca, to give	*ticmaca*	you give it to him/her	*oticmacac*	you gave it to him/her
paca, to wash	*nicpaca*	I wash it	*onicpacac*	I washed it

A2.2 *Class 2.* The greatest problem that Class 2 presents to the reader of texts is how to reconstruct the present, the dictionary form, starting from preterit forms which are truncated and transformed in various ways. The mere fact that a finite verb shows a stem ending in a consonant tends to suggest that one is dealing with the preterit of a Class 2 verb, to which one should add a vowel to get to the form in the dictionary. In the simplest cases, the operation is completed by adding the vowel, which will be *a* (more likely with transitives) or *i* (more likely with intransitives).

canque	remove *c-* object and *-que* plural, add *a* to *an*:	*ana*, to take: they took it
oyol	remove *o-*, sign of the preterit, add *i*:	*yoli*, to live: he/she lived

Class 2 preterit stems undergo some changes which are merely orthographic and entirely predictable but which do not for that reason cause students any less trouble. In the orthography of Molina and Carochi, there are three ways to write the sound [s]: before *a* and *o* (back vowels), *ç*; before *i* and *e* (front vowels), *c*; at the end of a syllable, *z*. The reader, seeing a *z* at the end of a stem, needs to reconstruct *ç* if the final vowel of the present is going to be *a*, *c* if it is going to be *i*. The sound [k] is written *qu* before *i* and *e*, and in other contexts *c*. A *c* at the end of a preterit stem will change into *qu* when you reconstruct a final *i* to get the dictionary form (there is no need to think of a final *a* here because all verbs in *-ca* belong to Class 1).

quitlazque	we reconstruct	*tlaça*	they hurled it
otinez	we reconstruct	*neci*	you appeared
yalhua omic	we reconstruct	*miqui*	he/she died yesterday

As these examples show, it is easy to distinguish between "he/she" and "they," and between "you" and "us" as subjects in the preterit because of the plural suffix. With stems ending in *c*, like *mic*, it is important to avoid the analysis *mi-c*; that is, a *c* like this one belongs to the stem and is not the *-c* preterit suffix seen in Class 1. For that reason the *c* is retained in the plural: *micque*, they died.

Some changes could be imagined as purely orthographic but nevertheless have a phonological aspect. In Nahuatl any voiced consonant becomes unvoiced at the end of a syllable. The inventors of Nahuatl orthography tried to suggest this process in the case of [w], writing *hu-* before a vowel and *-uh* before a consonant or at the end of a word. It is harder to recognize what is happening when *y* before a vowel is replaced by *x* at the end of a syllable, but the Nahuatl *x* [š] is indeed the approximate equivalent of an unvoiced *y* [y].

ye huecauh oticchiuhque	we reconstruct	*chihua*	We did it long ago.
oquimpix nototolhuan	we reconstruct	*pia*	He/she took care of my turkeys.

The two important verbs *pia*, "to keep, hold, have," and *chia*, "to await," are often written

---

[5]Despite the Carochi-derived orthography, *nemoa* contains *-hua* and could be written *nemohua*.

without a *y*, but basically they are *piya* and *chiya*. The traditional orthography of grammars and dictionaries (but not that of mundane texts) generally omits *y* between *i* and *a*.

Another change, in line with the general weakening of final consonants, is that *m* before a vowel becomes *n* at the end of a syllable, i.e., *m* [m] delabializes.

nican annenque	we reconstruct	*nemi*	you (pl.) lived here
yalhua otlan	we reconstruct	*tlami*	it ended yesterday

A final *n* in a preterit stem can be derived from either *m* or *n*. We already saw *canque*, "they took it," from *ana*. *Anque* is "they hunted," from *ami*.

The common verb *mati*, to know, belongs to Class 2, but has the peculiarity that in the preterit singular the final *t* is weakened to a glottal stop and thus disappears from the written form (*t* at the end of a word hardly occurs in Nahuatl). In the preterit plural the *t* is protected by a following suffix and survives.

onicma	I found out about it	*oticmatque* we found out about it

The verb *ma*, to catch, to take captive, belonging to Class 4, has the same form as *mati* (including the unwritten glottal stop) in the preterit singular, but not in the plural.

michin onicma I caught a fish	*michin oticmaque* we caught a fish	

A2.3. *Class 3.* In this class the verbs end in two vowels, either *ia* or *oa*, and the manner of forming the preterit is uniform. The final *a* is lost, and the glottal stop at the end of the preterit stem is not written. To reconstruct the dictionary form all we have to do is replace the final *a*. The apparent final vowel of the preterit stem makes for a similarity, in the written form, to Class 1, but verbs of Class 3 lack the -*c* in the preterit singular. Only in the plural is there room for confusion, since there both types seem to end in a vowel plus -*que*.

oquitlali	we reconstruct	*tlalia*	he/she put it down, issued it, ordered it
tictlalique	the same		we put it down, etc.
onicpolo	we reconstruct	*poloa*	I lost it, spent it, destroyed it
oanquipoloque	the same		you (pl.) lost it, etc.

It is good to remember that any verb in the applicative or causative, whether in the basic sense or as part of the reverential apparatus, behaves as if it belongs to Class 3.

ticnemitique	causative of *nemi*, Class 2	we maintained him/her/it
quicuilique	applicative of *cui*, Class 1	they took it from him/her
mochololti	rev. of *choloa*, Class 3	he/she fled
motlaqualtique	rev. of *qua*, Class 4	they ate
oanquimopialique	rev. of *pia*, Class 2	you (pl.) had it, kept it

A2.4. *Class 4.* This class also has an invisible glottal stop at the end of the preterit stem. In the rest it appears not to change, since it has no second vowel to remove. There is some danger of confusion between the present and the preterit singular. The class is very small. Aside from *qua*, "to eat," one frequently sees *ma*, "to catch," and *ihua*, "to send."

quiqua	he/she eats it	*otiquihuaque*	we sent it, have sent it
oquiqua, quiqua	he/she ate it	*otiquimma*	you took them captive
quiquaque	they ate it		

A3. *O and* ye *with the preterit.* The *o* which often accompanies the preterit and helps to mark it is a separate particle of antecessive time, perhaps with the original meaning of "already." It may be present or absent. Even when it is there, it does not affect the verbal complex properly speaking. We saw before that *qui* as a third person object prefix appears only when there is no vowel on either side of it, for when there is an adjacent vowel, the form *c* is used, as in *quicui*, "he/she takes it," and *niccui*, "I take it." But in the preterit we find *oquicuic*, "he/she took it," not *occuic*, so that a boundary exists between *o* and the verb. You will even see words, especially particles, intervening between *o* and the verb, as in the following example:

o huel quitlaçotlac in icihuauh	He really loved his wife.

In texts of the sixteenth and early seventeenth centuries, *o* is optional with the preterit. After having seen many examples, it seems to me that the version without *o* tends to be the simple past, and the version with *o* a perfect:

quimicti in iyaouh	He killed his enemy.
oquimicti in iyaouh	He has killed his enemy.

Nevertheless, no certainty has been attained in this matter, and translations should follow the context. Usage seems to have varied from speaker to speaker, region to region, and above all over time. *O* became ever less optional; in texts of the eighteenth century you will hardly find a preterit without *o*.

Somewhat similar to *o*, although it belongs even less to the verbal complex, is the particle *ye*, "already." Often it need not be translated; it simply reinforces the sense that something occurred in the past.

ye oquiz in tonatiuh	The sun has (already) risen.

With some expressions, *ye* and *oc*, "still," represent a complementary pair, *ye* for the past and *oc* for the future (which we will now proceed to study). *Oc* and *ye* will be treated more fully in a later lesson.

ye huecauh omochiuh	It happened a long time ago.
oc huecauh miquiz	He/she will die a long time in the future.
ye huiptla hualacic	He/she got here the day before yesterday.
(oc) huiptla hualaciz	He/she will get here the day after tomorrow.

B. *The future.* Future forms are much less complex than those of the preterit in Nahuatl, and though the future is a standard tense likely to appear in most documents of all kinds, the preterit is far more heavily used. The two tenses share some morphemes and have a somewhat similar history. Thus the future appears here almost as a footnote to the treatment of the preterit.

B1. *Future forms.* Compared to the preterit, the future is morphologically very uniform and simple. To start again with the historical evolution, it appears that at some time the future was formed by adding *z* to the root of the verb, which did not change, plus the same *-ca* that we saw in the ancient preterit. Thus *-ca* perhaps meant non-present time more than past time specifically. The singular of the future was *-zca*, the plural something like *-zca(h)*. As with the preterit, singular *-ca* weakened, first to *-que* and then to *-qui*, to disappear totally later, with the exception of some vestiges on the periphery of the Nahuatl speech area.[1] *-Ca(h)* plural became *-que(h)*, as with the preterit. The result of this process is that for the majority of verbs the future is formed using the unchanged present tense root as the stem, with the addition of *-z* in the singular and *-zque* in the plural.

aci	he/she arrives	*aciz*	he/she will arrive	*acizque*	they will arrive
yoli	he/she lives	*yoliz*	he/she will live	*yolizque*	they will live

---

[1] In the Tlaxcalan region a monosyllabic future often bore *-qui*, thus *yezqui*, "it will be." The same happened in the preterit: *oyaqui*, "he/she went, left."

Verbs of Class 3, as so often, lose the final vowel.

choloz	we reconstruct *choloa*	he/she will flee
quitlalizque	we reconstruct *tlalia*	they will put it down

The greatest difficulty that students have with identifying the future is that they tend to confuse it with the preterit. In the plural, the only difference between the future and the preterit with some verbs is a *z* hidden inside the word, and we get so used to *-que* as going with the preterit that we fail to realize that the form in question is in the future.

quimacaque	they gave it to him/her	*quimacazque*	they will give it to him/her
choloque	they fled	*cholozque*	they will flee
tlaquaque	they ate	*tlaquazque*	they will eat

With verbs of Class 2 the difference is more visible because of the modification of the root in the preterit.

ticpouhque	we read it, we counted it	*ticpohuazque*	we will read it, etc.
nenque	they lived	*nemizque*	they will live

Another frequent error is to think that the *z* of the preterit stem of a verb of Class 2 is the *-z* suffix of the future.

tlalpan quitlaz	He hurled it to the ground (i.e., this is the preterit stem of the verb *tlaça* and not a future).

B2. *Uses of the future.* If the morphology of the future tense turns out to be relatively simple, some difficulties lie in the fact that the future is used differently in Nahuatl than in English. The simple future as we know it does exist, of course.

iciuhca huallaz	He/she will come soon.

The future can represent an instruction or a very strong command, which also happens in English, although less frequently.

neltiz notlatol mochihuaz	My statement will be realized and carried out, or better, my statement is to be realized and carried out.

In Nahuatl the future is used in a dependent clause in which the action is to take place after the time of the main clause, regardless of the absolute time. In English we often use an infinitive or a "would" or "should" clause when the main verb is not in the present.

otlanahuati inic quipalehuizque	He ordered them to help him, that they should help him (lit. he gave orders how they will help him).
ma quimatican in ixquichtin in quittazque inin amatl	know all who should see this document (lit. who will see this document)

Nahuatl verbs lack an infinitive in the European style. The future makes up for it to a certain extent (consider in this context the *z* of *-liz*, the nominalizing suffix). In the first example immediately above, the future is used with *inic*, "how, that, in order that," in a way we often translate with the infinitive. Also with the verb *nequi*, to want, Nahuatl's main modal verb, the future functions in a fashion somewhat similar to the infinitive in English, although it continues to be a finite construction with its prefixes. The clause in the future acts as the object of *nequi*.

nicnequi niquittaz	I want to see it (lit. I-want-it I-will-see-it).
nicnequi ixquich ticmatizque	I want us to know it all (lit. I-want-it all we-will-know-it).

If the subject of both verbs is the same, the second clause can be incorporated within the first.

niquittaznequi	I want to see it.
cuix ticchihuaznequi	Do you want to do it?
ticochiznequi	We want to sleep.

This same construction with *nequi* can have the sense that the action is imminent:

| ye nimiquiznequi | I am about to die (lit. already I want to die). |
| xiniznequi in calli | The house is about to collapse (lit. wants to). |

C. *Examples.* Here are some examples of preterit and future verbs in sentences. In the first line, the particle *cuix* is literally "perhaps," but it is generally not translated as a separate word. It introduces a question to which the answer is yes or no. In the same example, the introductory particle *ca*, which we have seen before, has many uses. One of them is to introduce answers to questions. In the sixth example, *aço*, like *cuix*, is more or less "perhaps." When it introduces dependent clauses, it often translates as "whether" or "if."

cuix ye onacique ca amo yece iciuhca onacizque	Did they already get there? No, but they will get there soon.
aquin quinnemitiz nochcahuan	Who will maintain my sheep?
ticchihuaz in tlein nimitzilhuiz	You are to do what I (will) tell you.
ye huecauh oyolque ye huecauh onenque tocolhuan tachtonhuan	Our ancestors lived a long time ago.[1]
otiquittaque in tlein quichiuh	We saw what he/she did.
cuix oticma aço choloque	Did you find out whether they ran away?
amo nezque in tocihuahuan	Our wives didn't show up.
miec tomin quipolozque	They will spend a lot of money.
miec tomin quipoloque	They spent a lot of money.
cuix ticmonequiltia toconiz in atzintli	Do you wish to drink the beverage (pulque)?
cuix toconiznequi in atzintli	the same
aquin quichihuaznequi	Who wants to do it?
yalhua oquimonnamic in tlatoque	Yesterday he went to meet the rulers.
oquinhualpouh in imacehualhuan	He came to count his vassals.
in cuicani oquiyocox oquipic in icuic	The singer made up and invented his song.
tiquimmacaque taxca totlatqui iciuhca quicelique	We gave them our property; they quickly accepted it.
quimmomaquiliz quimonmocahuililiz in tlein oquimitlanilique	He/she is to give and leave them what they requested.
oquimacac in iconetzin ixquich in ical	She gave her child all her houses.

Cover the translations; analyze the sentences fully and retranslate. Reconstruct the dictionary form of all the verbs.

---

[1]More literally, "A long time ago lived (were quick), a long time ago lived (moved about) our grandfathers, our great-grandfathers."

7. Yet More on Verbs

Auxiliary verbs. The optative. Examples. An illustrative text.

A. *Auxiliary verbs.* Nahuatl has a very common construction in which the main verb is accompanied by an auxiliary verb adding a dimension or aspect to the statement. It may refer to the physical position of the subject of the main verb (standing, lying, spread out) or to the conditions under which the action takes place (on leaving, on arriving, in passing), or it can have an adverbial function (rapidly). But most frequently, even when it belongs to one of the types just mentioned, it acts as a progressive.

The main verb bears its normal prefixes and has its normal meaning, but it appears in a form identical to the preterit, i.e., it uses the preterit stem (with Class 1 omitting, of course, its suffix *-c*). After the main verb stem comes a ligature *-t(i)-* and at the end the auxiliary verb, which bears the suffixes indicating tense and number. The most frequent of the auxiliaries is *ca* (*cah*), "to be" in a stative sense, like Spanish *estar*. To say "I am awaiting him," the subject and object prefixes are the same as usual; the Class 2 verb *chia*, "to await," assumes the form of its preterit stem, *chix*; then comes the ligature *-ti-*, and finally the verb *ca*: *nicchixtica*. With a main verb from Class 1, "I am descending" would be *ni-*, "I," the preterit stem *temo* (which will be identical to the present tense or root), without its *-c*, and again *-ti-ca*: *nitemotica*. With a verb of Class 3, "I am running away" would be *ni-*, the preterit stem *cholo* from the verb *choloa*, and *-ti-ca*: *nicholotica*.

The key to identifying the construction is the ligature *-t(i)-*. You will get used to the rhythm of main verb, *-ti-*, and then a short verb as the basic characteristic of constructions of this type. It is also important to recognize that we are not dealing with a normal preterit: *ticchix* or *oticchix*, "you awaited her"; *ticchixtica*, "you are awaiting her."

The progressive *-tica* presents the additional difficulty that in the written form it is identical to instrumental *-tica*, that is, the relational word *-ca*, by means of, also with a *-ti-* ligature.

nechtolinitica	he/she is afflicting me, bothering me
tetoliniliztica	with affliction (from *tetoliniliztli*)
tlaquatica	he/she is eating
tlaqualtica	with food (from *tlaqualli*)

The basic thing to remember is that progressive *-tica* is always affixed to a verb, instrumental *-tica* always to a noun.

Many of the auxiliary verbs are irregular. Several have a present tense that is historically a preterit: thus *ca(h)*, "to be," with its plural *cate* (earlier they were *catqui* and *catque*). The preterit form having taken over the present tense, the preterit/imperfect form of the verb is also different: *catca*, "was," which is historically a pluperfect. Moreover, the verb uses a different root in many tenses: *ye*. The future is *yez*, "it will be." (If all this strikes you as strange, think of the verb "to be" in English, with forms as different as "is," "am," "was," and "be.")

quichixtica	he/she is awaiting him/her
quichixticatca	he/she was awaiting him/her
quichixtiyez (or- *tiez*)	he/she will be awaiting him/her

These constructions are less common in the future, but they do occur. We see here an orthographic difficulty. Since in any language and most especially in Nahuatl a [y] between [i] and a following [a] or [e] is not easily heard, the old masters such as Carochi and Molina did not usually write *y* between *i* and *a* or *e* (also often *o*), and we sometimes have to reconstruct it to recognize roots and tenses.

Other auxiliary verbs with preterit form and present meaning are *icac* (*ihcac*), "to be standing," and *onoc*, "to be lying, to be in a horizontal position." Their pasts are *icaca* or *icaya* and *onoca* or *onoya*; their futures are *icaz* and *onoz*.[1] The root of *onoc* is *o*; the *on* directional prefix has been added purely to keep the word from being so short. Since the compound form is longer, *-on-* is not needed there, so that with the ligature *onoc* appears as *-toc*; the *i* of *-ti-* is lost before *o*. An *i* is lost with *icac* as well, making *-ticac*. Students often get this form mixed up with the more general progressive *-tica*.

huetzcaticac	He/she is standing laughing.	*ticochtoc*	You are lying sleeping (i.e., you are sleeping).
huetzcaticaca,		*ticochtoca,*	
huetzcaticaya	He/she was standing laughing.	*ticochtoya*	You were lying sleeping.
huetzcaticaz	He/she will be standing laughing.	*ticochtoz*	You will lie sleeping.

With *icac*, a very irregular but quite common form is *itzticac*, "he/she is standing looking" (often translated only as "is looking"). It is derived from the verb *itta*, "to see," which in some combined forms has a root *itz-* (intransitive, though *itta* is transitive) with the meaning "to look."

Huitz, "to come," is also preterit in origin (it has a plural *huitze*, earlier *huitzque*), and moreover it is defective; the future tense is missing.

ticmamatihuitz	You are coming bearing it.
ticmamatihuitza	You came bearing it.

Also highly irregular, though not preterit in form, is *yauh*, "to go." Its preterit is *ya* (*yah*) and its future *yaz*. It has two roots, *ya* and *hui*; in some tenses one root appears, in others the other. (The present singular has both, but the present plural has *hui* only, at least in standard central area Nahuatl.) The form of *yauh* acting as auxiliary verb is *-tiuh*, which consists of the ligature *-ti-* and *-uh* (*hui* with loss of the final vowel). The most common meaning is to go along doing something, either literally or doing something bit by bit, but it can also have the sense of doing something upon leaving, which in testaments often is equivalent to doing something on dying.

titlaxtlauhtiuh	You are going along paying.
titlaxtlauhtia (*-tiya*)	You went along paying.
titlaxtlauhtiaz (*-tiyaz*)	You will go along paying.
oquimacatia in ipiltzin	He gave it to his child at death, or he left it to him.

Note that *-tia*, the preterit of *yauh* as an auxiliary verb, often is identical, in the written form, to the *-tia* causative suffix. This fact causes grief to students who have painfully learned to interpret all final *-tia* as causative. Generally, however, the stems of the two constructions will be different. Take *cahua*, to leave:

ticcahualtia	You make him leave it, stop it.
ticcauhtia	You went away leaving it, left it upon going.

Above we saw the irregular stem *itz-* from *itta*, "to see." *Yauh* as an auxiliary also occurs in a quite common form with *itz-*. *Itztiuh* means to go looking toward, i.e., to head toward, go toward. *Azcapotzalco nitztiuh* (or *nonitztiuh*), "I am headed for Azcapotzalco, I am on my way there."

Mani, for something to be spread out over a flat surface, is almost a regular Class 2 verb. The forms for the auxiliary verb are *-timani* present, *-timaniz* future, and sometimes *-timan* past, but much more often *-timanca* (pluperfect as preterit, as with several other irregular verbs). Its most frequent use is with meteorological phenomena.

---

[1] *Icaca* and *onoca* are formally pluperfects; *icaya* and *onoya* are imperfects from the old true present tenses *ica* and *ono*. There is little distinction of meaning between the two past formations. The futures are also based on the old presents. (See p. 63 for imperfect and pluperfect in general.)

There is an irregular (though not unparalleled) form with the verb *mana*, the transitive equivalent: *-timomana* with an unchanging reflexive prefix *mo* (in the other cases the auxiliary verbs do not bear their own prefixes). The sense is that a meteorological or general phenomenon presents itself, shapes up.

quiyauhtimani	It is raining.
quiyauhtimanca	It was raining.
tlahuactimomana	It gets dry, a drought comes.
tlahuactimoman	A drought came.

Nemi, "to live," like *mani*, often has the pluperfect instead of the preterit. It makes *-tinemi*, *-tinen* or *-tinenca*, and *-tinemiz*. The sense of the auxiliary verb is to go about doing something, to be involved in, engaged in something. If we ask how a verb "to live" can come to have such a meaning, the answer is that it originally meant "to go about, move"; the reduplicated form *nenemi* still has that sense.

quichiuhtinemi	He/she goes about doing it.
quichiuhtinenca	He/she went about doing it.

Ehua, "to depart," has the forms *-tehua*, *-tehuac*, and *-tehuaz*, a regular Class 1 pattern. The sense is to do something upon leaving or dying.

oquimacatehuac in itatzin in itlal	Her father gave her his land at death, left her his land.
niquitotehua	I say it on leaving, I leave it said.

Huetzi, "to fall," has the forms *-tihuetzi*, *-tihuetz*, and *-tihuetziz*, regular for Class 2. It is often mixed up with *-tihuitz*, the auxiliary "to come." The sense is to do something very rapidly. The train of thought seems parallel to that involved in our word "precipitous."

anquicuitihuetzi	You (pl.) quickly take it.
oanquicuitihuetzque	You (pl.) quickly took it.
anquicuitihuetzizque	You (pl.) will quickly take it.

As an independent verb, *quiça* (regular Class 2) has many senses: to emerge or come out, be born, end, and others. The most relevant sense here is to pass; as a helping verb it has the meaning of doing something in passing or quickly. It has the forms *-tiquiça*, *-tiquiz*, and *-tiquiçaz*.

tinechnamictiquiça	You meet me in passing.
otinechnamictiquiz	You met me in passing.
tinechnamictiquiçaz	You will meet me in passing.

You will remember that above we saw another kind of complex verbal construction, with *nequi*, "to want." To say "to want to do something" two clauses are constructed, the second in the future, acting as the object of *nequi*; the second can be incorporated in the first clause if there is no change of subject.

nicnequi niccahuaz	
niccahuaznequi	I want to leave it.

As you see, the ligature *-ti-* which appears in all these forms we have been talking about, and which is their clearest symptom, is lacking in the *nequi* quasi-infinitive construction.

Nequi is also almost an auxiliary verb in the reflexive form *monequi*, always in third person singular, with the sense "it is necessary." It also usually requires that the second clause be in the future, but not always.

monequi tiyazque	It is necessary that we go, we must go.
monequi mochihua	It needs to be done.

To say "I need something," the relational word -*tech* is used, i.e., "it is necessary to me."

> *notech monequi tomin*   I need money.

B. *The optative.* In English we have a not very well defined optative, or form for expressing wishes and veiled commands, "may they do it," or "let them do it," and a very well defined imperative, "do it!" In Nahuatl the two are combined, the second person of the optative being the imperative. The sign of the optative is the particle *ma*, placed before the verb; it appears where in English we would expect "may" or "let" (though the origin and grammatical function of the Nahuatl element bears no resemblance to those of the ones in English). In the majority of cases, the singular of the optative is identical to the present indicative; the plural adds the suffix -*can*. The most unusual thing about the paradigm is that in the second person the subject prefixes, *ti*- and *am*-, are replaced by the specifically imperative element *x(i)*-.

ma nicchihua	may I do it	*ma ticchihuacan*	may we do it
(*ma*) *xicchihua*	do it! (to one person)	(*ma*) *xicchihuacan*	do it! (to more than one)
ma quichihua	may he/she do it	*ma quichihuacan*	may they do it

Only in Class 3 is the stem distinct from the root. The final *a* is lost, as we have seen happens in most tenses other than the present.

ma nicholo	may I flee	*ma ticholocan*	may we flee
(*ma*) *xicholo*	flee!	(*ma*) *xicholocan*	flee!
ma cholo	may he/she flee	*ma cholocan*	may they flee

In the second person *xi* is enough to identify the form, so that *ma* can be omitted. *Ma* adds a modicum of courtesy, while the highest degree of politeness is expressed by replacing *ma* with another particle, *tla* ("if").

An optative future exists but will not be closely discussed here. It is fairly common in texts, but it differs from the indicative future only in having *ma* placed in front of the verb. Nor does a translation of the optative future usually come out any different from one of the optative present.

The optative can, of course, be used to make negative suggestions. Since nearly all the negative words in Nahuatl begin with *a* (*ah* is the basic negative particle), such as *amo*, not; *atle*, nothing; *ayac*, no one; *aic*, never; *acan*, nowhere, adding these to *ma* would result in a sequence of two *a*'s, which would represent an inconvenience in pronunciation. Hence in these cases a -*c*- appears almost as punctuation between *ma* and the following word, as in *macayac*, from *ma* and *ayac*, no one: "let no one." This *c* may be from a particle *ca* which is possibly negative itself. In the extremely common form *macamo*, "let not," the *a* does not bear the usual glottal stop of the negative; apparently the form must be analyzed *ma-ca-mo* (*mo* is a negative in its own right).

Ma can be used with nouns, giving the same optative sense, since any noun is residually an equative statement.

aquin yaz ma Juan	Who will go? Let it be Juan.
ma pilli ma macehualli ca tlaxtlahuaz	He is to pay, whether he be nobleman or commoner.

There is another *ma*, hypothetical, quite different in meaning and function from the optative *ma* (though probably related in origin). Although the hypothetical *ma* has a glottal stop and the optative *ma* a long vowel, they are written the same.

ayac ma aca oncan calaqui	No one, whoever it may be, goes in there.
atle ma itla nicpia	I have nothing, whatever it may be (absolutely nothing).
iuhquin ma nichichiton onechhuitec	He struck me as if I were a little dog.

C. *Some examples.* Note in the second example that the same change of *i* to *o* takes place with *xicon-* as with *nicon-* and *ticon-*, giving *nocon-*, *tocon-*, and *xocon-*, with no change of meaning.

ma xinechpalehui	Help me!
xoconcui in atl	Go fetch the water!
ma ticmacacan in tlalli	Let's give her the land.
macayac quinenpoloz in naxca in notlatqui	Let no one dissipate my property.
ma iciuhca nechhualmohuiquililican in noteponaz	Let them quickly bring me my log drum.
macamo xitechtlalcahuican	Don't abandon us!
tlatoanie tla ximocalaqui in mochan	O ruler, do please enter your home.
ma tlapanco xontlecocan	Climb up to the roof!
macamo nican timiquican	May we not die here.
ma mochihua in motlanequiliz	May your will be done.
macayac quicuiliz in nochpoch in itlal	Let no one take her land from my (grown) daughter.
ma iciuhca nican xaquican	Come in here quickly!
tla xicmocaquili in nocnotlatol	Please hear my humble words (petition).
ma ximotetlaçotilican	Love people! (Be loving!)
ma xicmomachili itla cenca mahuiztic nimitznolhuiliz	You must know something very marvelous that I will tell you.
macamo tiquimilcahuacan in icnotlaca ma tiquimpalehuican	Let us not forget the poor, let us aid them.
ma palehuilo nanimantzin	May my soul be helped.
macaic nechilcahuacan nopilhuan nox-huihuan	May my children and grandchildren never forget me.
macaocac nican hualcalaqui ca ye huel temi in calli	Let no one more come in here, for the house is already very full.
intlacamo[1] *tinechtlaxtlahuiz amo nicchihuaz in otiquitlan*	If you don't pay me I won't do what you asked.
intlacayac huallaz tochachan tiyazque	If no one comes, we will go to our homes.
intlacacan tipactinemi monequi tiquincaquiliz in intlatol in huehuetque in ilamatque	If you are happy nowhere, you need to listen to the words of the old men and women.

D. *An illustrative text.*

amixpantzinco in antlatoque ninoteilhuia in Juan Buenaventura mochipa motlapololti-tinemi tzatzitinemi ahuic motlalotinemi otlica cuicatiuh ixtomahuatiuh quemmanian mopetlauhtihuetzi tepan mitotitiquiça niman in ichan tlahuantoc quipolotica ixquich itlatqui in iquac miquiz atle quimmacatehuaz in ipilhuan ma canacan ma teilpiloyan quitlalican ma quimachtican in qualnemiliztli in nematcanemiliztli ca huel tlahueliloc iuhquin xolopitli nemi

Before you rulers I make a complaint. Juan Buenaventura is always going about out of his senses, shouting, and running this way and that. He goes along the road singing and making silly faces. Sometimes he quickly disrobes and passes by people dancing. Then he lies drinking at his home. He is destroying all his property; when he dies he will leave nothing to his children. Let them arrest him, let them put him in jail. Let them teach him good living, prudent living, for he is very perverse and lives like an idiot.

As usual, cover all the translations; analyze and retranslate the passages.

---

[1]The same "ligature" *-c-* or *-ca-* occurs after *intla*, "if," as after *ma*.

8. Practical Matters

A testament. The numbers.

A. *A testament.* The purpose of these lessons is to lead the student as quickly as possible to the reading and translation of actual texts in older Nahuatl. A great part of the quite large corpus of Nahuatl texts, perhaps as much as seventy-five percent of all that exist, consists of testaments. For that reason it is good to begin, even while a neophyte, to learn something about the formulas and vocabulary of the genre. Nahuatl wills follow the familiar European model but at the same time have their idiosyncrasies, for example repeated oral admonitions that would not be found in a testament in Spanish or English. The best way to learn how testaments are is to read one or two. The example that follows was, as an ensemble, made up, and it avoids the typical orthographical difficulties, but almost all the phrases were taken literally from archival documents.

icatzinco in itocatzin in Dios tetatzin in Dios tepiltzin in Dios Espiritu Santo ma quima-
0. In the name of   God the father,   God the child,   and   God the Holy Spirit,   know

tican in ixquichtin in quittazque inin amatl in quenin nehuatl Apolonia de la Cruz
     all who should see this document   how I,   Apolonia de la Cruz,

nican nochan in ipan altepetl Coatepec notlaxilacal Santa Maria Xaxalpan axcan nic-
whose home is here in the altepetl of Coatepec and my district is Santa María Xaxalpan,

chihua in notestamento in ça tlatzaccan notlanequiliz auh macihui mococoa in nonaca-
today make my testament,   my last will.   Although my body is ill,

yo yece pactica notlacaquiliz notlalnamiquiliz amo ninotlapololtia
nevertheless my understanding and memory are healthy; I have not lost my faculties.

inic centlamantli niquitoa in nanimantzin noconnomaquilia in totecuiyo Dios ca
1. First,   I say   that I give my soul to   God our lord,   for

itlachihualtzin ma quihualmaniliz auh in nonacayo nicmaca in tlalli ca itech .oquiz
it is his creature; may he come take it. But my body I give to the earth, for from it it emerged.

inic ontlamantli niquitoa ce missa nopan mochihuaz inic palehuiloz naniman ome
2. Second, I say that a mass is to be performed for me so that my soul will be helped;

pesos nohuentzin yez neltiz notlatol
two pesos is to be my offering; my statement is to be carried out.

iniquetlamantli niquitoa in nocal in iquiçayampa tonatiuh itzticac nicmacatiuh in
3. Third,   I say that as to my house that looks toward the east,   I am giving it to

nopiltzin itoca Juan auh in oc centetl nocal in icalaquiyampa tonatiuh itzticac nicmaca-
my child named Juan, and as to the other house of mine that looks toward the west, I am

tiuh in nochpochtzin in itoca Catalina in ixquich nocihuatlatqui quimocuiliz in nometl
giving it to my daughter named Catalina; she is to take all of my woman's things, my grinding stones,

in notecon in nocpauh auh in callalli concahuizque imomextin nopilhuan ayac quin-
my cups, and my yarn. And both my children are to share the house-land.   No one

43

cuiliz in tlein oniquinnomaquili
is to take from them what I have given them.

    inic nauhtlamantli niquitoa notlal oncan mani inahuac in otli inic hueyac ompo-
    4. Fourth,   I say that land of mine is close to the road,   forty units long

hualquahuitl inic patlahuac cempohualquahuitl nicnomaquilitiuh in nopiltzin itoca
      and twenty units wide;   I am giving it to my child named

Juan itech pohuiz ayac quicuiliz
Juan. It is to belong to him; no one is to take it away from him.

    inic macuillamantli niquitoa notlal oncan mani itocayocan Atlauhtlan inic hueyac
    5. Fifth,   I say that land of mine is at the place called Atlauhtlan,

cempohualquahuitl ommatlactli inic patlahuac cempohualli nicnocahuililitiuh in
  thirty units long   and twenty wide;   I am leaving it to

nochpoch itoca Catalina ayac quiquixtiliz
my daughter named Catalina; no one is to take it away from her.

    inic chiquacentlamantli niquitoa totlaçomahuiznantzin Santa Maria nicnopialia
    6. Sixth,   I say that I have our precious honored Mother St. Mary;

nicnomaquilitiuh in nopiltzin itoca Juan auh onca ce caltepiton chalcopahuic itzticac
I give her to my child named Juan. And there is a little house that looks toward Chalco;

icaltzin totlaçonantzin oncan quimotequipanilhuiz in onicteneuh nopiltzin intla qui-
it is our precious Mother's house, and my child whom I mentioned is to serve her there, if

mochicahuiliz in Dios
God gives him health.

    inic chicontlamantli niquitoa aoctle itla nicnopialia amo no nitetlahuiquilia auh in
    7. Seventh,   I say that I have nothing else at all, nor do I owe anything to anyone.

nalbaceashuan yezque in ipan motlatoltizque in nanimantzin in quintlamamacazque
As those who will be my executors, who will look after my soul and distribute things to

in nopilhuan niquimixquetza notlatzin itoca Francisco de Santiago ihuan nachtzin
my children, I appoint my uncle named Francisco de Santiago and my older brother

Gaspar de los Reyes ma qualli ic quimochihuilican intequiuh ye ixquich notlatol
Gaspar de los Reyes. May they do their duty well. That is all of my statement.

    imixpan omochiuh in testigos Francisco de Santiago Gaspar de los Reyes cihuatzi-
    8. It was done before the witnesses Francisco de Santiago and Gaspar de los Reyes, and

tzintin Ana Petronila Maria Agustina auh in nehuatl niescribano niquitoa ca qualli
the women Ana Petronilla and María Agustina, and I the notary say that the sick person

melahuac inic oquimochihuili in cocoxcatzintli in itestamento auh inic nelli nican
    made her testament well and correctly.   And to [show that it is] true I set down

nictlalia nofirma notoca axcan ic chicomilhuitl metztli mayo de 1583 años in ipan in
here my signature and name. Today the 7th day of the month of May of the year 1583, in

altepetl tlacpac omito
the altepetl mentioned above.

nixpan omochiuh		Pedro de Paz	escribano de republica
9. It was done before me,		Pedro de Paz,	notary of the commonwealth.

The following comments do not analyze absolutely everything, but concentrate on especially difficult or typical elements:

0. *icatzinco in itocatzin in Dios tetatzin in Dios tepiltzin in Dios Espiritu Santo* — *i-ca-tzin-co*: *ca*, relational word "by means of, etc."; *tzinco* reverential of a relational word; *i-* third person singular possessive prefix, referring to *itocatzin*; although properly speaking it says "through" the name of God, it is generally translated in wills as "in." *itocatzin*: *tocaitl*, name; *-tzin* reverential of a possessed noun; *i-* third person singular possessive prefix referring to *Dios*. The three *in*'s punctuate the series of the three manifestations of God. *tetatzin, tepiltzin*: as we saw in an earlier lesson, *te-* as an indefinite possessive prefix creates something like absolute forms of kinship terms. *tepiltzin* does not specify the gender of the child.

ma quimatican in ixquichtin in quittazque inin amatl — *ma quimatican*: third person optative plural of *mati*, to know. *in ixquichtin*: all (pl.), subject of the preceding verb. *in quittazque*, from *itta*, to see, future plural; with *in* preceding a verb, we suspect that the meaning is relative and know for sure that the clause is dependent. *inin amatl*, this paper, document, or letter.

in quenin nehuatl Apolonia de la Cruz — *in quenin*: how; with *in* preceding, it is dependent, not interrogative. The long clause introduced by *in quenin* is the object of the verb *mati*. According to the general rules of Nahuatl it should be *nehuatl niApolonia de la Cruz*, but very rarely is such a thing seen. It may be understood as *nehuatl (notoca) Apolonia*, "I whose name is Apolonia"; the form with *notoca* frequently occurs.

nican nochan in ipan altepetl Coatepec notlaxilacal Santa Maria Xaxalpan — *i* of *ipan* refers to *altepetl*. The rest proceeds by verbless reciprocal crossreference of nouns. An altepetl is a sovereign sociopolitical unit in Nahua style. Sometimes in English it is called a town, although it implied no urban structure; the Spanish *pueblo* is rather better. But it was such a special and central concept that many recent translations have begun to leave the Nahuatl word as it is.

axcan nicchihua in notestamento in ça tlatzaccan notlanequiliz — *notestamento* and *no-tlanequiliz* are equivalent. *ça tlatzaccan*, a fixed phrase, is derived from *tzaqua*, to close, block off, etc., but it functions more or less adjectivally, "last."

auh macihui mococoa in nonacayo — *auh* sometimes translates as "and," sometimes as "but," and sometimes it is best left untranslated because its effect is conveyed by the period of the previous sentence and the capital letter of the new one; it is an invaluable marker of a new independent clause. *nonacayo* is the subject of the reflexive verb *mococoa*.

yece pactica notlacaquiliz notlalnamiquiliz amo ninotlapololtia — *pactica*; the verb *paqui*, to be happy, with the progressive *-ti-ca*; in this form it often means for something to be healthy, sound, as it should be. *notlacaquiliz*, my understanding, derived from *caqui*, to hear, understand. *notlalnamiquiliz*, my memory, imagination, mind, derived from *ilnamiqui*, to remember, think of something. *amo ninotlapololtia*, a fixed phrase, "I am in control of my faculties," more literally "I am not losing things (rev.)."

1. *inic centlamantli* — The paragraphs or items of a testament are often introduced by the formula of *inic* (which creates ordinal numbers); a number assimilated to what follows; and *tlamantli*, a separate thing or block.

niquitoa in nanimantzin noconnomaquilia in totecuiyo Dios — *niquitoa*: "I say, declare," an almost universal element at the beginning of each bequest of a will. *nanimantzin*, "my soul"; the Spanish word *ánima* developed a final *n* when it became a loanword in Nahuatl, a reflection perhaps of the final glottal stop on all words ending in a vowel that were taken from Spanish.

ca itlachihualtzin ma quihualmaniliz — *ca* is the introductory particle, here "for." *itlachihualtzin*: *tlachihualli*, creature, thing made or produced, possessed by *Dios*. *quihualmaniliz*: *qui-hual-m-ani-liz*, from *ana*, to take.

auh in nonacayo nicmaca in tlalli ca itech oquiz — The entire formula comes from European testaments. *nonacayo*: *no-naca-yo*, "my-flesh-suffix of inalienable possession." Only the suffix *-yo* distinguishes "body" from "meat." A word for "body" is not much used in Nahuatl, and when it is it often refers to a corpse. *ca*: "for" again. The *i* of *itech* refers to *tlalli*.

2. *inic ontlamantli niquitoa ce missa nopan mochihuaz* — *nopan mochihuaz*, "will be said (made) for me."

inic palehuiloz naniman — *inic*: "so that." *palehuiloz*: "will be helped," a passive form that we have not yet seen.

ome pesos nohuentzin yez — *nohuentzin*, from *huentli*, offering, alms. *yez*, future of *ca*.

neltiz notlatol — "My statement will be carried out," one of the admonitive formulas so frequent in Nahuatl wills.

3. *iniquetlamantli niquitoa in nocal in iquiçayampa tonatiuh itzticac nicmacatiuh in nopiltzin itoca Juan* — *iniquetlamantli*: the equivalent of *inic e-tlamantli*, "third thing." *in iquiçayampa tonatiuh itzticac*: *in . . . itzticac*: *in* creates a relative clause and has the effect "which" (in reference to *nocal*, "my house"); *i-quiça-yam-pa tonatiuh*, "its-emerging-place-toward" ("its" refers to the irregular noun *tonatiuh*, the sun), "toward the place from where the sun comes out, toward the east." *nicmacatiuh*, with *yauh* as auxiliary verb, *-ti-uh*; it is likely but not yet quite firmly established that in wills it means "to do on dying" rather than "to go along doing." *nocal* is the direct specified object of *nicmacatiuh*, *nopiltzin* the indirect specified object.

auh in oc centetl nocal in icalaquiyampa tonatiuh itzticac nicmacatiuh in nochpochtzin in itoca Catalina — The sentence is parallel in everything to the preceding one. *oc centetl*: *oc* with a number is "more," and "one more" is "another." *icalaquiyampa tonatiuh*: this time the phrase contains *calaqui*, "to enter, go in," so that the meaning is "toward the west." The house looking east is to be found on the west side of the patio, and the one looking west on the east side. Houses, smallish buildings normally containing one nuclear family, were almost always oriented around a patio that is not mentioned.

in ixquich nocihuatlatqui quimocuiliz in nometl in notecon in nocpauh — *nocihuatlatqui*: *cihuatlatquitl*, household goods, but conceived as belonging to a woman, woman's things. *nometl*, from *metlatl*; *notecon*, from *tecomatl*; *nocpauh*, from *icpatl*.

auh in callalli concahuizque imomextin nopilhuan — *callalli*, from *calli* and *tlalli*, "house-land," arable land, the primary support of the residents, much more than a lot. *concahuizque*, from *oncahuia*, for two people to do something jointly or share something; *-on-* is not the directional prefix but from *ome*, two. One also sees *ecahuia*, for three people to do something, *nauhcahuia*, for four, etc. *imomextin*: this is an example of a construction including a possessive prefix, a number, and *xti(n)*, which means all those designated by that number. Here the number is two, so that the meaning is "both." *nopilhuan* is the subject of *concahuizque*.

'*ayac quincuiliz in tlein oniquinnomaquili* — *ayac quincuiliz,* a much used formula. *in tlein:* the whole clause beginning thus is the object of *quincuiliz; in* keeps *tlein* from being interrogative.

4. *inic nauhtlamantli niquitoa notlal oncan mani inahuac in otli* — *oncan,* there, only anticipates *inahuac in otli* and does not need to be translated. *i-* of *inahuac* refers to *otli. mani,* to be spread out, translates as "to be" (in a locative sense) with *tlalli,* "land." With chinampas, strips of land in shallow water, one says *temi,* literally to fill up (the water).

inic hueyac ompohualquahuitl inic patlahuac cempohualquahuitl — *inic* or *ic* plus *hueyac,* long, or *patlahuac,* wide, and a number forms expressions equivalent to so-and-so long, so-and-so wide. *ompohualquahuitl:* from *ome, -pohualli,* and *quahuitl,* "two-count (score)-stick"; one count is twenty, two are forty. *Quahuitl* is the name of a very common unit of measurement, generally in the range of seven to ten feet, that the Spaniards called a *braza de indios* because it was larger than the Spanish *braza* of six feet. Sometimes we use "braza" to translate it.

nicnomaquilitiuh in nopiltzin itoca Juan — The direct object of *nicnomaquilitiuh* is *notlal,* "my land," above.

itech pohuiz ayac quicuiliz — Two clauses. The prefix *i-* of *itech* refers to Juan.

5. *inic macuillamantli niquitoa notlal oncan mani itocayocan Atlauhtlan* — *macuillamantli:* from *macuilli* and *tlamantli; l* and a following *tl* always make *ll,* so that at times we have to reconstruct the *tl* to get dictionary forms. *oncan:* merely anticipation, just as above. *itocayocan: i-toca-yo-can,* "its-name-suffix of inalienable possession-locative suffix" (*i-* refers to Atlauhtlan), that is, "place with the name of." Here Atlauhtlan is the name of a settlement, but it means "next to the ravine." It is difficult, at times impossible, to distinguish between established names of settlements and ad hoc descriptions of physical features in Nahuatl sources.

inic hueyac cempohualquahuitl ommatlactli inic patlahuac cempohualli — *ommatlactli,* "plus ten," which with twenty makes thirty. The thing counted is often compounded with the larger number, followed by *om-* and the smaller number without any repetition of the word for what is being counted. *inic hueyac, inic patlahuac,* literally "how long, how wide," in effect "in length, in width."

nicnocahuililitiuh in nochpoch itoca Catalina — *nicnocahuililitiuh;* the direct specified object is *notlal* above, the indirect object *nochpoch.* Note the two *-li*-'s, one belonging to the reverential apparatus and the other a true applicative.

ayac quiquixtiliz — *quixtia,* to take out, remove, is the causative of *quiça,* to come out, emerge. *ayac* is the subject of *quiquixtiliz,* which contains a true applicative; the direct object is the land, the indirect object Catalina.

6. *inic chiquacentlamantli niquitoa totlaçomahuiznantzin Santa Maria nicnopialia* — The construction *totlaçomahuiznantzin* comes from *tlaçotli, mahuiztli,* and *nantli,* and most often refers to the Virgin Mary, sometimes to another female saint. Nahuatl testaments frequently speak of saints without mentioning words like "image." *nicnopialia:* reverential of *pia,* already with the meaning, affected by Spanish, of to have (although it still has much of its original sense, to keep, guard, be in control of).

nicnomaquilitiuh in nopiltzin itoca Juan — The image is the direct object of the verb, Juan the indirect object. If we do not understand that we are dealing with an image, it is difficult to decide which is the direct object, which the indirect.

auh onca ce caltepiton chalcopahuic itzticac icaltzin totlaçonantzin — *onca:* the verb *ca,* stative "to be," with the directional prefix *on-*, means "there is." It is necessary to keep in mind the distinction between *onca* and the particle *oncan*, there (despite the fact that in texts they are often written the same, both without *n*, or even both with it). *chalcopahuic*: from Chalco, *-pa*, and *-huic*, both meaning toward: "toward Chalco," here "toward the south." Instead of generic names for north and south, Nahuatl texts use names of nearby settlements, mountains, etc. *itzticac*, "which looks, looking," as above. The house is on the north of the patio. *icaltzin totlaçonantzin*: *i-* of *icaltzin* refers to *totlaçonantzin*.

oncan quimotequipanilhuiz in onicteneuh nopiltzin — *quimotequipanilhuiz*: reverential, with reflexive and applicative, of *tequipanoa*; subject *nopiltzin*, object *totlaçonantzin*. *onicteneuh*: "whom I mentioned," a relative clause placed before the noun that it modifies. We recognize it because it is a verbal complex inserted between *in* and the noun to which it refers.

intla quimochicahuiliz in Dios — subject *Dios*, object *nopiltzin*. *Chicahua*, "to strengthen," with God as the subject, means for the object of the verb to be in good health and more basically to live longer.

7. *inic chicontlamantli niquitoa aoctle itla nicnopialia* — *aoctle itla*: *atle*, "nothing," with *oc*, "still or more," infixed in it, yields *aoctle*, "nothing more." *itla*, "something," reinforces "nothing."

amo no nitetlahuiquilia — *amo no*, "not also," i.e., "nor, neither." *nitetlahuiquilia*: the applicative of *huica*, to take, be responsible for, is the most common expression in texts for owing money.

auh in nalbaceashuan yezque in ipan motlatoltizque in nanimantzin in quintlamamacazque in nopilhuan — *in . . . yezque*, "those who will be." *in ipan motlatoltizque*: *in* introduces a relative clause; *ipan* refers to *nanimantzin*; *ipan tlatoa* (here in the reverential) is an idiom meaning to be in charge of, see to, look after. *in quintlamamacazque*: with *in*, another relative clause; *quintlamamacazque*, distributive of *maca*, "to give," i.e., "to distribute to"; subject the executors, direct object *-tla-*, indirect object the children.

niquimixquetza notlatzin itoca Francisco de Santiago ihuan nachtzin Gaspar de los Reyes — *niquimixquetza*: object the names that follow, but the whole preceding clause about the executors is in apposition: "(as) those who will be executors I name . . ." *nachtzin*: *n-ach-tzin*; *-ach* is the older brother of a woman specifically.

ma qualli ic quimochihuilican intequiuh — *chihua* in the reverential, third person plural optative. *qualli ic*: "well." *intequiuh*: from *tequitl*; translated "duty" above, it could also be "charge," "office," or other things, since *tequitl* has so many implications.

ye ixquich notlatol — The words *ye ixquich* are important; they almost always indicate the end of the body of the document.

8. *imixpan omochiuh in testigos Francisco de Santiago Gaspar de los Reyes cihuatzitzintin Ana Petronila Maria Agustina* — *im-* of *imixpan* refers to the witnesses. Often the men and the women are enumerated separately, in two groups, as here; in Spanish testaments women generally were entirely absent as witnesses. It can be difficult to establish how many women there are; many bore two names, but it sometimes happens that humble people, men as well as women, had no more than a single name.

auh in nehuatl niescribano niquitoa ca qualli melahuac inic oquimochihuili in cocoxcatzintli in itestamento — *ca*: here it is not causal "for" but merely introduces the clause; we can translate it as "that," though it is not what makes the clause dependent. *inic*: here referring to manner, "how"; it causes us to translate *qualli* and *melahuac* adverbially. *cocoxcatzintli*: reverential of the preterit agentive noun *cocoxqui*, sick person, but given the original sense of the word, the reverential sense is inverted to give "poor sick person."

auh inic nelli nican nictlalia nofirma notoca — *inic nelli*: "how it is a true thing"; logically something like *inic nicneltilia*, "in order for me to verify it," seems to be needed, but it is rarely seen. The "signature" was the rubric and the "name" the name written alphabetically, but the two words became a double formula typical of Nahuatl.

axcan ic chicomilhuitl metztli mayo de 1583 años in ipan in altepetl tlacpac omito — *ic*: the same thing as *inic*, it makes "seven" ordinal. The months and years are almost always given in Spanish, and sometimes the day as well. *tlacpac*: *tla-cpac*, from *icpac*, on top of. *omito*: *o-m-ito*, from *itoa*, to say. *tlacpac omito* is a translation of the Spanish *susodicho*, aforementioned.

9. *nixpan omochiuh Pedro de Paz escribano de republica* — *nixpan omochiuh*: translation of the Spanish "pasó ante mí," "it occurred before me." *Pedro de Paz*: It seems that it ought to say *niPedro de Paz*, but as with testators' names,[1] such mainly fails to happen. *escribano de republica*: The indigenous municipal corporations were called *repúblicas*, which means a commonwealth or sociopolitical organization and not republic as we understand it today.

After closely studying the materials related to this sample testament and having attained a basic understanding, it would be advisable to begin reading some authentic documents, trying to analyze them and translate them in the same fashion.[2] Of course there is a great deal of grammar left to learn. But some things are learned better, or only, from experience and from the simple context, and what is so learned stays in the memory better. Moreover, you need to believe that this whole process leads to something, and you will find that reading real documents is more fun. At the same time, it is worth your while to keep up with the formal lessons and later with more detailed grammars. The best thing is to combine the two methods.

B. *The numbers.* Nahuatl has four basic numbers; after that it says five and one, ten and two, fifteen and three, etc., until it reaches twenty, "a count." Then everything is repeated in the same style up to four hundred and after that to eight thousand. All the simple numbers larger than four are normal nouns with an absolute singular ending (which they lose when compounded with other nouns). The four basic numbers have no singular absolute, but they can take an absolute plural ending when they refer to people, animals, etc.: *ome*, two; *omen* or *omentin*, two (people).

1 ce	2 ome	3 yei (ei)	4 nahui	5 macuilli
6 chiquace[3]	7 chicome	8 chicuei	9 chiucnahui	10 matlactli
11 matlactli once	12 matlactli omome	13 matlactli omei	14 matlactli onnahui	15 caxtolli
16 caxtolli once	17 caxtolli omome	18 caxtolli omei	19 caxtolli onnahui	20 cempohualli

As is seen here, the element *om-* (before a vowel or a labial consonant) or *on-* (before the other consonants), which means "plus," is very important. It is also important to avoid confusing *om-* the connector with *ome*, two. *Omome* is "plus two" and is easily understood, but beginners have a strong tendency to translate *omei*, "plus three," as "plus two" as well. *Cempohualli*, "twenty," consists of *cem-*, the combining form of *ce*, one, and *-pohualli*, count, from *pohua*, to count.

---

[1] See the comments on the name of Apolonia de la Cruz above, p. 45, section 0.

[2] Appendix 2 leads the student through such an exercise, and some practice texts are in Appendix 3.

[3] The numbers from six through nine are not based on *macuilli*, five, but use an element now appearing variously as *chiqua-*, *chic-*, and *chiuc-*, which once must have been or been related to an older way of saying five.

The combining forms of the basic numbers appear constantly in the larger numbers. They are:

basic forms:		assimilated forms:	
	ce , one		*cem-*, *cen-*
	ome, two		*om-*, *on-*
	yei, ei, three		*ye-, e-, yex-, ex-*
	nahui, four		*nauh-*

The final consonant of any of the assimilated forms (except for *yei/ei*) can become *p* by further assimilation, as in *nappa,* four times.

From twenty to forty the first series is repeated, beginning each time with *cempohualli om-*. *Cempohualli oncaxtolli,* twenty plus fifteen, i.e., thirty-five, and so on. Forty is *ompohualli,* two counts, sixty is *yepohualli,* etc. Nothing changes until we reach four hundred, *centzontli,* "a headful of hair." The multiplication continues as before: *ontzontli,* eight hundred, etc. With the larger numbers, *ipan* is often used instead of *om-*. For example, *centzontli ipan caxtolpohualli ipan nauhpohualli omome,* 400 plus 300 plus 80 plus 2: 782. *Ihuan,* "and," is also found instead of *ipan.* Things continue in this fashion until we reach *cenxiquipilli,* "a bag (full of cacao beans)," 8,000. By multiplying, numbers even larger can easily be made (*onxiquipilli,* 16,000, etc.), but they are hardly found in documents.

Nahuatl originally had a set of elements for counting things in different categories: round things, flat things, etc. By the sixteenth century the system had decayed and changed to the point that there were very few "counters." *Tetl,* earlier only for round hard things (*tetl* means "stone, egg"), acted as a counter for houses and many other things: *yetetl calli,* "three houses." *Tlacatl,* "person," was also used in this way: *nahui tlacatl icnocihuatl,* "four widows," and there were some others, especially for quantities larger than twenty. But things were also counted directly, as in English or Spanish. When a counter appears, it bears the entire numerical apparatus as though it were a number itself; it is never in the plural:

1 centetl	2 ontetl	3 (y)etetl	4 nauhtetl	5 macuiltetl
6 chiquacentetl	7 chicontetl	8 chicuetetl	9 chiucnauhtetl	10 matlactetl
11 matlactetl once	12 matlactetl omome	13 matlactetl omei	14 matlactetl onnahui	15 caxtoltetl
16 caxtoltetl once	17 caxtoltetl omome	18 caxtoltetl omei	19 caxtoltetl onnahui	20 cempohualtetl

To say "times," an assimilated number is combined with the relational word *-pa: ceppa,* once; *oppa,* twice; *expa, yexpa,* three times; *nappa,* four times; *macuilpa,* five times, etc. We already saw that to make ordinal numbers *ic* or *inic* is placed before the number: *inic centetl, ic centetl,* "the first thing"; *inic caxtoltetl omei,* "the eighteenth thing," etc.

9. Mainly on Nouns

> *Nominal plurals. Agentive nouns. Direct plural objects of verbs together with the indirect. Examples.*

A. *Nominal plurals.* The first thing to be said is that before the middle of the sixteenth century Nahuatl generally did not indicate the plurality of nouns for inanimate things by means of subject prefixes and suffixes, and although Spanish influence gradually made itself felt, Nahuatl has never gone over to consistent marking of all plurals. *Calli* can be a house, a complex of houses, or several complexes, and the same with *tlalli*, "land." "The clouds disappear" would be *polihui in mixtli*, with both noun and verb in the singular. Even when plurality is expessed by numbers, a plural suffix does not appear:

> *chicontetl nochinan nicmacatiuh in nopiltzin*   I give seven chinampas of mine to my child.

At times a plural is suggested by the use of the distributive (reduplication of the first consonant and first vowel of a word, with a glottal stop at the end of the new syllable thus created): *yaque immimilpan*, "they went to their various or respective fields."

Nevertheless, many plurals were marked from the beginning, for animate things play a large role in human languages. Plurality of nouns is expressed primarily by suffixes, divided into absolute and possessive. We already know the plural possessive suffix *-huan*, the same in all cases and clearly related to the now vestigial singular possessive suffix. The plural absolute suffixes are the ones causing the trouble, because they vary so, their distribution is not very fixed and predictable, and they have no well established relation to the singular absolutive suffix. (At times we have spoken here almost as though the singular form were the only absolutive, largely because it is the one found in the dictionary.)

A1. *Plurals of nouns with -tli/-li/-tl singular endings.* The three plural absolute suffixes of normal nouns are *-tin*, *-me(h)*, and *-(h)*, the last of which is only exceptionally written down, although it can be recognized by the absence of the singular absolutive suffix in an unpossessed noun. There is no difference of function or meaning between them. We can, however, detect some tendencies as to their distribution. *-Tin* occurs only after consonant stems.

macehualli	(he/she is a) commoner	*macehualtin*	(they are) commoners
quauhtli	(it is an) eagle	*quauhtin*	(they are) eagles
xolopitli	(he/she is an) idiot	*xolopitin*	(they are) idiots

-Me tends to come after a vowel, but unfortunately for consistency it is sometimes found after consonants too.

ichcatl	(it is a) sheep	*ichcame*	(they are) sheep
tototl	(it is a) bird	*totome*	(they are) birds
pitzotl	(it is a) pig	*pitzome*	(they are) pigs

Some regions prefer *-tin*, others *-me*, and variation has also occurred over time. The only nouns that are almost never found with a *-me* plural in older texts are those with a stem ending in a glottal stop, as with *xolopitin* above.

By its nature the invisible suffix *-(h)* can only come after a vowel. The nominal element *-ca-tl*, inhabitant of, has this plural, so that it is found in many names of peoples.

tlacatl	(he/she is a) person	*tlaca*	(they are) people
cihuatl	(she is a) woman	*cihua*	(they are) women
pochtecatl	(he is a) merchant	*pochteca*	(they are) merchants
mexicatl	(he/she is a) Mexica	*mexica*	(they are) Mexica

Since their roots end in a vowel, many of these words can also appear with a plural in -me. After all, for the reader of documents the variation is no great matter. If you can recognize all three absolute plural suffixes, you can interpret them correctly every time they occur, no matter what noun they are suffixed to.[1]

A2. *Plurals of other kinds of nouns.* Until now we have been acting as though all normal nouns have a singular absolute in -tli/-li/-tl. Nevertheless, there is another absolute ending, -in. The majority of the nouns in -in are words to describe smallish animate beings: birds, insects, small animals. In the plural this class is no different from other nouns, taking the suffixes -tin and -me (never -[h], because all the roots of these words end in a consonant).[2]

totolin	turkey hen	*totoltin, totolme*	turkey hens, turkeys
ocuilin	worm	*ocuilme, ocuiltin*	worms

A few normal nouns have no absolute ending in the singular, but their plurals are standard.

chichi	dog	*chichime*	dogs

It is possible that most of the nouns of this type earlier belonged to the -in group, for final *n* was very weak and subject to loss.

Another quite large group of nouns without a singular absolute ending consists of Spanish loanwords. When referring to animate beings, they can take absolute plurals of various types: the same suffix as in Spanish, -s or -es, the suffixes -tin or -me, or double plurals. They never have -(h) because the root of any noun originating in a Spanish word and ending in a vowel acquires a final glottal stop in Nahuatl (lost before *s*, however).

cahuallo	horse	*cahuallos, cahuallotin, cahuallome,*
		cahuallostin, cahuallosme horses

The possessive plural of Spanish loan nouns can also be simple or double. Not often is the plural found without -huan.

      icahualloshuan, icahuallohuan   his/her horses

Only rarely would we expect to see the form *icahuallos*.

A3. *Reduplication in the plural.* The plurality of nouns is also expressed by the reduplication of the first syllable, as with the distributive mentioned above, but this time with a long vowel instead of a glottal stop at the end of the new syllable. The construction includes one of the absolute plural endings as well. Some common words always form the plural in this way, but with many nouns reduplication is optional, and it hardly occurs with the plural possessive.

teuctli	(he is a) lord	*teteuctin*	(they are) lords
tlacotli	slave	*tlatlacotin*	slaves
coyametl	pig	*cocoyameme* (also *coyameme*)	pigs
maçatl	deer	*mamaça*	deer (pl.)
teotl	god	*teteo*	gods
ticitl	healer	*titici*	healers
tochin, tochtli	rabbit	*totochtin*	rabbits
çolin	quail	*çoçoltin*	quail (pl.)

---

[1] For those interested in regional variation and tendencies across time, of course, the variations are important. Regions can be mapped on the basis of such differences.

[2] That is, they effectively end in a consonant today. Historically the *i* belonged to the root. The absolute ending was once *n* only (before that probably *m* followed by a vowel), and some words ending in -an (like *chian*, "chia") originally belonged to the same class; now this *n* has been reconceived as belonging to the root, leaving such words apparently without a singular absolute ending.

The important thing from the point of view of the reader is to recognize the reduplication and remove the first syllable, because the reduplicated form often cannot be found in the dictionary.[3]

A pair of common nouns has an exceptional reduplicated plural:

ichpochtli	(she is a) maiden	*ichpopochtin*	(they are) maidens
telpochtli	youth	*telpopochtin*	youths

As you see, in these cases it is the second syllable that is reduplicated. Perhaps *pochtli* is the basic noun and the first syllable only a modification to specify the gender.

A4. *The plural of* -tzin *and* -ton. The nominal reverential *-tzin* and the diminutive *-ton* have their own reduplicated plural (the first syllable is short in this case) in addition to the usual plural suffix, which is always *-tin*.

macehualli	(he/she is a) commoner	*macehualtin*	(they are) commoners
macehualtzintli	poor commoner	*macehualtzitzintin*	poor commoners
piltzintli	child	*pipiltzitzintin*	children
tochtontli	little rabbit	*totochtotontin*	little rabbits

These elements (and some similar ones found less frequently in the sources) act almost as though they were animate nouns modified by the nouns with which they are bound. At times they are seen with a plural suffix, or at least with reduplication, even when the noun they are associated with is not animate.

tecomatotontin, or *tecomatoton* (from *tecomatl*)	little jars or cups

A5. *Quantifiers.* The Nahuatl words somewhere between nouns and pronouns that we call quantifiers cannot be possessed and have no absolutive suffix in the singular, but they can take nominal absolutive plurals when they refer to animate beings. One of these is our familiar *-tin*; the other is a more unusual *-n*.[4] When a quantifier ends in a vowel it can take either a simple plural in *-n* or a double plural in *-ntin*. When it ends in a consonant it takes *-tin* only. (Note that *miec* adds an *i* in the plural to become a vowel stem.)

ixquich	(it is) everything, all, a certain amount	*ixquichtin*	(they are) all
mochi	all	*mochin, mochintin*	all (pl.)
cequi	a part, some	*cequin, cequintin*	some (pl.)
miec	much	*miequin, miequintin*	many

You may remember that number words, which after all are also quantifiers, can take the same *-n* and *-ntin*: *yein, yeintin,* "three (animate beings)."

B. *Agentives.* Nahuatl has agentives of two types (an agentive is a noun derived from a verb that means the person [or thing] carrying out the action of the verb, like "worker.") Both reflect the object prefixes of the original verb. The form that is less basic and less ancient, though simpler, is the present agentive, which is formed from the root of the verb plus *-ni* (a verbal suffix for habitual action). The plural of the absolutive is formed with *-me*, or occasionally with *-(h)*.

cuica	to sing	*cuicani*	(he/she is a) singer	*cuicanime*	(they are) singers
miqui	to die	*miquini*	mortal	*miquinime*	mortals
te-machtia	to preach	*temachtiani*	preacher	*temachtianime*	preachers
te-tla-maca	to dispense communion	*tetlamacani*	dispenser of communion	*tetlamacanime*	dispensers of communion

---

[3]Sometimes it can be. Molina's dictionary gives quite a few plurals of this type as entries.

[4]*-Me* is rare, but I have seen *ixquichime* instead of *ixquichtin* in some texts from Tlaxcala.

The agentives in -ni reveal their recent origin in the fact that they lack a possessed form and cannot be bound to other nouns. For these purposes Nahuatl resorts to its other, older and better developed, agentive noun, the preterit agentive. The latter is formed from the preterit stem of the verb or in a sense simply is the verb's preterit, in many cases with the addition of a suffix in the singular. The reader will remember the four classes of verbs based on the preterit; the suffix varies with the class. Agentives derived from Class 1 verbs have the suffix -c, so that they are identical to the preterit of the finite verbs from which they derive. Agentives of Class 2 generally have a suffix -qui (an archaic preterit suffix which was briefly discussed above), so that they differ from the singular finite preterit verbs, which bear no suffix. Agentives of Class 3 most often lack a suffix, though sometimes, when animate, they have -qui. All have a plural in -que, exactly like preterit verbs. Preterit agentives from Class 4 are rare.

namaca	to sell	iztanamacac	salt seller	iztanamacaque	salt sellers
chihua	to make	tlaxcalchiuhqui	bread maker, baker	tlaxcalchiuhque	bakers
itoa	to say	tequitlato	tribute overseer	tequitlatoque	overseers

The preterit agentives are easily confused with the preterits of finite verbs; on the other hand, at times there is hardly any difference in sense and translation between the two forms.

tlanamacac	he/she sold something	tlanamacaque	they sold something
in tlanamacac	one who sold something (and other meanings)	in tlanamacaque	those who sold something (and other meanings)
tlanamacac	(he/she is a) vendor	tlanamacaque	(they are) vendors
tlapouh	he/she read	tlapouhque	they read
in tlapouh	one who read	in tlapouhque	those who read
tlapouhqui	(he/she is a) reader	tlapouhque	(they are) readers
temicti	he/she killed someone	temictique	they killed someone
in temicti	one who killed someone	in temictique	those who killed someone
temicti	(he/she is a) murderer	temictique[1]	(they are) murderers

When a preterit agentive is compounded with any other element to its right, the ligature -ca- appears, replacing any suffix on the agentive form, for essentially this -ca- is not a mere ligature but the original preterit suffix, which we saw when we studied the history of the preterit, here protected from reduction by its internal position.

iztanamacac	(he/she is a) salt seller	iztanamaca-ca-tequitl	(it is) salt seller's work
tlaxcalchiuhqui	baker	tlaxcalchiuh-ca-tzintli	baker, rev.
tequitlato	tribute overseer	to-tequitlato-ca-uh	our tribute overseer
qualanqui	one who angers	qui-qualan-ca-itta	He looks at him angrily.

As was mentioned above, the possessed form of a present agentive in -ni is based on the corresponding preterit agentive, even if the latter is not otherwise in use and is not found in the dictionary.

temaquixtiani	savior
notemaquixticauh,	my savior
notemaquixticatzin	my savior, rev.

When you find notemaquixticatzin in a document, you would first reconstruct temaquixti or temaquixtiqui, but when you fail to find these forms, you would begin to think of an analogous form in -ni and look it up. It too might be missing in the dictionary, but as long

---

[1]Of course if the optional antecessive particle o were added, the difference between the finite and the agentive forms would be greater. Remember, though, that in actual texts it is usually hard or impossible to tell what letters are part of what words by spacing alone.

as the original verb has an entry, you have a good chance of arriving at the meaning.

The same switch from present to preterit agentive occurs with -*ni* forms compounded with other nouns. "His fatigue, effort, or suffering as savior" would be *itemaquixtica-tlaiiyohuiliztzin*.

One of the most familiar -*ni* agentives, *tlatoani*, "ruler, king, chief," has not only the possessed and compounded forms, but also the absolute plural based on the preterit agentive, although the preterit form is no longer used in the absolute singular.[2]

tlatoani	ruler
tlatoque	rulers
notlatocauh	my ruler
notlatocatzin	my ruler, rev.
tlatocatlalli	ruler's land, royal land

A good grasp of how the agentives work, and especially an ability to recognize the -*ca*- of the preterit combining form and draw the proper conclusions, is an important part of one's equipment for dealing with Nahuatl texts. Experience shows, however, that students even into advanced stages are often stumped by -*ca*- and its implications. The topic will richly reward extra effort and concentration.

We have by now seen four basic elements of the language which are written with the letters *ca*. One is an introductory particle which sometimes remains untranslated, sometimes has causal force. It may come quite far into an utterance, but it always immediately precedes a potentially independent clause.

ca qualli	Okay (agreeing to an interlocutor's proposal).
axcan niyauh ca huel notech monequi niyaz	I'm leaving now, because I really have to go.
in yehuatl ca atle ic nechpalehuia	As to that fellow, he doesn't help me with anything.

Second is the stative verb *ca* (actually *cah*), "to be a certain way or at a certain time or place." In the proper persons it bears subject prefixes, and unlike most Nahuatl verbs, it tends to come last in an utterance. It is also common as an auxiliary verb preceded by -*ti*-.

Martin mochipa imilpan ca	Martin is always at his fields.
nican nica	I am here.
oncan ca	He/she is there.
poliuhtica	It is disappearing.

Third is the instrumental relational word -*ca*, which will either be possessed or tied to a noun by -*ti*-, making it look like the progressive -*tica* from the verb *ca*, but as has been mentioned before, the relational word will be attached to a noun, the verb to another verb.

ica tlaltepoztli onechhuitec	He struck me with a hoe.
metica quitzaqua in otli	They block off the road with magueys.
tlamahuiçoltica omonexiti	She appeared by a miracle.

Fourth is the -*ca*- we have just been talking about, illustrated by examples on this and the preceding page. It occurs between what looks like the preterit stem of a verb, actually a preterit agentive noun, and a following noun, nominal suffix, or sometimes a main verb; do not forget that even something as unprepossessing as the singular possessive ending -*uh* is still a nominal suffix and has -*ca*- before it. Once you have identified this -*ca*-, you still need to find in the dictionary either the preterit agentive noun itself, or failing that the verb from which it is derived.

---

[2] *Tlatoani* is derived from the verb *itoa*, "to say," with *tla*- indefinite object, and means literally "one who speaks."

The preterit -ca- appears in one other kind of construction, closely related to the form seen in compounds, with an adverbial sense. The word is derived in exactly the same way as a preterit combining form but is not directly attached to anything else. It has apparently kept the ancient -ca, complete with its long vowel, because such words virtually always appear before verbal complexes, being protected by the fact that they are in the first part of a phonological phrase.

iciuhca oquichiuh	He/she did it quickly.
yocoxca nemi	He/she lives peacefully.
tlamatca tlatocati	He rules prudently, peacefully.

These words can be analyzed just like normal preterit agentives. *Iciuhca* derives from the verb *icihui*, "to hurry," preterit *iciuh*. One can hypothesize the preterit agentive *iciuhqui*, one who hurries, which in fact is in the dictionary in the sense of one who is hurried. It would be harder to connect *yocoxca* with a current sense of a verb or an agentive in use. In any case, many constructions of this type are in Molina's dictionary just as they are, including all three of the examples just given (the last one as part of a set phrase). These adverbial words can also be incorporated into a noun exactly like a normal preterit agentive: *tlamatcanemiliztli*, "quiet, prudent living." In cases like this you should first presume a standard agentive noun and reconstruct *tlamatqui*; not finding it, you reconstruct the original verb. When *mati* doesn't work, you think of weak i and go to *imati*, which points toward the right sense, but a bit obliquely. As a last option you look directly for the unchanged form as an adverbial particle of preterit agentive origin and find it.

C. *Direct plural objects of verbs together with the indirect.* In previous lessons we have seen that Nahuatl has forms to indicate the plurality of the objects of verbs; among the object prefixes there are plurals as well as singulars. But we also know that Nahuatl suppresses the direct object when a verb has an indirect object: *tamechmaca*, "we give it to you (pl.)." How would the plurality of the object be expressed in such a case? How would one say "we give them to you (pl.)" (presuming that "them" refers to animate beings)? Recall the third person plural object prefix, *quim*. It consists of *qu-* (actually the same -c- as in the third person singular) plus -*im* plural. In situations where an indirect object is present and the direct object is plural, -*im*- appears after the object prefix (which here expresses the indirect object): *tamechimmaca*, "we give them to you (pl.)." Thank goodness, cases like this are not common in the sources, but one will from time to time come up against an apparently inexplicable -*im*- or -*in*-, and to prepare you for that eventuality this minimal explanation is included here.

D. *Some examples.*

micqui	(he/she is a) dead person
miccatzintli	dead person, rev.
mimicque	dead people
mimiccatzitzintin	dead people, rev., or poor dead people
nomiccauh	my dead person (a relative who has died)
nomiccatzin	my dead person, rev.
miccatepoztli	dead person-iron, i.e., bell
cuix nimicqui	Am I a dead person? (Am I dead?)
cuix onimic	Have I died? (Am I dead?)
teopixqui	friar, priest
noteopixcauh	my friar
teopixcatzintli	friar, rev.
teopixcatzitzintin	friars, rev.
teopixcatequitzintli	a friar's office or duty (rev.)

yolqui	living thing, animal, large domestic beast
noyolcahuan	my beasts
yolque	beasts

quiyolcatlatique — They burned him alive.

in macehualtin quintequipanoa in impillohuan[1] — The commoners serve their masters, lords.

miequintin oniquimma in totochtin in mamaça in mimichtin — I caught many rabbits, deer, and fish.

intlacamo qualli totlachihualiz in tlatlacatecolo mictlan techhuicazque — If our deeds are bad, the demons will take us to hell.

tianquizco tiquimittaz in panamacaque in connamacaque in nepapan tlanecuiloque — In the market you will see the sellers of medicines and pots, and the various kinds of dealers.

macamo xiquimilcahuacan in mimiccatzitzintin in otechcauhtehuaque — Do not forget the dead who have left us behind.

ma xinechmaca in totolin in otinechcuili — Give me the turkey hen you took from me.

ma xinechimmaca in nototolhuan — Give me my turkeys.

aic titechincuiliz in topilhuan — You will never take our children from us.

---

[1] In general, all the possessed forms of *pilli* refer to offspring; the absolute reverential and diminutive forms refer to small children.

nopiltzin	my child (simple *nopil* is hardly seen)
nopilhuan, nopiltzitzinhuan, (also) *nopilhuantzitzin*	my children
piltzintli, piltontli	a (small) child
pipiltzitzintin, pipiltotontin	(small) children
pilli	nobleman
pipiltin	noblemen
cihuapilli	noblewoman
cihuapipiltin	noblewomen

Pilli and *cihuapilli* in reference to nobles never occur with the *tzin* reverential.

In the case of the present example, the addition of *-yo*, which because of assimilation becomes *-lo*, to the root *-pil* attains a form of the word which can at the same time be possessed and have the sense "noble." Another such form is *nopiltzintzine*, in the vocative with a double *tzin*, meaning "O my nobleman or noblewoman, lord or lady."

Note that *-pillo* also, and very commonly, means the niece/nephew of a woman.

10. The Uses of *In*

The particle in *with verbal clauses. The particle* in *with nouns. The demonstratives* in *and* on.

A. *The particle* in *with verbal clauses.* In Nahuatl texts the particle *in* is seen repeatedly on every single page; few sentences will be found that lack this apparently innocuous little element. The beginner, who has much to think about, tends to ignore *in* as a secondary element, ubiquitous and to all appearances almost without meaning. For morphology, which becomes the beginner's whole life, *in* is of no particular interest; but for syntax, the understanding of whole clauses and sentences, *in* is basic. It is Nahuatl's general subordinator. A clause containing a verb and not beginning with *in* is probably independent, the main clause; a verbal clause beginning with *in* is dependent within a larger structure.

In is, then, of tremendous utility to the reader, but the indications that it gives us are very general and often ambiguous. *In* before a verb can result in a phrase indicating the person who does something, the fact that someone does it, or the time at which it is done.

quichihua	he/she does or makes it
in quichihua	dependent clause ambiguous without more context

Let us consider some examples:

in quichihua amo qualli amo yectli ca xolopiyotl   What he's doing is not good; it's a stupidity.

The dependent clause in itself could very well have the meaning "one who does it"; only on reaching the clause "it is a stupidity" do we grasp the intended sense, since a person can be stupid, but hardly a stupidity. If this clause had been *ca xolopitli*, "he/she is an idiot," the translation would have been "the person who is doing it is bad, an idiot." In this example we have another element very useful in understanding Nahuatl syntax, the already familiar introductory particle *ca*. Here it is like a semicolon, preceding the punch line. It also often means "for, because," and introduces answers to questions.

The most important function of *ca*, however, is to indicate where the main clause in an utterance begins when something else has been preposed. *Ca* in this function usually needs no translation. Note also that this *ca* is not the stative verb *ca(h)*. Used this way, *ca* is a bit like "why" in some English usage:

in yehuatl ca amo ixcoyan itoca quimati   As to that fellow, why he doesn't know his own name.

In other words, as *in* points to dependent clauses, *ca* in a complementary way tends to indicate independent clauses.

To return to *in*, in the following example *in quichihua* could equally well be "what he/she does" or "the one who does it" until we see that the subject of the main clause is a person. We learn here also that, unfortunately, *ca* does not always mark the main clause when something precedes it, though *in quichihua ca huel tlamatini* is equally possible.

in quichihua huel tlamatini   The one who does it is very wise.

In before a verbal clause in the present tense rarely has a temporal meaning, but when the verb is in the preterit, that meaning should be the reader's first hypothesis.

in oquichiuh niman ya   When he/she had done it, or having done it, (then) he/she left.

At times, in addition to *in*, the particle *iuh*, literally "thus," is inserted between *o*, the sign of the preterit (which virtually always accompanies it when the meaning is antecessive), and the body of the verb, and then we are sure of the antecessive temporal sense; the effect is that of a past perfect.

in o iuh quimacac in tlalli omic	After she had given him the land, she died.

Even in the preterit, the other senses are possible:

in oquichiuh ca cenca mahuiztic	What he/she did was (or is) very splendid.
in oquichiuh amo niquiximati	I don't know the person who did it.
in oichtec huallaz teilpiloyan	The one who stole (the thief) is to be brought to jail.

A very important type of dependent verbal clause signaled by *in* is relative in nature; a relative sense is especially likely to be involved when the clause immediately follows a noun.

in cihuatl in oquichiuh in tlaxcaltzintli ca nohuepoltzin	The woman who made the tortillas is my sister-in-law [a man is speaking].
in calli in oniquittiti ca huel huei calli	The house that I showed him is a very large house.

In Nahuatl the relative clause can come before the noun it modifies, as in German or Greek; we recognize it when we see a verbal clause inserted between *in* and a noun.

iz catqui in otinechicuilhui amatl	Here is the letter that you wrote me.
omochiuh in ipan in tlacpac omoteneuh xihuitl	It happened in the year above mentioned.

Nahuatl has some interrogative words similar to those of English; they also serve to introduce and define dependent clauses. The whole difference between the two functions is the presence or absence of *in*; without *in*, these words are interrogative, and with *in* in front they are not. Among the most common are *ac* or *aquin*, "who?"; *can* or *canin*, "where?"; *campa*, "from where, to where?"; *tle* or *tlein*, "what?"; *quen* or *quenin*, "how?" The synonymous pairs come from the incorporation of a subordinating *in*: *tle in ticnequi*, "What is it that you want?", leads to *tlein ticnequi*, "What do you want?"

aquin oquichiuh ca amo nicmati	Who did it? — I don't know.
ye niquitta in aquin oquichiuh	Now I see who did it.
canin tica	Where are you?
in canin tica in nehuatl amo nicnequi niyez	I don't want to be where you are.
campa tiyazque	Where are we to go? (What will come of us?)
amo nicmati in campa oya	I don't know where he/she went.
tle motequiuh tlein ticnequi	What's your business? What do you want?
in tlein notequiuh in tlein nicnequi aic ticmatiz	You will never know what my business is and what I want.
tleica tinechtolinia	Why are you pestering me?
amo quilnamiqui in tleica nechtolinia	He doesn't remember why he's pestering me.
tle ipampa quinquixtilique in pipiltzitzintin imaxca intlatqui	Why did they take their property away from the children?
in tle ipampa amo macho aço quinquixtilique in ipampa cenca tlahueliloque tlatlacoanime	The reason is not known; maybe they took it from them because they are very wicked and great sinners.

Other words too vary in sense or function according to the presence or absence of *in*. *Iquac* is "at that moment" in an absolute sense, but *in iquac* is "when," introducing a dependent clause.

iquac hualla	He/she came at that time.
in iquac hualla onechpalehui	When he/she came, he/she helped me.

Oncan is "there"; *in oncan* introduces a dependent clause and can often be translated "where."

oncan nemi teopannahuactzinco	He/she lives (there) close to the church.
huel ohuican in oncan nemi	Where he/she lives is a very difficult place.

There are many other cases of this type; with a whole series of words, Molina considers *in* so important that he includes it in the entry and alphabetizes the constructions under *i/y*, as opposed to other entries without *in*.

In is often used to change the emphasis, turning the main clause into a dependent clause. Remember that almost any Nahuatl word can be a main clause.

nican hualaci	He/she arrives here.
nican in hualaci	Here is where he/she arrives.
mitica chimaltica oquicuique in intlal	They took their land by war (by arrows and shields).
mitica chimaltica in oquicuique in intlal	It is by war that they took their land.

Here are some more sentences to illustrate the use of *in* in complex sentences:

cenca miequintin in itech pohui in itlan nemi in tlatoani[1]	Very many are those who belong to and are dependent on the king.
cuix tiquimiximati in yalhua ohualacique	Do you know those who arrived here yesterday?
in oncan nemi mochintin quinnamaquiltiaya iztatl in otlica nenenque[2]	Those who live there all would sell salt to those who traveled on the road.
amo çan tlapohualtin in immilpan tlaai tlatoca[3]	Innumerable are those who cultivate and sow on their fields.
in o iuh ammohuicaque hualacique in tlapixque in quimmocuitlahuia in noyolcahuan in ipan tlatoa inic ayac quitlacoz in nocal in notlal amo no nechcuiliz notlatqui in calitic onoc	After you (pl.) had gone, there arrived the guards who care for my beasts and see to it that no one does damage to my houses and lands nor takes from me my property that is in the houses.
cuix moztla onaciz in toteopixcatlatocauh obispo in teoyotica techmopialia	Will our priestly ruler the bishop, who is in charge of us in matters of the sacraments, get there tomorrow?
intla totecuiyo Dios quimochicahuiliz aço moztla anoço huiptla onmaxitiz in oticmotenehuili auh intla itla cocoliztli quimocuitiz aço huecahuaz inic onmaxitiz	If God our lord gives him health, perhaps he whom you mentioned will get there tomorrow or the next day, but if he should contract an illness, it may be a long time before he arrives.

B. In *with nouns*. At the beginning of these lessons I occasionally rather casually spoke of *in* as an "article." A certain correspondence exists between the distribution of *in* and the definite article in English. A noun complex preceded by *in* is somewhat more likely to refer to a specific thing or being, a noun without it to be indefinite. Often *in quahuitl* will translate as "the tree," simple *quahuitl* as "a tree." The further we advance, however, the more we see that nouns with *in* are often indefinite or generic, and that nouns without it often have a specific reference. *In* occurs before independent pronouns and possessed nouns.

in nehuatl amo iuh nicchihua	I don't do it that way.
amo otlato in nochpoch[4]	My daughter didn't speak.

The parallel between *in* and any kind of article, as we know articles in English, becomes tenuous.

Having spoken of *in* as a subordinator of verbs, or let us say, of clauses that contain

---

[1] Here two consecutive relative clauses both refer to *miequintin*; also, both relational words refer to *tlatoani*.

[2] Here *nenenque* could be understood as a preterit agentive or as a finite preterit verb without large implications for the sense.

[3] *Amo çan tlapohualtin* is a set phrase, literally "not just they-counted thing-pl."

[4] Some Romance languages, notably Italian, use the definite article in this position.

a verb as nucleus, we may ask if it has the same function with nouns. It seems possible that in principle it indeed does have that function. Already in the first lesson we saw that every noun is before anything else an independent or main clause; it needs to be subordinated for larger clauses to be constructed. *Tlalli* is a clause "it is land"; *notlal* is a clause "it is my land." If we place *in* in front of *tlalli* to create a dependent clause, "that which is land," we can form *in tlalli ca notlal*, "that which is land is my land," i.e., "the land is mine." Following this line of thought, the innumerable examples of *in* appearing before nouns in texts would be not articles but signs of subordination. That would readily explain the particle's use before pronouns and possessed nouns. Nevertheless, consistency is lacking; not all incorporated or dependent nouns, by any means, are accompanied by *in*. It seems that with nouns *in* can always be omitted without affecting the basic sense. In general, it is best not to worry too much about the presence or absence of *in* before a noun. The one thing that appears to be consistent is that though a noun can be subordinated with or without *in*, it cannot be an independent statement in itself if *in* precedes; *ca tlalli* is plausible and idiomatic as "it is land," whereas *ca in tlalli* is incomplete and leaves us waiting for the rest of the sentence.

A capital function of *in* with nouns is punctuation. It was mentioned in an earlier chapter, apropos of *ihuan*, that Nahuatl does not usually say "and" to end a series of nouns. The Nahuatl way is to place *in* before each one, no matter how many there are.

mochi tlacatl oquicuic in cocoliztli in pipiltzi-
   tzintin in ichpopochtin in telpopochtin in
   toquichtin[5] *in cihua in ilamatque in huehuetque*
	Everyone got sick: the children, the maidens,
	   the youths, the men, the women, the old
	   women, and the old men.

Also the noun pairs so typical of Nahuatl generally have an *in* placed before each.

iuh oquichiuhque in tocolhuan in tachton-
   huan
	Thus did our ancestors (grandfathers and
	   great-grandfathers).

ma achitzin nicnomacehui in mixitl in tlapatl	May I enjoy a bit of pulque (two hallucinogenic substances).
in quiyahuac in ithualco nitlapia	I am in charge of the household (the exit, the patio).

macamo nictequipacho in amix in amoyollo	May I not bother, perturb, or upset you (pl.)
	   (may I not cause concern to your spirits
	   [your faces and hearts]).

ayamo aca techilhui in motenyo in motlatollo	before anyone told us of your fame and story

C. *The demonstratives* in *and* on. The ubiquitous *in* subordinator has a short vowel. Another *in*, demonstrative, with a long vowel, means "this." It occurs most often in the combination *inin*, which consists of the subordinator plus the demonstrative.

ce cihuatl ohualla auh inin cihuatl miequintin
   iconehuan
	A woman came, and this woman had many
	   children.

inin aic nicceliz	This I will never accept.

huei momacehuallo auh inin cenca teixco
   teicpac tinemi
	You are very common; and another thing, you
	   are very rude and disrespectful.

In makes a complementary pair with *on*, "that," which like its fellow is most often seen in combination with the subordinator as *inon*.

inon tlalli hueca mani amo huelitiz ompa
   niyaz inic nitlatocaz
	that land is distant; I won't be able to go
	   there to sow.

---

[5]When men spoke of men in general or of groups of men, they said "we men."

Inin and *inon* appear perhaps most often either before a noun or independently. But the demonstrative can also be placed after an independent pronoun, a quantifier, a verb, or a relational word, always in its simple form, which in the case of *in* can be very difficult to recognize, that is, to distinguish from *in* the subordinator. The most frequently seen forms are *yehuatl in*, this, and *yehuatl on*, that.

in oquito yehuatl in	what he/she said is this: . . .
cenca ninococotica auh ipampa in	I am very ill, and because of this I will
amo niyaz tianquizco	not go to the marketplace.
ixquich in inic nimitznotolinilia	This is all with which I am bothering you.

Demonstrative *in* can sometimes be recognized in the original documents or a true transcription thereof by the orthography. The vowel [i] was generally written *y* at the beginning of a phrase, *i* inside it. Postposed *in* goes with what precedes it, so that it was normally written "in," whereas the subordinator *in* usually begins a phrase and was written "yn." The first example just above would be written, at least in many practiced hands, as "yn oquito yehuatl in."[1] The combination *inin* would most often appear as "ynin."

In texts of the sixteenth and early seventeenth centuries, *inin* and *in* are so much more frequently seen than *inon* and *on* that one could easily forget entirely about the latter, but as time goes on the second set becomes ever more common.

For exercises, analyze and retranslate all the examples in the usual fashion, this time with more attention to syntax.

---

[1]Those who tried to use spaces between letters to create meaningful solid strings (not all did, and few consistently) tended to write "yehuatlin," not "yehuatl in."

11. Even More on Verbs

The imperfect and the pluperfect. Irregular verbs. Texts and examples.

A. *The imperfect and the pluperfect.* We have already encountered the present, future, and preterit tenses of the indicative (not to speak of the present of the optative mode). Two tenses still missing are the imperfect and the past perfect or pluperfect. Of these the more frequently seen is the imperfect, which is all in all quite easy both to recognize and to understand. It is formed in all cases by adding -*ya* to the root, i.e., to the present tense. Its sense corresponds closely to that of the imperfect in such a language as Spanish; in English, the most common renderings are "was doing, would do, used to do." It usually speaks either of an action ongoing and not complete when another action (expressed by the preterit) took place, or of something customary in the past. The only complication is orthographic, owing to the practice of the old masters of not writing *y* between *i* and *a*, so that we have to reconstruct *y* to capture the uniformity of the imperfect. (In actual documents, this *y* was in fact frequently written).

1	2	3	4
naci, I arrive	*niyoli*, I live	*nicholoa*, I flee	*nitlaqua*, I eat
nacia (*naciya*), I was arriving	*niyolia* (*niyoliya*), I was living	*nicholoaya*, I was fleeing	*nitlaquaya*, I was eating

As with the present tense, the plural of the imperfect consists of only a glottal stop, so that there is no written difference between singular and plural.

nitlaquaya	I was eating	*titlaquaya*	we were eating
titlaquaya	you were eating	*antlaquaya*	you (pl.) were eating
tlaquaya	he/she was eating	*tlaquaya*	they were eating

At times this tense is found with the preterit *o* prefixed, without any apparent effect on the meaning. It is true that when the imperfect has the effect of a pluperfect, as it sometimes does, the *o* is somewhat more likely to be seen.

yalhua hualla don Juan Cuetlaxcoapan ohuia   Don Juan came back yesterday; he had gone to Puebla.

The pluperfect or past perfect properly speaking is also relatively easy, that is, easy if we can presume that the preterit with all its difficulties has already been grasped, because it is consistently formed by adding -*ca* to the preterit stem. The preterit suffixes are removed, of course, because this -*ca* is the same element that gave rise to all of them; it is the ancient -*ca* of the preterit, frozen and preserved in this specialized function.

1	2	3	4
(o)*nacic*, I arrived	(o)*niyol*, I lived	(o)*nicholo*, I fled	(o)*nitlaqua*, I ate
(o)*nacica*, I had arrived	(o)*niyolca*, I had lived	(o)*nicholoca*, I had fled	(o)*nitlaquaca*, I had eaten

Just as with the imperfect, there is no written distinction between singular and plural because the glottal stop of the plural was not written down.

onitlaquaca	I had eaten	*otitlaquaca*	we had eaten
otitlaquaca	you had eaten	*oantlaquaca*	you (pl.) had eaten
otlaquaca	he/she had eaten	*otlaquaca*	they had eaten

As to the meaning of this tense, often it functions exactly like the pluperfect in English, to indicate an action occurring before another action already past, or before a past time. But it can also simply indicate a remote time without reference to anything else. Perhaps the most difficult thing about this tense is that it is so rare in the sources that one tends to interpret it as an error or as a singular preterit verb followed by the particle *ca*. Nevertheless, it does appear now and then, especially in texts showing strong Spanish influence. In Lesson 9, p. 55, we saw four different types of *ca* that need keeping apart; we now have a fifth, or at least a different use of the fourth (preterit -*ca*- in compounds and adverbially).

B. *Irregular verbs*. We have already encountered the irregular verbs in the section on auxiliary verbs, because the two sets are nearly the same, but it is worthwhile reviewing a topic so miscellaneous in itself and which experience shows that students' minds resist with great tenacity. We can also now speak of these verbs' reverential forms, so hard to recognize.

B1. *Conjugation of some irregular verbs*. The most common of the irregular verbs are *i(h)cac*, "to be (standing)"; *onoc*, "to be (in a horizontal position)"; *mani*, "to be (spread out)"; *ca(h)*, "to be (more generally, but still stative)"; *yauh*, "to go," and *huallauh*, "to come." They have two general tendencies seen also in the irregular verbs of other languages. First, for many of them the present tense is formally a preterit, and the formal pluperfect consequently can be the simple past or imperfect (true of *icac*, *onoc*, and *ca*, with strong tendencies in that direction in *mani*). With these verbs there is sometimes no distinction at all between preterit and imperfect, and even when there is, the past tenses usually have the thrust of an imperfect, for they are mainly verbs expressing states, not actions. Second, the two most common of the irregulars, *ca* and *yauh* (with its twin *huallauh*), are suppletive, i.e., they have two different roots with different historical origins which appear in different tenses and numbers.

As to the verbs with preterit as present, *icac* and *onoc* belong to Class 1, so that their -*c* is the preterit singular suffix. They have plurals in -*que* like any other preterit: *icaque* and *onoque*. As we would expect, their pluperfects act as preterits: *icaca* and *onoca*. They also have true imperfects based on the original forms of the present, now lost, which would have been *ica* and *ono*: *icaya* and *onoya*. It is difficult to detect any difference in use between *icaca* and *icaya*, *onoca* and *onoya*.

Ca is also formally preterit, but it is harder to recognize as such. The lost present must have been *cati*, Class 2.[1] Its preterit must have been *cat* singular, *catque* plural, although in addition to *cat* there was a variant with the archaic singular -*qui*, *catqui*, which still exists in some frozen phrases (*iz catqui*, "here is," is the most common). As Nahuatl will not long tolerate a final *t*, *cat* became *ca(h)* in the same way that the preterit of *mati*, "to know," *mat*, became *ma(h)*. The *t* of the plural, protected by a suffix, survived, but perhaps because of the ultra-frequency of the word, the consonant of the suffix was lost, so that instead of *catque* we now see *cate*. Starting with *cat* as the preterit stem, the pluperfect *catca* is regular, and it is used as a preterit/imperfect (no other past is in common use in standard Nahuatl). At times it appears with the *o* preterit sign: *ocatca*.

It will be worth our while to look at paradigms of the three verbs in present and past:

nicac	ticaque	nonoc	nonoque	nica	ticate
ticac	amicaque	tonoc	amonoque	tica	ancate
icac	icaque	onoc	onoque	ca	cate
nicaca, nicaya	ticaca, ticaya	nonoca, nonoya	tonoca, tonoya	nicatca	ticatca
ticaca, ticaya	amicaca, amicaya	tonoca, tonoya	amonoca, amonoya	ticatca	ancatca
icaca, icaya	icaca, icaya	onoca, onoya	onoca, onoya	catca	catca

---

[1]The original meaning of *cati* was probably "to sit," for verbs of identical shape have that meaning in some other Uto-Aztecan languages, and no verb with that sense appears in the Nahuatl irregular set.

The future of *icac* and *onoc* is regular on the basis of the lost presents: *icaz* and *onoz*. But the future of *ca*, which is constantly seen, is based on the verb's second root, *ye*.

niyez, niez	*tiyezque, tiezque*
tiyez, tiez	*anyezque*
yez	*yezque*

The optative too is based on *ye* (*ma niye, nie*, "may I be"), as well as the form with the helping verbs (*yetiuh*, "he/she goes being") and the impersonal (*yeloa*, "things are").

Mani, "to be (spread out)" is perhaps in transition toward becoming one of the verbs of which we have been speaking. The present is still normal, although in documents from the Cuernavaca region the form *manic* is sometimes seen, a preterit for the present as though *mani* were a Class 1 verb. The past is most often the pluperfect *manca*, although the normal preterit *man* may also sometimes occur.

The verb *yauh*, "to go," is the most irregular of all. It does not have a preterit for a present, but its two roots, *ya* and *hui*, alternate in a fashion even more capricious than with *ca*. The present singular contains both; *yauh* consists of *ya* and of a *hui* that has lost its last vowel. The plural of the present has only *hui*.[2]

niyauh, niauh	*tihui*
tiyauh, tiauh	*anhui*
yauh	*hui*

This arrangement at least has the advantage of distinguishing the plural from the singular in writing, which is not possible with a normal present tense.

The preterit is based on the root *ya: ya(h), ya(h)que*. The imperfect comes from *hui*, the future again from *ya*.

niya, nia	*tiyaque, tiaque*	*nihuia*	*tihuia*	*niyaz, niaz*	*tiyazque, tiazque*
tiya, tia	*anyaque*	*tihuia*	*anhuia*	*tiyaz, tiaz*	*anyazque*
ya	*yaque*	*huia*	*huia*	*yaz*	*yazque*

The optative is based on *hui*; the plural is irregular, without the *c* of the suffix -*can*; *xihuian*, "go (pl.)!" The impersonal is also from *hui*, *huiloa*. The imperfect and impersonal have variants based on *ya* (*yaya, yaloa*), but they are not often seen in documents.

Huallauh, "to come," runs parallel to *yauh* in everything, since it is merely *hual-yauh* plus automatic assimilation. Thus the present is *nihuallauh, tihualhui*, preterit *nihualla*, imperfect *nihualhuia*, future *nihuallaz*, optative *ma nihualhui*, etc.

B2. *Reverentials of irregulars.* The reverentials of some of the irregular verbs can hardly be recognized on first sight as coming from the same root. But in most cases they do.

icac	*miquiltia, miquiltiticac*
onoc	*monoltia, monoltitoc*

In fact, *miquiltia* is a normal reverential, if we start with the ancient present tense *ica*: the *o* of the *mo*- reflexive cedes to *i* because a glottal stop follows; -*ltia* is causative; *a* of the root becomes *i* as so often; *c* becomes *qu* to preserve the pronunciation. *Monoltia* has the same structure and is more transparent. In one respect it is irregular. Earlier we saw that the root of the verb is *o* and that *on*- is the directional prefix, which is missing in the auxiliary form, -*toc*. Here it is included, but after the reflexive and not before as the order of prefixes dictates. In this case *on* has been considered part of the root. Both *icac* and *onoc* have reverential progressives in which the verb acts as its own auxiliary; these forms, given just above along with the other reverentials, are the most frequent.

The reverential of *ca* is *moyetztica*. Again the verb is its own auxiliary. The rest can-

---

[2]In documents of some regions the plural *yahui* is seen.

not be analyzed in the normal style. Perhaps it was once *mo-ye-ti-*, another reverential with the causative, and the *-ti-* became *-tz-*. In the absence of certainty here, the best thing is simply to learn to recognize the form, because it is of high frequency in the sources.

We have already seen the reverentials of *yauh* and *huallauh, mohuica* (to take oneself) and *hualmohuica* (to bring oneself).

Mani is not found in texts in reverential form, perhaps because it rarely refers to people.

C. *Some illustrative texts and examples.*

C1. *ye oxin in calli in nican icaya tlalpan onoc in quahuitl in tetl aoc itla oncan icac auh in calli itlallo çan çacayotimani nohuiyan cactimani ye hueca oyaque in oncan nemia ye ayac ichan ayac iaxca amo tlamani in iuh tlamania ca oncan icaya yetetl calli in xochimilcopahuic itzticaya itech çaliuhticatca in tonatiuh iquiçayampa itzticaya auh in icalaquiyampa tonatiuh itzticaya çan nonqua icaya in cale oncatca icihuauh huel qual-nezqui ihuan yei ipilhuan mochipa mahuiltiaya motlaloaya in ithualco in imilpan qualli ic omochiuh in centli in icuezcon huel temia imiltempan mamania xocoquahuitl no miequintin ipitzohuan miecpa tetlaqualtiaya mochipa tlachixticatca inic huallazque in icnihuan inic cuicazque mitotizque huel mahuiztic in ical catca auh inic qualli quauhxinqui in cale Mexico oya ompa miec tomin quixtlahuia mochintin quinhuicac icihuauh ipilhuan ma hualhuian ma quiquetzacan oc centetl calli ma oc ceppa mahuil-titiecan in pipiltzitzintin*

The house that used to stand here has fallen in. The wood and stone lies on the ground. Nothing is standing there any longer. And the land belonging to the house is just gone to grass. Everything is abandoned. Those who used to live there went far away; now it is no one's home and belongs to no one. Things are not as they used to be, for three houses stood there. The one looking toward Xochimilco (south) abutted on the one looking east, and the one looking west just stood by itself. The owner of the house had a very good looking wife and three children. They were always playing and running in the patio. On his fields the maize yielded well; his grainbin was very full. At the edge of his fields were fruit trees here and there (or all along). He also had many pigs. He would often feed people; he was always looking for his friends to come to sing and dance. His was a splendid house. And since the owner of the house is a good carpenter, he went to Mexico City. There they pay him a lot of money. He took everyone, his wife and children. Let them come back, let them build another house; let the children be playing again.

tlalpan: belongs with the following. Throughout the text remember that adverbial elements are always put in front of what they refer to if possible, that is, if they are short enough.

çacayotimani: *çaca-*, from *çacatl*, grass, weeds, dried grass for hay; *-yo*, nominal suffix, "covered with." The unusual thing about the construction is that it looks like a noun with a helping verb; it appears that this *-yo*, which is of verbal origin, still counts as a verb in certain contexts.

cactimani: this whole construction is to be found in the dictionary, but not the main verb it derives from; it could be an old intransitive verb related to *cahua*, "to leave." The word also has the sense of stillness, and our passage could be translated "It's quiet all around."

tlamani: *tla-* with an intransitive verb is not an object but forms an impersonal.

in xochimilcopahuic, etc. In this whole section about the three houses, *in* is basic for the structure.

in cale oncatca icihuauh: *onca* is "there is," saying that something exists. The old

Nahuatl way of saying "to have something" was first to specify the possessor, follow it with *onca*, and then its subject, a possessed noun referring back to the possessor; *in nehuatl oncate nopilhuan*, "to me there are my children," i.e., "I have children." The verb *pia* as an equivalent of "to have" soon began to replace phrases of this type in some respects, but many vestiges are found in the texts as long as Nahuatl was written.

qualli ic: *ic* can make adverbial constructions of adjectival substantives.

omochiuh: the reflexive of *chihua*, aside from functioning as a passive and meaning "to happen," has the sense "to ripen, yield."

mamania: it may appear strange to use "to be spread out, stretched out," for something as vertical as a tree, but the trees as a group are indeed spread out. The distributive (the reduplication) expresses that the trees are at intervals.

mochintin quinhuicac icihuauh ipilhuan: in Nahuatl a quantitative word can refer to a whole collection of things, however miscellaneous, so that it is possible to say "he took all his wife and children," even though there is only one wife. Such an utterance is possible because the quantifier, here *mochintin*, stands in apposition to whatever its crossreferent is, here *icihuauh ipilhuan*.

C2. *in nonamictzin omoyetzticatca nicchihuilizquia ce missa ma iciuhca mochihuaz auh in cruz in nocalnahuac miquiltiticac ca naxca macayac quiquixtiz ye ixquich in in namechnolhuilia in nican ammonoltitoque*

I was going to have a mass said for my late spouse; let it be said soon. And the cross that stands near my house is my property; let no one remove it. This is all that I say to you who are assembled here.

nicchihuilizquia: this is the first time that we have seen the tense called the conditional; note how similar it is to the conditional in Spanish, being closely related to both the future and the imperfect (*-zqui* is the archaic future; the imperfect *-ya* is hidden a bit by the orthography). This construction can be found with true conditional meaning ("I would do it"), but in texts it much more frequently has another sense, of an action that was planned or even begun but that after all was never carried out. "Was going to do" is the indicated translation.

ye ixquich in: this is the demonstrative *in* placed after *ixquich*. The following *in* is the subordinator. In an actual document, the passage would probably have been written *ye ixquich in yn namechnolhuilia*.

ammonoltitoque: reverential plural of *onoc*; despite the fact that the members of the audience are probably not in a horizontal position, this form often refers to a congregated group.

C3. Some forms of irregular verbs:

icazque	They will stand.
in notatzin moyetzticatca	my late father
monoltitoz	He/she will lie.
amo tihuia	We weren't going, we hadn't gone.
Quauhnahuac moyetztiyezque	They will be in Cuernavaca.
otiyaque in oncan ye huecauh yaca	We went where he/she had gone long ago.
ma xihualhuian	Come! (pl.), or Return!
in campa tihui	where we are going
anyaque	You (pl.) went, left.
miquiltiticaca	He/she or they stood.
timonoltitoca	You (sing.) lay.
canin timoyetztica	Where are you?

iciuhca omohuicac	He/she quickly went, left (rev.).
yalhua ohualmohuicac	He/she came or returned yesterday (rev.).
ya	He/she left.
tiyazque	We will go.
nican tiyezque	We will be here.
tiyaque	We went.
tecpantzinco onoque	They live, dwell, in the palace.
nican oticatca	We were, or you (sing.) were here.
onihualhuia	I was coming, returning, had come.
quemman tihualmohuicaz	At what time will you (sing.) come (rev.)?
oncan onicaca, onicaya	I stood there, was standing there.
canin onoya in cuchillo	Where was the knife?
canin icaz in calli	Where will the house stand?
choloca yece çatepan ohualla	He had fled, but afterward he came back.
Coyoacan mohuicaz	He/she will go to Coyoacan (rev.).
ye huiptla ammohuicazquia yece oc nican ammoyetztica	You (pl.) were going to leave (rev.) the day before yesterday, but you're (rev.) still here.

12. Some Nominal Suffixes

The -yo abstractive, collective, and indicator of inalienable possession. The nominal suffixes meaning "possessor of." Text and examples.

A. *The suffix* -yo. Nouns can take a suffix -yo (with a long o not detectable in the written form), which is added directly to the noun stem, in front of any absolutive ending. The addition creates a new noun which always takes an absolutive ending of -tl in the singular and by its nature hardly ever appears in the plural. When possessed, it does not take the ending -uh despite presenting a vocalic stem. The y of -yo may assimilate to the preceding stem in various ways, disguising itself as -lo, -ço, and -cho.

qualli	a good thing	*qual-yo-tl*	becomes	*quallotl*	goodness
mahuiztli	fear	*mahuiz-yo-tl*	becomes	*mahuizçotl*	honor, respect
oquichtli	male, man	*oquich-yo-tl*	becomes	*oquichchotl*	valor

These assimilations do not function automatically. Often the unassimilated forms will be seen, as well as forms in which the consonant at morpheme boundary is not written double, like *mahuiçotl* and *oquichotl*.

A noun in -yo means in the first instance the abstract quality of the noun from which it derives. English nouns in "-ness," "-ity," "-hood," and "ship" are similar, for example "badness" from "bad," "nobility" from "noble," "parenthood" from "parent," and "friendship" from "friend." Here are some parallel words in Nahuatl. They sometimes come in pairs with an overall meaning a bit different from that of either member of the pair.

pilli	noble	*pillotl*	nobility
teuctli	lord	*teucyotl*	lordship
tlatoani	ruler	*tlatocayotl*	rulership
amantecatl,		*amantecayotl,*	
toltecatl	artisan	*toltecayotl*	artisanry
nantli	mother	*nanyotl*	motherhood, maternity
tatli	father	*in nanyotl in tayotl*	parenthood

English abstract nouns act also as collectives and may have other more concrete senses, and so it is with -yo nouns as well. *Pillotl*, "nobility," can refer not only to the abstract quality but also to a particular assembly of nobles or to the entire class. Likewise, *teucyotl* can mean all the lords. *Tlatocayotl* is not used in the sense of all the kings, but it has the sense of the office, powers, and appurtenances of the *tlatoani:* if we call him a king, the *tlatocayotl* is equivalent to the crown or throne; if a ruler, to the rulership; if a chief, to the chieftaincy, if as in Spanish a *cacique*, to the *cacicazgo*. *Teucyotl* can have the same thrust in relation to *teuctli*. The possible meanings are multitudinous. *Yaotl* is "enemy;" *yaoyotl* should by rights be "enmity," but it has the well established meaning of "war, combat." *Conetl* is "child"; *coneyotl*, in addition to "childhood," is "childishness, the act of a child." *Teotl* is "god," *teoyotl* "divinity, divine matters," or more specifically "the sacraments (especially marriage)." *Acatl* is "reed, something through which fluid flows"; *acayotl* can be "tubing, a set of pipes." *Chichihualli* is "breast," *atl* is "water"; *chichihualayotl* is "milk."

In the above uses, nouns in -yo will rarely be found in possessed form, but -yo is also used to indicate a particular kind of possession, of something which for any of various reasons cannot be separated from the possessor. This construction, sometimes called the form of inalienable possession, perhaps grows out of the collective sense of -yo nouns. *Eztli* means "blood," viewed simply as an object, perhaps the blood in a stain or a bucket of a butchered animal's blood. *Nezço* is "my blood," the blood coursing inside my veins.

69

Nacatl is "meat, flesh." *Nonac* would be "my meat," some meat I have bought and mean to eat. *Nonacayo* is "my flesh," equivalent to "my body" (or as close as the Nahuas got to that concept; the word in this form mainly refers to general bodily health and to dead bodies). From these examples you will see why this use of *-yo* is also called the form of organic possession, referring to something which is an inherent, natural part of something else. But the possession can be more decreed and less organic. The Nahuas tended to set up a certain amount of land to go with a residence as its support, in theory inseparable from it, which they called *callalli*, "house-land." *Ichinanyo in calli* would be the chinampas that go with the house and cannot be given away by whoever has it.

B. *The nominal suffixes meaning "possessor of."* Nahuatl seems once to have had some verbs that meant to possess something, but by the time the Spaniards arrived all that was left of them was a set of suffixes which betray by their plurals that they originated as preterit agentive nouns: *-e(h)*, plural *-e(h)que(h)*; *-hua(h)*, plural *-hua(h)que(h)*, and *–yo(h)*, plural *-yo(h)que(h)*. They also show their preterit agentive origin in the combining form, where the *-ca-* ligature appears. They attach directly to the noun stem: *tlalli*, land; *tlale*, land owner.

B1. *-E and* -hua. The suffixes *-e* and *-hua* basically indicate simple possession. No distinction of meaning can be detected between them, and it appears that they are descendants of the same element, having taken a different form in different contexts. *-E* is used mainly with consonant stems, *-hua* with vowel stems, but exceptions are quite numerous.

milli	*mile*	*mileque*	*milecatzintli*
field	field owner	field owners	field owner, rev.
cihuatl	*cihuahua*	*cihuahuaque*	*cihuahuacatzintli*
woman	possessor of a woman, married man	married men	married man, rev.
piltzintli[1]	*pilhua*	*pilhuaque*	*pilhuacatzintli*
child	person with children	people with children	person with children, rev.

Possessor constructions like this could be formed ad hoc with almost any noun, but many have become set vocabulary items, and as we see in the case of *cihuahua*, the sense often goes well beyond that of literally possessing the referent of the root noun.

topilli	*topile*
staff	possessor of a staff, officeholder
calli	*cale*
house	owner of a house, householder, head of a household
chan(tli)	*chane*
home	resident, citizen, person born in a certain place
ixtli nacaztli	*ixe nacace*
eyes, ears	one who has eyes and ears, one who is alert, sharp
altepetl, atl tepetl	*altepehua, ahua tepehua*
waters, mountains, sociopolitical unit called altepetl	possessor of waters and mountains, citizen of an altepetl or an officer of it
quaquahuitl	*quaquauhe, quaquahue*
horn (of an animal)	ox, bull, bovine animal
ilhuicatl, tlalticpac	*ilhuicahua tlalticpaque*
heaven, (on) earth	owner or master of heaven and earth, God

Of high frequency are *axcahua* and *tlatquihua*, both meaning a property owner and often

---

[1]The form with reverential is used here because only that form means "child," the simple form always meaning "noble." See Lesson 9, p. 57, n. 1.

used as a pair, from *axcaitl* and *tlatquitl*, property. (The latter originally referred to that which is carried and thus meant primarily movable property, but by the time of the texts the two words were often treated as equivalent.)

Students commonly have problems recognizing *-e* and *-hua* formations. *-E* is so small and innocuous that it is often simply ignored and the construction is taken to be the root noun. *-Hua* is sometimes confused with the possessive plural suffix of nouns, *-huan*; such confusion is even more likely in actual texts, where the final *n* of the latter suffix is often omitted. Observe the differences between the following:

pilhua	person with children	*nopilhuan*	my children
pilhuacatzintli	person with children, rev.	*nopilhuantzitzin,*	
		nopiltzitzinhuan	my children, rev.
tlale	land owner	*tlalli*	land, piece of land
tlalecatzintli	land owner, rev.	*tlaltzintli*	land, rev.

A source of confusion with the *-e* suffix is Nahuatl's vocative. The vocative, though doubtless frequently used in everyday speech, is a rare enough phenomenon in written texts, particularly those of a mundane nature, that it might be omitted from a set of lessons like the present one were it not for the fact that some students sooner or later get wind of it and take it for the *-e* possessor suffix, or more often vice versa.

B2. *Spurious similarity of the vocative.* The vocative divides in two according to gender. Both male and female vocatives involve a very unusual measure for Nahuatl, the entire omission of the subject prefix of nouns. It is the vocative used by males that causes the trouble. To create this form, *-e* is added to the noun plus absolutive ending if there is one, although if the absolutive ordinarily ends in *i*, that *i* is elided. The *-e* can also be added to possessed forms and to deverbal agentive nouns, as well as to names. If we could hear the vocative *-e*, we would be aware that it lacks the glottal stop of the possessor suffix and that it bears a final stress unique in Nahuatl, but as things are, in both cases we only see an *e* at the end of the word.

telpochtli	*telpochtle*	*telpopochtin*	*telpopochtine*
youth	O youth!	youths	O youths!
pochtecatl	*pochtecatle*	*pochteca*	*pochtecae*[2]
merchant	O merchant!	merchants	O merchants!
nopiltzin	*nopiltzine*	*nopilhuan*	*nopilhuane*
my child	O my child!	my children	O my children!
tlatoani	*tlatoanie*	*tlatoque*	*tlatoquee*[2]
ruler	O ruler!	rulers	O rulers!

Aside from the final *e*, these words are markedly distinct from possessor suffix constructions. A possessor *-e* construction would lack even the vestige of an absolutive or possessive nominal ending to the left of it. If we imagine (though it is a bit unrealistic) something like *tlatoani* appearing in the possessor construction in the meaning "one who has a ruler," since the *-ni* agentive cannot be combined, the preterit agentive would be resorted to and a *-ca-* ligature would appear; once *-ca-* was there the ending would in any case be *-hua*, not *-e*: *tlatocahua* (vocative *tlatoanie*). If someone felt it necessary to address his fields, he would say *mille*, O field!, with two *l*'s as opposed to *mile*, field owner.

The female vocative has nothing in common with the *-e* possessor suffix construction. The danger here is not even to recognize that a vocative is involved, for there is no suffix.

---

[2]At these points in mundane texts and even in some grammars and ecclesiastical texts an *h* is likely to be written, representing the glottal stop at the end of the nominal plural or merely punctuating between two vowels, and at times *y* appears instead, for intervocalic glottal stop sometimes becomes *y*: *tlatoquehe, tlatoqueye*, etc.

What looks at first glance like a third person form is addressed to the second person; only attention to the context will reveal the intention. Once the second person reference has been somehow caught, we know that we are dealing with the vocative because of the lack of a corresponding subject prefix on the noun. We also know a female is speaking.

Juantzin tla xihualmohuica	Juan, do please come here.
totecuiyo nimitzonnonepechtequililia	O our lord, I bow down to you.

B3. -Yo *constructions.* Quite distinct from -*e* and -*hua* is a -*yo* that invites confusion with the abstract -*yo* of section A above but can be distinguished from it in several ways. The abstract/collective -*yo* can take a standard nominal absolutive ending, which the possessor -*yo* as a preterit agentive cannot. We cannot detect in the written form that possessor -*yo* has a glottal stop, abstract -*yo* a long vowel, but we can see that the former often takes a plural in -*que* corresponding to its origins, whereas the latter is rarely pluralized, and if it should be, the ending would not be -*que*. Possessor -*yo* is rarely possessed, whereas the other form frequently is.

It can be said with a certain validity that -*yo* constructions mean "possessor of," but only in a restricted sense; they almost always mean that the subject of the noun is literally or figuratively covered with what the noun refers to.

teuhtli	dust	*teuhyo*	something dusty	*teuhyoque*	dusty beings
çoquitl	mud	*çoqui(y)o*	something muddy	*çoqui(y)oque*	muddy beings
tlalli	earth	*tlallo*	something covered with earth	*tlalloque*	beings covered with earth
tepoztli	metal	*tepozço*	someone covered with metal, in armor or chains	*tepozçoque*	armored men, or people in chains
tenyotl	fame	*tenyoyo*	someone covered with fame, famous	*tenyoyoque*	famous people

C. *A text and some examples.*

otlanahuati in tlatoani visorrey oquito monequi oncan Ocuillan in altepehuaque caleque cihuahuaque cexiuhtica huel ixquich nanahui pesos tlacalaquilli quimanazque auh cenca miec tomin amo huel mochihua cuix tOcuilteca titocuiltonoa titotlamachtia campa ticcuizque nanahui tomin çatepan nican oquihualihuaque ce juez inic quinechicoz yece in nican chaneque ixeque nacaceque cequintin quauhtla choloque oc cequintin oconnamicque in juez in iquac nican ohualcalac ça tzotzomatli intilma ica mapanque ça xalloque çoquiyoque catzahuaque inic ixpantzinco onezque in juez oquitoque tlatoanie totecuiyoe ma xitechmotlapopolhuili ca in ticaleque huel ticnotlacatzitzintin cenca titotolinia amo taxcahuaque amo titlatquihuaque atle totomin in huei tlacalaquilli ticmonechicalhuiznequi amo huel mocahuaz ma xiquimmocnoittili in tocihuahuan in topilhuan çan miquizque itlachihualhuan totecuiyo Dios amo iuh quimonequiltia in ilhuicahuacatzintli in tlalticpaquecatzintli niman ic çan onmocuep in juez amo oneltic itequiuh

The lord viceroy gave orders; he said, "it is necessary that there in Ocuillan the citizens who are married householders should pay a full four pesos each of tribute per year." But it is a great deal of money; it can't be done. Are we people of Ocuillan wealthy and rich? Where are we to get four pesos each? Afterward they sent a judge here to collect it, but the local residents are astute. Some fled to the forest. Others went out to meet the judge when he entered here; the cloaks in which they wrapped themselves were just rags; they were just covered with sand and mud and dirty when they appeared before the judge. They said, "O ruler, O our lord, pardon us, for we householders are very poor pitiful people, we are greatly impoverished and unpropertied; we have no money. The great tribute you want to collect cannot be delivered. Have pity on our wives and children; the creatures of our lord God will just die (or inevitably will die). The master of heaven and earth does not wish it so." Thereupon the judge just went back; his assignment was not carried out.

nanahui pesos: The reduplication of the first syllable of a number gives a distributive sense, that many each.

tOcuilteca: When a settlement's name ends in *-tlan* (of which *-lan* is an assimilated form), the name of an inhabitant of that place ends in *-tecatl*.

inic quinechicoz: *inic* here translates as "in order to."

ica mapanque: the *i-* of *ica* refers to *intilma*; we could say "with which," but "in which" is more idiomatic in English. *Mapanque* is a preterit and analyzes as *m-apan-que*.

inic ixpantzinco onezque: here *inic* could be translated "when," or it could be taken as referring to the manner in which they appeared.

atle totomin: "nothing is our money," "we have no money."

ticmonechicalhuiznequi: from *nechicoa*. The clause is subordinate even though not preceded by *in*, something you will see in texts again and again.

niman ic: a set phrase, "thereupon," indicating the next thing in a sequence of actions.

Some specific examples:

in teucyotl in tlatocayotl huel inemac don Antonio catca	The lordship and rulership was fully don Antonio's inheritance.
ixquich in pillotl in teucyotl nican mocentlalia	All the nobles and rulers are assembled here.
ye otimohuapauh amo ticmomacaz in pillotl in coneyotl	You have grown up now; you are not to give yourself to childish actions.
in tlatlacatecolo ixpampa ehua in quallotl in yecyotl	The demons flee from goodness.
cenca monequi tictomahuizmachilizque in nanyotl in tayotl	It is very necessary that we honor parenthood.
teoyotica omonamictique	They have married in the church, by sacrament.
in vacascocone miec intech monequi in chichihualayotl	Calves use/need much milk.
huei oquichotl oquinexti in yaotequihua	The war leader showed great valor.
mococoa in nonacayo	My body is ill.
cenca etic notlallo noçoquiyo	My earth and clay (my body) are very heavy (ill).
tlallo çoquiyo ohualcalac	He/she came in dirty and muddy.
amo nicnamacaz in ichinanyo calli	I will not sell the chinampas going with the house.
yaopan noquilo teezço[1]	In war people's blood is spilled.

---

[1] Both *e*'s are retained here because the *e* of *te-* is long.

13. Purposive Motion and Passive

Purposive motion forms. Passives and impersonals. Locatives in -yan and -can. Text and examples.

A. *Purposive motion forms.* We now meet another type of auxiliary; the set we have already seen, marked by the ligature *-ti-*, in various ways describes the mode of the action of the main verb (carried out with the actor in a certain position, in an ongoing fashion, quickly, on leaving, etc.). Our new set does not speak to such matters, but says that someone or something comes or goes to carry out the action of the main verb. For that reason these have been called the forms of purposive motion.[1] One form, with the roots *-quiuh* and *-co*, means to come toward the speaker (or sometimes the listener) to do something; the other, with the roots *-tiuh* and *-to*, to go away from the speaker to do something. They act as suffixes added directly to the full present tense or verb root; as with the future and the optative, the final *a* of Class 3 verbs is omitted to form a new stem. There are only two indicative tenses, one of which refers more to the future and present, the other more to the past. In fact, there are subtle differences between the two as to tense implications that need not concern us here. The forms run as follows:

nicchihuaquiuh	I am coming or will come to do it	*ticchihuaquihui(h)*	we are . . .
(o)nicchihuaco	I come or have come to do it	*(o)ticchihuaco(h)*	we come . . .
nicchihuatiuh	I go or am going to do it	*ticchihuatihui(h)*	we go . . .
(o)nicchihuato	I went to do it	*(o)ticchihuato(h)*	we went . . .[2]

For the student to get a good sense of the purposive motion forms, immediate illustration through examples is needed.

oquixquetzque ce juez nican Tlaxcallan otepohuaco	They appointed a judge; he came here to Tlaxcala to count people (carry out a census).
oc ce juez ompa Quauhnahuac otepohuato	Another judge went to Cuernavaca to carry out a census.
nocniuhtzin onechcuepilico in notomin in nechhuiquiliaya	My friend came to return me my money that he owed me.
campa tiyauh nictequitiuh xocotl in ipan ialahuerta nomontatzin	Where are you going? I am going to pick fruit in my father-in-law's orchard.
ticnechicoquihui in diezmo in itechtzinco pohui in teopixcatlatoani obispo	We are coming to collect the tithe that belongs to the priestly ruler the bishop.
Cuetlaxcoapan titomachtitihui organo tictzotzonazque	We are going to Puebla to learn to play the organ.
tle axtica in mocihuauh quin axcan oya oquito ye natlacuitiuh amo nihuecahuaz	What is your wife doing? Just now she left; she said, "I'm going to fetch water; I won't be long."
in o iuh nican Mexico tlalpoloco in españolestin iciuhca oc mieccan tepehuato	After the Spaniards had conquered Mexico City,[3] they soon went to many other places to conquer people.
yehuantin in quineltilico quichicahuaco in iiyotzin itlatoltzin Rey	They are the ones who came to carry out and confirm the orders of the king.
moztla nimitznamiquiquiuh	Tomorrow I will come to meet you.

---

[1] By J. Richard Andrews in his grammar of classical Nahuatl.

[2] These forms also have an optative/imperative which is very rarely seen in mundane documents but sometimes occurs in more formal texts: *-qui*, plural *-qui(h)*, and *(-h)* (after a vowel) or *-ti*, plural *-ti(h)* or *-tin*. *Ma xicuicaqui ma ximitotiqui*, "Come sing, come dance!" Students may take the *-qui* to be the preterit agentive suffix or even imagine it to be the object prefix of a following verb. The *-ti/ -tin* tends to look like a nominal plural.

[3] More literally, "after the Spaniards had come to destroy the land in Mexico City." The more experience you get with the purposive forms, the less you will translate them. Above, instead of "my friend came to return me my money," we had just as well say "my friend returned me my money."

The *-co* of *-quiuh/-co* is often confused with the *-co* locative suffix, but the first always attaches to a finite verb, the second to a noun (or in *-tzinco* to a relational word). More worthy of our attention is the confusion between the *-tiuh/-tihui* of purposive motion and the *-tiuh/-tihui* consisting of *-ti-* ligature and progressive auxiliary from *yauh*, "to go." The *i* of the first is long, that of the second short, but that avails us nothing in the written form. When the main verb belongs to Class 2, a difference in the stems of the two forms tells us which is which. The stem before the progressive auxiliary is shortened, whereas the purposive motion form is the full present tense root.

quitamachiuhtiuh in itlal altepetl	*quitamachihuatiuh in itlal altepetl*
He goes along measuring the land of the altepetl.	He goes to measure the land of the altepetl.

With Classes 1 and 3, however, the written form in itself tells us nothing. The stem of Class 1 never reduces. With Class 3, the final *a* of the present tense is missing in both forms; the remaining vowel is followed by glottal stop in the progressive, whereas it is long without a glottal stop in the purposive motion form, but none of this shows in writing.

quittatiuh incal intlal icoltzin icitzin	He/she goes to inspect *or* goes along inspecting the houses and lands of his/her grandfather and grandmother.
motlapololtitiuh tlahuanaliztica	He/she goes along out of his/her senses with drinking *or* he/she goes to befuddle him/herself with drinking.

With verbs of these classes (and 4 is like 3 in this respect) we must rely on the context, common sense, and probability, which together will solve most cases adequately.

So far the notion of purposive motion has served us well in dealing with the *-quiuh/-co* and *-tiuh/-to* forms. It does not, however, apply to all cases by any means. The forms are often used with inanimate subjects which could have no purpose in mind. In many of these cases the sense seems to be that of going as far as, reaching a definitive destination.

in notlal itech acitiuh in Tollocan otli	My land goes as far as, reaches up to, the Toluca road.
imil Agustin itech acico in notepanco	Agustin's field comes or came as far as my boundary.
in huei citlalin icalaquiyampa tonatiuh opolihuito	Venus (the great star) disappeared in the west.

This sense is not restricted to inanimates. Examples exist with human subjects in which any notion of purpose is inapplicable.

quin axcan onmopehualti in tlatoani arço-bispo inic Caxtillan onmocuepaz çan Tecamachalco omomiquilito	Just recently the lord archbishop set out to return to Spain, but he got as far as Tecamachalco and died.
inteyacancauh catca don Luis çan hual-mocuepato	Their leader was don Luis, but he went a certain way and came back.
huei apan omomiquilico	He died on the ocean at some point on the way here.

One finds *-tiuh/-to* used this way more than *-co*. With another kind of use, *-co* is seen much more frequently. Apparently the forms can refer to movement over time; with *-co* the reference is to movement from the past toward the present, and with *-tiuh* apparently from the present into the future (though unambiguous examples are still lacking).[4]

iuh otlamaniltico in huehuetque tocolhuan tachtonhuan	So did our ancient forebears (lit., the ancients our grandfathers and great-grandfathers) order things.

Don't be overly concerned, especially at this stage, about the subtleties of meaning of

---

[4]Much the same thing is seen with the directional prefixes, *hual-* to express the passage of time from the past in the direction of the present, and *on-* from the present forward, fully parallel with their use in relation to space.

the *-quiuh/-co* and *-tiuh/-to* forms. They are often not crucial to a translation, and even the most advanced scholars do not yet understand them fully. The important thing is to recognize what they are in general and be able to get back to the dictionary form of the main verbs they are attached to.

B. *Passives and impersonals.* The passive of verbs is not used in Nahuatl texts as much as one might expect, in large part perhaps because of the frequent use of the active reflexive in a passive sense, as well as active verbs in the third person plural forming a kind of impersonal or passive equivalent.

ye omocauh in tlacalaquilli	The tribute has been delivered.
amo mitoa in tiquitoaya	What you were saying is not said.
quiquixtilizque in imil	They will take his fields from him.
	(equivalent to: His fields will be taken from him.)

Nevertheless, true passive forms and the closely related impersonals are indeed found in texts frequently enough to warrant our attention. They can be recognized in part by their endings (*-lo, -o, -hua, -ihua, -ohua*). But the thing that should by now strike you most about a passive (a true passive is possible only with a transitive verb) is the lack of any specific object prefixes.

    niquitta in calli   I see the house.   *in calli ittalo*   The house is seen.

The passive in Nahuatl works much as in English, with one major exception. In Nahuatl the agent is never expressed in connection with a passive construction. Such a sentence as "the boat was lifted by ten men" would have to be in the active voice in Nahuatl.

    Far and away the most common passive ending is *-lo*. It is added to the full present tense, except that with Class 3, as we have seen happen so often, the final *a* is omitted.

quichihua	He/she makes it.	*chihualo*	It is made.
quitoa	He/she says it.	*itolo*	It is said.
quitlalia	He/she puts it down.	*tlalilo*	It is put down.

The second most frequent ending of the passive is just *-o*, which in fact is shortened from *-lo*.[1] The last vowel of the verb root is also lost. Many passives exist in both the longer and shorter version, some in the shorter alone. Verbs in *-ca* are especially likely to have an abbreviated passive. There is no need to worry about it, as long as you can recognize either type.

quimaca	He/she gives it to him/her.	*maco*	It is given to him/her.
cana	He/she takes it.	*ano, analo*	It is taken.
quitta	He/she sees it.	*itto, ittalo*	It is seen.

As we expect from English, in the Nahuatl passive the object of the active verb becomes the subject. We may be a little surprised to see that the indirect object can also be the subject, but when we think about it, English sometimes does the same.

onechmacac in tlaltepoztli	He gave me the hoe.
onimacoc in tlaltepoztli	I was given the hoe, the hoe was given to me.

With the passive as with the active, Nahuatl is concerned to see that each element in the verbal complex is adequately represented. The verb *maca* always has two objects, one direct and one indirect. With this verb, the indirect is accounted for in the passive by

---

[1]This is the same phenomenon we saw with *-liztli* nouns, the omission of a vowel and a consonant at morpheme boundary. In *macalo*, "it is given to him/her," the *a* at the end of the stem and the *l* at the beginning of the derivational suffix are omitted to give *maco*. See also pp. 15, 28.

becoming the subject. The original direct object must be represented either as a noun outside the verb complex or as an indefinite object prefix within the complex.

otechmacac in Martin in petlatl	Martin gave us the mat.
otimacoque in petlatl	We were given the mat.
otitlamacoque	We were given something.

If the subject (the original indirect object) also is not specified, an indefinite prefix will replace it as well, giving in effect an impersonal:

otetlamacoc	Something was given to someone, things were given to people.

If the verb is of the type that takes an obligatory reflexive prefix, that fact will be indicated by *-ne*, the indefinite reflexive prefix.[2]

onechmocuitlahui nohueltihuatzin	My older sister took care of me. [A male is speaking.]
oninecuitlahuiloc	I was taken care of.

Verbs in derived forms, specifically in the applicative and causative, can be and often are put into the passive. You need to recognize the relevant endings and take them off before looking for the verb in the dictionary and finally considering what the statement means.

in Juan miecpa nechcuilia in notlaquen	Juan often takes my clothing from me.
miecpa nicuililo in notlaquen	My clothing is often taken from me.
in visorrey quicahualtiz don Francisco inic alcalde	The viceroy is to make don Francisco relinquish his post as alcalde.
don Francisco cahualtiloz inic alcalde	Don Francisco is to be removed from office as alcalde.

An intransitive verb cannot be passive in the same sense as the transitives we have been discussing, but it can be impersonal, in which case it has no specific subject, but is always in the third person singular with a subject which cannot be narrowly defined. The main ending of the impersonal is *-hua*, which has affected vowels preceding it in various ways, giving endings apparently in *-ihua* and *-ohua* (often confusingly spelled *oa* in Carochi and Molina); the close relationship to the passive is seen in the fact that some impersonals end in *-lohua* (*-loa*).

nemi	he/she lives	*nemoa, nemohua*	there is living, life goes on
yoli	he/she lives	*yolihua*	there is living, life goes on
choca	he/she weeps	*chocoa, chocohua*	there is weeping, weeping occurs
yauh	he/she goes	*huiloa, huilohua*	there is going, people in general go or a large group goes
aci	he/she arrives	*axihua*	there is arrival

English has no well defined impersonal construction, so translations are not easy for us. It is much simpler in Spanish (*se vive, se llora, se va,* etc.). Note in the last example that the *c* of *aci* becomes *x* in the impersonal just as it does in the applicative and causative. *T* and *tz* also often become *ch* as they do in that context. The same thing happens with the shortened passive from transitives: *mati,* "to know"; *macho,* "it is known."

When all of the objects of a transitive verb are represented by indefinite prefixes in the passive, it becomes essentially an impersonal. We already saw an example above: *tetlamaco,* "giving of things to people goes on."

All passives and impersonals belong to Class 1, i.e., they never lose their final vowel in other tenses. With *-lo* (and its short form *o*) this is because the *o* is long; with *-hua* we do not know the reason, but so it is, and the knowledge can be useful. The preterit of an *-ohua* impersonal can be recognized even if it is spelled *-oa; nemoa* will have the preterit

---

[2] See the discussion of the use of *ne-* with *-liztli* nouns in Lesson 5, pp. 28–29.

nemoac, not *nemo* as a Class 3 verb would.

A different way of forming an impersonal is to add what we otherwise know as the indefinite object prefix, *tla-,* to an intransitive verb.

amo iuh tlamani in Xochimilco in iuh nican tlamani	Things in Xochimilco are not as they are here.

As in this case, the sense is usually inchoate, that is, people even taken indefinitely or en masse do not act as the subject of the verb.

C. *Locatives in* -yan *and* -can. A series of locative nouns ending in *-yan* is so closely related to the passive and impersonal that the constructions are often confused. These nouns add *-yan* to a form identical to the impersonal or to the passive of transitives with all its obligatory prefixes (i.e., the impersonal form of the passive). Since *-ya* is the imperfect tense ending of verbs, only the single letter *n,* often omitted in real texts, distinguishes the forms.

tlachihualoya	making things was going on	*tlachihualoyan*	place where things are made
tlaqualoya	eating was going on	*tlaqualoyan*	eating place, dining room
axihuaya	arrival was going on	*axihuayan*	a place of arrival

These locative nouns based on the impersonal are never possessed. Another type of *-yan* locative is always possessed. It is based on active verbs, usually intransitive (or transitive with indefinite prefixes rendering them intransitive), and in this case too the imperfect of the verb is nearly identical to the locative construction, but here the possession makes the distinction easy.

nicochia (nicochiya)	I was sleeping	*nocochian (nocochiyan)*	my sleeping place, bedroom
nitlachiaya	I was looking	*notlachiayan*	place I look from

Locative nouns are also formed by the addition of *-can,* resulting in constructions much like the *-yan* impersonals in that they are absolute and cannot be possessed, but they are added to the preterit stem of the verb or to preterit agentives (including historical preterit agentives like the possessor suffixes). The *-ca-* of *-can* may be the *-ca-* "ligature."

cacchihua	he/she makes footwear	*cacchiuhcan*	place where footwear is made
altepehua	citizen of an altepetl	*altepehuacan*	place where altepetl citizens are (usually the whole countryside)

-Can attaches to many kinds of elements other than verbs and seems to be the same element in origin as the interrogative *can* meaning "where."

qualcan	a good or opportune place	*mieccan*	in many places
acan	nowhere	*oncan*	there
nican	here	*can*	where
canin	where is it that	*campa*	to or from where, where

Many locatives, especially the possessed *-yan* forms and forms like those listed immediately above, can refer to time as well as space, and one must always be alert for this possibility.

ipehuayan xihuitl	(at) the beginning of the year
itlamian xihuitl	(at) the end of the year
in oncan titztihui	where we are headed, i.e., in the future
qualcan oquichiuh	He did it at an opportune time.
notlacaquian omochiuh	It happened when I was there (to hear it), or during my lifetime.

A word such as *quemmani(y)an* is a locative by origin, but it will be found only in a temporal meaning: sometime, sometimes, at times.

D. *A text and some more examples.* In the following text notice above all the use of -*quiuh/*-*co* and -*tiuh/*-*to* forms.

yalhua ompa oniya teopan missa niquittato mochi tlacatl otlamahuiçoto ipampa ca ilhuitzin tosantotzin in onacito calitic ononcalac cuicaco in teopantlaca ihuan oqui-nechico in tohuentzin in fiscal no ihuan otemachtico in totatzin achi ohuecauh inic otlamico çatepan nochan onihualnocuepaco miec tomin nohuentzin onicpoloto amo iciuhca oc ceppa missa niquittatiuh

Yesterday I went to church to hear mass. Everyone went to admire (see what was going on) because it was the day of our saint. When I got there, I went inside. The cantors came to sing, and the fiscal came to collect our offerings. And also the priest came to preach; he took rather a long time before he finished. Afterwards I came back home. I gave out a lot of money as my offering; I won't go again soon to hear mass.

ompa: does little more than anticipate *teopan*.
missa niquittato: In Nahuatl one mainly saw rather than heard mass, probably because the expression was established at a time when there was little chance that the audience would understand anything that was said.
teopantlaca: "church people," the whole body of church attendants and employees, but in effect often mainly the musicians.
fiscal: the fiscal was the highest indigenous member of the church organization, a general steward of the church, the priest's right hand man, and a community leader.

Here are some additional examples.

ye oquetzaloc in calli ye otococ in xinachtli	The house has been built and the seed sown.
anozque teilpiloyan tlalilozque	They are to be arrested and put in jail.
ma ittocan ma cacocan in techtemoco	May those who have come to seek us be seen and heard.
cuix oammachtiloque in cuicatl in netotiliztli	Have you (pl.) been taught singing and dancing?
opiloloque yeintin ichtecque	Three thieves were hanged.
techquixtilique taxca totlatqui	They took our property from us.
otiquixtililoque taxca totlatqui	Our property was taken from us.
otitlaquixtililoque	Things were taken from us.
in ilamatzin otlaquixtililoc	Things were taken from the old woman.
otetlaquixtililoc	Things were taken from people (or from someone).
ma yectenehualo in itocatzin totemaquix-ticatzin	May the name of our redeemer be praised.
quimmocuitlahuia toyolcahuan	They take care of our beasts.
necuitlahuilo toyolcahuan	Our beasts are taken care of.
oquito in amo itolo	He said what is not said.
ye huecauh cenca otetlacamachoya oteima-caxoya otemahuiztililoya otetlaçotlaloya in axcan amo iuh mochihua	Long ago there used to be much obedience, fear, respect, and esteem; today it doesn't happen that way.
pololoque in huexotzinca miequintin cho-loltiloque oc cequintin maloque	The people of Huejotzingo were defeated. Many were put to flight; others were captured.
çaniyo in tianquizco tlacohualoz tlanama-coz amo tecacalco tiamicoz	There is to be buying and selling only in the marketplace; trading is not to go on in people's individual houses.
çan ceppa yolihua amo mochipa nican yeloaz	There is living only once; not always will there be being here. I.e., we live only once; we will not always be here.
intlacamo quiyahui intla tlahuaqui niman mayanalo	If it doesn't rain, if it's dry, then there is famine.

in huei çahuatl ca cocoliztli ic micoa	Smallpox is a disease from which people die.
cuix moztla hualaxihuaquiuh	Will there be arrival tomorrow? I.e., will the group or a group get here tomorrow?
ohuilohuac chichimecatlalpan	A party went to the land of the Chichimeca.
in canin otlacat amo huel macho	Where she was born is not well known, or cannot be found out.[1]
ma tequitihua macamo cochihua	Let there be work, not sleep, or let everyone work and not sleep.
intla cenca nepohualoz poliohuaz	Much bragging brings destruction, or if people brag a lot they will be destroyed.
ohuallaque in teopixque otetlamacoc	The friars came and communion was dispensed (things were given to people, people were served).
tetlamacoco	A group came to dispense communion, or to serve at table.
in quauhtla icochian maçatl	The sleeping place of the deer is in the woods.
nocochian nechmictico	They came to my bedroom to beat me.
ocnamacoyan miec nemacehuilo in octli	At a pulquería much pulque is enjoyed.
mochintin tianquizco tlacohuato	They all went to the marketplace to buy things.

---

[1]This is one of those cases where *huel* can be interpreted either as an intensifier or as meaning ability. With the annalist Chimalpahin, the meaning was ability, but others were different.

14. Word Order

The elements of standard order. Particles as guideposts. Anticipation. The role of in. *Texts.*

A. *The elements of standard order.* We have in a piecemeal fashion seen various aspects of Nahuatl word order. Now let us attack the subject a bit more systematically. The discussion cannot be truly systematic, however, because the order of components in a Nahuatl utterance is extremely fluid, and today we lack the clues of varying stress and tone that could explain the implications of each variation on the standard order. The very term word order is hardly applicable; in the preceding lessons we have long since learned that most Nahuatl verbs and nouns as used in utterances contain many discrete meaningful elements and are more like phrases and clauses than words in English.

At the core of most Nahuatl sentences is a nuclear complex; it is most often a verbal complex, the verb stem plus all its prefixes and suffixes, but it can also be a noun stem with any affixes it may bear. This complex is the statement proper. Other complexes, subordinated to it, may be present to specify its meaning further. Particles and short adverbial elements may be present and modify the nuclear complex directly.

The normal, or unemphasized, or unmarked order in Nahuatl, at least in the standard Nahuatl of the sixteenth to eighteenth centuries, is as follows: 1) particles and adverbial elements; 2) the nuclear complex; 3) the specified subject and object in the form of nouns or verbal clauses in various orders depending on their weight—the longer a constituent of this kind is, the further back from the nuclear complex it will usually stand. Constituents to be focused on or emphasized violate this order by being brought to the front.

Let us immediately look at some utterances illustrating the above. Note the following three points. First, Nahuatl does not make a thorough distinction between adverbs and conjunctions; both are particles and have the same position in the order. Second, when a constituent is preposed, the particle *ca*, as we have seen before, sometimes marks the place where the preposed element ends and the nuclear complex begins.[2] Third, preposing is so frequent that the degree of emphasis attained thereby cannot have been very strong.

huel tinocniuhtzin	You are really my friend.
cuix amo nimocniuh	Am I not your friend? (Aren't we friends?)
aço otetlamacac	Maybe she gave something to someone.
aço quitlamacac in Juan in Andres	Maybe Juan gave something to Andrés (though it could be that Andrés gave it to Juan).
aço oquimacac in Juan in Andres in tlaltepoztli	Maybe Juan gave Andrés the hoe.
nehuatl amo nicmacac in Andres in tlaltepoztli	I didn't give Andrés the hoe.
nehuatl amo nicmacaz in tlaltepoztli in Andres	I won't give Andrés the hoe. (I.e., order by relative weight is not infallible.)
in Andres amo onechmacac in tlaltepoztli	<u>Andrés</u> didn't give me the hoe.
in tlaltepoztli amo onechmacac in Andres	As to the hoe, Andrés didn't give it to me.
in Juan aço oquimacac in Andres in tlaltepoztli	Maybe it was Juan who gave Andrés the hoe.
in yehuatl tlaltepoztli in onimitzmacac cuix catepan oticmomaquili in Andres	That hoe I gave you, did you later give it to Andrés?
in tlatquihua ca amo in Juan	As to who is owner of the property [i.e, the hoe], it's not Juan.
inin tlaltepoztli aquin achtopa oquicouh cuix Andres cuix noço in Juan	This hoe, who first bought it? Was it Andrés? Or was it Juan?
in nocaltzin ca no tehuatzin mocaltzin	My house is your house too.
amo niquelehuia in ixquich monemac in omitzmomaquilitehuac motatzin	I don't desire all your inheritance that your father left you.

---

[2]Unfortunately, *ca* can also introduce dependent clauses, especially after factitive verbs.

in ixquich monemac in omitzmomaquilitehuac motatzin ca amo niquelehuia	As to all your inheritance that your father left you, I don't desire it.
yalhua onechixtlahui ce peso in Francisco Ignacio	Yesterday Francisco Ignacio paid me a peso.
yalhua onechixtlahui in Francisco Ignacio centzontli ipan caxtolpohualli pesos	Yesterday Francisco Ignacio paid me seven hundred pesos.
in notlatzitzinhuan ca nican cate	As to my uncles, they are here (i.e., don't forget that I have uncles who can protect me).

B. *Particles as guideposts.* A good part of the secret of handling Nahuatl sentences is to recognize preposed elements as such. We have already seen that *ca* is a very strong clue, but there are others. If particles and adverbial elements of almost any description are found well into the sentence, look for the possibility of the nuclear complex following immediately. The optative *ma* is a particularly good indication.

huel ticnextia momacehuallo	You really display your commonness.
momacehuallo huel ticnextia	(same translation, more stress on commonness)
huel nimocniuh	I am really your friend.
in nehuatl huel nimocniuh	I am really your friend.
macayac nechitlacalhuiz in notlatol in nican ipan amatl onictlali	Let no one go against my statement that I have put on paper here.
in notlatol in nican ipan amatl onictlali macayac nechitlacalhuiz	As to my statement that I have put on paper here, let no one go against it.
cenca nechpalehuia Martin	Martín helps me very much.
in Martin cenca nechpalehuia	As to Martín, he helps me very much. (Or) Martín helps me very much.
ma nechtlaçotlacan in notatzin in nonantzin in ixquichtin in nohuanyolque	May my father and mother and all my relatives love me!
in notatzin in nonantzin in ixquichtin nohuan-yolque ma nechtlaçotlacan	(same, somewhat different emphasis)
axcan nicmacatiuh in notlal in nochpochtzin	Now I am giving my land to my daughter.
in nochpochtzin axcan nicmacatiuh in notlal	To my daughter I am now giving my land.

Particles are guideposts in general, not only in relation to preposing. If we had no idea of their normal disposition, we could easily make a hash of the meaning of the following two passages, but as soon as we take it that particles normally precede and introduce nuclear complexes, we can find our way without too much trouble.

in otimocuep niman toconittaz in monantzin auh in o iuh tiquittac niman tianquizco tiyaz titla-cohuatiuh niman ic oc ceppa nican tihualmocuepaz yequene tinechmacaz in motlacohual cuix huel oticcuic otican ixquich in notlatol

When you have returned, then you are to go see your mother, and when you have seen her, then you are to go to the marketplace to buy things; next you are to come back here again; finally you are to give me your purchases. Have you fully grasped all I have said?

onitlato oniquilhui in callalli in tinechcuiliznequi ca naxca notlatqui amo motech pohui itech justicia nictlaliz notetlaitlaniliz çan onechnanquili ca qualli ma iuh xicchihua aquen nicmati çan ic oya

I spoke and said to him, "The house-land you want to take from me is my property; it doesn't belong to you. I will place my petition with the law." But he answered me, "Fine. Do it. I don't care." With no more than that he left.

Note the word *auh* in the first example. It is one of the few particles in Nahuatl that does not partake of the general ambiguity between adverb and conjunction. It can definitely be considered a conjunction. Its placement is the usual, but it refers to sentence-level phenomena only. We translate it sometimes as "and," occasionally as "but," and often not at all except as a preceding period or semicolon, but it tells us that the previous statement is complete and that a new one is beginning. *Niman*, "then," is also extremely useful in indicating a distinct, following, more or less independent utterance, but it is not as reliable, for it can mean "quickly, immediately" and function as a simple adverb. The first part of the first passage immediately above could be taken to mean "When you have returned, you are to go see your mother right away." *Niman ic*, however, always means "thereupon, next, etc.," and introduces another statement in a series of statements. *Çan*, of extremely high frequency, sometimes means "but," more often "only, merely," and is embedded in a hundred idioms where it no longer has any detectable individual meaning.

C. *Anticipation.* As much as Nahuatl wants to put adverbial elements in front of the nuclear complex, it runs up against its great reluctance to unbalance the complex by preposing anything weighty (as opposed to preposing a specified object or subject, which constitutes a whole separate complex and does not interfere with the nuclear complex as a phrase). The solution is to have it both ways, to put a short anticipatory adverbial element in front and specify it more fully as a noun complex or the like afterward. The words most associated with this phenomenon are *oncan* and *ompa*. Both mean "there," with *ompa* in principle farther away. In practice one learns that a great deal of the time they are used as equivalents, alternated apparently for stylistic variation. To make the statement "they sent him to Tecamachalco," it might be just possible to say *Tecamachalco oconihuaque*, but we are much more likely to see *ompa oconihuaque Tecamachalco*. Here are some more examples.

oncan mani in tlalli otenco atlauhtitech	The land is at road's edge next to the ravine.
ompa tihualehua Tlaxcallan ihuan Cholollan	We are coming from Tlaxcala and Cholula.
achtopa oncan oniya teopantzinco çatepan	First I went to the church; afterward I made
ompa onitlacouh Tlatelolco tianquizco	purchases in the Tlatelolco marketplace.
ompa niyaznequi in ompa timoyetztica	I want to go to where you are.[1]

As you can see, I tend to favor not translating the anticipatory locative indications at all in most cases, any more than we would say "I see her, the maiden," for *niquitta in ichpochtli*. After all, the inclusion of subject and object prefixes in front of the verb stem, to be filled out by whole phrases afterward, is Nahuatl's greatest example of anticipation. Translate "there" if you insist; the important thing is to realize that the short locative expression points forward to the remaining, more specific part of the statement. Students often not only translate *oncan* and *ompa*, but stop at that point and imagine that the cumbersome locative expressions coming later are something else, starting a new sentence, which is far from being the case.

    Anticipation also frequently affects the quantifiers, the quasi-nouns like "much," "little," "all," and also sometimes the numbers which are related to them in many ways. In English a quantifier is either a noun followed by a genitive, "all of something," or an adjective modifying what it quantifies, "all the women." In Nahuatl neither method is used. The quantifier is a substantive, it is true, but it stands in a kind of apposition to the thing quantified. *Miec tlaolli* means "much maize" by a complicated process in which two third person singular equative statements, "it is much" and "it is maize," crossrefer and depend on each other to make first a statement "that which is much is that which is maize," i.e., "there is much maize," and that in turn is subordinated into a larger statement as "that which is much maize," i.e., finally "much maize." Since the two elements crossrefer, there is nothing to prevent their being physically separated, and such

---

[1] *Oncan* and *ompa* can also refer to a place mentioned before, as in English. *Tollan onitlacat oncan ononoya inic nipiltzintli onicatca*, "I was born in Tula; I dwelt there when I was a child." Note the position of *onicatca* here; as was mentioned once before, with certain short irregular verbs, above all *ca(h)* and to a somewhat lesser extent *yauh*, the verb complex tends to come last in both main and dependent clauses.

happens constantly in Nahuatl, the shorter quantifier coming before the nuclear complex and the longer specification after, just as with the locatives.

cuix ye achi tiquelehuia in atzintli	Do you care for a little pulque?
çan niman atle nicpia tomin anoço teocuitlatl anoço chalchihuitl	I have no money at all, or gold or greenstone.
ixquich niquimmaca nocal notlal nochinan	I give them all of my houses, lands, and chinampas.
cuix ye achi oticmocuiti cocoliztli	Have you caught a bit of illness?
achi nicnomacehuia in itechicahualiztzin in totecuiyo	I enjoy a bit of the health of our lord.
ye etetl oticquetzque huei tecpancalli	We have built three large palaces.

Relational words are also an important part of the overall process of anticipation. The relational word itself is usually short enough to go in front of the nuclear complex; what it refers to can readily come after, at any distance, for the relational word's possessive prefix creates a firm tie to the rest.

icpac onitlecoc Popocatepetl	I climbed up on top of Popocatepetl (Smoking Mountain, the famous volcano).
ipan nimitzmati in notatzin	I look upon you as my father.
intech nicpohua notomin in nopilhuan Antonio ihuan Maria	I assign my money to my children Antonio and Maria.

It lies in the nature of things that this kind of construction appears primarily in the third person. In the first and second, the referent of the possessive prefix is normally not spelled out, so there is no question of anticipation. Even so, the relational word is generally short enough to go in front of the nuclear complex, and that is where we look for it first. Only weightier words will ever be found postposed.

notech pohui centetl calli in oquicauhtehuac in nocoltzin	A house that my grandfather left belongs to me.
ma topan mochihua missa	May a mass be said for us.
amopampa tlatoa in ialbacea amotatzin	The executor of your (pl.) father speaks on your behalf.

The word *iuh*, which much of the time seems like a particle, "thus, in a certain way," but which has a variant *iuhqui/iuhque* that is more of a substantive, also functions importantly in an anticipatory fashion. Its effect is to signal that a clause is to come later specifying the object of the verb of the nuclear complex, when that verb has to do with saying something or is otherwise factitive. The anticipated clause may or may not be introduced by *ca*.

iuh quitoque moztla tihuallazque	Thus they said: "We will come tomorrow." I.e, They said, "We will come tomorrow."
iuh quitoa ca moztla nihuallaz	He says, "I will come tomorrow."
iuh nechilhui aic quicahuaz in itequiuh in fiscal don Antonio de Tapia	He told me that the fiscal don Antonio de Tapia will never relinquish his office.
iuh ninomati ca ye huecauh omomiquilique	I think that they died a long time ago.

The *iuh* in front of the verb does much the same thing done in English by "that" after it. When the sentence contains a verb of saying, it is tempting to translate these constructions as indirect discourse. That is in fact done in the third example just above because it is in the third person, but the clause is probably literally the statement originally made by the speaker's informant and could be in quotes, without "that."

The emphasis in this section has been on adverbial elements as preposed anticipators of longer more specific phrases, but after all the quantifiers are not adverbial, and *iuh* hardly qualifies either. Anticipation is part of a larger process in which Nahuatl tries to put any and all short words in front of the nuclear complex, so that the nuclear complex with its unstressed preceding elements *is* the sentence, and any other constituents, whether in their normal postposed position or preposed for stress or focus, merely spell out the details.

Other things that always or virtually always come in front are indefinite pronouns, interrogative words, and independent pronouns; as elements that can bear stress they are not part of the phrase including the nuclear complex but are phrases of their own.

ayac ohualla	No one came.
aquin ohualla	Who came?
yehuatzin ohualla	That honored person came.

But despite the difference in structure, these elements too often take part in anticipation. The nature of the crossreference is the same as that discussed above with quantifiers.

ayac ohualla tlaxcalchiuhqui	No tortilla maker came.
aquin ohualla pochtecatl	Who came who was a merchant? What merchant came?
yehuatzin ohualla in tlatoani don Antonio	The honored ruler don Antonio came.

For reasons not yet well understood, the specification can sometimes come in front of the nuclear complex just behind the element that anticipates it; the opposite, however (the postposing of the anticipatory element), does not happen.

D. *The role of* in. A whole lesson was devoted to *in* above. Now let us put some of what was learned there in the context of the order of constituent parts of an utterance.

When *in* introduces an antecessive temporal clause, that clause almost always precedes the nuclear complex; being an adverbial element, well it might. The length of the clause is irrelevant.

in oquihuitec iciuhca quiyahuac oquiztihuetz	When he had struck him, he quickly came out the exit (or outside).
in o iuh monamicti ichan imontatzin omohuicac	After she had married, she went to her father-in-law's household.

A relative clause introduced by *in* most often follows directly after what it refers to.

ocholo in ichtecqui in martestica onechcuili notomin in cenca notech monequia	The thief who on Tuesday took my money that I badly needed ran away.
amo nican huecahuaz in teuctli in quin axcan ohualacico	The lord who just recently got here won't stay here long.

Since *in* can subordinate any phrase or clause, its distribution can be crucial in determining what the nuclear complex of a given sentence is. Subordination of what started as the nuclear complex may or may not involve a change in constituent order.

tictlapachozque in ical Juan	We will roof Juan's house.
ical Juan in tictlapachozque	It is Juan's house that we will roof.
huel iciuhca ichan yauh	He goes home very quickly.
huel iciuhca in ichan yauh	It is very quickly that he goes home. [1]
achtopa mohuica in cihuapilli	The lady goes first.
achtopa in mohuica in cihuapilli	It is first that the lady goes.
nican moyetztica in oticmochiali	Here is the one you have awaited.
oticmochiali in nican moyetztica	You have awaited the one who is here.

---

[1]This sentence is ambiguous; the *in* might be taken as applying to *ichan* alone and change nothing from the previous example. It is when *in* directly precedes a verbal complex that we can be most certain of the intent.

E. *Two texts.* Our treatment of word or constituent order has relied for illustration on individual sentences and short passages. The student will still most likely feel disoriented when faced with the flood of words and clauses, sometimes going on for a remarkable time before coming to a full stop, that is found in some kinds of Nahuatl writing. Here are two sections from the work of the great early seventeenth-century annalist called Chimalpahin today (he was actually known to his fellows mainly as don Domingo de San Antón). Only the orthography has been changed.

In ipan axcan miercoles ic matlaquilhuitl once mani metztli abril de 1601 años iquac quimotlaxilique yn huei cruz cenca hueyac catca in icaca San Francisco ithualco in quimoquechilitiuh totlaçotatzin fray Pedro de Gante quateçontzin maestro ihuan in matlactin omomentin teopixque in achto yancuican maxitico nican Mexico auh in tlaquetztli ipan xihuitl de mil 531 años auh in huehuexiuhtlapohualli matlactlomei acatl ye iuh matlacxihuitl omei acico in españolesme in iquac moquetz auh in oicaca in cruz yepohualxihuitl ipan chiucnauhxihuitl ipan etetl metztli ipan matlaquilhuitl once mani metztli Abril auh in ohuetzico in omotlaz ye iuh nauhpohualxihuitl ipan onxihuitl ihuan yei metztli ipan matlaquilhuitl once cahuitl in acico españoles // miequintin in tlatoque in ipan omicque virreyesme oidoresme in otlatocatico Mexico ihuan in Mexica tlatoque pipiltin ihuan obispome yhuan tlatocateopixque in omonemiltico nican Mexico Tenochtitlan

Today, on Wednesday, the 11th day of the month of April of the year 1601, was when they took down the big cross, very high it was, that stood in the churchyard of San Francisco, that was raised by our precious father fray Pedro de Gante, the lay friar and teacher, along with the twelve friars who first arrived here in Mexico City. Its raising was in the year of 1531, 13 Reed in the old year count; when it was put up, it had been thirteen years since the Spaniards arrived. The cross had stood for 69 years and three months on the 11th day of the month of April. When it fell and was taken down, it had been a time of 82 years, three months, and 11 days since the Spaniards arrived. — Many were the lords who died in its time [while it was standing], viceroys and Audiencia judges who came to rule in Mexico City, and Mexica rulers and nobles, and bishops, and friars in authority who came to live here in Mexico Tenochtitlan.

axcan: Chimalpahin maintained the convention that the entries were written on the day of the event, but most were in fact written or at least rewritten from a later perspective.
mani: used to say "it is" a certain day, but with repetition it has become not a verbal clause but something like "on," and generally hardly needs translation.
quimoquechilitiuh: translated here as a passive so that it can come before the long following dependent phrases and clauses.

huel iquac peuh in tlapaquiyahuitl inic momanaco huel ipan in ivisperatzin San Augustin chicueilhuitl in quiyauhtimanca cemilhuitl cecenyohual huel tetlaocolti in topan mochiuh ihuan nohuian tlatlaxicac in tochachan in timacehualtin ihuan castilteca ihuan in teopan nohuian atl nenez molon in atl in San Francisco in San Augustin in Santo Domingo in la Compañia Teatinos auh inic cecemilhuitl ihuan in cecenyohual quiyauh ca nohuian inic moch ipan Nueva España iquac nohuian molon motlatlapo in aoztotl inic cenca miec oncan oquiz atl ihuan in intech tetepe nohuiampa hualtemoc in atl auh inic nohuian ipan Nueva España mieccan in atocohuac ihuan netlapacholoc xixitin in calli ihuan iquac cequi hualmomimilo in cepayahuitl hualixxitin in Iztactepetl // auh oc cenca nican Mexico in ipan ohualtemoc in tepetitech atl inic cenca ipan

*otemico ic polihuizquia in altepetl auh inic nohuiampa hualtemoya in hualla-
miequiliaya in atl huel huei inic macoc auh mieccan papachiuh xixitin in calli ihuan
aapachiuh acallac in calli ic mocalcauhque in chaneque ihuan in otli nohuian popoliuh
ihuan in chinamitl huel nohuian poliuh auh in Atlixocan tlamelahua otli huei atezcatl
huei atl mochiuh auh in inchan españoles nohuian molon in atl ic cenca omomauhtique
miequintin ic mocalcauhque ic quitlalcahuique in altepetl Mexico ic nohuiampa altepetl
ipan yaque ompa motlalito auh in ixquich otli in huehuei otli mochi apachiuh cocoton
in Tepeyacac in Cohuatlayauhcan in San Miguel otli in Tlacopan Azcapotzalco huel
nohuian apachiuh*

A fine, lasting rain began to set in right at that time, right on the eve of [the feast of] San Agustín. For a week it kept raining, all day and all night; what happened to us was really pitiful. And it leaked in our houses everywhere, those of us commoners [indigenous people] and those of the Spaniards, and in the churches; everywhere water appeared and sprang up, at San Francisco, San Agustín, Santo Domingo, the Jesuit church. And since it rained every day and night, everywhere in all New Spain at this time water cavities [springs] sprang up and opened, so that very much water came out of them, and from the mountains everywhere water descended, and in many places all over New Spain people were drowned or buried; the houses fell in. And at this time some of the snow came rolling down on Iztactepetl; its surface came falling in [there was an avalanche]. — And the water from the mountains descended especially to Mexico City here, so that it greatly filled up, and the altepetl was about to perish because of it. Since from everywhere the water came descending and increasing, it rose very greatly, and in many places the houses collapsed and crumbled, and they were flooded over and went under water, for which reason the residents left their houses. And the roads everywhere disappeared, and also the chinampas disappeared absolutely everywhere. The road going straight to Atlixocan became a great pool or sea, and water sprang up in the homes of the Spaniards everywhere, by which they were greatly frightened; many for that reason left their houses, abandoned the altepetl of Mexico, and went to the [various] altepetl in the country all around to stay there. And the roads, the highways, were all flooded. The roads [going to] Tepeyacac, Cohuatlayauhcan, and San Miguel, and to Tacuba and Azcapotzalco were cut. It was flooded absolutely everywhere.

cemilhuitl cecenyohual: Cemilhuitl is literally "one day," often taken to mean "all day." *Cecenyohual* should mean "all night, each night," or "all night, night after night." This is probably the kind of reduplication that means a steady, ongoing series, not the distributive kind referring to separate manifestations. Chimalpahin's intention both times was probably "all day and night, every day and night," which is what we usually mean by "day and night."
tlatlaxicac in tochachan: I(h)xica is "to leak"; *tlaxica* is the *tla-* inchoate impersonal, "it leaks"; *tlatlaxicac* is the distributive, achieved by reduplicating not the first syllable of the verb root but the *tla-* itself, and means "it leaked in various places." *Tochachan* is also a distributive, "in our various houses." Throughout this passage reduplication is used repeatedly to suggest plurality and varied occurrence. The topic will be discussed more directly in the following lesson.
Iztactepetl: "White mountain," the peak next to Popocatepetl now called Iztaccihuatl.
macoc: Not the passive of *maca,* to give, but the active preterit reflexive of *acocui,* to raise.
Tlacopan Azcapotzalco huel nohuian apachiuh: In the translation above it is assumed that *Tlacopan Azcapotzalco* is an afterthought. As they stand, these words really do not look like part of the preceding sentence. The intention may well have been "In Tacuba and Azcapotzalco it was flooded absolutely everywhere."

15. Some Difficult Things

Verbs in -tia from nouns. Verbs in -ti from nouns. Nonactive agentives. Distributive and other reduplication.

ALL OF THE PHENOMENA included in this lesson are reasonably common in texts and as important for general comprehension as many topics that came much earlier in the book. After some experimentation, however, I found that at the earlier stages they were not being absorbed and were even causing a more general confusion, sometimes because of their resemblance to other better understood things, sometimes because of internal difficulties. A brief treatment of them is included here; they should later be studied further in more detailed grammars.

A. *Verbs in* -tia *from nouns.* The difficulty with this form is that students perennially mix it up with the causative from verbs. Apparently almost everyone studying Nahuatl deeply will go through a phase when any word ending in *-tia* is happily recognized as a causative. Possibly you are now past this stage and can entertain the notion of another kind of *-tia* verb.

The construction starts with a noun, to which one adds *-tia*, creating a transitive Class 3 verb. Its meaning is to provide the thing described by the noun to the object, the object usually being a person or other animate being.

calli	house	*ni-c-cal-tia in María* — I provide a house to or for María (which can mean I build her one, or I house her).
		quicaltia in Alonso — He makes or provides a house for Alonso.

The sense is the same when the verb is reflexive.

ni-no-cal-tia — I get a house for myself, build myself a house.

Many of these constructions are spontaneous, but others become a standard part of the vocabulary and are in the dictionary as verbs, sometimes with translations that seem to veer from the primary sense, but the structure remains the same, and the meaning too is always there beneath the surface. From *-namic*, "spouse," comes *namictia*, universally translated as "to marry," but we can also understand it as "to provide with a spouse."

ninonamictia	I marry, provide myself with a spouse
omonamicti Barbara Antonia	Bárbara Antonia married.
nicnamictiz Barbara Antonia	I will marry off Bárbara Antonia, provide her with a spouse.

One expects the last example to mean "I will marry Bárbara Antonia," but to get that sense we must extend the construction: an object prefix indicates the direct object, the thing provided, which as a specified external phrase stands in a kind of apposition to the incorporated noun, and a reflexive prefix indicates to whom it is provided.

nicnonamictiz Barbara Antonia	I will marry Bárbara Antonia, I will provide Bárbara Antonia to myself as a spouse.
quimonantia in doña Juana	She takes doña Juana as her mother.
otictaxcatique in caltepiton	We appropriated the little house, provided it to ourselves as property.
cuix oticmocniuhti in quin axcan ohualla	Did you make friends with the recent arrival, did you provide the one who just recently came to yourself as a friend?
nicnocaltia in oztotl	I make the cave my house.

All of our examples so far have used the unmodified noun stem as a basis; sometimes the nominal suffix *-yo* is added before *-tia.* Very common are *tocayotia* and *firmayotia.*

> *oquitocayoti oquifirmayoti*   He signed it (providing name and signature).

Let us now consider how we can distinguish this construction from the verbal causative. The overwhelmingly important consideration is that the causative *-tia* is preceded by a verb stem, this *-tia* by a noun stem. In fact, the two are so different in this respect that it is quite hard to find a pair similar enough to cause confusion. It is true that they conjugate the same and can have the same kind of prefixes, but look closely to the roots, as in the group following here, with causatives on the left, denominal verbs on the right.

nicchihualtia, I cause him/her to do it	*chihua*	*niccaltia,* I provide him/her a house	*calli*
onicaxiti, I brought it to its goal	*aci*	*onicnaxcati,* I made it my property	*axcaitl*
nechnemitia, he/she maintains me	*nemi*	*nechmiltia,* he/she makes me a field	*milli*

One might feel justified in confusing the denominal *namictia,* to marry, with the causative *namiquitia* or *namiquiltia,* to make something meet or match, since a causative such as *namiquitia* is sometimes further reduced by the loss of the final vowel of the verb stem, and *-namic,* "spouse, mate, match," is closely related to *namiqui,* "to meet, match." The common *tlaqualtia,* to feed, to have as a dinner guest, could probably be derived from either *tlaqualli,* food, or *qua,* to eat, in its intransitive form as *tlaqua.* (The latter is apparently always the correct interpretation.) But generally speaking, if you only have somewhere in the back of your mind the mere fact there is such a thing as a denominal verbal construction in *-tia* meaning "to provide," you will not fail to recognize it.

B. *Verbs in* -ti *from nouns.* At a remote time there must have been a verb *ti* meaning "to be or become." Verbs can still be formed by adding this *ti* to a noun stem, creating a word meaning to be, become, or act as the thing described by the noun. These verbs can belong to Class 1 or Class 2 depending on the nature of the stem. Some have become frozen as vocabulary items, such as *tlacati,* to be born, i.e., to become a person.[1]

don Andres Tetzcoco yauh gobernadortitiuh	Don Andrés is going to Tetzcoco to be governor.
ayamo nilamati	I haven't become an old woman yet.
in don Luis ca amo tetlaçotla amo tetatzin atle quimati aic tlatocatiz	Don Luis doesn't esteem people, isn't fatherly to them, knows nothing; he will never become ruler.
in iquac jueztia don Juan de Mendoza miequintin quintlatzontequiliaya tlatlacoleque	When don Juan de Mendoza was judge he used to sentence many wrongdoers.
cuix otitochtic otimaçatic	Have you become a rabbit and a deer? (Have you become bestial?)

Some verbs exactly like these end in *-tia* rather than *-ti;* by origin this ending is *-ti-ya,* the *-ya* being a durative, the same element that in a different use has become the imperfect ending of verbs. The ending is indeed often seen written *-tiya.* It is not uncommon for the *-ti* and the *-tia* form to exist side by side with the same noun stem; thus both *cualti* and *cualtia,* "to become good," are seen. The preterit of *-tia* may be either *-tiac* (Class 1) or *-tix* (Class 2, as with *chia/chix*).

nitlatlacoani onicatca yece ye niqualtia niyectia in huel oniqualtix aço nicihuahuacatiz	I was a sinner, but now I am becoming good; when I have become fully good, maybe I will become a married man.

---

[1]In all probability the denominal *-tia* construction is based, historically speaking, on this *-ti* construction. The *a* of so many transitives in Nahuatl is what remains of an ancient causative.

This *-tia/tiya* unfortunately adds another to our list of forms ending in *-tia*. Since both *-ti* and *-tia* forms are intransitive, they should be quite easy to keep apart from the causatives and denominal *-tia* verbs. The imperfect of a *-ti* verb, however, looks like the present of a *-tia* verb. In any case, let us review the different possibilities.[1]

present tense causative	*nicquixtia*	I remove it, cause it to come out.
present tense denominal	*niccaltia*	I provide him/her a house.
preterit of *yauh* auxiliary	*onicchiuhtia*	I went along doing it, or did it when I went.
imperfect of *-ti* verb	*alcaldetia*	He was acting as alcalde.
present of *-tia* verb	*qualtia*	He/she is becoming good.

Even in grammars, the last two may be written *-tiya*; in actual texts, any of them may be.

An outgrowth of *-ti* verbs is a large set of preterit agentives, nouns which are as close to adjectives as Nahuatl gets, ending in *-tic* (plural *-tique* where applicable). In many cases the *-ti* verb itself no longer exists. *Tetl* is stone, *teti* or *tetia* is to harden, and *tetic* is something which has hardened, something hard.

quahuitl	tree, stick, wood	*quauhtic*	something tall
mahuiztli	fear, respect, awe	*mahuiztic*	something honored, magnificent, splendid
camotli	camote, edible root	*camotic*	something soft
tlilli	soot, black substance	*tliltic*	something black (later an African)

Other *-tic* words lack even any extant noun source; for *alactic*, something slippery, there is only the somehow related reflexive verb *alahua*, to slip or slide. All of these words, as much as they may seem to shade into adjectival use, remain preterit agentive nouns, and when they are bound to anything else the *-ca-* ligature appears: *mahuizticatzintli*, "someone or something splendid (rev.)."

C. *Nonactive agentives.* We already know the present agentives, the ones in *-ni*, of which *tlatoani*, ruler, is the most famous example. All the ones we have seen are based on the active form of the verb. Other *-ni* nouns are based on the passive and impersonal forms. Small distinctions in their external shape have large implications for their meaning. Let us start with the passive of the transitive verb. *-Ni* with the finite passive as a stem gives a noun meaning something on which the action of the verb can be carried out, as with our adjectives in *-able* and *-ible*. But if all the normal object prefixes are added in their indefinite form to the *-ni* noun, it signifies the means by which the action can be carried out, i.e., is instrumental, and may refer to an actual instrument or tool.

quitequi	he/she cuts it	*teco*	it is cut
teconi	something that can be cut, is cuttable		
tlateconi	an instrument for cutting, an axe		
quitlapoa	he/she opens it	*tlapolo*	it is opened
tlapoloni	something openable		
tlatlapoloni	a key (opener)		
quitzaqua	he/she shuts it	*tzaqualo*	it is shut
tzaqualoni	something shuttable		
tlatzaqualoni	a lock or latch (closer)		
quitlamachtia	he/she teaches him/her something	*tlamachtilo*	he/she is taught s.t.
tlamachtiloni	someone teachable		
tetlamachtiloni	teaching aid		

---

[1] I almost hesitate to mention the fact that students sometimes mix up the *-ti* of the *-ti* verbs and the *-ti-* ligature in the auxiliary constructions. Generally speaking, the simplest distinction is that the *-ti* of these verbs comes last, whereas the *-ti-* of the ligature is always internal. The *-ti* of the denominal verbs is internal only before the purposive motion forms; *jueztitiuh*, "he goes to be judge," *jueztico*, "he came to be judge," etc. Progressives are very rare (*jueztitica*, "he is being judge"). The most salient distinction again is that one is attached to a noun stem, the other to a verb stem.

Here are some instances used in sentences.

in ticmonequiltia aço elehuiloni çaniyo amo chihualoni	What you want may be desirable, only it is not feasible.
in quahuitl ca huel teconi yece oiçoliuh in tepoztlateconi	The wood is very cuttable, but the (metal) axe has gotten old.
niccohuaz in etl in tlaolli in chilli in cacahuatl in huauhtli in ixquich qualoni	I will buy beans, shelled maize, chile, cacao beans, amaranth, everything edible.
itech monequi tetlacuitlahuiltiloni	He needs a means to force people to do things.

D. *Distributive and other reduplication.* Reduplication in Nahuatl mainly affects the first syllable of a noun, number, or verb (sometimes that first syllable is a prefix), placing a copy of the first consonant and first vowel in front of what therewith becomes the second syllable; if the word begins with a vowel, only that vowel is reduplicated.

inchachan	at their various homes	from *-chan*, (at) one's home
oome	two each	from *ome*, two
quimmamaca	he/she distributes it to them	from *maca*, to give
tlatlatzoma	she sews various things	from *itzoma*, to sew
in teteo	the gods	from *teotl*, god

There are actually two different types of reduplication. In one the new syllable contains a short vowel and a glottal stop; in the other, it contains a long vowel and no glottal stop. Though crucial, this distinction is invisible in texts, so that a relative neophyte cannot penetrate very deeply into the topic before attaining a great deal more experience. Even the old grammarians, who observed the system at first hand and heard the distinctions, despaired of discovering consistency in it. Let us confine ourselves to a few essentials. At least we can get attuned enough to reduplication to be prepared to get back to the dictionary form of the word.

The most common meaning of reduplication, aside from its use in simple plurals, is distributive, that is, saying that something happened several separate times, one instance at a time, or one occurrence for each subject or object involved. The most common bearers of distributive reduplication are the numbers.

cecenpeso ihuan oome tomin tlacalaquilli quimanazque	They are to pay a peso and two reales each as tribute.
nanahuintin impilhuan oquimpiaya	They had four children each.
quexquichtin inyolcahuan aço matlatlactin anoço cacaxtoltin	How many beasts do they have? Maybe ten[2] each, or fifteen each?
oniquimmamacac in tlalli in caleque nanauhtetl milli oniquimmacac	I distributed the land to the householders; I gave them four fields each.

Much the same meaning can attach to reduplication with verbs and nouns.

tiquintlapaloa	We greet them.
tiquintlatlapalotihui	We go along greeting them one after the other, or here and there.
onechhuitec onechtelicçac	He struck me and kicked me.
onechhuihuitec onechtetelicçac	He struck me and kicked me various times, or again and again.
oquitlatique incal inyaohuan	They burned the houses of their enemies.
oquitlatlatique incacal inyaohuan	They burned the various houses of their enemies in various separate actions.

At times, however, especially with nouns, the main thrust of the reduplication seems to

---

[2]With *matlactli* it is the second syllable that reduplicates.

be to bring out the plurality of words that would otherwise be hard to pluralize, for long into the postcontact period Nahuatl remained reluctant to put plural suffixes on nouns referring to inanimate things.

incacal ca huel tetepiton auh ihuan incuecuezcon amo tenticac	Their houses are very small, and also their grainbins aren't full.
immimilpan nohuian mamani huehuei tetl	On their fields there are big rocks everywhere.

Look back at the second passage by Chimalpahin at the end of Lesson 14, and you will see more examples. Even cases like this seem to have a choppy, distributive flavor.

All of the reduplication we have been discussing is normally of the type with short vowel and glottal stop. You may remember that far back, in Lesson 9, we discussed reduplication as a normal part of certain nominal plurals, with no implication of a distributive sense, as in *teteo*, gods. Here a long vowel is used. Apart from this, the great majority of reduplication one will see in texts is in some way distributive and involves short vowel and glottal stop. Long vowel reduplication (other than in formal plurals) did occur, however, and could have the sense of a steady, orderly repetition in an ongoing series. In that same passage of Chimalpahin, when he speaks of the rain going on *cecemilhuitl ihuan cecenyohual*, "all day and all night," he was probably using long-vowel reduplication, and surely the sense is what we associate with it, not the interrupted, here and there motion of the distributive.

At any rate, you should now not be shocked when you see reduplication in texts, and with a little experimentation you should be able to reconstitute the unreduplicated forms of the words so that you can deal with them in the normal way.

16. Some Crucial Particles
Ic and *inic*. *Iuh*. *Oc* and *ye*. *Çan*. *Huel*. *Particles in general*.

A WHOLE LESSON has been devoted to the particle *in*, and *ca* has also been discussed repeatedly here. A few more of these wordlets are so ubiquitous, so multifarious in meaning and function, and so hard to deal with without some guidance, that it is not advisable to put even a provisional end to our grammatical studies without facing them head on.

A. *Ic* and *inic*. The reader of texts will not go long before becoming aware of *inic*, which is likely to appear several times on almost any page of Nahuatl. A little less common is *ic*.[1] The two are the same in origin, the longer one merely having the subordinator *in* attached to it, and though some distinctions can be observed, which will duly be discussed here, virtually no meaning or function of one is entirely lacking in the other.

Ic/inic as we know it is indeed a particle in the sense that it never inflects and is usually placed in front of verbal and nominal complexes. It gives every indication, however, of having once been a relational word, now frozen in the third person form (its long *i* being the third person singular possessive prefix), with only *c* left of the word itself. It seems to crossrefer with nouns and verbal clauses like a relational word, always of course in the third person. One can even speculate that it evolved by reduction from the instrumental -*ca*, for it continues to have instrumentality as one of its meanings.

onechmacac in nonantzin chicome tomin ic cueitl onicnocohui	My mother gave me seven reales, with which I bought myself a skirt.

Inic has so many applications, senses, and nuances that students and even experienced readers are well advised to suspend judgment on first encounter with an instance of its use until the context gradually gives a better chance to find an adequate solution.

Let us simply start enumerating some of the uses, illustrating them with examples. The first thing that comes to mind with *inic* is purpose, the translation frequently being "in order that," "in order to." The clause introduced by *inic* in this sense is usually in the future, which as we have seen before has certain similarities to the English infinitive.

cemilhuitl nelimiqui inic niquintlaqualtiz nopilhuan	All day I cultivate in order to feed my children.
omomiquili in toteculyo inic titlapopolhuilozque	Our Lord died so that we would be forgiven.
nican otihuallaque inic tamechpalehuizque	We came here to help you (pl.).

A major use of *inic* has to do with expressions of time. Often it means "when."

inic ichan acito ye huel tlayohuaya	When she got home it was already very dark.
inic Mexico nitlatequipanoaya oc nitel- pochtli onicatca	When I was working in Mexico City I was still an unmarried young man.

But frequently it translates as "since," "from one time to another," or "until" (in the last meaning often in association with *ixquich cahuitl*, literally "the whole time").

inic otimohuicac omonamicti momachtzin	Since you went away your niece/nephew got married [the person spoken to is male].
inic oquiz tonatiuh inic ocalac nican onicatca	I was here from when the sun rose until it set.
ixquich cahuitl otichualhuicac centli inic in cuezcomatl huel tenticaca	We brought ears of maize until the grainbin was really full.

---

[1] I ignore here the interrogative *ic*, "when (in terms of time spans longer than a day)?"; though it is of exactly the same shape down to its long vowel and has an interesting meaning, it differs vastly from the element discussed here in having no crossreferent. It also happens to be rare in real texts.

Like English "since," *inic* can indicate the reason for something.

inic huel motoliniaya çan xacaltzintli oquimocaltique	Since they were very poor, they took a humble straw hut as their house.

Another sense of *inic* is in the general area of "how."

inic mochihua molli ca amo ohui çan monequi chilli cacahuatl	As to how *mole* is made, it isn't hard; you just need chiles and cacao.
inic nimitznopalehuiliz miec tomin nimitznomaquiliz	The way I will help you is that I will give you a lot of money. (Or: In order to help you . . .)
inic hueyac in huepantli	How long the beam is!

This "how" shades into "that," usually after verbs of saying, thinking, and the like.

otechilhui inic moztla onmopehualtiz in obispo	He told us how, that the bishop will depart tomorrow.
huel ticmati inic mochipa nimitzpalehuia	You know well how, that I always help you.
ohualla tlatolli inic miequintin Japontlaca ompa oacico Acapolco	News came that many Japanese arrived in Acapulco.

The clause-introductory "how" seems to lead on into a number of applications in which *inic* is associated with a single noun word.

huel oquinexti inic oquichtli	He really showed how he is a man, is brave.
nictlaçotla inic nocniuhtzin inic alcalde amo cenca nictemachia	I esteem him as, in the capacity of, my friend; as alcalde I don't have much confidence in him.
quimpanahuia in oc cequintin ichpopochtin inic qualnezqui	She surpasses the other young women as one who is good looking, i.e., she surpasses them in good looks.
in tlalli inic hueyac ompohualli inic patlahuac matlactli	the land is forty [units] as something long, ten as something wide; i.e., it is forty in length, ten in width.

Perhaps related is the use of *inic* to create ordinal numbers.

cempohualli	twenty	*inic cempohualli*	twentieth
caxtolli tlacatl	fifteen people	*inic caxtolli tlacatl*	the fifteenth person
ontetl nocal	two houses of mine	*inic ontetl nocal*	my second house

As to *ic*, it was already said above that *ic* can, depending on the time, place, and inclination of the writer, do pretty much anything done by *inic*. *Ic* is seen especially often in two of the uses just mentioned.

ic caxtolli tlacatl	the fifteenth person	*ompohualli ic hueyac*	forty units in length

The most common and important use associated with *ic* more than *inic* is to refer back to a previous clause saying "for that reason," "because of that," "in payment for that," etc.

amo naxcahua amo nitlatquihua ic amo no nicihuahua	I have no property, for which reason I have no wife either.
intla tiquintlacamatiz motatzin monantzin ic timahuiztililoz	If you obey your parents, you will be honored for it.
in aquin çan ichan quinamacaz in cacahuatl ic tlatzacuiltiloz ic teilpiloyan huallaz ic polihuiz in itlatqui	Whoever sells cacao at home will be punished for it, will be brought to jail for it, his/her property will be forfeited for it.

With so much else to survey and analyze, students are prone to ignore this type of *ic*, but it is often the key to the sentence, holding the clauses together.

Sometimes *ic* works in conjunction with an *inic* purpose clause, standing before the nuclear complex and anticipating the later clause.

ic otihuallaque inic timitztopalehuilizque	The reason we came is in order to help you.

Unlike *inic, ic* is often seen placed after a substantive and referring to it alone. The meanings are several.

miec ic tiquintlayecoltia	With a great deal we serve them.
qualli ic xinemican	Live well! (I.e., *ic* creates an adverbial expression.)
quahuitl ic oninomotlac	I hurled myself against, hit up against a tree.
cuix itla ic titlanahuatia	Are you giving some order?

In this last case, *ic* is used as a way of providing an object for a verb that is in effect intransitive. *Nahuatia,* to order, is used very often with the indefinite prefix *-tla,* after which it can no longer take a specific object. What *itla ic titlanahuatia* says is "you give orders with something, or about something."

The above are by no means all the uses of *ic* and *inic,* but they will do for now. Don't let yourself be overwhelmed by this pair and give up on them, as many before you have done. Getting a reasonable mastery of them is not in the end a matter of memorizing a multitude of unrelated applications and somehow spotting them in sentences. The most salient use of *ic,* to point back giving a reason, is almost the same thing, in reverse, as the most salient use of *inic,* to point forward giving a purpose. English "so that" comes close to doing both. Though the relationships would be hard to express succinctly, gradually all the uses will fall into place in your mind and seem a natural, logical continuum.

Before we go on to the next particle, consider the variety of uses of *inic* and *ic* in the following passages from a letter sent by the municipal council of Huejotzingo in 1560 to the king in Spain (a few words have been altered).

in momoztlae topan aci topan mochihua in netolin_iliztli in netequipacholiztli inic titochoquilia inic titotlaocoltia

Every day poverty and affliction reach us and are visited upon us, so that we weep, so that we mourn.

atle neci in totech monequiz in otlica in acalco in ticquazque ihuan inic titetlaxtlahuizque inic huel motechtzinco tacizque

What we would need to eat on the road and on the ship and to pay for things in order that we would be able to reach you is not available.

toteᵒ Dios techyolloti inic timitztotlatocatizque inic motechtzinco tipohuizque

Our lord God inspired us to take you as ruler and to belong to you.

ticcuitlahuiltique inic tlapalehuiz ihuan tictlacahualtique inic amo quinyaochihuaz

We pressed [the Tlaxcalan] to help, and we held him back so that he would not make war on them.

titechmotlaocolili inic techmachtico in padresme in evangelio inic techmachtico in tlaneltocaliztli inic techiximachitico in icel teotl in Dios toteᵒ

You granted us the favor that the fathers came to teach us the gospel, that they came to teach us the faith, that they came to make us acquainted with the sole divinity God our Lord.

huel ica tocializ totlanequiliz oticcuique oticanque in santo evangelio ayac ic techmamauhti ayac techcuitlahuilti ayac ma pilli anoço macehualtzintli ic toliniloc

With all our will we received and took the holy gospel; no one intimidated us about it, no one forced us, no one whether noble or humble commoner was mistreated over it.

miequintin altepehuaque cuitlahuiltiloque ic toliniloque in aço piloloque in anoço tlatiloque inic amo quicahuaznequia in tlateotoquiliztli

Many citizens were forced and were mistreated over it, who were hanged or burned because they did not want to relinquish idolatry.

miecpa techilhuiaya inic mixpantzinco topan tlatoz mitzmomachitiliz in ixquich ic otimitztopalehuilique inic otimitztotlayecoltilique

Often he would tell us how he would speak on our behalf before you and inform you of all with which we helped you, with which we served you.

aço itla oticmocaquiti in totlahuelilocayo inic cenca huei axcan topan huetz inin tlacalaquilli

Perhaps you have heard something of our wickedness, so that now this very great tribute has fallen upon us.

amo huecahuaz inic cempolihuiz inic xiniz in mociudad

It will not be long until your city will entirely disappear, until it will crumble.

B. Iuh *and its variants.* At first *iuh* may seem to be an ordinary particle usually meaning "thus, so, like," but before long we come to realize that *iuh* is part of a constellation of forms with many uses and meanings. There seems once to have been a verb *ihui*, "to be a particular way"; *ihui* is still seen in certain phrases, though no longer as a verb. *Ihui* gave rise to a preterit agentive *iuhqui* (plural *iuhque*), "one who or something which is a certain way." The word can still appear with virtually that thrust.

amo tiuhque	We're not that way.
nican mochi tlacatl iztlacati cuix ame-huantin amiuhque	Here everyone lies; are you (pl.) like that?
cuix ticmiximachilia in doña Francisca huel iuhcatzintli in mochpochtzin	Do you know doña Francisca? Your daughter is just like her.

The form *iuh* was presumably arrived at by the loss of *-qui* in *iuhqui*, as eventually happened with all Class 2 verbs, although it could also have arisen through the loss of the final *i* of *ihui* after it had become a particle rather than a finite verb. In the time of older Nahuatl as we know it, *iuh* was the dominant form. A final variant is *iuhquin*, apparently contracted from *iuhqui in*, used mainly in comparisons.

A word on pronunciation, a topic that has been religiously avoided until now, for it has little relation to our ability to understand texts. We do need to say words out loud to one other, however, merely in the process of learning and communicating, and sometimes we want to read a passage aloud in a class. If our pronunciation is too very barbarous, it leaves a bad taste. Generally speaking, just pronouncing the written forms as though they were Spanish, being sure to treat *x* as [sh], will do very well. But for some reason, most beginners mispronounce *iuh*, coming up with something like English "you." In fact, the vowel, the single vowel, in *iuh* is [i]; *-uh* is an unvoiced [w]. The *-uh* is hard; to pronounce *i* as the single syllabic vowel is the main thing.

The basic translation of *iuh* is "thus, so," but as we learn more we use "thus" and "so" less and less. That rendition is most likely in a back reference.

don Pedro ye huehuentzin aocmo tlacaqui in nehuatl no iuh ninomati	Don Pedro is already a little old man (senile); he no longer understands things. — I think so too.
in Ana Luisa mochipa quichihua itequiuh intla iuh tinemiz in titlaçotlaloz	Ana Luisa always does her duty. If you live thus (or so, or this way), you will be cherished.

Even in contexts of this kind, however, we will find ourselves saying "it" or "that," or "the same thing" instead.

mochintin in caleque huecapa cholozque ma iuh quichihuacan	All the householders will run far away. — Let them do it. (Or just: Let them.)
cuix nelli oquito in Antonio ca aic nochan ninocuepaz ca quemaca iuh oquito	Is it true that Antonio said,"I will never return home"? Yes, he said it. (Or: That's what he said.)
oquitlaxtlahuique ma no iuh nopan mochihua	He got paid. — May the same thing happen to me.

More often, *iuh* gets involved in the connecting of whole clauses, and is translated "as, like." When used this way it is generally preceded by *in*.

ma quimmaca in atl in licenciado Altamirano in iuh yeppa quimmacaya	Let licenciado Altamirano give them the water as he gave it to them before.
nicnequi timonemitiz in iuh ye huecauh timonemitiaya	I want you to live as you used to live a long time ago.

Even more common is a pattern of *iuh . . . in iuh*, "as . . ., so," or *no iuh . . . in iuh*, with the addition of *no*, also: "as . . ., so also." Even the examples just above could do with *iuh* before the verb in the first clause.

iuh oncan tlamaniz in quiyahuac in ithualco	So things are to be in the household as they

in iuh axcan tlamani	are now, i.e., things in the household are to stay the same as they are now.
in iuh tiquitoa no iuh nehuatl niquitoa	As you say so say I too, i.e., I say what you say.
no iuh choloa in iuh choloa maçatl	As a deer leaps, so too does he; he leaps like one.

Iuh is part of an often used idiomatic expression, *iuh ca -yollo*, literally "thus is someone's heart," meaning to have a certain intention, to be of a certain disposition, to have a certain understanding of something; also to be easy in one's mind.

iuh ca noyollo ca amo nimitztlaxtlahuiz	I'm of a mind not to pay you.
iuh ca moyollo ca mochipa tinemiz	You think you'll live forever.

Let us not forget two applications of *iuh* that we have studied before and should be considered as part of the panoply of possibilities. One is its use to anticipate dependent clauses, especially after factitive verbs. In these cases we will usually use the word "that" in the translation, whether or not it is thought of as rendering *iuh*.

iuh quitoque aca iciuhca huallaz inic tech- palehuiz	They said that someone will soon come to help us.
iuh ninomati ca huel timococoa	I think that you are very sick.

The other use is the placement of *iuh* between the preterit *o* and the rest of a verb complex, giving a pluperfect sense.

in o iuh yecauh in teopancalli niman opeuh oncan mochihua missa	After the church building had been finished, mass began to be performed there.
in o iuh niteniçac huel cemilhuitl onipixcac	After I had had breakfast, I harvested [maize] the whole day long.

The longer, older form *iuhqui* can still be used on occasion in virtually any of the ways shown for *iuh*. It especially often means "like."

ye tiquinnenehuilia in macehualtin in iuhqui quiqua in iuhqui quimoquentia ye no iuhqui totech ca	We are the same as the commoners; as they eat and dress, so it is with us too (they eat and dress like we do, or we like them).

Because of its length, *iuhqui* can receive more stress than *iuh* (but it would not be impossible to have *iuh* instead of *iuhqui* in the second sentence here just below).

quin axcan oniquittac ce coatl ome itzon- tecon	Just now I saw a snake with two heads.
acan iuhqui oniquittac	Nowhere have I seen the like.

Iuhqui is used in phrases with the implication "as though," which in turn verges on "almost."

iuhqui napizmiqui	It's as though I were dying of hunger; I'm almost dying of hunger.
iuhqui ye xiniznequi ye polihuiznequi in maltepetzin	It is as though your altepetl were about to crumble and perish; your altepetl is almost ready to crumble and perish.[1]

A special idiom is *in ye iuhqui*, meaning when the situation is right, when preparations have been made, when things are ready.

in ye iuhqui mochintin oquintlaqualtique in inhuanyolque in imicnihuan	When things were ready, they fed (held a banquet for) all their relatives and friends.

The form *iuhquin* is quite specialized. It is usually associated with noun comparisons;

---

[1] *Iuhqui* used this way resembles the horrible colloquial "like" that has developed in American English in recent decades, as in "she was, like, running the show." The Nahuatl is different in flavor.

often *ma (mah)* is placed after it, and then the sense is highly hypothetical.

| in Juanton iuhquin chichimecatl tzatziti-nemi tlamotlatinemi | Little Juan goes around screaming and throwing things like a Chichimec. |
| iuhquin ma nitlacauh nechtolinia | He mistreats me as though I were his slave. |

The oldest of these forms, *ihui*, is quite rare. It is seen sometimes at the end of particle strings: *ma ço nel ihui*, "although"; *çan ye no ihui*, "in the same fashion, the same thing." It appears quite frequently before the demonstrative *in: ihui in*, "like this." Some instances, however, are written *ihuin*, which may be simply a different pronunciation and spelling of *iuh in*.

| miecpa onechittaco nechyectenehuaya nechmacaya cacahuatl xochitl cozcatl ihui in nechtlauhtiaya | He came to see me often. He would praise me, he would give me cacao, flowers, jewelry; like this he did me favors. |

C. *The particles* oc *and* ye. Here we are dealing with two pure particles, at least as they existed in the language of the sixteenth through eighteenth centuries, both temporal in basic meaning, though one of them, *oc*, goes far beyond its origins. They are a pair, *oc* meaning first of all "still," speaking of something past continued into the time being discussed, while *ye* is "already," speaking of something in existence prior to the time or action in question.

oc ichpochtli ocatca inic omomiquili	She was still a young unmarried woman when she died.
ye huehue ocatca inic omomiquili	He was already an old man when he died.
ayamo[1] nimiqui oc nonnemi	I'm not dead yet,[1] I'm still going on living.

In the negative, the sense of *oc* is naturally "no longer." When combined with negative words, *oc* is not added to them (unless they are of one syllable) but inserted in the middle in a way that never fails to puzzle or alienate English speakers at first. In addition to the simple *aoc*, "no longer," *amo* plus *oc* gives *aocmo*, with the same meaning; *atle* plus *oc* gives *aoctle*, "nothing any longer"; *ayac* plus *oc* gives *aocac*, "no one any longer."

| in Clara Elena aocmo nican onoc | Clara Elena no longer lives here (doesn't still). |
| aocac itech pohui in tlalli | The land no longer belongs to anyone. |

Temporal *oc* is, however, often given another slant, implying that something will continue only for a while, until something else happens, so that it comes to mean "first."

| oc achitzinca nican nicehuiz çatepan in milpan namechonnamiquiz | First I will rest here for a little while; later I will go meet you (pl.) at the fields. |
| ma oc xicmochiali quin yohuac ma ximohuica mochan | Wait for her a while and go home afterward, in the evening. |

Just as frequent as the temporal application of *oc* is its use to mean additional quantities. In English we often say "still more" or "yet more," but here "still" actually means "more." When the quantity is one, the resulting translation is "the other," "another." When it is one time that is in question, the result will be "again," i.e., another time.

| huallaque noteachcauh ihuan oc ce tlacatl | My older brother and another person came. |
| motlapanaz in naxca tlaco itech pohuiz in Juan Antonio in oc tlaco itech pohuiz in Diego Francisco | My property is to be divided. Half is to belong to Juan Antonio; the other half is to belong to Diego Francisco. |

---

[1]The *ya* in *ayamo*, "not yet," is an older form of *ye*, kept from moving to [ye] by the preceding [a]; *ayamo nimiqui* says literally "not already I die."

yohuatzinco onicpalehui nahuitzin texiliz-tica teotlac oc ceppa onicpalehui	Early in the morning I helped my aunt with grinding maize; in the afternoon I helped her again.

Even when the quantities are larger than one, the translation can still be "other."

iz catqui ontetl metlatl cuix motechtzinco monequiz oc ontetl	Here are two metates. Do you need another two?
nauhcan mani in notlal ceccan nicaquia no-meuh auh in oc excan niccui centli etl	My lands are in four places; in one place I plant my maguey, and from the other three places I get ears of maize and beans.
cequintin iuh quitoa Tepoztlan oya in tlato-ani oc cequintin iuh quitoa ca Mexico oya	Some say that the ruler went to Tepoztlan; others say that he went to Mexico City.

But soon we will find ourselves translating *oc* as "more," both with quantities larger than one and with indefinite quantities.

cuix oc achi ticmomacehuiz atzintli	Will you have a bit more pulque?
oc yei ilhuitl nicchiaz niman niyaz	I'll wait for him three more days, then I'll go.
cuix oc itla tiquilnamiqui	Do you remember anything more?
quemaca ca oc miec tlamantli niquil-namiqui	Yes, I remember many more things.

From meaning "more" *oc* has come to play a role in formal comparative structures in which one party exceeds another in some way. One or two words, often quantitative, follow *oc*, then perhaps *inic* plus the quality being compared, followed by *in amo*, not, and the loser in the comparison.

oc achi miequintin in tlaxcalteca in amo in huexotzinca	The people of Tlaxcala are more numerous than the people of Huejotzingo.
in Apolonia oc hualca inic qualnezqui in amo in Maria	Apolonia is (much) better looking than Maria.
in tocal oc achi inic huei in amo in amocal	Our house is bigger than yours.

A good deal more vocabulary is involved in similar expressions, and there are several other ways to make formal comparisons, but for our present purposes the topic is not worth going into. It is remarkable how few such comparisons are found in extant texts. A single somewhat related expression, *oc cenca*, "especially," will probably appear in texts you see more than all the comparative structures put together.

monequi nacatl tlaolli chilli oc cenca monequi cacahuatl	Meat, shelled maize, and chiles are needed; cacao is especially needed.

As has been mentioned before, in several types of expressions *oc* and *ye* are systematically paired, *oc* referring to the future and *ye* to the past.

(oc) huiptla nimitzonnottiliz	I will go see you the day after tomorrow.
ye huiptla oniquimonnottili	I went to see them the day before yesterday.
oc huecauh mochihuaz	It will happen a long time in the future.
ye huecauh omochiuh	It happened a long time in the past.
oc ome ilhuitl oncan nontlatequipanoz	I will keep working there for two days more.
ye ome ilhuitl oncan onitlatequipano	I have worked there for two days.[2]

You will see *ye* as often as *oc*, both being of high frequency, but *ye* is much simpler because it hardly goes beyond the temporal function. It by no means always needs to be or

---

[2] *Ye* is not obligatory here. The speaker has stopped working; otherwise the present would be used. The frequent construction *imoztlayoc* means "the day before" when it is accompanied by *oc* and the day after when it is not. *Ye* is not usually involved. *Oc imoztlayoc ilhuitzin totlaçonantzin*, "the day before the feast of our Precious Mother"; *imoztlayoc ilhuitzin*, "the day after her feast day."

should be translated as "already." That will have to depend on your sense of the context. In the following situations it should be.

ayamo tlatlalchipahua auh ye oiçaque in pipiltzitzintin	It's not light yet, and the children have already woken up.
nicnequi nicalaquiz in oncan moyetz- tica in tlatoani	I want to go in where the ruler is.
omochiuh ototlahueliltic ye omomiquili	Alas, he has already died.

Otherwise, *ye* precedes a huge number of preterit verbs, all equipped with the *o* preterit sign as well, and usually seems merely to emphasize the pastness; with some writers it may have been on the way to becoming a part of the normal preterit formation. It seems to be used by some writers to help distinguish a perfect sense from a simple past narrative sense. I would recommend leaving *ye* with preterits untranslated unless there is some compelling reason to do the opposite.

With expressions of duration in the present tense, *ye* can stress that an action has been going on for a time, giving a sense which in English is often expressed by the present perfect. *Ye* will precede a word dealing with the amount of time passed.

ye matlacxihuitl in nemi	It is already ten years that he/she lives, i.e., he/she has been alive for ten years.
ye nauhilhuitl nican titlatequipanoa	We have been working here for four days.

With a simple present tense verb, *ye* can translate as "already," or "is beginning to," or "now," or in yet other ways. In the present it is more likely to need translation than in the preterit, but the thrust is often subtle and tenuous.

ye Tollan itztiuh	He is already heading for Tula.
ye atlatataca in macehualtin	The commoners are beginning drainage excavation.
ye niquitta in tleica oticmocniuhti in nochpochtzin	Now I see why you made friends with my daughter.

Ye is used when something is impending, but generally some other facet of the sentence already tells you that. The most common is the construction in which *nequi*, literally "to want," incorporates a future verb. *Ye* is rarely lacking.

ye momiquiliznequi	He/she is about to die.
ye polihuiznequi in altepetl Tenanco	The altepetl of Tenango is at the point of perishing.

The particle string *çan ye no ihui* or *çanyenoihui*, "in the same fashion," was mentioned above in connection with *iuh/ihui*. *Ye* is a crucial component of this varying phrase, for just *çan no* means "likewise," and *no iuh* is part of "so . . . as" constructions.

ye miecpa onichtequililoc çan ye no iuh nopan omochiuh	I have often been robbed. — The same thing has happened to me.
in ipan xihuitl de 1613 años nican mayanaloc çan ye no ipan xihuitl otepohualoco	In the year of 1613 there was a famine here. In the same year they came to carry out a census.
yei hora tzilini onacico auh ye no iquac acico in nohueltihuatzin	I got here at three o'clock, and my older sister got here at the same time. [A male is speaking.]

D. *Çan*. The basic sense of this much used particle is "only, merely, just," putting a limit on something, stressing that more was not done or that the thing does not belong to a higher category. Often it is somewhat derogatory.

amo teuctli amo pilli amo no quauhpilli çan macehualli	He is not a lord, not a noble, not even a noble by merit. He is just a commoner.

cuix çan chiltzintli quiltzintli ticquazque	Are we to eat just chile and greens?
niman ic çan oya	Thereupon he just left (too abruptly).

In other cases it has no derogatory implication.

çan ce huel nelli Dios	only one very true God

In a turn not entirely unfamiliar to English speakers, *çan* comes to mean "simply, absolutely," somewhat as when we say, "I just know it," or "I just have to go." [1]

ahueliti in ticmottiliz in obispo	It is not possible for you to see the bishop.
oc ceppa niquitoa çan niquittaz	Again I say, I am simply going to see him.

Many Nahuatl expressions are accompanied by *çan* so often that doubt arises whether it really still means anything or should be acknowledged in a translation. *-Cel,* "alone, by oneself," is preceded by *çan* more often than not.

çan nocel onihualla	I have come alone (more literally, I have just come by myself).

Çan has a way of getting attached to other words so firmly that the new combination acquires a special meaning and is like a word in its own right. *Çan* plus *no,* "also," has come to mean "likewise," and will be found in dictionaries as a unit, *çanno.* For our purposes the parts will continue to be separated, for when you see them in an actual original text, you will have to make the decision about their status for yourself; particles are normally all run together in older orthography.

in noxhuiuh Ana Clara nicmacatiuh chicon-	To my grandchild Ana Clara I am giving seven
tetl chinamitl auh inic ome tlacatl noxhuiuh	chinampas, and to my second grandchild
itoca Apolonia çan no chicontetl nicmaca	named Apolonia I likewise give seven.

The word *iyo,* "alone," behaves much like a particle even though it originated as a preterit agentive noun and still has an *iyoque* plural. It rarely if ever means to be by oneself, but almost always comes together with *çan* in the meaning "only, exclusively," a sense less frequently associated with unaccompanied *çan.*

cihuapan çan iyoque calaqui in ichpopochtin	Only maidens and girls enter the women's
in cihuapipiltzitzintin	quarters.

Ixquich is a word often added to *çan* without bringing about much change other than creating a longer phrase which can receive greater emphasis. Students often concentrate on the larger word, which usually means "everything, all," neglect the innocuous *çan,* and arrive at an entirely false interpretation. *Ixquich* happens to mean "a certain amount" as well as "all," and it is probably that sense that is involved here.

in pipiltin inquaquauhecahuan oquinhual-	The nobles brought their oxen; the commoners
mohuiquilique in macehualtin çan ixquich	brought only digging sticks and sod breaking
huictli huitzoctli oquihualhuicaque	sticks.

Çan plus our now familiar friend *iuh,* "thus," becomes a dictionary word meaning for something to be its natural condition, unchanged, unimproved.

aocmo elimiqui in itlalpan çan iuh mani	He no longer cultivates his land; it lies fallow.
in Diego Buenaventua ayamo monamictia	Diego Buenaventura isn't married yet; he lives
çan iuh nemi	as a bachelor.

Çan plus *niman,* "then, next," is used to intensify all sorts of negative expressions.

çan niman aic niquilcahuaz	I will never ever forget her.

---

[1] Carochi seems to limit this meaning to *ça,* but in mundane texts written *çan* figures as well.

çan niman atle oquichiuhque	They did nothing whatever.
cuix aca ticmottilia çan niman ayac oniquittac	Do you see someone? — I haven't seen anyone at all.

The words *amo çan tlapohualli* (not just something-counted) constitute an invariable phrase—though it can be in the plural—meaning "something innumerable."

amo çan tlapohualtin in ilhuitica papaqui	Innumerable are those who celebrate on the feast day.

Without losing its role as an adverbial particle meaning "only, just," *çan* often veers in the direction of being an adversative conjunction governing whole clauses, i.e., translating as "but." Such a situation should be quite easy for us to understand. Consider a sentence such as "I'd like to go, only I have to take care of the kids." Often *çan* can be rendered equally well as "only, just," or as "but."[1]

chichimecatlalpan yazquia çan hualmocue-pato	He was going to go to the land of the Chichimeca, but after starting he came back.
ca quemaca nimitzpalehuiz çan oc achtopa monequi niquinchihuiliz molli nonamictzin nopiltzitzinhuan	Yes, I'll help you, but first I need to make *mole* for my spouse and children.
amo yaoyotica otiquinnamicque in espa-ñoles çan matca çan ihuian in nican taltepeuh ipan ocalacque	We did not meet the Spaniards with war, but (or rather) they entered our altepetl here peacefully.

E. *Huel.* Perhaps *huel* does not belong in the company of the other particles in this lesson in respect to general importance in the structure of Nahuatl sentences. It is equally frequent, however, and it causes students an almost equal amount of trouble.

Nahuatl once had a common noun *hueli*, without absolutive ending as far as we know, meaning "power, ability." A vestige is the expression *ixquichihueli*, "omnipotent" as an attribute of God, which although usually written solid is really *ixquich i-hueli*, "everything it-his-power." From this noun is derived a *-ti* verb still very much in use, *hueliti*, "for something to be possible." It can be used impersonally or with a personal subject.

cuix hueliti (or *huelitiz*) *motlapachoz in nocal*	Is it possible for my house to be roofed?
amo nihueliti axcan nimitznopalehuiliz	I can't help you now.

From *hueli* evolved the reduced form *huel*, a particle with two meanings both derived from the original. The more common is that of intensification, much as in the English of the nineteenth-century American frontier: "That's a powerful big gun." The other meaning still has to do with ability.

As an intensifier *huel* causes no other difficulty than the minor one of just how to translate it. Often it is virtually synonymous with the other main intensifier, *cenca*.

cenca tomahuac in moteachcauh	Your older brother is very stout.
huel tomahuac in moteachcauh	

The second example could be given the same translation; often, though, *huel* translates as "really," so we could say "your older brother is really stout."

Huel is used more widely than *cenca*, with all kinds of constructions, sometimes with the sense "that very," as in *huel iquac*, "at that very moment."

---

[1] An important variant of *çan* is *ça* (with a long vowel compensating for the loss of the *n*). In many ways the two remain very similar, but some distinctions have arisen. The topic will not be treated here because in actual texts the two are so often written the same: *çan* appears without its *n* much of the time, and one can even find *n* added to *ça*. For a discussion of the use of *ça* see Carochi.

huel oquixixini in xacalli	He completely demolished the hut.
huel achtopa niquitoa	First of all (or the very first thing), I say . . .
cuix oquichiuh in Alonso ca huel yehuatl oquichiuh	Did Alonso do it? — He's the very one who did it.
huel ipan ilhuitzin Santiago	right on the feast day of Santiago

Since *huel* is constantly seen in uses like the above, it is easy to forget the other sense, of possibility. Moreover, little or nothing about the possibility construction distinguishes it from the use of the word as an intensifier. *Huel* is simply placed in front of a verb, often in the future but sometimes in other tenses. *Huel quimictiz* could equally well mean "he will really beat or kill him" or "he will be able to beat or kill him." If you are alert to both alternatives, the larger context will usually (not quite always) allow you to make the right interpretation. Here are a few examples of *huel* meaning possibility.

yequene huel otlayahualoque in cofradesme	Finally the members of the cofradía were able to go in procession.
cuix huel calacohuaz in ichantzinco in tlatoani	Can people go into the house of the ruler? Or: Is it possible to go into the ruler's house?
nican Mexico miec in huel mochihua	Here in Mexico City many are the things that can be done.

The possibility meaning is more likely to be involved when the expression is in the negative; when, as quite often, the shortened form of the negative *amo, a- (ah-)* is used, you can be sure. This *a-* is attached directly to *huel.*

nican ahuel timocalaquiz	You can't come in here.
in ticmonequiltia ahuel nicchihuaz	I can't do what you wish.

F. *Particles in general.* Several other Nahuatl particles are nearly as common and nearly as complex and varied in their use as the ones we have been talking about. Eventually you will need to become deeply familiar with all of them, but meanwhile take the ones you have now been exposed to as a guide for the new ones you meet in texts. Don't expect them to act exactly like either adverbs or conjunctions of the kind you know from European languages. They are somewhere in between, a little of both, perhaps because the Nahuatl nuclear complex is somewhere between a word and a sentence. Particles often show characteristics of older forms from which they evolved; we have seen them still behaving in part like preterit agentive nouns and relational words. And indeed, relational phrases are not only adverbial but sometimes behave much like particles.

Nahuatl particles are forever clustering, then scattering again; the clusters become very significant, and we cannot handle the language without taking advantage of them, yet they never really become "words" as we know them in English. As definite a thing as *amo*, Nahuatl's main way of saying "not," can have *ya* inserted right inside it to make *ayamo*, "not yet," and both *a* and *mo* function as separate negatives in some contexts. We have seen that the notion of "the same" can be conveyed, doubtless with subtle differences that escape us, by different combinations of some of our most used particles: *çan ye no ihui, çan ye no iuh, çan ye no, ye no.* When this way of modifying nuclear words begins to seem natural to us, we are making real progress in understanding how Nahuatl utterances are built, and we are on our way to grasping their meaning more readily.

To this day the most detailed, enlightening treatment of the corpus of Nahuatl particles is the section in Carochi's grammar on "adverbs." You can study it repeatedly with profit, especially if you concentrate on the examples. The limitation of Carochi's adverb section is that a good many of the particles he discusses have little occasion to appear in extant texts, and some that do are not discussed.

17. Orthography

General orthography. Variations within standard orthography. Overbars and abbreviations. Variations over time. Punctuation. The principles of writing by Nahuas. Common deviances from standard orthography. Stage 3 changes. A selection from a text.

A. *General orthography.* Having arrived in Mexico in force in 1519 and achieved something approaching the conquest of the central part of the country in 1521, by the 1530's the Spaniards, or those of them (mainly ecclesiastics) who were interested in seeing Nahuatl written alphabetically, were arriving at the system that would predominate from that time to this. In this book we have essentially been using a version of that system developed by the grammarian Horacio Carochi in the mid-seventeenth century (minus some diacritics which never became a part of the writing practice of the Nahuas). You are already familiar with this manner of writing, but let us briefly discuss some facets of it, as used here and more generally, that you may not have noticed. The system is based on Spanish practice, with overall the same values for letters in both orthographies. (In the sixteenth century Spanish *x* was pronounced [sh], as in "shoe," and it was used for that sound in Nahuatl, even after Spanish itself began to pronounce *x* differently.)

Pronunciation as such is quite secondary to us as readers and interpreters of texts, but some aspects of it affect syllabification and word formation. Spanish *ll* represented an indivisible sound, [l̄] or [lʸ], but in Nahuatl writing *ll* was used for a true double *l*, each part of which was pronounced separately, so that syllables can divide between the two, and major morphological divisions can occur at that place, as in *cal-lal-li*, "house-land." Spanish lacked *tz* and *tl*, which correspond to unitary sound segments in Nahuatl, so it used two letters, a digraph, for the one sound. Thus even though we have seen that a Nahuatl word cannot end in two consonants, *tlacatl*, "person," or *huitz*, "he/she comes," are acceptable, because in each case the final two letters represent only one consonant. These conventions should not bother us, for our own writing system has digraphs. In Nahuatl writing *ch* works exactly the same way as *tz* and *tl*, but seems more familiar to us because it has the same value in Spanish and English. (Our *sh*, *th*, and *ph* are also digraphs.)

B. *Variations within standard orthography.* Some aspects of the Nahuatl phonetic system that were not present in Spanish were simply ignored in the Spanish-based Nahuatl orthography. The representation of vowel quantity, a basic feature of Nahuatl phonology, is hardly seen outside Carochi's circle. Such things make it harder in general to read and understand Nahuatl writing, but that is simply a fact of life and not something to occupy us here. What does become relevant is that though the glottal stop, inherently as important as any other consonant of Nahuatl, was generally left unwritten, attempts were made from an early time to represent it by *h*. Some of the most prominent early philologists used *h* this way, though never consistently. Although the convention did not become part of the standard canon, the tradition of it never entirely disappeared, either among Spanish ecclesiastics or among the Nahuas themselves. Thus in texts of any type you may suddenly be confronted with examples like the following:

tlahtoque, tlatohque, or *tlahtohque* <u>for</u>	*tlatoque*	rulers
tlahxilacalli	*tlaxilacalli*	district, constituent part of an altepetl
notahtzin	*notatzin*	my father
iuhquin mah piltzintli	*iuhquin ma*	as though he/she were a child

This *h* is not to be confused with the same letter in the *hu/uh* that represents [w]. It will generally be found at the end of a syllable, i.e., before a consonant, or in a particle preceding a nuclear word. Rarely indeed does it occur at the end of a nuclear word; for that reason I did not include *tlahtohqueh* as a possibility with our first example just above. Sometimes it appears between two vowels, especially when they are rearticulated in the distributive, almost as punctuation between them, but also when the glottal stop is a normal part of the word.

ohome ilhuitica	two days each, or every two days
yehica	wherefore, for which reason

Since the use of *h* for glottal stop, although perennial, never became standard, neither did its placement. Both Nahuas and Spaniards seem to have perceived the combination of a vowel and a following glottal stop as an inseparable unit, which led to putting the *h* before the letter for the vowel rather than after it.

hamo (ahmo)	not
nothatzin (notahtzin)	my father

From the early seventeenth century forward, in texts of ecclesiastical origin, primarily printed works, you may find a grave accent over a vowel, indicating a glottal stop after that vowel.

àmo	not
notàtzin	my father

Any voiced consonant in Nahuatl is devoiced, merely aspirated, when it comes at the end of a syllable or a word. Standard orthography reflects this phenomenon by representing [w] as *hu* when voiced, *uh* when unvoiced. As readers of texts this concerns us mainly in that we must know how to convert the unvoiced version to the voiced to arrive at the word's citation form. We have learned that Class 2 preterits in *-uh* correspond to present tenses in *hu-*, as in *oquichiuhque*, "they did it," and *quichihua*, "they do it." The same thing can happen in reverse. *Quauhtli*, "eagle," and *ihuitl*, "feather or down," can be combined to make "eagle feathers or down," which might be spelled *quauhihuitl*, as we have been writing such things here, but in either ecclesiastical or mundane texts it might appear equally well as *quahuihuitl*, for Nahuatl pronunciation took any consonant before a vowel within a word as the starting point of a new syllable, regardless of where stems may divide.

quaquauheque	<u>or</u>	*quaquahueque*		oxen
chalchiuhatl	<u>or</u>	*chalchihuatl*		jade water

An attempt was made very early in the game, associated with the grammarian fray Andrés de Olmos, to give [l] much the same treatment as [w], i.e., to write *l* before a vowel and *lh* syllable-finally, as in *icalh*, "his/her house," for *l* too is voiced before a vowel, unvoiced before another consonant or word-finally. Even Olmos and the Tlaxcalan circle associated with him never wrote *l/lh* consistently, and the convention soon faded, but echoes of it will be found here and there.

What never reached uniformity among writers of either the ecclesiastical or the mundane world was how to write [kʷ] syllable-finally. Before *e* and *i*, it was always *cu*, and before *a* it was long almost unanimously written as *qu*, until in the late period many began to write *cu* instead. But at the end of a syllable or word, there were three conventions: *cu*, *uc*, and *cuh*. In these lessons we have used *uc*, following Carochi.

[tēkʷtli], "lord"	*tecutli*	Molina and others
	teuctli	Carochi and some others, mainly ecclesiastic
	tecuhtli	the most widespread convention

Even these three variants do not exhaust the possibilities; the great and well educated seventeenth-century annalist Chimalpahin wrote *uhc: teuhctli*. The problem with *cu* is that you are likely to interpret the *u* as a vowel, when it merely represents the rounding of the consonant [k]. The *cuh* variant is the most logical, calling to mind the *uh* used normally to represent an unvoiced or aspirated [w], and the aspiration of [kʷ] in syllable-final position must have had a very similar effect.

In Nahuatl speech, all syllable-final consonants were weakened, devoiced where relevant, sometimes losing their point of articulation, and often assimilated to the following, syllable-initial consonant. Thank goodness, not much of all this is represented in standard orthography. But even in writing under ecclesiastical auspices, the letter for a fricative or affricate (*x, z, ch, tz*) could be omitted before another one, especially before *tz* and most frequently before the reverential -*tzin*. No writer ever carried out such omissions consistently, which in a way makes it all the harder for us. You must always be prepared to meet cases like the following:

itetzinco pohui	for	*itechtzinco pohui*	It belongs to him/her.
nochpotzin		*nochpochtzin*	my daughter
totetlaçotlalitzin		*totetlaçotlaliztzin*	our love

A more pedantic, less often seen usage concerns the writing of *n* before sibilants, mainly *c/ç*. According to Carochi, [n] assimilates to following [s], so that when an *n* is followed by *c/ç* within a phonological phrase (not his terminology), the *n* should be written *z*, as in *izcihuatl* for *in cihuatl*, "the woman." Neither Carochi nor anyone else ever did this more than sporadically, but it does occur in texts under ecclesiastical auspices, usually causing considerable puzzlement.

It is generally agreed that Nahuatl has four vowels, well represented as *a, e, i,* and *o*, each of which occurs both long and short. Spanish lacked quantity but had one more letter and sound, *u* [u], and those who devised the orthography often thought they heard it in Nahuatl words. Soon, however, *u* came to be used much less than *o*. Carochi does not use vocalic *u* at all and specifically denies that Nahuatl has that vowel; more importantly, long before him many of the best writers of both ecclesiastical and mundane texts had nearly abandoned *u* as a syllabic vowel. Nevertheless, it continued as a minority phenomenon in texts of all kinds, above all for long *o*, but for short *o* too. In Molina's great dictionary *o* is the main convention, but many important words are in *u* as well, as with *xuchitl* in addition to *xochitl*, "flower," and *teutl* in addition to *teotl*, "god."

In the pronunciation of Nahuatl, there was no systematic distinction between [ia] and [iya] or [oa] and [ohua]. As a result, the inventors of the Nahuatl orthography and their successors had to deduce from other forms of a word whether to write *y* between *i* and *a* or *hu* between *o* and *a*. For example, with the verb *tlalia*, "to place, etc.," since no *y* was ever pronounced in tenses of the verb where *a* was missing, the deduction was that no *y* was involved, leading to the standard spelling of Class 3 verbs without it. With *pohua*, "to count, etc.," since a [w] showed up in the preterit, *pouh*, the result was to spell the present tense with *hu*. The grammarians and the whole body of writers strongly influenced by ecclesiastics eventually reached a reasonable uniformity on *ia/iya* (hardly writing *iya*) and *oa/ohua*. However, a capital fact for the reader of texts, who will spend much time looking in Molina's dictionary, is that Molina's general (though not exceptionless) policy was to write *oa* not only for Class 3 -*oa* verbs but also in situations where Carochi and most others would write *ohua*; thus he has "to count" as *poa* (see Appendix 1).

The reader must also be prepared for variation on some related matters which were never quite settled. Carochi refused to write *iya* under almost any conditions, and he insisted on *ia* when *i* of a verb stem met -*ya*, the ending of the imperfect tense, (i.e., *nemia* for "he/she was living" instead of *nemiya*), but even highly orthodox writers often wrote this *y*. Carochi and some others wrote *coatl*, "snake," but there is no way to test the presence or absence of *hu*, and *cohuatl* will be seen in texts with a standard flavor. When the *hua* of an impersonal verb meets a stem in *o*, again there is no possibility of a check; even Carochi hesitated between *-oa* and *-ohua*, leaning toward the former, as with *nemoa*, "there is living, life goes on." Nor did he and those like him ever quite decide whether to write *y* between *i* and *o*. We see *-çoquio*, "one's physical or earthly aspect," containing the *yo* of inalienable possession, but also *totecuiyo*, "our Lord." The variation in standardizing texts in this respect, however, is nothing to what is seen in mundane texts, so a thorough discussion of the matter will be reserved for a little later.

I have used here the Carochi standard of writing vocalic [i] as *i* and the glide [y] as *y*. Molina's dictionary follows the same convention. But even in texts of ecclesiastical provenience one will see another convention (or at least hints of it) which was normal in secular Spanish writing and came to dominate in mundane Nahuatl texts as well. In this scheme, [y] was always *y*, but [i] could be either *y* or *i* depending on its position. In Spanish, at the beginning of a word *y* was often written whether the letter represented a glide or a syllabic vowel, thus *ya*, "already," with the glide, and *yglesia*, "church," with the vowel. In Nahuatl, *y* came to be used not so much at the beginning of a word as at the beginning of a word complex or phonological phrase; thus the particle *in*, which starts a million phrases, was usually *yn*; *ihuan*, "along with it, and," was often *yhuan* for the same reason. Traces of this usage can be found even in Carochi himself; in other texts done under ecclesiastical auspices it is usually more pronounced than in Carochi, and sometimes even dominant.

C. *Overbars and abbreviations.* It was a standard feature of Nahuatl orthography that an *n* after a vowel could be represented as a line over that vowel. The practice was carried over from Spanish calligraphy; it had been especially prominent in the Latin orthography with which the ecclesiastics who invented the Nahuatl system were familiar. The line actually means any nasal consonant, so that sometimes we may want to write *m* in resolving the line, which we call an overbar. In the originals it is usually curved upward in the middle and extends well beyond the single letter it is intended for; here it will be shown as a straight line directly above the letter for the vowel (not to be confused with the same sign as used by Carochi to show a long vowel and then called a macron). Some writers used it mainly to save space, and it is likely to be seen more frequently as the right margin approaches, but others spread it liberally over their pages. As time went on the overbar was used less, but it never entirely disappeared during the time that Nahuatl was written.

> ī ātlatoque amopāpatzīco nicnotlalilia huētzītli
> in antlatoque amopampatzinco nicnotlalilia huentzintli
> On behalf of you rulers I make an offering.

In the large number of Spanish words in Nahuatl texts the tilde over *n* (ñ) often appears, and it has been represented here in the standard way. In actual texts it often cannot be distinguished from the overbar except by the fact that it stands over an *n* and not over a vowel. Indeed, in many older printed books and some of today, the tilde is used to represent the overbar (ã, etc.).

Another bit of Latin calligraphic lore that came into Nahuatl writing for a time was a series of marks over *q* to indicate *que*, *qui*, and *qua*. The first was shown by a generally horizontal, though somewhat curving line, the second by a vertical line, also usually curved, and the third by a zigzag line looking a good deal like *w*. Here they are represented as q̃ for *que*, q̇ for *qui*, and q̃ for *qua*. The first was by far the most common and lasted the longest, probably because it was the only one practiced by secular writers of Spanish. The other two are rarely seen beyond about 1580 or done by writers other than those directly trained by ecclesiastics. Another way of abbreviating *que* was a combination that looks for all the world like *qz* and can be so represented.

> *otlatoq̃ oq̇toq̃ ma q̇çacā ī pipiltzitzītī ma tlaq̃cā*
> *otlatoque oquitoque ma quiçacan in pipiltzitzintin ma tlaquacan*
> They spoke and said, "Let the children come out, let them eat."
>
> *q̃uhnahuac oq̇zqz*
> *Quauhnahuac oquizque*
> They came out of Cuernavaca.

As to abbreviations in the usual sense, shortened forms of whole words, the vast majority to be found in Nahuatl texts are of Spanish loans, treated the same as in Spanish texts, and we will discuss those in the next chapter. With Nahuatl words you may occasionally see *a⁰* for *amo*, not; *tlalᵖᵃᶜ* for *tlalticpac*, "the earth, on earth," and the reverential element of relational words abbreviated by a final superscribed *ᶜᵒ*, as in *ipampaᶜᵒ* for *ipampatzinco*, "because of it." A few other short forms may appear here and there; usually you can figure them out ad hoc from unabbreviated instances of the same word. The one great Nahuatl abbreviation is *tote⁰*, *tte⁰*, *tt⁰*, or the like for *totecuiyo*, "our Lord." Indeed, if you relied on actual Nahuatl texts for instruction, it would probably be a long time before you would ever see *totecuiyo* written out and discover what it is.

D. *Variation over time.* Once standard orthography in Nahuatl had jelled, by perhaps 1570 or 80, it showed great stability as practiced in ecclesiastical circles; what happened in mundane circles we will discuss later. Some important extant texts, to which you may well be exposed in due course, contain features from the time before relative uniformity had been attained. The marks on *q* that we just discussed are rife in the very earliest Nahuatl texts and rapidly diminish, especially after about 1560, becoming something of a rarity after about 1580. The very first texts also still lack one important feature of the definitive system; [s] had not yet been distinguished from [tˢ], i.e., *tz* had not yet been invented. In the large corpus of Cuernavaca region census records from the late 1530's and early 1540's we can see such things as:

çe ipilçin		*ce ipiltzin*	He has one child.
ayac ipilzin	for	*ayac ipiltzin*	He has no children.
quiqueza		*quiquetza*	He raises it.

It took quite a while to come to a uniform convention on writing [w]. At first *v*, *u*, and *hv* or *vh* were written alongside *hu* for [w] before a vowel. The circle of fray Bernardino de Sahagún, responsible for many important texts, wrote *ho* or *o*, and continued to do so into the late sixteenth century. The word *ihuan*, "along with it, and," could be written any number of ways. Leaving out of account that either *y* or *i* could represent the first vowel, that some were not so sure the final *n* should be written, and that even if it was an overbar could be used, we still have the following:

> *ivan   iuan   ihuan   ihvan   ivhan   ihoan   ioan*

The notion of writing syllable-final [w] differently is present, though not consistently, even in the earliest documents. Soon the main forms seen syllable-finally were *vh* and *uh*, with *uh* gaining ground quickly, but sometimes *hv* was retained. The word *omochiuh*, "it happened," can be seen in the following ways:

> *omochiuh   omochivh   omochihv*

All of the variants retained some adherents to 1600 and beyond, mainly people who had learned early and never changed, but by 1580 *hu* had become dominant before a vowel, probably because the same thing had happened in secular Spanish orthography, and even before 1560 *uh* was the usual way of representing the syllable-final sound.

After 1640 or 50, in the third of the three stages into which the evolution of post-contact Nahuatl falls, some further important changes took place, but they were confined largely to mundane texts, which by that time were the overwhelming majority of all being produced, and they will be discussed under the tendencies of Nahua writers.

E. *Punctuation.* Among secular Spaniards in the sixteenth through eighteenth centuries, handwritten texts were hardly punctuated at all, nor was capitalization or spacing in the least consistent. Among the ecclesiastics who devised Nahuatl orthography, all these things were somewhat closer to modern practice, but by no means identical with it. Even the ecclesiastical practices were not successfully carried over to the bulk of indigenous writers in Nahuatl, so that all in all punctuation cannot be counted on as an aid in understanding written Nahuatl. That is why the texts and examples in these lessons have not been punctuated at all.

From the very beginning of Nahuatl writing, texts will be found which literally have no punctuation-like marks, and that in the end became the predominant style at the level of sentences and phrases. Paragraphs and items in wills were often introduced by a mark like a *v* over a line (v, approximately; here I have used a hyphen), and a diagonal (/) or double diagonal (//) sometimes indicated changes of subject.

Very early in the game there appeared a convention adapted specifically to Nahuatl syntax, in which the "word" is not as distinct as in European languages, and subordinated clauses all in all do not stand out as clearly from independent clauses, but the complexes around nuclear words, mainly verbs and nouns, have overwhelming importance as the building blocks of sentences. A tendency developed, instigated by whom it is not certain, to put a dot, or sometimes a diagonal, between each complex and the next. When carried out consistently, this system is perhaps the best way to punctuate Nahuatl texts ever invented. Consistency was never attained, however. Many writers spread the dots about so sparsely and so arbitrarily that it would be much better had they done nothing. Others developed meaningful but idiosyncratic ways of using the system. Chimalpahin was still decorating his lines quite liberally with dots in the early seventeenth century. The tradition continued to wither, but some vestige of it remained as long as Nahuatl was being written.

Here is the most consistent example I have ever seen, done in Mexico City in 1565.

In iquac . quinmomaquilia topili . ȳ alldes . mexico . ȳ visorrey . q̓nmolhuilia . yn
When / he gives the staff to / the alcaldes / of Mexico City, / the viceroy / says to them:

amehuantin . alldes ye anmochihua . yn axcan achtopa . cenca . ypan xitlatoca . ȳ
"You / alcaldes who are being appointed / now for the first time, / greatly / see to / the

doctrina x̄p̄iana . ma mochi tlacatl . quimati . yn itlayecoltillocatzin . ȳ tote⁰ . dios
Christian doctrine; / let everyone / know / the service of / our lord / God.

Auh çatepan . ypan ātlatozque . yn itlayecoltilloca . ȳ totlatocauh . ȳ Su mag^t . ȳ tleyn
And after that / you are to see to / the service of / our ruler / His Majesty; / what

quimonequiltia . yn itetzinco . monequi . ypan ātlatoz̄q̄ . huell anquimocui-
he desires, / what by him / is needed / you are to see to, / you are to take good

tlahuizque auh yn ixquich tlacatl . ȳ macehualtzintli . huell āquimocuitlahuiz̄q̄ .
care of.   And as to all / the poor commoners, / you are to take good care of them,

anquitlaçotlazā . ayac çā tlapictli . anquitlatzōtequilizā . yhuan . huell anqui-
/ you are to treat them with esteem; / no one without reason / you are to judge, / and /

mocuitlahuizā . ynic mochi tlacatl . Elimiquiz . ayac tlatziuhtinemiz .
you are to take good care / that everyone / cultivates, / no one goes about in idleness."

The distribution of dots here is even more methodical than it at first seems, for the writer takes it that *auh* automatically signifies a break and does not put a dot before it. Also, in the framework of this text some weighty particles probably received enough emphasis to be considered complexes themselves and hence are marked off in a way we might not usually expect.[1]

In circles closely dominated by ecclesiastical philologists, punctuation soon went beyond complex-marking to a full system featuring the comma, semicolon, colon, period, at times capitalization after a period, and even sometimes question marks. All books published in Nahuatl during the postconquest centuries manifest these signs, and so do many important manuscripts of the time done under ecclesiastical auspices, including those done in the circles of fray Bernardino de Sahagún and Horacio Carochi. Here is a passage from Book Twelve of the Florentine Codex, done under Sahagún's direction, with its original orthography and punctuation.

Auh in ie iuhqui in o mochi munechico in teucuitlatl. Nimā ie ic quīoalnotza, quī-oalnenotzallani in ixquichtin in pipiltin in Malintzin: tlapanco oalmoquetz, atenanticpac: Quitoa. Mexica xioalhuian ca cenca ie tlaihiovia in Españoles: xiqualuicā in tlaqualli, in chipaoac atl, yoan in ixquich monequi, ca ie tlaihiovia, ie quiciavi, ie quihiovia, ie mociavi, ie mihiovia: tleica in amo anoallaznequi? ic neci ca anqualani.

And when the collection of all the gold was completed, thereupon Marina summoned to her, had summoned, all the noblemen. She stood on a flat roof, on a roof parapet, and said, "O Mexica, come here, for the Spaniards are suffering greatly. Bring food, fresh water, and all that is needed, for they are suffering travail, are tired, fatigued, weary, and exhausted. Why is it you do not want to come? From that it appears that you are angry."

If you read many texts done this way you will soon begin to see that the distinction between the meanings of comma, semicolon, and colon is tenuous, and a period does not always mean the end of the sentence, even when the next letter is capitalized. What one will often find is that though not so intended, the full punctuation system in the hands of Nahua amanuenses moved back in the direction of simply marking the beginning and end of a large number of small complexes or phonological/syntactic phrases, much like the dots.

A particular kind of punctuation is the convention of putting a space between each group of letters considered to be a word. We today are so accustomed to this procedure that we can hardly imagine things without it. Yet writing among sixteenth-century secular Spaniards did entirely without any such convention, typically running letters into each other all the way across the page; ecclesiastical writers usually made spaces, but not quite like those we know today. Nahuatl texts done under ecclesiastical auspices usually make some gesture toward spacing, but they often include particles with the main following word (our complex again) and are never very consistent. Mundane texts by Nahuas vary from a practice resembling that of ecclesiastical writers to a habit of leaving a small

---

[1]A facsimile of this passage appears in Lockhart, *The Nahuas*, p. 340. Some text using dots and diagonals in the same way can be seen at the beginning of Appendix 3.

space after every single syllable regardless of words and complexes; many followed the secular Spanish practice of simply running everything together until the end of the line comes or the ink runs out. Oddly enough, non-spacing or arbitrary spacing causes less trouble than one would expect for those who are reasonably well prepared in Nahuatl morphology.[2]

The upshot is that though in some kinds of texts you may find some familiar-looking punctuation marks and spacing, you are more likely not to find them, and even when they are there they may mislead more than help you unless you treat them with considerable suspicion and sophistication. Generally speaking, you yourself are responsible for dividing the letters into something like words and establishing the larger units.

F. *The principles of writing by Nahuas.* When left to themselves, and to the extent that they were left to themselves even when working under Spanish auspices, Nahua writers had a very different outlook on what they were doing than did their Spanish counterparts. Spaniards were spelling words; in general, they wrote a given word the same way every time they used it, employing the same standard spelling,[3] in relative independence of how they might pronounce it. To the Nahuas, the word, insofar as they were even aware of it, was a constantly changing entity with fluid borders. What they were doing when writing was reproducing the flow of speech, a sound/letter at a time, regardless of any standard or abstract notion of how a given "word" was written. Although they were limited by what the orthography expressed, within that framework they were simply recording speech, much like a tape recorder. Nahuatl pronunciation could vary greatly from place to place and time to time, and such variations will be found reflected in written texts.

A marvelous early corpus of Nahuatl writing is the set of census records from the Cuernavaca region in the late 1530's and early 1540's. Here we can find the word *ichpochtli*, "girl past puberty, unmarried young woman," written as *chipochtli* and even as *chipochitl*, because that was the pronunciation of some people in the area at the time.[4] Presented with such things, we are at the mercy of our ingenuity and good luck, but it will not hurt to remember that short *i* was Nahuatl's least stable vowel, often merely holding the slot, so to speak, for something else to take its place, not really representing a full vowel at all but merely serving to make a word pronounceable and equally likely to come before a given consonant or after it. Other frequent items in the census are *ya monamicti* and *yaquene*, for Molina's *ye monamicti*, "a year ago," and *yequene*, "finally." Here the lesson is that in many words originally having *ya* [ya], the [a] assimilated to the [y] in speech and became [e]. Even when *e* is now the standard, *a* may be found at any time, and vice versa; thus *mi(y)ec* or *mi(y)ac*, "much," *pi(y)a* or *pi(y)e*, "to keep, hold, have," etc.

You cannot anticipate all such things or even necessarily understand the pattern in them, but you can be prepared, and you can grasp the general principle. In a great many cases the letter causing puzzlement represents a sound very close to the sound represented

---

[2] I have not attempted to duplicate the experience for the student by printing passages, or even a sample passage, with no spaces. The effect on a printed page is much more frightening than the actuality. Some people when first presented with an unspaced handwritten page hardly even realize the lack of spacing but immediately start reading elements and words as though they were spaced. Also, the purely paleographic problem of recognizing letters is much less severe with Nahuatl calligraphy than with Spanish.

[3] With some equally standard variations or equivalences.

[4] Similar in its origins is the word *mocchotia*, frequently met with in the Cuernavaca-region records in the meaning "she marries, takes a man." It derives from *oquichtli*, "man," with the *i* of the root omitted: *m-oquich-(y)o-tia*, "she provides herself with a man." But though seen infrequently in the Valley of Mexico, this verb is actually in Molina's dictionary.

by the letter more usually seen in that position, indicating that in speech the two sounds have merged or one has replaced the other. Let us take some sets that are frequently inter-changed: *ch* and *x*, and *tz* and *z*. *Ch* is for [tsh] and *x* for [sh]; *tz* is for [ts] and *z* for [s].[1] Nahuatl consonants in syllable-final position were always weakened in some way or other. In these two sets, the [t] attack might be omitted, leaving the other sound, so that *x* would be written for *ch*, *z* for *tz*. If a writer pronounced the stronger two (affricates) as the weaker two (fricatives), they were then identical, and there was no reason not also to write *ch* for standard *x*, *tz* for standard *z*.

noxpox	= standard	*nochpoch*, "my daughter"	*meztli*	= standard	*metztli*, "month"
chiyauh		*xiyauh*, "go away!"	*imiquitzpan*		*imiquizpan*, "at the time of his/her death"

G. *Some common deviances from standard orthography.* Here are briefly discussed and illustrated some of the most common features of writing by Nahuas, resulting from their writing like they talked, that make things harder for you than when dealing with per-fectly standard orthography.

G1. *Omission and insertion of nasals.* Perhaps your biggest shock when you face real texts will be that a vast number of *n*'s (and some *m*'s) present in standard spellings are missing, and on the other hand many *n*'s are present that are missing in standard forms. The phenomenon occurs only in syllable-final position, where [n] appears to have been Nahuatl's weakest consonant. Even in ecclesiastical circles it was common to write *ihua* for *ihuan*, "and, with it," and *-ti* for *-tin*, the absolute plural ending of nouns. When you see *oca*, it may be *o ca*, summing up a preceding presentation, but it may also mean *onca*, "there is," and the most likely of all, *oncan*, "there" (not to speak of *occan*, "in two places"). In the Cuernavaca census records what is written as *ymaque* appears often; it turns out to be equivalent to *in m-anque*, "that they took each other, i.e., got married."

In Lesson 20 you will face a champion example of deviance with respect to *n*. For now let us be content with the following small sample, from Huejotla in 1634:

yn iquac oquichihuiqueleccio çan oca oquichhuique ynztacia ometi huell otlahuaque auh tehuati amo ticnequi ca huel toca mocacayahua ynn alcates oquitlali çequicaya-nis ynhua tzahuiqui amo quimocopirmalhui yn totlatocatzin

in iquac oquichiuhque eleccion çan oncan oquichiuhque estancia omentin huel otla-huanque auh tehuantin amo ticnequi ca huel toca mocacayahua in alcalde oquitlali cequi igañan ihuan tzauhqui amo quimoconfirmarhui in totlatocatzin

When they held the election, it was only two people who were very drunk who held it at the estancia. We don't want [the governor], because he greatly deceives us. As al-calde he installed someone who is his hired man and a weaver. Our ruler (the viceroy) has not confirmed him (the governor).

It is clear enough that if the Nahuas pronounced syllable-final [n] barely or not at all, they would be inclined not to write *n* in that position. But why did many of them write so many syllable-final *n*'s where they don't seem to belong at all? It begins to appear that since *n* represented the weakest Nahuatl consonant usually written, some writers used it to represent any weak consonant. Thus sometimes it falls in the place of a glottal stop, including the one that always came at the end of Spanish loanwords apparently ending in a vowel, and sometimes for the first, weakened member of a consonantal pair.

---

[1]The sound [s] was also represented by *c* before *e* and *i* and by *ç* before any vowel, especially *a* and *o*, but since *c* and *ç* as [s] are not written syllable-finally, they do not come into play here.

otlanto	for	otlato (otlahtoh), "he/she spoke"
molan		mula (mulah), "mule"
canli		calli, "house"

But that hardly begins to explain the profusion of extra *n*'s appearing in some texts. We are almost driven to think that some writers had real trouble figuring out where there was an [n] and where there wasn't and were just guessing. In some texts the correspondence between the presence or absence of an [n] in standard speech and the presence of absence of *n* is far under fifty percent. At any rate, when you fail to find a word in the dictionary, start removing and adding syllable-final *n*'s in the form you are working with.

G2. *Single and double consonants.* In real texts by Nahuas you must expect any medial double consonant to appear single at any time, and any medial single consonant to be doubled.[2] It may be that the weakened, syllable-final component in a set of two identical consonants was so nearly inaudible that it invited omission. On the other hand, it seems that Nahuas often liked to use a consonant to finish the preceding syllable as well as to begin the next, leading to doubling. The two tendencies together seem to have erased all distinction between single and double consonants for some speakers (and writers). We can not entirely explain the phenomenon, but we can learn to expect certain things. In texts you will see cases like the following:

onicuic	=	oniccuic, "I took it"	occ onaciz	=	oc onaciz, "he/she will get there"
tlali		tlalli, "land"	nictlallia		nictlalia, "I place it, etc."
y nopiltzin		in nopiltzin, "my child"	innic		inic, "so that, etc."

You will have noticed in the examples just given that doubling and singling can occur either within a word complex in the narrower sense or between preliminary particles and that complex. The latter type tends to cause more difficulty for readers, but it is also more instructive. Doubling and singling occurs only within the complex broadly construed, within a single phonological/syntactic phrase, so that when it occurs between the nucleus and something to the left of it, we are being told that that element belongs in the complex. In an earlier example we saw *huell anquimocuitlahuizque*, "you are to take good care of it." The *ll* of standard *huel* tells us beyond all doubt that *huell* belongs syntactically with the following verb. The element most involved in this sort of manipulation is the subordinator *in*, doubling its *n* when a vowel follows and losing it when followed by another *n*. By rights these assimilated elements should be written solid with what follows (as they always are in actual texts), for example *ynopiltzin*, "my child," but experience shows that such a policy causes readers undue trouble.

The consonants vary in their proneness to this kind of variation. *L* is probably the most involved, especially in the reduction of the *l-li* at the end of nouns and the doubling of the *l* of the *-lia* ending of verbs, as in our examples just above. Second would come *n*, mainly on the strength of *in*, and third *c*, though it is reduced much more frequently than it is augmented. With most of the other consonants too reduction is more frequent.

cepa	=	ceppa, "once"	mota	=	motta, "it is seen"
meço		mezço, "your blood"	ixoxouhqui		ixxoxouhqui, "green-faced"[3]

Generally speaking *m* is not much involved, but one may see such a form as *immixpan* for *imixpan*, "in their presence."

G3. *The behavior of glides.* The semiconsonantal sounds [y] and [w] are used in many

---

[2]In sequences of two unlike consonants, the first may quite frequently be omitted, but that phenomenon does not become such a major feature of the corpus. *Tl* is never doubled.

[3]As was seen above, p. 106, the letter for the first of two consecutive affricates or fricatives may be omitted even in standard orthography and even when they are not identical.

languages as a transition between two consecutive syllabic vowels and in this capacity are called glides. In Nahuatl writing the letters for the glides, usually *y* and *hu*, will be found not only where the dictionary indicates them, but anywhere that two vowels come together within a phonological phrase. They can have the same effect of tying a phrase together as do the reduction and augmentation of consonants.

ohuacico	= *oacico*, "he/she arrived"	*huey yotli*	= *huei otli*, "big road, highway"
tlayolli	*tlaolli*, "shelled maize"	*tlayi*	*tlaai*, "he works the land"

But the main problem with the glides is in one particular kind of context: with *y* between *i* and *a*, with *hu* between *o* and *a*. Any given writer is likely to interchange *ia* and *iya*, *oa* and *ohua*, regardless of the form you may find in a dictionary.

monamictiya	= *monamictia*, "he/she marries"	*iyachtzin*	= *iachtzin*, "her older brother"
tlatohuani	*tlatoani*, "ruler"	*quicoa*	*quicohua*, "he/she buys it"

An example of *ia* for *iya* is not included in the set just given because the sequence *iya* is so rare in fully standard orthography. All in all, the variants with the glides tend to predominate in mundane texts, but you will find plenty of examples in both modes.

The phonological reason for all this, in case it should help you, is as follows. The natural glide to insert between *i* [i] and *a* [a] is *y* [y], just as *hu* [w] is the natural glide to insert between *o* [o] and *a* [a]. Some Nahuas seem to have pronounced the intermediate sound in all cases of these combinations, others never, others possibly did or didn't indifferently, but no one made a consistent distinction between the presence and absence of the glide, causing a high degree of inconsistency in writing it down.

H. *Stage 3 changes.* It will emerge more clearly in Lesson 18 that Nahuatl underwent three successive distinct phases in its adaptation to Spanish influence: Stage 1, 1519 to 1540 or 1545, during which Nahuatl hardly changed and alphabetic writing was just being developed at certain centers; Stage 2, from then until 1640 or 1650, a hundred years during which the primary change was the borrowing of a large stock of Spanish nouns; and Stage 3, from that time forward, when a substantial mass of bilingual Nahuas integrated a wide spectrum of Spanish phenomena into the language.

The corpus of extant Nahuatl texts belongs overwhelmingly to Stages 2 and 3, those of Stage 1 being of great intrinsic interest but almost negligible in quantity. The standard orthography used in these lessons is a Stage 2 product, and in discussing the variations upon it in this lesson I have had that phase primarily in mind. Actually, virtually all of these phenomena continued strong in Stage 3, but some relatively minor differences surface which it will be well to take into account.

Nahuatl documents of the late seventeenth and the eighteenth centuries look different from their predecessors. Capitals are seen much more frequently (though distributed quite haphazardly, often in the middle of a root); the letters, especially *l*, are higher, and they slant more. In such things Nahuatl calligraphy was following the trend in Spanish writing, to which those who wrote Nahuatl were ever more exposed.

The single most substantial change in Stage 3 Nahuatl orthography, involving the representation of the sound [s], also has to do with Spanish writing. When the Spaniards came to Mexico in the sixteenth century, [s] was written in their system as *c* or *ç* before a front vowel, [e, i], as *ç* before a back vowel, [a, o, u], and as *z* syllable-finally. Those values came into the Nahuatl system and were the norm during the whole of Stage 2; they are incorporated into the standard orthography used here.

Spanish writing had a letter *s*, but it represented a retroflex or apical [s] that was so close to [sh] that it alternated with the *x* representing [sh] in sixteenth-century Spanish orthography (thus Suarez or Xuarez). Consequently, if you find an *s* in a text written by Nahuas during Stage 2, it will usually represent [sh], as in *isquich* for standard *ixquich*, "everything." A few writers wrote *s* quite consistently before a consonant, *x* anywhere else, thus *ascan* for *axcan*, "now," but *cuix*, "perhaps," and *xihuallauh*, "come!"

By mid-seventeenth century, Spanish *s* was coming to be pronounced as a true [s], falling together with the *c/ç/z* series, and it quickly began to be merged with them in writing, before long nearly displacing them, so that even well educated Spaniards would write *crus* for *cruz*, "cross," or *pareser* for *parecer*, "to appear." No sooner had this begun to happen than the Nahuas followed suit in their own texts. In Stage 3 texts we can expect such things as the following.

nesi	=	*neci*, "he/she appears"	*selilo*	=	*celilo*, "it is received"
quisa		*quiça*, "he/she comes out"	*messo*		*mezço*, "your blood"
totlasomahuisnantzin		=	*totlaçomahuiznantzin*, "our precious revered mother"		

The change was progressive. In earlier Stage 3 texts the two conventions may coexist or *s* for [s] may not appear at all. The set *c/ç/z* never entirely faded from memory, but by the eighteenth century *s* was the norm and anything else an exception.

Another change in Spanish around this time has left far fewer but still noticeable traces in Nahuatl texts. In sixteenth-century Spanish, the sounds represented by *ll* and by *y* were distinct (as they are indeed in much Spanish pronunciation to this day). By the later seventeenth century some people in Mexico were beginning to pronounce the two spellings identically, and we can see in Spanish texts, usually by the less well educated, such things as *cullo* for *cuyo*, "whose," and *jolla* for *joya*, "jewel." In other words, *ll* was being used as an equivalent of *y*. The same thing occurs as an undercurrent in Stage 3 Nahuatl texts, thus *llehuatl* for *yehuatl*, "he/she/it, that." In the practice of a few writers, *ll* was reserved for [y], and [ll] was always written as a single *l*, thus *lleica* for *yeica*, "therefore," and *tlali* for *tlalli*, "land." Whether for this reason or not, the writing of single for double *l* picks up greatly in Stage 3.

Aside from the superficially changed appearance of the texts and the one major shift with [s], Stage 3 texts differ little from those of Stage 2 and can be read using the same skills.

I. *A selection from a text.* Here is reproduced an example of some of the most deviant Nahuatl writing I have ever seen, from the Toluca region in the eighteenth century. It is, however, far from hopeless.

This writer, like others of the time and region, was weakening syllable-final consonants drastically. Final *tl* [tl] had become *l* [l], as it still is in the Nahuatl speech of much of the region. Many final consonants are simply omitted; failing that, they may be followed by an *i*; in speech the writer apparently actually pronounced an [i] so that the consonant would not be syllable-final and could be pronounced as well. Normal *hu* is written *chu* here.

In such a form as *ninotlatlatilia*, the writer has omitted a *c*, the object prefix (in speech it may have been a glottal stop or other weak sound), and a *uh* from standard *nicnotla-tlauhtilia*, "I implore him." Final *c* [k] and *uh* [w] are omitted throughout the manuscript. On the other hand, we see *ylchuicaqui Calitiqui* for standard *ilhuicac calitic*, "inside heaven"; the final *i*'s represent the writer's pronunciation of an [i] so that the [k] sound would not be final and hence could be pronounced (and also written).

Everything in the writer's practice can eventually be understood as normal and rational within his own system of speech and orthography. His writing is simply a further development of the principles and processes discussed in the body of this chapter.

- ax^{c}a viernes a 15 de junio de 1731 año Nica nicchichua notestame^{to} nechual ni-cocoxiqui Notoca Lusia maria Ca ninotlatlatilia noteotzin Notlatocatzin y tt^o dios nocychua ninotlatlatilia notlasomausnatzin Santa maria Nocychua ninotlatlatilia yn S^{n}toti ycha S^{n}tati yn motemiltiticate ylchuicaqui Calitiqui nopa motlatoltisque yn nechimotlapopolchuilisque yn notlatlacol yni onimoyoloytlacalchuili yn tt^{o}cuio gesus Risto Ca ninocemaquilitzinnochua y noyolia noanimatzin ytla ninomacechuis yntlasomiquilistzin yn tutecuio dios ypallechuiloca noanimatzin Ce misa Ynca Resposos nopa mitos y ncehimopalechuilis noteopixicatzin padre ministro Ca Sann ixiquichi[1] niSonquixitia nocococatlatol Ynpa yaltepetzin S^{n}to S^a Lucas EnBange-lista ca yechuatzintzin notestigos

- axcan viernes a 15 de junio de 1731 años nican nicchihua notestamento nehuatl nicocoxqui notoca Lucia Maria ca nicnotlailauhtilia noteotzin notlatocatzin in tote-cuiyo Dios no ihuan nicnotlatlauhtilia notlaçomahuiznantzin Santa Maria no ihuan niquinnotlatlauhtilia in santotin ihuan santatin in motemiltiticate ilhuicac calitic nopan motlatoltizque in nechmotlapopolhuilizque in notlatlacol inic oni-noyolitlacalhuili in totecuiyo Jesus Cristo ca nicnocenmaquilitzinoa in noyolia nanimatzin intla nicnomacehuiz itlaçomiquiliztzin in totecuiyo Dios ipalehuiloca nanimatzin ce misa ica responsos nopan mitoz ic nechmopalehuiliz noteopixcatzin padre ministro ca çan ixquich in[3] nictzonquixtia nocococoxcatlatol ipan ialtepetzin Santo San Lucas Evangelista ca yehuantzitzin notestigos[huan]

- Today, Friday the 15th of June of the year 1731, here I make my testament, I the sick person named Lucía María. I implore my god and ruler our lord God; I also implore my precious honored mother Santa María; I also implore the male and female saints who fill heaven to speak for me and forgive me my sins through which I have offended our lord Jesus Christ, for I give him my spirit and soul entirely. If I experience the precious death of our Lord God, the aid of my soul will be that one mass with responses will be said for me; with this my priest, the father minister, will help me. This is all; I conclude my sick person's statement, in the altepetl of the saint San Lucas Evangelista. My witnesses are:[2]

---

[1] Possibly the intention is *ixquich ic*, which would result in a translation "This is all with which I conclude . . ."

[2] The entire text is reproduced in Lockhart, *Nahuas and Spaniards*, pp. 122–40, along with some similar ones and an exhaustive analysis of the orthographic and phonological implications.

18. Spanish Influence in Nahuatl Texts

The Stages. Orthography of Spanish loanwords. Stage 1 and 2 contact phenomena. Stage 3 phenomena. A selection from a Stage 3 text.

A. *The Stages.* Let us discuss in a bit more detail the three-step process by which Nahuatl adapted to the presence of Spanish speakers over the centuries. As a result of this progressive change, you will find certain kinds of words and constructions of Spanish origin in the texts of a given period and not in those of a different period. It is always well to have an idea what to expect. The overall nature and rationale of the process are not hard to understand; at first rarely coming into close daily contact with Spaniards, the bulk of the Nahuas gradually became ever more intermeshed with them, so that the degree of Spanish influence increases greatly over time.

In the first generation, Stage 1, 1519 to perhaps the early 1540's, Nahuatl adopted essentially no ordinary Spanish words, instead using familiar words for Spanish introductions, as in *maçatl*, "deer," for horse, or describing them with neologisms invented out of the resources of Nahuatl, as in *tlequiquiztli*, literally "fire whistle or trumpet," for a firearm. Proper names, however, were taken in, above all as the baptismal names of the Nahuas themselves, but also in reference to Spaniards. Some of them included titles verging on normal words, such as *don*, an approximate equivalent of "sir." One proper name, for the place the Spaniards came from, Castile (Castilla) was used not only to refer to that country but above all to modify Nahuatl words in naming Spanish introductions, as in *Caxtillan centli*, "Castile maize," for wheat. As you see, Spanish words were from the beginning pronounced and interpreted within the Nahuatl framework. Here Spanish retroflex or apical [s] was pronounced as Nahuatl [sh], Spanish [ĺ] as Nahuatl [l-l], and an [n] was added. The last was not just phonological; the Nahuas took *Castilla* to be a place name like their own and even with one of their own endings, *-tlan/-lan*, "place of."

By 1540 or 1545, perhaps because a new generation was growing up that had had some exposure to Spanish almost from birth, a fundamental change took place. In Stage 2, stretching forward in time to 1640 or 50, Nahuatl accepted a wide range of Spanish words into the language as what we call loans; what we really mean is that after whatever changes Nahuatl phonology imposed on them, the contributions from Spanish became Nahuatl words like any others, a permanent part of the vocabulary. Many of the Stage 2 loanwords displaced Stage 1 descriptions; thus *maçatl* for horse faded out in favor of *caballo*. In Nahuatl the word was probably pronounced with a [w] for the [β], [ll] for [ĺ], and a glottal stop at the end; it might be written either *cahuallo* or as the Spaniards did it: *caballo, cavallo,* or *cauallo.*

The impact on the culture was quite massive; you may get some sense of it from the kind of loanwords that have been included in texts and examples here. The impact on the language proper was quite limited. All the words borrowed were nouns; a few that seem to be adjectives were interpreted as nouns too. Pronunciation appears to have been little affected; by all indications the Nahuas continued to use native sounds for those lacking in their language when pronouncing words from Spanish. Gradually over this time some Spanish verbs, especially *tener*, "to have," began to affect the meaning of some Nahuatl vocabulary (*pia* moving toward *tener*), but Spanish verbs were not borrowed.

In Stage 3, beginning of course as Stage 2 ended, around 1640 or 1650, and extending forward indefinitely in time, the barriers were broken, apparently because of the rise of a large group of Nahuas able to speak and understand Spanish, and Nahuatl accepted Spanish verbs and particles (from the Spanish point of view, prepositions and conjunctions) into the language. It translated whole Spanish idioms using Nahuatl vocabulary

117

(in what we call calques), began marking plurals of nouns more as Spanish does, adopted Spanish words for close kin relationships, and in general established open channels by which it could take anything needed from Spanish. From the point of view of the reader of texts, perhaps the most important single component of the Stage 3 revolution was that Nahuatl speakers acquired most or all of the Spanish sounds missing in their own language and began to write Spanish loanwords (the newer ones, at least) more like the Spaniards did.

B. *The orthography of Spanish loanwords.* Nahuas writing Spanish words might use either of two procedures: the Spanish method, whereby the spelling of a particular word was learned, memorized, and thenceforth mechanically written the same way every time, or their own method of transcribing the sounds they produced as they pronounced the word. Let us first look at what happened when they followed the Spanish model.

The first Nahuas to write alphabetically were trained by Spaniards, and apparently many of them learned a repertoire of standard spellings of common loans. *Dios*, "God," overwhelmingly appears in the normal Spanish form, though the Nahuas probably pronounced it [ti(y)ōsh], and in a few manuscripts outside the mainstream *tiox* and *tiyox* can in fact be found. Above all the Nahuas learned a number of abbreviations current among the Spaniards, starting with some names, of which the following are among the most often seen:

ju^o	Juan	ju^a	Juana	p^o	Pedro	d^o, di^o	Diego	dg^o Domingo
m^a	María	al^o	Alonso	$fr^{co}, fran^{co}$	Francisco	$x\overline{po}bal$	Cristóbal	$\overline{min}$ Martín

You see here the two main ways of making abbreviations. The first and most common consists of writing a few letters of the beginning of the word in the normal way, skipping some of the body of the word, and writing the final letter or a few of the final letters at the end, superscribed. The word *justicia*, "justice, the law, officer of the law," is generally seen both in Spanish and in Nahuatl texts as *just^a*. *Majestad*, "majesty," then spelled *magestad* in Spanish, virtually always occurs abbreviated and in the phrase "his Majesty," *su mag^{dad}*. The possibilities are many, but usually abbreviations of this type can be figured out in context, and they are mainly limited to much used words of Spanish origin and legal or religious nature. Just how the short form of "Juan" came to be I am not sure, but it never varies.

The second way of making abbreviations was to begin as before, with the first letter or several letters of a word and also as before end with some final letters, but in this case not superscribe the last part, instead putting a line over the place where letters are missing. The abbreviation for Martín just above is of this type. So is the one for Cristóbal, but it involves another Spanish convention, of writing *cristo*, "Christ," as *x$\overline{po}$*, a normal abbreviation of this type except that following tradition the first two letters are as they would appear, or almost as they would appear, in Greek script, *x* representing *Ch* and *p* standing for *r*. The word for church, *iglesia*, is often seen abbreviated this way, usually *yg$\overline{li}$a*. The word for alcalde is the most common item of this type, with the line drawn backward from the *d* through the two *l*'s; it may be represented in print as *al̶l̶de*.

Over the whole time that Nahuatl was written, then, many Spanish loanwords were represented no differently in Nahuatl texts than the Spanish originals would have been in Spanish texts. But very often writers of Nahuatl treated words of Spanish origin just as they would native vocabulary, and that is where the trouble really begins for the present-day reader. Indeed, I would say that for both beginners and those with the greatest experience in these matters, figuring out the Spanish loanword hiding behind an unfamiliar set of letters is often the hardest thing that one has to do, the last to be solved.

The principle is simple enough; when a Spanish word had a sound lacking in Nahuatl, Nahuas pronounced it using the sound they did have that most closely approximated to the new one, and therefore they wrote it using the letter for that sound. Later, in what we call hypercorrection, having been exposed to the entire Spanish alphabet, they would use the letter for the new sound also to represent their approximation, since after all they could detect no difference between the two.

Nahuatl lacked the voiced stops present in English and Spanish; it lacked a voiced labial [b], having only the corresponding unvoiced [p]; it lacked the voiced dental [d], having only [t]; and it lacked the voiced velar [g], having only [k]. It also lacked the unvoiced labiodental fricative [f], [p] being again the closest thing. Thus we can expect the following kinds of substitutions:

p for *b*	*patan*	for	*batán*, "fulling mill"
t for *d*	*ton*		*don*, "sir"
c for *g* [g]	*copelnatol*		*gobernador*, "governor"
p for *f*	*pixcal*		*fiscal*, "church steward"

Of the two liquids in Spanish, [l] and [r], Nahuatl had only [l]; consequently *l* was often substituted for *r*.

l for *r*	*lexitol*	for	*regidor*, "municipal councilman"

Among the vowels, since Spanish had [o] and [u], Nahuatl only [o], *o* was sometimes substituted for *u*.

o for *u*	*mola*	for	*mula*, "mule"

These are the great basic substitutions, and getting a grasp of them will take you far in being able to decipher words of Spanish origin in Nahuatl texts. But you will find in addition many refinements and lesser phenomena.

Spanish retroflex or apical [s] was so close to [sh] that *x* for *s* hardly counts as a substitution, but to the eye it appears to be one.

x for *s*	*xolal*	for	*solar*, "lot"

Although Nahuatl had both [i] and [e] just as Spanish did, it appears that unstressed Spanish [e] often struck Nahuas as [i]; thus we can expect *i* for *e* in that position.

i for *e*	*gomiz*	for	Gómez

As seen above, *p* is the expected substitution for *b*. But when Spanish *b* (and also *v*, for many speakers) occurred in medial position, between two vowels, it was weakened and pronounced as a voiced bilabial fricative [β]. For this sound either [p] or [w] might be substituted, each retaining one of the basic features of the Spanish pronunciation and sacrificing the other, leading to either *p* or *hu* (and other ways of writing [w]) for *b/v*.

p for *b/v*	*capilton*	for	*cabildo*, "municipal council"
hu for *b/v*	*cahuallo*	for	*caballo*, "horse"

Hu can replace *b/v* even when it is not medial, as in the common word *huacax* from *vaca(s)*, "cow." (Perhaps initial Spanish *v* was not always pronounced [b] as is thought.)

Likewise although *t* is the primary substitution for *d*, when it is in medial position sometimes *l* is used instead, for Spanish *d* like *b* was pronounced as a fricative medially.

l for *d*	*melio*	for	*medio*, a coin, half a real

As in the case of *hu* for *b/v*, here too the substitution is occasionally found when *d* is not medial, as in Lionicio for Dionisio.

The pronunciation of the Spanish phonemes represented by *j* and *g* before *e* or *i* seems to have been in flux in the sixteenth and seventeenth centuries. They apparently were something like voiced alveolar fricatives or affricates, about to be devoiced. The normal, though rare, Nahuatl substitution was *x* [sh].

x for *j*	*xontera*	for	*juntera,* "carpenter's plane"
x for *g*	*rexitor*		*regidor,* "municipal councilman"

The Spanish palatalized [ñ] written as *ñ* was lacking in Nahuatl. It is not hard to recognize the Nahuatl substitution of [n] or [nn] (*n, nn*), as in *dona* or *donna* for *doña.* Sometimes, however, *y* was substituted, the [y] representing only the palatal aspect of the sound. The same thing could happen with Spanish double *ll* [ĺ].

y for *ñ*	*toya*	for	*doña,* "lady"
y for *ll*	*cavayo*	for	*caballo,* "horse"

Let us pass over some further subtleties of this kind to look at an aspect of Nahuatl writing that can puzzle the reader of texts greatly, namely the reversal of all the substitutions we have been discussing, a phenomenon we call hypercorrection. Since Nahuas initially heard no difference between [p] and [b], and were introduced to two letters, *p* and *b*, it was natural to assume that they were two different ways of writing the same sound and could be used interchangeably. Hypercorrection is the mirror image of primary substitution; it is perhaps most common when both letters in a substitution pair occur in the same word, as in *bueplo* for *pueblo.*

b for *p*	*bablo*	for	Pablo
g for *c*	*garlos*		Carlos
d for *t*	*daça*		*taça,* modern *taza,* "cup"
f for *p*	*falacio*		*palacio,* "palace"
r for *l*	*morino*		*molino,* "mill"
u for *o*	*desurello*		*tesorero,* "treasurer"

The letters representing sounds not in Nahuatl are also found replacing one another, as in *babia* for Fabián (which appears as *papia* as well).

All the usual Nahuatl propensities, such as inserting glides and omitting or inserting nasals, occur in the writing of loanwords as well.

ypaxiyotzin	for	*ipasiontzin,* "his passion or suffering"
ypilman		*ifirma,* "his signature"
tanxacio		*tasación,* "assignment of quotas"

Some transformations of loanwords go beyond the substitution of letters and do not properly belong to orthography, but since they affect the spelling, they may be discussed here. The Nahuas naturally if illogically identified the *in-* at the beginning of some Spanish words as their own subordinator/article *in* and hence did not consider it a part of the word. Moreover, since they merged unstressed Spanish *e* and *i* and were notably casual about syllable-final nasals, they acted the same when the word began with *en-* or *i-*, especially before a nasal consonant.

telocadorio	for	*interrogatorio,* "questionnaire"
comendero		*encomendero,* "holder of a grant of tribute and labor"
maxe		*imagen,* "image"

We also see an intermittent tendency to omit the second of two final vowels in a word of Spanish origin, perhaps because in Nahuatl the only such words were verbs.

matrimoni	for	*matrimonio,* "matrimony"
audienci		*audiencia,* "high court"

Nahuatl could not allow a word to begin or end with two consonants. Spanish also lacked final consonant clusters, but it had initial clusters, and Nahuatl had to respond to them either by omitting something or by adding something. One member of the cluster was often [r], a sound which caused the Nahuas problems even when occurring alone. In many cases *r* would simply be left out. The other solution was to take the vowel nearest to the cluster and insert a copy of it between the two consonants (epenthesis).

quixtiano	<u>for</u>	*cristiano*, "Christian"
coloz		*cruz*, "cross"
palacixco		*Francisco*

In Stage 3 texts, both primary substitutions and hypercorrections become much less numerous, because the Nahuas had acquired the Spanish sounds and were able to match them with the letters in the Spanish fashion. Nevertheless, some writers who were less in touch continued somewhat in the old vein, and above all, common words which had been borrowed with sound substitutions in Stage 2 had been frozen in that form; they were pronounced and often written as they had always been.[1]

C. *Stage 1 and 2 contact phenomena.* The lexical, morphological and syntactic reaction of Nahuatl to Spanish over the postconquest centuries is a topic of great interest and significance. A full understanding of it can lead to more accurate translations, a better grasp of cultural interaction, and the ability to place a given text within the framework of a long progressive evolution. Our aim here, however, is to get past the preliminary difficulties in reading Nahuatl texts, and the truth is that the orthography of loanwords causes readers far more trouble than all the other contact phenomena put together. Once you have identified a Spanish word or even a Spanish-influenced meaning, you will generally immediately understand it intuitively even if some of the linguistic and cultural implications escape you. Overall Spanish linguistic influence, then, can be given a very light treatment here.

That is especially true for Stage 1, first on the grounds that, alphabetic writing being one of the main symptoms of Stage 2, there are very, very few Stage 1 texts to work with,[2] and second because the chief characteristic of the texts of that stage is the minimal Spanish influence on them. The most important thing about Stage 1 for one interested in reading the general run of Nahuatl writings is that some vocabulary items arising at that time survived into Stage 2 and beyond, including some of the imaginative names for animals, such as *ichcatl*, first "cotton," then "wool," and finally "sheep," or *quaquauhe*, "one with head-wood, horns," for bovine creatures. But after all, you can find these in the dictionary the same as any other word. *Caxtillan* as a modifier long continued on an ad hoc basis to describe items of European origin; these expressions, however, are largely self-explanatory, as with *caxtillan tlilli*, "Castile (i.e., Spanish, European-style) ink." With the recommendation that you read more about Stage 1 elsewhere, let us pass on to Stage 2.[3]

As we have already seen, the primary characteristic of Stage 2 was the borrowing of a large number of Spanish nouns. Knowing this and having mastered the expected letter

---

[1] The whole topic of the orthography of Spanish words in Nahuatl is discussed in greater detail and more systematically, with many additional examples, in Karttunen and Lockhart, *Nahuatl in the Middle Years*, pp. 1–15.

[2] Cline, ed., *The Book of Tributes*, contains a whole volume of the Cuernavaca-region census records, and Lockhart, ed., *We People Here*, contains a selection from the Annals of Tlatelolco. No other large-scale writings with fully Stage 1 characteristics are known.

[3] You will find a detailed exposition of Stage 1 phenomena, a good deal of it deduced from archaic items in Molina's dictionary, in Lockhart, *The Nahuas*, pp. 263–84.

substitutions, you are essentially equipped to deal with words of Spanish origin in Stage 2 texts. But let us touch upon some phenomena on the edges of noun borrowing.

You will find certain loan nouns in texts in forms different from Spanish which are not explained by letter substitution alone. Some of the variations we have already mentioned. Another is that certain words, either place names or nouns referring to something with a spatial dimension, may be seen with *a*, "to," prefixed to the Spanish form. Nahuatl had no prepositions, and it expressed motion to or from within the verb complex, so that when Nahuas heard such an expression as *vete a la huerta*, "go to the orchard," they took it that the "to" was in *vete* and that the noun was *a la huerta*. Thus arose words like the following:

alahuerta	orchard (Sp. *huerta)*	alachina	the Philippines (Sp. la China)
alaera	threshing floor (Sp. *era)*	alaflorida	Florida (Sp. la Florida)
alaguna	lake (Sp. *laguna)*[1]		

From the first, Spanish nouns were taken into the language without any of the native absolutive singular endings, although an unwritten glottal stop was added to any word ending in a vowel (and this glottal stop was retained in any derived or combined form, i.e., it was part of the root). There were a few exceptions, however. If a word was normally possessed, as with a kinship term or a word for an item of clothing, it was easy to lose track of its absolutive form and then reconstitute the normal Nahuatl absolutive in the relatively few cases when the word was not possessed. Thus arose a few words like these:

camixatli	shirt (Sp. *camisa)*
comadretli	female ritual coparent (Sp. *comadre)*
compadretli	male ritual coparent (Sp. *compadre)*

These words take *-tli* rather than *-tl* because they end in a consonant, the glottal stop just mentioned. After a short time no other Spanish loan nouns were given this treatment, though the words that acquired *-tli* in the early period have retained it to this day.

It took Nahuas some time to adjust to the Spanish way of pluralizing nouns. There were two distinct problems, first to recognize the Spanish plural ending as such, and second to decide whether to use the Spanish ending, a native ending, or both to mark plurality on loan nouns. Also, Nahuatl had two kinds of plural endings, absolutive and possessive, whereas Spanish had only one for all purposes. At first Spanish *-s* or *-es* was in fact often not recognized as a plural. With words for things that come in herds, flocks, or pairs, the *-s* might be taken as part of the root and incorporated permanently.

huacax	a cow (*vacas)*
patox	a duck (*patos)*
çapatox	a shoe (*çapatos*, modern *zapatos)*

In general, however, the Nahuas soon distinguished the Spanish plural, leaving it off the singular form of loan nouns. At first all the different options for showing plurality appear: from *regidor*, "municipal councilman," *regidorme*, with only the native *-me*; *regidores*, with only the Spanish *-s*; and *regidoresme* or *regidorestin*, with both.[2] The use of the single native plural ending soon went out of fashion, and in the absolutive one sees either the normal Spanish plural or a double plural. As time went on the Spanish plural came to be more and more predominant, but certain common words kept their double plurals, such as *españolestin*, "Spaniards."

With possessed nouns, Nahuatl insisted on adding the plural *-huan*, sometimes to the

---

[1]The Spanish phrase would have been *a la laguna.*

[2]Though probably pronounced mainly as [sh] during Stage 2, the Spanish plural ending was most often written with an *s* from an early time.

bare stem, sometimes to a form already equipped with the Spanish -*s*. The latter mode soon came to be more common.

nalbaceahuan or *nalbaceashuan*   my executors (the executors of my will)

Nahuatl, as we have learned, marked the plural only on nouns for beings that were animate or imagined as such. In general that continued to be the practice with loanwords as well. Some texts, however, show a recognition of Spanish usage without incorporating it into Nahuatl grammar. That is, they may show a plural as it would be written in Spanish but otherwise treat the item as singular in the sentence. In the following example a Spanish plural is the subject of a singular verb.

monequi miec moquetzaz iglesias   It is necessary that many churches be constructed.

Identifying a Spanish loanword in a Nahuatl text usually solves the question of its meaning, which can be expected to be much the same in Nahuatl as in Spanish. Otherwise, why borrow the word? Nevertheless, the Nahuas had their own slant on these terms, which once borrowed were Nahuatl vocabulary and subject to reinterpretation. Keep your eyes open for semantic differences between the original Spanish word and the Nahuatl loanword. Here are some of the most common.

Nahuatl   *tomin, tomines,* "money, cash"   Spanish   *tomín,* a specific coin or value
            quixtiano, "Spaniard"   *cristiano,* "Christian"
            señora, xinola, "Spanish woman"   *señora,* "lady"

During Stage 2 Spanish speech heard by Nahuas was affecting Nahuatl in some ways not reflected in loanwords, especially in beginning to alter the meaning of certain native verbs in the direction of Spanish verbs. At the center of this development was *pia,* a Nahuatl verb meaning "to keep, guard, have custody of, hold," which began to move in the direction of Spanish *tener,* "to have."

Traditional Nahuatl: Stage 2 Spanish-influenced expression

oncate yeintin ipilhuan,   *quimpia yeintin ipilhuan,*
   "Three who are his children exist."   "He has (his) three children."
ye matlacxihuitl in nemi,   *quipia matlacxihuitl,*
   "It is already ten years that he lives."   "He has ten years, i.e., is ten years old."

At one point the applicative of *pia, pialia,* began to approach the meaning of Spanish *deber,* "to owe (money) to someone," but that sense was taken over more definitively by *huiquilia,* the applicative of *huica,* "to take, accompany, be responsible for."[3]

D. *Stage 3 phenomena.* The primary diagnostic characteristic of Stage 3 texts is the occasional presence of Spanish loan verbs. A single example of a loan verb goes back into the late sixteenth century, and there are a few in the early seventeenth, but as 1640 or 1650 approaches they become a standard feature, with regular mechanisms of formation and inflection.

The entire Spanish infinitive was used as a base, and to it the element -*oa,* which already made verbs from nouns in Nahuatl, was added. -*Oa* bears all the inflection, and prefixes are added as appropriate, as with any other verb. From *presentar,* "to present," comes *presentaroa.* We can expect forms such as the following (like other -*oa* verbs, loan verbs belong to Class 3):

nicpresentaroa   I present it   *onicpresentaro*   I presented it
oticpresentaroque   we presented it   *mopresentaroz*   it is to be presented

---

[3] See pp. 17, n. 2; 25, note.

Coming in as they do mainly during Stage 3, loan verbs tend to be written as in Spanish, but there are exceptions, especially with the popular word *pasearoa* from *pasear*, "to stroll, parade about," which must have been one of the first verbs borrowed. It is often seen as *paxialoa*, with three typical substitutions: *x* for *s*, *i* for unstressed *e*, and *l* for *r*. It first appears in a text in the form *oquipassealoltique*, "they paraded him about," with the *-ltia* causative. Reverentials may occur using this causative: *oquimopresentarolti*, "he presented it." An early example, from 1634, already quoted in Lesson 17, uses the applicative instead of the causative (remember that the applicative of *-oa* is *-huia*) as a reverential in *quimocopirmalhui*, "he confirmed him," from *confirmaroa* (note that *p* is substituted for *f* and *l* for one *r*).

The second great symptom of Stage 3 is the presence of loan particles. Sometimes they act as conjunctions, more often as prepositions. They represent a revolution in Nahuatl grammar, but they are easy for us to understand, because they work just as in European languages. The two most common are *hasta*, "until, up to, as far as," and *para*, "(destined) for, in order to." Here are some examples with *hasta*.[1]

oquimohuiquili yn onpa mexico asta oc motlatitlanili caxtillan ynic motta tleyn mochihuas	He took him to Mexico City <u>until</u> word should be sent to Spain to see what was to be done.
ompa huey otlipan asta oncan san lasaro teopan	on the highway <u>as far as</u> the church of San Lázaro
muchi quintecuiliyaya . . . asta axnotzitzin quintecuiliyaya	They took everything from them . . ., they took <u>even</u> the donkeys from them.

Sometimes you will find that the text includes a traditional Nahuatl word of related meaning as well as the Spanish particle. In the first example, *oc*, "meanwhile, provisionally," is an echo of what might have been said before the introduction of *hasta*. *Para* as "in order to" is sometimes accompanied by *inic* or *ic*, with nearly the same meaning.

Some of the Nahuatl verbs which were moving in the direction of Spanish verbs of somewhat related meaning attain in Stage 3 what I call equivalence relationships with those verbs, automatically able to reproduce any meaning of the Spanish verb. *Pia* can mean anything that *tener* can, leading to such an expression as *tlein ticpia*, equal to *¿qué tienes?*, "What's the matter with you?" The verb *pano*, originally meaning "to cross or pass over a flat surface," became also an equivalent for the Spanish verb *pasar*, "to pass," so that we can find such a sentence as *opanoc yei ilhuitl*, "three days passed." In this way much Spanish idiom entered the language.

In Stage 3, Nahuatl began to go in the direction of Spanish in marking more plurals of inanimates. You may see such things as *caltin*, "houses," and *quauhtin*, "trees." Even so, most of the traditional singulars for inanimates were retained.

For the rest, keeping in mind that Stage 2's *c/ç/z* will mostly be written as *s*, all you have learned about Stage 2 Nahuatl will prove relevant in reading Stage 3 texts as well.[2]

E. *A selection from a Stage 3 text.* The transcription is followed by a version written in our standard orthography. Note that sometimes *x* = ch, *h* = ch, syllable-final *c* = uh, *ll* = y, *tz* = c (s here), *hu* = uh.

Sano ipan tonali Omotenehu in icuac Oniquincaquili in tlaxilacaleque intlatol ihuan Oniquitac in nehuatle ni Jues G^{or} *ihuan moxtintzitzin Ofisiales de Republica inic allac*

---

[1]Given also in Karttunen and Lockhart, *Nahuatl in the Middle Years*, p. 35, with additional discussion.

[2]The phenomena of Stages 2 and 3 are presented and analyzed in considerable detail in Lockhart, *The Nahuas*, pp. 284–318.

quiContradisiroa in posesion quimotlania in tlalcoccatzintle Onicnotzi in Jues de Sementeras ihuan Onicnahuati iCa yhuelitzin tohuitlatocatzin Rey N. S^r quitamachihuas
in tlali ahu inic Oriente ihuan poniente quipix onpohuali brasadas inic Oriente mo-
Cuaxohnamiqui yca itlal Bartholome de Bargas ahu inic poniente ica in otli llahu
Cuahupanahuasco yhuan itlaltzin OCacca in Dios Oquimohuiquili Sr Andres Gonsales
axcan quipixticate in ipilhuantzitzi ahu inic patlahuac Oquipix de norte a Sur Sen-
pohuali brasadas moCuaxohnamiqui inic norte ica intlal tlaxilacaleque S^n Simon
poxtlan ahu inic Sur moCuaxohnamiqui ica intlal St^o Domingo huexotitlan tlaXilacaleque ahu in tlalCuahuitl inic omotamachihu Ca llehualtl in quipie ome bara yhuan tlaco
motenehua tzennequetzalpan ahu llotlan Omotamachihu Onicnonochili in Sr D^n Antt^o
Gonsales tersero yhuan yca in ihuelitzin Rey N. S^r onicnocalaquili inpan posesion
Omotlamochili Omotlaxihutemili Omopaxialolti ipan in itlalcoaltzin inesca Ca lloQui-
mocuyli posesion Cualllotica allac Otlachalani Otlapalolo

çan no ipan tonalli omoteneuh in iquac oniquincaquili in tlaxilacaleque intlatol
ihuan oniquittac in nehuatl ni juez gouernador ihuan mochtintzitzin oficiales de
Republica inic ayac quicontradeciroa in posesion quimotlania in tlalcouhcatzintli
onicnotz in juez de sementeras ihuan onicnahuati ica ihuelitzin tohueitlatocatzin Rey
nuestro señor quitamachihuaz in tlalli auh inic oriente ihuan poniente quipix ompohualli brazadas inic oriente moquaxochnamiqui ica itlal Bartholome de Vargas auh
inic poniente ica in otli yauh Quauhpanahuazco ihuan itlaltzin ocatca in Dios oquimohuiquili señor Andres Gonçalez axcan quipixticate in ipilhuantzitzin auh inic patlahuac
oquipix de norte a sur çempohualli brazadas moquaxochnamiqui inic norte ica intlal
tlaxilacaleque San Simon Pochtlan auh inic sur moquaxochnamiqui ica intlal Santo
Domingo Huexotitlan tlaxilacaleque auh in tlalquahuitl inic omotamachiuh ca yehuatl
in quipia ome vara ihuan tlaco motenehua cennequetzalpan auh [in] otlan omotamachiuh onicnonochili in señor don Antonio Gonçalez tercero ihuan ica in ihuelitzin Rey
nuestro señor onicnocalaquili ipan posesion omotlamochili omotlaxiuhtemili omo-
pasearolti ipan in itlalcohualtzin inezca ca oquimocuili posesion qualyotica [quallotica]
ayac otlachalani otlapalolo

On the same day aforementioned, when I the judge-governor and all the municipal
officials had heard the words of the district citizens and seen how no one contradicts the
possession that the land purchaser requests, I summoned the lands judge, and with the
power of our great ruler the king our lord I ordered him to measure the land. And from
east to west it measured 40 brazas, on the east abutting on Bartolomé de Vargas's land and
on the west on the road going to Quauhpanahuazco and the land that belonged to señor
Andrés González, whom God took, that now his children have. And in width it measured
20 brazas from north to south. It abuts on the north on lands of the citizens of the district
of San Simón Pochtlan, and on the south it abuts on the lands of the citizens of the
district of Santo Domingo Huexotitlan. And the unit of land measurement with which it
was measured is the one that is $2^1/_2$ yards long, called "one full height." And when the
measurement was finished I summoned señor don Antonio González, member of the
Third Order, and with the power of the king our lord I introduced him into possession. He
threw stones, [collected?] grass, and strolled about on his purchased land signifying that
he took possession properly; no one disputed it, it was accepted.[3]

---

[3]The larger text of which this passage is a part, done in Azcapotzalco in 1738, is to be found
transcribed and translated in the 1976 edition of Anderson, Berdan, and Lockhart, *Beyond the
Codices*, Doc. 17, pp. 100–09. A second edition is planned.

19. Two Real Texts

Petition of Leonor Magdalena, 1613. Petition of don Gerónimo Márquez, ca. 1610.

NOW WE ARE at last getting to the point of attempting what our whole course of study has been aimed at, namely to read texts written by Nahuas, in their entirety, as originally cast and spelled. Even now, though, we will proceed gradually. The faithful (or as we say, diplomatic) transcription is followed by another one using the orthography that was used in the rest of the book. Look there for a more familiar rendering of anything that initially puzzles you; not only will words be spelled in the way you by now probably expect, but abbreviations will be resolved and proper names consistently capitalized. In one respect, this whole lesson can be thought of as an extended exercise for Lesson 17 on orthography, which you might review before proceeding. The first of the two texts here is not far from the Carochi standard; the second deviates from it a bit more.

In both transcriptions the letters continue to be divided by modern criteria, as they are in this whole book. To deal with the original spacing you will need to work extensively with handwritten texts either in the original or in photocopies. Print cannot do justice to the matter. Don't worry, with what you have behind you, you will soon get the hang of it, but never forget that any word division we arrive at is our own interpretation. If a passage is hard to translate, respacing it (which amounts to reanalyzing it) often brings the solution.

The emphasis in this lesson is double: to get accustomed to facing real writing, and to work with the analysis and decipherment of some actual texts more independently than you have been doing. The commentary goes into detail on many features of the orthography, except for standard ones like the use of *y* for *i*, overbars, and abbreviations (which you can check against the second transcription). Several comments are given on salient features of the translation as well, but you are largely left to figure out for yourself how the Nahuatl text comes to mean what is given in the English translation here. By all means carry out this task; analyze the morphology and syntax of each text as fully as you can. Work directly from the unstandardized transcription if you find it possible.[1]

A. *Petition of Leonor Magdalena to the governor of Coyoacan, 1613.* Let us discuss some instructive aspects of the way this document is written even before you look at it as a whole.

Perhaps the most outstanding feature of the orthography of this text is that instead of *hu/uh* we sometimes see *hv* or *vh*; once even *vuh*. Remember that [w] was often written *v* in the first documents in Nahuatl, and that a virtual equivalence of *u* and *v* was a long tradition in Latin writing, carried over by Spanish ecclesiastics into the Nahuatl system to a certain extent. By the time of this document, *v* and *hv/vh* had long since largely given way to *hu/uh*, but clearly they were not entirely gone. The writer actually doesn't seem to master the old convention fully (and also uses just *u* a couple of times), but that needn't concern us here. If you are interested in subtleties, notice *where* this convention is used. The second and third paragraphs use *hu/uh* in exactly the way you are acquainted with. All the instances of *hv/vh* occur in the first and fourth paragraphs. The middle sections are the petition proper, written by one person on Leonor Magdalena's behalf, and the first and last sections are remarks set down on the page later by another person, the clerk of

---

[1]The two texts used in this lesson appear in Karttunen and Lockhart, *Nahuatl in the Middle Years*, pp. 103–06, in transcription and translation, with some commentary. The archival locations of the documents are also given there.

126

the governor's court. That much one could deduce from the transcription alone without ever seeing the original.

- *çenpoali* for *cempohualli,* "twenty." Note three things that you will meet again and again. First, despite Carochi, Nahuas more often wrote *n* than *m* before *p*; second, as we have seen before, any *oa* can appear as *ohua* at any time, and vice versa, an important fact for dictionary work; third, *l* for *ll* is an instance of the constant reduction of double consonants found in texts (and perhaps most common of all with *l*).

- *metzitli* for *metztli,* "month." Possibly a simple error, possibly a weak *i* this writer actually pronounced. The important thing is, don't take what you see as canonical; rather, if you don't find it in the dictionary cast about for something similar.

- *huizmingari,* later *huitzimengari.* Ignore the variation and the whole case, which is absolutely exceptional, for Huitziméngari is a Tarascan name.

- *tin^{te}* for *teniente,* "deputy." An example of how unstressed *e* and *i* in Spanish words are often switched in Nahuatl texts.

- *nicteylhuiya* for *nicteilhuia,* "I accuse her." The lesson here is that *ia* and *iya* are just like *oa* and *ohua*; either can appear for the other as known in standard orthography, and we have to treat them as equivalent and alternate (see pp. 113–14). The text has several more examples of *iya* for standard *ia,* as well as some *ia* that is standard.

- *pedronilla* for *petronilla,* "Petronilla." A *d* for *t,* a typical hypercorrection.

- *nomiccacihuamo* for *nomiccacihuamon,* "my daughter-in-law, etc." Typical omission of a syllable-final (and here also word-final) *n.* You would have no chance of finding *mon(tli),* "son-in-law," the basic word here, if you didn't reconstruct the *n.*

- *tlata* for *tlatta,* the verb *itta,* "to see," with the indefinite object prefix. Another example of reducing a double consonant to single. The form *quita* a little later does the same thing with the same verb; the standard would be *qu-itta,* "she sees it." Still later comes *motaz* for *mo-ttaz,* "it will be seen." In *oquimotily* for *o-qui-mo-tti-li,* "he has seen it (rev.)," only *t* is left of *itta,* a common occurrence for this familiar verb.

- *quimimaqcaxilia* for *quimimacaxilia,* "she fears, respects it." You must recognize that *qc* is impossible in the Nahuatl system and draw your own conclusions. This case is no doubt a simple error; the writer started to do something else, then found the right solution but didn't correct the error.

- *tlathocayotl* for *tlatocayotl,* "rulership." Here the glottal stop that in speech comes after the first *o* is written before it instead. The same thing happens in the same root below in *motlathocatequitzin,* "your rulerly or royal office, duty, or task." In the absolute, though, this word appears as *tlathohuani.* In this case there is actually no glottal stop after the *o*; maybe the *h* is meant to represent the other glottal stop after the first *a,* or maybe the writer just got used to *tho* in this word; it isn't our business at this point, just as long as we are not deterred by the slight deviation from the standard spelling.

Above we saw *oa* for standard *ohua*; in *tlathohuani* we see *ohua* for standard *oa.* As with *ia/iya,* we have to treat the two as equivalent and go looking under both possibilities until we find something. Another case of *ohua* for standard *oa* is found below: *ninopilohua.*

- *caxtonlli* for *caxtolli,* "fifteen." Not only is *n* often omitted, it is often inserted where it does not belong in standard orthography. If you don't find something in the dictionary, start omitting *n*'s, that is, in syllable-final position, because *n* before a vowel is as stable as any other consonant. Here we know that something is up because Nahuatl never has three consonants in a row. The *n* here probably represents a weakening of the first, syllable-final *l* of the *ll* cluster.

- *onechtzacuilli* for *onechtzacuili,* "she intercepted me." Just as *ll* is often reduced to *l,* single *l* is often doubled. The text contains other examples of the doubling of *l,* as well as yet other cases where it stays single.

- *nechpalostahuiya* for (possibly) *nechpalosdahuia*, "she gives me blows." This is a unique formation that only someone with a good deal of experience of both Nahuatl and Spanish would likely be able to decipher, but you would be on the way if you suspected that something of Spanish origin is involved here (the *s* would be a hint), thought of letter substitution, and came up with *d* as the most likely possibility for the *t*, so that you would have "palos da," somehow related to *palos dar*, "to administer blows to someone."

Although in context we would probably translate this verb in the past tense, it is formally a present; the *huiya* at the end we would see in standard writing as *huia*. We may be used to thinking of *-ya* endings as most often indicating the imperfect tense, but that is not true in real texts.

- *onechtzatayanili* for *onechtzatzayanili*, "she ripped something of mine." This must be a simple error of *t* for *tz*; real documents don't have "[sic]" to guide you. Our main clue would be not finding anything like *tzatayana* in the dictionary, whereupon we might think of reduplication; in this case the reduplicated form is the more common and is actually listed in a dictionary entry. We might also remember that *t* before *a* inside a root is quite rare.

26 de junio 1613
nican ypan altepetl vᵃ de coyovhacan çenpoali onchicuaçen mani metzitli junio de mill y seisçientos y treçe años yxpantzinco don constanᵒ huizmingari juez gᵒʳ nican ypan altepetl yuan ixquich ytlauilanalpan ycatzinco xᵗᵒbal de molina pisa tinᵗᵉ yxiptla marques del valle omopouh ynin petiçion yn oquiteyxpanti nican tenevhtica

Nehuatl leonor magdalena notlaxilacal tenanitlan mixpantzinco ninocnopechteca chicahuacatica nicteylhuiya yn pedronilla nomiccacihuamo Auh ynic nictecpana yn noneteylhuil niquitohua amo tle ypan tlata Amo quimimaqcaxilia yn totecuiyo dios yhuan yn tlathocayotl justicia atle ypan quita yn ipan lunes caxtonlli yn ipan metztli ynin junio atlauhco onechtzacuilli onechmicti onechtetelicçac yhuan nechpalostahuiya nechquatlatlapanaz yhuan no ceppa Sacramēto ylhuitzi onechmicti nohuipil onechtzatayanili yuhqui ce loca omocu[ep] cenca quitepexihuiya yn ianimā quitlamamaltiya huel ymacehualyo ynic huel huey justicia yc tlatzacuiltiloz teyxpan

Cenca nimitznotlatlauhtilliya yn tehuatzin tlacatl tlathohuani ma xicmocelili testigos tlatolmelahuazque quineltilizque yn noneteylhuil ypanpa cenca chicahuac justicia ticmotlatzacuiltilliz yhuā oncan mixcuitizque yn oc cequintin auh ypanpa ynin noquerella juramētotica nicneltillia camo niccocoliya amo nictentlapiquiya ca çan justicia motlathocatequitzin nocontennamiqui ytech ninopilohua

leonor magⁿᵃ

avuh yn oquimotily juez gᵒʳ ynin petiçion omotlanahvatilly quineltiliz yca ynformaçion yn ineteylhuil avh yn oquitemacac ynformaçion yquac motaz neltiz yn tleyn jusᵃ yc tlaytlani yxquich ynic omotlanahvatilli avh oquimofirmayotilli

don constanᵒ huitzimengari

26 de junio 1613
nican ipan altepetl villa de Coyoacan cempohualli onchiquace mani metztli junio de mil y seiscientos y trece años ixpantzinco don Constantino Huitzimengari juez gouernador nican ipan altepetl ihuan ixquich itlahuilanalpan icatzinco Cristobal de Molina Pisa teniente ixiptla Marques de Valle omopouh inin peticion in oquiteixpanti nican teneuhtica

Nehuatl Leonor Magdalena notlaxilacal Tenanitlan mixpantzinco ninocnopechteca chicahuacatica nicteilhuia in Petronilla nomiccacihuamon auh inic nictecpana in no-

neteilhuil niquitoa amo tle ipan tlatta amo quimimacaxilia in totecuiyo Dios ihuan in tlatocayotl justicia atle ipan quitta in ipan lunes caxtolli in ipan metztli inin Junio atlauhco onechtzacuili onechmicti onechtetelicçac ihuan nechpalosdahuia nechquatlatlapanaz ihuan no ceppa Sacramento ilhuitzin onechmicti nohuipil onechtzatzayanili iuhqui ce loca omocu[ep] cenca quitepexihuia yn ianiman quitlamamaltia huel imacehuallo inic huel huei justicia ic tlatzacuiltiloz teixpan

Cenca nimitznotlatlauhtilia in tehuatzin tlacatl tlatoani ma xicmocelili testigos tlatolmelahuazque quineltilizque in noneteilhuil ipampa cenca chicahuac justicia ticmotlatzacuiltiliz ihuan oncan mixcuitizque yn oc cequintin auh ipampa inin noquerella juramentotica nicneltilia camo niccocolia amo nictentlapiquia ca çan justicia motlatocatequitzin nocontennamiqui itech ninopiloa

Leonor Magdalena

auh in oquimottili juez gouernador inin peticion omotlanahuatili quineltiliz ica informacion in ineteilhuil auh in oquitemacac informacion iquac mottaz neltiz in tlein justicia ic tlaitlani ixquich inic omotlanahuatili auh oquimofirmayotili

don Constantino Huitzimengari

June 26, 1613.

Here in the altepetl and town of Coyoacan, the 26th of the month of June of the year 1613, before don Constantino Huitziméngari, judge-governor here in the altepetl and all its dependency through Cristóbal de Molina Pisa, lieutenant and representative of the Marqués del Valle, was read this petition which the here mentioned presented:

I Leonor Magdalena of the district of Tenanitlan bow down before you and strongly accuse Petronilla, my daughter-in-law, widow of my late son. As to how I order my accusation, I say that she respects nothing; she does not fear our lord God, and she thinks nothing of rulership and justice. On Monday, the 15th of this month of June, she intercepted me at the ravine and beat me, repeatedly kicked me, and gave me blows that almost split my head. And again on the day of the Sacrament she beat me and ripped my blouse (huipil) and became like a crazy woman. She is very much hurling her soul into an abyss and placing a load on it, and great is her commonness, so that with very great justice she should be punished for it in public.

I greatly implore you, O lord ruler, to receive witnesses who will tell the truth and verify my accusation, because it is very strong justice that you should punish her, and the others will take an example from it. I attest to my complaint by oath. I do not hate her, I am not fabricating it about her, it is simple justice. I salute your office as a ruler and cling to it.

Leonor Magdalena.

And when the judge-governor had seen this petition, he gave orders that she verify her complaint by formal proof, and when she has presented proof, at that time it will be seen, and whatever she requests with justice will be carried out. That is all he ordered, and he signed.

Don Constantino Huitziméngari.

Now some comments on the Nahuatl itself:

- *tenevhtica*: although the dictionaries give *tenehua*, "to mention," only as a transitive verb, this form alone, with a *-ca* auxiliary and no object prefixes, proves that it can be intransitive as well. Many transitive verbs in *-hua* have an intransitive related form in *-hua* or *-hui* with a (middle) passive meaning, here "to be mentioned." We actually cannot be sure if the verb involved is *tenehua* or *tenehui*, but the meaning is clear.

- *nomiccacihuamo*. As mentioned above, the last element is standard *-mon*, which is usually translated "son-in-law," but it may be that it originally meant "child-in-law," since -*cihuamon*, "female child-in-law," means "daughter-in-law." The preterit agentive noun *micqui*, "dead person," can be incorporated into in-law terms. They then mean not that the mentioned in-law is dead, but that the blood relative through whom the relationship was established has died. Thus this word means "my daughter-in-law, whose husband, my son, through whom she came to be my daughter-in-law, is dead."

- *amo tle ypan tlata*, "she respects nothing, she looks upon things as nothing." This expression may strike you as a bit irregular, seeming to have a specific substantive, *amo tle*, in crossreference with the indefinite *tla* of *tlat(t)a*. Nevertheless, all is well. *Amo tle* crossrefers with the *y*- of *ypan*, and *tla*- is the self-contained object of *itta*, taking the same place as *justicia* in the second use of this idiom just below. The clause says, then, that "She sees things in general (expressed by *tla*-) as (*ypan*) nothing."

- *nechpalostahuiya*. This construct is surely based on Spanish *palos dar*, but it is not an example of the normal Stage 3 convention for borrowing verbs, -*oa* plus the infinitive of the Spanish verb. Indeed, it would be rather too early for that, though one or two known attestations do go back this far. The -*huia* used here is actually related to -*oa* in the sense that verbs in -*oa* have applicatives ending in -*huia*. Affixed to nouns, it means to wield the thing named on some object: *tepozhuia*, "to use an axe on someone or something, etc." It can also be used with adverbial expressions, such as *achtopa*, "first": *tlaachtopahuia*, "to do something first." Here apparently the whole unanalyzed but quite well understood Spanish phrase *palos da*, with a third person singular verb, "he/she administers blows," plays the same role relative to -*huia* as *achtopa* does in *achtopahuia*, yielding a verb meaning "to do blow-giving on someone." Nothing like this example is so far attested in any other Nahuatl text known to me. It is congruent, however, with the strong influence of colloquial Spanish felt in the petition.

- *yuhqui ce loca*. Here again we feel the closeness of Spanish conversation; the Spaniards were always talking of someone behaving like a lunatic or crazy person (*loco*). Here *loco* is managed properly for gender even as a loan; actually, Nahuatl sometimes took the masculine and feminine genders of a word as separate items, as it did with *santo* and *santa*, male and female saint. The phrase *yuhqui ce loca* translates easily as "like a crazy woman." The following verb is obscured by a smudge but is at least compatible with *omocuep*, "she became."

- *tlacatl tlathohuani*. These words appear to be in the feminine vocative.

B. *Petition of don Gerónimo Márquez to the regional administrator, Cuernavaca, ca. 1610.* This time have a good look at the text before you resort to the analysis given below of its orthography.

Nomahuitztlatocatzine mixpātzico onihualla y nehuatl nicnotlacatl auh onicno-tlanehui molla onichuiccazquiya mexico otziyahuito ocotevec auh oca onicpatlac o-niquilhui melchior ma chinechmopallehuilli notelpoçe ma oc nica xicmovielli yni molla auh ca noconatiquiçaz huiptla auh nomahuitztlatocatzine onichuicac mexico yn icahuayo auh onichualhuicac yn oca ycha ocotevec auh yehuatl onicpiyaltitiquiz notlatlanehuel ayocac oquipollo ça nexilhuiya ochollo auh onihualla y nica mo-chatzinco quauhnahuac nima ye nitlatemoa yn opa ytlaquaquaya çacatla yey metztli otictemoque ayac netzin auh ye yxquich cahuitli yn oquipollo Axca ye chicome metztli auh nocotetemohuā ayac nechmonextillia ça motlatia yehuatl melchiol auh yn achca onicanilito yn icahuayo ma itla yztlacatlatoli ticmocaquiti ynic mohuictzinco onihualla tinechmovallehuilliz y tinotlaçomahuitztlatocatzi

    dō geronimo marques

Nomahuiztlatocatzine mixpantzinco onihualla in nehuatl nicnotlacatl auh onicno-
tlanehui mula onichuicazquia mexico otzinyahuito Ocotepec auh oncan onicpatlac o-
niquilhui Melchor ma xinechmopalehuili notelpochtze ma oc nican xicmopieli ynin
mula auh ca noconantiquiçaz huiptla auh nomahuiztlatocatzine onichuicac mexico in
icaballo auh onichualhuicac in oncan ichan Ocotepec auh yehuatl onicpialtitiquiz
notlatlanehuil ayocac oquipolo çan nechilhuia ocholo auh onihualla in nican mochan-
tzinco Quauhnahuac niman ye nitlatemoa yn ompa itlaquaquayan çacatla yei metztli
otictemoque ayac neci auh ye ixquich cahuitl in oquipolo axcan ye chicome metztli auh
nocontetemoa ayac nechmonextilia çan motlatia yehuatl Melchor auh in axcan onic-
anilito yn icaballo ma itla iztlacatlatolli ticmocaquiti inic mohuictzinco onihualla
tinechmopalehuiliz in tinotlaçomahuiztlatocatzin

    don Geronimo Marquez

O my honored ruler, humble person that I am I have come before you. I rented a mule
and was going to take it to Mexico City. At Ocotepec it got a pain in its flank, and I ex-
changed it there. I said to Melchor, "Help me, my son; keep this mule here for a while, and
I will come by the day after tomorrow to take it." And O my honored ruler, I took his
horse to Mexico City and brought it back to his home at Ocotepec. But [the mule] I rented
that I gave him to guard when I passed through was no longer there; he lost it. He just told
me it ran away. I came here to your home, Cuernavaca; then I searched in its pasture in
the grasslands. For three months we have sought it, and it has not appeared. It has now
been seven months since he lost it. I go on searching for it repeatedly. That Melchor does
not show himself to me, but hides. Now I have gone to take his horse from him. Lest you
hear some lying statement, I have come to you. You will help me, you who are my dear
honored ruler.

    Don Gerónimo Márquez.

Like the first document, this one veers from the Carochi standard on *l* vs *ll* and on the
ia/iya question. You are now equipped to deal with those problems.

The first document had one or two missing or inserted *n*'s, but it hardly prepared us for
what we see here. Only a couple of *n*'s are inserted, but many, many are omitted. Indeed,
we could say that not a single standard syllable-final *n* is notated in the entire text were it
not for the overbar in *mixpātzico*. This writer possibly did not pronounce final *n* and
surely did not usually write it down. Read the text through once, specifically concentrating on an attempt to reconstruct lost *n*'s so you can recognize words or find them in
the dictionary. They have all been restored in the second transcription.

Such treatment of *n* is rife in the Nahuatl documentary corpus. A bit rarer, but indicative of the unusual orthographic phenomena you may find at any time, is the handling
here of *z/tz* and *x/ch*, which are merged. That is, the two members of each pair are treated
as equivalents; they may appear where we expect them, or they may substitute for each
other. As seen in Lesson 17, the combinations make phonological sense, for *z* represents
the dental fricative [s] and *tz* the dental affricate [ts], while *x* represents the palatal
fricative [sh] and *ch* the palatal affricate [tsh]. In other words, it appears that the writer
has a hard time distinguishing between the fricatives and affricates articulated at the
same position. Even without quite grasping the technicalities, you may intuit some of
this, and it may help decipher the intention. If not, morphological analysis and dictionary work can set you on the right track. When you see *ma chinechmopallehuilli* you will
surely recognize it as a verb, and not long thereafter as a Class 3 verb in the optative. If
you run down the possible prefixes, *ni* for the first person, *xi* for the second, and nothing
for the third, you are bound to pick *xi*, and from there on it will get easier. Also, some

words are written both ways; standard *axcan*, "now," appears as both *axca* and *achca*.

- *notelpoçe*, "my son." This form is a case of the phenomenon we were just talking about, with *ç* for standard *tz*. *-Tze* is a shortened, somewhat less reverential form of *-tzine*, reverential *tzin* plus vocative *e*. Even that, however, would not get us to the fully standard form, *notelpochtze*. Remember the omission of the letter for a fricative or affricate before another, mentioned in Lesson 17.

- *molla* for *mula*, "mule." We expect *o* for *u* in Spanish words, since Nahuatl had no [u] distinct from [o].

- *ocotevec* for Ocotepec. We expect hypercorrection, the use of a letter not corresponding to anything in Nahuatl for one that does, primarily in Spanish loanwords. Once in a while it will infect the writing of native vocabulary as well. Here we have *v* for *p* rather than the more often seen *b* for *p*; it must have happened because *v* and *b* were treated by many as equivalent in Spanish writing. This writer was quite enamored of *v* for *p*; he spells Ocotepec the same way a second time, and uses *v* also in *palehuia*, "to help."

- *notlatlanehuel*, "that which I borrowed or rented." The last *e* should be *i* in standard orthography and even in the writing of most Nahuas. It may be a simple error, but *e* for *i* as an actual reflection of speech is not unheard of.

- *ayocac*: most often we see *aocac*, but since this comes from *ayac*, "no one," and *oc*, "still," it is not far off.

- *cahuitli*. Here we seem to have an extra *i* which may or may not have corresponded to the writer's pronunciation. Or possibly the intention was *cahuitl in*, with the postposed demonstrative, meaning "this time," but that doesn't fit very well with the context.

Some comments on the Nahuatl:

- *onichuicazquiya*, standard *onichuicazquia*. The "conditional," with the usual meaning "was going to." In this case the antecessive *o-* is attached, something quite rarely seen.

- *otziyahuito*, for *otzinyahuito*. This form contains the past of the purposive motion form *tiuh/to* and the verb *tzinyauh*. Rarely if ever have I seen a form of the verb *yauh*, "to go," used with *tiuh/to*. I would have expected *yato* (with the same stem as the future of the verb) but given the rarity of the case and the fact that we are dealing with a compound, *yahuito* may fall within standard usage. Molina's dictionary gives a slightly different definition of *tzinyauh*, and it functions grammatically slightly differently than it does here, but close enough that one can arrive at the translation given above.

- *ayac nechmonextillia*. The verb looks like a normal reverential, but that would give the sense "no one makes me appear," and in any case throughout this text the writer does not use reverential forms in reference to Melchor. All the elements of the verb complex have semantic significance here; "he makes himself appear to me." Both in this phrase and once above, in *ayac netzi*, the writer seems to be using *ayac*, "no one," or "someone is absent," as very nearly the same thing as *amo*, "not."

- *ma itla yztlacatlatoli ticmocaquiti*, "may you not hear some false tale, beware lest you hear some false tale." This is the vetitive of the verb, *ma* plus an ending which here has the shape *-ti*; we have not studied it in these lessons because of its relative rarity in texts.

20. A Stage 3 Text

Will of don Nicolás de Silva, San Francisco Centlalpan, 1736.

IN THIS DOCUMENT you will encounter a feast of inserted and omitted *n*'s, of which I believe I have never seen the equal, though many texts show all the same tendencies. You should by now be prepared for just about all of this writer's orthographic conventions. He tends to omit some consonants syllable-finally (*c* several times and *l* once), often before *tz*, perhaps reflecting a corresponding weakening in speech. He also goes his own way in writing the *-tl/-tli* singular absolutive, sometimes putting *-tl* after a consonant (mainly weak consonants) and *-tli* after a vowel. Possibly his *caltlaltzintl*, "house-land," reflects speech in its failure to assimilate an [ltl] sequence to [ll] as in the standard *callaltzintli*.

Here each section of the text is followed by another transcription in standard orthography and a translation.

YCa yn itocatzin yn Dios tetatzin y Dios ypiltzin y Dios espirito santo ma mochitin quimatinCan yn aquiq̃ quitasq̃ quipohuasq̃ ynin amatlaCuiloli yn quenin nehuatl notoCan dⁿ Nicolas de silva Nican nichanen yn ipan Barrio San Diego chalcatepehuaCan ompa nipohui yn ipā San Franᶜᵒ altepetl toCabeseran auh masihui y ninoCoCohua y notlallo nosoquiyo auh y notlamachilis y notlalnamiquilis aq̃ mochihua ca sa huel pactica chicauhtica ycatzinco yn ttᵒ dios auh yese yn axCa Ca huel ninoseneltoquitia yn sa setzin huel neli teutl dios yn ttᵒ Jesus christo yhua y ye mochi quimoneltoquitia y tonatzin santa ygˡᵃ Catolica Roma – yhua Ca yehuatli y nicchihua y nictecpanā y notestamento yn sa tlatzancCan notlanequilis

Ica in itocatzin in Dios tetatzin in Dios ipiltzin in Dios espiritu santo ma mochintin quimatican in aquique quittazque quipohuazque inin amatlacuilolli in quenin nehuatl notoca don Nicolas de Silva nican nichane in ipan barrio San Diego Chalcatepehuacan ompa nipohui in ipan San Francisco altepetl tocabecera auh macihui in ninococoa in notlallo noçoquiyo auh in notlamachiliz in notlalnamiquiliz aquen mochihua ca çan huel pactica chicauhtica icatzinco in totecuiyo Dios auh yece in axcan ca huel nicnocenneltoquitia in çan cetzin huel nelli teotl Dios in totecuiyo Jesus Christo ihuan in ye mochi quimoneltoquitia in tonantzin Santa Iglesia Catolica Roma – ihuan ca yehuatl in in nicchihua in nictecpana in notestamento in ça tlatzaccan notlanequiliz

In the name of God the father, God his child, and God the Holy Spirit, let all know who see and read this document how I named don Nicolás de Silva, citizen here in the district of San Diego Chalcatepehuacan, belonging to the altepetl of San Francisco, our head-town, though I am sick [in] my earthly body, yet nothing has happened to my understanding and memory, but they are very sound and strong through our lord God. Now I most firmly believe in only one very true divinity God, our lord Jesus Christ, and in all that our Holy Catholic Mother Church of Rome believes. And this is my testament and final will that I make and order.

Note: Here the Spanish *cabecera*, which refers to a capital town ruling subject towns, has been virtually equated with *altepetl*, i.e., it includes the whole entity.

- huel achtopa niquitoa y [n]anima Ca ysenmactzinCo nicnoCahuilia yn ttᵒ dios y[eica] huel yehuatzin omquimochihuili yhua onquimomaq[uixtili yca] yn itlasopasiyotzin yhua yn itlasoessotzin ynic quimo[huiquiliz yn i]chantzinco yn il[hui]Cac auh y nona-[ca]yo Ca nicmaca y tlali ye[ica oncan o]quis ca huapo

- huel achtopa niquitoa in [n]anima ca icenmactzinco nicnocahuilia in totecuiyo Dios

y[eica] huel yehuatzin oquimochihuili ihuan oquimomaq[uixtili ica] in itlaçopasiontzin ihuan in itlaçoezçotzin inic quimo[huiquiliz in i]chantzinco in il[hui]cac auh in nona-[ca]yo ca nicmaca in tlalli ye[ica oncan o]quiz ca [i?]huampo

- First of all I declare that I leave my soul entirely in the hands of our lord God because he himself made it and redeemed it with his precious passion and his precious blood in order to take it to his home in heaven. And as to my body, I give it to the earth, because it emerged from there and is [the earth's?] companion.

Note: *Nicnocahuilia* appears to need another *li* to mean "I leave it to him." Similar constructions below sometimes bear a double *li*, sometimes not.

- *yhua niquitoa yn iquac q[. . .] Ninomiquilis ompa nitoCos y [San Diego? y]chantzinco y mochihua y nosepoltora*

- *ihuan niquitoa in iquac q[. . .] ninomiquiliz ompa nitocoz in [San Diego? i]chantzinco in mochihua in nosepultura*

- And I declare that when [. . .] I die, I am to be buried at the home [church] of [San Diego ?], [which] becomes my tomb.

- *yhua niquito[a nochantzin?]Co ninocahua y nopilhuatzintzinhua D^n domigo de Silban [. . .] D^n Panblo Coztantino d^n lureso de silban D^n Juan Gervansion [. . .] yhuantzin y no-namictzin y nonamic D^oa sebastiana Gentrodis [. . .] yhua oc omme tepitoto getrodes an^tta yehuatzintzin nechmoquimilhuisq̄ yhua nechmotoquilisq̄ quimotenmaquilis y huetzintl yhua yn ipan y notlachicueytilis sen misa de requia nopan mitos ypanlenhui-loca y nanima auh sano yehuantzintzin y nopilhuantzitzinhua yn oniquinotenehuili quimotenmaquilisque yhuetzin y notococa onme peso y nomisa yey peso – 3 p^os – yhua ynic tzinlinis yhua yn iserantzin y santa Cofrandi sa ninocnoma ypaltzinco y tt^o Dios*

- *ihuan niquito[a nochantzin?]co ninocahua in nopilhuantzitzinhuan don Domingo de Silva [. . .] don Pablo Constantino don Lorenzo de Silva don Juan Gervasio [. . .] ihuantzin in nonamictzin in nonamic doña Sebastiana Gertrudis [. . .] ihuan oc ome tepitoton Gertrudis Antonia yehuantzitzin nechmoquimilhuizque ihuan nechmotoquilizque qui-motemaquiliz in huentzintli ihuan in ipan in notlachicueitiliz cen misa de requiem nopan mitoz ipalehuiloca in nanima auh çan no yehuantzitzin in nopilhuantzitzinhuan in oniquinnotenehuili quimotemaquilizque ihuentzin in notococa ome peso in nomisa yei peso – 3 pesos – ihuan inic tziliniz ihuan in iseratzin in santa cofradia çan ninocno-ma[ti?] ipaltzinco in totecuiyo Dios*

And I declare that [at my home?] I leave behind my children don Domingo de Silva [. . .], don Pablo Constantino, don Lorenzo de Silva, don Juan Gervasio [. . .], and my spouse—my spouse is doña Sebastiana Gertrudis—[. . .] and two other small children, Gertrudis and Antonia. They are to shroud and inter me and make the offering, and a week after I have died a requiem mass is to be said for me, for the help of my soul, and likewise my children whom I mentioned are to make the offering for my burial, 2 pesos, and for my mass 3 pesos, and so the bells will toll and for the candles of the holy cofradia. I humbly [ask it?] for the sake of our lord God.

Note: *Ninocahua* is irregular for the meaning "I leave them"; we would expect *niquincahua* or in the reverential *niquinnocahuilia*. There was a problem with this same verb just above; perhaps it was taking on some peculiarities in this local speech area. Yet this meaning is handled more normally in the next paragraph.

The form *notlachicueytilis* is a possessed *-liztli* noun apparently from the verb *tlachicue(i)tilia* (though a *-li-* seems to be missing). By its structure the base verb ought to mean "to cause something to be eight, to bring it to eight." In Spanish eight days means a week later; probably the verb had come to mean "to arrive at the same day a week later."

This writer is not the only one in this book to double the *-huan* in *-piltzitzinhuan*.

- *yhua niquitoa y niCann ipan yn iquiya[hua]ctzin ythuatzin y tt^o Dios Ca onca ninoca-huilitihui y nonamitzin D^a Sebastiana Getrodes yhua y nopiltzin dⁿ domi[ngo] de silban Ca omca quimotequipanilhuisque yn mahuiztic santo sⁿ diego ca ayac quimotehuililis y quename nestica yn ipan yn itestametotzin y nopilitzin maria Gacoben nica nechmoCa-huilitihui yhua mochititzintzin y santos nica quimotequipannilhuisque y queni tlamani san iuhqui tlamanis*

- *ihuan niquitoa in nican ipan in iquiahuactzin ithualtzin in totecuiyo Dios ca oncan nicnocahuilitiuh in nonamictzin doña Sebastiana Gertrudis ihuan in nopiltzin don Domingo de Silva ca oncan quimotequipanilhuizque in mahuiztic santo San Diego ca ayac quimmotecuililiz in quenami neztica in ipan in itestamentotzin in n[ach]piltzin Maria Jacoba nican nechmocahuilitiuh ihuan mochintintzitzin in santos nican quin-motequipanilhuizque in quenin tlamani çan iuhqui tlamaniz*

- And I declare that here at the entryway and patio of our lord God [i.e., here in my house-hold] I am leaving my spouse doña Sebastiana Gertrudis and my child don Domingo de Silva; there they are to serve the marvelous saint San Diego. No one is to take it away from them. As appears in the testament of my great-grandmother María Jacoba, she left it to me here along with all the [images of] the saints. They are to serve them here, and things are to remain as they are.

Note: Several times this text uses a verb *tehuilia* in the meaning "to take away from." This is the verb *cui*, "to take," in the applicative, with the indefinite object prefix *te-* absorbed into the stem. The consonant [k^w] sometimes weakens to [k], but here it has weakened to [w].

The form *-pilitzin*, standard *-piltzin*, may be a mistake for *-achpillitzin*, standard *-achpiltzin*, found further on in the text, to mean "great-grandmother." I have not seen this word elsewhere, but other words beginning *ach-* do refer to great-grandparents.

- *yhua niquitoa y Caltlaltzintl quelenmiqui nahui yonta motoca tlacoton tlaonli o-niquinocahuililitihui i nonamictzin ihua i nopiltzin in oniquinotenehuili tlacpac ayac quimotehuilis ymaxCan*

- *ihuan niquitoa in callaltzintli quelimiqui nahui yunta motoca tlacoton tlaolli oni-quinnocahuililitiuh in nonamictzin ihuan in nopiltzin in oniquinnotenehuili tlacpac ayac quinmotecuiliz imaxca*

- And I declare that I have left the house-land, which four yoke of oxen cultivate and on which a fourth of a fanega of maize is sown, to my spouse and child whom I mentioned above. No one is to take their property from them.

- *yhua niquitohua y nohermanatzin D^a madanlennā de silban ommonamictitzinno santiago ayanpanCo Ca ye panCa yoCoxca omtotlaxelhuique ynn ome termanos do nico-las de silvan yn achto titepilhuan yn ipan sen matrimoni in totatzin Dⁿ domigo de sil-ban yn inamitzin D^a madalenna Buena auh inic ompan matrimonion onquimosihuac-titzinnoCa D^a Sebastiana maria ompan channen yn ipan Barrio Sⁿto res auh omqui-mopeli ipilhuatzitzinhuan ytetzinco y motenenhua tochanhuanatzin yeytin – ynic sen Dⁿ Fran^{co} de silban ynic omme Dⁿ Diego de silvan ynic yey dⁿ domingo de silban auh paCa yoCoxca ontitonotzque y nohermanatzin D^a madalenna de silban ytechcacopan ynic ompā tohermanotzintzinhuan yn omotenech quitlani tlen onqui[mo]Cahuilitehuac yn totatzin Dⁿ domigo de silban Canel amo [oqui]mochihuili testamento auh quitlani yn tlenn imaxCan [. . .] y noparten Ca ye onquisenlli medianega senbra[dura y]n axcan ypan*

*nococolis ca san ic omosihuac[titzino yn] tiachCauh Dⁿ franᶜᵒ de silba auh yni tlali
onCa mani yn [itoca]yocCan tlilan ytech y hueyy otli Calaqui amaquemeca Can[in?]
tlami ompitzanto auh yn oc sentlali ytoCayoncan conmaxanlan tlaConton motoCa
tlaolli conmanillia Dⁿ diego de silban auh Sano yohqui yn ipartetzin y nohirmanatzin
quimomaquilis medianegan senbradoran onpan tlanpechhuanCan yn otocatenehua-
lonque tlacpac tohermanos ynic ye moyonlalia acmo senpa tlen quimitlanilisque yn
topilhuan yn opan tonitztihui*

*- ihuan niquitoa yn nohermanatzin doña Magdalena de Silva omonamictitzino San-
tiago Ayapanco ca ye pacca yocoxca otitotlaxelhuique in omen tihermanos don Nicolas
de Silva in achto titepilhuan in ipan cen matrimonio in totatzin don Domingo de Silva
in inamictzin doña Magdalena Buena auh inic oppa matrimonio oquimocihuatitzinoca
doña Sebastiana Maria ompa chane in ipan Barrio Santos Reyes auh oquimopiali ipil-
huantzitzinhuan itechtzinco in motenehua tochahuanantzin yeintin – inic se don Francisco de Silva inic ome don Diego de Silva ynic yei don Domingo de Silva auh pacca yocoxca ontito[no]notzque in nohermanatzin doña Magdalena de Silva itechcacopa inic
oppa tohermanotzitzinhuan in omoteneuh quitlani tlein oquimmocahuililitehuac in
totatzin don Domingo de Silva canel amo oquimochihuili testamento auh quitlani in
tlein imaxca [. . .] in noparte ca ye oquiceli media fanega sembradura in axcan ipan
nococoliz ca çan ic omocihua[titzino in] tiachcauh don Francisco de Silva auh inin tlalli
oncan mani in [itoca]yocan Tlillan itech in huei otli calaqui Amaquemecan can[in]
tlami opitzacton auh in oc centlalli itocayocan Conmaxallan tlacoton motoca tlaolli
conmanilia don Diego de Silva auh çan no iuhqui in ipartetzin in nohermanatzin quimomaquiliz media fanega sembradura ompa Tlapechhuacan in otocatenehualoque
tlacpac tohermanos[huan] inic ye moyollalia aocmo ceppa tlein quimitlanilizque in
topilhuan in ompa tonitztihui*

- And I declare that as to my sister doña Magdalena de Silva, who married in Santiago Ayapanco, we two siblings, she and I, don Nicolás de Silva, being children of the first marriage of our father don Domingo de Silva, his spouse being doña Magdalena Buena, already amicably made division between us. And in second nuptials he married doña Sebastiana María, citizen of the district of Santos Reyes, and by our said stepmother he had three children: first, don Francisco de Silva; second, don Diego de Silva; third, don Domingo de Silva. And my sister doña Magdalena de Silva and I agreed amicably about how our aforementioned second siblings demand what our father don Domingo de Silva bequeathed them at death; since he did not make a will, they demand what belongs to them. The eldest brother, don Francisco de Silva, just recently during my illness already received my part and got married with it, [land] on which half a fanega of grain can be sown, and this land is at the place called Tlillan next to the highway entering Amecameca, where a narrow little road ends. And don Diego de Silva is taking another piece of land at the place called Conmaxallan, where a fourth of a fanega of maize can be sown. And likewise my sister is to give him her part, [land] where half a fanega can be sown at Tlapechhuacan. With this our siblings whose names were mentioned above are satisfied. They are not to ask anything of our children again in the future.

Note: In *omtotlaxelhuique*, standard *otitotlaxelhuique*, *tito-* has been compressed to *to-* by the omission of the *it* in between, a procedure common and valid enough to be mentioned in the old grammars, though it is not seen very often in texts.

With *ynn ome termanos*, standard *in omen tihermanos* or *termanos*, not only has Spanish terminology been taken into Nahuatl for close kinship terms, something that did not happen in Stage 2, but the most basic principle of the Nahuatl use of the terms, that they must always be contingent and never collective ("the brothers," "the sisters," "the cousins," etc.), has been abandoned. The traditional Nahuatl use of subject prefixes is also violated here. By general Nahuatl principles *omen* should be preceded by *ti*, and just after this don Nicolás's name should be preceded by *ni*.

- *yhua niquitoa y D*^a *ma[nue]llan de silban yhua ynamitzin D*ⁿ *antt*^o *fran*^{co} *yhua y D*^a *madalenna de silban ynamictzin D*ⁿ *panblo Coztatino yhuan D*^a *josepha de silban yn inamictzi D*ⁿ *lureso de silban yhua D*^a *Domiga de silban yhuan ynamitzin d*ⁿ *Juan Gervansion de santiago auh niquitoa nicnopieli tlaltzintl tlilan quipie sen anega senbradoran auh niquitoa motlaCoCotonas y tlaco quimoCoCotonisque y nomotzintzinhuan yn oniquinotennehuili tlacpac san panrenjan auh yn oc tlaco Comanilis y nonamictzin d*^a *Sebastiana Gentres yhua y nopiltzin D*ⁿ *domigo de silban ayac quimotehuilis ypa quimoscaltilisą y pipiltzintin yhuan y tlalli yn oc monemiti[s] y nonamictzin oc quimopielis yquac yn Dios quimohuiquilis quimomaquilis y nomotzitzinhua*

- *ihuan niquitoa in doña Manuela de Silva ihuan inamictzin don Antonio Francisco ihuan in doña Magdalena de Silva inamictzin don Pablo Constantino ihuan doña Josefa de Silva in inamictzin don Lorenzo de Silva ihuan doña Dominga de Silva ihuan inamictzin don Juan Gervasio de Santiago auh niquitoa nicnopialia tlaltzintli tlillan quipia ce fanega sembradura auh niquitoa motlacocotonaz in tlaco quimococotonizque in nomontzitzinhuan in oniquinnotenehuili tlacpac san pareja auh in oc tlaco conmaniliz in nonamictzin doña Sebastiana Gertrudis ihuan in nopiltzin don Domingo de Silva ayac quimmotecuililiz ipan quimozcaltilizque in pipiltzitzintin ihuan in tlalli in oc monemitiz in nonamictzin oc quimopializ iquac in Dios quimohuiquiliz quinmomaquiliz in nomontzitzinhuan*

- And I declare, as to doña Manuela de Silva and her spouse don Antonio Francisco, and doña Magdalena de Silva spouse of don Pablo Constantino, and doña Josefa de Silva spouse of don Lorenzo de Silva, and doña Dominga de Silva and her spouse don Juan Gervasio de Santiago: I declare that I have a piece of land at Tlillan where a fanega of grain can be sown, and I say that it is to be divided in half. My sons-in-law whom I mentioned above are to divide one half among them equally, and my spouse doña Sebastiana Gertrudis and my child don Domingo de Silva are to take the other half. No one is to take it from them. With it they are to raise the small children. While my spouse still lives she is to have the land; when God takes her, she is to give it to my sons-in-law.

- *yhuan Niquitoa nicnopielia oc sententl tlaltzintl ytoCanyoncan yanpan quipie tlacoton motoca tlaoli yn tonalli yąsanyanpan yCuetetzinco yn D*ⁿ *diego de S. migel auh yn tonalli yanquiyanpan yCuetetzinco yn D*ⁿ *Juan de silban auh ynic amilpanCopaCopan yCuetetzinco y D*ⁿ *Juan belasquis amaquemeCan auh ynic tlacpacCopa ytech tlami in atlauhtl Ca ninomaquilia y nonamictzin yhua y nopiltzi onniquinotenehuili tlacpac ayac quimotehuililis*

- *ihuan niquitoa nicnopialia oc centetl tlaltzintli itocayocan Yappan quipia tlacoton motoca tlaolli in tonalli iquiçayampa icuententzinco in don Diego de San Miguel auh in tonalli iaquiyampa icuententzinco in don Juan de Silva auh inic amilpancopa icuententzinco in don Juan Velasquez Amaquemecan auh inic tlacpaccopa itech tlami in atlauhtli ca nicnomaquilia in nonamictzin ihuan in nopiltzin oniquinnotenehuili tlacpac ayac quinmotecuililiz*

- And I declare that I have another piece of land at the place called Yappan where a quarter of a fanega of maize can be sown, to the east at the edge of a field of don Diego de San Miguel, and to the west at the edge of a field of don Juan de Silva, and toward the irrigated fields (to the south) at the edge of a field of don Juan Velásquez of Amecameca, and in the upper direction (north) it ends at the ravine. I give it to my spouse and my child whom I mentioned above; no one is to take it from them.

- *yhuan niquitoa sen salan omnicpieyan ye onxixitin auh moCahua sen yehua ysintiyon ompa moCaltitihua y nopilhuantzintzinhuan yn oniquiteneuh onnechmoCahuililitehuac y notatzin Dⁿ domigo de silban moch ica ypantiyo yhua sen cabanllerisia niquinocahuillilia y nonamitzin yhua y nopilhuatzitzinhua yn oniquiteneuh tlacpac ayac quitehuilis*

- *ihuan niquitoa cen sala onicpiaya ye oxixitin auh mocahua ce yegua isitio ompa mocaltitihu[i?] in nopilhuantzitzinhuan in oniquinteneuh onechmocahuililitehuac in notatzin don Domingo de Silva moch ica ipatio ihuan ce caballeriza niquinnocahuililia in nonamictzin ihuan in nopilhuantzitzinhuan in oniquinteneuh tlacpac ayac quintecuiliz*

- And I declare that I used to have a large dwelling room that collapsed, but a place for mares remains; there my children whom I mentioned are sheltered. My father don Domingo de Silva left it to me when he died, complete with its patio and a stable. I leave it to my spouse and children whom I mentioned above. No one is to take it from them.

- *yhuan niquitoa tlalmanalCo Calli quimopielia Dⁿ franc^{co} Diego anticpac quimomaquilis Cu[. . . no]pilhua yhuan yn oc nesis ypan yBentario yhuan [. . . qui]chipanhuasque*

- *ihuan niquitoa Tlalmanalco calli quimopialia don Francisco Diego Aticpac quimomaquiliz [. . . no]pilhuan ihuan in oc neciz ipan inventario ihuan [. . . qui]chipahuazque*

- And I declare that don Francisco Diego of Aticpac has a house [of mine] at Tlalmanalco; he is to give it to [. . . my] children along with whatever else appears in the inventory, and they are to clear [the title?].

- *Ca ye yxquich yn onicteneuh [. . .] auh y nopilhuantzintzinhuan yhuan [. . . Dⁿ] juan de silban noalbanse[ashuan . . .] Niquino[tlatlauhtilia ma ipan] motlatoltisque y noanima ytla quali quim[ochihuilis]q̄ yc quimocnelis y Dios*

- *ca ye ixquich in onicteneuh [. . .] auh in nopilhuantzitzinhuan ihuan [. . . don] Juan de Silva noalbace[ashuan . . .] niquinno[tlatlauhtilia ma ipan] motlatoltizque in naniman intla qualli quim[ochihuiliz]que ic quimmocneliliz in Dios*

- That is all I have said. [. . .] And I [implore] my children and [. . . don] Juan de Silva, my executors, to speak [on behalf of] my soul; if they do it well, God will favor them for it.

    auh ynn ax[ca]n ipan tonali [. . .] ynic Caxtoli yhua yey tonalli mani metztli sentien[bre] yn ipan xihuitli de 1736 años yn onicchiuh y notestamento ymixpantzinco yn aalCaltt hor^{or} por Su^{dad} yhuatzin fiscal santa ygelcia yhuan ymixpantzinco y testigos yhuan nicfirmarohua
    Don nicolas de silva

    auh in axcan ipan tonalli [. . .] inic caxtolli ihuan yei tonalli mani metztli septiembre in ipan xihuitl de 1736 años in onicchiuh in notestamento imixpantzinco in alcalde ordinario por Su Magestad ihuantzin fiscal santa iglesia ihuan imixpantzinco in testigos ihuan nicfirmaroa
    don Nicolas de Silva

    Today on the 18th day of the month of September of the year 1736 I made my testament before the alcalde ordinario through His Majesty and the fiscal of the holy church, and before the witnesses, and I sign it.
    Don Nicolás de Silva.

Niquitoa y nehuatl Commo alCalde hordinario yn ipan altepetl s. franᶜᵒ zentlalpan ca huel melahuac y tlen yn oquimotenehuilli yn itestametotzin yhua oniquitac yn itestametotzin y dᵃ maria jancoben yn iachpillitzin ytocayonCan XochmolCo auh ticfirmarohua mochi y testigos

Dⁿ Juan Mendes Alde rodinario   D Juan de Silva   Dⁿ Anttᵒ franᶜᵒ fiscal Dⁿ diego franᶜᵒ de santiago   Dⁿ anttᵒ Bernaber alcalde pasado   Diego de s. migl

niquitoa in nehuatl como alcalde ordinario in ipan altepetl San Francisco Centlalpan ca huel melahuac in tlein in oquimotenehuili in itestamentotzin ihuan oniquittac in itestamentotzin in doña Maria Jacoba in iachpiltzin itocayocan Xochmolco auh ticfirmaroa mochin in testigos

don Juan Mendez alcalde ordinario   don Juan de Silva   don Antonio Francisco fiscal don Diego Francisco de Santiago   don Antonio Bernabe alcalde pasado   Diego de San Miguel

As alcalde ordinario in the altepetl of San Francisco Centlalpan I declare that what he said as his testament is entirely true, and I saw the testament of doña María Jacoba, his great-grandmother, from the place called Xochmolco, and all we witnesses sign it.

Don Juan Méndez, alcalde ordinario. Don Juan de Silva. Don Antonio Francisco, fiscal. Don Diego Francisco de Santiago. Don Antonio Bernabé, past alcalde. Diego de San Miguel.

Niquitoa y nehuatl esⁿᵒ de la repobliCan yhuan y testigos niquitoCatenehuan pedro matias rexidor anttᵒ pasqual Juan domingo Dⁿ Nicolas galicia juan anttᵒ

niquitoa in nehuatl escribano de la republica ihuan in testigos niquintocatenehua Pedro Matias regidor Antonio Pascual Juan Domingo don Nicolas Galicia Juan Antonio

I declare that I am notary of the municipality and I name as witnesses Pedro Matías, regidor, Antonio Pascual, Juan Domingo, don Nicolás de Galicia, and Juan Antonio.

Niquitoa y nehua esⁿᵒ repoblican yn ipan altepetli S. franᶜᵒ zen[tlal]pan Ca nixpan onquichiuh yn itestanmento y CoCoxcantzintl Ca huel quali onquitecpan yn itlatoltzin Ca huel ycamactzinco onquis Ca moch ionqui onnictlali onniquicuilli yn ipan tonalli martes a 18 de setienbre yni año de 1736 años auh y nicneltilia yca y notoCa y nofirma
SenBastian thomas esⁿᵒ de repuᶜᵃ

niquitoa in nehua escribano republica in ipan altepetl San Francisco Centlalpan ca nixpan oquichiuh in itestamento in cocoxcatzintli ca huel qualli oquitecpan in itlatoltzin ca huel icamactzinco oquiz ca moch iuhqui onictlali oniquicuili in ipan tonalli martes a 18 de septiembre inin año de 1736 años auh in nicneltilia ica in notoca in nofirma
Sebastian Tomas escribano republica

I, municipal notary of the altepetl of San Francisco Centlalpan, declare that the sick person made his testament before me. He ordered his statement very well; it issued from his very mouth, and just so I put it all down and wrote it, on the day of Tuesday, the 18th of September of this year of 1736, and I verify it with my name and signature.

Sebastián Tomás, notary of the municipality.

Epilogue

HAVING COME TO the end of these lessons, you are by no means done with grammar. The structure of the conditional sentence and the imperfect optative tense of the verb, so important to conditional statements, have not been mentioned at all; nor have the passive abstract nouns in -oca or the -tzinoa reverential. The vetitive mode appears only in a footnote or two. When you go into full-scale grammars, as you eventually must, you will find much that is new to you (you will also find that you already know about some relevant matters not treated there). The important thing is that you by now understand enough and have enough experience to work with Nahuatl texts independently, and the best way to learn more grammar and vocabulary is not merely to pore over grammar books, but to alternate between texts and grammars, gradually giving the texts ever more of your time. The three appendixes are meant as aids in your transition to this next stage.

What you might do first of all, though, is to go right back through this book from beginning to end. If you are like many who have repeated these lessons in one form or another (and the experience is not confined to this particular set of lessons or to Nahuatl), you will be surprised at several things: how natural and easy much of the material seems; how much more you understand than you did the first time around; how much better it sticks in your memory. The very best thing you could do is to find an eager learner and lead him or her through the lessons, for not only does one study more deeply and learn more when one has the responsibility of teaching and explaining, it is a great boost to the morale to deal with someone who knows even less than oneself.

In saying that you should go on to texts, I do not necessarily mean handwritten originals in the archives or even photocopies of them—though exposure to such materials carries with it an unparalleled excitement and hence a great learning opportunity, and in the long run you will need to turn to them. Meanwhile published texts will be important, and if you continue with this kind of thing they will always be important, for you cannot by yourself find, transcribe, translate, and put into easily readable form the whole larger corpus that is emerging, each part of which bears on all the rest. Nearly all published Nahuatl texts contain translations. Take advantage of them. It isn't cheating; you have already seen that an immense amount of intellectual effort separates a Nahuatl original from an idiomatic English translation of it. You have plenty to do simply to figure out how the translation was achieved. Once you have done that, you can begin to go beyond it. Any translation is for a particular purpose; it reveals many things about the original but is bound to leave other things hidden. The hidden part will now be open to you. You can see for yourself what school the orthography belongs to, how the word order reflects focus and emphasis, what words and what kinds of words are Spanish loans. You might want to translate some words or passages differently. You may even find cases where the translation is in out-and-out error. If you do find an error, draw the proper conclusions, but don't gloat. It is safe to say, in view of the relative newness of the whole modern enterprise of translating Nahuatl texts and the relatively few that have been translated, that no work of translation has yet been published without some errors, and it is unreasonable to expect that any will be for at least a generation or two.

*　　*　　*

Now let us look at some publications containing texts of interest. All of them include both transcriptions and translations. In all of them the Nahuatl is respaced according to modern criteria. Given that it is good to look at many different kinds of texts, still there is, I think, something like an ideal progression for a student's further reading, at least until reaching the point of relative independence. The order in which I list the items here represents what I would consider a good sequence for approaching them.[1] Many of them are rare today, but they are in the best libraries, and most are well worth photocopying in whole or in part.

Cline, S. L., and Miguel León-Portilla, eds. 1984. *The Testaments of Culhuacan.* UCLA Latin American Center Nahuatl Studies Series, 1. Los Angeles: UCLA Latin American Center Publications.

Here is included in its entirety one of the largest known collections of Nahuatl wills, and surely the largest to have existed as a single collection from the beginning. The sixty-five wills and some related materials were generated within a few years of one another in a period of epidemics, mainly in 1579–81. Nahuatl writing was entering a golden age at this time, and the collection is highly revealing on human and family matters, indeed on a wide variety of topics having to do with households in a Valley of Mexico altepetl in the heart of Stage 2. The fact that the same couple of notaries wrote so many of the testaments makes it possible for the student to read a large number of them more quickly than might otherwise be possible. The transcription changes the original only in resolving overbars. Commentary is provided for each document, and translations face the transcriptions. The volume has long been out of print, and plans exist for a second edition.

Karttunen, Frances, and James Lockhart. 1976. *Nahuatl in the Middle Years: Language Contact Phenomena in Texts of the Colonial Period.* University of California Publications in Linguistics, 85. Berkeley and Los Angeles: University of California Press.

This linguistic monograph contains an appendix of ten mundane Nahuatl documents of various types across the postcontact centuries, translated and in a transcription which departs from the originals in nothing but spacing. Some linguistic and orthographic commentary is provided for each document. Three of the ten texts are reproduced in full in this book, in Lessons 19 and 20. The others too are strong on human as well as historical and linguistic interest.

Lockhart, James, Frances Berdan, and Arthur J. O. Anderson. 1986. *The Tlaxcalan Actas: A Compendium of the Records of the Cabildo of Tlaxcala (1545–1627).* Salt Lake City: University of Utah Press.

The book contains a long analysis of the only known set of Nahuatl municipal council records and a summary of all the sessions reported in the original document. Most relevant here is Part III, "Selected Sessions," in which twenty-five session reports are transcribed and translated in full, each with an individual commentary. The texts date from 1548 to 1627, most falling between 1550 and 1561. Some are brief; others are longer presentations, debates, and speeches, well developed and often colorful. The transcription resolves overbars but is otherwise diplomatic.

Lockhart, James. 1991. *Nahuas and Spaniards: Postconquest Central Mexican History and Philology.* UCLA Latin American Center Nahuatl Studies Series, 3. Stanford, Calif.: Stanford University Press and UCLA Latin American Center Publications.

One section of this collection of essays contains five pieces with transcriptions (overbars unresolved) and translations of Nahuatl documents in facing format. Among the documents are petitions, testimony, wills, land sales (one of them in dialogued form), and other land proceedings. The texts are from Stage 2 and Stage 3. Some of the documents are very colloquial, and all are accompanied by a great deal of commentary.

---

[1]In its present form, *Beyond the Codices*, now quite far down in the sequence, represents a considerable challenge to a student. If and when the second edition comes to pass, with comments about orthography, translation difficulties, and substance for each document, I would put it at the top of the list as the most indicated place to go when you are through with the present book. At this writing, new translations and transcriptions exist, as well as notes for the commentary.

Sousa, Lisa, Stafford Poole, C. M., and James Lockhart, eds. and trans. 1998. *The Story of Guadalupe: Luis Laso de la Vega's* Huei tlamahuiçoltica *of 1649*. UCLA Latin American Center Nahuatl Studies Series, 5. Stanford, Calif.: Stanford University Press and UCLA Latin American Center Publications.

In 1649 Luis Laso de la Vega published a Nahuatl version of the story of the apparition of the Virgin of Guadalupe to a humble indigenous person, Juan Diego, together with a set of miracle narratives and some other materials. It now begins to appear that Laso de la Vega largely wrote the book himself, basing the apparition story mainly on a previous book in Spanish by his friend Miguel Sánchez. He even made some errors in the Nahuatl. Nevertheless, the book is in a beautiful Stage 2 Nahuatl, flowing, understandable, sometimes even humorous. This publication includes a complete diplomatic transcription and a facing translation, with a substantial preliminary study.

Karttunen, Frances, and James Lockhart, eds. 1987. *The Art of Nahuatl Speech: The Bancroft Dialogues*. UCLA Latin American Center Nahuatl Studies Series, 2. Los Angeles: UCLA Latin American Center Publications.

It was apparently in Tetzcoco, a great altepetl of the Valley of Mexico, around 1570–80, that a Franciscan friar (or friars) got a Nahua aide (or aides) to help put together a set of speeches and dialogues meant to teach ecclesiastics the refinements of polite conversation among the Nahuas. Later, sometime in the first half of the seventeenth century, the collection came into the hands of the great grammarian Horacio Carochi, who had it recopied by someone in his circle with the diacritics he used to indicate vowel quantity and glottal stop. Today only this form is extant. Here it is published complete with the diacritics, with two separate translations, one more flowing and idiomatic, the other sticking close to the literal meaning and order. A second more rudimentary translation is helpful to the student when it comes to elevated speech, for without much preparation one could think that the pragmatic translation has no relation to the original at all. An analytical introduction discusses among other things the meaning of much of the special vocabulary in the text.

Lockhart, James. 1999. *Of Things of the Indies: Essays Old and New in Early Latin American History*. Stanford, Calif.: Stanford University Press.

Chapter 9 of this book, called "Between the Lines," contains complete transcriptions and translations of two Nahuatl wills, which are also included in the *Testaments of Culhuacan* and *Nahuatl in the Middle Years* respectively. The transcriptions resolve abbreviations and overbars and use capitalization in the modern way. On the other hand, the wills are accompanied by extraordinarily detailed commentary, item by item, concentrating more on ultimate meanings than on the linguistic avenues used to attain them. These sections can be useful to those who wish to go on to use Nahuatl texts for general historical research.

Sahagún, fray Bernardino de. 1950–82. *Florentine Codex: General History of the Things of New Spain*. Trans. by Arthur J. O. Anderson and Charles E. Dibble. 13 parts. Salt Lake City and Santa Fe, N. M.: University of Utah Press and School of American Research, Santa Fe.

Through much of the sixteenth century the Franciscan Sahagún worked with a team of Nahuatl writers and interviewers who produced, under his direction, a survey of Nahua civilization in twelve books. The work is monumental and of vast significance, but much of it stands apart from the rest of the Nahuatl written corpus, betraying Sahagún's quite direct intervention in various ways. Book Six, full of elaborate speeches in an approximately preconquest Nahua style, and Book Twelve, on the conquest, contain a great deal of connected prose and authentic Nahua manner of presentation, as opposed to the encyclopedia style found in much of the work.

Anderson and Dibble provide a fine transcription, virtually identical to the original except for a certain number of spacing changes. Their translation is also erudite and deeply considered. It is more literal than most recent work by translators of Nahuatl, but for that very reason it can be very helpful in guiding the student, who as I say is often hard pressed to tell what part of a translation corresponds to what part of an original text. The original work has two columns, one the Nahuatl written by Sahagún's aides, and the other a Spanish translation and commentary dictated by Sahagún. Anderson and Dibble include only the Nahuatl and their English translation of it. Sahagún's Spanish would be most useful, but for most of the work it can be seen together with the Nahuatl only in a facsimile edition of 1979.

Lockhart, James, ed. and trans. 1993. *We People Here: Nahuatl Accounts of the Conquest of Mexico.* UCLA Center for Medieval and Renaissance Studies, *Repertorium Columbianum*, 1 (gen. ed. Geoffrey Symcox). Berkeley and Los Angeles: University of California Press.

The volume assembles six texts or extracts of texts written by Nahuas in Nahuatl in the first or second postcontact generation about the conquest of Mexico. Of these by far the largest is Book Twelve of Sahagún's Florentine Codex, reproduced here in its entirety, with the original Nahuatl and Spanish columns and English translations of each, all facing on the same two pages. The translation is considerably less literal than that of Anderson and Dibble. A certain amount of commentary is provided in an introduction and footnotes. The transcription is fully diplomatic.

Kirchhoff, Paul, Lina Odena Güemes, and Luis Reyes García, eds. 1976. *Historia tolteca-chichimeca.* México: Instituto Nacional de Antropología e Historia.

The so-called *Historia tolteca-chichimeca* is a set of annalistic material from Cuauhtinchan in the eastern part of Nahua territory, with a pronounced and beautiful pictorial element, done probably in the 1560's, most of it referring to the preconquest period. It is notable for being a large-scale treatment of precontact sociocultural matters done without the kind of Spanish supervision so clear in the Florentine Codex. The transcription standardizes somewhat, but you can look directly at the clear writing in the color facsimile. The Spanish translation is as good as can well be achieved with such exotic material.

Bierhorst, John, ed. and trans. 1992. *History and Mythology of the Aztecs: The Codex Chimalpopoca.* Tucson: University of Arizona Press.

_____, ed. 1992. *Codex Chimalpopoca: The Text in Nahuatl with a Glossary and Grammatical Notes.* Tucson: University of Arizona Press.

This is a substantial set, containing two famous and significant writings originally done around 1570 or 80: a set of annals of Quauhtitlan (present Cuauhtitlan), an altepetl north of Mexico City and closely associated with the Mexica, and a mythological text usually called "the legend of the suns." Both deal primarily with preconquest matters. The Nahuatl ranges from straightforward to extremely difficult and metaphorical. The transcription is exceptionally good, retaining not only the original capitalization or lack thereof, the spellings, abbreviations, and diacritics, but even the original punctuation. The translation is superb overall, with of course some of the dubious renderings to be found in any product of this kind done in the present generation; the translator is not very familiar with the corpus of mundane Nahuatl documentation, and that shows at times.

An apparent great disadvantage of the set is that instead of the usual facing transcription and translation, we find the translation in one volume, the Nahuatl text in the other. In fact, however, the situation is far from hopeless. The volumes are compact, so that it is not hard to keep them both open side by side or half overlapping, and they are keyed to each other line for line. There is even the advantage that, once having reviewed the original and the translation of a passage together, the student can wrestle with the Nahuatl in total independence.

Cline, S. L., ed. and trans. 1993. *The Book of Tributes: Early Sixteenth-Century Nahuatl Censuses from Morelos.* UCLA Latin American Center Nahuatl Studies Series, 4. Los Angeles: UCLA Latin American Center Publications.

In the course of these lessons there has been more than one occasion to mention the census and tax records from the Cuernavaca region in the late 1530's and early 1540's, the largest known corpus with Stage 1 characteristics. The material can seem dry and repetitious, but it records one family after another, specifying the names of all members, the relationships between them, their land, and their tax duties. Many of the people were not yet even baptized, much less married in the church. Here we have a large preliminary study together with the transcription and translation of an entire volume of the three extant. The transcription is diplomatic except for resolving overbars.[1]

Anderson, Arthur J. O., and Susan Schroeder, eds. and trans. 1997. *Codex Chimalpahin,* vols. 1 and 2. Norman: University of Oklahoma Press.

The greatest known writer of Nahuatl was an annalist from Amecameca who was active in Mexico City in the early seventeenth century. He was born Domingo Francisco, was called in his prime don Domingo de San Antón, and today is known as Chimalpahin from the name of an alleged ancestor that he took to himself. Much of his most important work was first published by Günter Zimmermann without translation.[2] The present two volumes, with a fully diplomatic transcription and an English translation, contain material in Chimalpahin's hand that was quite recently found. Just how much of it is to be attributed to Chimalpahin, how much is more or less openly copied from others, remains to be seen, but much of it is representative of Chimalpahin's vocabulary and style. The translation is not as literal as Anderson and Dibble's rendering of the Florentine Codex.

A future volume of this set is to include a series of annals entries mainly concerning Mexico City in Chimalpahin's own time, a sort of journal that has come to be known as his *Diario.* The editors and translators will be James Lockhart, Doris Namala, and Susan Schroeder. A preliminary translation has been completed as of this writing.

Chimalpahin, don Domingo Francisco de San Antón Muñón. 1998. *Las ocho relaciones y el memorial de Colhuacan.* 2 vols. Ed. and trans. by Rafael Tena. México: Consejo Nacional para la Cultura y las Artes.

A very large proportion of Chimalpahin's total corpus, with the weight on preconquest times, is contained in this set. The transcription uses modern capitalization and punctuation and resolves overbars and abbreviations, otherwise retaining the original spellings; typographical errors are not lacking, and spacing is not entirely reliable. The translation is far the best of Chimalpahin's work to appear to date in Spanish and very good by any standards; it was reviewed before publication by Luis Reyes.

Anderson, Arthur J. O., Frances Berdan, and James Lockhart, eds. and trans. 1976.

---

[1]See also Elke Hinz, Claudine Hartau, and Marie-Luise Heimann-Koenen, eds. and trans., *Aztekischer Zensus. Zur indianischen Wirtschaft und Gesellschaft im Marquesado um 1540: Aus dem "Libro de Tributos" (Col. Ant. Ms. 551) im Archivo Histórico, México,* 2 vols. (Hanover: Verlag für Ethnologie, 1983). The publication is of the same order of significance and has many of the same characteristics as Cline's (which it does not overlap with as to the original material), but of course the translation and commentary are in German.

Beyond the Codices. Berkeley and Los Angeles: University of California Press and UCLA Latin American Center Publications.

This publication was meant as an introduction to mundane Nahuatl writing. It contains a broad variety of selections from various genres, from the sixteenth, seventeenth, and eighteenth centuries. The texts are all the more valuable because they have been used in subsequent historical scholarship on the Nahuas. The whole area of mundane Nahuatl texts was just being opened up at this time, and the translations contain a certain number of errors discovered since. The transcriptions resolve overbars but are otherwise faithful reflections of the originals. An introduction discusses the corpus generally, but individual documents are not commented upon. Plans exist for a second edition which will retain the same documents and their numbering, correct known translation errors, and provide detailed comments on the texts.

Zapata y Mendoza, don Juan Buenaventura. 1995. *Historia cronológica de la Noble Ciudad de Tlaxcala.* Ed. and trans. by Luis Reyes García and Andrea Martínez Baracs. México: Universidad Autónoma de Tlaxcala and Centro de Investigaciones y Estudios Superiores en Antropología Social.

Writing in the second half of the seventeenth century in Tlaxcala, Zapata was an annalist like Chimalpahin and is the only Nahuatl author who can be put in at all the same class. His large set of annals is here transcribed and translated in its entirety. Some of the Nahuatl is of exceeding difficulty, much of the rest more readily understandable. The transcription resolves abbreviations and overbars and standardizes capitalization but otherwise seems to stick very close to the original. The Spanish translation is excellent, especially for the first rendering of a text of this magnitude, and many of the problems are discussed in notes.

Lockhart, James. 1992. *The Nahuas After the Conquest: A Social and Cultural History of the Indians of Central Mexico, Sixteenth Through Eighteenth Centuries.* Stanford, Calif.: Stanford University Press.

The appendix contains four documents of different types with a fully diplomatic transcription and facing translation. Two of the items supersede versions published earlier in *Beyond the Codices.* One is also in *Nahuas and Spaniards.* The appendix contains no commentary beyond some footnotes, but the texts are frequently referred to in the body of the book.

Reyes García, Luis, ed. and trans. 1978. *Documentos sobre tierras y señorío en Cuauhtinchan.* Colección Científica, Fuentes, Historia Social. México: Centro de Investigaciones Superiores, Instituto Nacional de Antropología e Historia.

Along with Spanish material, this volume includes several documents ranging from historical to mundane and from an early date into the eighteenth century. The transcriptions are good, though somewhat standardized, and the translations are generally excellent.

---

[2]Not until you are very far along should you work with this book, which contains the core of Chimalpahin's legacy: Chimalpahin Quauhtlehuanitzin, don Domingo Francisco de San Antón Muñón, *Die Relationen Chimalpahin's zur Geschichte Mexico's,* ed. by Günter Zimmermann (2 vols. Hamburg: Cram, De Gruyter, 1963–65). Zimmermann first made us see the thrust of Chimalpahin's work by rearranging much of it chronologically by entry. The original groupings, of course, are lost. There is no translation at all, but some footnotes in German address certain puzzling passages and give additional information. The transcription resolves overbars and many abbreviations and changes the punctuation scheme to one approaching the modern. Some of the spacing betrays a misunderstanding of the structure of the Nahuatl. Overall, however, the transcription is reliable. The edition represents a fine opportunity and challenge for the advanced student.

Sullivan, Thelma D. 1987, ed. and trans. *Documentos tlaxcaltecas del siglo XVI en lengua náhuatl.* México: Instituto de Investigaciones Antropológicas, Universidad Nacional Autónoma de México.

This substantial volume consists primarily of transcriptions and translations of sixteenth-century litigation in Nahuatl from Tlaxcala. Written records of Nahuatl litigation being comparatively rare, the volume is valuable on that score alone. The material is often colorful, and preconquest situations are meaningfully reflected in some of the suits. Despite capitalization and resolution of abbreviations, overbars, and other diacritics (of which early Tlaxcalan writing was full), the basic orthography is well retained, and no punctuation is added. The translation is overall excellent and sensitively expressed. The fact that there are some demonstrable errors does not separate this volume from other first-rate works of the kind.

Rojas Rabiela, Teresa, Elsa Leticia Rea López, Constantino Medina Lima, et al., eds. 1999. *Vidas y bienes olvidados: Testamentos indígenas novohispanos.* Vol. 1. México: Centro de Investigaciones y Estudios Superiores en Antropología Social (CIESAS) and Consejo Nacional de Ciencia y Tecnología (CONACYT).

Included in this volume is among other things a collection of over 45 Nahuatl wills and fragments from the Ocotelulco section of Tlaxcala, originally written between 1572 and 1673, with the great majority dating from the last fifteen years of the sixteenth century. They were originally brought together in connection with a lawsuit, so that they have a bit of the sort of coherence seen in the Culhuacan testaments; they combine the advantage of originating in the golden age of high Stage 2 with the novelty of being from the Tlaxcalan region, from which we otherwise have almost everything but a mass of testaments. The transcriptions resolve abbreviations and overbars, respell *v*, and capitalize by modern principles; otherwise the main lines of the original orthography are retained, and very little punctuation is added. Some mistakes have been made in spacing. The Spanish translations are primarily those made at the time, with occasional supplementation by the editors. Like other translations of this kind, the present ones are at the same time very useful, lacking in subtlety, and often incomplete. The materials should be easy for advanced scholars to use and learn virtually everything they need to know. Students will need to exert themselves to question and analyze both transcriptions and translations, but they should be able to do so and to learn much from the experience.

Further volumes in the series are expected.

Horcasitas, Fernando. 1974. *El teatro náhuatl.* México: Universidad Nacional Autónoma de México.

Containing a large number of Nahuatl plays of a religious nature, this is an attractive, significant publication. The transcriptions rest mainly on previous late transcriptions, many of them quite dubious, and in addition the orthography is inconsistently standardized using the modern Mexican system. The translations are reasonable but rather uneven. There is little or no comment on the language proper.

Bautista, fray Juan. 1988. *Huehuehtlahtolli.* Facsimile of the 1600 edition, with introduction by Miguel León-Portilla and transcription and translation by Librado Silva Galeana. México: Comisión Nacional Conmemorativa del V Centenario del Encuentro de Dos Mundos.

In addition to a facsimile of the original work, this publication contains over 200 pages of transcription and translation of the Nahuatl in it, consisting of traditional Nahua speeches of advice by elders to their juniors, with a large element of Christian preaching added. The material is comparable to that in Book Six of the Florentine Codex but generally much less complex, in shorter units, and more readily understandable. The transcription modernizes the orthography and punctuation considerably. The translation is a serious effort, and there are many explanatory notes.

Celestino Solís, Eustaquio, Armando Valencia R., and Constantino Medina Lima, eds. 1985. *Actas de cabildo de Tlaxcala, 1547–1567.* México: Archivo General de la Nación.

A full transcription and translation into Spanish of a unique major documentary corpus. The transcription is somewhat standardized, and the translation has rough edges. It would be well to get to know *The Tlaxcalan Actas,* above, before approaching this work.

Sahagún, fray Bernardino de. 1993. *Psalmodia Christiana (Christian Psalmody).* Ed. and trans. by Arthur J. O. Anderson. Salt Lake City: University of Utah Press.

Adapting the desperately obscure, difficult form and vocabulary of precontact Nahuatl song for Christian hymns, Sahagún composed or had composed by his aides a considerable corpus, and published it in 1583. The material is not inordinately difficult. The transcription is diplomatic, the translation flowing. Commentary and analysis are minimal.

Sahagún, fray Bernardino de. 1986. *Coloquios y doctrina cristiana.* Ed. and trans. by Miguel León-Portilla. México: Universidad Nacional Autónoma de México and Fundación de Investigaciones Sociales, A. C.

In the late sixteenth century Sahagún and his aides composed a dialogue which they imagined to have taken place in 1524 between indigenous Nahua priests and the first Franciscan friars to arrive in Mexico City. To the dialogue proper they appended a general presentation of Christian doctrine; this catechism-like part either was left incomplete or has been partially lost. The luxurious edition of these materials includes a facsimile, a diplomatic transcription, a good translation, and copious explanatory material. In the transcription and translation the words are divided into short lines giving the appearance of verse. Such was not the nature of the original, but you can see that for yourself by looking at the facsimile.

Carrasco, Pedro, and Jesús Monjarás-Ruiz, eds. 1976–78. *Colección de documentos sobre Coyoacán.* 2 vols. México: Centro de Investigaciones Superiores, Instituto Nacional de Antropología e Historia.

Well over half of the documents reproduced in this collection are in Spanish. The second volume contains transcriptions and translations, without comment, of a substantial number of Nahuatl documents originating in Coyoacan, mainly in the sixteenth century. The transcriptions are quite rough and ready. In many cases Spanish translations done at or near the time of the documents are included; though interesting, they are not adequate. When no such translation was available, new ones were provided, and these, apparently done by Luis Reyes, are good. The Nahuatl documents overlap partly with material in *Beyond the Codices* but include items not found there.

Kellogg, Susan, and Matthew Restall, eds. 1998. *Dead Giveaways: Indigenous Testaments of Colonial Mesoamerica and the Andes.* Salt Lake City: University of Utah Press.

The book is an anthology of articles on testaments of indigenous people in various times, places, and languages, with reproduction of sample testaments. Four Nahuatl wills are transcribed and translated with extensive commentary and analysis. The translations (and even the transcriptions) vary greatly in quality. There is much to learn here, but be careful.

Ruiz de Alarcón, Hernando. 1984. *Treatise on the Heathen Superstitions that Today Live Among the Indians Native to this New Spain, 1629.* Trans. and ed. by J. Richard Andrews and Ross Hassig. Norman: University of Oklahoma Press.

The book proper was originally written in Spanish by the secular priest Ruiz de Alarcón. The interest of the publication here stems from Ruiz de Alarcón's inclusion of Nahuatl incantations of preconquest type still preserved among the Nahuas of his time. Ruiz de Alarcón himself hardly understood them. The edition gives the original form of the Nahuatl, which is often quite bizarre, a translation of Ruiz de Alarcón's own translation, then a regularized version of the Nahuatl using the orthography of Andrews' grammar and a new translation of it. The extra transcription and translation are much needed. This is a whole subterranean area of the Nahuatl language with its own vocabulary and almost its own grammar. Extensive introductory commentary and appendixes introduce you to the special religious and botanical terms.[1]

*　　*　　*

And now let us discuss the grammars you should consult. It is not a matter of deciding which is best. As Arthur Anderson used to say, when you are learning the language you profit from reading all the grammars you can get your hands on, and later if you have them on the shelf there is no telling when some obscure matter of interest will turn out to be discussed in one of them that in general wasn't very useful. In the long run, you will use grammars less and less, turning to them only when at the end of your rope, and Carochi will stand out ever more from the rest for the original materials contained there.

Carochi, Horacio. 1983. *Arte de la lengua mexicana con la declaración de los adverbios della.* Facsimile of 1645 edition, with introduction by Miguel León-Portilla. México: Instituto de Investigaciones Filológicas, Instituto de Investigaciones Históricas, Universidad Nacional Autónoma de México.

The grammar of the great Italian Jesuit Horacio Carochi easily eclipses all the others produced in a golden age of Nahuatl philology in the sixteenth and seventeenth centuries. It covers virtually the entire morphology of the language in a subtle, lucid, often definitive fashion. It gains vastly from a unique, extensive discussion of what Carochi calls adverbs—particles, relational words used adverbially, and a host of more or less adverbial expressions. It is made irreplaceable by a very large number of examples in sentence form, culled often from texts now lost and just as often from Carochi's daily conversations with Nahuas. The examples illustrate Carochi's points as nothing else could, and his translations of them and comments on them represent unique subtle analysis of complex Nahuatl sentences by someone who was immersed in the milieu and could question the speakers. Because Carochi marked vowel quantity and glottal stop through diacritics, the only figure of his time to do so at all systematically, the examples are also the source of most of our knowledge today of these important features of older Nahuatl. Even after you reach a high plateau of comprehension of Nahuatl, you will want to keep the Carochi grammar as your primary work of reference for anything that may puzzle you in working with texts.

---

[1] I recommend that you wait before studying John Bierhorst, ed. and trans., *Cantares Mexicanos: Songs of the Aztecs* (Stanford, Calif.: Stanford University Press, 1985). It contains a fine transcription of the largest collection of Nahuatl song, arranged in such a way as to allow the original units to be seen. The translation is often ingenious, and profits from a systematic compilation of similar meanings and expressions for the whole corpus. But it suffers greatly from Bierhorst's belief that the compositions were "ghost songs" like those of the North American plains Indians of the nineteenth century. (See my discussion of Bierhorst's work in Lockhart, *Nahuas and Spaniards*, pp.141–57.) The earlier editions of many Nahuatl songs by Angel María Garibay were transcribed in such a way as to obscure their organization and symmetries utterly. It is my belief that no one in the world can presently translate older Nahuatl song with anything approaching the degree of reliability we can expect for other genres. See my general remarks on the song corpus in Lockhart, *The Nahuas*, pp. 392–401. By all means look at the transcriptions of some of the songs in Bierhorst, but I advise you to leave them largely alone until you are at a very advanced stage in your study of Nahuatl.

For a modern reader, however, the original, even in a clear facsimile, is very hard to use. The print is not easy to read, and when it comes to the tight italics in which the examples are reproduced, problems mount. Only readers with special experience and training are able to grasp the seventeenth-century language and the Latinate grammatical terms readily. In a few aspects, such as his description of Nahuatl phonology and his analysis of the preterit, Carochi has been superseded to the extent that students should not simply absorb his teachings as they can in most of the book. The diacritics are an invaluable resource, but they are anything but consistently used. Only a thorough, systematic, large-scale analysis can arrive at what Carochi really intended in the way of vowel length.

Carochi, Horacio. 2001. *Grammar of the Mexican Language, with an Explanation of its Adverbs.* Bilingual edition by James Lockhart. UCLA Latin American Center Nahuatl Studies Series, 7. Stanford, Calif.: Stanford University Press and UCLA Latin American Center Publications.

In this edition I have attempted to obviate the difficulties mentioned in the preceding paragraph. The original Spanish and Nahuatl are reproduced as exactly as they can be, but more legibly. On facing pages is an English translation of the Spanish; the Nahuatl on this side regularizes the diacritics, as well as altering the spacing whenever Carochi's practice veers from the modern. Extensive footnotes give a more contemporary analysis of matters such as phonology, the history of the language, and the classification of the preterit, and attempt to elucidate Carochi's meaning in cases where it may not be clear. Since many of Carochi's translations of examples are highly compressed, and readers may not quickly see how they correspond to the Nahuatl, some examples are retranslated in footnotes, more fully and literally. Students coming directly from the present set of lessons should find my edition of Carochi immediately intelligible and useful.

Andrews, J. Richard. 1975. *Introduction to Classical Nahuatl.* Austin: University of Texas Press.

Andrews began the rediscovery and reanalysis of Carochi which has been so important in the whole Nahuatl philological movement of the last quarter of the twentieth century. In this work he was the first to publish a version of the definitive classification of the preterit (and of verbs in general), which escaped Carochi because he thought of a word ending in a glottal stop as ending in a vowel. Andrews also systematized and made explicit a crucial, basic aspect of Nahuatl that had been at most implied in Carochi: that every Nahuatl noun bears the subject prefixes exactly like the verbs and that every noun is inherently an equative statement. Andrews goes on to an analysis of morphology at least as complete as Carochi's and even touches somewhat on syntax. He does not, however, go as deeply into the "adverbs."

The problem for beginning or intermediate students attempting to use Andrews is his complex, rigid, forbidding terminology and his equally complex, rigid method of analyzing words. Also, although the order of topics in the book is logical, it is not adapted to pedagogical needs. Some readers are frightened by the massiveness of the book. Experience shows that the insights of Andrews are appreciated mainly by relatively advanced students.

Launey, Michel. 1979. *Introduction à la langue et à la littérature aztèques,* vol. 1: *Grammaire.* Paris: L'Harmattan.

_____. 1992. *Introducción a la lengua y a la literatura náhuatl.* Trans. by Cristina Kraft. México: Universidad Autónoma de México.

Launey's grammar, while on a somewhat less grand scale, has many of the virtues of Andrews without the terminological and other barriers. Launey has a feeling for pedagogy. It is also a plus that he stays closer to Carochi's orthography. If you know some French, you might give this grammar a try at a relatively early stage. If you do not, by all means try the Spanish translation, although it seems to contain a certain number of errors not in the French original.

Campbell, R. Joe, and Frances Karttunen. 1989. *Foundation Course in Nahuatl Grammar*. 2 vols. Austin: Institute of Latin American Studies, University of Texas at Austin.

Intended for an intensive summer course, this set of lessons covers all of the basics of Nahuatl morphology and some of the subtleties, and it explains phonological aspects fully. The presentation is lucid, pedagogically excellent. A vast number of exercises are included, with a key in the second volume. Students at the beginning and intermediate levels could profit greatly from the book. Most of the vocabulary and virtually all of the general structures described apply to older Nahuatl, but some of the syntax used does not. You will find particles regularly placed after verbs, contrary to older Nahuatl practice, forms of questions not used in older Nahuatl, and other things never seen in older texts.

Olmos, fray Andrés de. 1972. *Arte para aprender la lengua mexicana*. Ed. by Rémi Siméon. Facsimile of 1875 Paris edition, with prologue by Miguel León-Portilla. Guadalajara: Edmundo Aviña Levy Editor.

Olmos was the first Spanish grammarian of Nahuatl whose work has come down to us, and he is also among those whose analyses we can still take seriously today. The presentations here fade in comparison with Carochi, but the experienced scholar of Nahuatl will find useful examples and some interesting individual insights. All in all, this item is more likely to confuse than to help the relative neophyte.

Molina, fray Alonso de. 1945. *Arte de la lengua mexicana y castellana*. Facsimile edition. Madrid: Ediciones Cultura Hispánica.

Published in 1571, the same year as his great *Vocabulario*, this work is, as a grammar, a slight and rudimentary work, less distinguished and less comprehensive than the grammar of Olmos. Also, the facsimile is quite hard for the uninitiated to read. Nevertheless, the work contains some interesting examples and insights of the author on certain grammatical points and especially on pronunciation/orthography. Like the Olmos grammar, this publication is mainly for the advanced.

Anderson, Arthur J. O. 1973. *Rules of the Aztec Language: A Translation with Modifications of Francisco Xavier Clavigero's* Reglas de la lengua mexicana. Salt Lake City: University of Utah Press.

Clavigero's eighteenth-century grammar is one of the latest and slightest of the Jesuit descendants of Carochi, all trying in some way to simplify. The short chapters are fragmentary and many of the statements made are prima facie misleading. Despite a few changes, Anderson did not basically alter the nature of Clavigero's work. The book is, however, in a readable English. Its main use would be as a review of certain grammatical elements after one has already achieved a good grasp elsewhere.

Garibay K., Angel María. 1970. *Llave del náhuatl: Colección de trozos clásicos, con gramática y vocabulario, para utilidad de los principiantes*. 3rd. ed. México: Porrúa.

The work begins with a 117-page "Noticia gramatical" which touches in some fashion on most of the basic matters of Nahuatl grammar, extending even to syntax, but in such chaotic, undeveloped fashion and with so many out-and-out errors, some of them egregious and of large implications, that scholars of Nahuatl at any level would hardly turn to it for instruction today. Nevertheless, the book had a great impact in its time (the first edition came out in 1940). It was my own first text. Moreover, despite frequent mistakes and highly arbitrary procedures, Garibay did in his way understand the language very well and had some notions ahead of his time. For example, he was on the verge of grasping that any Nahuatl noun is in principle an equative statement. An experienced student who has quite fully mastered Nahuatl grammar as it is understood today can gain something from reading Garibay's grammatical section, concentrating on the examples he gives and carrying on an internal critique of the more general statements.

A number of selections from well known annals and song collections are less treacherous ground for the student, but the transcriptions evince arbitrary and inconsistent practices of spelling, spacing, and punctuation, involving partial modernization, so that the neophyte can easily be thrown off, and the same is true to a lesser extent of the translations. It is best to avoid the book's glossary entirely.

The reader must be able to separate an appreciation of the work's vast importance in the revival of Nahuatl studies in the twentieth century from its manifest, indeed grotesque failings seen in the light of the attainments of either Carochi and Molina or today's Nahuatl grammarians and philologists.

Sullivan, Thelma D. 1976. *Compendio de la gramática náhuatl.* México: Instituto de Investigaciones Histórica, Universidad Nacional Autónoma de México.

This book (although Andrews' *Introduction to Classical Nahuatl* appeared one year earlier) precedes the late twentieth-century revolution in Nahuatl grammar based on a full understanding of Carochi and a wider reading of texts. One could say indeed that it is the best grammar produced between 1800 and the onset of that revolution. But from the perspective of today's scholarship it contains shocking errors (maintaining that *quauhtli* has an [au] diphthong in it, that *tecutli* contains a [u] vowel followed by a glottal stop, that *ihuan* is a conjunction, that *ça* and *çan* are the same, etc.); the verb classes are unrecognized, and indeed the book is weak in any kind of useful generalization. Nevertheless, Sullivan was a true expert on the Nahuatl of the sixteenth century, especially the traditional corpus of formal texts with preconquest emphasis, of which the Florentine Codex is the greatest. The grammar abounds in paradigms which taken individually are correct and helpful, and above all in illuminating examples consisting of phrases, clauses, and passages, mainly taken directly from the texts she specialized in, well and idiomatically translated.

Appendix 1
The Dictionaries and How to Use Them

THROUGHOUT THESE LESSONS I have hammered at the importance of being able to find things in the dictionary. The emphasis has been on how to analyze strings of letters in order to be able to reconstruct citation forms, beginning with the inflected forms found in texts. A complementary skill, hardly less essential, is to know how to find your way around in the dictionaries. Perhaps the following discussion of the dictionaries available, with some hints as to their nature and special qualities, can get you started.

Molina's *Vocabulario* is in a class by itself, if only because it was done in the sixteenth century, and other dictionaries have to depend on it. Most students of older Nahuatl in the end use Molina far more than any other dictionary. If you are going to continue your Nahuatl studies, you have no alternative to acquiring a copy of Molina. The book is periodically reprinted in Mexico, but it also periodically becomes rare, and in this country expensive. No matter, it is worth whatever trouble and expense you have to go to. Some students have photocopied the Nahuatl-to-Spanish half of the book as a stopgap measure, and even that form has served them well.

1. Molina's *Vocabulario.*

This large compilation of 1571, containing a first section with entries from Spanish to Nahuatl and a second section from Nahuatl to Spanish, grew out of an earlier publication going from Spanish to Nahuatl only. By the time of its appearance the Franciscan fray Alonso de Molina, who himself had grown up in Mexico and was surely one of the two or three Spaniards in the country who understood Nahuatl best, had been working with Nahua consultants for at least a couple of decades. The coverage, authenticity, and correctness of the work are astounding. Despite its auspices it has no notable ecclesiastical bias. To this day our best hope of understanding a rare meaning in a Nahuatl text is to find something related to it in Molina. Of course, anything new happening after the publication date will not be reflected. Things as common in the Nahuatl of Stages 2 and 3 as *pia* to mean "to have" and *huiquilia* to mean "to owe" are not to be found in Molina. One is constantly surprised, though, how often a puzzling term in an eighteenth-century text can be elucidated by some sixteenth-century Molina entry.

Most of us use Molina's dictionary in the 1970 Mexican edition, which has often been reprinted: fray Alonso de Molina, *Vocabulario en lengua castellana y mexicana y mexicana y castellana* (1571) (México: Porrúa). This edition is sometimes called a facsimile, and it is, in the sense that the contents of the individual columns and pages are the same as in the original, that all spelling, spacing, and punctuation reproduces the original exactly, that even original typographical errors are reproduced, but the book is not a photographic facsimile. It has been reprinted with a type face much more readily readable than that of the original. The one problem that neophytes sometimes have is that they think the high *s* used in the Spanish is an *f*: if you will look closely, you will see that the *s* is crossed only on the left side (and lightly), the *f* only on the right.

In the majority of his conventions, Molina agrees with Carochi and the standard orthography employed in this volume. Among other things, he uses *c/ç/z* for [s] (*centli*, "ear of maize"; *çacatl*, "grass, straw"; *oninez*, "I appeared"); *qu* for [kʷ] before *a* (*tlaqualli*, "food") and *cu* for [kʷ] before *e* and *i* (*cueitl*, "skirt"; *cui*; "to take"); *i* for the syllabic vowel [i] (*iuh*, "thus") and *y* for the glide [y] (*ye*, "already");[1] *uh* for syllable-final [w] (*onicchiuh*, "I did it"). He takes no account of vowel length. Overall, you should feel quite at home.

Some differences, however, may cause you trouble for a while. Syllable-final [kʷ] is *cu*, not *uc: necutli*, "honey." Like many of the earlier Nahuatl philologists, Molina writes [w] before a vowel as *u*, not *hu*. *Chihua*, "to do, make," will be *chiua*. When the [w] is word-initial, it is written *v* (still pronounced [w]), as in *vel* for *huel*, the intensifier. But sometimes *hu* will be found too, mainly after a consonant; it is regularly seen after *l*, as in *ilhuitl*, "day," and Molina has *ithualli*, "patio." We also find the independent pronouns with *hu* (*nehuatl*, etc.); possibly here the *h* represents the glottal stop after the *e*.

For although in general Molina does not notate the presence of a glottal stop, he occasionally does so with an *h*. This occurs most often between two vowels (*aehecatl*, "wind that brings a rainstorm or comes from the sea"; *yehica*, "wherefore"), but even in such cases the *h* by no means always appears (*eecatl*, "wind").

Molina's largest deviance from Carochi and from most Stage 2 Nahuatl writing is that for Carochi's two representations, *oa* and *ohua*, he has only one, *oa*. He was right that there was no real difference in pronunciation, but he was going against the stream of orthography in ecclesiastical circles, where the distinction was maintained based on whether a [w] showed up in some other form of the word or not, and also contrary to practice in mundane Nahuatl writing, which used both representations almost indifferently, with *ohua* predominating. At any rate, if anything is written *ohua* in Carochi, in this book, or in a text, it will be found with *oa* in Molina. Our *pohua*, "to read, count, etc.," corresponds to Molina's *poa*; our *cohua*, "to buy," to Molina's *coa*. The convention is carried out consistently in all related forms; *tlapohualli*, "count, something counted or told," will be *tlapoalli*.

With *ia* and *iya* Molina does exactly the same thing, i.e., he writes only *ia*, but that doesn't strike us as different because Carochi, ecclesiastical circles in general, and our orthographic standard here all follow that convention too. No one including Molina is absolutely consistent with it. When it comes to *io* and *iyo*, Molina joins the others in often preferring *io* but also using *iyo* (see his entry *çaniyo* and just below it another, *çanio*, saying that the two are the same).

As was already mentioned in the body of the lessons, Molina mainly writes *o* for Nahuatl's [o], but also sometimes *u*; he has both *xochitl* and *xuchitl*, "flower." The common *tepoztli*, "metal, iron, copper," is under *tepuztli* only. A *u* for [w] will always be followed by a vowel; this syllabic *u* will almost always be followed by a consonant.

In spacing Molina is quite inconsistent; sometimes he approaches modern standards, printing each smallest particle separately, but just as often, more in the vein of his own time, he runs particles together with one another and with the following nuclear word. Thus we see *çanyenoyehuatl* for what would appear here as *çan ye no yehuatl*, "the same one." On the same page, *çanic nemi intenauatia* is glossed as "a boss who is constantly giving many orders"; as almost always, Molina is right, but the Nahuatl is actually a sentence which would be written here as *çan ic nemi in tenahuatia*, "he lives just therewith that he orders people," i.e., "all he is engaged in is giving orders, or all he does is give orders." There is an entry *inaxcan*, "now," and another *iniquac*, "when."

The most special feature of Molina's entries is his manner of citing verbs. The present-tense form of the body of the verb, which amounts to the root, is given first. Then, after a period (with or without a space), come the relevant prefixes, using the first person as one does with Latin, except when the verb or that meaning of the verb never occurs in the first person. If the verb is intransitive, only *n(i)* will be given. If it is transitive, an object prefix will be added: *nic*,[2] or *nitla*, or *nite*. In the case of *nite* we know for sure that this verb

---

[1] Occasionally *y* is found for the syllabic vowel, for example three times in *Yauh ytlaqual yn tanima.*, "the sustenance of our souls (lit. the water and food of our soul)."

[2] This may be *niqu* if *e* or *i* follows, thus *Itta. niqu.* "to see something."

or this use of the verb has only people as objects; *nic* usually means that the object can be either a person or a thing, and *nitla* should mean that the object can only be a thing, but in fact that doesn't quite work out. If the verb or that use of the verb is reflexive without any other object, Molina will put *nin(o)*. If it takes both a normal object prefix and a reflexive, the entry will have *nicno* or sometimes *ninote* or *ninotla*. Needless to say, we are expected to turn the entries around, to understand that *Nemi. ni.* will appear in utterances as *ninemi*, "I live," etc.[1]

Neci. ni. to appear.	intransitive
Cui. nic. to take something or someone.	transitive, presumably any kind of object
Tequi.nitla. to cut something.	transitive, presumably nonhuman object
Tlaçotla. nite. to love someone.	transitive, human object
Eua. nin. to get up from sleep, etc.	reflexive
Maceuia. ninotla. to attain something.	two objects, one of them reflexive

If a verb or a meaning of a verb occurs only in the third person, no subject prefix will be given. If the subject must be plural, the prefix will usually be *ti*. If the verb or the use of the verb is reflexive and always in the third person, the entry is most likely to appear under *mo*, not under the verb proper followed by *mo*.

Cepayaui. for it to snow.
Cepanoa,tito. for people to unite in friendship or agreement.
Monequi. to be necessary.

With this manner of citation, basically the same verb may appear three, four, or many more times consecutively, perhaps once with a human object, once with a nonhuman object, once reflexive, and then as involved in various idiomatic expressions and in derived forms. Newcomers to Molina may look at only one entry, find that it doesn't match their need, and give up, when the right answer is only a line or two away. Once you are accustomed to Molina's style, you will realize that it is extremely convenient. Here is what you will find under *Eua*.

Eua. nic. to be able to lift something.
Eua. amonic. not to be able to lift something.
Eua. nin. to get up from sleep or from lying down.
Eua. nite. to lift someone who is lying.
Eua. non. to depart for someplace.
Eua. n. for a bird to rise in flight.
Eua .noquich. to attack valiantly.
Eua. nouic. for something to disgust someone, for food to nauseate a sick person.
Eua. tecan. to rush against someone. (The whole expression equals *teca neua*.)
Eua. nitenauatit. for one who is departing or dying to leave something ordered. (I.e., here *eua* is an auxiliary; the main verb is *nauatia*.)
Eua. quitot. for a person in that condition to leave something said. (This time the third person is used.)
Eua. teuicn. the same thing as *teca neua*.
Eua. teuann. to be a partisan, belong to a party.

At this point you will be tempted to stop, for the next several entries are based on the nominal root *ehua-*, Molina's *eua-*, having to do with skin, leather, bark, etc. But a little further on, interspersed with more "skin" entries, comes the following:

---

[1]The procedure of reproducing elisions, as in *Eua. n.*, can lead to the loss of a vowel at the beginning of a verb root and an alphabetization of the word where you would never expect it. The important verb *itlacoa*, "to harm, spoil, ruin, do wrong, mess up," appears once as *Tlacoa.nitla*, because its initial *i* is in fact normally elided after *tla-*; fortunately there is also an entry *Itlacoa. nitla*. But *itzoma*, "to sew something," appears only as *Tzoma.nitla*.

Eualtia.nite. to pursue someone, denigrate a favor received.
Eualtia. nitla. to make something leave, or to dispatch bearers, and the like. (*-tla* despite usual-
ly specifying a nonhuman object can refer to a whole human group.)
Euatica. n. to be seated.
Euatiquetza . nitla. to raise something, like a banner or pole.
Euatitlalia . nin. for someone lying in bed to rise in order to take a seat.
Euatitlalia . nitla. the same as *euatiquetza.*

And many entries later,

Euhteua. n. to leave for someplace quickly.
Euhteua. nin. to rise from bed quickly.

Molina's verb entries end by giving the preterit form, with the same prefixes as at the
head of the entry, but this time turned around, in the normal speech order.

for *cui*, "to take something"	*pre.oniccuic.*
for *chiua*, "to make, do something"	*pret. onicchiuh.*
for *itoa*, "to say something"	*Pret. oniquito.*
for *qua*, "to eat something"	*Preteri. onitlaqua.*

You will notice that the four verbs just cited belong respectively to Classes 1, 2, 3, and 4.
Thus you not only learn exactly what form the preterit takes but, by in effect being told
the class, you can predict what form the verb will take in other tenses. In this way Molina
disambiguates some uncertainties left by his practice of writing only *oa* where we are
used to two spellings, *oa* and *ohua*. The entry *nemoa*, the impersonal of *nemi*, "to live," by
its initial appearance might be a Class 3 *oa* verb. But when we read *Pre. onemoac* we see
that it belongs to Class 1 and will soon realize that it is an impersonal in unreducing
-hua. *Poa*, "to count," looks like a Class 3 verb initially, but its preterit *onicpouh* reveals
that it belongs to Class 2.

Nouns are generally listed in their simplest form, the third-person singular absolutive, and in that case they present little problem, as with the word for "house," listed
predictably as *Calli*. Difficulties arise because certain Nahuatl words are virtually
always possessed, and Molina is likely to list them in that form, under *te-*, "someone's,"
n(o)-, "my," *t(o)-*, "our," or even *i-*, "his/her/its" or *im-/in*, "their." Thus the word for
"spouse" is listed not as *Namictli* but as *Tenamic*, "someone's spouse." The common
deverbal noun *-nenca*, "one's sustenance," is listed as *Nonenca* and *Tonenca* only. Body
parts are often under *to-*, sometimes *no-*. The Spanish loanword *anima*, "soul," which
was treated essentially as a body part, appears as *Tanima* and *Teanima*, but not as
Anima. Try looking for the root anyway, for quite often Molina goes against usage and
lists the absolutive singular in the name of convenience, as with *Tatli*, "father," despite
the fact that you can read hundreds of pages of Nahuatl without ever seeing such a form.
(*Tetatzin* is also an entry.) Sometimes the possessive form is used, but even so the word is
listed under the root, with the possessive prefix afterward, as with the verbs. (*Nencauh.
no.*"my servant.") If this had been the normal procedure, things would have been
considerably simpler for us.

Absolutive plurals and to an extent possessed and combining forms of Nahuatl nouns
are not predictable, but these aspects of nouns are not given as part of the entry, as the
preterit is with verbs. Sometimes the absolutive plural, especially if it is unusual, is given
in a separate entry. Thus *Teotl.* "god" is one entry, and *Teteo.* "gods," alphabetized in its
proper place pages later, is another. The same thing sometimes happens with possessed
forms. *Maitl*, "hand/arm," appears separately as *Maytl*, *Noma*, and *Toma*. Sometimes
the gloss varies considerably between the absolutive form and the possessed form, as
with *Tequitl.* "tribute or work," and *Notequiuh.* "my charge or office." At any rate, despite

useful windfalls you cannot depend on getting information on plurals or possessed forms, and the only way you can find out about combining forms is if a compound using the word you are interested in appears in an entry. Thus from *Camapiqui. nino.* "to close the mouth," we know that the combining form of *camatl*, "mouth," is *cama-* even though the possessed form is *-can* (a fact we cannot verify in Molina).

What we often consider to be adjectives are treated in every way like nouns, as indeed they are in Nahuatl itself, whether they are morphologically normal noun words or agentives: *Qualli.* "a good thing"; *Tomauac.* "a fat, thick, or corpulent thing."

Particles present few difficulties; since they do not vary in shape, they are easy to find. Even when they are part of complex expressions, they usually come first and are found where you expect them. One thing to watch for is that many words which introduce dependent clauses are under the *in* that always precedes them, as *Inaxcan.* "now." Many particles and adverbial expressions will likewise be found under *ça* and *çan,* "only."

Distributives are listed as separate entries, alphabetized however they fall: thus *Oome.* "each two, or two at a time, or two to each one."

Relational words, always possessed or combined with a noun in usage, are rarely alphabetized under the root in Molina. We do find the instrumental *-ca,* simply called a "preposition"; glosses are under *Ica, Noca,* and *Teca. -Nahuac* is for once *Nauac. no.* "near me or with me," although we see *Inauac.* and *Tenauac* as well. Generally speaking, relational words will be found under *i-, no-, to-,* and *te-,* the third person singular, first person singular, first person plural, and indefinite personal possessive prefixes respectively.

Merely finding a relational word is not the point. Molina's glosses of words of this type are not very enlightening, and a brief gloss can rarely do them justice in any case. To get the simple meaning of a relational word—which in most cases you probably already know—you had better go elsewhere, best of all to Karttunen's dictionary and then the appropriate sections of Carochi's grammar. Idiomatic use is what we are seeking here. Molina often gives us a large set of idioms in which the relational word is used in conjunction with a verb or sometimes a noun to give a meaning that would be hard or impossible to deduce from the roots alone. *-Tech,* the general connector, is used in a welter of idioms, many of which are listed under *Itech, Notech,* and especially *Tetech. -Pan,* "on, in, for, etc.," is almost as rich, under *Ipan, Nopan, Topan, Tepan.*

The entire dictionary is full of idiomatic expressions listed under whatever word and whatever form of that word they happen to start with. Many of them we find mainly by good fortune. Under *Q* is *Quinepanoa yn noyollo.* "to attain certainty on something one had been in doubt about, or to hit upon something one had forgotten." Under *O* is *Oticmihiouilti.* "Welcome!" But we are helped by the nature of Nahuatl word order, which as we have seen likes to put adverbial expressions and any small elements in front of the nuclear complex. That is why so many idioms appear under the possessed forms of the relational words. Certain other short words also typically begin idioms, so that collections can be found under them, for example *atle,* "nothing," and *aquen,* a negative hard to get a sense of except by looking at the expressions in which it appears. The words *-yol* and *-yollo,* literally "heart" but often used for the mind, the emotions, and volition, figure in a large number of Nahuatl idioms. You will find a group of eleven of them in Molina under *Noyol* and *Noyollo.*

With experience you will get a feeling for, or perhaps a subliminal memory of, such caches and many other aspects of this remarkable work. One part of the education of an expert in older Nahuatl is to read through Molina's *Vocabulario* much as you would read through a grammar or a text, absorbing not only the lexical content but lore about the book and Molina's procedures. Over the years you may do it several times.

Of course once you have found the right entry, you still have to understand Molina's gloss. People who have reasonable Spanish, and as I have said before virtually all who try to learn Nahuatl do, usually get seventy-five or eighty percent of Molina's sixteenth-century Spanish from the start. But for one who knows only the modern form of the language much remains hidden, or may not mean what it seems to. Whenever you have doubts, look in any modern Spanish dictionary, which will contain many of the less common terms and meanings. Others, however, have entirely disappeared. Some of them can be found in the three-volume *Diccionario de autoridades,* a facsimile of an eighteenth-century set published in 1984 by Editorial Gredos, Madrid. When searching in recent dictionaries, remember to convert Molina's ç to z and to experiment with his b/v and consonant u, which may convert into either b or v in modern Spanish. He often omits an initial h now seen on a word or has an h now missing.

Note that Molina uses some Latin words in his glosses; the most common are *vel,* "or" (exactly the same way he writes the Nahuatl particle *huel*); *idem,* "the same," and *et sic de aliis,* "and the same way concerning other things." This he uses when instead of an analytical definition of a word he gives an example of its use, relying on the reader to imagine other similar examples. (He writes &c with the same meaning.) You will also frequently see an s. or .s. which apparently stands for *scilicet,* "if you will." At any rate, he uses it before remarks clarifying the previous part of the gloss; often it would translate best as "for example."

Once you understand how Molina writes words, puts them into entries, and glosses them, you still must know how he alphabetizes. The overall order he uses is the one we all use today, with one major exception; y is equated with i, and both come in the order at the point where we expect i. Like modern practice in English and unlike Spanish practice today, Molina's alphabetization ignores digraphs. Today in a Spanish dictionary there is a whole section for words beginning ch as opposed to c, and even word-internally ch is placed after c. In Molina ch is simply among the c's, and any word containing ch is alphabetized after a similar word containing ce and before one containing ci. Tl and tz get the same treatment, so that the t section takes up a huge proportion of the whole work. We today are not familiar with ç; Molina includes it with but after c. At the beginning of words he sometimes proceeds in blocks: a whole list of words in ca, for example, then a whole list in ça. Other times ç is interspersed word by word among the c's accordingly as the individual letters fall. The reader has to be prepared for both possibilities. Take advantage of the headings to each page which categorize the contents of the page, like "Q. ANTE VI, ET T ANTE A." (Note that the v here means u—u is automatically printed as v when it is capitalized or word-initial—and the et is Latin "and.")

Everything said so far concerns the second, Nahuatl-to-Spanish section, which we use infinitely more than the first, Spanish-to-Nahuatl section. If you own a Molina for some years, you will begin to see the second section get tattered and discolored while the first remains pristine. Nevertheless, the first section has important uses once you have come to know Nahuatl and Molina better. When you are more advanced, you can read straight through the first section and gain as much as with the second. The two parts have different histories and are far from mirror images of each other. The greatest utility of the first section is to check out hunches. Suppose you have formed from its context a theory of what a particular word means but cannot locate it in the second section, either because it is actually not there or because you haven't hit on Molina's way of putting it into an entry. When I was first beginning, working with Frances Berdan on the will of the Tlax-calan lord don Julián de la Rosa, it became clear from repeated occurrences that something like *namictli* must mean "wife" or "spouse," but we didn't yet know about *te-*. We could have found out what we needed by looking under *Esposo.* and *Esposa.* in the first section of the *Vocabulario*. (In fact, we were enlightened directly by Arthur Anderson.) Since then I have often used the first section as a tool in achieving a final solution to half-resolved puzzles. You must be sure to try all the related Spanish vocabulary you can think of, remembering the vagaries of Molina's Spanish orthography.

2. Siméon's *Dictionnaire*.

Siméon, Rémi. 1963. *Dictionnaire de la langue nahuatl ou mexicaine*. Facsimile of the 1885 edition. Graz, Austria: Akademischer Druck- u. Verlagsanstalt.

_____. 1977. *Diccionario de la lengua náhuatl o mexicana*. Trans. by Josefina Oliva de Coll. México: Siglo Veintiuno.

With entries from Nahuatl to French only (and in the 1977 edition to Spanish), this work is overwhelmingly based on Molina's *Vocabulario*, apparently the Nahuatl-to-Spanish section exclusively. A small number of additions come from the grammars of Carochi and Olmos, Sahagún's Florentine Codex, and lesser miscellaneous sources.

The orthography of Molina is preserved intact. Some attempt was made to rationalize Molina's use of syllabic *u*; for example, Siméon consolidates Molina's *xochitl* and *xu-chitl* entries into one under *xochitl* (still giving the *u* variant). But *tepoztli* appears as *tepuztli* only. In respect to orthography, then, you can proceed as if you were using Molina. Siméon also employs largely the same manner of alphabetization, including putting *y* in with *i*. The only difference is that he treats *ç* consistently, in the French manner, interspersing the *ç* among the *c* in detail; i.e., *çan* comes immediately after *can* and is followed by *cana*. Siméon also keeps Molina's entire apparatus for citing verbs with their prefixes and giving their preterits.

By this time you may wonder if there are any substantial differences between Molina and Siméon at all. The one large, basic, obvious difference is that Siméon changes Molina's atomistic entry policy in favor of consolidation of all or at least most uses of a word in a single entry, much as most modern dictionaries do. Under a given verb you will find both its simple transitive and its reflexive form, if it has both, plus any other prefix combination it manifests, followed by idiomatic expressions it is involved in. In a way things are made much easier; with a verb like *mati*, "to know," idioms in Molina under *tetech*, *ipan*, *aquen*, *iuh*, and many other initial words are consolidated, brought together in one place. In searching for an idiom in Siméon one must take its nuclear words, its verbs and nouns, as the handle, not its particles and relational words as with Molina. Siméon's method seems to have obvious practical advantages, but my own experience and my vicarious experience through students is that, confronted with an entry half a column, a column, or a column and a half long, not typographically differentiated, not alphabetically organized, you are even more likely to miss things than in Molina.

Siméon changes Molina's policy of citing relational words and many nouns under their possessed forms. -*Namic*, "spouse," will be found under *namictli*; Molina's *Tenamic* is abandoned. -*Tech*, "next to, etc.," is listed as *tech* and given a definition fuller than in Molina, but all the other ramifications of the word, its uses in holding a hundred idioms together, are lost. The phrases listed in Molina under whatever word or prefix comes first are rearranged under major words they contain. Often, however, they are simply lost. Molina's invaluable *Oticmihiouilti*. "Welcome!" should be in Siméon under his *ihiouia* or *ihiouiltia*, but it is not.

People react differently to the Molina and Siméon systems. Some have become so used to modern dictionary organization that they always continue to prefer Siméon. Others immediately prefer Molina. Most who become expert in older Nahuatl find Siméon useful for a year or two and then gradually go over to using primarily Molina. I was surprised not long ago to read a statement by Arthur Anderson that he wasn't quite sure whether

Molina or Siméon was best. I do know from personal observation that his copy of Molina was much more bedraggled. I myself use Siméon only when I am desperate.

A major problem with Siméon is that being a great pioneer with no immediate antecedents, he was just beginning to reconstitute the lore of Nahuatl grammar. He edited Olmos, rediscovered Carochi and Sahagún, and translated some of Chimalpahin, but the grammatical sketch at the beginning of his dictionary is awkward, sometimes in out-and-out error. Siméon's project of listing the constituent roots of compound words in his entries was a good one, but he made many, many errors in root identification. Some of the glosses too seem misleading. They are in any case for the most part French translations of Molina's originals by a person who had little or no other knowledge about the word involved than Molina's gloss. The upshot is that when you are doing serious research or translation you almost always want to go back and check what Molina says on the matter, so that in the end you are not saved a search through Molina after all.

If you are not very familiar with French, you can turn to the Spanish translation of Siméon. The problem is that though it is a good translation in modern Spanish, it re-translates from French a translation from Molina's original sixteenth-century Spanish and gets even more distant from the original gloss. It does appear that sometimes the translator went back to Molina for guidance, but a large element of uncertainty remains. The Spanish edition can, however, be very helpful to students during the early stages.

3. Karttunen's *Analytical Dictionary*.

Karttunen, Frances. 1983. *An Analytical Dictionary of Nahuatl.* Austin: University of Texas Press. (Reprinted in 1992 by University of Oklahoma Press, Norman.)

The primary purpose of this very useful work, which if you continue to study Nahuatl you should acquire, is to record attested vowel quantity and glottal stop in Nahuatl words, since Molina and Siméon (along with the whole Nahuatl writing tradition) ignore vowel length entirely and notate only a few cases of glottal stop. Karttunen used Carochi's grammar—a great mine of attestations—and a manuscript written in Carochi's circle (published as *The Art of Nahuatl Speech*, ed. by Karttunen and Lockhart, described in the epilogue), plus two modern local dictionaries, to make dictionary entries for all words therein attested with the relevant data (entries in the other direction, starting with English, were not called for). It proved possible to include nearly all of the more common roots and many quite rare items, but the coverage is of course far more limited than in Molina or Siméon. Even though vowel length and glottal stop hardly surface in the corpus of Nahuatl writing, almost all of us who work with that corpus sooner or later come to realize the importance of these matters, and to learn about them this dictionary is the principal work of reference.

The entries are set up following modern lexical principles and are self-explanatory. Possessed nouns and relational words are listed under the root; particle clusters are listed under the first particle, written solid. Some absolutive plurals and possessed and combining forms are specified in the noun entries. The reflexive and simple transitive versions of a verb are both treated within a single entry, but the entries are concise, not becoming seas of confusion as in Siméon. As one would expect from the basic nature of the work, it does not include many idiomatic expressions of sentence length.

Many of the glosses (which are given in both English and the usually original Spanish) go back to Molina, but an important contribution of this dictionary is that Karttunen explored Carochi's grammar exhaustively, including his large and rich section on "adverbs," and delivers many items and meanings from that source not present in Molina and Siméon. Even if you have a Molina, you would be well advised to look here first for particles and relational words. Karttunen also integrates words and meanings from modern dictionaries of Tetelcingo and Zacapoaxtla, some of which are relevant for working with older texts.

Karttunen uses an orthography first developed by J. Richard Andrews; it will be discussed here because Karttunen's dictionary supersedes the glossary of Andrews' grammar as a work of reference. Much is the same as in the standard orthography used here. In accordance with modern Mexican principles of transcription, based on practice in modern Spanish, [s] before [a] and [o] is written z, not ç; *çacatl* is *zacatl* here, *çoquitl zoquitl*. The sound [kʷ] is written as *cu*, not *qu*, before [a]; you will see *tlacualli*, not *tlaqualli*. In matters more internal to the writing of Nahuatl, *ia/iya* is treated the same as *oa/ohua*; i.e., if evidence of [y] shows up in some form of the root, *y* is written throughout; instead of *pia* and *chia* you will see *piya* and *chiya*. The glottal stop is consistently written as *h*, the same representation adopted in these lessons whenever a glottal stop is notated. A macron over a vowel says that it is long; the lack of one says it is short. A weak vowel, one which is dropped when adjacent to another vowel in an affix or a bound form, is put in parentheses.

Alphabetization is generally the same as in modern English; *y* comes before *z*, not with *i* as in Molina and Siméon. The greatest difficulty is that the glottal stop *h* counts in alphabetizing an item. Words beginning with four digraphs, *ch*, *cu*, *tl*, and *tz*, have been separated out and put in sections like those devoted to the single letters. This distinction, however, does not carry on into the entry lists inside sections, which are arranged strictly by the alphabetical order of individual letters as in English.

The work is overall highly reliable as well as easily usable. Some specifications of vowel length may be erroneous because of the occasional necessity of relying on extremely few attestations, and some English glosses are opaque or wrong, often because of the same qualities in the sources. Karttunen analyzes the final vowel of Class 3 verbs as long on the basis of the indisputable fact that it is long in the imperfect and the customary present. I disagree with the analysis, however, finding that the final *a* otherwise behaves like a short vowel (i.e., it is often omitted) and that analysis shows the preceding vowel more likely to have been long historically. The long *a* in the two exceptional forms could be explained by quantity metathesis and by the influence of Class 4.[1]

4. Campbell's *Morphological Dictionary.*

Campbell, R. Joe. 1985. *A Morphological Dictionary of Classical Nahuatl: A Morpheme Index to the* Vocabulario en lengua mexicana y castellana *of fray Alonso de Molina.* Madison: The Hispanic Seminary of Medieval Studies.

This huge work (nearly 500 8½ by 11 pages in two columns of small print) lists everything in the Nahuatl-to-Spanish section of Molina's *Vocabulario* by root. Each entry contains every single instance of the use of that root in the whole second section of Molina, arranged alphabetically according to however it appears in the original. Each subentry consists of Molina's original Nahuatl, a full breakdown into its morphological components, a translation of Molina's gloss into English, and a reproduction of Molina's Spanish gloss.

The book is potentially as useful as it is big. For one thing, those dubious about the meaning of any of Molina's glosses, and we all are sometimes, can see how they are rendered into English by an expert in both Spanish and Nahuatl who is deeply familiar with Molina.[2] The greatest potential advantage is that Campbell offers a virtually fool-

---

[1]See my detailed discussion in Lockhart, *Of Things of the Indies* (Stanford: Stanford University Press, 1999), pp. 294–98.

[2]Though the translations are overwhelmingly correct, Campbell is no more immune to error in

proof way of finding a given word or expression in Molina, if it is in the second section at all. Nouns normally possessed are listed under the third person singular absolutive form.[3] Relational words are listed under the root, and with them all the idioms including them. If you run into some form of the expression -tech huetzi in noyollo, "to become enamored of someone or something," you can be sure of finding it under tech, uetzi, and yollotli.

Orthographically, Campbell changes ç into z but retains, as far as I can see, all of Molina's other spellings, including qu before a, and in the subentries he also leaves Molina's spacing unchanged. No attempt is made to indicate vowel length and glottal stop, and indeed it would be impossible, for in many cases the information is not available. Campbell realphabetizes y to its usual place according to modern practice, creating a section for it, and of course there is a section for z. He does not make cu, tl, and tz into separate sections. His alphabetization follows modern English practice in all details.

There is no denying that in several ways Campbell delivers useful information from the most consulted section of Molina in a form much easier to locate and understand than in the original. The reason that the book has not simply replaced Molina is that putting all items containing a given root in a single entry results, with the more common roots, in an undifferentiated paragraph going on for a whole column, several columns, or in many instances for several pages. Since within that framework the items are alphabetized by however they began in Molina, one must read with the closest attention. It is very easy to miss what you are looking for, even if it is there, after spending several minutes concentrating closely. I must admit that for that reason I have not made heavy use of the book. Nevertheless, I recommend it to readers. I am sure that with experience one would acquire the same instincts and ability to operate quickly as with the *Vocabulario* itself. If a specific item is crucial to a translation or a scholarly project, persistence will find it here if it is in the original, whereas one can search forever and never find a given item among the infinitely varied citations of Molina. Campbell's book can also be invaluable in various kinds of research on the language.

5. Andrews' Vocabulary.

J. Richard Andrews' 1975 *Introduction to Classical Nahuatl* (described in the epilogue) contains a 69-page vocabulary that was the best place to find out about a word's status as to vowel length and glottal stop until the appearance of Karttunen's larger and more systematic compilation in 1983. The vocabulary is still a substantial resource, representing not so much a work of reference as a body of material instructive about how Nahuatl words are built and how a large number of particular roots and morphemes, including many of the most common and basic in the language, relate to one another. Entries contain a basic word and then if needed a long paragraph or sometimes a page of other words using the same root, many of them often not beginning with the same initial letter at all. A modified version of Molina's classification of verbs through specification of prefixes is used. Each tiniest morpheme is separated from the next by a hyphen, incorporated elements are italicized, stems are enclosed in parentheses, zero ending markers are used liberally, derived forms are separated from basic forms by the > sign, and in general the vocabulary is a bristling, incomprehensible mass until you master its conventions. Once you do, it can be very informative.

---

understanding Molina's Spanish than the rest of us. He gives *pasarse el papel* as "for paper to fade," rather than the intended "to soak through," and he gives "screw" rather than "lathe" for *torno*.

[3] Our test word -namic, "spouse," however, does not appear as namictli or as a separate entry at all. It is subsumed under the verb namiqui, "to meet, match, etc."

Andrews glosses and gives vowel length and glottal stop information on quite a few items not in Karttunen; although they are not exactly attested, the analyses made through analogy and extrapolation seem very reliable in general. Occasionally Andrews differs from Karttunen on a word; for some reason he lists *ixquich* with a short initial vowel, though ample evidence from Carochi and elsewhere shows it to be long.

Orthography, alphabetization, and grouping are nearly the same as in Karttunen, whose practice is modeled on Andrews'.[1]

4. *Dictionaries of modern Nahuatl.*

The introduction of Spanish vocabulary into Nahuatl has continued apace over the whole time since the language ceased to be a written medium in the late eighteenth and early nineteenth centuries. The language gradually fragmented, with each local variant no longer in contact with the others, so that some are no longer easily mutually intelligible. The result is that something in modern Nahuatl cannot automatically be presumed to have been the same, or even present, in the older form of the language. Yet no one can deny that much has survived, and among the survivals are some items and meanings not in Molina or Carochi. It is hardly worth the while of a neophyte to go looking in modern dictionaries, but they will occasionally clarify a word or expression in an older text that would otherwise remain obscure.

Dictionaries of modern Nahuatl inevitably have to be restricted to a particular town and its immediate surroundings. Many have been done by Protestant missionaries with little knowledge of the broader language or even of lexical principles. Nevertheless, they can contain much of value. Two that I know and have used are:

Brewer, Forrest, and Jean G. Brewer. 1971. *Vocabulario mexicano de Tetelcingo, Morelos.* 2d printing. México: Instituto Lingüístico de Verano.

Key, Harold, and Mary Ritchie de Key. 1953. *Vocabulario mejicano de la Sierra de Zacapoaxtla, Puebla.* México: Instituto Lingüístico de Verano.

The core words and meanings of these two compilations are incorporated in Karttunen's *Analytical Dictionary* in a much more easily understandable form, but you can still find things of interest in the full original entries. Of the two, the Tetelcingo dictionary is much the better, but even so the other work contains unique material.

Jonathan Amith, who has long worked with the modern Nahuatl of Guerrero, is at this writing far advanced on a large and elaborate dictionary of the language as spoken in a town of that region. When the work is completed and is available, it will provide a resource for modern Nahuatl at a higher level and more compatible with the works on the older language.

*   *   *

I believe I have made sufficiently clear that the proper use of the dictionaries is crucial to your progress and to the quality of your translations. Yet it is best in the long run not to get too very dictionary-reliant. I have known a Nahuatl expert who carried a Molina with her everywhere she went, like a fetish. Eventually you will reach the point where nine out of ten puzzles you meet concern the reanalysis of lore already in your head, not a lexical item really unknown to you (though of course that constantly happens too). By then it is better to go to dictionaries only after you have searched your mind thoroughly.

---

[1]Although it can be of interest to true experts, I do not recommend for most readers John Bierhorst's *A Nahuatl-English Dictionary and Concordance to the Cantares Mexicanos* (Stanford: Stanford University Press, 1985). It presents many pitfalls and purveys a considerable amount of misinformation connected with Bierhorst's notion that the Cantares Mexicanos were "ghost songs."

Appendix 2: "P. 64"

ONCE YOU HAVE learned a good deal of Nahuatl grammar and vocabulary, you need to assimilate the knowledge and make it useful by working over a few texts in the greatest imaginable detail, accounting for every smallest prefix and suffix as well as the roots and the larger flow of syntax and idiom. Essentially you must do this for yourself, but it is sometimes hard to get started. Here is a section of a text (part of p. 64 of the 1976 edition of *Beyond the Codices*, by Anderson, Berdan and Lockhart) which I have given the full treatment as a sample. The exercise has proved helpful and enlightening to students at a certain stage. Before that it is incomprehensible; after that, it can be extremely tedious, even holding you back from developing necessary speed and facility. At some intermediate stage, it is just what one needs, and some people at a certain juncture can better absorb the general points expounded here (most already made in the lessons) apropos of a specific passage in a specific text than within a more systematic grammatical presentation.

The text, written in 1622, runs as follows:

yca yn itocatzin tote⁰ dios ma yxquich tlacatl quimati yn quenin nictlalia ynin memoria testamento yn ça tlatzacan notlanequiliz yn nehuatl don Ju⁰ de guzman nichane nican ypan altepetl villa cuyohuacan ypan tlaxillacalli sᵗtiago xuchac niquitohua ca nicnoneltoquitia yn santissima trinidad dios tetatzin dios tepiltzin dios espiritu sᵗ⁰ can ce huel nelli dios yxquichihueli yn oquiyocux yn oquimochihuili yn ilhuicatl yn tlalticpac yn ixquich ytalo yhuan yn amo ytalo ca mochi nicneltoca yn ixquich quimoneltoquitia yn tonantzin sᵗᵃ yglessia catolica

yn axcan cenca ninococotica huel mococohua y nonacayo amo pactica yece yn notlamachiliz cenca pactica yn iuhqui nechmomaquili yn tote⁰ dios amo nitlapolohua auh yn axcan yntla nechmohuiquiliz dios yntla ninomiquiliz ca ymactzinco noconcahua yn noyolia yn naniman ma quihualmaniliz ca cenca nicnotlatlauhtilia yn tlaçocihuapilli sᵗᵃ mᵃ cemicac ichpochtli ma nopan motlatoltiz yn ixpantzinco ytlaçoconetzin tote⁰ Jesu x⁰ ma nechmocnoyttiliz ca nopampa omomiquili cruztitech omamaçohualtiloc oquimonoquili yn itlaçoyezçotzin ynic ninomaquixtiz yhuan yehuatzin sᵗ Ju⁰ bapᵗᵃ nosantotzin ma nopan motlatoltiz yn ixpantzinco dios

- ynic centlamantli nitlanahuatia niquitohua yn iquac yntla oninomiquili ompa ninotocaz yn huey teupan sᵗ Ju⁰ bapᵗᵃ

In the name of our lord God, may everyone know that I am issuing this memorandum and testament as my last will; I don Juan de Guzmán, citizen here in the altepetl and town of Coyoacan, in the district of Santiago Xochac, declare that I believe in the most holy Trinity, God the father, God the child, and God the Holy Spirit, but only one very true God omnipotent who created and fashioned the heaven and the earth, all that is seen and not seen; I believe all that our mother the holy Catholic church deems true.

Now I am very sick, my body is very ill and not healthy, but my understanding is very sound, as our lord God gave it to me, and I am not confused. If God takes me now and I die, I leave my spirit and soul in his hands; may he come take it, for I greatly implore the precious lady St. Mary, eternal virgin, to speak on my behalf before her precious child our lord Jesus Christ; may he view me compassionately, because he died for me; he was stretched out on the cross and spilled his precious blood so that I might be redeemed; and may also San Juan Bautista, my saint, speak for me before God.

- First I order and declare that when I have died I am to be buried at the main church of San Juan Bautista . . .

163

¹*yca* ²*yn* ³*itocatzin* ⁴*tote*ᵒ ⁵*dios* (in our standard orthography *ica in itocatzin totecui-yo Dios*), "In the name of our lord God," more literally "its-through the his-name our-lord God."

<u>Word 1</u>. *yca*. *i-* third person singular possessive prefix plus relational word *-ca*, "through, by, with," and other instrumental meanings. The prefix varies with the referent: *i-ca*, "his/her/its-through, through him/her/it," *no-ca*, "my-through, through me," *in-ca*, "their-through, through them," etc. In Nahuatl, words like this, with a function close to that of English prepositions, never occur alone but are always preceded by a possessive prefix or a noun, the two bound together as a single word. For this reason they are sometimes called postpositions; Andrews calls them "relational nouns," which I think is better. I call them relational words. They are hard to find in Molina, where they are usually given only bound to one of the possessive prefixes. (It is now time to begin consulting Molina directly in addition to the vocabulary of this volume.) The job of the reader is not done until the referent of the prefix bound to the relational word has been identified. Here the referent is the noun "name," word 3.

<u>Word 2</u>. *yn*. *in*, the Nahuatl "article," subordinator, punctuator, marker of syntactic beginnings. In this document, as in many Nahuatl texts, following a Spanish practice of the time, the syllabic vowel [i] is written sometimes *y*, sometimes *i*, according to its position. At the beginning of a unit, the spelling is usually *y*; inside the unit, *i*. The unit may be something we recognize as a word (as with *yca* just above), but Nahuatl functioned in terms of a phonological phrase often containing a number of particles in front of the nuclear word. Here it is clear that the writer takes *yn itocatzin* as a unit, with the first [i] *y* and the following ones *i*. At this point in your studies you may not be too interested in the nature of Nahuatl phonological phrases, but the occurence of *y* and *i* can help you a great deal in discerning word division in documents where you most often cannot deduce it from the arbitrary or nonexistent spacing of letters.

<u>Word 3</u>. *itocatzin*, "his name, the name of . . ." Third person singular possessive prefix *i-* referring forward to words 4 and 5, "our lord God." Again, the reader's task is to identify the referent and hook it to this form. In fact, as you work through, it is probably best to think of something like *itoca* as "the name of . . ." rather than as "his name" so that you will be forced into the realization that you aren't through until you've found out whose name it is. The possessed noun here is *toca(i)-tl*, name, with the absolutive ending taken off, as that suffix always is when a noun is possessed. A few common nouns lose not only the *-tl* but the preceding vowel as well. The point is to reconstruct the form with the absolutive so that you can find it in the dictionary. At the end of word 3 is *-tzin*, indicating the reverential. It comes immediately after the noun stem, before the absolutive suffix if there is one and last if there is no absolutive. Seeing *-tzin* in final position is a good indication that one is dealing with a possessed noun.

<u>Word 4</u>. *tote*ᵒ for *totecuiyo*, "our lord." *to-* first person plural possessive prefix. *Tecu-tli*, *teuc-tli*, even *tecuh-tli*, noun, "lord." *-yo* abstract or collective nominal suffix, here much like English "-ship"; "lordship." The simple possessive of *teuctli*, without *-yo*, is virtually not seen. Absolutive suffix missing because possessed. (The *u* in *tecutli* is not a vowel, as can be seen from the *-tli* suffix, used only with consonants. The *cu* is a single consonant [kʷ], and the word is written in the Carochi tradition [and here] as *teuctli*. *-tecui-* is an archaic stem form generally used with *-yo* rather than *tecu-*.)

<u>Word 5</u>. *dios*. Borrowed from Spanish; like most Spanish loan nouns it lacks the absolutive suffix even when not possessed.

¹*ma* ²*yxquich* ³*tlacatl* ⁴*quimati*, "may/let all persons know (the contents of the

following clause)."

Word 1. *ma*, "may, let, would that, etc." Particle used with (and to the left of) verbs in the optative/imperative.

Word 2. *yxquich, ixquich*, "all, everything." A quantifier usually invariant in the singular (though it can take a plural, *ixquichtin*, and forms such as *tixquichtin*, all of us, may be seen occasionally).

Word 3. *tlaca-tl*, noun, "person (of either sex)." No subject prefix, hence third person. Has absolutive, not being possessed; can be found in the dictionary exactly as it is. Although animates usually have overtly marked plurals in Nahuatl, Nahuatl retains the singular form much more than English, here because a whole class is in question (many languages do this).

Word 4. *qui-mati*, "(he)-it-know, know it," the "it" being what follows, so that one could translate "know that . . ." No subject prefix, hence third person subject. *qui-* third person singular object prefix attached to transitive verbs. Tells you that the stem of the word is a transitive verb. Refers forward to the following clause. *-mati*, the transitive verb "to know," to be found in Molina as *mati, nic*. The optative singular has no special ending for most classes of verbs.

¹*yn* ²*quenin* ³*nictlalia* ⁴*ynin* ⁵*memoria* ⁶*testamento*, "that I am issuing this memorandum (and, of) testament," "the how I-it-issue this memorandum testament."

Word 1. *yn. in*, here subordinating a whole clause. The following word, *quenin*, is interrogative when not preceded by *in*. Many words work this way: *aquin*, "who?"; *in aquin*, "he who," or "whoever."

Word 2. *quenin*. Interrogative word, "how?" *Quen* by itself means "how?" The rest of the word is the subordinating particle *in*, which originally went with the following clause ("how is it that . . .?"), but was so frequent that it came to be felt as part of the question word, and the longer form is now much more common than simple *quen*. When introducing a subordinate clause, although the word can always be translated as "how" in some sense, the effect is often "that." (Spanish *como* is much the same in this respect.)

Word 3. *ni-c-tlalia*. "I-it-put down, order, issue," "I issue it," "it" being the testament just to be mentioned.

Word 4. *ynin. inin*, "this," consists of the subordinator *in* plus another *in* which is the proximate demonstrative proper and sometimes occurs without the introductory subordinating *in*. The demonstrative *in* has a long vowel that is invisible in the written form.

Word 5. *memoria*. The Spanish word for memorandum, here a loanword in Nahuatl.

Word 6. *testamento*. Another Spanish loanword, "testament, will." The full Spanish phrase runs "memoria de testamento," memorandum of testament. Even when taking an entire unanalyzed Spanish phrase, Nahuatl would sometimes omit its prepositions, since as we saw above it lacked that part of speech. It would be hard to say whether here we are dealing with a unitary, unanalyzable block, with a two-noun set in which the second modifies the first, or a set in which each of the nouns is taken to have much the same meaning and refers to the same thing (a very common Nahuatl device).

¹*yn* ²*ça* ³*tlatzacan* ⁴*notlanequiliz*, "my last will," "the just last-place my-wanting." In apposition to *testamento* just above.

Word 1. *yn*. "article" or subordinator.

Word 2. *ça*. (has closely related form *çan*.) Particle, "just, only," hence "very" (as in "very last"), and many other meanings. Often doesn't need translating into English at all.

Word 3. *tlatzacan*, standard spelling *tlatzaccan*. (Reduction of double *c*'s is endemic in

Nahuatl texts, and any double consonant at all may be reduced to a single one.) The whole thing is in the dictionary, "finally, at the end," also used in effect adjectivally, "last, final." Consists of *tla-* indefinite nonpersonal object, "something"; *tzaqua*, "to close, finish, follow," in shortened combining form; and *-can*, place of an action. Virtually always preceded by *ça*.

Word 4. *notlanequiliz*, "my wanting, willing (will)." This form is easy to mistake for a verb because the root is verbal and the ending looks like a future applicative, but nevertheless we are dealing with a possessed noun. To get the dictionary form we remove the possessive prefix from the front and add the absolute suffix to the back; *tlanequiliztli*. Even if it were not in the dictionary we could arrive at its meaning. Adding *-liz(tli)* to a verb makes a noun which means the performance of the act denoted by the verb, like "-ing" in English. If the verb is transitive, Nahuatl adds an indefinite object prefix to show the transitivity and what kind of an object the verb takes. *Tla-*, "something"; *-nequi-*, "to want"; *-liz-*, "-ing"; *-tli*, absolute suffix. Word 4 is introduced by *no-*, first person singular possessive prefix, hence lacks the absolute suffix. Do not forget that the lack of a subject prefix means that this word has a third-person subject or referent.

¹*yn* ²*nehuatl* ³*don* ⁴*ju⁰* ⁵*de* ⁶*guzman*, "I don Juan de Guzmán."

Word 1. *yn*. The "article" is used to indicate the beginning of units in many places where English would use neither the article nor a conjunction, and it is often not translated.

Word 2. *nehuatl*. "I," one of the series of emphatic independent pronouns for each person and number. If anything complementary follows them it must ordinarily bear the attached pronominal prefix in addition, not only if it is a verb (*nehuatl nicchihua*, "I do it"), but also if it is a noun (*nehuatl nipilli*, "I (am a) nobleman") and even twice in the case of a noun plus free-standing "adjective" (*tehuatl timahuiztic titlatoani*, "you [are a] revered ruler"). It should be, strictly, in the classical language, *nehuatl ni-don ju⁰*; but as in this case, such often fails to happen in postconquest texts, especially when Spanish names are involved. One explanation is that many early texts have the equivalent of *nehuatl notoca don ju⁰*, "I my-name don Juan," "I, whose name is don Juan." Phrases like this one can be seen as eliding *notoca*, "my name."

Word 3. *don*. the Spanish honorific title, sometimes seen in early texts as *ton* and *to*.

Words 4-5-6. *ju⁰ de guzman*. All baptized Nahuas had Spanish-style first names and often surnames as well. Sometimes these are spelled just as in Spanish, as here; sometimes there are variant spellings, representations of pronunciations assimilated to Nahuatl, which can make them hard to recognize. The abbreviation *ju⁰* for "Juan" is standard in both Spanish and Nahuatl texts.

¹*nichane* ²*nican* ³*ypan* ⁴*altepetl* ⁵*villa* ⁶*cuyohuacan*, "I am a citizen here in the altepetl (state) and town of Coyoacan (I-home-owner here its-in altepetl town Coyoacan)"

Word 1. *ni-chan-e* "I-home-owner." *ni-*, first person singular subject prefix, plus noun *chan(-tli)*, "home," (as opposed to *cal-li*, "house"), plus nominal suffix *-e* (with a final glottal stop almost never written), "possessor of (whatever is designated by the preceding noun stem)." The absolute suffix of the noun is omitted, and *-e* replaces it (another, no doubt related suffix of identical meaning, *-hua*, also with an invisible glottal stop, used mainly with vowel stems, works the same way). The verb "to be" is not used in equative statements in Nahuatl; the structure is verbless, i.e., "I-big", "I-little", "I-man", "I-woman." This is one of the hardest things for an English speaker to grasp about Nahuatl, especially in the third person where there is no attached subject prefix. What looks to us like one or two simple nouns may be one or more equative statements. For example, *don ju⁰ amo qualli tepachoani çan cochpal çan xolopitli*, "don Juan not (he-)good (he-)governor just (he-)dullard just (he-)idiot," i.e., "don Juan is not a good governor; he is just a dullard, he is just an idiot."

Word 2. *nican*, "here," a particle. The element -*can* is a general indication of place appearing in many kinds of locative expressions.

Word 3. *ypan* "in . . . (its-in)." *y*- third person singular possessive prefix referring forward to *altepetl*, plus -*pan*, relational word meaning "on, in, at, for," etc.

Word 4. *altepe-tl*, "state, regional ethnic state, city-state, sovereign sociopolitical entity, etc." Unpossessed third person noun complete with absolutive ending. A compound, or doublet, originally *a-tl*, "water," and *tepe-tl*, "mountain, hill." One still sees *atl tepetl*, as well as *iauh itepeuh*, his/her altepetl, and *ahua tepehua*, citizen.

Word 5. *villa*, Spanish title of "town" given to Coyoacan, in apposition with *altepetl*. Very often Nahuatl texts give both the Nahuatl and the Spanish of something. A good hypothesis about an ununderstood Nahuatl word next to a Spanish word is that it refers to the same thing.

Word 6. *cuyohuacan*, Coyoacan. In general Nahuatl does not distinguish between [u] and [o] per se. By the Carochi standard only *o* is used, and in actual texts it certainly predominates, but *u* can appear written for standard *o* at any time. One sees *u* most frequently when the *o* is long. What Molina writes as *oa* is often seen as *ohua* in texts, i.e., with a written indication of a [w] glide between the two vowels that some people probably always pronounced. Molina: *poa, coa, tlatoa*. Many texts: *pohua, cohua, tlatohua*. The first two actually have a [w] as a basic part of the word, while the third does not, as one can tell from their preterits (*pouh, couh, tla(h)to(h)*), but any given text will usually treat them all the same, either all *oa* or all *ohua*, or sometimes alternate haphazardly.

¹*ypan* ²*tlaxillacalli* ³*sᵗtiago* ⁴*xuchac*, "in the barrio, district of Santiago Xochac."

Word 1. *y-pan*, as in the above paragraph.

Word 2. *tlaxillacalli*, standard *tlaxilacal-li* without first double *l*, "barrio," subdivision of an altepetl. A third person singular noun with absolutive, being some sort of compound built on *cal-li* "house," but the first part of the word, *tla(h)xila-*, is not yet understood. Much, much more common than *calpolli* in postconquest Nahuatl texts.

Word 3. *sᵗtiago*, "Santiago."

Word 4. *xuchac*, Nahuatl toponym, name of a sociopolitical entity; most places of barrio size or larger had a double name, saint's name plus a Nahuatl one. Again *u* for a long *o*: *xoch(i)-tl*, "flower," plus *a(-tl)*, "water," plus -*c*, "place where," "place of flowery water."

¹*niquitohua* ²*ca* ³*nicnoneltoquitia* ⁴*yn* ⁵*santissima* ⁶*trinidad* ⁷*dios* ⁸*tetatzin* ⁹*dios* ¹⁰*tepiltzin* ¹¹*dios* ¹²*espiritu* ¹³*sᵗᵒ*, "I say that I believe in the most holy Trinity, God the father, God the son (child), God the holy spirit."

Word 1. *ni-qu-itohua* "I-it-say, I say that . . ." Transitive verb in present tense. *ni*- first person singular subject prefix; -*qu*- third person singular object prefix. Spanish-style orthography puts -*qu*- before *e* and *i*, -*c*- before *a, o, u* for the same sound [k], obscuring the identity of the object prefix [k]. Another source of confusion is that Nahuatl adds -*i* to [k], making *qui*-, whenever this is necessary for pronunciation, that is, if there is not a vowel on one side or the other. For example, one could not pronounce *c-maca*, "he/she gives it to him/her," so Nahuatl says *qui-maca*. If the verb begins with *i*, one cannot know beforehand whether the *i* is part of the prefix or of the verb, that is, in this case, whether the verb is *tohua* or *itohua*. One must check both possibilities in the dictionary. In fact it is *itohua*, standard *i(h)toa* "to say." In Molina as *itoa, niqu.*

<u>Word 2</u>. *ca.* clause-introductory particle. Here English would say "that," though the grammatical function is very different. In many cases *ca* has the effect "for, because." In others, English needs no translation. Most of the examples of *ca* that one sees in texts are this particle, and very few are the verb *ca(h)*, "to be (in a certain place, time, or condition), i.e., *estar*." The particle comes before the phrase, the verb (unlike most verbs) almost always comes at the end of it and at least is never absolutely initial.

<u>Word 3</u>. *ni-c-no-neltoqui-tia*, transitive verb in present tense reverential, "I believe (the following) (reverential)," "I-it-myself-believe-cause." *ni-* first person singular subject prefix; *-c-* third person singular object prefix; *-no-* first person singular reflexive prefix. The order of these elements is always the same as it is here; subject-object-reflexive, or subject-reflexive when there is no other object (*ni-no-*, *ti-to-*, etc.) or object-reflexive when there is no subject prefix, in third person (*qui-mo*). Here the reflexive is used not for actual reflexive meaning ("myself") but as part of Nahuatl's reverential equipment. (That is, at a remote time the present construction would have meant "I cause myself to believe it," but gradually this more complex form was taken simply as a fancier way of saying "I believe it," and the actual original meaning of the complex construction faded.) The reflexive pronoun is placed before the verb stem, and the applicative (*-lia*) or the causative (*-tia*) suffix goes after the verb stem; the two together (i.e., the reflexive plus one of the suffixes) constitute the normal reverential of verbs. When used this way they cancel each other out as to actual meaning. Example: *chihua* "to do"; *qui-chihui-lia* "he/she does it for him/her," with the true applicative meaning of "for" because the reflexive is missing; *mo-chihua* "it does itself, i.e., is done, happens," with the true reflexive meaning because the applicative is missing; *qui-mo-chihui-lia* "he/she does it (reverential)," with the two canceling each other. ("He/she does it [non-reverential]" is *qui-chihua*.) *-neltoqui-*, the stem of the verb, from *neltoca*, "to believe, believe in." When a verb ends in *-a*, adding the applicative (*-lia*) suffix normally causes the *a* to change to *i* (the same often happens with the *-tia* causative, though when it is *-ltia* the *a* may be retained). If the preceding consonant is *c*, this will undergo the standard orthographic change to *qu* to retain the [k] sound: *toca, toquilia; maca, maquilia*, etc. In seeking the dictionary form of a causative or applicative verb, however, one does not automatically change the final *i* of the stem to *a*. Many verbs end in *i*, and they remain unchanged: *nemi, nemitia*. The essential art with a verbal complex like this is to know how to strip off the affixes exactly down to the root (not right on into the root; remember a verb <u>can</u> begin *no-* like the first person singular reflexive, etc.), reconstructing the form that can be found in the dictionary. This process in the present case leads us to *neltoca* or *neltoqui*, of which the former proves right. Sometimes the root fails to appear in the dictionary because it is a compound. *Nel-toca* consists of *nel-li*, "a true thing," and the verb *toca*, "to follow, to consider as." This compound is so common and has such a special meaning that in fact it is in dictionaries as such, but in many cases one must break what appears to be the root down into smaller elements, identify them, and use their meaning as a guide to the meaning of the larger construct. Remember that most verbs in Nahuatl end in *a* or *i*; most of those in *a* are transitive, and most of those in *i* are intransitive, though there are many exceptions.

<u>Word 4</u>. *yn.* the "article."

<u>Words 5–6</u>. *santissima trinidad.* Spanish loan phrase.

<u>Words 7–8</u>. *dios te-ta-tzin* "God the father," "God someone's-father-reverential." *dios* as before. *te-* indefinite personal prefix used as an object on verbs but also functioning as an indefinite possessive prefix attached to nouns, "someone's"; with terms of kinship

te- is used just like English uses "the," that is, when the context is already set. Suppose a text says *nican omentin telpopochtin ipaltzinco nemi intatzin itoca Lorenço,* "here two young men live under the roof of their father, named Lorenzo." It might go on, *auh yn tetatzin quimmaca in ixquich in intech monequi,* "and the father gives them everything they need." *ta(h)(-tli),* noun, "father." *-tzin,* reverential suffix, positioned as usual just to the right of the noun stem. No absolute suffix because the noun is possessed, as kinship nouns are in the vast majority of cases.

Words 9–10. *dios te-pil-tzin* "God the child," "God someone's-child-reverential." Same as the phrase of words 7–8 except that the noun is *pil-li* "child (of either sex)." In reconstructing the form with absolutive in order to find it in the dictionary remember that noun stems ending in *-l* ordinarily take *-li,* which is the form that *-tli* assumes when it comes up against *-l-*. The combination *l* plus *tl* always becomes *ll* wherever the two meet in a Nahuatl word, however fleetingly. *Hual-,* directional affix, "in this direction," plus *tlamelahua* "to go straight," makes *hual-lamelahua* "comes straight in this direction." Note also that *pilli* has another meaning, "noble person," which causes great confusion for the relative beginner. Most of the time, the possessed form means "child," the nonpossessed form "noble person." When either is in the state not most common for it, there are attempts to disambiguate. In the absolute, the diminutive suffix *-ton* makes it definitely "(little) child," *pil-ton-tli,* and *pil-tzin-tli* is the same, *-tzin* having originally been a diminutive; in the possessed vocative (marked by *-e* when a male is speaking) what looks like a double reverential signals that the meaning is "noble": *no-pil-tzin-tzin-e,* "O my nobleman" (a polite form somewhat like English "milord").

Words 11–12–13. *dios espiritu s^{to}* (equals *santo*), "God the holy spirit." All Spanish loan words, 12 and 13 apparently an inseparable set phrase.

¹*can* ²*ce* ³*huel* ⁴*nelli* ⁵*dios* ⁶*yxquichyhueli* "just one really true God omnipotent (all-his-power)."

Word 1. *can* for *çan,* "just, etc.," more frequent than the slightly different *ça* mentioned above. The cedilla on *c* is fairly often omitted in Nahuatl texts just as it was in Spanish ones. One hardly knows whether to call it a mistake or not, but in any case you have to recognize somehow what has happened and replace the cedilla to get to the word in the dictionary. *Çan* is often (and properly) left unaccounted for in English translations. Often, as here, it has a sense close to "but" or "rather."

Word 2. *ce,* the number word "one." Often incorporated into following nouns or even verbs, then becomes *cem/cen.*

Word 3. *huel,* particle, much-used intensifier "really, very, fully," etc. Comes from *hueli,* "power," as though one said "powerful true, or mighty true"; also can indicate the ability to do something when used with verbs, a source of much ambiguity. Note that *huel* is in Molina as *vel.* For prevocalic [w] Molina mainly uses *v* at the beginning of a word and *u* inside it. (The *v* is to be pronounced [w] just like the *u.*)

Word 4. *nel-li,* noun word often used more or less adjectivally, "a true thing, true." There is no special form for adjectives in Nahuatl; some are like ordinary nouns, some are like substantives made from verbs. It may be that they are not truly adjectives; this example may involve a verbless equative phrase "true thing-God." Anyway, we can often translate them into English as adjectives. When an "adjective" which is a noun word stands free from the word it appears to modify, it bears an absolutive ending just like any other noun.

Word 5. *dios,* "God," as before.

Word 6. *yxquich-y-hueli* "omnipotent," "all-his-power," an equative statement frozen and used somewhat like an adjective. *yxquich*, "all," as above; *-y-* third person singular possessive prefix "his"; *-hueli*, archaic noun "power" never seen any other way than possessed, and therefore we don't know what its absolutive suffix might be, or if it could be said to have one. In fact *hueli* fails to appear in Molina as such, but one can deduce its meaning from many complex words starting *veli-*. It is often necessary to resort to this procedure in using Molina and other dictionaries, because many words in texts are without entries in the dictionaries.

[1] *yn* [2] *oquiyocux* [3] *yn* [4] *oquimochihuili* [5] *yn* [6] *ilhuicatl* [7] *yn* [8] *tlalticpac*, "who created, who made the heaven and the earth," "the he-it-created, the he-it-made the heaven the earth."

Word 1. *yn*. Here the particle is an indicator of subordination, unambiguously recognizable as such because it precedes a verb rather than a noun. What kind of subordination is involved has to be figured out from context. Sometimes the whole following clause is the subject or object of a verb, or crossreferent with a noun phrase in an equative statement; then English adds "what," "that which," or "that," "the fact that"; *in oquito ca amo qualli*, "<u>what</u> he said is bad" (open also to other interpretations). Sometimes the relationship is more temporal, and English may supply "when": *in oquito iciuhca oniya* "<u>when</u> he had said it, I quickly left." If a sentence has no specified subject, *in* may imply that the subject of the main clause is specified only as being the person who performed the action of the subordinate clause, in which case English adds "he who" or "whoever": *in oquichiuh quimati* "he who (whoever) did it knows it." Other cases are quite similar except that the subject of the verb in the subordinated clause has already been specified (as it has been for Words 1–2), making the construction relative, and then English adds "who" only: *ye oya in cihuatl in oquichiuh* "the woman <u>who</u> did it already left." There are many other possibilities, and these structures are often irresolvably ambiguous unless the full context is known. Remember above all that *in* introducing a verbal clause probably indicates some sort of subordination in a system very unlike the English one.

Word 2. *o-qui-yocux*, transitive verb in the preterit, "he created it (something to follow)." *o-*, the sign of the preterit, sometimes separated from the verb proper by one or more particles; also frequently omitted altogether, for the essential preterit formation is in the way the present tense stem is modified at the other end, the rightward side or back, and how suffixes are added there. No subject prefix, hence third person subject. *-qui-* third person singular object prefix. In a moment we will see that there are two specified objects, but Nahuatl usually uses the singular object prefix even if the object is semantically plural, if that object is inanimate. Note that we have *qui* rather than *c* despite there being a vowel to the left that would make it pronounceable. *o-* doesn't count as part of the word for this purpose, so *ocyocux* doesn't happen, not in older Nahuatl at least. *-yocux*, preterit of the verb *yocoya*, "to create." *u* for standard *o* as often happens. This preterit is more regular than it appears to be. The normal way to make a preterit in Nahuatl is to drop the final vowel of the present tense (Class 2), though a large number of verbs for various reasons are prevented from losing the vowel and remain unreduced in the preterit, this being Nahuatl's older system (Class 1). That is, a standard Class 2 verb is *yoli*, "to live," *yol* preterit. But since voiced consonants occur only before vowels in Nahuatl, the consonant which is now final after loss of the vowel will be devoiced and undergo other kinds of weakening. *Hu-* is written *-uh* to indicate its voicelessness: *chihua*, *chiuh*. *M* is delabialized as well as devoiced, i.e., becomes *n*: *nemi*, "to live," *nen*. Devoiced *y* merges with *x* (like Eng. *sh*), and is so written: *yocoya*, *yocox*; *pi(y)a*, "to keep, hold," *pix*; *chi(y)a*, "to await," *chix*, etc. Word 2 is unambiguously singular. In the present tense, plural forms are distinguished from singular ones only by a final glottal stop in the plural, which is almost never written in texts, so that singular and plural look alike except for different subject prefixes, of which the third person has none, while first person plural and second person singular are both *ti-*. In the preterit there is the plural *-que(h)*; if it is lacking, the form is singular.

Word 3. *yn.* another subordinator for a second phrase equivalent to the one of words 1–2, inserted even before the object common to the two verbs has been specified. The two phrases mean virtually the same thing, a common facet of Nahuatl texts and an invaluable aid in translation. If one of two parallel Nahuatl constructions is opaque, we can often crack it by assuming it means the same as the one with which it is paired. Even if we don't decipher it in terms of dictionary roots, we've already got the basic sense.

Word 4. *o-qui-mo-chihui-li*, transitive verb in the preterit reverential, "he made it (something to follow)." The Nahuatl reverential is not like Spanish *usted*, to be used automatically if used at all; rather enough verbs and nouns are put in the reverential to get across the general notion of respectful speech (not always in relation to the person addressed), and many others are left unadorned. In this whole larger string only this word is in the reverential. *o-*, sign of the preterit; no subject prefix, third person singular; *-qui-* third person singular object prefix; *mo-* third person reflexive, here one half of the reverential formula; *-chihui-*, the verb stem, changed from *chihua*, "to make," in view of the following applicative suffix; *-li*, preterit singular form of *-lia* applicative suffix, here the other half of the reverential. There is a Class 3 of verbs, in *-ia* and *-oa*, whose preterits look in texts like those of Class 2 (i.e., they lose the final vowel), but which in fact add a glottal stop (*-ih*, *-oh*). Since this is almost never written, it need not occupy us here.

Word 5. *yn.* "article" before a noun.

Word 6. *ilhuica-tl*, unpossessed third person singular noun with absolutive ending, "heaven, heavens, sky." As was mentioned before, throughout this text *y* and *i* alternate as representations of the syllabic vowel [i]. Let us not forget the consequences, which can become important for you when you begin reading handwritten documents. The general practice, followed in this text too, was to put *y* at the beginning of strings of letters, *i* internally. Since the text has been divided here into smaller units, the practice is hard to see, but what was usually done was to write in quite large units including the preceding particles with the following larger word. Words 5–6 would have been *ynilhuicatl*. What is given as *yn itocatzin* would have been *ynitocatzin*.

Word 7. *yn.* "article" before a noun again, but there is a bit more to it. When Nahuatl gets a series of two, three, or more nouns, it only occasionally specifies "and" as English does, but rather just piles them up, each preceded by *in*. The succession of *in*'s says the same thing we do in English with "and" or commas with "and" before the last item.

Word 8. *tlal-t-icpac*, "the earth," "earth-(ligature)-upon." *tlal-li*, noun, "land, earth, soil, ground," here without the absolutive suffix, which is lost when a relational word is suffixed. *-t-*; the "ligature" *-ti-* appears between the noun stem and the relational word in a rather unpredictable way, that is, often it is not there at all, but when it is we can recognize it. If the relational word begins with *i*, one of the two contiguous *i*'s is lost. *-icpac*, relational word, "upon." The proper meaning of the form is "upon the surface of the land, on earth," and it was still used that way for the most part, but the whole thing becomes a new noun meaning "the earth, the world," and as such can serve as subject or object of verbs and receive the absolutive suffix, *tlalticpac-tli*.

172 – Appendix 2 –

¹*yn* ²*ixquich* ³*ytalo* ⁴*yhuan* ⁵*yn* ⁶*amo* ⁷*ytalo,* "everything seen and unseen," "the everything it-is-seen its-with the not it-is-seen."

Word 1. *yn.* "article," with implications of subordination.

Word 2. *ixquich,* "all, everything," as before.

Word 3. *yta-lo,* standard spelling *ittalo* or in texts *yttalo* (reduction of a double consonant again), "it is seen," third person (no subject prefix) passive of the verb *itta,* "to see." The most common way to form the passive is simply to add *-lo* to the active. But there is also *itt-o* with the same meaning, in which *-al-* has been left out. English speakers have great trouble recognizing the Nahuatl passive. Remember that if a transitive verb lacks an object prefix of some kind at the front, it must be passive; *quitta,* "he/she sees it," *ittalo,* "he/she is seen"; *ni-qu-itta,* "I see it," *n-itto,* "I am seen."

Word 4. *y-huan,* "and," "its-with," relational word. *y-* third person singular possessive prefix, *-huan* relational word "with" and related meanings. The referent of *y-* is the phrase *yn amo ytalo.* The total effect is often "and," but by no means always. The meaning can be "additionally," "along with," and the form varies according to the referent: *no-huan,* "with me," "my-with."

Word 5. *yn.* the subordinator. Before a verb, especially before a passive or impersonal verb as here, the particle *in* like the English article can indicate the creation of a substantive, as in English "the hurt," "the divided," etc., yet essentially this is the same as the "one who" or "that which" construction.

Word 6. *amo (aʰmo),* negative particle "not," precedes what it modifies as in English.

Word 7. *ytalo.* same as word 3. Words 5–6–7 mean "that which is not seen, the unseen."

¹*ca* ²*mochi* ³*nicneltoca,* "and/for I believe everything (that) . . .," "and/for everything I-it-believe."

Word 1. *ca,* the clause-introductory particle again, this time renderable somewhere in the range of "and" and "for," though not exactly either.

Word 2. *mochi,* "all, everything," another quantifier invariant except for taking a plural (together with a subject prefix) when appropriate, like *ixquich,* which means so nearly the same thing that in this case the two quantifiers are in crossreference.

Word 3. *ni-c-neltoca,* transitive verb in present tense, "I believe (it, i.e., 'everything' as specified by *mochi* and to be further specified in the following clause)." Not reverential. *ni-* first person singular subject prefix; *-c-* third person singular object prefix; *neltoca,* verb stem, "believe," seen before.

¹*yn* ²*ixquich* ³*quimoneltoquitia* ⁴*yn* ⁵*tonantzin* ⁶*sta* ⁷*yglessia* ⁸*catolica* ". . . that our mother the holy Catholic church believes," "the everything (she-)it-believes the our-mother-rev. holy church Catholic."

Word 1. *yn.* "article"/subordinator.

Word 2. *ixquich* "everything," as before. Repeats the previous *mochi* in a way English would not and which is ignored in an idiomatic English translation. Nahuatl often puts a short hint of something to come in front of the verb, then spells it out in full weighty detail after the verb. The apparent duplication makes English speakers uncomfortable, but the practice is actually crossreference or apposition. *Ayac neci oc ce tlacatl* "no one appears another person," i.e., "no one else appears"; *atle onca itomin iaxca* "nothing there is his money his property," i.e., "he has no money." The first part of the construction is usually more general, and the second is included within it. "No one—and getting down to specifics within that, another person—appears."

Word 3. *qui-mo-neltoqui-tia,* present tense transitive verb in reverential, "(she) believes (it, everything)." no subject prefix, hence third person subject; *qui-* third person singular object prefix; -mo- third person reflexive prefix, half of the reverential formula; -neltoqui-, verb stem from *neltoca*, "to believe," *a* changed to *i* before *-tia*; and *-tia* causative suffix, here constituting the other half of the reverential formula.

Word 4. *yn.* "article."

Word 5. *to-nan-tzin* "our mother (reverential)." *to-* first person plural possessive prefix "our"; *nan-(tli),* noun, "mother"; *-tzin,* reverential suffix positioned immediately after noun stem; no absolute suffix because possessed.

Words 6–8. *s^{ta} iglessia catolica, santa iglesia catolica.* "Holy Catholic church," loan phrase.

¹*yn* ²*axcan* ³*cenca* ⁴*ninococotica,* "now I am very sick", "the now very I-myself-hurt-(progressive)."

Word 1. *yn* "article"/subordinator. Despite preceding the particle "now," *in* does not have a clearly subordinating effect on the clause in this case. *In* can always be primarily an indication of a beginning or a subtle distributor of degree of emphasis. The only thing it can be said to subordinate here is the particle *axcan* itself, which does have an un-particle-like tendency to be an independent statement, and in that capacity is sometimes found after the verb instead of in front where one expects a particle to be (in that case it is almost always preceded by *in*).

Word 2. *axcan,* particle as just discussed, "now, today."

Word 3. *cenca (cencah),* particle, "very, much," frequently used all-purpose intensifier. At one time this item must have been a sentence or verb phrase, *cen-,* "one, entirely," combined with *cah* "it is *(está)*", i.e., "it absolutely is (that way)." As here, particles of whatever nature normally precede the main or nuclear word, whether verb or noun.

Word 4. *ni-no-coco-ti-ca,* "I am sick (progressive)." *ni-* first person singular subject prefix "I"; *-no-* first person singular reflexive prefix "myself"; *-coco-* (*cocoh*) from *cocoa,* "to hurt (transitive)," which when reflexive means "to be sick." Note that for once the reflexive means something beyond being part of the reverential, since it is not paired with a causative or applicative suffix. The verb is in a shortened form looking like a preterit, which is the combining form in general, and especially before a certain kind of auxiliary verb tied to the main verb by the same *-ti-* ligature seen with relational words: verb in preterit plus *-ti-* plus auxiliary verb. There are several helping verbs used this way, most of them short and irregular; the sense of the whole construction is often some sort of progressive, ongoing action. The verb here is *ca(h),* "to be *(estar)*." A persistent problem for beginning translators is that the *-ti-ca(h)* progressive, added only to verbs, looks like the form in which the relational word *-ca,* "through, by, with," is placed after a noun: *qui-chiuh-ti-ca,* "he/she is doing it"; *te-ti-ca* "with a rock." Since the rightward forms are identical in writing, one must rely on the leftward forms to indicate whether it is a question of a noun or a verb, and once that is decided, the interpretation of *-tica* is automatic: progressive if a verb; instrumental if a noun (actually, it must be admitted that there is, alas, a construction in which a noun word and the progressive verb construction can appear together, but thank goodness, it is quite rare, it mainly applies to adjective-like words, and it is perhaps most frequently used in the future tense where it looks nothing like the nominal-instrumental *-ti-ca: qual-ti-yez* "it will be good").

¹*huel* ²*mococohua* ³*y* ⁴*nonacayo,* "my body is very sick," "really (it-)itself-hurts the my-body."

Word 1. *huel.* the intensifier, as before, characteristically placed before the verb.

Word 2. *mo-cocohua,* standard *mococoa,* reflexive verb in present tense, "(it-)itself hurts, is sick." no subject prefix, hence third person subject; *mo-* third person reflexive prefix, <u>not</u> part of the reverential this time because not paired with an applicative or causative suffix; *-cocohua (cocoa)*, as before, "to hurt"; "to be sick" when reflexive, as seen above. The specified subject of the verb follows, as it does more often than not. Nahuatl constituent order (that is, order of the larger constituents) is quite free, but the standard order for a sentence or clause containing a verb is: first any particles, second the verbal complex, third any specifications of subject and/or object, just as in this example. Putting the subject or object first emphasizes or focuses on it.

Word <u>3</u>. *y (yn, in)*. the "article." Nahuatl frequently puts this element before a possessed noun, "the my (something)," reminiscent of Italian but not English. An *n* has been lost from *yn* in the text. That is, one is there, but it belongs to the possessive prefix attached to the following noun. In other words, one *n* is made to serve for two. The reader must be constantly aware of this and of similar problems. In actual texts, "words" are rarely divided out from each other systematically, and particles are usually written in with the following larger word, as well they might be, since the phonological phrase containing both particles and a nuclear word is the true unit. Suppose one is presented with the string of letters *ynextli* and figures out correctly that it must be a noun in the absolute preceded by the article. The first stab would be *yn extli*, but there is no such thing; the only way to find the noun in the dictionary is to assign the *n* to it, which yields *nex-tli*, "ash." *n* is constantly being omitted from texts, perhaps most expectedly when two *n*'s run together as here, but also when alone, whenever *n* comes at the end of a word or before a consonant; for example, *noco* for *no-con* (from *comitl*), "my pot"; *nicnepoloa* for *nicnenpoloa*, "I waste it," etc. When there is trouble, one standard part of the search for a solution is to try putting *n* after any vowel that lacks one, or two *n*'s where there is only one between vowels.

Word <u>4</u>. *no-naca-yo*, possessed noun, "my body," "my-flesh(-collective)." no subject prefix, hence third person subject, something we tend to forget about with nouns, many of which could never have first or second person subjects, that is, human beings as subjects, so we often simply leave the subject out of consideration, but it is always there in some sense, even when the noun is possessed. The form here basically means "it is my body." Two third person nouns can constitute an equative statement through crossreference: *huei tecpancalli in ical*, "his house is a great palace." *no-* first person singular possessive prefix; *naca-(tl)* "meat, flesh"; *-yo* nominal suffix seen before as abstract or collective. *-yo* is also used as a sign of things which are a part of someone or something, inalienable "possessions," so that the *-yo* form of this kind has a special organic meaning (forms with this meaning are seen only possessed): *omi-tl*, "bone"; *i-omi-yo*, "(the totality of) his/her bones (the ones in his/her body)"; *ez-tli*, "blood"; *i-ez-yo* (also assimilated as *i-ez-ço*, "(all of) his blood (now in his body)." In some cases, as in the present one, English uses an entirely different word for the collective-inalienable form: *naca-tl*, "meat"; *i-naca-yo*, "his/her body." Word 4 lacks an absolute suffix because it is possessed.

[1]*amo* [2]*pactica*, "it is not healthy," "not (it-)is glad(-progressive)." The specified subject is still the preceding "body."

Word <u>1</u>. *amo*. the negative particle, as before.

Word <u>2</u>. *pac-ti-ca* "it is not healthy, sound," intransitive verb in present progressive. No subject prefix, so third person; *pac-* preterit of *paqui* "to rejoice, be happy, content," thus shortened to combine with a progressive auxiliary verb; *-ti-* the ligature, as before; *ca(h)* the auxiliary verb "to be." The progressive forms sometimes become quite frozen and get special meanings; *pactica* almost always means "be healthy, sound, as something should be." See *pactinemi* in Molina, defined as "tener salud," which is the same formation except with *nemi*, "to live," as the auxiliary verb. In general, when you don't find exactly what you are looking for in the dictionaries, consider well the possible relevance of similar and conceivably related forms.

¹*yece* ²*yn* ³*notlamachiliz* ⁴*cenca* ⁵*pactica*, "but my understanding is very sound," "but the my-something-knowing very it-is-being-happy."

Word 1. *yece (yeceh)*, clause-introductory particle "but, however, nevertheless," etc.

Word 2. *yn.* the article before a possessed noun again.

Word 3. *no-tla-machi-liz*, possessed noun, "my understanding," "my-something-know-ing." *no-* first person singular possessive prefix "my"; *tla-* indefinite object prefix "something," used in this form because even though nominal it comes from a transitive verb; *-machi-*, the stem of the nominalized verb, from *mati*; as mentioned before, some verbs change their final consonant when *-lia* and *-tia* suffixes follow them. This often holds for the *-liz* suffix meaning "-ing" as well. In such cases *t* and *tz* may change to *ch*, *c* (before *e* and *i*) and *ç* to *x*: *mati, machilia; notza, nochilia; a(h)ci, a(h)xi-lia*. The reason for these changes is that at one time there was a vowel preceding *-lia*, *-tia*, and *-liz(tli)* which was pronounced quite far back in the mouth and drew the preceding consonant back further along with it; i.e., *t* [t] and *tz* [ts] are farther forward than *ch* [ch]; *c/ç* [s] is farther forward than *x* [sh]). *-liz*, again the suffix making action nouns from verbs, "ing"; no absolute ending because possessed.

Word 4. *cenca.* the intensifying particle as before.

Word 5. *pactica* as before, specified subject this time "understanding."

¹*yn* ²*iuhqui* ³*nechmomaquili* ⁴*yn* ⁵*toteᵒ* ⁶*dios*, "as (or like) our lord God gave it to me," "the thus (he-)to me-it-gave the our-lord God."

Word 1. *yn.* here functions to indicate subordination of this entire clause to the previous clause.

Word 2. *iuhqui*, particle (originally a preterit verbal form), "thus," also seen as *iuh*. But especially in the longer form and especially when preceded by *in*, it almost always refers backward or forward, tying things together, often comparing, having the effect "like, as," etc. Here almost "the way that . . ."

Word 3. *nech-mo-maqui-li*, transitive verb in the reverential preterit, "he gave it (my understanding) to me." Notice that *o-*, the sign of the preterit, is missing here, as it often is; useful though its presence is, one cannot count on it to determine whether a verb is in the preterit or not. No subject prefix, third person; *nech-* first person singular object prefix "me," "to me"; Nahuatl makes no formal distinction between direct and indirect object for the most part, but when the indirect object is present the direct object prefix isn't, so there is no "it" in this form (however, the plurality of a direct animate object can be indicated even though there is an indirect object: *nech-im-maca* "he gives them to me"). *-mo-* third person reflexive prefix, first half of the reverential formula; *-maqui-*, the verb stem, from *maca*, "to give," vowel changed to *i* before *-lia*, *-c-* written *-qu-* for orthographic reasons; *-li (-lih)* preterit singular of applicative suffix *-lia*, the second half of the reverential formula.

Words 4–5–6. *yn toteᵒ dios* "(the) our lord God," as seen above.

¹*amo* ²*nitlapolohua*, "I have not lost my judgment, I am rational," "not I-something-lose."

Word 1. *amo*, negative particle, placed in front as usual.

Word 2. *ni-tla-polohua* "I lose, get rid of something or things," with the specific meaning

"I lose command of my senses." Transitive verb in present tense; *ni*- first person singular subject prefix "I"; *-tla-* indefinite object "something, things"; *polohua* (Molina, Carochi, *poloa*), verb, "to lose, destroy, efface, cause to disappear."

¹*auh* ²*yn* ³*axcan* ⁴*yntla* ⁵*nechmohuiquiliz* ⁶*dios*, "(And) now if God takes me," "And/ but the now if (he-)will take-me(-reverential) God."

Word 1. *auh*, clause-introductory particle, coming out in English sometimes as "and," sometimes as "but," often not to be translated at all, or one could say that it is translated as a period; that is, it generally implies that there was a full stop immediately preceding and that this is a new beginning. In general, *auh* punctuates between whole clauses, *(i)huan* "and, along with" between individual constituents or words. But alas, there are exceptions.

Words 2-3. *yn axcan*, subordinator plus particle, "(the) now." As before, the *yn* here is not indicating that the whole following clause is subordinated, but refers only to *axcan*. Apparently what happens is something like this: like Nahuatl nouns, *axcan* in and of itself is an equative statement "(the time is) now"; *in* subordinates this statement: "(at the time which is) now."

Word 4. *yntla*, clause-introductory particle, "if." Consists of *in-* as subordinator and *-tla* optative particle. *tla* also occurs by itself with the same meaning. Unlike English "if," *tla* and *intla* often do not necessarily imply any uncertainty about the outcome, are in effect more like English "when"—but not always.

Word 5. *nech-mo-huiqui-liz*, transitive verb in reverential future, "he will take me." If-clauses have the verb in the future more often in Nahuatl than they do in English; the future in fact is used to indicate all manner of hypothetical dependent statements, like "should," "would," or the infinitive in English. No subject prefix, hence subject third person, later specified as "God"; *nech-* first person singular object prefix "me"; *-mo-* third person reflexive prefix, here first half of the reverential formula; *-huiqui-*, verb stem, changed from *huica*, "to take, carry, accompany" (exactly like *-maqui-* from *maca* just above); *-liz*, future singular of *-lia* applicative suffix, here the second part of the reverential formula. The future is made by adding *-z* singular, *-zque(h)* plural, to the present tense form, which remains unchanged except that Class 3 verbs (*-ia, -oa*) lose their final *a: -lia, -liz*, but *choca*, "to cry," *chocaz*; *nemi*, "to live," *nemiz*. The Class 3 verbs lose their second vowel in several positions when the present tense stem of all other verbs remains unchanged. The big thing is to be prepared to reconstruct the *-a* to get the dictionary form after removing the suffix.

Word 6. *dios*, God, as before; the specified subject of *nechmohuiquiliz*.

¹*yntla* ²*ninomiquiliz*, "if I die (reverential)." Another clause with nearly the same basic meaning as the immediately preceding one.

Word 1. *yntla*, "if," as before.

Word 2. *ni-no-miqui-liz*, verb in the future reverential, "I will (should) die." *ni-* first person singular subject prefix; *-no-* first person singular reflexive prefix "myself," "to myself," here the first half of the reverential formula; *-miqui-*, the verb stem, being the entire unchanged intransitive verb *miqui*, "to die" (again, not all verbs before *-lia* have had *-a* changed to *-i*; some end in *-i-* in the first place, like this one); *-liz* future singular of *-lia* applicative suffix, here the second half of the reverential formula. This entire verb complex is transitive because *-lia* adds transitivity; but the *-no-* reflexive and the *-lia* applicative cancel each other out and we know that this is an essentially intransitive verb even if we have never seen it before. If it were truly transitive there would be some further indication of object, like *-c-* or *-tla-*. Knowing about transitivity not only helps you interpret the sentence, it is a hint in dictionary search, because as already mentioned, despite exceptions the majority of transitive verbs in Nahuatl end in -a, the majority of intransitive verbs in -i. Close attention to transitivity also allows you to distinguish between related verb forms of quite different meaning. Intransitive *pohui* is "to belong," transitive *pohua* is "to assign (cause to belong)" and other meanings: *mo-pohui-lia*, "he/she belongs (reverential)," from *pohui*; *qui-mo-pohui-li-lia*, "he/she assigns it to him/her (reverential)," from *pohua*. Intransitive *nemi*, "to live": *mo-nemi-tia*, "he/she lives (reverential)" (intransitives especially often use the causative for the reverential suffix instead of the applicative); *qui-nemi-tia*, the true causative, "he/she causes him/her to live, maintains him/her"; *qui-mo-nemi-ti-lia*, the causative reverential, same meaning again, "he/she maintains him/her." Some grammarians have expressed the notion that an intransitive verb with a first person subject cannot be reverential, that first person verbs can be reverential only if they are transitive and the honorific aspect can be referred to the object. That will indeed most often be the case, but nevertheless, here we have a first person intransitive in the reverential; it is one more indication that the Nahuatl reverential is not at all like the European system, which primarily concerns the relative position of interlocutors, but refers to the entire occasion or to particular objects or events which have a certain status regardless of the speaker.

[1]ca [2]ymactzinco [3]noconcahua [4]yn [5]noyolia [6]yn [7]naniman, "I deliver my spirit and soul into his hands," "why his-hand-into (rev.) I-it-deliver the my-spirit the my-soul."

Word 1. *ca*, clause-introductory particle, not needing translation into English here. In this case, as often, *ca* signals that the introductory, topicalized, or subordinate matter has ended and the main statement is about to begin. Compare English "why." *Intla ticmonequiltiz ca nicchihuaz*, "If you want me to, why I'll do it." *In aquin oquichiuh ca huel nehuatl*, "As to who did it, why it was me myself."

Word 2. *y-ma-c-tzin-co* "in his hands," "his arm/hand-at/in-reverential-at/in." This is a difficult form to explain to the neophyte. It appears to and in fact does have the same element -*c*/-*co*, a locative relational word (or suffix, since it is never seen except attached to a preceding noun), two times in the same complex, but with a different function each time. First of all, -*c*/-*co*, "at, in, place where" alternates on the same principle as the absolutive suffix -*tl*/-*tli*; that is, the short form occurs after a vowel stem, the long form after a consonant stem where the extra vowel is needed for pronunciation. The first -*c* in the present form is attached to the noun *ma(i)-tl*, being -*c* rather than -*co* because *ma-* ends in a vowel. (Beginners find -*c* very hard to recognize. When they see *ymac* they may not unnaturally take it for a preterit verb, a particle, or a possessed noun *mac-tli*, rather than *y-ma-c*, possessed noun plus locative suffix.) Second, the frozen structure -*tzin-co* is part of Nahuatl's overall reverential system. -*tzin* is added to words of several different kinds, in slightly different ways which help tell the reader what part of speech he is dealing with; -*tzinoa* (preterit -*tzino*, future -*tzinoz*) is added to a verb; plain -*tzin* appears mainly on possessed nouns or absolutiveless proper names; -*tzintli* is for unpossessed nouns; and -*tzinco* tells you that what is to the left is most likely a relational word: for example, *i-ca*, "its-through, through it"; *i-ca-tzin-co*, the same in the reverential; *i-pal*, "for the sake of, by means of," *i-pal-tzin-co*, the reverential. In this combination -*co* no longer has locative meaning, but merely says that the preceding is a relational word rather than a regular noun. All this remains true even when a noun is compounded with the relational word: *cal-li*, "house"; -*nahuac*, relational word, "close to"; *cal-nahauc-tzin-co* "close to a or the house (reverential)." One might say that in *i-*

chan-tzin-co, "at his/her home," *-tzin-co* is a true locative reverential suffixed to a noun, but I think not. *-chan,* "home," is an anomalous noun always possessed in texts, always locative and partaking of the nature of a relational word; *i-chan* means "at his/her home" all by itself, and one never sees *i-chan-co.* With place names, *-tzin-co* has actual locative meaning and also is not reverential, but indicates a settlement named after another, usually being smaller than the parent community and sometimes close to it: Teocal-co, Teocal-tzin-co. Even here the *-co* is added regardless of whether or not the original had it, and usually to something with a relational word: Tlaxcal-lan, Tlaxcal-lan-tzin-co. Word 2 is of the type of a noun plus a relational word, with the noun possessed in addition: *y-* third person singular possessive prefix "his," referring back to "God" in an earlier clause; *-ma(-itl),* noun, "arm, forearm, hand as instrument," without the absolutive, which is replaced by a relational word (*maitl* is never in the plural in classical older Nahuatl even if the meaning seems plural, but acts like the inanimates, as do body parts in general); *-c-,* relational word, here meaning "in"; *-tzin-co,* reverential for relational words as just discussed.

Word 3. *no-c-on-cahua,* transitive verb in present tense, "I deliver it (the following)," "I-it-in outward direction-leave/deliver." *no-* looks like either the first person singular reflexive prefix "myself" or the first person singular possessive prefix "my," but it is neither, being instead the form that *ni-,* first person singular subject prefix "I" usually (not always) takes when it is followed by the combination *-c-on* (i.e., the *i* of *ni* assimilates to the *o* of *on* across the consonant *c*); *-c-* third person singular object prefix "it," later to be specified as "soul"; *-on-* directional affix to verbs indicating motion outward, away from the speaker. *on* pairs with *hual,* mentioned once above, which is the same kind of affix indicating motion inward, toward the speaker. The two also refer to time; *on* to something going on from now into the indefinite future, and *hual* to something going on from a past time in the direction of the present. There are also more subtle uses and connotations, and *on* especially is sometimes used more to add a reverential tone than for its stricter meaning. It is also used to make too-short verbs long enough, as in *onoc,* "to lie," and *oni,* "to drink." So many subtleties are involved that in effect we often ignore the directional affixes in translation; but we must at least be able to identify them and distinguish them from the verb stem before we can disregard them. Both are assigned to the same invariable position among the verbal prefixes, immediately after the object if there is one and just before the reflexive if there is one (the reverential of *noconcahua* would be *no-c-on-no-cahui-lia*). *-cahua,* "to leave (in almost all the same senses as the English verb), to deliver."

Word 4. *yn,* "article" before possessed noun.

Word 5. *no-yoli-a* "my spirit, soul." Human constituent parts are always possessed in Nahuatl; the most usual way to say "the soul" is "our soul," so this word like more physical parts is to be found in Molina under "our," *toyolia* (likewise *to-yac* "our nose," etc.) However, the word is regularly derived from a verb, and many such constructions are not to be found in dictionaries at all, leaving it up to the reader to figure out the sense independently. Without going into what this form really is (a deverbal instrumental substantive), it always starts with a possessive prefix, followed by a verb in the imperfect (i.e., the present tense form plus *-[y]a),* and it signifies the thing by means of which the possessor carries out the action of the verb. *no-* first person singular possessive prefix; *-yoli-* "to live"; *(y)a* imperfect ending, or at least something that looks just like the imperfect ending (when a verb stem ends in *-i,* the *y* of the *ya* imperfect is often not written). The signified thing, the spirit, is in some sense what its possessor lives with. The expression may or may not have been invented specifically as a counterpart to or definition of Spanish *ánima*.

Word <u>6</u>. *yn*. Again the second "article" in quick succession hints "and," i.e., that what follows will be paired with or identical to Word 5.

Word <u>7</u>. *n-animan* "my soul," possessed loan noun. No subject prefix, hence third person subject. *n-* first person singular possessive prefix "my," since the *o* of *no-* is usually elided before any vowel other than *i*; *animan*, Spanish loan noun "soul." Intrusive *n*'s occur constantly in Nahuatl texts; one must delete them to get at dictionary forms. With *anima*, the added final *n* is so common that one can well consider it standard. The word is sometimes seen in texts as *āīa*. A general convention of Spanish writing was that any syllable-final nasal could be represented by a line over the preceding vowel, and this pervades Nahuatl writing: *ipā*, *ipan*, "in (something)"; *nomō*, *nomon*, "my son-in-law," etc. The extreme weakness of [n] in spoken Nahuatl may have had something to do with the pervasiveness of this convention in Nahuatl writing. In this text the overbars have been resolved into *n*'s and *m*'s.

¹*ma* ²*quihualmaniliz*, "may he (come) take it (my soul)."

Word <u>1</u>. *ma*, optative particle, "let, may," as before.

Word <u>2</u>. *qui-hual-m-ani-liz*, transitive verb in optative future reverential; no subject prefix, hence third person subject; *qui-* third person singular object prefix "it"; *-hual-* directional prefix "in this direction," in this case quite important to the overall meaning, necessitating that an English translation add "come"; *-m-* the third person reflexive *-mo-* reduced because of the following vowel, here the first half of the reverential formula (note that the three prefixes are in their normal order); *-ani-* verb stem, changed from *ana* the transitive verb "to take" because of the following *-lia*; *-liz*, future and optative future (there is no difference) singular of *-lia* the applicative suffix, here the second half of the reverential formula. When *mo-* reduces to *m-* before a verb beginning with a vowel, there is no way of being sure beforehand whether the *m* is part of the verb or not. One must check both possibilities in the dictionary. In fact, there is a verb *mana*, "to offer, etc.," and except for a vowel-length difference which does not show up in texts or Molina, *mana* would work perfectly well here. Its final *-a* would also change to *i*; the applicative suffix, not being balanced by the reflexive, would have the true applicative meaning; the form would be translated "that he (come) offer it for or to him." But this translation doesn't fit the larger context here, so we decide in favor of *ana*, and will find it confirmed in similar texts in less ambiguous form. At any rate, remember that verb roots apparently beginning *m-* may actually begin with the following vowel (and the same in first person singular, with *n-* from *no-* and first person plural *t-* from *to-*: *nicnaquilia*, "I insert it (rev.)," from *aquia*; *nicnanquilia*, "I reply to him/her," from *nanquilia*.

¹*ca* ²*cenca* ³*nicnotlatlauhtilia* ⁴*yn* ⁵*tlaçocihuapilli* ⁶*s*^{ta} ⁷*m*^a ⁸*cemicac* ⁹*ichpochtli*, "for I greatly implore the precious lady Saint Mary, forever virgin, that . . .," "for greatly I-her-implore (rev.) the precious-woman-noble Saint Mary forever maiden."

Word <u>1</u>. *ca*, clause-introductory particle, here translatable as "for." By "particle" is meant any word which does not accept prefixes and suffixes to show different states, numbers, tenses, etc., but is always invariant; in other words, just about everything in the language that is not a noun word, verb, or relational word. Most of the particles in Nahuatl have the functions of adverbs and conjunctions in English (the relational words having those of our prepositions), but we don't call them by the English grammatical terms because there is hardly any distinction between them (*çan*, for example, is like an adverb when it means "merely," like a conjunction when it means "but"). As mainly small, weightless words or half-words, they cluster in various combinations at the beginning of clauses and phrases, half-attached to the larger noun or verb complexes which they precede. Normally they refer forward.

Word 2. *cenca*, intensifying particle, seen above, here "greatly, very much."

Word 3. *ni-c-no-tlatlauhti-lia*, transitive verb in present tense reverential, "I implore her (the following person)." *ni-* first person singular subject prefix "I"; *-c-* third person singular object prefix, here "her" (Mary); *-no-* first person singular reflexive prefix used as part of the reverential formula; *-tlatlauhti-*, the verb stem, from *tlatlauhtia*, "to pray, implore, speak to in supplication, address formally" (Class 3 verbs, that is, *-ia* and *-oa* verbs, lose the final *-a* before the applicative, causative, and passive suffixes); *-lia* applicative suffix, completing the reverential formula.

Word 4. *yn.* "article."

Word 5. *tlaço-cihua-pil-li*, compound noun further compounded with adjective/noun, "precious lady." *tlaço-*, a noun incorporated adjectivally into the noun, from *tlaço(h)-tli* "a thing which is precious, dear, expensive, fine, high, etc." Noun words which function as adjectives, like this one, can either stand apart from what they modify, retaining the absolutive, or they can be incorporated into the modified noun, losing the absolutive suffix, as here. *-cihua-*, from the noun *cihua-tl*, "woman," having lost its absolutive to be combined with a following noun. Nahuatl has few gender-specific nouns and tends to add *cihua-* for the specifically female, *oquich-*, "male human being," for the specifically male. As in this case, two nouns neither of which by any stretch of the imagination is an adjective can be freely combined in Nahuatl; the modifier comes first and loses its absolutive, while the term modified comes second and retains the absolutive: *cihua-ocelo-tl*, "woman-jaguar, female jaguar"; *ocelo-cihua-tl*, "jaguar-woman." (However, when one of the two terms is abstract and the other concrete, Nahuatl generally makes the concrete one modify the abstract one, contrary to English practice: *tlal-cohualli* "land-purchased thing," which we would call "purchased land.") *-pil-li*, noun, "noble person," with absolutive suffix as being unpossessed. *cihuapilli* is unambiguously "lady" rather than "female child," which would be *cihuapiltzintli* or *cihuapiltontli*. Some of the most inherently reverential nouns in Nahuatl do not appear in overtly reverential form: *pilli*, "nobleman"; *cihua-pilli*, "noblewoman, lady"; *tlatoani*, "ruler, king"; *teuctli* "lord."

Words 6–7. *s^{ta} m^a*, standard abbreviation for *santa María*.

Word 8. *cemicac*, a particle, "forever, eternally." Some particles are more recently evolved than others and still reveal the elements of which they are made; this one is originally a verb phrase: *cem-*, "one," which attached to verbs means "entirely, once and for all, forever"; *i(h)cac*, irregular verb, "it stands."

Word 9. *ichpoch-tli*, third person singular unpossessed noun with absolutive suffix, in apposition with "Mary." The meaning is close to that of Spanish *doncella*, young unmarried woman, with some implication of virginity. When possessed it means "daughter," but specifically one who is grown up: *no-chpoch*, "my daughter," (note characteristic loss of initial *i* after a possessive prefix).

¹*ma* ²*nopan* ³*motlatoltiz* ⁴*yn* ⁵*ixpantzinco* ⁶*ytlaçoconetzin* ⁷*tote^o* ⁸*jesu* ⁹*x^o*, "that she speak for me before her dear child our lord Jesus Christ," "may my-for she-speak (rev.) the his-before her-dear-child (rev.) our lord Jesus Christ."

Word 1. *ma*, the optative particle "let/may" as before, here introducing a subordinate clause with no overt indication that it is subordinated except that the object of the verb in the previous clause was left unspecified until now, this clause therefore being what is implored.

<u>Word</u> <u>2</u>. *no-pan*, relational word bound with possessive prefix, "my-for, for me." *no-* first person singular possessive prefix "my"; *-pan* "on, in," also as here "for."

<u>Word</u> <u>3</u>. *mo-tla-to-ltiz*, transitive verb in optative future reverential, "(she) speak." No subject prefix, hence third person; *mo-* third person reflexive prefix, here half of the reverential; *-tla-* indefinite nonpersonal object prefix "something." These two elements are in their normal order; whereas the specific object (*-c-*, etc.) goes before the reflexive, the indefinite object comes after it, the last thing before the verb stem. *-to-*, the verb stem, from *i(h)toa*, "to say"; the *i* is elided being adjacent to the *a* of *tla-*; the *h* is left unwritten; at the other end, as normal with Class 3 verbs, the final *-a* is dropped before the causative, leaving only *-to-*. *tla-* forms of transitive verbs act in effect like intransitives and often even get different translations: *tla-toa* "to speak," in all the senses of the English verb; *itoa* with a specific object, "to say (some particular thing)." *-ltiz*, (optative) future singular of *-ltia*, variant of the causative suffix, here the second half of the reverential.

<u>Word</u> <u>4</u>. *yn*. the "article," often used before relational words.

<u>Word</u> <u>5</u>. *ix-pan-tzin-co*, possessed compound relational word in reverential, "before, in the presence of (the following person)." *ix(-tli)* "face, sight, eye," noun, combined with *-pan*, the relational word "in, on" seen just above, the two becoming a new compound relational word "in the presence of," etc. This form takes possessive prefixes like any other (*n-ixpan* "my-before, before me"), but when the affix is third person singular, the *i-* falls together with the vowel of the root as a single written *i*. We know the possessive *i-* is intended because relational words are always bound with something, either a noun or a possessive prefix. *-tzin-co*, the reverential of relational words, as seen before.

<u>Word</u> <u>6</u>. *y-tlaço-cone-tzin*, possessed noun with adjective/noun compounded to it, in reverential, "her dear child." *y-* third person singular possessive prefix "her"; *-tlaço-* "dear," adjectival noun word combined with noun, hence following the possessive prefix and lacking its own absolutive suffix, which it does have when independent; *cone(-tl)*, "child"; often differs from *pil(-li)* in being specifically the child of a woman, as here; *-tzin* reverential suffix; no absolutive suffix because possessed.

<u>Word</u> <u>7</u>. *tote*[o] "our lord(ship)," standard abbreviation for *totecuiyo* as before.

<u>Words</u> <u>8</u>–<u>9</u>. *jesu x*[o], "Jesus Christ." *x*[o], or more frequently *xpo̅*, was the standard abbreviation for *christo* in older texts, based on the appearance of the first letters of the word in Greek; the full form is hardly ever seen in either Spanish or Nahuatl texts.

[1]*ma* [2]*nechmocnoyttiliz*, "that he view me compassionately," "may (he-)me-poor-see (rev.)."

<u>Word</u> <u>1</u>. *ma*, optative particle "may/let," here in effect "that," same construction as the preceding clause, except that it is left up to the reader to figure out without external indication that the subject has changed to "Jesus Christ" and this clause is dependent upon the one immediately preceding rather than parallel to it.

<u>Word</u> <u>2</u>. *nech-mo-cno-ytti-liz*, transitive verb in optative future, in reverential, "he have pity on me." No subject prefix, hence third person subject; *nech-*, first person singular object prefix "me"; *-mo-*, third person reflexive prefix, here half of the reverential formula; *-cno-* from *icno(-tl)*, noun, "poor or humble person, orphan," which is freely combined with various verbs, adding to them the sense of performing the act with humility or compassion. It causes endless trouble for beginning verb analyzers, because the *i* is elided after any vowel, as it is in this case, and what is left, *-cno-*, looks like the object prefix *-c-* plus the first person reflexive *-no-*, and is even in the

correct order, in itself. One must look carefully at the rest of the verb complex; the present case is an easy one, since there could not be two different reflexive prefixes affixed to the same verb; nor could the -c- represent the object, since it comes after the reflexive prefix -mo- instead of before, aside from there already being another object prefix. The first person forms get somewhat more dizzying: "I will have pity on him/her (rev.)" would be ni-c-no-cnoittiliz. -ytti-, the verb stem, changed from itta because of the following applicative suffix (and with y for i despite the general tendency to write i unit-internally [at least it is root-initial]); first vowel not elided as it would usually be because the preceding o is long. Actually many of the verbs compounded with icno- are so common and have such special meanings that the whole compound will be found in the dictionary, as will this one, as icnoitta, nite, "apiadarse de." -liz, (optative) future singular of the applicative suffix -lia, here the second half of the reverential formula.

^{1}ca ^{2}nopampa ^{3}omomiquili, "for on my behalf he died (rev.)."

Word 1. ca the clause-introductory particle, here translatable as "for."

Word 2. no-pampa, possessed relational word, "my-behalf, my-(be)cause; because of me, on my behalf." no- first person singular possessive prefix "my"; -pampa, relational word, "cause, concern, behalf, for"; the last meaning is the same as one of the meanings of the relational word -pan, already seen above, and in fact -pampa is -pan plus -pa, "toward" (and other meanings). i-pampa, with -pampa bound to the third person singular possessive, the latter referring to a whole clause, is Nahuatl's most frequent way of saying "because."

Word 3. o-mo-miqui-li, intransitive verb in preterit reverential, "he died." o- sign of the preterit; no subject prefix (which would come in this position), hence third person subject; -mo- third person reflexive, here half of the reverential; -miqui-, verb stem, unchanged from miqui "to die" because although followed by the applicative it already ends in -i; -li, preterit singular of the applicative -lia, here the second half of the reverential formula.

^{1}cruztitech ^{2}omamaçohualtiloc, "he was stretched out on the cross," "cross-joined-to he-was-made-to-arm-spread-out (distributive)."

Word 1. cruz-ti-tech, loan noun with relational word suffixed, "cross-joined-to," "on the cross." The beginner would be much inclined to assign this word to the previous clause: "he died on the cross." This is in fact not utterly impossible; only reading the following clause will entirely convince one that cruztitech belongs with it. However, the result does conform to general expectations, since not only particles but all kinds of phrases used more or less adverbially usually precede the verb they modify unless they are long enough to spoil the balance of the sentence. cruz-, loan noun "cross," behaving like any other Nahuatl noun except that it has no absolute suffix to lose in the first place; -ti-, ligature between noun and relational word; -tech, relational word, "next to, stuck to, at, on," etc., used in all kinds of situations calling for connection, part of countless idioms with verbs.

Word 2. o-ma-ma-çohua-lti-loc, transitive verb in passive preterit, "his arms were spread out," "he was made to arm-(distributive)-spread out." o-, sign of the preterit; no subject prefix, hence third person; no object prefix, hence, once we have figured out the main verb of the construction is transitive, it must be in the passive; skipping past -ma-ma- for the moment, -çohua- (Molina çoa) is the transitive verb "to spread out, extend"; back to -ma-, combining form of the noun ma(i)-tl, "arm," added to çohua gives ma-çohua "to extend the arm(s)," a compound verb which itself will be found in

Molina; since *ma-* is the object of *çohua*, the verb as a whole is intransitive. *-ma-ma-* is distributive; both nouns and verbs can reduplicate the first syllable to indicate, with nouns, mainly plurality, with verbs mainly varied or repeated action. Whichever way we take it, as reduplication of the incorporated noun or, more likely, of the verb as a whole, the effect is the same, to spread out both arms. Reduplication has many subtle and difficult aspects; the main thing about it at this point is to be alert to recognize it as such in order to be able to reduce the root to its simple form, in order in turn to find it in the dictionary. *-lti-* from *-ltia* the causative variant, minus its *a* before the passive suffix; this for once is a true causative, not paired with a reflexive pronoun as the reverential; the whole verb *mamaçohualtia*, now transitive again, means "to make someone spread both arms out." *-loc*, preterit singular of the passive suffix, reversing the semantic direction, so that the whole construct comes to mean "he was made to spread out both arms."

¹*oquimonoquili* ²*yn* ³*itlaçoyezçotzin*, "he spilled (rev.) his precious blood (rev.)" The clause is parallel to the previous two, all of them following upon *ca*, "for."

Word 1. *o-qui-mo-noqui-li*, transitive verb in preterit reverential, "he spilled (it, the following)." *o-*, sign of the preterit; no subject prefix, hence third person subject; *-qui-* third person singular object prefix; *-mo-* third person reflexive prefix, here half of the reverential formula; *-noqui-*, the verb stem, from *noquia*, "to spill, pour out," which as a Class 3 verb loses the final *a* before the applicative; *-li*, preterit singular of applicative suffix *-lia*, here the second half of the reverential.

Word 2. *yn*. the "article."

Word 3. *i-tlaço-yez-ço-tzin*, possessed noun with incorporated adjective/noun and collective-inalienable suffix, in reverential, "his precious blood"; acts as specified object of the preceding verb. No subject prefix, third person subject. *i-*, third person singular possessive prefix "his"; *-tlaço-* the incorporated adjectival noun word without its absolutive, as seen before; *-yez-*, noun stem, variant form of *ez(-tli)*, "blood." Not in Molina with the *y-*, but frequently so seen. Both of the glides, [y] *y* and [w] *hu-, u-, v-*, occur with great irregularity in Nahuatl; any word that has them in the dictionary may appear without them in texts, and almost any word without them may occur with them in texts. *y* varies more, and especially when it is before *e* (not to speak of when it follows syllabic *i* before another vowel): *eztli* or *yeztli*, "blood"; *etl* or *yetl*, "bean," *yei* or *ei*, "three"; *yehuatl* or *ehuatl*, "that one," etc. One of the standard things to do when you can't find a stem in the dictionary is to start adding and subtracting *y*'s. *-ço-*, nominal inalienable/collective suffix, from the *-yo-* discussed above, which may assimilate to the preceding stem; if it ends *-z-*, *-yo* may become *ço* ; if *-l-*, *-lo*. Molina, by the way, alphabetizes *y* with *i*, just after *h*. *-tzin* reverential suffix (*-yo* forms a new noun stem and thus precedes *-tzin*); no absolutive suffix because possessed.

¹*ynic* ²*ninomaquixtiz* "so that I might be redeemed," "so-that I-myself-will-redeem."

Word 1. This clause depends on the previous one, giving the reason or purpose for the earlier mentioned action, that being among the most common of the many functions of the often clause-introductory word *ynic*. One hesitates to call it a particle not only because it consists of the particle *in* plus *ic* and the *ic* can appear alone with most of the same meanings, but above all because *ic* itself is apparently a relational word *-c*, "purpose, means, manner," bound to the third person singular possessive prefix *i-*. Nevertheless, it never appears in any other person, and being invariant is very particle-like. *ic* and *inic* have so many meanings and uses that it is hopeless to try to deal with them here. The notion of purpose is at least a good start.

Word <u>2</u>. *ni-no-ma-quix-tiz*, transitive verb in reflexive future, "I will be redeemed," "I-myself-will-redeem." *ni-* first person singular subject prefix "I"; *-no-* first person singular reflexive prefix "myself"; as in this case, the most common use of the reflexive, when it is not part of the reverential, is to create a semantic passive, just as in Spanish, which is used at least as much as the "true" passive in *-lo* and *-o*. *-ma-quixti-*, though a compound, is the effective verb stem here, from *maquixtia* "to save, redeem," to be found in Molina as such, which as a Class 3 verb loses its final *a* before the future (singular) suffix *-z*. Analyzing the compound, *ma-* is the combining form of the noun *ma(i)-tl*, "arm," here apparently indicating instrumentality; *-quix-* verb stem from *quiça*, "to emerge, come out." We saw above that the last consonant of several verbs is modified when the applicative or causative suffixes are added; *ç* becomes *x* in these cases, as here. Also, before the causative specifically, some verb stems not only change final vowels (*a* to *i*), but lose the final vowel entirely, which has happened here. *-tia*, the causative suffix. The compound means "to cause to emerge (from trouble, captivity) by using the arms, to lift one out of trouble," hence "to save, redeem (including to get out of hock)." Word 2 is quite tricky in that despite the pairing of reflexive and causative it is not the reverential of intransitive *maquiça*, "to escape" (which exists). *Maquixtia* is treated as an unanalyzable simple transitive verb, something that one could establish with certainty only from having seen many other cases of the use of this verb in similar contexts.

[1]*yhuan* [2]*yehuatzin* [3]*s^t* [4]*ju^o* [5]*bap^{ta}* [6]*nosantotzin* [7]*ma* [8]*nopan* [9]*motlatoltiz* [10]*yn* [11]*ixpantzinco* [12]*dios*, "and may San Juan Bautista, my saint, speak for me before God," "its-with he (rev.) San Juan Bautista my-saint (rev.) may my-for he-speak (rev.) the his-before (rev.) God."

Word <u>1</u>. *y-huan*, relational word bound with possessive prefix, "and," "its-with." As said above, this construction ties nouns together more often than whole clauses, as it seems to here; however, the latter does happen. Nevertheless, it is possible that the referent of *y-* is Saint Mary, so that *yhuan* would be "her-with," "in addition to her."

Word <u>2</u>. *yehua-tzin*, "he," "that one," emphatic pronoun, third person singular, in reverential. *ye(h)hua-tl* is a noun word, with an absolutive suffix, but does not behave entirely like ordinary nouns; it cannot be possessed, and when the reverential *-tzin* is suffixed to it the absolutive suffix disappears despite there being no possession involved. *ye(h)hua* also occurs, and also *ye(h)*, the shorter forms getting correspondingly less emphasis and being more nearly incorporated into what follows. The forms can and often do refer to a person or thing specified at some distance, but sometimes, as here, they are placed immediately before the referent. The nonreverential versions can convey a reserve toward the person, as English "that" can: *yehuatl ichtequi* "that thief"; but more frequently it is respectful or neutral, and then English simply leaves it untranslated.

Words <u>3</u>–<u>4</u>–<u>5</u>. *s^t ju^o bap^{ta}*, standard abbreviation for *san(t) juan baptista*.

Word <u>6</u>. *no-santo-tzin*, possessed loan noun in reverential, "my saint." *no-* first person singular possessive prefix "my"; *-santo-*, loan noun "saint"; *-tzin* reverential suffix; no absolutive suffix on two counts, since the form is possessed and even more to the point in this case, since the Spanish loan noun has no absolutive ending to begin with. No subject prefix, so the construct as a whole is in the third person.

Words <u>7</u>–<u>8</u>–<u>9</u>–<u>10</u>–<u>11</u>–<u>12</u> *ma nopan motlatoltiz yn ixpantzinco dios*, "may he speak for me before God." Identical to a clause discussed above (p. 180), except for the last word. In this case, however, the clause is not dependent on a preceding one in which the subject was specified; rather it is an independent clause in which the specified subject of the verb (San Juan Bautista) has been removed from its expected place after the verbal complex and put in front, emphasizing it and singling it out as the topic for discussion. If a string of words appears to be a unified independent clause and there is anything in front of the particle or particles, that element is being made the focus. Constructions like "the dog I'm going to feed him" or "the child let them not forget him" are typical of Nahuatl and not uncommon in Spanish, but less characteristic of English, so English speakers need to attune themselves to focus through preposing.

¹*ynic* ²*centlamantli*, "first," "how (or with-it) one-separate thing."

Word 1. *ynic*, the particle-like word referred to above, with so many senses having to do with purpose or means, also sometimes translatable as "how." One of its many uses is to create ordinal numbers; that is, placing *inic* in front of a cardinal number makes it ordinal: *ce*, "one"; *inic ce*, "first"; *ome*, "two"; *inic ome*, "second," etc. *ic* by itself has the same effect: *ic ce*, "first."

Word 2. *cen-tlaman-tli*, number word compounded with a noun acting as classifier or base for numerals, "one separate thing, one item." *cen-*, combining form of *ce-*, "one"; *tlaman-tli*, third person singular noun in absolutive, "matter, item, separate thing or group," possibly derived from the verb *mani* "to be (spread out over a flat surface)," or more likely from its transitive counterpart *mana*. Nahuatl uses (optionally) a set of classifiers in counting, like English "ten head of cattle." The one most seen is *tetl*, which is also a noun meaning "stone," originally for counting round things but then greatly extended: *nauh-tetl metlatl*, "four metates." *tlamantli* is another of them, with a rather large range of things it can count, but above all matters to be discussed, things to be taken care of, demands, requests, subheadings in a larger discourse, etc.; it seems to occur especially with the ordinal numbers. The items of a will or the paragraphs of a petition are standardly introduced by *(yn-)ic* (number in combining form-)*tlamantli*, which we could handle as "first item," "second item," but usually can do justice to in English simply with "first," "second," etc.

¹*nitlanahuatia* ²*niquitohua*, "I order, I say (that) . . .", "I-something-order, I-it-say." A verb with *tla-* and no specific object prefix cannot have a specified object, not even a whole clause. Here as so often, Nahuatl puts first the general, then the specific which illustrates it. "I give orders (or an order): (and getting down to cases) I say (that) . . ."

Word 1. *ni-tla-nahuatia*, transitive verb in present tense, "I order, command, give orders." *ni-* first person singular subject prefix "I"; *-tla-* indefinite nonpersonal object prefix "something"; *-nahuatia*, the verb. The *-tia* on the end does bear some relation to the causative *-tia*, but the meaning is not, or at least no longer, "I cause something to perform an act denoted by the verb *nahua*." Though such an analysis is perfectly reasonable and in fact quite indicated for the novice, it is not borne out in dictionary work. Not finding any verb *nahua*, one asks if this could be a different *-tia* (of which there are several types), or if, as very often happens, an originally causative suffix has been permanently incorporated into the verb. Many dictionary verbs ending in *-tia* and *-lia* are causatives or applicatives by origin but have been frozen in that form, while the stem preceding them has disappeared from independent use. *tla-nahuatia* is in effect an intransitive verb and almost always means "to order"; the same verb with a specific object, very frequently seen, varies in meaning more; it can mean to order someone to do something, but also to notify, announce, advise, etc.: *nicnahuatia* "I inform him/her" (or, possibly, "I instruct him/her to . . .").

Word 2. *ni-qu-itohua*, transitive verb in present tense, "I say (that) . . .," "I-it-say," as analyzed above (p. 167); the entire following main clause with its dependent clauses is the specified object.

¹*yn* ²*iquac* ³*yntla* ⁴*oninomiquili,* "when I die," "when I have died," "the when if I-have-died (rev.)."

<u>Word 1</u>. *yn.* *in* preceding a temporal particle indicating that its meaning is contingent and that the clause is subordinate.

<u>Word 2</u>. *iquac (ihquac),* particle, "when." Unlike English "when," *iquac* does not necessarily introduce a dependent clause (and is not at all interrogative); when it is not preceded by the subordinator *in*, it can mean "at that time (as given by the general context)", or "(that was the time) when."

<u>Word 3</u>. *yntla,* particle, "if"; as seen and discussed above, it does not necessarily imply uncertainty, especially when used with the preterit and paired with *iquac* as it is here. The combination of the two does <u>not</u> mean what English does with "when and if."

<u>Word 4</u>. *o-ni-no-miqui-li,* intransitive verb in preterit reverential, "I have died." *o-*, sign of the preterit; *-ni-* first person singular subject prefix "I"; *-no-* first person singular reflexive prefix, here the first half of the reverential formula; *-miqui-*, the verb stem, unchanged from the verb "to die" as already ending *-i* as we have seen before; *-li* preterit singular of *-lia* the applicative suffix, here the second half of the reverential.

¹*ompa* ²*ninotocaz* ³*yn* ⁴*huey* ⁵*teupan* ⁶*s*ᵗ ⁷*ju*ᵒ ⁸*bap*ᵗᵃ, "I will be buried at the great church of San Juan Bautista," "there I-myself-will-bury the big church San Juan Bautista."

<u>Word 1</u>. *ompa,* particle, "there." With places, as with many other kinds of elements (as we have already seen), Nahuatl will often prepose a brief hint that a place designation is coming, and only later specify the place fully; most typical is to position a word like "there" before the verb, as here, with the full specification after it; or the designation may follow "there" immediately. In either case it is, from the point of view of idiomatic English, redundant, and need not be translated. *ompa* consists originally of *on*, the demonstrative "that," and *-pa*, "toward." It may indicate a place more distant than *oncan*, which is also "there" but in a more neutral sense (i.e., *ompa* is like Spanish *allá*, *oncan* like *allí*); yet in fact the two are often used as substitutes for each other in stylistic variation.

<u>Word 2</u>. *ni-no-toca-z,* transitive verb, in future, reflexive, "I will be buried," "I-myself-will-bury." The reflexive as a passive equivalent again. *ni-* first person singular subject prefix "I"; *-no-* first person singular reflexive prefix "myself"; *-toca-* the transitive verb "to bury"; *-z* future singular ending. Since there is no applicative suffix, the reflexive has its true force rather than being part of the reverential.

<u>Word 3</u>. *yn.* "article."

<u>Word 4</u>. *huey,* noun word/adjective, "something large, big, great." Standard orthography *huei*. Never has an absolutive ending in the singular, but in the plural may be seen as *(hue)hue(y)-in-tin,* sometimes without the final *-tin*. When combined directly with the following noun or other element it may become *hue(h)-*.

<u>Word 5</u>. *teupan* (standard *teopan*, *u* for *o* again), "at the church," a noun plus relational word combination that has taken on a special meaning and has gone four-fifths of the way to becoming a new noun in a new sense. *teo-(tl)* "holy thing, god"; *-pan,* relational word "in, on, for," etc., seen above, also as here "where anything is," the whole construct meaning "where a god or holy things are," and hence specifically "at the church" (in preconquest times "at the temple"). This expression then begins to mean the church or church precinct itself, can be used as the specified subject or object of verbs, and in this use can even (though not necessarily) take an absolute

suffix as *teopan-tli*. Nevertheless, "at the church" is still just *teopan*, not *teopanco* or some such (the reverential is *teopantzinco* as with any other compound relational word). *teopan* is only one of many *-pan* compounds which act like nouns part of the time.

Words 6–7–8. *s^t ju^o bap^{ta}*, standard abbreviations for *San(t) Juan Baptista* or *Bautista*, "San Juan Bautista." As so often, Nahuatl has no need to say "of" ("church of").

*   *   *

Here I have stopped. At one time I meant to go on for at least the rest of the page, perhaps the whole document. But many of the basic elements have already been repeatedly illustrated, and the most essential general points have been made. Perhaps, too, I should have chosen a different kind of text for the purpose (though this one is very beautiful Nahuatl and does seem to serve, all in all). At any rate, sooner or later the totally guided approach must be halted and the student must face texts without a specific guide. In working with new texts, proceed at first in steps:

1. Analyze each word, or what you originally take to be a word (without worrying too much at this point that in Nahuatl the real unit is the phrase). Establish what part of speech the supposed word is, verb, noun, quantifier, or particle. The affixes and lack thereof are the best clues. Identify and peel off all the affixes. Reconstruct the dictionary form of the word used as stem and try to find it in the dictionary if you don't recognize it. If the text is in its original handwriting, there will be the additional problem of separating the particles from the inflected nuclear words.

2. Carefully assess the meaning of all the affixes (including missing ones) in relation to one another and to the stem. Now form a first hypothesis about the overall meaning of the word. If there is an attached possessive or subject or object prefix, don't stop until you have found the further specification of the referent, or as much specification as is given.

3. After you have done this for a string of several words, use notions of standard word order and agreement between words, plus the presence and absence of key particles like *in*, *ca*, and *auh*, as well as your intuition of the semantic thrust, of what should be being said, to decide where the clauses begin and end and which are subordinate to which, not stopping until you have an idiomatic English equivalent of the entire statement.

Understanding Nahuatl texts of almost any description depends on the simultaneous exercise of two apparently very different skills, the first involving constant attention to every last scrap of grammatical information, omitting nothing, taking no leaps, registering each detail fully in the face of endless repetition, and the second involving attention to the pragmatics of what is being said, feeling the thrust of the overall statement, remembering what was said before and nearly anticipating what is going to be said next. It's as though two separate antennae were taking in the flow, and with the triangulation between them the statements jell and take on dimension. Actually, one might divide the work of the pragmatic antenna in turn into three parts. First, one can do a great deal simply with the instincts and patterns of thought we as humans share with the Nahuas. Second and not to be neglected are the repeating phrases, vocabulary, and format of each specific genre: a will, a petition, a sale, an annals entry. And third there are the quirks of the writer of the particular document, which once he has revealed them in the hard going of the first few paragraphs should present us with few difficulties in the remainder of the text. The present example has very few idiosyncrasies, compared to the bulk of Nahuatl documentation.

Eventually, the absorption of the more strictly grammatical information becomes nearly automatic, leaving the conscious mind free to concentrate on the developing sense. But for a long time one must divide the steps. In reading the Nahuatl of p. 64, first get the grammar for a clause, then contemplate its meaning. You can usefully do the same thing in reading the analytical comments. Read through once, concentrating on what is said about parts of speech, morphology, etc., and then read through again concentrating on the meaning of the roots, constructs, and phrases. Also read whole phrases or sections of the text after reading the relevant comments. Later read the entire original page concentrating on the grammar; right after that read it thinking only what it means, how it runs in large chunks. Do all the different types of reading repeatedly, and if you do it with your mind alive and not in a spirit of routine, you will find that you get more each time. The all-important thing is that in directly confronting the text itself you bring up out of your own mind, with a sense of discovery and inner comprehension, the proper analysis. What you don't have this experience with you will not remember.

Then work on the rest of the document in the same way. You now have to expect some new and unknown things, maybe ones not accounted for by any dictionary or understood fully by any person now living. There are two basic things to realize about dealing with new material. First, insoluble puzzles should not impede your progress. Don't dally over a detail forever; you may get it later from a complementary or parallel passage, you may see it differently when you return to it after an interval, or you may just have to live for some hours, months, or years with a puzzle. Of course you'd like to solve it eventually, but remember that what is not yet solved in no way detracts from anything which is firmly understood either as a general principle or as a specific point, and rarely does anything important for the mind turn upon a single isolated word or passage. Second, *most* of what follows will be like what went before; it will have the same morphemes and order, it will yield to the same kinds of analysis, it will in a word be almost boringly familiar, as Nahuatl, in its manner of construction. But it will not revert to being English or Spanish. In the neophyte, the English or Spanish models are so infinitely more deeply embedded than the Nahuatl equivalents that he or she will go back to them again and again, as automatically as a bird flying against the glass. Don't. Expect the inexorable unending repetition of the things I have spent so many pages illustrating. Every Nahuatl noun is either possessed or not possessed, and its shape varies accordingly; although it doesn't matter in either Spanish or English, every last time we are confronted with a Nahuatl noun we must ask whether it is possessed or not. Even very unfamiliar kinds of Nahuatl texts, from distant times and places, will be found to work the same way once you get used to some exotic superficial phenomena.

In case you are eager to try your hand right away, here is material corresponding to the rest of p. 64 of the 1976 edition of *Beyond the Codices*, plus some of p. 65. You will notice that after more than twenty years there are still a couple of words I have not figured out. It may interest you to know that the don Juan de Guzmán of this will and the doña Juana mentioned on p. 189 are the same ones figuring in section 7, pp. 199–201, of Appendix 3.

- *ynic centlamantli nitlanahuatia niquitohua yn iquac yntla oninomiquili ompa ninotocaz yn huey teupan s^t Ju^o bap^{ta} oncan yxpantzinco Entierro ymiquiliztzin tote^o dios oncan tonetocayan oncan mochintin toctitoque notatzin noteachcahuan noteyccahuan mocahuaz huentzintli yn iuh ca tlatecpantli yhuan hualmohuicaz ce totatzin capa quimotlaliz nechmaniliquiuh yhuan teupantlaca mocahuaz huentzintli yn iuh mocahuani ynic tlatziliniz auh ynin catley onca tomines nicpia ca ytech quiçaz calli monamacaz ompa mani tetla ycalteputzco s^{or} don ju^o cortes yhuan yni tlalli mochiuhtica temilli ypan mamani tzapoquahuitl yhuan metl yhuan tecomuli oncan mamani durasnos yhuan atlacomulli yhuicallo yez in calli yhuan oncan quiçaz yc nitlaxtlahuaz notech ca missas chiquacentetl huehuey misas cantadas ypampa yaniman Doña ysabel micatzintli quauhtitlan cihuapilli yhuan ypampa ynamic catca don hernando estrada*

- *yhuan niquitohua nicmelahua nicnocuitia ca nechpialtitia 8 p^os ylamatzin Ana ytoca catca ye omomiquili ycnocihuatl chane tlacopac*
- *yhuan niquitohua nicnocuitia yn yehuatzin nohueltihuatzin catca doña Ju^a de guzman xuchmillco namiqueticatca ynamic catca don p^o de sotomayor yei missas cantadas mochihuiliz ypampa yAniman ye huecauh omomiquili*
- *yhuan niquitohua ca yn nonamictzin catca doña fran^{ca} ye huecauh momiquili ytech catca ytomin magdalena ynamic catca español luys hidalgo mocahuaz teupan chiquacen p^os missas yc mochihuiliz yn omoteneuh magdalena*
- *yhuan nitlanahuatia niquitohua ca yn ompa tetla mani huerta peras oncan mani yhuan ahuacatl higos oncan pehua ynic tontemo yuhqui teatlauhtli ompa onnaci yn techinamitl mani ymil catca miguel ayeuhtzin oniccohuili concahuizque yn omentin nochpochuan doña Ana dona m^a tepotzontlan*

- First I order and declare that when I have died I am to be buried at the main church of St. John the Baptist, facing the [altar of] the burial and death of our lord God; there is our burial place, where my father, my older brothers, and my younger siblings all lie buried. The offering is to be made as it is in the schedule, and a priest is to come wearing a cloak to take me, along with the cantors; the offering usually given will be made to ring the bells; and seeing that I have no money, [the payment] is to come from the sale of a house located at Tetla behind the house of señor don Juan Cortés; and this land has become a [rocky?] field, on which are zapote trees and maguey and [a rocky depression?], and there are peach trees spread around on it and a well; it will go with the house, and from there will come the means to pay for the masses incumbent on me: six high masses to be sung for the soul of doña Isabel, deceased, a lady of Quauhtitlan, and for her late spouse, don Hernando Estrada.
- And I declare, affirm, and acknowledge that an old woman whose name was Ana lent 8 pesos to me. She is dead now; she was a widow, citizen of Tlacopac.
- And I declare and acknowledge that my late older sister doña Juana de Guzmán was married in Xochimilco; her spouse was don Pedro de Sotomayor. Three masses are to be sung for her soul; she died long ago.

- And I declare that my late spouse doña Francisca, who died long ago, owed money to Magdalena, who was the spouse of a Spaniard, Luis Hidalgo. Six pesos are to be given to the church for masses to be said for the aforementioned Magdalena.
- And I order and declare that at Tetla is an orchard, where there are pears, as well as avocados and figs; it begins there as you go down toward something like a [rocky ravine?]; it goes as far as a stone enclosure. It was the field of Miguel Ayeuhtzin, and I bought it from him. My two daughters, doña Ana and doña María at Tepotzotlan, are to share it.

Appendix 3: Selections from Texts

The following selections are meant both to give you an immediate opportunity for further independent work and to point you toward publications where you can find more similar material. No explanatory notes are included except in a case or two where I was especially puzzled, although some doubtful words are discussed in the vocabulary.

1. From the early Cuernavaca-region census and tax records, ca. 1535–45?.

For the context of these passages and much more of the same see S. L. Cline, ed. and trans., *The Book of Tributes: Early Sixteenth-Century Nahuatl Censuses from Morelos*, described in the epilogue, p. 144.

- *y nican icha / ytoca nochhuetli. / aᵒ mocuateꞯa yn izivauh ytonca . tlaco . / aᵒ mocuateꞯa . / ayac ypilzin y maꞯ . ya matlacxivitli . / yz ca yteycauh / y nochhuetli . ytoca . tēçozōmoc haᵒ mocuateꞯa / yn izivauh / ytoca tla haᵒ mocuatequia / ayac . ypilzin . / y maque ya monamicty . yz ca yn imil . ōpulhualli / yz ca yn itequivh y napohualtyca . quicahua . / zeçotli / y cuauhnavacayotli . yz ca yn itetlacualtil / zeçotli / cānahuāc / ça ya yo yn iteꞯvh / y nica acticate / naviti y cetetli / calli y cate —*

- Here is the home of one named Nochhuetl; he is not baptized. His wife is named Tlaco; she is not baptized. He has no children. They married (took each other) ten years ago. Here is his younger sibling, named Teçoçomoc; he is not baptized. His wife is named Tla[co]; she is not baptized. He has no children. They married last year. Here is his field; it is forty [units of measurement in length]. Here is his tribute that he delivers every eighty [days]; it is a quarter-length of a Cuernavaca-style [cloak or cloth]. Here is his provisions tribute; it is a quarter-length of a narrow [cloak or cloth]. That is all of his tribute duty. Here four people are included who are in one house.

- *yz ca ya quin ohualaque omotlatlaEcoltiaya / ytocayocā cuauhvizla / y ōca huell icha / y vizilla / ytoca pᵒ tezauh yn izivauh / ytoca / maꞯ . dalena . xoco . / omety yn ipilhuā y ce tlacatli / ytoca pᵒ nochhuetli / yn tlacat ya chicuhnauhxivitli / ynic ometi / ytoca pᵒ tlilli / y tlacat ya chicuexivitli yz ca yn imil / matlacmatli / yz ca yn iteꞯvh / çeçotli canavac / atley . tlacalaꞯlli ça ya yo yn iteꞯvh / y nica / acticate / naviti . / ȳ cetetli calli y cate*

- Here are [some people] who just came; they had been making a living in various ways at the place called Quauhhuitztlan. His real home is in Huitzillan. His name is Pedro Tetzauh. His wife is named Magdalena Xoco. He has two children. One of them is named Pedro Nochhuetl, who was born nine years ago. The second is named Pedro Tlilli, who was born eight years ago. Here is his field; it is ten units [in length]. Here is his tribute; it is a quarter-length of a narrow [cloak or cloth]. There is no tribute [in provisions]. That is all of his tribute duty. Here four people are included who are in one house.

2. From the Testaments of Culhuacan, ca. 1580.

For many other wills in the rich extant collection from this time and place see S. L. Cline and Miguel León-Portilla, eds., *The Testaments of Culhuacan*, described in the epilogue, p. 141. Note the consistent use of dots; those apparently missing usually would have come at the end of a line.

thomas de aquino sᵗᵃ mᵃ magᵈ cihuatecpā

Tomás de Aquino of Santa María Magdalena Cihuatecpan

- *In ica . ytocatzi . toteᵒ . Jesu x̄p̄o . yhuā . yn*

- In the name of our lord Jesus Christ and

itlaçonantzi . yn ilhuicac . çihuapilli Sancta maria . mochipa . ychpochtli . ma mochinti . quimatica . yn ixquichti . yn quitazque . yn quipohuazque . ynin amatl . y nehuatl . thomas . de aquino . nicā . nocha . sancta maria . mathalegna . çihuatecpa . maçonelihui . ỹ ninococohua . heçe . y noyolia . y nanimā amo quē catqui . çā huel pactica . auh ca huel melahuac . ynic nicnoneltoquitia . yn santissima . trinidad tetatzin . tepiltzin . dios espū sancto . ça çe yn iyeliztzin . yhuā . ca mochi . nicneltoca . yn ixquich . quimoneltoquitia . Sancta yglesia . de roma . auh ypāpa . yn axca yn ica . ynotzaloca . ytlatlauhtiloca . yn toteᵒ . dios . nicchihua yhuā . nictecpana . y notestamēto . y notzōquizcatlanequiliz . macayac quitlacoz .

- Ynic centlamātli . niquitohuā . y noyolia . y nanimā . ca nicnomaquilia . yn toteᵒ . dios . heyca . ca oquimochihuilli . yhuā . ca oquimomaquixtili . yn ica . yn itlaçohezçotzi . y nicā . tlalticpac . auh y nonacayo . ca nicmaca . yn tlali . heyca . ca ytech . oquiz . auh yn iquac oquiz . y nanimā . y nonacayo . onpa tocotiuh . yn toteopācha . S. Juᵒ . Euagᵗ .

- Ynic ōtlamantli . niquitohua . ca onicchiuh . yn huētzintli . onicnomaquilito . y-yomatcatzinco . yn totlaçomahuiztatzin . priyor fray Juᵒ . nunez . nicnolhuili notlaçotatzine . ca yz catqui . nohuētzi nicchihua . vi . pᵒs . noyolocacopa . amo ma ytla ypāpa . amo ma oniquichtec ca niquitohua . yn ixquich cahuitl . yn oninonemiti yn onechmomaquilliaya . yn toteᵒ . yn ixquich . y notech . omonequia . ma no yuh nicnocuepilliti

- Yhuā . niquitohuā . yn nocaltzin . yn ōca . onicatca . yn tonatiuh yquiçayāpa . ytzticac . nicmacatiuh . y nonamic . Juanā tiacapā amo no ac quicuiliz . yhuā . yn nocalnepanol . yn xochmilcopa . ytzticac . ça mochi itech çeyez . y nonamic . yhuā . yn yehuatl . teoyotica . noconetzin . y nicnonapalhui . yn itocā . casbar . yn ipiltzi . marcos morales . ychā . cohuatla . tenāco

- Auh yn chinamitl . yn ipa . onitequitia . yn ōpa . temi . yn itocayoca . tequacuilco . vii . tlachicōtepohualli . yhuā . y nicā . yn ātētlali . çan ic açi . yn chicontetl . nicma-

of his precious mother, the heavenly lady Holy Mary, eternally virgin, know all who see and read this document that I, Tomás de Aquino, whose home is here in Santa María Magdalena Cihuatecpan, even though I am ill, nevertheless my spirit and soul are serene and sound. And I truly believe in the most holy Trinity, father, child, and God the holy spirit, of just one essence. And I believe all that the holy church of Rome believes. Therefore now with invocation and supplication of our lord God, I make and order my testament and last will. Let no one violate it.

- First I say that I give my spirit and soul to our lord God because he made it and redeemed it with his precious blood here on earth. And my body I give to the earth because from there it came. And when my soul has left my body, it will be buried at our church of San Juan Evangelista.

- Second I say that I have made an offering: I went to give it to our dear honored father, prior fray Juan Núñez, in person, and I said to him, "My dear father, here is my offering of six pesos that I am making voluntarily, for no special reason at all, nor did I steal it, but I say that during all the time that I have lived, our Lord gave me all that I needed; let me return it to him in the same fashion."

- And I say as to my house where I have been, which faces to the east, I give it to my spouse, Juana Tiacapan. Nor is anyone to take it from her. And as to the two-story house of mine, facing toward Xochimilco, all of it together will belong to my spouse and my godchild that I adopted (embraced), named Gaspar, child of Marcos Morales, whose home is in Coatlan Tenanco.

- And as to some chinampas on which I paid tribute in the place named Tequacuilco, which count as seven, and only with the land here at the edge of the water do

catiuh . y nonamic . yhuā . niquitohuā . y nochina . yn ōpa temi . tecuitlaapa . matlactetl . çecenpohualhuiyac . ymiltitech . mīn . çā quicuiz . yhuā . nicmacatiuh y nonamic . Juanā . tiacapā . amo ac . quicuiliz . yhuā niquitohuā . y nonamic . yn ipilhuā . ca cenca . onechmocuitlahuique yn izquipa . oninococohuaya . ca cenca . onechtlaçotlaque . auh niquitohuā . çā nica ytlantzinco . moyetztiyezque . yn innātzin

- Auh yn oniquitoca . yn tlacpac . y nocalnepanol . yn onicmacaca . yn teoyotica noconetzin . yn casbar . ca oyçoliuh . yn quauhtzintli . auh yn axca . niquitohua . ma çan itlatzi . quimomaquiliz . y nonamic yn piltzintli . yc mohuapahualtiz . yntla monemitiz . yntla noço momiquiliz

they reach seven, I am giving them to my spouse. And I say that there are 10 chinampas of mine in Tecuitlaapan, each one 20 [units of measure] long, next to the field of Martín. My spouse Juana Tiacapan is just to take them, and I give them to her. No one is to take them from her. And I say that my spouse's children took care of me a lot every time I was sick, and they showed me much affection (treated me very well), and I say that they are to remain here next to their mother.

- And as to the two-story house of mine that I had mentioned above that I gave to my godchild Gaspar, the wood has deteriorated. Now I say, let my spouse give some small thing to the child with which he will be brought up, if he lives, or, if he dies . . .

3. From the Tlaxcalan Actas (municipal council records), 1560.

No other Nahua cabildo seems to have left summaries and minutes of its sessions as the council of Tlaxcala did in the sixteenth century. This episode and other selections can be seen in James Lockhart, Frances Berdan, and Arthur J. O. Anderson, *The Tlaxcalan Actas: A Compendium of the Records of the Cabildo of Tlaxcala*, described in the epilogue, p. 141.

tlanavati cabᵒ ȳ axcā nicā mocētlaliya ȳ . / ipanpa ȳ tlatouani visorei dō luis de velasco q̇moneq̇ltiyaya in tlaxcalteca . ōtzōtly ōmatlactecpātly . namiq̄hq̄ ōpa mochātlalizqz ȳ chichimecatlalpā itocayocā Sāt miguel / auh ȳ achto . uel q̇celihca in tlatoq̄ inic ōpa yalouazque Sāt miguel . Auh in çatepā . oq̇taq̄ . ȳ cēca tetolini mochivaz intla yaloua / ȳ aq̇q̄ yazqz / ȳ nicā ȳtlal yvā ȳcal . aquin . q̇cuiz . yc neixnamicoz / yvā in çoatl piltzintli q̄nī nenemiz ohtlipā . aquī . q̇tq̇z yn ihtac . / yvā in aq̇q̄ yazqz , çan ipā q̇tazq̄z . ȳ tecocoliliztly . yehica yc cē yazque . Auh yehica q̇mitavilique cabildo tlaca / ayc yuhqui omoteq̇ti[c?] . ȳ ya yxq̇chcauhtica yc valaq̄ spañoles . ȳ çoatl piltzītli . yahqui canahpa . uehca // auh maço miecpa . oyaoq̇xivac ȳ uehca yn itēcopa Rey . totlatocauh . yuh q̇mativi . ȳ tlaxcalteca . ȳ q̄xq̇ch ōpa miq̇z Auh in oc q̄xq̇ch mocavaz . valmocuepaz amo çāmā yc cē yavi . Auh ipāpa ȳ o-

The cabildo ordered that now the following be summarized here: because the lord viceroy don Luis de Velasco wanted a thousand married Tlaxcalans to establish their homes in Chichimeca country at a place called San Miguel, at first the lords entirely accepted the going to San Miguel, but later they saw that going would cause much affliction. Who would take the land and houses here of those who went? There would be contention over it. And how would the women and children travel on the road? Who would carry their provisions? And those who went would view [the assignment] as [the result of?] hate, for they would be going forever. Hence the cabildo members said, "Never has such a duty been undertaken ever since the Spaniards came, that women and children went to some far distant place. And though many times groups have gone far away to war by order of the king our ruler, the Tlaxcalans went knowing that some would die there, but the rest would be left, would return and not go forever." Therefore the

quimitavilią cab⁰ / ma tictotlatlauhticā
yn sr⁰ visorei . ynic techtlaocoliz . ȳ amo
yalouaz Sāt miguel / nimā yehuā ąm-
ixątzą in ju⁰ ximenez aɫlde yvā dō Alonso
maldonado . ju⁰ de avalos . ju⁰ maldonado
regidores . ōpa yahca . mex^co / yxpantzīco
sr⁰ visorei . / Auh yc quinnāąly uel ą-
paccaçeli . ynic ąmotlatlauhtilią . inic
amo yalouaz Sāt miguel . ąmilhui . maca⁰ .
quītequipacho tlaxcalteca / amo yazą Sāt
miguel . ypāpa achi uehca ątzticate . /
yehvā oniąnmacac xilotepec tlaca ōpa
motlalitivi . ypanpa amo uehca ątztoque /
quitoą cab⁰ ypāpa ȳ otechicneli sr⁰ visorei
. ȳ amo yalouaz / Auh nicā ticteneua tią-
toą ȳ aąą . ąpixtazą . atl tepetl . tl̄xn / ȳ
at ąmaniȳā . ytlah tinavatilozą ytechcopa
rrei monequi . / ma oc achto uel ąmotilicā
ȳ cuix uel ticchivazą . maca⁰ yçiuhca . ące-
lihtiuetzizą yehica ȳ çatepā yc tech-
pinauhtiya . inic ticnequi ȳ macaocmo .
cepa yuh mochivaz / yn ihçiuhca / mo-
celitihuetz ȳ tlē moneą ēc

ynic ōtlamātli mocētlaliya ipāpa in
omohololozqz macevalli ąxiniz ycal .
quicauhtevaz ycuē . miec tlamātli yc mo-
tolinizqz / Auh yehoatl ju⁰ ximenez . aɫlde
yvā bu^ra vñade regidor . ątlatlauhtito
mex^co sr⁰ visorei ynic aya⁰ uel mochihuaz
. ȳneçeçētlaliliz ma oc ąxąch cahuitl / yuhqui vel ąpaccaceli yn tlatouani visorei .
ynic aya⁰ mochiuaz . necētlaliliztli . çan oc
yuhtiyez . centetl mandami⁰ ąualcuią . /

cabildo members said, "Let us request the
lord viceroy to grant us that there be no
going to San Miguel." Then they appointed
Juan Jiménez, alcalde, and don Alonso
Maldonado, Juan de Avalos, and Juan
Maldonado, regidores, who went to Mexico
City before the lord viceroy. And he replied
that he accepted very gladly what they
asked of him, not to go to San Miguel, and
he said to them, "Let it not trouble the
Tlaxcalans; they are not to go to San Miguel, because they live quite far away. I
have assigned it to the people of Xilotepec
to go to settle there because they live not far
away." The cabildo members said, "Because of this the lord viceroy granted us the
boon that there will be no going. But here
we declare and say to those who will have
keeping of the altepetl of Tlaxcala [in the
future] that if sometime we are ordered to
do something required for the king, let
them first consider well whether we can do
it; let them not quickly rush to accept it,
for afterward it will bring us shame, so
that we wish it never to be done again that
what is needed is hastily accepted, etc."

The second thing summarized here is
about the commoners to be congregated;
they will take apart their houses, they will
leave their fields behind, and they will be
afflicted in many ways. And Juan Jiménez,
alcalde, and Buenaventura Oñate, regidor,
went to Mexico City to request the lord
viceroy that their congregation not be per-
mitted to be carried out yet; let a little more
time [pass]. The lord viceroy accepted very
gladly that the congregation not yet be
carried out and things stay as they are for
now; [the emissaries] brought back an
order [to that effect].

4. From Book 12 of the Florentine Codex, ca. 1550–80.

The Spanish conquest, or rather the part the people of Tlatelolco and Tenochtitlan played in
that episode, is the topic of Book 12 of Sahagún's Florentine Codex. The entire book will be found,
with the Nahuatl, the Spanish, and translations of both, in James Lockhart, ed., *We People Here*,
described in the epilogue, p. 143.

Auh niman in iehoan Españoles, qui-
tlalique in quauhtematlatl in mumuz-
ticpac, inic quintepachozą in macevaltin.
Auh in oquicencauhque, in ie quitlaçaz-

And then those Spaniards installed a
catapult on top of an altar platform with
which to hurl stones at the people. And
when they had it ready and were about to

que, cenca cololhuitinemi, cēca omma-
piloa, quinmapilhuia in macevalti, om-
mapiloa in vmpa omocenquixtiq̄ in a-
maxac, in ie ixquich macevalli, cenca
quimōmottitia, ommaçoa in Españoles,
inic impan contlaçazque conmaiavizque,
in iuhqui quintematlavizque: nec quima-
lacachoa nec quitevilacachoa: nimā ic
meoatiquetz in quauhtemalacatl in i-
quauhio. Auh in tetl amo vel vmpa ia in
ipā macevalli, çan ie icampa iteputzco in
vetzito tianquiztli xumolco.

Auh ic vncā mixnamicque in iuh nezque
Españoles iuhquin mixmapilxixili, cenca
chachalaca. Auh in quauhtematlatl mo-
cuecuepa avic iaiauh, çan ivian motlame-
lauhcaquetztia: niman ic vel nez in iiacac
catca in tematlatl cenca tomaoac in me-
catl, inic mecaio: niman ic quitocaiotique
quauhtematlatl:

auh ie no ceppa quicentlazque in Españoles: yoā in ixquich tlaxcaltecatl, nimā ie
ic motecpana in iacaculco, yoan tecpancaltitlan yoan copalnamacoia: nimā ie
vmpa atecocolecan quiniacana in ixquich
techiaoalotoc, cencan ivian in onotiui.
Auh in tiiacaoan valmomātivi, vel mochi-
chicaoa, vel moquichquetza, aiac tlacue-
cuetlaxoa, aiac tlacioatlamachtia: quitoa.
Xioalnenemican tiiacavane, aquique in
tenitotonti, tlalhuicatotonti. Auh in tiia-
cavan avic vivi, ixtlapal huivi, aocac tla-
melauhca icac, motlamelauhcaquetza

(auh miecpa motlacacuepaia in Españoles, amo monextiaia in iuh mochichioa
nican tlaca: no iuh mochichioaia, tlaviztli
cōmaquiaia, tilmatli pani quimolpiliaia,
inic mixpoloaia, çan motetoctitivitz, çan
ic quiteimachitia, in o aca quiminque, ne-
pacholo, tlaltech viloa, cenca tlachialo,
cenca mixpepetza in campa ie vallauh, in
campa ie valitztiuh in tepuzmitl, vel
mimati, vel motlachielia in tiiacaoan in
Tlatilulca:)

shoot it off, they gathered all around it,
vigorously pointing their fingers, pointing
at the people, pointing to where all the
people were assembled at Amaxac, showing
them to each other. The Spaniards spread
out their arms, [showing] how they would
shoot and hurl it at them, as if they were
using a sling on them. Then they wound it
up, then the arm of the catapult rose up. But
the stone did not land on the people, but
fell behind the marketplace at Xomolco.

Because of that the Spaniards there
argued among themselves. They looked as
if they were jabbing their fingers in each
other's faces, chattering a great deal. And
the catapult kept returning back and forth,
going one way and then the other; bit by bit
it righted itself. Then it could be seen
clearly that there was a stone sling at its
point, attached with very thick rope. Then
because of that they named it a "wooden
sling."

And again they sent out the Spaniards
and all the Tlaxcalans. Then they formed
up at Yacacolco, Tecpancaltitlan, and Co-
palnamacoyan. Then at Atecocolecan [the
Spaniards] led all those who surrounded
us; very slowly they proceeded. And the
[Mexica] warriors came in formation,
working up their spirits, taking a manly
posture; no one was faint of heart, no one
was like a woman. They said, "Come running, O warriors! Who are these little bar-
barians, these little backlanders?" And the
warriors went this way and that, sideways;
no one stood straight, raised up straight.

(And often the Spaniards took on the
appearance of their enemies, not showing
themselves. They got themselves up as the
local people do, putting on devices, tying
cloaks on to disguise themselves, coming
hiding behind the others. The only way
they made people aware was when they
shot someone. Then everyone crouched
down and hit the ground; everyone looked
and searched closely to see where the iron
bolt came from, which way it was aimed.
The Tlatelolca warriors were very alert,
kept very good watch.)

Auh cencan yiolic in techxocotivi, in techcaltechpachotivi.

Very slowly they went along throwing us back, pushing us against the wall.

5. From Book 10 of the Florentine Codex, ca. 1540–1580.

Book 10, called by Anderson and Dibble "The People," treats a wide variety of topics, mainly among the Nahuas themselves, but a section late in the book deals (largely in terms of stereotypes, as you will see) with some other peoples of the larger region. Anderson and Dibble's multivolume edition of the Florentine Codex contains the Nahuatl and an English translation of it for all the books (see the description in the epilogue, pp. 142–43).

In teuchichimeca, in quitoznequi, vel nelli chichimeca, anoço molhui chichimeca, in ioan intoca çacachichimeca, in quitoznequi, çacatla, quauhtla in nemi: ca iehoantin in veca nemi, in quauhtla, in çacatla, in ixtlaoacan in texcalla nemi: inique in, acan vel inchan, çan quiztinemi, çan otlatocatinemi, çan panotinemi, ça ça ie vi in ie vi, in canin inpan iooatiuh: vncan quitemoa in oztotol, in texcalli, vncan cochi.

The Teochichimeca, which means real true Chichimeca, or out-and-out Chichimeca, who are also named Çacachichimeca, which means that they live in the grasslands and forests, for they live far away in the forests, grasslands, plains, and rocky crags—these have no real home, they just go passing through, traveling, crossing [the plains and streams]; they just go wherever they go. Wherever night catches them they seek a cave or crag and sleep there.

* * *

* * *

Iz catqui, in iiolizmatiliz inique y, chichimeca, ca tlatecque, ca cenca vel quiximati in tecpatl, in itztli, in iiacac quiquetza, quitlalia in acatl, in mitoa mitl: auh ioan cenca vel quiximati in tezcatl, ca mochintin quititlani in tezcatl, mochipa intzintempan quimana: auh in iquac canapa vi, in vtlatoca, ça ce in teiacana çan motecpana, ça cenpanti, vmpa vnmotztivi in tezcac in intzintempan mamantiuh: ioan quixima, quichiqui in xivitl, in teuxi[vi]tl in incozqui, in incuecueioch in inpipilol:

Here are the arts of these Chichimeca. They are cutters of stone, for they are very well acquainted with flint and obsidian; they set and place it at the tip of a reed, called an arrow. And they are also very well acquainted with mirrors, for they all use mirrors. They always put them on their lower backs, and when they go somewhere, as they go along, only one leads the way, and they go in order, in single file; they go along seeing themselves in the mirrors that go placed on their various lower backs. They also shave and scrape turquoise, fine turquoise, to be their necklaces, earrings, and pendants.

ioan quiximati in xiuitl, in tlanelhoatl in quenami, in quen ihiio, iehoantin intlaiximach in mitoa peiotl: inique, y, in quiqua in peiotl, vctli ipan in quipoa, in anoço nanacatl, mocentlalia cana ixtlaoacan, monechicoa: vncan mitotia, cuica ceioal, cemilhuitl: auh in imuztlaioc, oc ceppa mocentlalia choca, cenca choca, quil mixpaca, ic quichipaoa in imixtelolo:

They are also acquainted with herbs and roots, their nature and emanations. They are the ones who [first] knew of what is called peyote. These people eat peyote; they consider it in the same light as pulque or mushrooms. They assemble and gather somewhere on the plains; there they dance and sing all night and all day. The next day they assemble again, weeping, greatly weeping. It is said that in that way they wash their eyes, they cleanse their eyeballs.

ioan hiviçaloque, amanteca, ca quichi-

They are also gluers of feathers, feather

oa, ca quiçaloa in coçoiaoalolli: ioan cue-
tlaxoaoanque, tlaiamanilique: ipampa in
ixquich imeoaquen chichimeca, ioan im-
eoacue in incioaoa, ca iehoantin quiia-
mania, quioaoana:

auh in aço itla tlaqualli quixca, quitle-
oatza, anoço quipaoaci: amo iehoan qui-
tequipanoa in oquichtin, çan iehoan in
cioa: ipampa cenca quimalhuia in imixtelolo, amo quititlani in poctli, quil
quimixitlacoa, ca cenca veca tlachia inique, y, chichimeca: ioan cenca tlatlame-
lauhcaittani, ca in tlein quimina, amo
oppa, expa, quitlaxilia çan cen: in manel
cenca tepiton, amo quineoa, in manel noço
veca ca, vel quimina, amo quineoa, amo no
quezquipa in quintlaxilia.

Iz catqui in intlaqual chichimeca:
nupalli, nochtli, cimatl, tlanelhoatl, tzi-
oactli, nequametl, icçoxuchitl, icçonenecu-
tli, menecutli, xiconecutli, pipioli, quauh-
necutli: ioan in tlein quiximati tlanelhoatl, in tlallan onoc, ioan in ie ixquich
nacatl, tochin, coatl, maçatl, tequani: ioan
ixquich in patlantinemi.

Inique in chichimeca: inic iuhqui intlaqual, y, aic cenca mococoa, cenca ve-
caoa, çan veve miqui, tzoniztaztivi, qua-
iztaztivi: auh intla aca cocoliztli itech
motlalia, in ie omilhuitl, ie eilhuitl, in ie
navilhuitl, amo pati: niman mocentlalia
in chichimeca, quimictia, totomitl iquech-
tlan conaquilia, ic onmiqui: ioan in aquin
o vel veuetic, in o vel ilamatic, çan no quimictia: inic quimictia cocoxqui, manoço
veve, quil ic quitlaoculia, quil ipampa in
amo motoliniz tlalticpac: ioan inic amo
quintlaocultiz: auh inic quitoca, cenca
quimaviztilia, omilhuitl, eilhuitl in mic-
caoati, mitotia, cuica:

inic iuhqui intlaqual y, in ioan amo
cenca quexquich intlaque, vel chicaoaque,
vel pipinque, vellalichtique, ioan cenca
ichtique, tlaloatique, ioan tlamolhoati-
que, ioan cenca paina inic vi, inic tepe-

workers, for they make and glue together a
round device of yellow parrot feathers.
They are also curers and softeners of hides,
because all the clothing of the Chichimeca
is of leather, and their women's skirts are
leather; they (the women) soften it and
scrape it.

When there is some food they roast it,
broil it, or boil it. The men do not work at
it, only the women, because they (the men)
take great care of their eyes, they do not
expose them to smoke; it is said that it
harms their eyes. For these Chichimeca see
very far, and they see very truly. Whatever
they shoot an arrow at they do not let loose
at twice or three times, but only once.
Though it be very little, they do not miss it,
or though it be far away, they hit it straight
on. They do not miss, nor do they shoot at
things more than once.

Here is the Chichimeca's food: nopal
cactus, tuna, cimatl roots, tzihuactli cactus, [fruit of?] a palm tree, yucca flowers
and juice, maguey juice, honey from large
bees and other bees, sap from trees, and the
roots they know of that are in the ground,
and all the meats—rabbit, snake, deer,
large predators, and all the things that fly.

Since these Chichimeca's food is such,
they never get very sick. They live a long
time; they die only when old, when they go
about white haired, white headed. If someone gets sick for two, three, or four days
and doesn't get well, then the Chichimeca
assemble and kill him. They put an arrow
in his throat, from which he dies. They
likewise kill whoever has become a very
old man or a very old woman. When they
kill the sick person, though an old man, it
is said that thereby they do him a favor. It
is said that it is so that he will not suffer on
earth and he will not arouse pity in them.
When they bury him, they pay him great
honor; for two or three days they hold
obsequies, dancing and singing.

Since their food is like this and they
don't wear very much clothing, they are
very strong, tough, stringy, wiry, sinewy,[1]
and they run very fast when they move;
when they climb mountains, it is really as

tleco, vel iuhquin ecatoco: ipampa [a]mo ceceioque, amo[2] tzotzoltique, inic atle quimelleltia

though they were being carried off by the wind, because they are not covered with fat, but[2] thin, so that nothing holds them back.

6. From the Bancroft Dialogues, originally ca. 1570–80, redone in the 17th century.

A set of conversations and speeches done by Nahua aides under ecclesiastical auspices and recopied in the circle of Horacio Carochi tells us much about Nahuatl elevated speech. Here a macron over a vowel (ˉ) means the vowel is long, a breve (˘) that it is short, and a grave (ˋ) that it is followed by a glottal stop. An unmarked vowel is more likely to be short, but not always, for some long vowels are left unmarked. Some diacritics are erroneous. The whole set, with a second more literal translation, is in Karttunen and Lockhart, eds., *The Art of Nahuatl Speech*, described on p. 142.

Lo que dicen despues de comer à su Madre dos niños.

What two boys say to their mother after eating.

Ōtlācāuhqui in īyōllòtzin totēcuiyo nopiltzīntzīne cihuāpille, ca īhuiān yōcoxcā ō motechtzīnco monec in tlamātzoaltzintli in ātēxātzintli: auh ōtomācēhualtic ōtocnōpiltic in īcōcōcàtzin in tlācatl in totēcuiyo: mā cencà īc tictoyēctēnēhuilīcan. Auh ōtitēchmocnēlili tlācàtle cihuāpille nopiltzīntzīne.

Our lord has been generous, my noble lady; in peace the food has been consumed at your table. The goods of our Lord have been our good fortune; let us greatly praise him for it. Thank you, oh personage, oh lady, oh my noble person.

[A boy greets his uncle.]

Quēn ōtimotlathuitì, quēn ōmitzmotlathuittili in tlācatl in totēcuiyo? cuix tepitzin ticmomàcēhuitzīnoa in ītēchicāhualiztzīn? cuix nocè ītlà ītēmoxtzin ièēcatzīn mopantzīnco quihuālmihuālìznequi? canel àmo ticmatì inīc techmonemītilia in ītlālticpactzīnco in ilhuicahuà in tlālticpaquè in īpalnemoani.

How did you feel on rising, how did our Lord cause you to feel on rising? Are you enjoying a bit of his health? Or is he about to send some of his afflictions upon you? For we do not know how the master of heaven and earth, the giver of life, is causing you to fare on his earth.

R[a.]

Reply.

Ōtinēchmocnēlili nomāchtze: mācihui in ōninohuēhuètili izçā nihuihuītōntìnemi in ītlālticpactzīnco in tlācatl in totēcuiyo: tel achìtzīn nichuelmati in tlālli izçōquitl, īhuan huel onyauh in ātēxātzīntli in tlamātzohualtzīntli nechmomaquilia māhuītzīn.

Thank you, my nephew. Though I have grown old and am just tottering along on our Lord's earth, still I am tolerably well in body, and the food and drink your aunt gives me agree with me.

Dos uiejos principales saludan à unos Cantores

Two elderly noblemen greet some singers.

Anmotolīnià noxōcōyōhuāne, òanquìīyōhuìquè: àço ōti[tla]tlàcàtiliquè tlā çā yè pēhua in huēhuētl, īc huālìçaz in tlācatl, canel īpāc in cuīcatl.

You are suffering [standing here waiting in the cold ?], O my youngest ones; greetings. Perhaps we have gotten behind schedule; just let the drum begin, with which the lord will awaken, for he is a lover

---

[1] I have not identified "tlamolhuatique." In view of the nature of this passage, it is probably close in meaning and structure to "tlaoatique," which derives from *tlalhuatl*, "sinew," with the preterit agentive *-tic*.

[2] Since *tzoltic* means "narrow, thin," I can only come to the conclusion that the *amo* before it is an error for some other particle such as *çan* or *ca*.

Respondenles los cantores.

Nopiltzīntzīne tlàtoānie ōanquimiȳyō-huiltìque, cĕcuīztli amotlantzīnco aqui, ca qualcān in ōanmàxitīcò, ca çã oc achi yohuatōnco, quin ye huālmoquetza in tlāhuizcalli, auh in tlācatl mocēhuitzinòtoc: ōtontlàtlăcaquito in īyĕyāntzinco, tlamattimani, ayāc mà nāhuati: ȳhuān in tōpīlèquè calìtic motlacuitlahuia, ayamo quihuāllapoà. Quēn yè ōamechmotlathuiltìli in totēcuiyo? cuix tepitzin yēctli qualli ōanquimomàcēhuitzīnòque in īyohualtzin, cuix nocè ītlà ītēmoxtin īĕĕcatzinco ō amopantzinco ōquihuālmihuāli? canel àmo ticmati inīc òtlatoca in yohualli in tlàcàtli in īcemilhuitzin in tlācatl in totēcuiyo, nopiltzīntzīne, cocoliztli tamēchtocuītilīzque: Mā yè nicān ximohuetziltīcan in amoyeyāntzinco in amocpalpantzinco.

Ohua nōxōcōyōhuāne ōannechmocnēlilìquè, auh ōanquimocnēlilìquè in nomachtzin: ca tepitzin quēntēltzin ōtēchmohuēytlathuiltìli in tlācatl in totēcuiyo in īpalnemoāni, ca tepitzin tictomàcēhuià in ītēchicāhualiztzin.

Vnos principales saludã à su Gou^{or.} despues de leuantado de la cama auiendo cantado antes à su modo.

Tlācatle, tlàtoānie timitzontonepechtēquililià, àço ōtimitztotzonteconēhuilìquè: quēn ōmitzmotlathuiltìli in tlācatl in totēcuiyo? cuix tepitzin huel onyà in cochiztli? canel miec inic conàmana in mixtzin in moyōllòtzin in ītcōca in ī-māmaloāca in ātl in tepētl. Tlā īxquich motlàpaltzin xoconmochīhuili, tlā onixtlāhui, tlā ompōpohui in tēucyōtl in tlàtòcāyōtl, auh in nānyōtl in tàyōtl. Ca ye imman īn, àço toconmāniliz in mocxitzin, inic tonmohuīcaz īchāntzinco totēcuiyo: ca ye iz moch mitzmochialìtoquè in motēchīuhcāhuān.

of song.[1]

The singers answer them.

O my nobleman, O ruler, greetings; you must be cold [on this chilly morning]. You have arrived in good time, for it's still quite early, dawn has just come, and the lord lies resting. We have listened around his quarters, and it's quiet, no one's talking, and the officials who take care of things in the house haven't come yet to open up. How did our Lord cause you to feel on rising? Did you enjoy his night somewhat well, or did he send something of his afflictions down upon you? For we do not know how our Lord's day, both nighttime and daytime, marches along. We [do not wish to] make you ill; do sit down here in your places, your seats.

[Reply.]

Ah, my youngest ones, I thank you on my behalf and on behalf of my nephew here. Our Lord the Giver of life caused us to rise tolerably well, and we are enjoying a bit of His health.

Some noblemen greet their governor after he has risen from his bed, first having sung to him in their fashion.

O personage, O ruler, we bow down to you; we [hope we have not] given you a headache [with our singing]. How did the lord our Lord cause you to rise? Did your sleep go somewhat well? For you disturb your spirit greatly with the governance of the altepetl. Exert all your effort, let lordship, rulership, and parenthood be as they should be. It is late, perhaps you should hasten (stretch your feet) to go to the house of our Lord, for all your progenitors (aides) are awaiting you here.

---

[1] In *īpāc in cuīcatl*, *-pāc* is a still not fully identified noun that must be related to *pāqui*, "to be happy." In Molina we find "ciua impac," "one with a fondness for women." Thus the possessive prefix refers to the thing liked, not to the person who likes it. Apparently *-pāc* means not the fondness but the person who likes something, as though it were an agentive.

Respondeles el Gou^or.

Ōannēchmocnēliliquè nopiltzīntzīne: ōtlācāuhqui in amoyōllòtzīn: ca tepitzīn ōnomàcēhualtic in ītēchicāhualiztzin totēcuiyo. Auh huel ōnonnotlamachtī, huel īc ōnompāc inīc ōnichuālcactoca ōanconmēhuiliquè yāōcuīcatl īc pōyōmicquè Ācōlhuàquè tlaxcallān yāōtēpānco, ye achi quēxquich cāhuitl in niquelēhuia nonconcaquiz. Auh in yè amèhuantzitzīn anmotolīnìtzīnoà, àço cēcuiztli amotlantzīnco àqui, ca oc yohuac in ōanhuālmohuīcaque, yhuān ca inīc cēhuatoc. Cuix nō achitzīn anquimomàcēhuìtzinoà in ītēchicāhualiztzin in tloquè nāhuàquè in īpalnemoāni? cuix nocè cēmè amopantzīnco quihualmihuālia in ītētzīn in īquàuhtzīn in ītēmoxtzīn in īèècatzin?

Respondele uno por todos.

Otitēchmocnēlili nopiltzīntzīne tlàtoānie, ca timochtīn tocepaniān oc quēntēltzin tocontomàcēhuià in ītēicnēliltzīn in tlācatl totēcuiyo

The governor answers them.

Thank you, O my noblemen, you have spoken generous words. I have enjoyed a bit of the health of our Lord. And I truly enjoyed and rejoiced in lying listening to you sing the war song about the Acolhuaque [people of the Tetzcoco region] dying by treachery at the Tlaxcalan war boundary; for some time now I've been wanting to hear it. You are suffering [standing here], perhaps you are getting cold, for you came early, and it is chilly. Are you also enjoying a bit of the health of the All-pervasive, the Giver of life? Or has he sent down upon one of you his punishments and afflictions?

One answers him for all.

Thank you, O my nobleman, O ruler, we are jointly all tolerably enjoying the beneficence of our Lord.

7. From testimony of don Juan de Guzmán, Xochimilco, 1586.

In 1586 the indigenous authorities of Xochimilco held voluminous proceedings invalidating the testament of doña Juana de Guzmán, a lady of Coyoacan who had married into the highest circles of the Xochimilco ruling group. Among the papers is the testimony of her brother don Juan de Guzmán, of which the following is a part. His whole statement and substantial commentary are in James Lockhart, *Nahuas and Spaniards* (described in the epilogue, p. 141).

auh yn iquac ye oconmotlaqualtilique yn iehuantin señoratin, ye oaçic chicome oras motzilinia ye yohua. Niman ye quinmolhuilia yn iehuantin señoratin yn iehuatzin çihuapilli doña juana de guzman oannechmocnelilique otlacauhqui yn amoiollotzin aço ça yyoppa yn onamechnotlanehuitzino yn ascan / aço moztla ninotocaz: ca tel ohualmohuicac yn nicuhtzin don ju^o de guzman ynic onicnotemolitoya ynic oninentlamatoya. ca cenca yc oninoyollalli, auh ma oc xinechtlalcahuilicā ca oc oncā nicnōnochiliz çentlamantli ypampa: auh nimā moquixtique yn señoratin conmonahuatiliq̄ yn cihuapilli, niman ye yaque Ynon ye cuel açitiuh chicuhnahui oras, Niman yc nechhualmonochili yspan yn itoca Mīn de rosas yhuan yn icuhtzin ytoca grabriel de s^ttiago yhuan ypilotzin don diego de velasco yn omoten-

And when those Spanish women had finished feeding her, seven o'clock was already ringing and it was dark. Then the lady doña Juana de Guzmán said to the Spanish women: "Thank you for your generosity; perhaps this was the last time I will tarry with you, perhaps tomorrow I will be buried; but my younger brother don Juan de Guzmán has come, whom I was looking for and languishing after, and it has put my mind to rest. So do please leave me now, for I must talk to him about something." And then the Spanish women came out; they took their leave of the lady, then departed. That was already at nine o'clock. Then a person named Martín de Rojas came to call me to her, along with her younger brother named Gabriel de Santiago and her nephew don Diego de Velasco who was mentioned above, from

euh tlacpac chane xallatlauhco Niman
oquimolhuili yn itoca Mīn de Rosas.
Martintzin tla oc xitechmotlalcahuili, tla
oc ximoquixti. Auh yn nehuatl ni don juº
de guzman niman yc nonniquani, tla-
pechtenco, nōnotlali, auh in iehuatzin
çihuapilli yn nohueltihuatzin doña juana
de guzmā: mohuetzititoc. Niman ye ic nic-
nolhuilia Totecuioe Cihuapille, nimitznotlatlauhtilia aço nelli yn ie oticmotlalili
yn motestamentotzin ma achiton çan mo-
tlatolticatzinco niccaqui yn quenin oticmotlalili yn ipampa yn itecpancaltzin catca sºr don pedro de sotomayor yn ttoteº
dios oquimohuiquili yn motlaçonamic-
tzin catca, quen oticmitalhui quen otimo-
tlanahuatili yn ipan motestamētotzin.
Auh nimā nechmonanquilili quimitalhui.
tle ypampa yn timotlatlania. Niman nicnolhuili ca çan ypampa yn nicmatiznequi,
aço ytla yc otimotlatlacalhui yn ipan in
tlatocacalli, yhuan yn ipan ysquich tlatocatlalli, milli, chinamitl, ma achitzin
niccaqui, quenin catqui. Niman oquimitalhui ynin calli yn mochi ymanian ca
mochi monamacaz: auh yn quexquich
neçiz tomines yn ipatiuh mochihuaz ca
mochi teupan callaquiz, yc missa topan
mittoz yn tonehuan notlaçonamictzin
moyetzticatca dios oquimohuiquili señor
don pedro de sotomºr ca nel ayac çe to-
conetzin monemiltia / ca yntla onca çe
momahtzī ca nel mochi ytech pohuiz ytech
niccauhtiaz ypampa yn, ca nel ayac, y-
pampa yn yn mochi monamacaz yhuā yn
isquich yn tlatocatlalli, yhuā yn quexquich onicnotzinquixtili niscoyan ynic
onitlatlaxtlauh yn isquich yn quimi-
tlacalhuitiuh yn notlaçonamictzin ca çenca miec ynic onitlaxtlauh yhuā tel mochi
oncatqui amatl cartas de pago yn onech-
macaque yn tlatquihuaque. Auh yn iquac
yn oniccac yn isquich yn oquimitalhui
cihuapilli. Nimā onicnonanquilili, Onicnolhuili. Ca çenca otimotlatlacalhui ca
amo qualli yn oticmochihuili Cuix amo
oncate tepilhuā, temachhuā, teyshuihuā,
Cuix amo cenca mitzonmahuilizque yntla
dios omitzmohuiquili, mitzonmotlatel-
chihuililizque Cuix amo huey pleito mo-

Xalatlauhco. Then she said to the person
named Martín de Rojas, "Dear Martín, do
please leave us, do go out." And I, don Juan
de Guzmán, changed my place and sat down
at the edge of the bed where the lady my
older sister doña Juana de Guzmán was
lying. Then I said to her, "O my mistress, O
lady, I ask you, is it true that you have
already made your testament? Let me hear
a bit just in your words how you have dis-
posed concerning the former palace of
señor don Pedro de Sotomayor whom our
lord God took, your dear late spouse, what
you have said and ordered in your testament." And then she answered me and
said, "Why do you ask?" Then I said to her,
"Just because I want to know if you have
done something wrong about the ruler's
house and all the ruler's lands, fields, and
chinampas; let me hear a bit how it is."
Then she said, "This house and everything
that goes with it is all to be sold, and
however much money is raised from what
turns out to be its price will all be delivered
to the church and masses will be said with
it for both of us, my dear late spouse señor
don Pedro de Sotomayor, whom God took,
and me, since no child of ours is alive, for
if there were a nephew or niece of yours,
certainly it would all belong to him or her
and I would leave it to that person, but
since there isn't anyone, because of that
everything is to be sold, with all the ruler's
lands, [aside from] however much I have
reduced it myself, with which I have paid at
various times all the debts my dear spouse
left, for I have paid a great deal, and there
are all the papers, the bills of payment the
creditors gave me." And when I heard
everything the lady said, then I replied and
told her, "You have done very wrong; it is a
bad thing you have done. Aren't there
children, nephews [and/or nieces],
grandchildren, and won't they complain
greatly of you when God has taken you, and
curse you for it? Won't there be a great
lawsuit after you are gone? Won't there be

chihuaz ӯ micampatzinco cuix amo tlatza-
tzatziz ycahuacazque yn imachtzitzinhuā
catca yn ttote⁰ dios oquimohuiquili sᵒʳ dō
peᵒ de sotomᵒʳ yn mopilotzitzinhuā ӯ
nemi ascā, yhuā cuix yca huel mopampa-
tzinco quimotlatlauhtilizque yn ttote⁰
dios Yhuan onicnolhuili: auh yn nehuatl
yntla oc çemilhuitzintli nechmochicahui-
liz ttote⁰ dios yhuan yn mopilotzin ca o-
quichtzintli yn onechmotlauhtili ttote⁰
dios yhuā yn nonamic ӯ mopilotzin ca
mochipa nican hualmohuicatiuh yn chi-
chicohometica yn ipā sabado, auh intla
quenmanian nican topan oyohuac campa
tontohuicazque campa tontocallaquizque
cuix tepan ticacallaquizque, ca o no çenca
titechmotolinili, ca yuhquin ma titechmo-
telchihuilitehuac ynic nican ayocmo ceppa
tihuallazᾱ, tihualcallaquizque yn nicā
ytic tecpancalli auh ynin ca çenca otitech-
motolinili.

shouting and discord among the nephews of the late señor don Pedro de Sotomayor, whom God took, your nephews as well, who are now alive? And because of this will they be able to pray to our lord God on your behalf?" And I said to her, "And what about me? If our lord God gives life a while longer to me and the boy your nephew, whom our lord God has granted me, and my spouse, your niece, why she always comes here every week on Saturday, and if nightfall catches us here sometime, where are we to go, where are we to take shelter? Are we supposed to go to other people's houses? You have greatly mistreated us too, it is as though you had scorned us, so that we are not to come here ever again, to enter inside the palace here. In a word, you have greatly mistreated us."

8. From Chimalpahin's Mexico City journal, ca. 1600–1630.

The great Nahua annalist Chimalpahin generally specialized in collecting indigenous antiquities, often preconquest and often about his birthplace, Amecameca, but one of his most interesting writings is a long set of entries about events mainly in Mexico City where he lived and mainly during his own lifetime. The whole set is to published by James Lockhart, Doris Namala, and Susan Schroeder with University of Oklahoma Press.

- Auh yn ipan axcan yc 21 . mani metztli
Setiembre de 1607 . años . yquac ypan
ylhuitzin quiz . Sant . Matheo apostol .
yquac mochi tlacatl . oquittac . ce citlalli
popocaya : ohualnez ylhuicatitech . ye nipa
hualitztia mictlampa y norte . yhuicpa yn
azcapotzalcopa . auh can [sic] ihuian
huallotlatocatia ynic nican motlallico .
tonatiuh ynepillohuayan . yn iquac calla-
quia tonatiuh . yn onpoliuh . niman hual-
necia yn popocaya citlalli . hualmoque-
tzaya ycuitlapil . yn itlanex . cenca huiac .
çan iuhquin ayauhpoctli . yn hualmoque-
tzaya . ynic hualnecia . ypocyo . mochipa
yuh hualnecia . yn maca çan hualma-
pillohuaya . ye nican tocpacpa . yn qui-
hualquetzaya ycuitlapil . tonatiuh yquiça-
yampa onitzticaya .

Today, the 21st of the month of September of the year 1607, was when the feast day of San Mateo the apostle was celebrated and when everyone saw a comet that appeared in the sky; it headed this way from off to the north, from toward Azcapotzalco. It came along slowly, settling at the place where the sun descends; when the sun went down and disappeared, the comet became visible. The light of its tail took shape, very long, its smoke appearing like vapor as it shaped up. It always appeared that way, not just pointing toward us, but putting its tail here over our heads, looking toward the east.

- Auh çan no ypan in yn ipan ilhuitzin
quiz . Sant . Matheo . oncan ye no nicuel
ceppa missa mito . yn ihtic teopancalli
Sancto Domingo . ye otlayecchichihualoc .

Also in this [month], when the feast day of San Mateo was celebrated, mass was said again inside the church of Santo Domingo. Things had been fixed up, and

ye qualcan yn ihtic . yn ipampa yc tla-
tlanauhca . atl yn manca yhtic . // Auh yn
la compañia de Jesus . ye quin ça tepan
Domingo . yn motlapo teopancalli . ypan
ylhuitzin catca . yn ichpochtli Sancta
Vrsula . ca ça tzauhcticatca . ynic ye no
yehuantzitzin teopixque . omotlayecchi-
chihuillique . yn tlalpātli Oquimaco-
cuillique . ynic no cenca tentimanca atl
teopan . // Yhuan yn ypan in omoteneuh
metztli miyequintin atlan micque yn
matlanhuique macehualtin . yhuan yn
ipan in omoteneuh metztli Setiembre .
ynic tlamico . huel hualnecia ynic popocaya citlalli .
- Auh niman ic hualmoma yn metztli .
octubre . mochi yn ipan in popocaya citlalli . yhuan yn ipan in metztli ça quez-
quilhuitl . yn onquiyauh . ye ytlacoyoc
ynepantla . yn oquiçaco quiyahuitl. // auh
çan no yquac yn ipan in omoteneuh
metztli octubre de 1607 . años . yquac o-
hualla tlahtolli yn ompa españa . oma-
chiztico . nican mexico . ye ce xihuitl çan
no yehuatl . ypan yn omoteneuh metztli
octubre de 1606 años . yn ipan omomiquilli in yehuatzin tlahtocapilli Don diego
luis de moteuhcçoma yhuitltemoctzin . yn
ipiltzin tlacatl Don Pedro de moteuhcçoma
tlacahuepantzin . ye omito yuh machiztico
ye ce xihuitl yn omomiquilli . ynin Don
diego luis de moteuhcçoma yhuitltemoctzin ye yxhuiuhtzin yn tlacatl catca huey
tlahtohuani emperador . Moteuhcçoma-
tzin xocoyotl . auh in yehuatzin Don diego
luis de moteuhcçoma yhuitltemoctzin . yn
ompa españa oquincauhtia ynamic huel
española yn cihuapilli ytoca Doña franca
de la cueba yhuan ypilhuantzitzin chiqua-
cemī mestiçoti . yehica ye omito yn
innantzin ca huel española . nahui o-
quichtli . ome cihuatl .
- ynic ce ytoca Doña Maria miyahua-
xochtzī
- ynic ome ytoca Don Pº desifun de la cueba
de moteuhcçoma auh yn oc cequintin amo
huel momati yn intoca . yn ipilhuantzitzin
Don diego luis de moteuhcçoma yhuitl .
temoctzin .
Auh niman hualmoman in metztli No-

the inside was good [for walking on]; the reason why it had become unusable was that water was inside. // The Jesuit church was opened later, on Sunday, the feast day of the virgin Santa Ursula; it had been closed while those religious too fixed things up and raised the floor, because that church too was very full of water. // And in the aforementioned month many commoners (indigenous people) died in the water and drowned. And at the end of the aforementioned month of September the comet was still fully visible.

Then came the month of October, during all of which the comet was there. During this month it rained for only a few days; in the middle of the month the rain stopped. // In this same month of October of the year 1607 was when word came from Spain and it became known here in Mexico City that a year before, likewise in the aforementioned month of October, of the year 1606, there had passed away the royal nobleman don Diego Luis de Moteucçoma Ihuitltemoctzin, child of the lord don Pedro de Moteucçoma Tlacahuepantzin. As was said, it became known that he had died a year before. This don Diego Luis de Moteucçoma Ihuitltemoctzin was the grandchild of the late lord high ruler and emperor Moteucçoma the Younger. Don Diego Luis de Moteucçoma Ihuitltemoctzin left behind in Spain a wife, a noblewoman who is fully Spanish named doña Francisca de la Cueva, and six children who are mestizos, because, as was said, their mother is fully Spanish. Four of them are male, two female.

The first is named doña María Miyahuaxochtzin.

The second is named don Pedro [Tecifón?] de la Cueva de Moteucçoma, and the names of the other children of don Diego Luis de Moteucçoma Ihuitltemoctzin cannot be established.

Then came the month of November of

uiembre de 1607 . años, yn iquac ypan in ça yquezquilhuiyoc yn onpolihuico . yn popocaya citlalli . tonatiuh ycallaquiyampa temoc . ynic poliuh .
- Auh yn axcan yc 5. mani metztli nouiembre de 1607 . años. yquac ye no nicuel oquinmonahuatili . yn visurrey ỹ nauhcame chalca . ynic ompa quauhtequizque . quauhquixtizque . yn quauhtla quauhtemohuizq̄ . yehuatl quinmotequitilli yn quamimilli yn motenehua morrillos . auh ynic nenque yn quauhtecque . chalca . mochi yn ipan metztli nouiembre .

the year 1607. A few days into this month the comet disappeared; it went down and disappeared toward the west.

Today, the 5th of the month of November of the year 1607, was when the viceroy again ordered the people of the four parts of Chalco to cut trees in the forest and remove them; he gave them the duty of bringing down the round logs called *morillos*. The Chalca cutting trees worked at it during the whole month of November.

9. From bachiller Luis Laso de la Vega's *Huei tlamahuiçoltica*, 1649.
This publication about the legendary apparitions of the Virgin of Guadalupe, apparently written largely by Laso de la Vega himself, was well known at the time and has become even more famous today. The whole book is contained in Lisa Sousa, Stafford Poole, C. M., and James Lockhart, eds. and trans., *The Story of Guadalupe: Luis Laso de la Vega's* Huei tlamahuiçoltica *of 1649*, described in the epilogue, p. 142. Note that a grave accent generally means a glottal stop after the vowel on which it is placed, but it marks the vocative *e* as well.

In imoztlayoc Lunes in iquac quihuicazquia in Iuan Diego in itla inezca inic neltocoz, aocmo ohualmocuep: yeica in iquac àçito in ichan çe itla catca itoca Iuan Bernardino o itech motlali in cocoliztli, huel tlanauhtoc, oc quiticinochilito, oc ipan tlàto, yece aocmo inman ye huel otlanauh: auh in ye yohuac quitlatlauhti in iTla in oc yohuatzinco, oc tlàtlayohuatoc hualquiçaz, quimonochiliquiuh in oncan Tlatilolco çeme in teopixque inic mohuicaz, quimoyolcuitilitiuh, ihuan quimoçencahuilitiuh, yeica ca huel yuh ca in iyollo ca ye inman, ca ye oncan inic miquiz ca aoc mehuaz aocmo pàtiz.

Auh in Martes huel oc tlàtlayohuatoc in ompa hualquiz ichan in Iuan Diego in quimonochiliz teopixqui in ompa Tlatilolco, auh in ye àçitihuitz inahuac tepetzintli tepeyacac in icxitlan quiztica òtli tonatiuh icalaquianpa in oncan yeppa quiçani, quìto intla çan nicmelahua òtli manen nechhualmottiliti izçihuapilli ca yeppa nechmotzicalhuiz inic nichuiquiliz tlanezcayotl in teopixcatlàtohuani in yuh onechmonànahuatili; ma oc techcahua in

On the following day, Monday, Juan Diego did not return when he was supposed to take some sign in order to be believed, because when he reached the home of an uncle of his, whose name was Juan Bernardino, a sickness had come upon him and he lay gravely ill. First he went to summon a physician for him, who looked after him for a while, but it was too late; he was already mortally ill. When night had come his uncle asked him that while it was still very early in the morning and dark everywhere, he should come to Tlatelolco to summon one of the friars to go hear his confession and prepare him, because he was fully convinced that it was now time for him to die and that he would not rise again or recover.

It was Tuesday, still very dark everywhere, when Juan Diego left his home to summon a friar in Tlatelolco. When he came by the hill of Tepeyacac, at the foot of which the road that he took previously passes to the west, he said, "if I just go straight along the road, I am afraid that the Lady may see me, for before you know it she will detain me in order that I should carry the sign to the priestly ruler as she instructed me. May our affliction

*tonetequipachol, ma oc nicnonochilìti-
huetzi in teopixqui motolinia in notlàtzin
àmo ça quimochialìtoc. Niman ic contla-
colhui in tepetl itzallan ontlècoc ye nepa
centlapal Tonatiuh yquiçayanpa quiçato
inic içiuhca açitiuh Mexico inic àmo
quimotzicalhuiz in ilhuicac Çihuapīlli in
momati ca in ompa ic otlacolo ca àhuel
quimottiliz, in huel nohuiampa motzti-
lìtica: Quittac quenin hualmotemohui
icpac in tepetzintli ompa hualmotztìlitoc
in ompa yeppa conmottiliani, conmo-
namiquilico in inacaztlan tepetl, conmo-
yacatzacuililico, quimolhuili. Auh noxo-
coyouh, campa in tiyauh? campa in titz-
tiuh? Auh in yèhuatl cuix achi ic mel-
lelmà? cuix noçe pinahuac? cuix noçe ic
miçahui, momauhti? ixpantzinco mopech-
tecac, quimotlàpalhui, quimolhuilì, nochpochtzinè, noxocoyohuè, Çihuapillè ma
ximopaquiltitie quen otimixtonalti? cuix
ticmohuelmachitia in motlaçònacayotzin
noTecuiyoè, nopiltzintzinè; nictequipa-
choz in mixtzin in moyollòtzin, ma xicmo-
machiltitzino nochpochtzinè, ca huella-
nauhtoc çe momaçehualtzin noTla huei
cocoliztli in itech omotlali ca yeppa ic
momiquiliz, auh oc nonìçiuhtiuh in mo-
chantzinco Mexìco noconnonochiliz çeme
in itlaçòhuan toTecuiyo in toTeopixcahuā,
conmoyolcuitilitiuh, ihuā conmoçenca-
huilitiuh, ca nel yè inic otitlacatque, in
ticchiaco in tomiquiztequiuh. Auh intla
onoconnellìlito, ca niman nican oc ceppa
nihualnocuepaz, inic nonyaz noconitquiz,
in mìiyotzin in motlàtoltzin Tlacatlè,
Nochpochtzinè, ma xinechmotlapopolhui-
li, ma oc ixquich ica xinechmopaccaiyo-
huilti càmo ic nimitznoquelhuia, noxocoyohuè, nopiltzintzinè, ca niman moztla
niquiztihuetziquiuh.*

*Auh in o yuh quimocaquiti itlàtol in
Iuan Diego quimonanquilili in icnohuà-
caçenquizcaichpochtzintli: Ma xiccaqui
ma huel yuh ye in moyollo noxoco-
youh macatle tlein mitzmauhti, mitzte-
quipacho, macamo quen mochihua in mix
in moyollo, macamo xiquimacaci in cocoliztli, manoçe oc itlà cocoliztli cococ
teòpouhqui, cuix àmo nican nicà nimo-*

leave us first; let me first hurry to summon
the friar. My uncle is in need and he can't
just lie waiting for him." Thereupon he
went around the hill, climbing through an
opening and coming out on the other side
to the east, so that he would quickly reach
Mexico City and the heavenly Lady would
not detain him. He believed that if he went
around there, she who sees absolutely
everywhere would not be able to see him.
He saw her coming down from the hill
where she was watching, where he had seen
her before. She came to meet and intercept
him on the hillside, saying to him, "Well,
my youngest child, where are you going?
Where are you headed?" And wasn't he a bit
bothered by it? Or ashamed? Or startled
and frightened by it? He prostrated himself
before her, greeted her, and said to her, "My
daughter, my youngest child, Lady, may
you be content. How did you feel on awakening? Is your precious body in good
health, my patron, my very noble lady? I
am going to cause you concern. You must
know, my daughter, that a poor subject of
yours, my uncle, lies very gravely ill. A
great illness has come upon him, of which
he will soon die. And first I am hurrying to
your home of Mexico City to summon one
of those beloved of our Lord, our friars, to
go hear his confession and prepare him,
for what we were born for is to come to
await our duty of death. When I have carried this out, then I will return here again
so that I may go to carry your message, O
personage, my daughter. Please forgive me
and meanwhile have patience with me. I
am not doing it on purpose [or I am not
fooling you?], my youngest child, my very
noble Lady. I will come by quickly tomorrow."

When she had heard Juan Diego's words,
the compassionate, consummate Virgin
answered him, "Understand, rest very
much assured, my youngest child, that
nothing whatever should frighten you or
worry you. Do not be concerned, do not fear
the illness, or any other illness or calamity. Am I, your mother, not here? Are
you not under my protective shade, my

Nantzin? cuix àmo noçehuallotitlan, nè-
cauhyotitlan in ticà? cuix àmo nèhuatl in
nimopaccayeliz? cuix àmo nocuixanco,
nomamalhuazco in ticà? cuix oc itlà in
motech monequi? macamo oc itlà mitz-
tequipacho, mitzàmana, macamo mitzte-
quipacho in icocoliz moTlàtzin càmo ic
miquîz in axcan itech ca; ma huel yuh ye in
moyollo ca ye opàtic:

shadow? Am I not your happiness? Are you
not in the security of my lapfold, in my
carrying gear? Do you need something
more? Do not let anything worry you or
upset you further. Do not let your uncle's
illness worry you, for he will not die of
what he now has. Rest assured, for he has
already recovered.

10. From a Stage 3 set of annals of Puebla, last quarter of the seventeenth century.

An anonymous Nahua of Puebla wrote a set of annals of his time, the second half of the seventeenth century, with an unusual expressiveness; the entries were widely copied and integrated into
other sets. The bulk of the selections here is also included in James Lockhart, *The Nahuas After the
Conquest*, Chapter 9. Another section is in Frances Karttunen and James Lockhart, *Nahuatl in the
Middle Years*, described in the epilogue, p. 141. The second passage here speaks of a solar eclipse.

niman ticalaque metztli de septiembre auh
niman oncan omononotzque onpualli om-
matlactli caxtilteca yni[c] san yehuantin
quichihuasą̃ yn pantzin niman otlecoque
yxpan alcalde mayor ynic omobligaroque
ynic san yehuantin quichihuasque pan
ynic quitlacualtisque yn siudad de loz an-
geles auh niman yn justisiatlaca oquin-
notzque yn masehualtzitzintin ynic quin-
quixtilisque ȳ tlaxcalchihualistli oncan
oquinpenatique ynic tonalli oquimacaque
termino ynic amo quichihuas yn pantzin
san oc yehuantin yn caxtilteca yn omix-
quesque quichihuasque auh amo huel o-
quisustentaroque sann ica ome tonalli
ynic omochiuh yn itec siudad ynin ome
tonalli ye yc oapismicoaya ypan tonali
lunes yc senpuali ose 21 tonali mani
metztli septienbre huel ypan ylhuitzin san
matheo lunes yhuan martes yn ohuapis-
micohuaya aocmo nesia ma pan ma tor-
tillas yn tianquisco ma tienda auh yn
aquin ychtaca oquimochihuili yn se mita
caca[xt?]li yn conaxitiaya yn tianquisco
ma toltilla san ypan omomictiaya yn cax-
tilteca manel huel momahuistilia aocan
quipoaya masehualtzintli yn aquin ach-
to[p]a sa yehuatl quihuicaya yn tlaxcalli sa
choquistli omania auh niman onca o-
macomanque ynic muchi tlacatl yuhqui
teopixque yuh caxtilteca yuhqui mase-
hualtzintzintin ynic mochi tlacatl ynpan
omomanque ym masehualtzitzintin oqui-
macaque se amatl oquichiuhque mase-

Then the month of September came, and
then at that time fifty Spaniards agreed
that only they would make [wheat] bread.
Then they went up before the alcalde mayor and obliged themselves that only they
would make bread to feed the City of the
Angels. Then the law officers summoned
the commoners [i.e., "Indians"], [telling
them] that they were taking breadmaking
from them; they set a fine for them, giving
them a deadline for not making bread, that
only those Spaniards who made the offer
should make it. But they couldn't keep it
up. It was done for only two days in the
city, and in those two days people were
already starving because of it. On Monday,
the 21st day of September, the very day of
San Mateo, Monday, and on Tuesday,
people were starving. Neither wheat bread
nor tortillas could be found, neither in the
marketplace nor in shops. And if someone
secretly made half a carrying frame full
and took it to the marketplace, even if it
was tortillas, the Spaniards just fought
over it. Even though it was someone of very
high standing, the commoners no longer
paid them respect. Whoever was first got
the bread. There was nothing but weeping.
And then everyone became disturbed,
priests and Spaniards as well as commoners, so that everyone took the commoners' side. The commoners personally
gave a letter that they wrote to the alcalde
mayor. When the alcalde mayor was going

huacltzitzintin ymatica yn alcalde mayor yquac ye ontleco alcalde mayor ypalasio niman muchin pipiltzitzintin yhuan sequintin huehuey tlaca oquitzatzilique oquilhuique pan pan pa señor capitan ye tapismiquisque ye tapismiquisque auh in iuh oquicac yn alcalde mayor yhuan oquipohuilique yn amatl yn iuhqui oquitotia ynic mochi polihuis yn itequipanolocatzin yn tohueytlatocatzin Rey yntla techcahualtisque yn toofisio yn tlaxcalchihualistli ma yehuantin yn caxtilteca quichihuacan yn quexquich tlatequipanolistli yhuan in tlacalaquili auh yn iuhqui oquicac yn alcalde mayor niman isiuhca otlanahuati mochihuas yn acto ynic niman omotlastihuetz pregon ynic quichihuasque yn masehualtzitzin yn pantzin auh yn caxtilteca otlatequiuhti quintzatzaquasque auh yn yehuantin niman ocholoque yn caxtilteca yn omixquetzca

* * *

Oaçic yn chiucnahui hora niman OÇentlayuhtimoman Oquinenehuili yn chicome hora yohuac auh huel çe quarta ora ynic huecahuac yn otlayohuatimania auh y tototzitzintin yn cacalome y tzotzopi[lome] niman muchin tlalpan huetzque Ça papatlacatinemia huel otlaocoltzatzique auh yn tetepeh yuhquin costic tlemiyahuatl ynpan motecaya yn popocatzin yuhqui yn tlepoctli yn ipan catca auh yn tlatlaca niman Çan yuhqui yn omotlapoltique teopan Çequintin omotlaloque Çequintin omauhcahuehuetzque auh Çan yey yn niman omomiquilique yn iquac Ça choquis[tli] omania aocmo omiximatia yn tlatlaca . . . auh yn Çemilhuitl yeyecapitzactli oquistoya ca huel çeçec auh ypan yey ora asta ypan nahui ora teotlac oquiauhticaya temamauhti yn oquimochihuili ÿ tloque nahuaque totecuiyo Dioz ypan on teotlactli jueues

up to his palace, all the children together with some adults shouted to him, telling him, "Bread, bread, bread, lord captain, we'll starve, we'll starve!" And when the alcalde mayor heard it, and they read him the letter saying that the service of our great ruler the king would perish, that if they were going to forbid us our trade of breadmaking, let the Spaniards do the different services and pay the tribute, when the alcalde mayor had heard it, he quickly ordered a decree to be prepared, and then it was quickly proclaimed that the commoners could make bread, and he ordered that the Spaniards be jailed, and then the Spaniards who had made the offer fled.

* * *

At nine o'clock it became entirely dark, like seven o'clock at night, and it was dark for a full quarter of an hour. Then the little birds and the crows and buzzards all fell to the ground and went fluttering about, crying out in distress. Something like yellow tongues of fire lay over the mountains, and there was something like fire and smoke over the volcano. It was as though people had lost their senses. Some ran to the church, some fell down in fright, and three simply died right away. There was nothing but weeping, and people no longer knew each other. . . . All day there were very cold windstorms, and from three to four o'clock it rained. It was fearful what the lord of the near and the close, our lord God, did on that Thursday afternoon.

Vocabulary

THE FOLLOWING vocabulary is specifically for this volume and does not give words not therein contained unless required for the understanding of words that are; nor does it necessarily give all the meanings of the words listed. Before using the vocabulary you would do well to read the guiding material presented here immediately below.

Vowel quantity and glottal stop. I take the position that it is important to learn to handle texts as they were actually written, with little or no indication of vowel quantity and glottal stop, yet at the same time I believe in the importance of those elements for an understanding of the language and even in the long run for the ability to decipher texts. Therefore they are indicated in this vocabulary even though they were not shown in the body of the book. A long vowel bears a macron (ā, ē, ī, ō); any vowel without a macron is understood to be short. We are told that long vowels were in general not pronounced as long at the end of a word. Nevertheless, simply in order to convey necessary information, final long vowels are indicated here in the primary citation; in inflected forms and phrases in the body of an entry, they are not.

The presence of a glottal stop is indicated by an *h* smaller than the surrounding print: *huēhueh*. Aside from the macron and the *h*, words appear here in the standard orthography used in examples in the lessons.

Whenever questions of vowel quantity or the presence and absence of glottal stop go beyond my personal knowledge, I have relied on Karttunen's *Analytical Dictionary*. In a very few cases I have disagreed with that work. When I consider the situation as to these matters uncertain or simply do not know and cannot find out, I have said so.

Spanish loanwords. Loanwords were pronounced and written with a great variety of substitutions. Generally these are ignored in reproducing them here and the standard modern Spanish form is used, but two known facts are represented: that a vowel stressed in Spanish was long in Nahuatl, and that any Spanish word ending in a vowel (except for particles, possibly) had a glottal stop added. In a few exceptional and well established cases the form representing the Nahuatl pronunciation more closely is given, as with *cahuālloh* for horse; in such cases the standard Spanish is also listed.

Alphabetization: The letters are alphabetized as though they were in English words, treating any digraph (*ch, tl, tz, qu* or *cu*) simply as the two consecutive letters of which it consists. The one thing that may cause you a little difficulty until you get used to it is that THE SMALL *h* USED TO REPRESENT THE GLOTTAL STOP DOES <u>NOT</u> COUNT IN ALPHABETIZATION, for you will be looking up words as they are in the examples and texts, without any representation of glottal stop. The macron showing a long vowel also does not count unless two words are identical except that one has a short vowel, another a long vowel in the same position, and in that case the long vowel comes second: first *toca*, then *tōca*. Likewise *c* and *ç* are intermingled, with *ç* coming after *c* only when the items are otherwise the same: first *ca*, then *çā*.

Weak vowels: Initial weak vowels, which in many contexts are elided, are indicated by being put in parentheses, thus *(i)cnēlia*. In fact, these weak initial vowels are always *i*. Weak vowels at the end of noun stems are indicated by separating the stem proper from the weak vowel plus the absolutive singular prefix, thus *āxcā-itl, cuīc-atl*.

Verbs: The verb entries are modeled on Molina, i.e., they give the present tense form of the root, followed after a comma by the proper prefixes in the first person unless the first person is not applicable, but they do not follow his practice in every detail.[1] With the entry *nemi, ni*, you are being told as with Molina that *nemi* is intransitive. With *āna, nic*,

---

[1] To see how Molina cites verbs, read the section on the topic in Appendix 1, pp. 153–55.

you know that the verb is transitive. The prefix *c/qu* is used widely here to indicate transitivity without specifying whether the object is human or nonhuman; the great majority of transitive verbs can have either type of object under certain circumstances. The prefix *tla-* is used not to indicate nonhuman objects per se but to specify that the verb at least in that sense is literally used with *tla-*, as in *(i)ħtoa, nitla,* "to speak"; i.e., the form *nitlaħtoa* means "I speak." With the prefix set *nino*, you know that the verb at least in that meaning is reflexive. The prefix set *nicno* means that the verb in that meaning takes both a normal object prefix and a reflexive prefix. The directional prefixes are also included as appropriate.

When a verb is used with different prefix combinations in different meanings, here as in Molina the different forms are in separate entries, but they are numbered so that looking at one you will know there are others, as in *mati* (1), *nic*, followed by an entry *mati* (2), *nino*. Under special circumstances, such as relative rarity in usage, a different prefix combination and its meaning may be given in the main entry. If the transitive form of a verb is in the list, the reflexive form is listed only if it translates differently than the normal meanings of the reflexive, action back on the subject or a passive sense.

With each verb its class is indicated after the gloss, and its preterit is given in the same fashion as with Molina, in the first person singular in the normal order, with the ō preterit sign prefixed even though it will not always be there in actual usage. When the same verb has more than one entry, only the first gives this information. With applicatives and causatives of verbs that have their own entries, unless the derived form has taken on a radically unexpected meaning, the preterit is not given. In any case, all applicatives and causatives belong to Class 3.

Nouns: Nouns are normally cited in the third person singular absolute form, as with Molina. The stem used for possessed and combining forms is indicated by a hyphen between it and the rest, which will in most cases be merely the absolute singular ending, as with *quāuh-tli*, where you will understand that the possessed form is *-quāuh* and the combining form *quāuh-*. When the final vowel of the root is weak, omitted in other forms, the hyphen comes after the stem, as in *quahu-itl*. You will understand that the possessed form is *-quauh* and the combining form *quauh-*. As in this example, automatic orthographic and phonological changes discussed in the body of the lessons are taken for granted. When the combining form differs from the possessed form, the combining form is given in addition. From *nac-atl* you know that the possessed form is *-nac*; an additional remark tells you that *naca-* is the combining form. It is assumed that consonant stems will have no possessive suffix and vowel stems will have *-uh*, i.e., that the possessed form of *cal-li* is *-cal* and that the possessed form of *ā-tl* is *-āuh*. At the same time it is taken for granted that nouns with a stem ending in a long vowel followed by a weak *i* before the absolute ending will not add *-uh*, thus the possessed form of *cuē-itl* will be *-cuē*. The same is true of derived nouns ending in *-yō-tl* or its assimilated forms (*-lō-tl, -çō-tl, -chō-tl*).

Absolute plurals are specified only when they are out of the ordinary (i.e., no simple *-meh* or *-tin* plurals). Possessed plurals are not taken into consideration because they are almost never irregular.

Kinship terms and other nouns that always or nearly always appear in possessed form are listed (against my own inclinations) with an absolute singular ending for convenience in finding them, thus *huezhuah-(tli)*. The parenthesis around the absolute ending indicates that it is virtually a hypothetical form. A few inalienably possessed forms, such as *-nacayō*, are given without an absolute ending because even in theory it is inapplicable or would change the meaning. A very few nouns have no absolute singular at all, thus *chichi*.

Preterit agentive nouns and the possessor nouns in -*eh*, -*huah*, and -*yoh* are understood to have absolutive plurals in -*queh* and combining forms in -*cā*- (which means that the possessed form will be -*cāuh*).

Relational words. With verbs and nouns, their glosses and in most cases their morphological equipment make the part of speech sufficiently clear, so it is not further specified. Relational words are specifically labeled as such. They are listed by the bare root, thus -*tech*, preceded by a hyphen to remind you that they are always possessed or have a noun bound to them. Idiomatic expressions including them, when listed at all, are mainly under the principal accompanying verb or noun; thus -*tech quīça*, "to emerge from," is in the *quīça* entry.

Quantifiers. These words, like *miec*, "much," are also specifically labeled as such. It is understood that they cannot be possessed but can take absolutive plurals and first and second person subject prefixes. Numbers, which share these qualities, are not labeled because the nature of the word is clear from the gloss.

Interrogatives. Although some of these words act like particles (*quēn*, "how"), some like quantifiers (*quēxquich*, "how much"), some like indefinite pronouns (*āc*, "who"), they are simply identified as interrogatives, along with the fact that in certain circumstances they introduce dependent clauses instead.

Particles. Words which do not inflect in any way are considered particles here (except for some invariant locative nouns and absolute relational words) and are so labeled in the entry. They usually act adverbially or as conjunctions, or very often both. With them the convention of reproducing a final long vowel apparently also corresponds to practice in speech, for since they were normally attached to a following verb or noun complex in a single phonological phrase, a final long vowel was not reduced to short as it would have been with the following nuclear word.

In accord with the policy in the body of the lessons of writing each identifiable part of a particle cluster separately, such an item as *çan ye no* will be found in the *çan* entry. Nevertheless, a very few combinations are so universal and special that they are printed solid and alphabetized accordingly, thus *çātēpan* (also under *tēpan*, however).

Attached elements. Important derivational and inflectional elements are listed as separate entries, mainly because the student does right to look up absolutely everything when it comes to a Nahuatl construction, and in the early stages it is hard to keep track of the great flurry of often nearly identical elements in Nahuatl morphology.

Analysis of components. When the component roots of a compound word are known (and sometimes even when they are a bit uncertain), they are specified at the end of the entry. The intention is to help you understand how the Nahuatl lexicon is built up and what the original meaning of many words was, as well as to provide a sort of cross-reference.

Abbreviations. The abbreviations used in the entries are very few:

abs.	absolutive	pret.	preterit
obj.	object	sing.	singular
pl.	plural	Sp.	Spanish

*　　*　　*

-*h*. pl. ending for verbs in the present and some other tenses; abs. pl. ending for some nouns with vowel stems; also part of some other pl. endings, such as *-meh, -queh*.

ah-, particle. not. always prefixed to something.

abrīl. April. Sp.

āc. who, interrogative, or preceded by *in* in relative, or one who, etc. has abs. pl. *āc ihqueh*, in which *ihqueh* takes any subject prefix.

acah. someone. indefinite pronoun. sometimes seen with pl. *acahmeh*.

ācalaqui, ni. to go beneath the level of the water. Class 2: *ōnācalac. ātl, calaqui*.

ācalli. boat, ship. *ātl, calli*.

ahcān, particle. nowhere. *ah* negative, *-cān*.

āca-tl. reed. *ātl, -ca-tl* inhabitant of.

ācayōtl. piping, tubing, urinary equipment of a male. *ācatl, -yōtl*.

-āch. older brother of a female.

-āchcāuh. see *-tēāchcāuh*.

achi, quantifier. a little, some, a good deal. *oc achi, oc achi miec*, more (in comparative constructions).

achihtzīnca, particle. a very short time, a little while. *achi, -tzīn-*, a *ca* that often concludes compound adverbial particles.

achpil-(li). unusual word meaning great-grandmother. *ach-* as in *achtōn-(tli), pilli*.

achto, particle. first. the root *-ach* must mean first, oldest, etc. In *tēāchcāuh*, etc., however, the root with a similar meaning has a long vowel.

achtōn-(tli). great-grandfather.

★*achtopa*, particle. first. *achto, -pa*.

ahci. arrive, get somewhere. *-tech ahci*./ reach as far as. Class 1; *ōnahcic*. very frequently seen with the directional prefixes, the purposive motion forms, or both. *-pan ahci*, to find a person or thing there on one's arrival.

ahco. above. also often *ahcopa*.

ahço, particle. perhaps, if.

ahcocui (1), *nic*. to raise. Class 2 irregular: *ō-nicahcoc. ahco, cui*.

ahcocui (2), *nin*. to rise.

ācōlhuah. inhabitant of the Tetzcoco region. abs. pl. *ācōlhuahqueh*.

ahcomana, nin. to get disturbed, worked up. Class 2: *ōninahcoman. ahco* above, *mana*.

āctoh. see *āutoh*.

ahhua, nic. to scold, upbraid, argue with, complain of someone. Class 1: *ōnicahhuac*.

āhuah tepēhuah. inhabitant of an altepetl. *ātl, tepētl, -huah*.

āhuaca-tl. avocado.

ahhuachia, nic. to sprinkle someone or something. often with *tla-* obj. prefix. Class 3: *ō-nicahhuachih*. probably related to *ātl*.

ahhuel, negated particle. not possible, i.e., for the action of the following verb not to be possible. *ah, huel*.

ahhuīc, particle. back and forth from one side to the other. possibly contains *-huīc*.

āhuīl-li. play, frivolity.

āhuiltia, nin. to amuse oneself, play. Class 3: *ōnināhuiltih*.

āhui-(tl). aunt. lacks *-uh* possessive.

āi, n (āyi). to do something. also with *tla-*, generally in the sense of cultivating the land. Class 2: *ōnāx, ōnitlaāx*.

aīc, particle. never. *ah-* negative, *īc*.

alactic. something slippery. related to *alāhua* to slide; contains *-tic*.

alahuērtah. Orchard, intensively cultivated garden. Sp. *huerta*.

albacēah. executor of a will. Sp. *albacea*.

alcāldeh. alcalde, first instance judge on a municipal council. sometimes in the set phrase *alcāldeh ordinārioh*, to distinguish this officer from an alcalde mayor. Sp.

alcāldeh mayōr. chief Spanish magistrate of a large district. Sp.

āltepēhuah. inhabitant or official of an altepetl. *āltepētl, -huah*.

āltepēhuahcān, locative noun. in the various altepetl. almost always in a collective sense, amounting to the countryside. *āltepētl, -huah, -cān*.

āltepē-tl. local ethnic state, sovereign sociopolitical unit, pueblo, altepetl. normal possessed form *-āltepēuh*. is actually a noun doublet, *ātl* and *tepētl*, in which the first is weakened but still bears a vestige of the absolutive ending. still occurs at times with the same meaning as *ātl tepētl* or *in ātl in tepētl* and even as possessed *-āuh -tepēuh*.

am-. you (pl.), 2nd person pl. subject prefix; also your (pl.), form of *amo-*, 2nd person pl. possessive prefix, before certain vowels.

ahmana, nic. to disturb, unsettle. Class 2: *ōnic-ahman. ah-* up, *mana*. closely related to *ahco-mana*.

āmantēcatl. artisan, sometimes specifically featherworker. abs. pl. *āmantēcah*. originally meant inhabitant of Āmantlān.

Āmaquēmehcān. Amecameca, an altepetl. *ā-matl, (tla)quēmitl, -eh, -cān*, in reference to an often snow-topped mountain nearby.

āma-tl. paper, document, letter, book.

amēch-. you (pl.), 2nd person obj. prefix of verbs.

amehhuān-tin. you (pl.), 2nd person pl. independent pronoun.

āmi, n. to hunt for game, go hunting. Class 2: *ōnān*.

āmīl-li. irrigated field(s). *ātl, mīlli*.

amo-. your (pl.), possessive prefix.

ahmō, particle. not. *ahmō quēn*, the same as *ahquēn*. contains two negatives, *ah-* and *-mō*.

ahmōl-li. soap.

āmox-tli. codex, book.

an-. form assumed by am-, you (pl.), 2nd person pl. subject prefix, when followed by a non-labial consonant.

āna (1), nic. to take; to seize, arrest; to stretch. Class 2; ōnicān.

āna (2), nin. to stretch, grow.

ānah(3), tito. to take each other (in marriage).

anēgah. see fanēgah.

-ānima(n). soul. Sp. ánima.

ahnoço, particle. perhaps, or. ahço with particle no inserted. Not nō, also, because of length.

añoh. year. Sp.

aoc, particle. no longer. ah- negative, oc.

aocmō, particle. no longer. ahmō, oc.

aoctle(h), negated quantifier. nothing more. ahtle(h), oc.

āpachihui, n. to be inundated, submerged. Class 2: ōnāpachiuh. ātl, pachihui.

ahpāna, nin. to gird oneself with, wrap oneself in something. Class 2. ōninahpān.

āpīzmiqui, ni. to starve, be very hungry, "be dying of hunger." Class 2: ōnāpīzmic. āpīztli hunger, miqui. the length of the i in the element meaning hunger is in doubt.

ahquēn, particle. negative expression used in certain idiomatic phrases. ahquēn cah, or ahquēn mochīhua, for nothing to be wrong with something, for someone to be serene and normal. ahquen nicmati, not to care (a whit) about something. ah negative, quēn.

aqui, n. to enter, to go or fit inside something, to be included. Class 2: ōnac.

aquia (1), nic. to put something inside something, to plant or transplant, etc. Class 3: ōnicaquih. from aqui.

aquia (2), nocon. to put on some tight fitting garment. Class 3: ōnoconaquih. In Molina the verb in this meaning is given as nonnaquia, reflexive with no other obj.

-aquiāmpa, -aquiyāmpa, complex relational word. rarer variant of -calaquiāmpa, which see.

āquin. who, interrogative; preceded by in, relative, or one who, whoever, etc. āc, in.

āquihqueh. manner of writing the abs. pl. of āc.

āsnoh. donkey. Sp.

at, particle. perhaps, whether. used especially in Tlaxcala. related to ah negative.

ahtenām-itl. parapet or projection on a roof or top of a wall; eave. contains tenāmitl. the h in the first element is speculative, suggested in view of some words in which ah has a sense of above.

ātexā-tl. something to drink with something ground in it, perhaps a gruel. tlamātzoalli ā-texātl, food, the fare. ātextli, something watery and ground, from ātl and teci, and ātl.

ātēzca-tl. (shallow) pool, puddle. ātl, tēzcatl.

ā-tl. water. ātl tepētl, altepetl. huēi ātl, ocean. see also ātzīntli.

ahtlāca-tl. bad or inhuman person, monster. ah negative, tlācatl.

ātlacomōl-li. well (source of water). ātl, tlacomōlli large hole or depression.

ātlacui, n. to fetch water. Class 1: ōnātlacuic. ātl, cui.

ātlan, complex relational word. in, into, under the water. ātl, -tlan.

ātlanhuia, nin. to drown. Class 3: ōninātlanhuih. ātlan, -huia.

ahtlapal-li. wing. part of the expression in cuitlapilli in ahtlapalli, metaphor for the common people.

ātlatataca, n. to dig in relation to water, usually to make excavations related to drainage. Class 1: ōnātlatatacac. ātl, tataca to dig.

ātlauh-tli. ravine.

ahtle(h), negated quantifier. nothing. ah negative, tle(h).

ātocō, n, verb in passive only. to be carried away by water or drowned. Class 1: ōnātocōc. ātl, toca.

ātocohua. impersonal of ātocō.

ātōyātl. river. contains ātl, probably twice.

ātzīn-tli. reverential of ātl, water, generally with the meaning beverage, often alcoholic and specifically pulque.

audiēnciah. high court of a large region; also any judicial court in session. Sp.

auh, particle. beginning of a new independent statement; indicates that a pause (a period) came just before, although exceptions are found. Generally translated "and," sometimes "but," often not translated except by a period and a capital letter.

āutoh. official act, decree. Sp.

āxcā-itl. property.

āxcān, particle. today, now. quin āxcān, just now, just recently.

āxcātia, nicno. to appropriate something. Class 2: ōnicnāxcātih. āxcāitl, -tia².

ahxīhua. impersonal of ahci.

ahxilia, nic. applicative of ahci.

ahxitia, nic. causative of ahci. (it is not certain whether it is ahxītia or not.)

ayāc, indefinite pronoun. no one; to be absent or nonexistent. ah, āc.

āyacach-tli. rattle.

ayamō, particle. not yet. sometimes translates as before. from ahmo and ya/ye.

āyauhpōc-tli. (water) vapor. āyahuitl, fog, low cloud; pōctli.

ayoc, ayocmō. same as aoc, aocmō.

Āzcapōtzalco. an important altepetl near Mexico City. āzcapōtzalli ant hill, -co.

bārrioh. district of an altepetl. Sp.

batān. fulling mill. Sp.

brazādah, braçādah. Spanish unit for measuring length, a fathom. sometimes used as equivalent of Nahua *quahuitl.*

-*c-.* him, her, it, 3rd person sing. obj. prefix of verbs when there is an adjacent vowel.

-*c.* the form assumed by the locative suffix -*co* after a vowel.

-*c.* the form assumed by the pret. sing. suffix of verbs after a vowel.

ca. clause-introductory particle with many uses. sometimes it indicates reason why, other times the beginning of the nuclear complex, or the beginning of an answer. *ca qualli* or *ca ye qualli,* that's fine, okay. *ca nel,* because, since, for, etc.

-*ca.* instrumental relational word. by means of, through, with, etc. *ī-ca-tzīnco,* in the name of.

-*c(a)-.* element, possibly itself a negative particle, used as a kind of ligature or punctuation between *mā, tlā,* and *intlā* and following negative particles and pronouns.

-*cā-.* element serving to link words originating as preterit agentives with other elements to the right. also the ending of adverbial particles originating as preterit agentives. by origin the ancient preterit suffix of verbs, protected in internal location.

çā, particle. merely, almost the same as *çan,* of which it is a reduced form, but it can imply that the now deprecated situation was not always so.

cah, ni. to be, stative. present pl. *cateh.* irregular verb. has second root *ye.* see also *oncah.* -*tech cah,* to be incumbent on, to be attached to, etc. *iuh -tech cah,* to be a certain way with, etc. past *ōnicatca.* future *niyez.*

caballerīzah. stable. Sp.

caballo, see *cahuālloh.*

cabecērah. capital or head town ruling others, the Sp. meaning, or used as the equivalent of *āltepētl.* Sp.

cabīldoh. municipal council, cabildo. Sp.

cacahua-tl. cacao.

cācālō-tl. crow (the bird).

çaca-tl. dry grass, hay, weeds, zacate.

çacatlah, complex relational word. grassland, uninhabited and uncultivated area. *çacatl,* -*tlah.*

cācāx-tli. carrying frame fitted to the back.

cahcayāhua, nino. to laugh at, mock, cheat someone. with -*ca.* Class 2: *ōninocahcayāuh.*

çacayoh. something covered with grass, grown over. *çacatl,* -*yoh.*

cacchīuhcān, locative noun. shop where footwear is made. *cactli, chīhua,* -*cān.*

cactimani. for silence to reign, for a place to be abandoned. probably related to an old intransitive form of *cāhua,* plus -*ti-, mani.* the root *cac-* is found only in constructions with auxiliary verbs. A form that looks like *cacti* in the Tetelcingo dictionary is the equivalent of *cactiuh. cactimani* is not attested in any other tense than the present, but presumably it would be the same as any other -*timani* auxiliary.

cac-tli. footwear, sandal.

✳ *cāhua* (1), *nic.* to leave, abandon, relinquish, deliver, let. Class 2: *ōniccāuh.*

cāhua (2), *nino.* to remain, survive, be left. mainly in third person.

cāhua (3), *tla.* see *tlacāhua*

cahuālloh. horse. Sp.

cāhualtia, nic. causative of *cāhua,* to make someone leave a place or position or stop doing something. Class 3: *ōniccāhualtih.*

çahua-tl. breaking out of the skin. *huēi çahuatl,* smallpox.

cāhu-itl. time, a time. *ixquich cāhuitl,* the whole time, as long as, generally in expressions with a sense related to "until."

calaco(hu)a. impersonal of *calaqui.*

calaqui, ni. to enter; to be delivered. Class 2: *ōnicalac.* from *calli, aqui.*

calaquia (1), *nic.* to put something inside, cause it to go in, deliver it. Class 3: *ōniccalaquih.* from *calaqui.*

calaquia (2), *nino.* acts as the reverential of *calaqui.*

-*calaquiāmpa, -calaquiyāmpa,* compound relational word. toward where something goes in. in the phrase *īcalaquiyāmpa tōnatiuh,* toward where the sun goes down, toward the west. from *calaqui,* -*yān,* -*pa.*

çālihui, ni. to be stuck to, abut on. Class 2: *ōniçāliuh.* with -*tech.* intransitive counterpart of *çāloa.*

caleh. householder, family head. *calli,* -*eh.*

cal-li. house, structure, container.

callāl-li. house-land, arable land going with the dwelling complex of a household. *calli, tlālli.*

calnepanōl-li. house of two stories. *calli,* patientive noun from *nepanoa* to join, put together.

çāloa, nic. to glue something, make things stick together. Class 3: *ōnicçāloh.* transitive counterpart of *çālihui.*

caltech-tli. side of a house, wall. *calli,* -*tech.*

caltēn-tli. sidewalk, space in front of a house. *calli, tēntli.*

cal-tia, nic. provide someone with a house. Class 3; *ōniccaltih. calli,* -*tia*[2].

cam-atl. mouth. combining form *cama-.*

camīxah-(tli). shirt. sometimes spelled *camīsah-(tli).* Sp. *camisa.*

camohtic. something soft, easy to spread. *camohtli, -tic.*

camoh-tli. an edible root much like a sweet potato.

cāmpa. to or from where. interrogative; with *in,* relative, dependent. *cān, pa.*

cān. where, interrogative.

-cān. place where an action is carried out, etc. preceded by a number, that number of places, or at that number of places.

-cān. optative pl. suffix of verbs.

çan, particle. only, just, merely, but. when *niman* intensifies a negative, the addition of *çan* intensifies it yet more. *çan iuh,* as it is, without improvement or change. *çan īxquich,* only. *çan nō,* likewise. *çan ye nō* (also *çan ye nō thui)* indicates sameness. see *çaniyoh.*

canāhuac. something narrow. pret. agentive from *canāhua,* to be or become narrow.

canel, particle. because, for, since (giving the reason for something). *ca, nel* secondary particle from *nelli.*

cānin. where, interrogative. preceded by *in,* relative, dependent. *cān, in.*

çaniuh. see under *çan.*

çaniyoh, usually particle. only (exclusively). can also function as an indefinite pronoun with abs. pl. *çaniyohqueh. çan, iyoh* (alone).

çanman, particle cluster. used in the records of Tlaxcala, perhaps shortened from *çan niman,* which intensifies negative phrases.

cāpah. cape, cloak. Sp.

çapātox, çapātos. a shoe, shoes. Sp.

caqui, nic. to hear, to understand. Class 2: *ōniccac.*

caquilia, nic. to hear the words, advice, etc., of someone. Class 3: *ōniccaquilih.* applicative of *caqui.*

caquizti. to sound, be heard. Class 1: *ōcaquiztic.* related to *caqui,* has *-ti.*

cārtah de pāgoh. bill of payment, receipt. Sp.

catca. past of *cah.* also late, deceased.

cateh. present pl. of *cah.*

çātēpan. afterward, later. *çā, tē-, -pan.*

cātle(h). interrogative what, which. the "catley" in Appendix 2 may be a version of this, or it may represent *ca ahtle in.*

catqui. archaic present sing. of *cah.* seen most often in set phrase *iz catqui,* here is.

catzāhuac. something dirty. pret. agentive from a verb *catzāhua,* to get dirty.

Caxtīllān. Spain. Sometimes written with s instead of *x.* reinterpreted Sp. loanword, from Castilla, Castile.

caxtīltēca-tl. Spaniard. Caxtīllān, *-tēcatl.*

caxtōl-li. fifteen.

cē. one. also sometimes used much like the indefinite article in English. combining form *cem-, cen-,* or even *cep-, cec-,* etc. through assimilation. incorporated in a verb, entirely, forever, etc. has pl. *cēmeh* which usually still translates as one (of a larger group). *īc cen,* forever.

ceccān, locative noun. in one place. *cē (cem), -cān.*

cecec. something cold. related to *cetl* ice, cold thing, and a combined form of similar meaning, *cec-.*

ceceyoh. something fatty, covered with fat. contains *-yoh* possessor suffix; related to *ceceyōtl,* animal fat. length of the *e*'s not known; there might be a glottal stop after the first.

cecuiz-tli. cold, being cold, having chills. *cetl* ice or cold thing, *cui, -liz-tli.*

cēhuallō-tl. shadow, shade. *cēhualli* shadow, *-yōtl.*

cēhua. for it to be cold. Class 2: *ōcēuh.* related to *cetl* ice, something cold.

cēhui, ni. to rest, cool off, abate. Class 2: *ōnicēuh.*

cēhuia, nino. to rest. Class 3: *ōninocēhuih.* related to *cēhui.*

-cēl, necessarily partially possessed indefinite pronoun. someone or something alone, by oneself or itself, only, unique. can have a pl. *-cēltin.*

celia, nic. to receive, to accept. Class 3: *ōniccelih.*

cēmeh. see *cē.*

cemihcac, particle. eternally. *cē, ihcac.*

cemilhui-tl. a day, all day. *cē (cem), ilhuitl.*

cempāntih, ti. to be or go in single file. *cē/cem, pāntli* row, *-ti.*

cempōhua (1), *nic,* to add something up. Class 2: *ōniccempōuh. cē (cem), pōhua.*

cempōhua (2), *mo.* for something to total a certain amount.

cen. combining form of *cē. īc cen,* forever, and other meanings.

cencah, particle. very, greatly, general intensifier. *oc cencah,* especially. from *cē (cem, cen)* and *cah.*

cencāhua, nic. to prepare, make ready, get fixed up. Class 2: *ōniccencāuh. cē/cem, cāhua.*

cennequetzalpan. see *nequetzalpan.*

cenquīçah, ti. to join together or assemble somewhere. Class 2: *ōticenquīzqueh.*

cenquīxtia, nic. to collect something scattered.

Class 3: *ōnicenquīxtih.* causative of *cenquīça.*

cenquīzqui. something perfect, whole, consummate. pret. agentive of *cenquīça,* from *cē/cem, quīça.*

centlapal, particle. on one side. *cē/cem, -tlapal* side.

centlālia (1), *nic.* to bring a group of things together; to summarize. Class 3: *ōniccentlālih.*

centlāliah (2), *tito.* to assemble, congregate. Class 3: *ōtitocentlālihqueh. cē* (cem), *tlālia.*

cen-tli. maize (in ears). also *cin-tli. Caxtīllān centli,* wheat.

cenyohual, particle. all night. *cē, yohualli.*

-cēpaniān, by origin locative noun. all jointly, together; *tocēpaniān,* all of us jointly. *cē, -pan, -i* creating verb *pani?, yān.*

cepayahu-itl. snow. contains *cetl* ice, something cold; related to *quiyahuitl, tlapaquiyahuitl.*

ceppa, particle. once. *oc ceppa,* again. *cē* (cem) plus *-pa.*

cequi, quantifier. some, a certain quantity, one part. *cequīn, cequīntin* pl., some, a certain number of people or animals. *oc cequīntin,* others.

cērah. beeswax, usually meaning wax candles to be burned in religious ceremonies. Sp.

chachalaca, ni. to chatter. Class 1: *ōnichachalacac.*

chāhuanān-(tli). stepmother. *chāhua-,* pejorative element characterizing secondary and irregular familial relationships, *nāntli.*

chalānia, nitla. to argue. Class 3: *ōnitlachalānih.* based on intransitive *chalāni,* for a vessel to crack, for music to be out of tune.

chālchihu-itl. greenstone, jade, etc. Some suspicion remains that the first *i* is long.

Chālco. a large region in the southeast of the Valley of Mexico.

chālca-tl. inhabitant of Chalco. abs. pl. *chālcah.*

chāneh. resident, citizen, person from. *chān(tli), -eh.*

chān-(tli). home, residence. almost always seen possessed, locative; without any other suffix it means "at one's home." acts like a relational word in every respect, including taking a reverential in *-tzīnco,* even when a noun is compounded to it, as in *īteōpanchāntzīnco,* "in his/her churchly home."

chia (1), *nic.* to await. Class 2: *ōnicchix.* historically the verb may have been *chīa* [*chīya*] pret. is sometimes *chīx,* and an irregular applicative is *chīlia.*

chia (2), *nitla.* usually to look.

chian, chia. chia, a plant from whose seeds an edible oil was secured.

chicāhua, ni. to be, become strong or old. Class 1: *ōnichicāhuac.*

chicāhua (1), *nic.* to strengthen, give health and life to, to encourage; to confirm. Class 2. *ōnicchicāuh.*

chicāhua (2), *nino.* to take a forceful attitude, to encourage oneself, work up one's spirits.

chicāhuac. something strong. pret. agentive of intransitive *chicāhua.*

chichi. dog.

chihchīhua, nino. to get outfitted, dress oneself, fix oneself up, etc. Class 2: *ōninochihchīuh.* distributive *chīhua.*

chīchīhual-li. breast. patientive noun based somehow on *chīchī* to suckle.

chīchīhualāyō-tl. milk. *chīchīhualli, ātl, -yōtl.*

chīchīltic. something red, crimson. *chīlli, -tic.*

chīchīmēca-tl. Chichimeca, indigenous inhabitant of north Mexico; anyone considered a barbarian. abs. pl. *chīchīmēcah.* from a place name Chīchīmān, *-(m)ēcatl* inhabitant of a place or unit whose name ends in *-mān.*

chicōme. seven. assimilated form *chicōm-, chicōn-.*

chicuēi. eight. assimilated form *chicuē-.*

chīhua (1), *nic.* to do, make, engender, perform, etc; to spend time; to pay or deliver tribute. Class 2; *ōnicchīuh.*

chīhua (2), *mo.* to happen, to become, to be appointed to an office, for a plant to grow and yield, etc. also often serves as passive of *chīhua* (1). *-pan mochīhua,* to happen to someone, or in someone's time.

chīhualtia, nic. causative of *chīhua.*

chīl-li. chile.

chīmal-li. shield. together with *mītl,* arrow, metaphor for war.

chinām-itl. chinampa (strip of built-up earth in shallow water for intensive cultivation); an enclosure of cane or other materials; a subunit of an altepetl.

chipāhua, ni. to become clean, pure. Class 1: *ōnichipāhuac.*

chipāhua, nic. to clean, purify something. Class 2: *ōnicchipāuh.*

chipāhuac. something clean, clear, light, beautiful; of water, fresh. from intransitive *chipāhua.*

chiquacē. six. combining form *chiquacem, chiquacen.*

chiucnāhui. nine. combining form *chiucnāuh-.*

Chiucnāuhtlān. an altepetl, "place of nine."

chōca, ni. to weep; for animals to make various sounds. Class 1: *ōnichōcac.*

choloa, ni. to flee, run away; to leap. Class 3; *ōnicholoh.*

chololiztli. running away, flight, leaping. *choloa, -liz-tli.*

chōquiz-tli. weeping. also *chōquiliz-tli. chōca, liz-tli.*

ciahui (1), *nic.* to earn one's way with effort; to get tired. Class 2: *ōnicciauh.* related to intransitive *ciahui,* to tire.

ciahui (2), *nino.* to tire.

cializ-tli, will. *cia, ceya,* to want, consent, *-liz-tli.*

cihuācal-li. "woman-house," sense not well understood; apparently at times simply a building occupied or inherited by a woman.

cihuāhuah. married man. *cihuātl, huah.*

cihuāmōn-(tli). daughter-in-law. *cihuātl, mōn-(tli).*

cihuāpan, compound relational word sometimes acting as noun. (in the) women's quarters. *cihuātl, -pan.*

✳ *cihuāpil-li.* lady, noblewoman. abs. pl. *cihuāpīpiltin. cihuātl, pilli.*

✳ *cihuā-tl.* woman. possessed form generally means wife. in compounds used to indicate the female of anything. abs. pl. *cihuah.*

cihuātlamachtia, nitla, probably an ad hoc construction. for someone, in this case specifically a warrior, to act like a woman. Class 3: *ōnitlacihuātlamachtih. cihuātl, tlamachtia* or *machtia* with *tla-,* in what sense is not clear.

cihuātlatqui-tl. woman's things, household goods.

cīma-tl. plant with an edible root, or the root.

cītlal-in. star. abs. pl. *cīcītlaltin. huēi cītlalin,* the planet Venus. with *popōca,* a comet.

cih-(tli). grandmother. also hare (usually not possessed).

ciudād. city. Sp.

-co. general locative suffix. *-c* after a vowel.

-co. present/past of the purposive motion form *-quīuh/-co* for motion in toward the point of reference. pl. *-coh*

cōā-tl. snake, serpent. perhaps it should be written *cōhuātl;* that the *ō* is long is dubious.

çohuā-tl. variant in Tlaxcala and other places of *cihuātl.*

cochi, ni. to sleep. Class 2: *ōnicoch.*

cochtlamelāhua, ni. to fall asleep right away. Class 2. *ōnicochtlamelāuh. cochi, tlamelāhua.*

-cochiān, -cochiyān, locative noun. where one sleeps, bedroom or bed. *cochi, -yān.*

cochiz-tli, also *cochiliz-tli.* sleep, sleeping. *co-chi, liz-tli.*

cocoa, nino. to be sick. Class 3: *ōninococoh.* based on transitive *cocoa's* sense of to hurt.

cocōc teohpōuhqui. set phrase meaning some sort of severe affliction or calamity. *cocōc* is in some way related to *cocoa; teohpōuhqui* is a pret. agentive from a probable verb *teohpō-hui* to be tormented or afflicted, in turn from *teōtl, pōhui,* though the semantic connection is not clear.

-cocōcāuh. property, goods, means for sustaining life. possessed reverential form *-cocōcah-tzīn.*

cocolia, nic. to hate. Class 3: *ōniccocolih.* related to *cocoa,* to hurt.

cocoliz-tli. sickness. *-tech motlalia cocoliztli,* literally for an illness to settle upon one, to contract an illness. related to *cocoya,* to be sick.

cocoxqui. a sick person. pret. agentive of *cocoya,* to be sick. *cocoxcātzīn-tli,* mock reverential, poor sick person.

coçoyahualōl-li. a round device made with the feathers of a yellow parrot. *coçōtl* a yellow parrot, patientive noun from *yahualoa.* the length of the second *o* is speculative.

cofradīah. lay religious sodality. Sp.

cōhua, nic. to buy. Class 2: *ōniccōuh.*

çōhua, nic. to spread something out, display it. Class 2: *ōnicçōuh.*

cōhuia, nicno. applicative of *cōhua,* used apparently mainly with the reflexive.

cōhuilia, nic. regular applicative of *cōhua.*

cōlhuia, nictla. see *tlacōlhuia.*

çōl-in. quail. abs. pl. *çōçōltin.*

cōl-(li). grandfather. *totahhuān tocōlhuān,* forebears, ancestors.

cōloa, nitla. to go in a curved path. Class 3: *ōni-tlacōloh.*

cōm-itl. pot.

comādreh-(tli). co-godmother, ritual co-parent. Sp. *comadre.*

cōmo (cōmoh?), loan particle. as, in the capacity of. Sp.

compādreh-(tli). co-godfather, ritual co-parent. Sp. *compadre.*

conē-tl. child (most often of a woman). abs. pl. *cōconeh.*

coneyō-tl. childhood, childishness, an act of childishness. *conētl, -yōtl.*

confirmāroa, nic. to confirm (in office). Class 3: *ōnicconfirmāroh.* Sp. *confirmar, -oa.*

contradecīroa, nic. to contradict. Sp. *contra-decir, -oa.*

-*copa*, suffixal relational word. in a certain manner, in a certain direction, etc. attaches to nouns and adds nuances to other relational words.

çoqui-tl. mud, clay. *tlālli çoquitl*, the earthly aspect of a person, the body.

-*çoqui(y)ō.* mud or clay belonging to something. -*tlāllo* -*çoqui(y)o*, one's earthly body. *çoquitl*, -*yō.*

çoqui(y)oh. something covered with mud. *çoquitl*, -*yoh.*

ço-tl. a quarter of a standard length of cloth as paid in tribute. length of the *o* not known; possibly long as in *çōhua*?

cotōna, nic. to break something off. Class 2: *ō-niccotōn.* transitive equivalent of *cotōni.*

cotōni, ni. to be broken off, cut. Class 2: *ōnicotōn.* intransitive equivalent of *cotōna.*

coyame-tl. pig, peccary. abs. pl. *cōcoyameh* or *coyameh.*

Coyōahcān, Coyōhuahcān. Coyoacan, an important altepetl. apparently *coyōtl* coyote, -*huah*, -*cān.*

cōzca-tl. necklace, jewelry. *a* changes to *i* in the possessed form, which is -*cōzqui.* combining form *cōzca-.*

-*cōzqui.* sing. possessed form of *cōzcatl.*

coztic. something yellow/red. contains pret. agentive -*tic*; noun of origin lost.

cristiānoh, cristiānah, adjective modifying Sp. words. Christian. Sp. see also *quixtiānoh.*

crīstoh (then always written christo). Christ. Sp.

cruz. (Christian) cross. Sp.

cuārtah. a fourth (of an hour). Sp.

cuchīlloh. knife. Sp.

cuehcuetlaxoa, nitla. to faint, flag. Class 3: *ōnitlacuehcuetlaxoh.* reduplicated form of *cuetlaxoa* with much the same meaning. the *h* in the first syllable is uncertain.

cuē-itl. skirt, especially one in indigenous style.

cuēl, particle. already, quickly. in Chimalpahin, *ye nō nicuēl*, again (origin of the *ni-* not well understood).

cuem-itl. furrow, turned soil; cultivated field.

cuepa (1), *nic.* to return something. Class 2: *ōniccuep.*

cuepa (2), *nino.* to go back, return, turn into.

cuepilia, nic. to return something to someone. Class 3. *ōniccuepilih.* applicative of *cuepa.*

cuetlāch-tli. wolf. abs. pl. *cuēcuetlāchtin.*

Cuetlaxcoapan. Puebla. (vowel quantities of *o* and second *a* not certain.) appears to contain *cuetlaxtli*, leather, hide.

cuetlaxhuahuanqui. curer of hides. *cuetlaxtli*, leather, cured hide; pret. agentive of *huahuana.* the second *a* of *huahuana* may be long.

cuezcom-atl. grainbin. related to *quā* and *cōmitl*?

cui, nic. to take, get, fetch, grasp. Class 1: *ōniccuic. cui, ana*, to understand, profit from what one is told. (It is possible that the *i* of *cui* was once long.)

cuīca, ni. to sing. Class 1. *ōnicuīcac.*

cuīcani. singer. *cuīca*, -*ni.*

cuīc-atl. song, singing. comb. form *cuīca-.* from *cuīca.*

cuiltōnoa, nino. to be wealthy; to be happy. Class 3: *ōninocuiltōnoh.*

cuītia (1), *nic.* causative of *cui.*

cuītia (2), *nicno.* to acknowledge a superior, to confess misdeeds; to confess or acknowledge something in general.

cuitlahuia, nicno. to take care of. Class 3: *ōnicnocuitlahuih.*

cuitlahuiltia, nic. induce or force someone to do something. Class 3: *ōniccuitlahuiltih.*

cuitlapil-li. tail. part of the expression *in cuitlapilli in ahtlapalli*, a metaphor for the common people. *cuitlatl*, excrement or extrusion, *pilli.*

cuix, particle. literally perhaps; generally creates a question to which the answer is yes or no; in dependent clauses it creates an indirect question, translating as whether, if.

cuixān-tli, more often *cuexān-tli.* the lapfolds of a loose garment used as something to carry things in. usually in the locative with -*co.* -*cuexānco* -*māmalhuāzco*, under someone's protection.

de, preposition. from, of. mainly in unanalyzed Sp. loan phrases. Sp.

diēzmoh. tithe. Sp.

Diōs. God. Sp.

doctrīnah. instruction in (Christian) doctrine. Sp.

domīngoh. Sunday. Sp.

don. honorific title, like Sir. Sp.

doña. honorific title, like Lady. Sp. (I doubt that *don* and *doña*, as particle-like elements receiving little stress and coming before nuclear words, had a long *o* or that a glottal stop was added to the latter.)

durāznoh. peach, peach tree. Sp.

-*eh.* possessor of. abs. pl. -*ehqueh.*

ehcatocō, n. verb in passive only. to be carried away by the wind. Class 1: *ōnehcatocōc.* root *ehca-* related to *ehēcatl, toca.*

ehcauhyō-tl. shadow, shade. first element may be related to *ehēcatl;* contains *-yōtl.*

ehēca-tl. wind, movement of the air. *tēmōxtli ehēcatl,* illness, pestilence.

ehēcapitzāc-tli. windstorm? breeze? Molina defines "pitzauac ehecatl" as "viento liuiano." *ehēcatl, pitzāctli.*

ēhua (1:1), *nic.* to raise; to sing a song. Class 2. *ōniquēuh.*

ēhua (2:1), *nihuāl.* to come from a certain place. Class 1. *ōnihuālēhuac.*

ēhua (1:2), *nin.* to rise, get up. Class 2. *ōninēuh.*

ēhua (2:2), *non,* to depart. Class 1: *ōnonēhuac.*

ēhuaquēm-itl. clothing of hides or leather. *ēhuatl* uncured leather, *(tla)quēmitl.*

ēi. three. also *ēyi, yēi, yēyi.* combining form *ē-, yē-, ēx-, yēx-.* (It is possible that instead of *ē-* the form is *eh-,* which definitely does occur at times.) abs. pl. *ēīn, ēīntin.*

elecciōn. election. Sp.

ēlēhuia, nic. to wish, desire. Class 3: *ōniquēlēhuih.*

ēlimiqui, ni or *nic.* to cultivate (land). Class 2: *ōnēlimic* or *ōniquēlimic.*

ēllelmati, nin. to be annoyed, pained, vexed by something. Class 2 irregular: *ōninēllelmah. ēllel-,* an apparently nominal combining form associated with various kinds of bad feeling; *mati.*

ēlleltia, niqu. to hinder, hold back. Class 3: *ōniquēlltih.* contains same *ēllel-* as *ēllelmati.*

emperadōr. emperor. Sp.

encomendēroh. holder of a grant of indigenous tribute and labor. Sp.

ērah, alaērah. threshing floor. Sp. *era.*

epāhuax-tli. cooked beans. compound patientive deverbal noun from *etl, pāhuaci,* to cook by boiling in a pot.

escribānoh. notary, official clerk. Sp.

español. a Spaniard. Sp.

española. Spanish woman or girl. Sp.

Espīritu Sāntoh. Holy Spirit. (I assume that because the phrase was always treated as a single entity there would not have been a glottal stop after *u.*)

estānciah. private legally sanctioned landed property of some size, usually for livestock. Sp.

etic. something heavy; sometimes refers to bodily sluggishness, illness. pret. agentive of *eti-(ya),* to be or grow heavy.

e-tl. bean(s).

evangēlioh. gospel. Sp.

ēx-. combining form of *ēi,* three. *ēxpa,* three times.

ez-tli. blood.

fanēgah. fanega, grain measure, about a bushel and a half. Sp.

fīrmah. signature, rubric. Sp.

fīrmāroa, nic. to sign something. Class 3: *ōnic-fīrmāroh.* Sp. *firmar, -oa.* Sp.

fīrmahyōtia, nic. sign something, make a rubric on it. Class 3; *ōnicfīrmayōtih.* Sp. *firma, -yōtl, -tia².*

fiscāl. church steward. Sp.

gañān. permanent employee, especially in a rural context. Sp.

gobernadōr. highest officer of an indigenous municipal government. also called *juēz gobernadōr.* Sp.

hāsta, preposition, adverb. until, as far as, even. Sp. possibly *hāstah.*

-hermānah. sister. Sp.

-hermānoh. brother, pl. brothers (and sisters). Sp.

hīgos, hīgox. a fig, fig tree. Sp. usually the Sp. plural was incorporated into the stem, but some Nahuas used the sing. and pl. as in Sp.

hōrah. hour, o'clock. Sp.

-huah. possessor of. abs. pl. *-huahqueh.*

huācax. cow. Sp. *vaca(s).*

huahuana, nic. to scrape, make stripes or striations in something, cure hides. Class 2: *ōnic-huahuan.* the second *a* may be long.

huāl-. directional prefix of verbs, signifying that the action is carried out in the direction of the speaker or point of reference.

huālcah, particle. nearer, in this direction. preceded by *oc,* more, much more. *huāl-, cah.*

huāllauh, ni. to come, come back, be brought. irregular verb consisting of *huāl-* and *yauh;* pret. *ōnihuāllah.*

-huāmpoh. someone or something that is the same in kind as something else, its fellow. *-huān, -poh* (which by itself has the same meaning when combined with any noun stem).

-huān, relational word. with, along with. 3rd person sing., *ī-huān,* and, in addition.

-huān. possessive pl. nominal suffix.

-huānyōlqui. relative. *-huān,* pret. agentive of *yōli.* The construction really consists of two words; the possessive prefix applies to *-huān* only, so that the abs. pl. is *-huānyōlqueh.*

huapāhua (1), *nic.* to raise, bring up someone. Class 2: *ōnichuapāuh.*

huapāhua (2), *nino.* to grow, grow up.

huāqui, ni. to get dry. Class 2: *ōnihuāc.* Often seen as *tlahuāqui,* for things to get dry, for there to be a drought.

huāuh-tli. amaranth (the seeds of which were eaten).

huehca, particle. distant. *huēi, -ca* ending of particles with adverbial sense.

huehcāhua, ni. to be, spend, or take a long time. Class 2: *ōnihuehcāuh* (also Class 1: *ōnihuehcāhuac*). *huēi, cāhua.*

huehcapa, particle. to or from a great distance. *huehca, -pa.*

huehcapan, particle. high, above; deep. *huehca, -pan.*

huehcāuh, particle. a long time. with *ye,* a long time ago. with *oc,* a long time in the future. *huēi, cāhuitl/cāhua.*

huēhueh, an old man, something old. abs. pl. *huēhuetqueh,* frequently elders, the ancients. combining form *huēhueh-* or *huēhuetcā-*; it may be that the constructions with the first are not really bound forms. related to *huēi.*

huēhuentzīn. mock reverential form, man in senility. form of *huēhueh, -tzīn.*

huēhuehti, ni. to become an old man, sometimes to grow old more generally. Class 1: *ōnihuē-huehtic. huēhueh, -ti.*

huēhuē-tl. drum, especially an indigenous upright cylindrical drum with a deerskin head.

huehuetzca, ni. to laugh (in peals). Class 1. *ōni-huehuetzcac.* reduplicated form of *huetzca.*

huēi, huēyi, perhaps sometimes pronounced *huēy.* someone or something big, large, great. abs. pl. usually *huēhuēin, huēhuēintin. huēi ātl,* ocean.

huel, particle. very, greatly, fully, completely, general intensifier; sometimes well. also can indicate capability, possibility. reduced from *hueli.*

-hueli. power. no abs. ending known.

hueliti (1). to be possible. Class 1: *ōhuelitic. hueli, -ti.*

hueliti (2), ni. to be able to.

huelmati, nic. to savor, enjoy. with a word referring to the body as obj., to enjoy bodily health. usually in the reverential. Class 2 irregular: *ōnichuelmah. huel, mati.*

huēltiuh-(tli). older sister or female cousin of a male. reverential *-huēltihuahtzīn.*

huen-tli. offering.

huehpāntli. large rough-hewn wooden beam. *huēi, pāntli* as in *tepāntli.*

huehpōl-(li). a sibling-in-law of the opposite gender; brother-in-law of a woman, sister-in-

law of a man.

huērtah, more usually *alahuērtah.* orchard, intensively cultivated garden. Sp.

huetzca, ni. to laugh. Class 1: *ōnihuetzcac. -ca huetzca,* to laugh at.

huetzi, ni. to fall. Class 2: *ōnihuetz.* as *-ti-* auxiliary verb, to do something quickly.

huetzītia, huetziltia, nino. causative reverential of *huetzi,* usually meaning to take a seat.

huetzītihtoc, nino. causative reverential of *huetztoc.*

huetztoc, ni. to lie (fallen), to be sick in bed. *huetzi, ti-, onoc.*

huexōtzīnca-tl. inhabitant of Huexōtzīnco, Huejotzingo. Huexōtzīnco, *-catl* inhabitant.

Huexōtzīnco. Huejotzingo, an important altepetl. *huexōtl* willow, *-tzīnco* referring to a secondary place.

huezhuah-(tli). sister-in-law of a female. non-reverential possessed form *-huezhui.*

huēy. see *huēi.*

hueyac. something long. also *huiyac, huiac.* a pret. agentive form probably derived from *huēi(y)a* to grow large. vowel quantity not well attested; originally long *e* probably neutralized before the glide, since it was being weakened to *i.* The *a* was possibly long.

huih. 3rd person present plural of *yauh.*

huihhuitōmi, ni. also *huihhuitōni.* to stagger. Class 2: *ōnihuihhuitōn.*

-huia. applicative of verbs in *-oa.* attached to a noun stem, gives a verb meaning to apply the thing denoted by the noun to something.

huiac. see *hueyac.*

-huīc, relational word. toward, from, in relation to. often in combination with *-pa.*

huīca (1), nic. to take, accompany, be responsible for. Class 1: *ōnichuīcac.*

huīca (2), nino. acts as the reverential of *yauh,* to go; similarly *huīca, nihuālno,* is the reverential of *huāllauh,* to come.

-huīcallō. something that goes along with something else. patientive noun from *huīca, -yō* of inalienable possession. seems to need *tla-.*

huic-tli. digging stick. length of *i* not known; probably long.

huīloa. impersonal of *yauh.*

huīpīl-li. long unfitted blouse worn by indigenous women.

huīptla, particle. the day after tomorrow. *ye huīptla,* the day before yesterday. *mōztla huīptla,* in the future.

huīquilia, nic. to be responsible to someone for

something; to owe money to someone. with *huāl-*, to bring something to someone. Class 3: *onichuīquilih.* applicative of *huīca.*

huītequi, nic. strike, hit. Class 2: *ōnichuītec.*

huītz, ni, defective irregular verb. to come. pret. *ōnihuītza.*

huitzōc-tli. sharp-pointed stick of hard wood for levering out and breaking sod. contains *huitztli*, thorn, something sharp-pointed.

huiyac. see *hueyac.*

ī-. his/her/its, 3rd person sing. possessive prefix.

ī, nocon. to drink. Class 1: *ōnoconīc.* (at times *ī* occurs without *on-*.)

īc, particle. in many ways acts like a 3rd person sing. relational word. for which reason, etc. creates ordinal numbers. gives an adverbial sense to adjectival substantives.

īc, interrogative. when, in terms of days, weeks, or longer periods of time.

ihça, ni. to wake up. Class 1: *ōnihçac.*

ihcac, ni. to be standing, vertical. irregular verb. pret. *ihcaca, ihcaya.*

ihçahuia, nin. to be startled, amazed. Class 3: *ōninihçahuih.* related to *ihça.*

(i)hcahuaca, ni. to make discordant sounds, to murmur. Class 1: *ōnihcahuacac.* more often seen with impersonal *tla-.*

-īcampa, relational word. behind, in one's absence. *-īcampa, -tepotzco,* behind one's back, when one is not there, usually meaning when one is dead. *īcan* with the same meaning, *-pa.*

iccāuh-(tli). younger sibling or cousin of a male. pl. possessed form *-iccāhuan,* because the *uh* of the stem was originally the possessive suffix. also seen as *-tēiccāuh.*

icçōneneuc-tli. yucca juice. *icçōtl* a type of yucca, *neuctli.* there may be a glottal stop after the first *e.*

icçōxōch-itl. yucca flower. *icçōtl* a type of yucca, *xōchitl.*

(i)chca-tl. cotton, sheep. abs. pl. varies.

(i)hchiqui, nic. to scrape, scratch. with *tla,* especially to harvest magueys. Class 2: *oniquih-chic.*

(i)chpōch-tli. maiden, girl who has reached puberty, young unmarried woman. possessed, (grown) daughter. abs. pl. *ichpōpōchtin.*

ichtacā, pret. agentive as adverbial particle. secretly. also bound to nouns and verbs. original verb not known. related to *ichtequi?*

ichtecqui. thief. pret. agentive of *ichtequi.*

(i)chtequi (1), *n.* to steal. Class 2: *ōnichtec.*

(i)chtequi (2), *niqu.* to steal something. Class 2: *ōniquichtec.*

īchtic. something stringy, sinewy. *īchtli,* maguey fiber or thread therefrom, and pret. agentive of *-ti.* The long *i* is not certain.

ihcihui, n. to hurry. Class 2: *ōnihciuh.*

ihciuhcā, pret. agentive as adverbial particle. quickly, soon. *ihcihui.*

(i)cnēlia, niqu. to favor, befriend. Class 3: *ōniquicnēlih. ōtinēchmocnēlilih, ōannēchmocnēlilihqueh,* thank you. related to *icnīuh(tli).*

(i)cnīuhtia, nicno. to make friends with someone. *icniuh(tli), -tia²*.

(i)cnīuh-(tli). friend; almost always possessed. the *-uh* was originally the sing. possessive prefix; the pl. is *-cnīhuān* (not *-cnīuhhuān*).

(i)cnōcihuā-tl. widow. *icnōtl, cihuātl.*

(i)cnōhuah. a compassionate person. *icnōtl, -huah.*

(i)cnōitta, nic. to take pity on, view with compassion. Class 1: *ōniquicnōittac. icnōtl, itta.*

(i)cnōmati, nino. to humble oneself. Class 2 irregular: *ōninocnōmah. icnōtl, mati.*

(i)cnōpilhuia, nic. to deserve, attain, get something. contains *icnōtl.* synonym of *mahcēhua.*

-(i)cnōpilti, no. for something to become what one deserves, i.e., for one to attain or enjoy it. in present tense *-(i)cnōpil* is used. same meaning and same construction as *-mahcēhualti,* which see, and with which it is often paired. Class 1: *ōnocnōpiltic. -icnōpil* that which one deserves, *-ti.*

(i)cnō-tl. orphan, poor humble person. extensively combined with verbs and nouns to add a sense of compassion or humility.

(i)cnōtlāca-tl. poor humble person, orphan. *icnōtl, tlācatl.*

ihçolihui. for something to get old, worn out through use. Class 2: *ōihçoliuh.*

-(i)cpac, relational word. on top of, above; on someone's head. see also *-īxco.*

(i)cpal-li. seat; sometimes a specific type of seat used by indigenous rulers.

(i)cpa-tl. thread, yarn. Some evidence points to the *i* being long, but since it is seen elided in some sources, for at least some speakers it must have been short, which fits better with the structure of the word, for initial *ī* in a simple root was rare and before two consonants much rarer.

(i)hcuilhuia, nic. applicative of *ihcuiloa.*

(i)hcuiloa, nic. to paint, write. Class 3: *ōniquihcuiloh.*

(i)cxi-tl. foot.

(i)cxiāna, nino. to hurry (walking or running along). Class 2: *oninocxiān. icxitl,āna.*

iglēsiah. church. generally the entire Christian church, not a building; often occurs with usual Sp. modifiers, such as holy, Catholic, Roman, etc. Sp.

ihuā, nic. to send, dispatch. Class 4: *ōniquihuah.*

ī-huān. 3rd person sing. possessed form of *-huān.*

ihui. unreduced form of *iuh.*

ihuiān, ihuiyān, particle. peacefully, uncontested, gradually, bit by bit. the same as *matcā.* from *iuh/ihui, -yān?*

ihhuiçāloh(qui). featherworker, one who glues feathers together. *ihhuitl, çāloa.*

ihhui-tl. feather(s), especially small feathers or down.

ihīyāc. something foul smelling. (the long *ā* is seen in Carochi.)

ihīyōcui, ni. to rest, refresh oneself, eat a bit. Class 1: *ōnihīyōcuic. ihīyōtl, cui.*

ihīyōhuia (1), *niqu.* to earn one's way with difficulty; to suffer lack, to tire. in 2nd person preterit, especially reverential, welcome, greetings. Class 3: *ōniquihīyōhuih. ihīyōtl, -huia.*

ihīyōhuia (2), *nino.* to be weary, fatigued.

ihīyōhuia (3), *nitla.* to suffer travail, become fatigued, expend effort.

ihīyō-tl. breath; emanation. *-ihīyo -tlahtōl,* someone's declaration, orders, message.

ilama. old woman. abs. pl. *ilamatqueh.*

ilcāhua, niqu. to forget something. Class 2: *oniquilcāuh.*

ilhuia, nictē. see *tēilhuia.*

(i)lhuia, niqu. tell someone something. Class 3: *ōniquilhuih.* functions as applicative of *ihtoa,* but not genetically related.

ilhuicahuah. possessor or master of heaven, God. usually paired with *tlālticpaqueh. ilhuicatl, -huah.*

ilhuica-tl. sky, heaven, heavens. most often seen in the locative form *ilhuica-c.*

ilhui-tl. day; also, especially when possessed, the feast day of a saint, god, etc.

ilnāmiqui, niqu. to remember something, think of something. Class 2: *ōniquilnāmic.*

ilpia, niqu. to tie; to put or keep someone in custody. Class 3: *ōniquilpih.*

-im-. rare verbal prefix indicating the plurality of the direct obj. when the full obj. prefix refers to the indirect object.

im-. their, 3rd person pl. possessive prefix. *-īn*

when before a nonlabial consonant.

īmacaci, niqu. to fear, respect. Class 2: *ōniquīmacaz.*

īmacaxilia, niqu. applicative of *īmacaci.*

ihmachītia, niqu. to make someone aware of something, alert. Class 3: *ōniquihmachītih.* causative of *ihmati.*

imāgen. image. Sp.

ihmati, nin. to be prudent; to be on one's guard, alert. Class 2 irregular: *ōninihmah.*

imman, particle. time to do something, late. probably originally *in, mani.*

in, particle. subordinator, "article," punctuator. many translations and often none.

-in-. form taken by *-im-,* indicator of plurality of the direct obj. when the full obj. prefix refers to the indirect obj., if a nonlabial consonant follows.

īn, demonstrative pronoun. this.

in-. form that *īm-,* 3rd person pl. possessive prefix, assumes before a nonlabial consonant.

ihnēhua, niqu. to miss something (in shooting at it). Class 2: *ōniquihnēuh.*

informaciōn. formal inquiry. Sp.

inīc, particle in some ways acting like a 3rd person sing. relational word. how, in order to, for which reason, that, since, until, because, etc. also creates ordinal numbers. subordinator *in* plus *-īc,* with which it shares many meanings.

inīn, demonstrative pronoun. this. abs. pl. *in ihqueh īn. auh inīn* introduces a new topic or prepares the listener for the ending formula of a speech. combination of subordinator *in* and demonstrative *īn.*

inman. see *imman.*

inōn, demonstrative pronoun. that. combination of subordinator *in* and demonstrative *ōn.*

interrogatōrioh. questionnaire. Sp.

intlā, particle. if, when. combination of subordinator *in* and optative particle *tlā.*

intlācahcān, combination of particle and negative locative expression. if nowhere. *intlā , c(a)* "ligature," *ahcān.* This word may actually be *intlācacān,* like *intlācamo.*

intlācamo, compound particle. if not. *intlā, c(a)* "ligature," *mō* negative.

intlācayāc, combination of particle and indefinite pronoun. if no one. *intlā, c(a)* "ligature," *ayāc.*

inventārioh. inventory. Sp.

īpalnemo(hu)ani. giver of life, the deity. *-pal,* instrumental noun from *nemi.*

ihquāc, particle. at that time. *in ihquāc*, when.

ihquania, nin. to move from one place to another. Class 3: *ōninihquanih*.

ihquiltia, nin; ihquiltihtihcac, nin. reverentials of *ihcac*.

ihtac-atl. provisions for the road, etc. combining form *ihtaca-*.

-(i)htec. older variant of *-ihtic*.

-(i)htahuilia, nic. older equivalent of *ihtalhuia*, found in the records of Tlaxcala and probably other peripheral regions.

(i)htalhuia, nic. applicative of *ihtoa*, used mainly as part of the reverential and not meaning to tell or say to someone, which is *ilhuia*.

-(i)tcōca. the carrying of something, the governing of something. often paired with *-māmalōca.* passive abstract noun from *itqui*.

ithual-li. patio. mainly seen in locative form, *ithual-co.* together with *quiāhuatl*, means household. apparently an irregular patientive noun from *itta* (earlier *ithua*), that which can be seen, an open place.

-(i)htic, relational word. within, inside of. *ihtitl, ihtetl,* belly, womb, *-co/-c*.

itlah, quantifier. something.

(i)htlacalhuia, nic. applicative of *ihtlacoa*.

(i)htlacoa, nic. to harm, damage, spoil, ruin, mess up, do something badly or wrong, go against. Class 3: *ōniquihtlacoh*.

(i)htlani (1), *niqu.* to request, demand. Class 2: *ōniquihtlan*.

(i)htlani (2), *nitla.* to ask (for information).

(i)htlania (1), *nic.* can act as the applicative of *ihtlani*, on which it is based. Class 3: *ōniquihtlanih*.

(i)htlania (2), *nictla.* to ask someone for information, to interrogate. with *-ca.* Class 3: *ōnictlahtlanih*.

(i)htoa (1), *niqu.* to say. *quihtōznequi,* it means (literally it wants to say, perhaps based on Sp. *quiere decir*). Class 3: *ōniquihtoh*.

(i)htoa (2), *nitla.* to speak. *-pan tlahtoa,* to see to, take care of, be in charge of, sometimes to speak for.

ihtōtia, nin. to dance. Class 3: *ōninihtōtih*.

(i)tqui, niqu. to carry, transport. Class 1: *ōniquitquic*.

(i)tta, niqu. to see; to inspect. Class 1: *ōniquittac*.

(i)ttitia, niqu. to show something to someone. Class 3: *ōniquittitih.* causative of *itta*.

itz-. irregular stem of *itta* in combined forms. usually intransitive in spite of *itta* being transitive.

(i)htzoma, nic. to sew. Class 2: *ōniquihtzon*.

itzticah, n. to be looking. *huehca(pa) niquitzticah,* to be looking at something from far away, i.e., to be distant from it. Note that here *itzticah* is transitive. pret. *ōnitzticatca* or *ōniquitzticatca. itz-* from *itta, -ti-, cah*.

itztiuh, n. to go looking toward, i.e., to head toward. pret. often with *on-* directional prefix. pret. *ōnitzti(y)ah. in ōmpa* (or *oncān*) *tonitztihuih,* in the future (where we are heading). *itta, yauh* as auxiliary.

ītz-tli. obsidian, sharp-bladed instrument of obsidian. It is not entirely certain that the *i* of the root is long.

-iuc. younger sibling or cousin of a female.

iuh, particle. thus, in such a way, like, that. *in iuh,* as. *ō iuh,* after. look also under *çan*.

iuhqui, particle, sometimes indefinite pronoun. thus, in this or that way, as, like, almost. *in ye iuhqui,* when things are ready. longer version of *iuh* with *-qui* pret. agentive suffix, can act as a substantive and take a *-queh* abs. pl.

iuhquin, particle. like (in comparisons). *iuhqui* plus *in. iuhquin mah,* as if it were, like.

(i)xca, niqu. to bake, roast. Class 1: *ōniquixcac*.

-īxco, complex relational word. at the face or surface of something or someone. *tēīxco tēicpac ninemi,* to be rude and disrespectful. *īxtli, -co*.

-īxcohyān. one's very own, as in *nīxcohyān notlatqui,* my very own property. behaves rather like a relational word, looks rather like a deverbal locative noun. constituent elements not clear.

īxcuītia, nin. to take an example (from something), model oneself (on it). Class 3: *ōninīxcuītih.* apparently based on *īxtli* and the causative of *cui*.

īxeh nacaceh. someone who is observant, acute, quick. *īxtli, nacaztli, -eh*.

(i)xhuītia, nino. to fill oneself. Class 3: *ōninoxhuītih*.

(i)xhuīuh-(tli). grandchild. pl. possessed form *-xhuīhuān,* not *-xhuīuhhuān,* because the *-uh* of the sing. was originally the possessive suffix.

(i)hxīca. to leak. Class 1: *ōihxīcac.* most often with *tla-* impersonal.

īximati, nic. to recognize, know, be acquainted with. Class 2: *ōniquīximat, ōniquīximah. īxtli, mati*.

īximachtia, nic. to make someone acquainted with something. causative of *īximati*.

īximachītia, nic. same as *īximachtia*.

īxmaḣpilxixili, niqu. ad hoc construction, to keep stabbing a finger in someone's face. Class 2: *ōniquīxmaḣpilxixil. īxtli, maḣpilli, xixili* to make a repeated stabbing or pounding motion. Vowel quantities are not known with *xixili,* and it may have a glottal stop after the first *i; iḣxili* (quantity of the second *i* unknown) is the basic verb to stab.

īxnāmiquiḣ, tit. to contend, differ, argue. Class 2: *ōtitīxnāmicqueḣ. īxtli, nāmiqui.*

īxīptla-tl. stand-in, representative, image. does not have *-uh* in the possessed form.

īxpāca, nin. to wash one's eyes. Class 1: *ōninīxpācac. īxtli, pāca.*

-īxpan, relational word. in the presence of, before, facing. *īxtli, -pan.*

-īxpampa, relational word. from or toward the presence of. *-īxpampa ēhua.* flee from. *īx-tli, -pan, -pa.*

īxpantia, niqu. to present or show something, put it before someone. takes both direct and indirect obj. Class 3: *ōniquīxpantiḣ. -īxpan, -tia.*

īxpepetza, nin. to look carefully all around, scrutinizing everything, "to keep your eyes peeled." Class and pret. unknown. may have a glottal stop after the first *e.* instance in the Florentine Codex is possibly an error for a reduplicated form of Molina's reflexive *īxpetzoa,* Class 2, with the same meaning. *īxtli,* some form of root *petz-* having to do with shining, polishing.

īxpoloa, nin. to disguise oneself. Class 3: *ōninīxpoloḣ. īxtli, poloa.*

īxquetza (1), nic. constitute, elect, name for a task or office. Class 2: *ōniquīxquetz. īxtli ?, quetza.* the length of the first vowel is not directly attested, but since *o* is elided before it, it must be long.

īxquetza (2), nin. to offer to do something.

īxquich, quantifier. everything, all, a certain amount, an equal amount. abs. pl. *īxquichtin,* all. *çan īxquich,* only. *ye īxquich,* that is all, important indicator that the body of a document or speech has come to an end and the final formula is beginning.

īxquichīhueli. one who is omnipotent. actually two words, *īxquich* and *-hueli* power.

īxteloloḣ-tli. eyeball, the physical aspect of the eye. *īxtli, teloloḣtli* ball, something small, hard, and round.

(i)xtlāhua, nic. to pay, pay back. Class 2: *ōniquixtlāuh.* bears *tla-* obj. prefix much of the time.

ixtlāhuacān, locative noun. plain or plains, unpopulated flat land. *ixtlāhua,* probably a verb meaning to be flat, *-cān.*

(i)xtlāhui, for something to come into its own, be as it should be. often but not necessarily with *on-.* synonymous with and often paired with *pōpohui.* Class 2: *ōixtlāuh.* intransitive counterpart of *ixtlāhua.*

(i)xtlāhuia, (i)xtlāhuilia, nic. applicative of *ixtlahua.*

īxtlapal, particle. sideways. *īxtli* (perhaps meaning facing), *-tlapal* side.

īx-tli. face; in compounds, sometimes refers to the eye, sometimes to the surface. *-īx -yōllo,* spirits, good or bad mood, etc. *quēn mochīhua -īx -yōlo,* to be worried. see also *īxeh.*

īxtomāhua, n. to make faces like a simpleton. Class 1: *ōnīxtomāhuac.* from *īxtli* and *tomāhua,* to grow fat.

īxtōna, apparently for the dawn to come. Class 1: *ōīxtōnac. īxtli, tōna.*

īxtōnaltia, nin. to feel a certain way on awakening in the morning. virtually always in 2nd person. Class 3: *ōninīxtōnaltiḣ.* causative reverential of *īxtōna.*

īxxoxōuhqui. someone with a green face, sickly. *īxtli,* pret. agentive of *xoxōhui(ya)* to turn green.

iyoḣ, pret. agentive noun becoming a particle. something alone. usually seen in *çan iyoḣ,* exclusively. as pret. agentive has abs. pl. *iyoḣqueḣ.* verb of origin now lost.

iyoḣpa, particle. *çā iyoḣpa,* this one last time, the last time, no more. *iyoḣ, -pa.*

iz, particle. here. rarer than *nicān.*

(i)zcaltia, niqu. to raise, educate children. Class 3: *ōniquizcaltiḣ.* causative of *izcalia,* to come to life, to come to the age of reason.

iztāc. something white. pret. agentive related in some way to *iztatl.*

izta-tl. salt.

iztanamacac. salt seller. *iztatl, (tla)namacac.*

iztlaca-. noun seen only in combining form, referring to falsity, lying, etc. apparently the equivalent of *iztlactli,* saliva, poison, lie.

iztlacahuia, niqu. to lie to, deceive, cheat someone. Class 3: *ōniquiztlacahuiḣ. iztlaca-/iztlactli, -huia.*

iztlacati, ni. to lie, tell untruths. Class 2: *ōniztlacat. iztlaca-, -ti.*

juēves. Thursday. Sp.

juēz. judge. often in combination *juēz gobernadōr,* the highest officer of an indigenous municipal government. Sp.

jūnioh. June. Sp.

juntērah. carpenter's plane, joining tool. Sp.

juramēntoh. oath. Sp.

justīciah. justice, the law, judge or judges, officers of the law. Sp.

-lia. applicative ending of verbs. also acts as causative of verbs in *-ti.* Class 3: *-lih.*

licenciādoh. licentiate. Sp. title.

-liz-tli. makes gerunds from verbs, like English words in -ing.

llāveh. key. Sp.

-lō. nonactive, mainly passive ending of verbs. Class 1: *-lōc.*

lōcah. crazy woman. Sp.

-ltia. causative ending of verbs. Class 3: *-ltih.*

lūnes. Monday. Sp.

mā. particle, sign of the optative, may/let.

mā, nic. capture, take, catch in hunting or fishing. Class 4: *ōnicmah.*

mah. particle to indicate something hypothetical. *iuhquin mah,* as if it were. *ahtleh mah itlah,* nothing whatever.

maca (1), *nic.* to give something to someone (always has both direct and indirect obj.). Class 1: *ōnicmacac.*

maca (2), *nitetla.* often to serve people at table, to dispense communion, but it can also mean simply to give something to someone as in *maca* (1).

māca, particle. with *çan,* not just. also in other negative expressions. *mā, ca* as in *mācamō* etc.

mācaīc, compound particle. may never. *mā, c(a)* "ligature," *aīc.*

mācamō, compound particle. may not. *mā, c(a)* "ligature," *mō.*

mācaocāc, combination of particles and indefinite pronoun. may no one any longer. *mā, c(a)* "ligature," *oc, ayāc.*

maçāti, ni. to become bestial, literally to turn into a deer. Class 1: *ōnimaçātic. maçātl, -ti.*

maçā-tl. deer; also used in Stage 1 for horse. abs. pl. *māmaçah.*

mācayāc, combined particle and indefinite pronoun. let no one. *mā, c(a)* "ligature," *ayāc.*

mahcēhua, nic. to deserve, attain, get, enjoy. with *tla-* obj. prefix, to do penitence. Class 2: *ōnicmahcēuh.* usually in the reverential as *mahcēhuia, nicno.*

-mahcēhual. what one deserves, what one attains or enjoys. patientive noun from *mahcēhua.*

-mahcēhualti, no. for something to become what one deserves, i.e., for one to attain or enjoy it. the incorporated noun is always possessed and the verb is always in the third person. not used in the present tense, where *-mahcēhual* appears instead. often paired with *-icnopilti.* Class 1: *ōnomahcēhualtic. -mahcēhual, -ti.*

mācēhual-li. common person, not noble; human being; after ca. 1600, sometimes indigenous person, referential equivalent of Indian (most often in pl. and often with *ti-* subject prefix). In pl., at times the people in general of a certain entity. In possessed form, subject, vassal.

mācēhuallō-tl. commonness, vulgarity. *mācēhualli, -yōtl.*

mahcēhuia, nicno. Class 3: *ōnicnomahcēuih.* reverential of *mahcēhua* (more common than *mahcēhua* itself).

-mach, secondary particle. intensifies dubitative particles and interrogatives, often can be translated as the devil, in the world, in heaven's name, etc.

machilia, nic. applicative of *mati.*

machītia, nic. to inform. a causative of *mati.*

machizti. to become known. Class 1: *ōmachiztic.* from a *liz-tli* noun based on *mati* plus *-ti.*

machō. passive of *mati.*

machtia (1), *nic.* to teach someone something. with *nitē,* usually to preach. Class 3: *ōnicmachtih.* causative of *mati.*

machtia (2), *nino.* to learn. reflexive of *machtia,* to teach.

mach-(tli). niece or nephew of a man.

mācihui, particle. although. *mā,* secondary dubitative particle *ço, ihui.*

māço, particle. although. *mā,* secondary dubitative particle *ço.*

māçōhua, ni. to spread the arms. Class 2: *ōnimāçōuh. māitl, çōhua.*

māçonelihui, particle cluster. although. *mā,* secondary dubitative particle *ço, nel* secondary particle derived from *nelli, ihui.* not written solid in the lessons.

mācuīl-li. five.

maēstroh, teacher; master of theology, etc. Sp.

mahuiçoa, nic, more frequently *nitla.* to marvel at, to see, behold. Class 3: *ōnicmahuiçoh.*

mahuiçō-tl. honor. also *mahuiçōtl, mahuizyōtl. mahuiztli, -yōtl.*

mahuizmati, nic. to honor, respect. Class 2: *ōnicmahuizmah. mahuiztli, mati.*

mahuiztic. something marvelous, splendid, fine, worthy of respect. *mahuiztli, -tic.*

mahuiztilia, nic. to honor, respect. Class 3:

ōnicmahuiztilih. mahuiztli, -ti, -lia.

mahuiz-tli. fear, respect, something that deserves respect. often combined with other nouns in a reverential sense. mahui to be afraid, -liz-tli.

mā-itl. hand, forearm, arm. Combining form sometimes mā-, sometimes mah.

majestād. majesty. seen only in the combination su majestād, His Majesty, in reference to the Spanish king. Sp.

malacachoa, nic. to make something revolve, spin, to wind it up. Class 3: ōnicmalacachoh. related to malacatl, spindle.

malhuia, nic. to take good care of something, handle it carefully. Class 3: ōnicmalhuih.

māmā, nic. to carry, bear. Class 4: ōnicmāmah.

mahmaca, niquin. to give various things to the members of a group, to distribute to. distributive of maca.

mahmāçōhua, ni. to spread out both arms. Class 2: ōnimahmāçōuh. māitl reduplicated, çōhua.

māmalhuāz-tli. backpack for carrying things. -cuexānco -māmalhuāzco, under someone's protection. patientive noun from māmā plus -huāz-tli tool.

-māmalōca. the bearing of something, the governing of something. often pairs with -itcōca. passive abstract noun from māmā.

māmaltia, nic. to load, burden. Class 3: ōnicmāmaltih. causative of māmā.

mahmauhtia, nic. to frighten, menace, intimidate. Class 3: ōnicmahmauhtih. distributive of mauhtia with much the same meaning,

mana (1), mo. for a certain condition, meteorological, epidemiological, or other general, to form, present itself, set in, shape up, break out, spread, etc. also for a group to form up in a certain way. as auxiliary, -timo-mana, with the same meanings. Class 2: ōmoman. transitive counterpart of mani.

mana (2), nic. to put flat things down or in place, to make things flat, to present offerings, tribute and the like.

mana (3), nino. with -pan, to take someone's side.

mandamiēntoh. official order. Sp.

mānel, particle. although. mā, nel.

mānēn, particle. let it not be that, beware lest, etc. less ambiguous and more emphatic than mā with the vetitive. mā, nēn in vain.

mani (1), (ni). to be extended over a flat surface, often translated simply as to be. used for "it is" a certain day of the month, usually trans-

lated as on that day. often employed as a -ti- auxiliary. irregular with present manic in some texts, and past usually manca (formally the pluperfect). intransitive counterpart of mana.

mani (2), tla. for things to be a certain way.

-maniān, locative noun. where something spreads out. mochi -maniān. as far as something goes, everything it includes. mani, -yān.

maniltia, nitla. to make things be a certain way, to rule or manage things. Class 3: ōnitlamaniltih. causative of mani.

mānoceh, particle. nor. mā, noceh.

mānoço, particle cluster. although. mā, noço.

mahpil-li. finger. māitl, pilli.

mahpilhuia, nic. to point a finger at someone. Class 3: ōnicmahpilhuih. applicative of mahpiloa.

mahpiloa, ni. to point with the finger. Class 3: ōnimahpiloh. mahpilli, -oa.

māquīxtia, nic. redeem, save, get out of hock. Class 3: ōnicmāquīxtih. māitl, quīça, -tia causative.

mārtes. Tuesday. Sp.

matcā, pret. agentive as adverbial particle. peacefully, bit by bit. the same as ihuiān. verb of origin not certain; from mati?

mati (1), nic. to know, to find out, to feel, taste. Class 2: ōnicmat, ōnicmah. pl. of pret. is always -matqueh, and the same with compounds built on mati. -pan nicmati, to consider someone or something a certain thing.

mati (2), nino. to have a certain opinion or feeling, to believe, to think.

mahtlac-tli. ten. distributive mahtlahtlactli.

matrimōnioh. matrimony, marriage. Sp.

mauhcā, pret. agentive as adverbial particle, fearfully. also combined with verbs and nouns in meaning in fear, fearful, with respect. from little used mahui to be afraid.

mauhtia, nic. to frighten. Class 3: ōnicmauhtih. causative of mahui to be afraid.

māyahui, nic. to hurl, hurl down. Class 2: ōnicmāyauh.

mayāna, ni. to be hungry. Class 2: ōnimayān. most often seen in impersonal, mayānalō, for there to be a general hunger or famine.

māyoh. May. Sp.

meca-tl. cord, rope.

mecayoh. something tied with rope.

-meh. abs. pl. ending of nouns, especially vowel stems.

mēdio, mēdia, adjective. half of anything, usually preceding a Spanish loanword and making a set phrase with it.

mēdioh. coin, monetary value, half a real or tomín. Sp.

melāhua (1), *nic.* to declare truly, explain; to straighten; also to go straight along something. Class 2: *ōnicmelāuh.*

melāhua (2), *nitla.* see *tlamelāhua.*

melāhuac. something straight, true, just. pret. agentive of intransitive *melāhua* to be, become straight etc.

memōriah. memorandum. Sp.

mestīzoh. mestizo. Sp.

me-tl. maguey.

metl-atl. metate, grinding stone for maize. combining form *metla-.*

mētz-tli. moon, month.

mēxihca-tl. Mexica. abs. pl. *mēxihcah.*

Mēxihco. the altepetl of the Mexica, Mēxihco Tenochtitlan, or Mexico City as it was considered by the Spaniards. sometimes also includes Tlatelolco, also inhabited by Mexica.

miccātepoz-tli. (church) bell. *micqui, tepoztli.*

mich-in. fish. abs. pl. *mīmichtin.*

miccā-. element prefixed to in-law terms to show that the person through whom the relation exists has died. also pret. combining form of *micqui* in general.

miccāhuahti, ni. to mourn for a dead person, to hold obsequies, to go in mourning. Class 1: *ōnimiccāhuahtic. micqui, -huah, -ti.*

micoa, micohua. impersonal of *miqui.*

micqui. dead person, dead body. abs. pl. *mīmicqueh.* pret. agentive of *miqui.*

mictia, nic. to kill, to beat. Class 3: *ōnicmictih.* causative of *miqui.*

mictlān. land of the dead, hell. some form of *miqui* or *micqui* and *-tlān.*

miec, quantifier. much. abs. pl. *miequīn, miequīntīn,* many. sometimes *miac,* also *miyec, miyac.*

mieccān, locative noun. in many places. *miec, -cān.*

miecpa, particle. often, frequently, many times. *miec, -pa.*

miequilia, nitla. to increase. Class 3: *ōnitlamiequilih.* based on *miec.*

miērcoles. Wednesday. Sp.

mīl. a thousand. Sp.

mīl-li. cultivated field, milpa.

mīllahca-tl. field worker. *mīlli, -tlah, -catl* inhabitant.

mimiloa, nino. to roll over repeatedly. Class 3: *ōnimimiloh.*

mīna, nic. to shoot someone. Class 2: *ōnicmīn.*

minīstroh. minister. Sp.

miqui, ni. to die. Class 2: *ōnimic.*

miquini. someone or something mortal. *miqui, -ni.*

miquiz-tli, miquiliz-tli. death. *miqui, -liz-tli.*

mīs(s)ah. (holy) mass. *mīsah cantādah,* high mass (sung mass). Sp.

mitād. half. Sp.

mī-tl. arrow, dart.

mitz-. you, 2nd person sing. obj. prefix of verbs.

mīxī-tl. hallucinogenic plant. used in a pair with *tlāpātl,* generally with reference to inebriation and pulque drinking.

mix-tli. cloud.

miyāhua-tl. tassel, especially of maize but also other things with a similar appearance. possessed form seems usually to add -*yō.*

mo-. your, 2nd person sing. possessive prefix; reflexive prefix for all the persons except the first and for both numbers.

mō, negative particle mainly seen as part of the negative *ahmō,* but occasionally independently or in other combinations.

moch. shortened form of *mochi, mochīn, mochīntin.*

mochi, quantifier. all, everything. has shortened form *moch.* abs. pl. *mochīn, mochīntīn,* all. *moch īca,* including, along with.

mōchilia, nictla. applicative of *mōtla.*

mochipa, particle. always. *mochi, -pa.*

mōlah. same as *mūlah.*

molhui. puzzling form apparently acting as some sort of intensifier. perhaps related to Molina's *molhuia* (apparently *mo-(i)lhuia*) for something to increase, grow.

molīnoh. mill. Sp.

mōl-li. sauce, something ground, mole.

molōni. for water to spring and bubble up, for fog to rise, etc. Class 2: *ōmolōn.*

mōmōztlaeh, particle. every day. from *mōztla.*

mōmōz-tli. platform or raised altar for sacrifices and displays in preconquest style, also used for similar items in later times. length of the *o*'s not certain.

mōntah-(tli). father-in-law. *mōntli, tahtli.*

mōn-(tli). son-in-law.

mōtla (1), *nitla.* to throw stones and the like. Class 1: *ōnitlamōtlac.*

mōtla (2), *nino.* to hit up against something (with a relational word like *-tech* or *-īc*).

mōztla. tomorrow. *mōztla huīptla,* in the future.

-*mōztlayōc.* the day after something. preceded by *oc,* the day before something. in effect always with the 3rd person sing. possessive prefix *ī-. mōztla, -yōtl, -co/-c.*

mūlah. (female) mule. Sp.

nac-atl. meat, flesh. combining form *naca-.*

-nacayō. someone's body. *nacatl, -yōtl.*

nacaz-tli. ear, corner, side.

-nāhuac, relational word. close to, near.

nāhuaihtoa, mo. to be said in Nahuatl. *nāhua,* with meanings such as clear, *ihtoa.*

nāhuati, ni. to speak out loud, to make a clear sound. Class 2: *ōnināhuat.*

nahuatia (1), nic. advise, notify someone, give instructions or orders to someone, take one's leave of someone. Class 3: *ōnicnahuatih.* apparently not based on *nāhuati.*

nahuatia (2), nitla. give orders. with *īc.*

nāhui. four. usual combining form *nāuh-.*

namaca, nic. to sell. Class 1: *ōnicmacac.* originally *na-* reciprocal prefix added to *maca.*

-namacac. see *tlanamacac.*

namaquiltia, nic. to sell something to someone. causative of *namaca;* it does not appear to have the sense expected in a causative, but so it is in the sources.

nāmictia (1), nic. to get someone married, marry someone off. Class 3: *ōnicnāmictih. nāmic(tli), -tia².*

nāmictia (2), nino. to get married. also for something to find a match more generally. *ye monāmictih,* a year ago (the time has matched).

nāmictia (3), nicno, to marry someone, get married to someone.

nāmic-(tli). spouse male or female; something equal and complementary, matching. related to *nāmiqui.*

nāmiqueh. a married person. *nāmic(tli), -eh.*

nāmiqui, nic. to meet. Class 2: *ōnicnāmic.*

nāmoyā, nic. to steal, tear away, take by force. Class 1: *ōnicnāmoyāc.*

nanaca-tl. mushroom. probably related to *nacatl.*

nānquilia, nic. to answer someone, respond to someone. Class 3: *ōnicnānquilih.* appears to be the applicative of a verb now lost.

nān-(tli). mother.

nānyō-tl. maternity. often in phrase *in nānyōtl in tahyōtl,* parenthood. *nān(tli), -yōtl.*

nāpaloa, nic. to take or carry something in the arms. Class 3: *ōnicnāpaloh.*

nāppa, particle. four times. *nāhui, -pa.*

nāuhcameh. four groups, (the people of) something divided into four parts. *nāhui, -ca* used in making a kind of ordinal number, *-meh.*

ne-. indefinite reflexive prefix, once reciprocal.

nec, particle. unidentified element that appar-

ently means then, the next thing. length of the *e* not known.

necentlāliliz-tli. assembly, bringing together. *ne-,* reflexive *centlālia, -liz-tli.*

nēch-. me, first person sing. obj. prefix of verbs.

nechicoa, nic. to collect, assemble, gather. Class 3: *ōnicnechicoh.*

nēci, ni. to appear; for money, tribute, etc., to be produced or available. Class 2: *ōninēz.*

-nehuān, complex relational word. with the pl. possessive prefixes. both, both together.

nehhuā-tl. I, independent pronoun. Shortened forms *nehhua* and *neh.*

neīxnāmicō. impersonal of reflexive *īxnāmiqui.*

nel. element in particle clusters derived from *nelli,* though it now rarely translates as true or truly. *ca nel,* because, since, for, etc. *mā nel,* although.

nel-li. something true.

nelti. to become true, to be carried out, realized, verified. Class 1: *ōneltic. nelli, -ti.*

neltilia, nic. to carry out, realize; to verify, authenticate. Class 3: *ōnicneltilih. nelti, -lia* (causative of *-ti* verbs).

neltoca, nic. to believe, believe in, consider true. Class 1. *ōnicneltocac. nelli, toca* (in its meaning of to consider).

nemac-(tli). inheritance, portion, that which is given to one. patientive noun from *maca,* with *ne-* representing the reflexive form of the verb.

nehmatcā, pret. agentive as adverbial particle. prudently, carefully. adverbial pret. agentive form of reflexive *ihmati.* also the latter's pret. agentive combining form.

nehmatcānemiliz-tli. a prudent way of life. *nehmatcā, nemi, -liz-tli.*

nemi, ni. to live, sometimes to be involved in something. Class 2: *ōninen.* as *-ti-* auxiliary verb, to go about doing something. sometimes has pluperfect *nenca* for pret., especially as auxiliary.

nemiliz-tli. life, living. *nemi, -liz-tli.*

nemītia, nic. to cause to live, to keep or maintain a person or animal. Class 3: *ōnicnemītih.* causative of *nemi.*

nemoa, nemohua. impersonal of *nemi.*

nenāmictiliztli. marriage. *ne-, nāmictia, -liz-tli.*

nehnehuilia, nic. to be equal to something, to resemble it. Class 3: *ōnicnehnehuilih.* probably built on reciprocal *ne-.*

nehnemi, ni. to go about, go along, travel. Class 2: *ōninehnen.* distributive of *nemi.*

nehnenqui. traveler, pilgrim. pret. agentive of

nehnemi.

nēntlamati, ni. to feel malaise, be unhappy, languish. Class 2 irregular: ōninēntlamah. nēn- in vain, tla-, mati.

nenōtzallani, nic. to send to summon someone. Class 2: ōnicnenōtzallan. nenōtzalli patientive noun from reflexive nōtza, -tlani to have something done.

nēnpoloa, nic. to waste, dissipate. Class 3: ōnicnēnpoloh. nēn- in vain, poloa.

nēpa, particle. there, at a distance, sometimes on the far side.

nepantlah, particle. in the middle. -nepantlah, complex relational word. in the middle of something. ne-, -pan, -tlah.

nepāpan. particle, originally an absolute relational word. various. ne-, -pan.

nepechtēquilia, nic. applicative of reflexive pechtēca.

-nepiloāyān, locative noun. place of suspension, descent. ne-, reflexive piloa, -yān.

nepōhualiz-tli. pride, bragging. ne-, pōhua, -liz-tli.

nequame-tl. type of tree like a palm. vowel quantity speculative.

nequetzalpan, complex relational word acting as noun. as high as a person can reach, used to name a particular measure of length. patientive noun from reflexive quetza, -pan.

nequi (1), nic. to want, desire, use. Class 2: ōnicnec. many modal uses.

nequi (2), mo. to be necessary, needed; to be used. with -tech.

netēcuitlahuiliz-tli, taking care of people. ne-, tē-, cuitlahuia, -liz-tli.

netēilhuīl-li. accusation, complaint. patientive noun from tēilhuia.

netequipacholiz-tli. worry, concern, etc. ne-, tequipachoa, -liz-tli.

netequipachōl-li. worry, concern, etc. patientive noun from tequipachoa.

netlacuitlahuiliz-tli. taking care of things. ne-, tla-, cuitlahuia, -liz-tli.

-netōcayān. someone's burial place. ne-, reflexive tōca, -yān.

netolīniliz-tli. affliction, poverty, bother, etc. ne-, tolīnia, -liz.

nehtōtiliz-tli. dancing. ne-, ihtōtia, -liz-tli.

neuc-tli. honey, also the drinkable saps and juices of various kinds of plants.

nēxītia, nino. alternate causative of nēci, to appear, mainly used as the latter's reverential.

nēxtia, nic. to show, to make something appear, to produce it. Class 3: ōnicnēxtih. causative of nēci.

nex-tli. ash(es).

-nēzca. sign of something. abstract noun from nēci; in the absolutive it would be nēzcāyōtl, with pret. agentive combining form plus -yōtl.

n(i)-. I, first person sing. subject prefix.

-ni. verbal suffix to indicate the habitual present and some optatives, but mainly it serves to form present agentives, as in tlahtoāni.

nicān, particle. here. nicān tlācatl, a person from here, a local person, an indigenous person. mainly in the pl.

niman, particle. then, immediately. niman īc, thereupon, next in a sequence. niman before a negative intensifies it.

nipa, particle. over there, to the side, etc.

nō, particle. also. ahmō nō, neither, nor.

no-. my, possessive prefix; myself, reflexive prefix.

noceh, particle. or. see also mānoceh. noço, a base -eh.

nōchilia, nic. applicative of nōtza.

nōch-tli. tuna, fruit of the prickly pear cactus.

noço, particle. or.

nocon-. sequence of verbal prefixes equal in meaning to nicon-.

nōhui(y)ān, particle. everywhere, all around. also nōhui(y)ampa, with the implication of movement. it is possible that the o is short.

nōnōtza (1), nic. to advise, warn, consult with, talk with. Class 2: ōnicnōnōtz. nōtza.

nōnōtzah (2), tito. to agree about something.

nōnquah, particle. separately.

nohpal-li. nopal, prickly pear cactus.

nōquia, nic. to spill. Class 3: ōnicnōquih.

nōrteh. north. Sp.

nōtza, nic. to call, summon, talk to. Class 2: ōnicnōtz.

-nōtzalōca. the calling of someone, someone's being called, invocation. passive abstract noun from nōtza.

noviēmbreh. November. Sp.

-oa. Ending of many of the verbs of Class 3. Class 3 derivational suffix that creates verbs from nouns meaning to put the thing named by the noun into action. also creates loan verbs by being added to the Sp. infinitive. pret. -oh.

obīspoh. bishop. Sp.

obligāroa, nin. to oblige oneself (legally). Class 3: ōninobligāroh. Sp. obligar, -oa.

oc, particle. still. with quantities, more, another.

-oc. auxiliary verb, the same as onoc.

occān, particle. in two places. *oc, -cān.*

occhōtia, nin. see *oquichōtia.*

ōcēlō-tl. jaguar; also sometimes ocelot.

ocnamacōyān. tavern, pulquería, place where pulque is sold. *octli, namaca, -yān.*

oc-tli. pulque.

octūbreh, October. Sp.

ocuil-in. worm.

oficiāl. practioner of a manual trade; officer (usually of the local municipality). Sp.

ofīcioh. trade, calling. Sp.

ohua, exclamation. ah, oh, etc.

ohuih. something difficult.

ohuihcān. a difficult, dangerous place to get around in; also such a situation. *ohuih, -cān.*

oidōr. civil judge of the Royal Audiencia, the high court. Sp.

ololhuiah, tic. to gather around something. Class 3: *ōticololhuihqueh.* applicative of *ololoa.*

ololoa, nic. to roll something up, to gather or collect something. Class 3: *ōnicololoh.*

om-. plus, followed by small numbers. also *on-.*

ohmaxalco. often a place name, but it means where a road forks. *ohtli, maxal-* something forked, *-co.*

ōme. two. in combined forms *ōm-, ōn-.* abs. pl. *ōmen, ōmentin.*

-ōmextin, -ōmexti. both. always half possessed, with a pl. possessive prefix. *-xtin* has the same sense with any number, the total. *īmēixtin,* all three, etc.

omi-tl. bone.

ōmpa, particle. there (more distant than *oncān*). *in ōmpa,* where. *ōn, pa.*

ōn, demonstrative pronoun. that.

on-. directional prefix, action goes in direction away from speaker or reference point.

on- with numbers; see *om-.*

oncah. there is (i.e., the subject of the verb exists). with a possessed noun subject, to have. *in cihuātl oncateh ōme īconēhuān,* the woman has two children. *on-, cah.*

ōncahuiah, tic. for two people to do something together or share something. *-cahuia* can be with any number; *ēxcahuia,* for three people to share something; *nāuhcahuia,* four, etc. Class 3: *ōticōncahuihqueh.* The construction consists of a number, a *-ca-* which arranges numbers in groups in a way not yet fully understood, and *-huia.*

oncān, particle. there; can also refer to a point in time. *in oncān,* where.

onoc, n. to lie (be in horizontal position); to dwell; in plural, especially in reverential, sometimes to be assembled. irregular verb. contains directional *on-,* which is dropped when it is used as a helping verb. pret. *ō-nonoca, ōnonoya.*

onoltia, nin; onoltihtoc, nin. reverentials of *onoc.*

ōppa, particle. twice. *ōme, -pa.*

oquichhuah. married woman, person with a man. *oquichtli, -huah.*

oquichōtia, nin. for a woman to marry. Class 3: *ōninoquichōtih. oquichtli, -yōtl, -tia².*

oquichō-tl, oquichchō-tl. manliness, valor. *o-quichtli, -yōtl.*

oquichtlatqui-tl. man's gear, the typical personal possessions of a man. *oquichtli, tlatquitl.*

oquich-tli. man, male person, used in compounds to indicate the male of anything. in verbal compounds it often refers to valor, etc. possessed form *-oquichhui.* men referring to groups of men or men in general often say *toquichtin,* "we men," without the speaker meaning to include himself in the reference.

ōrganoh. (musical) organ. Sp.

oriēnteh. east. Sp.

ohtlatoca, n. to go along the road, to proceed; to fare, get along in life. Class 1: *ōnohtlatocac. ohtli, tla-, toca* to follow.

oh-tli. road; channel for anything. possessed form *-ohhui.*

ohtlīca (ohtli ī-ca), phrase becoming a particle. on the road, on the way.

ōztō-tl. cave, cavity.

-pa, suffixal particle. toward or from the direction of. with a numeral bound to it, times. also serves to add nuances to other relational words, to which it is suffixed.

-pāc. someone who is a fancier of something, takes joy in it. *cihuah īmpāc,* one who likes women. word and construction not yet fully understood. apparently related in some way to *pāqui.*

pāca, nic. to wash something. Class 1: *ōnic-pācac.*

pāccā, pret. agentive as adverbial particle. gladly, willingly, peacefully. often in a pair with *yōcoxcā,* of similar meaning. also combined with verbs and nouns. *pāqui.*

pāccācelia, nic. to accept something gladly or with equanimity. Class 3: *ōnicpāccācelih. pāccā, celia.*

pāccāihīyōhuia, nic. to take something patiently. Class 3: *ōnicpāccāihīyōhuih. pāccā, ihīyō-huia.*

pāccāyeliz-tli. happiness, being happy. *pāccā, yeliztli.*

pachihui, ni. to fall in, collapse, sink. Class 2: *ōnipachiuh.* related to *tlapachoa.*

pachoa (1), *nic.* to press, to govern. Class 3: *ōnicpachoh.*

pachoa (2), *nino.* to bow or crouch down.

pācticah, ni. to be healthy, sound. *pāqui, cah.*

pāctinemi, ni. to be happy, content, be healthy. Class 2 irregular: *ōnipāctinenca. pāqui, nemi.*

pādreh. priest (Christian). Sp.

pāhuaci, nic. to cook something in a pot, boil it. Class 2: *ōnicpāhuaz. pā-* is a root meaning water and by origin the same as *ātl.*

pāīna, ni. to run fast. Class 2: *ōnipāīn.* vowel quantity speculative.

-pal, relational word. for the sake of, by means of.

palācioh. palace. Sp.

palēhuia, nic. to help someone. Class 3: *ōnic-palēhuih.*

-palēhuilōca. someone's help, aid, the help given to someone. passive abstract deverbal noun from *palēhuia.*

pālosdahuia, nic. rare construction; to give someone a beating. Class 3: *ōnicpālosda-huih.* Sp. *dar de palos, -huia.*

pām-itl, also *pān-tli.* banner.

-pampa, relational word. on account of, because of, on behalf of, concerning, for. *-pan, -pa.*

-pan, relational word. in, on, for, during, as, place of or among, etc. *-pan tlahtoa,* to see to, take care of, be in charge of, sometimes to speak for.

pān. wheat bread. Sp.

panahuia, nic. to surpass, exceed. related to *panō.*

pani, particle. on the surface, showing, on top. older abs. form of *-pan.*

panō, ni. to cross over some surface. in Stage 3, also equivalent to Sp. *pasar,* to pass. Class 1: *ōnipanōc.* related to *-pan.*

pān-tli, also *pām-itl.* banner.

pahpāqui, ni. to rejoice, celebrate, have fun. Class 2: *ōnipahpac.* distributive/frequenta-tive of *pāqui.*

papatlaca, ni. to flutter, tremble. Class 1: *ōni-papatlacac.* frequentative of *patlāni* to fly.

pāqui, ni. to be happy, content, to enjoy oneself. Class 2: *ōnipāc.*

pāra(h?), preposition. (meant) for, in order. Sp.

parējah. used in a text here apparently meaning equally. from Sp. *pareja,* pair, couple.

-pārteh. one's share. Sp.

pasādoh, loan adjective. past, referring to an official who has served in a previous year. Sp.

paseāroa, ni. to stroll, parade about. Class 3: *ōnipaseāroh.* Sp. *pasear, -oa.*

pasión. passion, suffering (of Jesus Christ). apparently usually possessed. Sp.

pahti, ni. to get well, recover; for some problem or the like to be fixed. Class 1: *ōnipahtic. pah-tli, -ti.*

pātioh. patio. Sp.

patiuh-(tli). value, price of something. virtually always possessed; final *uh* of the stem is by origin the possessive suffix. related to *patla.*

patlāhuac. something wide. pret. agentive from a verb *patlāhua* to grow wide.

patla, nic. to trade, exchange, replace. Class 1: *ōnicpatlac.*

patlāni, ni. to fly. Class 2: *ōnipatlān.*

pah-tli. medicine, potion, poison. originally same root as *ātl,* water.

pātox, pātos. a duck. Sp.

paxiāloa. see *pasearoa.*

pechtēca, nino. to bow down low. Class 1: *ōni-nopechtēcac. pech-,* element having to do with flatness, the ground, a base, and *tēca.*

pēhua, (1), *ni.* to begin. Class 2: *ōnipēuh.*

pēhua, nic. to conquer someone. Class 2: *ōnic-pēuh.* related to *pēhua* (1)?

pēhua (2), *non.* to depart.

pēnahtia, nic. to assign a fine to someone. Sp. *pena, -tia²*.

pērah. pear, also apparently pear tree. Sp.

pēsoh. peso, unit of monetary value. Sp.

petición. petition. Sp.

petl-atl. mat (of reeds). combining form *petla-.*

petlāhua, nino. to strip off one's clothes. Class 2: *ōninopetlāuh.*

peyo-tl. peyote. length of vowels unknown; *o* most likely long.

pia (piya) (1), *nic.* to guard, keep, hold, have. in addition to older meanings gradually becomes equivalent to Sp. *tener,* to have. Class 2: *ōnicpix,* often *ōnicpīx;* the *i* of *pia* was probably originally long.

pia (2), *nitlah.* to be on guard, in charge (with a locative expression). origin of *h* unknown.

pial-(li). usually possessed. custody, something in one's custody. patientive noun from *pia.* (why the usual *tla-* is missing is not clear.)

pialtia, nic. to have someone keep something, to lend something to someone. Class 3: *ōnic-pialtih.* causative of *pia.*

pie, nic. variant of *pia.*

pil-li. unpossessed nonreverential, noble(man). possessed, child of someone. unpossessed reverential or diminutive, with *-tzīn-* or *-tōn-,* (small) child. possessed, in vocative, with *-tzīntzīn,* O my noble (including female). abs. pl. *pīpiltin.*

-pillō. one's master, lord. the niece or nephew of a woman. *pilli, -yōtl.*

pillō-tl. nobility; also childishness *pilli, -yōtl.*

piloa (1), *nic.* to hang someone or something. Class 3: *ōnicpiloh.*

piloa (2), *nino.* to be suspended. *-tech ninopiloa,* to hang from something, to depend on it, count on it. *in tōnatiuh mopiloa,* the sun descends in the sky.

pīnāhua, ni. to be ashamed. Class 1: *ōnipīnāhuac.*

pīnāuhtia, nic. to shame, put to shame, bring shame upon, affront. Class 3: *ōnicpīnāuhtih.* causative of *pīnāhua.*

pipinqui. something strong, vigorous. pret. agentive of a verb now lost. situation with vowel quantity and glottal stop not known.

pipiol-in. a type of wild, honey-producing bee. vowel quantities unknown; conceivably there is a glottal stop after the first *i.*

pīqui, nic. to invent, make up, fabricate. Class 2: *ōnicpīc.*

pitzāc-tli. something long and thin. status of the *-tli* uncertain; may by origin be a pret. agentive related to *pitzāhua,* to grow thin.

pitzo-tl. pig. perhaps the *o* is long.

pixca, ni. to harvest. Class 1: *ōnipixcac.*

piya, nic. same as *pia.*

plēitoh. lawsuit, controversy. Sp.

pōchtēca-tl. merchant, trader. abs. pl. *pōchtēcah.* from Pōchtlān, name of a place or sociopolitical unit.

pōc-tli. smoke.

pōhua (1), *nic.* to count, read, relate, assign. Class 2: *ōnicpōuh. -tech pōhua,* to assign to. transitive counterpart of *pōhui.*

pōhua (2), *nino.* to brag, be proud.

pōhua (3), *nitē.* to carry out a census.

-pōhual-li. preceded by a number in combining form, twenty. *cempōhualli,* one twenty, i.e., twenty; *ōmpōhualli,* two twenties, i.e., forty, etc. patientive noun from *pōhua.*

pōhui, ni. to belong, count (as). Class 2: *ōnipōuh. -tech pōhui,* to belong to. *-pan pōhui,* to count as. intransitive counterpart of *pōhua.*

polhuia, nic. applicative of *poloa.*

polihui, ni. to disappear, be destroyed, be defeated, be spent. Class 2: *ōnipoliuh.* intran-

sitive counterpart of *poloa.*

poliohua. impersonal of *polihui.*

poloa (1), *nic.* to destroy, erase, spend, lose, defeat. Class 3: *ōnicpoloh.* transitive counterpart of *polihui.*

poloa (2), *nitla.* to be irrational, to have lost one's faculties. often in reverential.

ponīenteh. west. Sp.

Popōcatepētl. name of a famous large volcano. seems to be a sentence saying "the mountain smokes." *popōca* to smoke, *tepētl.*

Popōcatzin. name of the volcano now (and then) called Popōcatepētl. "he smokes, one who smokes," with verb *popōca* to smoke.

pōpōhui. for something to come into its own or be as it should be. often but not necessarily with *on-.* synonymous with and often paired with *ixtlāhui.* Class 2: *ōnipōpōuh.* reduplication of *pōhui.*

pohpolhuia, nictla. see *tlapohpolhuia.*

posesión. act of taking possession of property legally. Sp.

poyōmiqui, ni. to die through stealth or treachery. Class 2: *ōnipoyōmic.* contains *miqui.*

pregōn. proclamation, announcement. Sp.

presentāroa, nic. to present (a document in court, etc.). Class 3: *ōnicpresentāroh.* Sp. *presentar, -oa.*

priōr. prior (of a house of religious). Sp.

quā, nic. to eat something. Class 4. *ōnicquah.*

quāātēquia, nic. to baptize, sprinkle water on someone. Class 3: *ōnicquāātēquih. quāitl, ātēquia* to sprinkle or pour water on something, in turn based on *ātl, tēca.*

quahu-itl. wood, stick, tree, trees; unit for measuring land etc., often seven to ten feet. *tetl quahuitl,* punishment or disease.

quā-itl. human head, top or end of something. combining form most often *quā-,* sometimes *quah.*

quāiztaya, ni. for one's head to be or turn white. Class 1 or 2: *ōniquāiztayac* or *ōniquāiztaz. quāitl, iztaya* to whiten.

qualāni, ni. to get angry. Class 2: *ōniqualān.*

qualāncāitta, nic. to view something with anger, annoyance. Class 1: *ōnicqualāncāittac. qualāni* in pret. agentive combining form, *itta.*

qualcān. a good place, good time or opportunity. *qualli, -cān.*

qual-li. something good. *ca (ye) qualli,* very well, fine, okay.

quallō-tl. goodness. also sometimes *qualyōtl. qualli, -yōtl.*

qualnemiliz-tli. a good and proper way of life.

qualli, nemi, līz-tli.

qualnezqui. something or someone good-looking. qualli, nēci.

quālōni. something edible. quā, -lō, -ni.

qualtia, ni. to become good. Class 2: oniqualtix. qualli, -ti(y)a.

quammimil-li. round log or wooden column. quahuitl, (tla)mimilli related to mimiloa, to roll over and over.

quahquā, nitla. to nibble, graze. ōnitlaquahquah. distributive/frequentative of quā.

quāquahueh. bovine animal, ox. quāquahuitl, -eh.

quāquahu-itl. horn (of an animal). quāitl, head, and quahuitl, wood.

quāquauheh. equals quāquahueh.

quāteçon(tzin). someone with a scraped head, closely clipped hair; lay friar in one of the religious orders. quāitl, teçontli rough, scraped material.

quātēquia. see quāātēquia.

quauhcal-li. jail, or sometimes any wooden house or structure. quahuitl, calli.

Quauhnāhuac. Cuernavaca. "close to the woods." quahuitl, -nāhuac.

quauhnāhuacayōtl. something in Cuernavaca style. Quauhnāhuac, an a that is added to nāhuac when it is combined, -yōtl.

quāuhpil-li. nobleman through war deeds or other personal merit, not through descent. quāuhtli, pilli.

quauhtemātl-atl. ad hoc term invented to describe a catapult, literally wooden sling for throwing stones. combining form quauhtemātla-. quahuitl, temātlatl.

quauhtic. something tall. quahuitl, -tic.

quauhtlah, complex absolute relational word. forest, woods, wilds. quahuitl, -tlah.

quāuh-tli. eagle.

quauhxīnqui. carpenter. quahuitl, pret. agentive of xīma to shave, dress.

quāxoch-tli. boundary, border. the length of the vowels is not attested. the first element seems to be quāitl, but that could lead to either quā- or quah. the second element shows no semantic affinity to xōchitl, flower, and could be either long or short.

quechilia, nic. applicative of quetza.

quech-tli. throat, neck.

quelhuia, nic. applicative of queloa.

queloa, nic. with īc or çan īc, to do something on purpose. In the passage from Laso de la Vega, however, it may have the same meaning as nicquehqueloa, to laugh at, cheat, fool.

Class 3: ōnicqueloh.

quēmahca, particle. yes. quēn, ah negative, ca (adverbial ending or introductory particle?).

quēmman. at what time (of the day), interrogative. with in or even without, sometimes, at intervals. quēn, mani.

quēmmanian, particle. sometimes, sometime, ever. quēn, mani, -yān.

quēn. how, interrogative.

quēnamih. how, how constituted, interrogative. preceded by in, as, or dependent how. Can have an abs. pl. quēn amihqueh in which the second element bears the subject prefixes if any. quēn, a preterit agentive base amih.

quēnin. how, interrogative; preceded by in, dependent. quēn, in.

quēntēl, particle. tolerably, so-so. quēn, tēl.

quēntia, nicno. to wear. (tla)quēmitl, -tia².

querēllah. legal complaint. Sp.

quetza (1), nic. to raise, make stand up, erect (a building). Class 2: ōnicquetz.

quetza (2), nino. to stand, stand up, stop, appear.

quēxquich. how much, interrogative; preceded by in, dependent. also sometimes as a quantifier an indefinite amount, a little, a bit. abs. pl. quēxquichtin, how many. apparently related to quēn, īxquich.

quēzqui, interrogative and quantifier. abs. pl. quēzquīn, quēzquīntin. as interrogative, how much, how many; preceded by in, dependent. as quantifier, a certain number, a few.

quēzquipa, particle. a few times, several times. quēzqui, -pa.

-quēzquilhuiyōc, complex relational word. a few days after something. quēzqui, ilhuitl, -yō, -co/-c.

qui-. him, her, it; 3rd person sing. obj. prefix of verbs when there is no other supporting vowel on either side.

-qui, pl. -quih. optative ending of purposive motion form -quīuh/-co.

-qui. characteristic ending of many pret. agentive nouns, being the archaic pret. suffix. mainly on Class 2 verbs, some Class 3. abs. pl. -queh. combining form -cā-.

quiāhua-tl. exit, entryway. most often seen in locative, quiāhua-c, sometimes meaning outside. often spelled quiyāhuatl. together with ithualli, patio, denotes the household.

quiahui. see quiyahui.

quīça, ni. to come out, emerge, pass (by), end, leave, etc.; for a feast day to be celebrated. as a -ti- auxiliary, to do something in passing.

Class 2: *ōniquīz.* -*tech quīça,* to come out of. -*pan quīça,* to pass by.

-*quīçayāmpa,* compound relational word. toward where something emerges. in phrase *īquīçayāmpa tōnatiuh,* east (toward where the sun comes out). *quīça, -yān, -pa.*

quil, particle. they say, it is said that, reportedly.

quil-itl. (edible) greens.

quim-. them, 3rd person pl. obj. prefix of verbs.

quimiloa, nic. to wrap something in cloth, to put in a shroud. Class 3: *ōnicquimiloh.*

quin, particle. afterward, not until, just now. *quin āxcān,* very recently, just now.

quin-. form taken by *quim-* 3rd person pl. obj. prefix before a nonlabial consonant.

-*quīuh.* future of inbound purpose motion suffix -*quīuh/-co.* pl. -*quīhuih.*

quīxtia, nic. to remove something. Class 3: *ōnicquīxtih.* causative of *quīça.*

quixtiānoh. Nahuatl form of Sp. *cristiano,* usually meaning not a Christian as such but a person of European extraction, a Spaniard.

quiyahui. to rain. Class 2: *ōquiyauh.*

quiyāhua-tl. see *quiāhuatl.*

regidōr. councilman on a municipal council. Sp.

repūblicah. commonwealth, usually referring to the Spanish-style municipal organization of an altepetl. Sp.

respōnsoh. response (in ecclesiastical ritual). Sp.

rēy. (the Spanish) king; also sometimes means viceroy. Sp.

sābadoh. Saturday. Sp.

sālah. living room, large central room. Sp.

santīsima trinidād. holy Trinity. Sp.

sāntoh, sāntah. male saint, female saint. apparently considered separate words by the Nahuas. also occurs in many set loan phrases where the meaning is holy.

sembradūrah. sowing. Sp.

señōrah. lady, but usually any Spanish woman. often pronounced and written *xinōlah.* Sp.

se(p)tiēmbreh. September. Sp.

sepultūrah. grave. Sp.

sītioh. site, often but not always a large area originally granted for growing livestock. Sp.

sombrēroh. hat. Sp.

sūr. south. Sp.

sustentāroa, nic. to sustain, keep up. Class 3: *ō-nicsustentāroh.* Sp. *sustentar, -oa.*

tāçah. cup. Sp.

tamachīhua, nic. to measure something. Class 2: *ōnictamachīuh.* contains *chīhua.*

tamal-li. tamal.

tamalchīhualiz-tli. tamal making. *tamalli, chī-hua, -liz-tli.*

tasaciōn. assignment of quotas. Sp.

tah-(tli). father. *totahtzin,* a priest or friar.

tahyō-tl. fatherhood. with *nānyōtl,* parenthood. *taht(li), -yōtl.*

taza. see *tāçah*

tē-. indefinite personal obj. prefix. also indefinite personal possessive prefix of nouns.

-*tēāchcāuh.* older brother or cousin of a male. also independent *tēāchcāuh* meaning not only someone's older brother but anything preeminent. also occurs as -*tiāchcāuh* and *tāchcāuh.* must have been pronounced *tē-yāchcāuh;* the *ē* assimilated to the *y,* becoming *ī,* and the length of the *i* was neutralized; in this context the now short weak *i* led to yet another form, *tāchcāuh.* contains an incorporated *tē-* and -*āch-,* a root meaning first or elder; the remainder looks like the ending of a possessed pret. agentive noun.

tēca, nic. to spread or stretch something on a flat, usually low surface; with water, to pour. Class 1: *ōnictēcac.*

-*tēca-tl.* inhabitant of a place or unit whose name ends in -*tlān/-lān.* abs. pl. -*tēcah.*

tēch-. us, first person pl. obj. prefix of verbs.

-*tech,* relational word. joined to, next to; used as a general connector in verbal idioms with greatly varying translations depending on the verb.

-*techcacopa,* particle. fairly rare form equal in meaning to -*techcopa* and -*techpa.*

-*techcopa,* relational word. relating to, about, concerning. -*tech, -copa.*

tēchicāhualiz-tli. the strengthening or encouraging of people; health. health sense usually possessed, possessor God. *tē-, chicāhua, -liz-tli.*

-*tēchīuhcāuh.* one's progenitor, someone who engendered one; nonreverential form, often the aide of a ruler or lord. possessed form of the pret. agentive of *chīhua* with *tē* obj.

-*techpa,* relational word. relating to, about, concerning. meaning same as -*techcopa.* -*tech, -pa.*

teci, ni. to grind, especially maize. Class 2: *ōnitez.*

tēcocoliliz-tli. hate, abhorrence (of people, of someone). *tē-, cocolia, -liz-tli.*

tecolō-tl. owl. abs. pl. usually *tētecoloh*

tecom-atl. jar, cup, tecomate. *tetl, comatl* as in *cuezcomatl.*

tecomōl-li. rocky depression? *tetl, (tla)comōlli*

hole, depression?

tecōni. something cuttable. passive agentive of *tequi.*

tēcpan. palace, public governmental building. acts both as a locative, a complex relational word, and a full-fledged noun. *tēuctli, -pan.*

tecpāna, nic. literally to put in order or in a line, or to order something more abstractly. Class 2: *ōnictecpān.*

-tecpān-tli. preceded by a number, means that many twenties of people, just like *-pōhualli* in general. patientive noun from *tecpāna.* same word as *tlatecpāntli,* with a number replacing the *tla-.*

tecpa-tl. flint, knife of flint.

tēcuilia, nic. to take something from someone. Class 3: *ōnictēcuilih.* applicative of *cui* with *tē-* incorporated in stem.

-tēcuiyo. usual possessed form of *tēuctli.* archaic stem of *tēuctli* plus *-yōtl.*

-tēhua, auxiliary verb. to do something specified by the main verb on departing, dying. *-t(i)-* ligature, *ēhua* (2).

tehhuān-tin. we, independent pronoun. shortened form *tehhuān.*

tehhuā-tl. you, independent pronoun. shortened forms *tehhua, teh.* reverential *tehhuātzin.*

tehuilacachoa, nic. to make something revolve; to make something round. Class 3: *ōnictehuilacachoh.* situation with vowel quantity not known.

-tēiccāuh. more common form of *-iccāuh,* double possessed.

tēilhuia (1), *nic.* to accuse, denounce someone. Class 3: *ōnictēilhuih. tē-, ilhuia.*

tēilhuia (2), *nino.* to make a complaint or accusation, bring suit.

tēilpilōyān, locative noun. jail. *te-, ilpia* to tie, detain, *-lō, -yān.*

tēl, particle. but, however.

telchīhua, nic. to curse, scorn, deprecate someone or something. Class 2: *ōnictelchīuh.* element *tel-* often with a negative connotation, *chīhua.*

telicça, nic. to kick. Class 1: *ōnictelicçac.*

tēlpōch-tli. youth, adolescent, unmarried young man. possessed, (grown) son. abs. pl. *tēlpōpōchtin.*

tēma, nic. to put something into a container or the like, to fill it up. Class 2: *ōnictēn.* transitive counterpart of *tēmi.*

tēmachia, nic. to have confidence in, look to. Class 3: *ōnictēmachih.* ultimately based on *mati.*

tēmachtiāni. preacher, teacher. *te-, machtia, -ni.*

tēmahmauhtih. something that frightens people. pret. agentive of *mahmauhtia.*

tēmāquīxtiāni. redeemer. *te-, māquīxtia, -ni.*

temātlahuia, nic. to use a rock-hurling sling on something. Class 3: *ōnictemātlahuih. temātlatl, -huia.*

temātl-atl. sling for hurling stones. combining form *temātla-. tetl, mātlatl* net.

tēmi, ni. to be full, to displace liquid; with chinampas, to be (in a certain place). Class 2: *ōnitēn.*

tēmictih. murderer, someone who has killed or beat someone, something fatal. pret. agentive from *mictia.*

temīl-li. rocky field? *tetl, mīlli.*

tēmiqui, nic. to dream something. Class 2: *ōnictēmic.*

temō, ni. to descend. Class 1: *ōnitemōc.*

temōhuia, nic. to lower something, bring or take it down. also acts as applicative of *temō.* The *o* may not be long.

tēmoa, nic. to seek, look for. Class 3: *ōnictēmoh.*

tēmōx-tli. individual meaning not known, but the combination *tēmōxtli ehēcatl* means illness or pestilence.

tenām-itl. wall; rampart.

tenān-tli. the same as *tenāmitl.*

-tēncopa, complex relational word. by order of. *tēntli, -copa.*

tēnēhua, nic. to mention, to say, sometimes to promise. Class 2: *ōnictēnēuh. tēntli, ēhua.*

tēnēhua?, tēnēhui?, ni. to be mentioned. Class 2: *ōnitēnēuh.* intransitive counterpart of *nictēnēhua.*

tēnihça, ni. to have breakfast. Class 1: *ōnitēnihçac. tēntli, ihça.*

teniēnteh. deputy, often general lieutenant of the chief Spanish magistrate of a district. Sp.

teni-tl. barbarian, person from another country, newly arrived in the land. quantity of the *e* not known.

tēnnāmiqui, nic. to kiss. Class 2: *ōnictēnnāmic. tēntli, nāmiqui.*

Tenochtitlan. name of the altepetl at the center of the so-called Aztec empire, remaining as an indigenous entity within Mexico City in the time of the Spaniards. full name Mēxihco Tenochtitlan. the meaning and nature of *tenoch-* is not entirely clear despite general consensus that it refers to a type of cactus. the rest is *-t(i)-, -tlan.*

tēntlapīquia, nic. to give false testimony about

someone. *tēntli*, an applicative of *pīqui* with *tla-* incorporated.

tēn-(tli). lip(s), edge, word.

tēnyō-tl. fame. *tēntli*, *-yōtl*.

teōcuitl-atl. gold, precious metal. combining form *teōcuitla-*. *teōtl*, *cuitlatl*, extrusion.

teōpan. church, at the church. *teōtl*, *-pan*.

teōpantlāca-tl. church attendant, cantor. seen mainly in the pl. *teōpan*, *tlācatl*.

teōpixqui. friar, priest. *teōtl*, *pia* in pret. agentive.

teohpōhua, *nic.* to offend. Class 2: *ōnicteohpōuh*. *teōtl*, *pōhua?*

teō-tl. god. abs. pl. *tēteoh*. combining form most often *teō-*, sometimes *teoh*; combined form can mean fine, fancy, large, etc.

teōtlac, particle. in the afternoon.

teōyō-tl. divine thing, divinity, sacrament(s), sometimes the sacrament of marriage specifically. *teōtl*, *-yōtl*.

tepachoa, *nic.* to hurl stones at. Class 3: *ōnictepachoh*. *tetl*, *pachoa*.

tēpan, relational word in absolute form. when someone is already there, i.e., after someone, afterward. nearly always *çā tēpan (çātēpan)*. *tē-*, *-pan*.

tepān-tli. wall, fence, boundary. *tetl*, *pāntli* row, wall.

tepēcen-tli. maize grown on hills or other unwatered lands, relying on natural rainfall. *tepētl*, *centli*.

tepē-tl. mountain. sometimes has abs. pl. *tētepeh*.

tepehxihuia, *nic.* to hurl off a precipice, into an abyss, etc. Class 3: *ōnictepehxihuih*. *tepehxitl* precipice, *-huia*.

tepitōn, quantifier. a little, a bit, something little. *tepi-* little, *-tōn*.

-tepitōn. with a noun compounded to it, a little whatever it is.

tepitzīn, quantifier. a bit. *tepi-* little, *-tzīn*.

teponāz-tli. log drum. etymologically from *tepon-*, probably stump, and *-(hu)āz-*, tool.

-tepotzco, complex relational word. behind. see *-īcampa*. *tepotztli*, *-co*.

tepotz-tli. back.

tepozçoh. someone or something covered with metal. can refer to a person in chains, a man in armor, etc. *tepoztli*, *-yoh*.

Tepoztlān. a prominent altepetl, "place of copper." *tepoztli*, *tlān*.

tepoztlatecōni. axe. *tepoztli*, *tlatecōni*.

tepoz-tli. iron, steel, copper, workable metal.

tēquāni. fierce beast, large predator. *tē*, *quā*, *-ni*.

tequi-. element incorporated into verb stems to indicate intensification, large quantity.

tequi, *nic.* to cut; to pick fruit, etc. Class 2: *ōnictec*.

tequipachoa (1), *nic.* to cause someone concern, worry someone. Class 3: *ōnictequipachoh*. *tequi-*, *pachoa*.

tequipachoa (2), *nino.* to be concerned.

tequipanilhuia, *nic.* applicative of *tequipanoa*.

tequipanoa (1), *ni.* to work. sometimes with *tla-* obj. in same meaning. Class 3: *ōnitequipanoh*. *tequitl*, *-pan*, *-oa*.

tequipanoa (2), *nic.* to work for someone, serve someone.

-tequipanōlōca. the service done for someone. passive abstract noun from *tequipanoa*.

tequiti, *ni.* to work, do tribute duty, etc. Class 1: *ōnitequitic*. *tequitl*, *-ti*.

tequitia (1), *nic.* to assign a duty to someone, order someone to do something. Class 3: *ōnictequitih*. *tequitl*, *-tia²*.

tequitia (2), *nitla.* same as *tequitia (1)* except to assign the duty or give the order to everyone in general.

tequi-tl. task, work, tribute, duty, assignment, office, business, share, etc. *çan tequitl*, nothing but.

tequitlahtoh. tribute overseer. *tequitl*, *tla-*, pret. agentive form of *ihtoa*.

tequiuhtia, *nic.* same as *tequitia*, based on the possessed form of the noun *tequitl* as a stem.

tērminoh. deadline for doing something, term within which something must be done. Sp.

tesorēroh. treasurer. Sp.

testamēntoh. testament, will. Sp.

testīgoh. witness. Sp.

teti, *tetia*, *ni.* to grow hard. *teti* Class 1: *ōnitetic*; *tetia* Class 1 or 2: *ōnitetiac*, *ōnitetix*. *tetl*, *-ti* or *-ti(y)a*.

tetic. something hard. *tetl*, *-tic*.

te-tl. stone; counter for round hard objects and many other things. *tetl quahuitl*, punishment or disease.

tētlacahualtiliz-tli. stopping someone from doing something, making someone leave something. *te-*, *tla-*, *cāhua*, *-ltia*, *-liz-tli*.

tētlachīhuililiz-tli. ad hoc noun meaning doing things for people. *tē-*, *tla-*, *chīhua*, *-lia*, *-liz-tli*.

tētlaçohtlaliz-tli. love, charity, good treatment, hospitality, etc. *tē-*, *tlaçohtla*, *-liz-tli*.

tētlacuiliz-tli. taking something from someone. *tē-*, *tla-*, *cui*, *-liz-tli*.

tētlaihtlaniliztli. petition, request. *tē-*, *tla-*, *ihtlani*, *-liz-tli*.

tētlaōcoltih. something arousing pity. pret. agentive of *tlaōcoltia.*

tētolīnih. something that afflicts people, etc. pret. agentive from *tolīnia.*

tētolīniliz-tli. affliction, etc. *tē-, tolīnia, -liz-tli.*

tēuc-tli. lord. possessed form nearly always *-tēcuiyo.* abs. pl. *tētēuctin.*

tēucyō-tl. lordship. *tēuctli, -yōtl.*

teuh-tli. dust.

texcallah, complex relational word. rocky, craggy place. *texcalli* rock outcropping or crag, *-tlah.*

texiliz-tli. grinding (often maize). *teci, -liz-tli.*

tēx-(tli). brother-in-law of a male.

tēyacānqui. leader; lower sociopolitical official. *tē-,* pret. agentive of *yacāna,* to lead.

tēzca-tl. mirror.

t(i)-. you or we. 2nd person sing. subject prefix, or first person pl. subject prefix.

-t(i)-. element used as a ligature in certain kinds of constructions, specifically between main and auxiliary verbs and between nouns and relational words.

-ti, pl. *-tih, -tin.* optative ending of outbound purposive motion form *-tīuh/-to.*

-ti. derivational ending creating a verb meaning to be, become, or serve as the thing denoted by the noun stem to the left.

-tia. causative ending of verbs. Class 3: *-tih.*

-tia². added to a noun, creates a verb meaning to provide the thing denoted by the noun. Class 3: *-tih.*

-tia, -tiya. variant of *-ti* to be or become. pret. Class 2 or 1: *-tix* or *-tiac. -ti, -ya* durative.

-tiah, -tiyah. pret. of *yauh* as an auxiliary.

tiahcāuh. one valiant in war, warrior. pl. *tiahcāhuān.* originally *tēahcāuh,* possibly related to *tēāchcāuh.*

(-)tiāchcāuh. see *-tēāchcāuh.*

tiāmiqui, ni. to do business, trade. Class 2: *ōnitiāmic.*

tiānquiz-tli. marketplace. most often seen in locative, *tiānquiz-co.* originally a *-liz-tli* noun from *tiāmiqui.*

-tic. ending of many adjective-like substantives. *-ti, -c* pret. ending indicating pret. agentive. abs. pl. *-queh,* combining form *-cā-.*

tīci-tl. healer, physician. abs. pl. *tītīcih.*

tiēndah. shop, store. Sp.

tilmah-tli. man's cloak, cloth in general.

-tin. abs. pl. ending of nouns after consonant stems.

tītlani, nic. to send (messages, people on errands); in a Florentine Codex passage, appar-

ently to use and even to expose something to. Class 2: *ōnictītlan.*

tītlan-tli. messenger. patientive noun from *tītlani.*

-tiuh (ti-uh), auxiliary form of *yauh,* progressive, goes along doing. pl. *-tihuih.*

-tīuh. present of the purposive motion form away from the speaker, *tīuh/-to.* pl. *tīhuih.*

tla-. indefinite nonpersonal obj. prefix of verbs. also prefixed to relational words to make absolute forms. also prefixed to intransitive verbs to make impersonals.

tlā, particle. may, let, if, used with the optative of verbs instead of *mā* for maximum politeness.

-tlah, relational word always suffixed to a noun. place of abundance of something.

tlāça, nic. to hurl, throw down, let go (with an assault, etc.), issue. Class 2: *ōnictlāz.*

tlahcah, particle. in full day (late morning), toward midday.

tlācacuepa, nino. to go over to the other side in war; in a Florentine Codex passage, to take on the appearance of the other side. Class 2: *ōninotlācacuep. tlācatl, cuepa.*

tlacāhua -yollo. for someone to grant or concede something, to be generous; often said in a spirit of giving thanks, could be translated as thanks. The verb is *cāhua,* Class 2; since this is a set phrase, the preterit can take the archaic form *ōtlacāuhqui* with the obsolete preterit suffix.

tlacalaquīl-li. tribute, anything delivered. patientive noun from *calaquia.*

tlācamati, nic. to obey someone. Class 2: *ōnic-tlācamah. tlācatl, mati.*

-tlacaquiān, -tlacaquiyān, locative noun. when or where one was there to hear something, in one's lifetime or within one's reach. *tla-, caqui, -yān.*

tlacaquiliz-tli. hearing or understanding something; especially possessed, the hearing, the understanding, the mind. *tla-, caqui, -liz-tli.*

tlācatecolō-tl. demon, devil, specter. abs. pl. *tlā-tlācatecoloh. tlācatl, tecolōtl.*

tlācati, ni. to be born. Class 2: *ōnitlācat. tlācatl, -ti.*

tlahcahti. for it to get late in the day (though still full day). Class 1: *ōtlahcahtic. tlahcah, -ti.*

tlāca-tl. person, human being of either gender. also, especially before a noun referring to a high position, or in the vocative, honorific, like lord or lady, person of high degree. abs. pl. *tlācah,* in some places *tlātlācah.* possessed form serves as the possessed form of *tlācoh-tli*, slave.

tlahcah-tli, nominalized particle. the daytime, the central part of the day after early morning until into the afternoon. *tlahcah*.

tlachicueitiliz-tli. rare form meaning, when possessed, a week after one's death. See p. 134.

tlachīhualiz-tli. doing things, deeds. *tla-*, *chī-hua*, *-liz-tli*.

tlachīhual-li. something made, done, created; creature, artifact, etc. patientive noun from *chīhua*.

tlachīuh-tli. the same as *tlachīhualli*.

tlach-tli. indigenous ball court. length of the *a* not certain.

tlahco, quantifier. half.

tlacōhualiz-tli. act of buying something. *tla-*, *cōhua*, *-liz-tli*.

tlacōhual-li. something bought. patientive noun from *cōhua*.

tlacōlhuia, *nic*. to go around something. Class 3: *ōnictlacōlhuih*. applicative of *cōloa*, which with *tla-* means to go in a circular manner; here *tla-* seems to be absorbed in the stem.

Tlacōpan. Tacuba, an important altepetl near Mexico City. *tlacōtl* switch, stick, *-pan*.

tlaçohtilia, *nic*. applicative of *tlaçohtla*.

tlaçohtla, *nic*. to love, esteem, treat well. Class 1: *ōnictlaçohtlac*. built on *tlaçohtli*.

tlācoh-tli. slave. possessed form *-tlācauh*. abs. pl. *tlātlācohtin*.

tlaçoh-tli. a precious thing. most often seen combined with nouns to mean dear, precious, etc. possessed, can mean a person beloved by someone.

tlahcotōn, quantifier. a quarter of a measure of grain. *tlahco*, *-tōn*.

-tlahcoyōc, complex relational word. in the middle of something, half way through it. *tlahco*, *-yō*, *-co/-c*.

tlacpac. on top, above. *-icpac* plus *tla-*.

tlahcuilōl-li. document, painting, anything written or painted. patientive noun from *ihcuiloa*.

tlāhuāna, *ni*. to drink (alcoholic beverages). Class 2: *ōnitlāhuān*.

tlāhuānaliz-tli. drinking (alcoholic beverages). *tlāhuāna*, *-liz-tli*.

tlahuēlīlōc. scoundrel, rogue, bad person, evildoer. abs. pl. *tlahuēlīlōqueh*. passive pret. agentive noun from *tlahuēlia* to abhor, hate, be angry at.

tlahuēlīlōcāyōtl. evildoing, roguery, badness, wickedness. *tlahuēlīlōc*, *-yōtl*.

-tlahuēliltic, ōno, interjection. Woe is me. Also

used in 2nd person plural, *ōtotlahuēliltic*. pret. of a *-ti* verb with *tlahuēlilli*, probably meaning something hated or abhorred (and it also seems that the first *i* should be long), which is always in 3rd person at the same time that the noun has a 1st person possessive prefix; prefixes in other persons are quite rare. Usually preceded by *ōmochīuh*.

tlahuilānal-li. something dragged along. often in possessed form, meaning the dependency of something, especially of an indigenous municipality. patientive noun from *huilāna* to drag.

tlāhuizcal-li. the light of dawn. *tlāhuitl* red ochre, anything red or fire-like, patientive noun from *izcalia* to come to life.

tlāhuiz-tli. insignia. vowel quantity uncertain.

tlaihīyōhuiliz-tli. fatigue, effort, suffering. *tla-*, *ihīyōhuia*, *-liz-tli*.

tlaihtlan-tli. something requested. patientive noun from *ihtlani*.

tlaīximach-tli. something recognized. patientive noun from *īximati*.

tlālcāhuia, *nic*. to abandon, leave behind. Class 3: *ōnictlālcāhuih*. *tlālli*, an applicative of *cāhua*.

tlālchipāhua. for it to get light in the morning. Class 1: *ōtlālchipāhuac*. *tlālli*, *chipāhua*.

tlālcōhual-li. bought land. *tlālli*, patientive noun from *cōhua*.

tlālcōuhqui. land purchaser. *tlālli*, pret. agentive of *cōhua* with *-qui* ending.

tlalhuatic. something sinewy, wiry, etc. *tlalhuatl* sinew, *-ti* in pret. agentive form.

tlālhuīca-tl. inhabitant of Tlālhuīc, the lowlands and specifically the Cuernavaca region; hence a backlander. abs. pl. *tlālhuīcah*.

✳ *tlālia* (1), *nic*. to put, place, set down, issue, order, set up, install, etc. Class 3: *ōnictlālih*.

tlālia (2), *nicno*. to put something on, wear it.

tlālia (3), *nino*. to settle, make a stay somewhere; to sit down.

tlalichtic. something tough, like poorly cooked food. pret. agentive from a *-ti* verb now no longer recoverable.

tlāllan, particle-like complex relational word. in, under the ground. *tlālli*, *-tlan*.

tlāl-li. land, earth, soil. *tlālli çoquitl*, the earthly aspect of a person, the body.

-tlāllō. the land or earth belonging to something. *-tlāllo -çoquiyo*, one's earthly body. *tlālli*, *-yō*.

Tlālmanalco. an important altepetl. patientive noun from *tlālli*, *mana* to flatten, even out, plus *-co.*

tlalnāmiquiliz-tli. remembering something, thinking of something; especially possessed, the memory, the mind. *tla-, ilnāmiqui, -liz-tli.*

tlaloa, nino. to run. Class 3: *ōninotlaloh.*

tlālpan, complex relational word, on or to the ground, throughout the country.

tlālpan-tli. floor, ground. *tlālpan* nominalized.

tlālpoloa, ni. to carry out a conquest. Class 3: *ōnitlālpoloh. tlālli, poloa.*

tlāltepoz-tli. hoe, mattock. *tlālli, tepoztli.*

tlālticpac, complex relational word sometimes used as noun. on earth, the earth. occasionally appears with *-tli* ending. *tlālli, -ti-, icpac.*

tlālticpaqueh. possessor or master of the earth, God. usually paired with *ilhuicahuah. tlālticpac, -eh.*

tlamachiliz-tli. knowing things, knowledge; especially possessed, understanding, mind. *tla-, mati, -liz-tli.*

tlamachtia (1), *nic.* to enjoy something. Class 3: *ōnictlamachtih.*

tlamachtia (2), *nino.* to be wealthy; to be happy.

tlamahuiçōl-li. something wondered at, a marvel, a miracle. patientive noun from *mahuiçoa.*

tlaman-tli. a separate thing, an item. used as a counter, usually has a number or quantifier bound to it. related to *mani?*

tlamat- form of a main verb used with *-ti* auxiliaries. to be quiet. related to *mati?*

tlahmatcā. preterit agentive as adverbial particle. prudently, quietly, peacefully. also acts as a combining form. from a form of *ihmati.*

tlamatini. sage, wise person, scholar. *tla-, mati, -ni.*

tlamātzo(hu?)al-li. folded tortillas. *tlamātzoalli ātexātl,* food, the fare. appears to be a patientive noun from *mātzoa,* to knead, but that should give *tlamātzōlli.*

tlamelāhua, ni. to go straight. Class 2: *ōnitlamelāuh. tla-, melāhua.*

tlami, ni. to finish, end. Class 2: *ōnitlan.*

tlamolhuatic. probably something sinewy. See p. 197, n. 1. pret. agentive from a *-ti* verb.

-tlan, relational word. next to, below, among. often takes *-ti-* ligature after nouns, especially in proper names. *-tlan nemi,* to be the dependent of someone.

-tlān, relational word used only as suffix. place of. mainly in place names.

tlanahui, ni. to be gravely ill, worsen, be near the end, to be in bad shape. Class 2: *ōnitlanauh.* related to *-tlan.*

tlanamacac. vendor. *tla-, namaca, -c.*

tlanamac-tli. something sold. patientive noun from *namaca.*

tlanecuiloh. trader, retailer. pret. agentive from *necuiloa,* to trade.

tlanēhuia, nicno. to borrow or rent something. here *-c-* is the direct obj., *-no-* the indirect. Class 3: *ōnicnotlanēhuih.*

tlahnēhuia, nicno. to lend oneself to someone, to be in their presence. here *-no-* is the direct obj., *-c-* the indirect. in fact the indirect obj. is usually in the 1st or 2nd person.

tlanelhua-tl. root. analysis unclear, but *nelhua-* appears in many other words having to do with roots and foundations.

tlaneltoquiliz-tli. belief, faith, the Christian faith. *tla-, neltoca, -liz-tli.*

tlanequiliz-tli. will, wish. *tla-, nequi, -liz-tli.*

tlanēx-tli. light, radiance. patientive noun from some verb form related to *nēci.*

tlanēzcāyō-tl. This form in Laso de la Vega appears to be a mistake for *nēzcāyōtl,* sign, consisting of the preterit combining form of *nēci* and *-yōtl.* possibly the intention was *itlah nēzcāyōtl.*

tlaōcol-, combining form. sad, piteous. form of a noun *tlaōcolli* hardly seen independently, patientive noun from *tlaōcoya.*

tlaōcolia, nic. to favor someone, do someone a favor, to grant someone something. Class 3: *ōnictlaōcolih.* related to *tlaōcoya.*

tlaōcoltia, nic. to move someone to pity. acts as causative of *tlaōcoya,* though the final *-ya* is not reflected.

tlaōcoya, ni. to be sad, mourn. Class 2: *ōnitlaōcox.*

tlaōl-li. maize in dried kernels, shelled maize. from *ōya,* to shell.

tlapachoa (1), *nic.* to cover, roof something. Class 3: *ōnictlapachoh. pachoa* with incorporated *tla-.*

tlapachoa (2), *nino.* to be covered under falling material, etc.

tlahpalhuia, nic. applicative of *tlahpaloa.*

tlahpal-li. force, strength, energy. *īxquich notlahpal nicchīhua,* to exert all one's effort, do all one can. often in 2nd person optative, in which case it can also have the sense of keeping one's spirits up.

tlahpaloa, nic. to greet. Class 3: *ōnictlahpaloh.*

tlahpaltic. someone strong, forceful. *tlahpalli, -tic.*

tlapāna, nic. to break up, split, divide. Class 2: *ōnictlapān.*

tlapan-tli. (flat) roof. usually in the locative, *tlapan-co. tla-, -pan.*

tlapaquiyahu-itl. a long-lasting drizzle. con-- tains *quiyahuitl.* seems to have *pa* as in *cepa- yahuitl.*

tlāpā-tl. a hallucinogenic substance. used in a pair with *mīxītl* in connection with drunken- ness.

tlapech-tli. platform, bed, litter. based on *pech-* as in *pechtēca.*

tlapīc-tli. something falsely invented, made up. usually used in an adverbial sense, preceded by *çan,* meaning for false reasons, without good reason. in this sense also loses its ab- solute ending and acts like a particle, *çan tlapīc.* patientive noun from *pīqui.*

tlaħpixqui. guard, servant. from *pia.* origin of the glottal stop unknown.

tlapoa, nic. to open. Class 3: *ōnictlapoħ.*

tlapōhual-li. a count, something counted. *aħmō çan tlapōhualtin,* people or animals without number. patientive noun from *pōhua.*

tlapolōl-li. something lost, destroyed, etc. pa- tientive noun from *poloa.*

tlapololtia, nino. to be irrational, out of one's senses. Class 3: *ōninotlapololtiħ.* reverential of the less common *nitlapoloa,* which has the same sense.

tlapōlōni. something openable. passive agen- tive of *tlapoa.*

tlapoħpolhuia, nic. to pardon someone. Class 3: *ōnictlapoħpolhuiħ.* distributive applicative of *poloa.*

tlaqualiz-tli. eating. *tla-, quā, -liz-tli.*

tlaqual-li. food. patientive noun from *quā.*

tlaqualōyān, locative noun. dining room, eating place. *tla-, quā, -lō, -yān.*

tlaqualtia, nic. to feed someone; to have some- one for a meal. Class 3: *ōnictlaqualtiħ.* causa- tive of *quā.*

-tlaquaħquāyān. grazing area of some animal. *quaħquā, -yān.*

tlaquēm-itl. garment, clothing. mainly seen in possessed form, *-tlaquēn.*

tlaquetz-tli. something raised, erected. patien- tive noun from *quetza.*

tlatecōni. a tool for cutting, usually an axe or hatchet. instrumental noun from *tequi.*

tlatecpān-tli. something that has been ordered, arranged. patientive noun from *tecpāna.*

tlatecqui. one who works stones, often precious stones. literally, one who cuts things. pret. agentive of *tequi.*

tlatelōlca-tl. inhabitant of Tlatelolco.

Tlatelōlco. major altepetl, connected with the other and more famous Mexica altepetl Te- nochtitlan. *tlatelōlli,* analysis uncertain, plus *-co.*

tlateōtoquiliz-tli. idolatry. *tla-, teōtl, toca* to consider as without good reason, *-liz-tli.*

tlatequipanoliz-tli. service. *tla-, tequipanoa, -liz-tli.*

tlathui. for the dawn to come. Class 1: *ōtlathuic. tla-, ithui* variant intransitive counterpart of *itta,* so that the original meaning was for things to be seen.

tlathui(l)tia (1), *nic.* for someone (God) to cause someone to feel a certain way on rising in the morning. Class 3: *ōnictlathui(l)tih.* causative of *tlathui.*

tlathui(l)tia (2), *nino.* to feel a certain way on awakening in the morning. causative rev- erential of *tlathui.*

tlatia, nic. to burn something, someone. Class 3: *ōnictlatiħ.* based on intransitive *tlatla* to burn.

tlātia, nic. to hide something, someone. Class 3: *ōnictlātiħ.*

Tlatilōlco. variant of Tlatelōlco.

tlaħtlacoāni. sinner, wrongdoer, one who makes mistakes. *tla-, iħtlacoa, -ni.*

tlaħtlacōleħ. wrongdoer, sinner, one who has made a mistake. *tlaħtlacōlli, -eħ.*

tlaħtlacōlli. sin(s), wrong deed(s), mistake, fault. patientive noun from *iħtlacoa.*

tlatlanēhuīl-li. something borrowed, rented. patientive noun from *tlanēhuia.*

tlatlapōlōni. key (opener). instrumental noun from *tlapoa.*

tlatlātīl-li. something hidden. patientive noun from *tlātia.*

tlatlatzīniliz-tli. thunder. *tlatlatzīni,* to thunder, *-liz-tli.*

tlātlauhtia, nic. to implore, pray to someone, address someone. Class 3: *ōnictlātlauhtiħ.*

-tlātlauhtīlōca. the imploring of someone, someone's being implored. passive abstract noun from *tlātlauhtia.*

tlaħ-(tli). uncle. according to Carochi the pos- sessed form is *-tlā.* related to *taħ(tli).*

tlaħtoāni. ruler, king, also used in reference to various high Spanish officials. pl. may refer to a group of notables who are not rulers. the abs. pl. and all other forms are based on the pret. agentive *tlaħtoħ,* no longer used in the abs. sing. *tla-, iħtoa, -ni.*

tlaħtohcā-. combining form of *tlaħtoani* based on the pret. agentive of *iħtoa.*

tlahtohcāti, rule, serve as ruler or governor. Class 2: *ōnitlahtohcat. tlahtoāni, -ti*.

tlahtohcāyō-tl. rulership. *tlahtoāni, -yōtl*.

tlahtōl-li. word(s), statement, what one says, language, speech, news, lawsuit, etc. patientive noun from *ihtoa*.

-tlahtōllō. story, history. *tlahtōlli, -yō*.

tlahtōlmelāhua, ni. to tell the truth. Class 2: *ōnitlahtōlmelāuh. tlahtōlli, melāhua* to make straight.

tlahtohqueh. abs. pl. of *tlahtoāni*, based on the pret. agentive.

tlatqui-tl. property (sometimes movable, hence gear). patientive noun from *itqui*.

tlatzaccān, locative noun now virtually a particle. last place or time. part of set phrase *çā tlatzaccān*, used in effect like an adjective, last, final. *tla-, tzaqua* to close, *-cān*.

tlatzaqualōni. lock, latch (closer). instrumental noun from *tzaqua*.

tlatzihui, ni. to be idle. Class 2: *ōnitlatziuh*.

tlatzilīni. tla- impersonal of *tzilīni*, for the bells to ring generally.

tlatzontequilia. see *tzontequilia*.

tlauhtia, nic. to favor someone, do him/her favors, give him/her things. Class 3: *ōnic-tlauhtih*. length of the *a* uncertain.

tlaxcalchīhualiztli. bread making, tortilla making. *tlaxcalli, chīhua, -liz-tli*.

tlaxcalchīuhqui. baker, tortilla maker. *tlaxcalli*, pret. agentive form of *chīhua*.

Tlaxcallān. Tlaxcala, an extremely important, vast complex altepetl. *tlaxcalli, -tlān*.

tlaxcal-li. bread, tortilla(s). patientive noun from *ixca*.

tlaxcaltēca-tl. Tlaxcalan, inhabitant of Tlaxcala. Tlaxcallān, *-tēcatl*.

tlahxīca. see *ihxīca*.

tlahxilacalli. subdistrict of an altepetl. length of first *i* and second *a* not known.

tlahxilacaleh. citizen of a tlaxilacalli, sometimes an authority of one.

tlāxilia, nic. applicative of *tlāça*.

tlayahualoa. see *yahualoa*.

tlayamānilih. curer of hides, softener of something. pret. agentive of *yamānilia*.

tlayecoltia (1), *nic*. to serve someone. Class 3: *ōnictlayecoltih*.

tlayecoltia (2), *nino*. to try to make a living.

-tlayecoltīlōca. service of someone, performed for someone. final *ā* is probably long when anything follows. passive abstract deverbal noun from *tlayecoltia*.

tlayohua. for it to be or grow dark; for night to fall. Class 1: *ōtlayohuac. tla-* impersonal of *yohua* with same basic meaning.

tle(h). what, interrogative. preceded by *in*, that which. the glottal stop is not present when a vowel follows in the same phrase.

tlehcahuia, nic. to raise, hoist something. Class 3: *ōnictlehcahuih*. related to *tlehco*.

tlehcō, ni. to climb, go up, ascend. Class 1: *ōni-tlehcōc*.

tlehuātza, nic. to broil. Class 2: *ōnictlehuātz. tletl, huātza* to dry something out.

tle īca, tleīca. why, what for, interrogative unless preceded by *in. tle(h), -ca*.

tlein. what, interrogative; preceded by *in*, that which. *tle(h), in*.

tlen. shortened form of *tlein*.

tlepōc-tli. seems to mean smoke mixed with fire. *tletl, pōctli*.

tlequiquiz-tli. firearm. *tletl, quiquiztli*, horn, trumpet, whistle.

tle-tl. fire. related to *tlatla* to burn.

tlīl-li. soot, ink.

tlīltic. something black; a person of African descent. *tlīlli, -tic*.

tloqueh nāhuaqueh. possessor or master of that which is near, close, in reference to God or in preconquest times to powerful indigenous deities. *-tloc* relational word synonymous with *nāhuac; nāhuac*; and *-eh* twice.

t(o)-. our, first person pl. possessive prefix; ourselves, first person pl. reflexive prefix.

-to. past of the outward moving purposive motion suffix *-tīuh/-to*. pl. *-toh*.

-toc. auxiliary form of *onoc. ti-* ligature plus *onoc* minus *on-*.

toca, nic. to follow, pursue; to consider something to be something (usually incorporated in the verb), often without sufficient grounds. Class 1: *ōnictocac*. in texts externally indistinguishable from *tōca*.

tōca, nic. to sow, to bury. Class 1: *ōnictōcac*. in texts externally indistinguishable from *toca*.

tōcā-itl. name.

-tōcāyohcān, locative noun. place named . . . *tōcāitl, -yoh, -cān*.

tōcayōtia, nic. to name, sign. *tōcāitl, -yōtl, -tia²*.

tōch-in. older variant of *tōch-tli*.

tōchti, ni. to become bestial, literally to become a rabbit. Class 1: *ōnitōchtic. tōchtli, -ti*.

tōch-tli. rabbit. abs. pl. *tōtōchtin*.

-tōcōca. one's burial. passive abstract deverbal noun from *tōca*.

tocon-. sequence of verbal prefixes equal to *ticon-*.

tōctitoc, ni. to lie buried. *tōctli* something planted or buried, *-ti,* auxiliary form of *onoc.*

toctia, nicno. to take someone or something as something to hide behind. Class 3: *ōnicnotoctih.* analysis unclear. looks like a form based on a noun stem *toc-* with *tia²*.

tolīnia (1), *nic.* to afflict, oppress, mistreat, bother. Class 3: *ōnictolīnih.*

tolīnia (2), *nino.* to be poor, afflicted, bothered, in need of attention, etc.

Tōllān. Tula, a major altepetl extremely important as center of a legendary culture and empire. *tōlin* rush, reed, *-tlān.*

Tōllohcān. Toluca, an altepetl and a region. *tōlin* rush, reed, *-yoh, -cān.*

tōltēca-tl. inhabitant of or person from Tōllān, Tula; hence an artisan. Tōllān, *-tēcatl.*

tōltēcayō-tl. artisanry. can also mean anything in Tula style or the entity of Tula. *tōltēcatl, -yōtl.*

tomāhuac. something fat, thick.

tomīn. eighth of a peso, a coin worth that (a *real*), or cash or money in general. from Sp. *tomín,* which means only the coin and the specific value.

-tōn-. diminutive element inserted between a noun stem and the absolutive or possessive ending if there is one. supposedly pejorative but often doesn't seem to be in texts. has its own pl. *-totōn(tin).*

tōna. to shine, be hot. Class 1: *ōtōnac.*

tōnal-li. day, the sun. patientive noun from *tōna.*

tōnatiuh. the sun. irregular absolutiveless noun derived from *tōna* and *-tiuh, yauh* as auxiliary, thus it originally meant (one who) goes along shining.

tōpīleh. constable, lesser officeholder, person in charge of some function. *tōpīlli, -eh.*

tōpīl-li. staff, especially of office.

tortīllah. tortilla. Sp.

totē°. abbreviation for *totēcuiyo,* our lord.

tōtol-in. turkey hen; also sometimes chicken. pl. sometimes means turkeys male and female.

tōtō-tl. bird.

totōca, ni. to run fast, hurry. Class 1: *ōnitotōcac.*

tzacui. to be closed. Class 2: *ōtzauc.* intransitive counterpart of *tzaqua.*

tzacuilia, nic. to stop, intercept, detain someone. Class 3: *ōnictzacuilih.* applicative ? of *tzaqua.*

tzacuiltia, nictla. to punish someone. Class 3: *ōnictlatzacuiltih.* causative of *tzaqua.*

tzāhua, ni. to spin (yarn). Class 2: *ōnitzāuh.*

-tzālan, relational word. between, among, in the midst of. *tepētl ītzālan,* a valley, a place between mountains. possibly the second *a* of *-tzālan* is long too.

tzapo-tl. sapota, zapote, type of fruit.

tzaqua, nic. to block up, close, finish, pay for, etc. Class 2: *ōnictzauc.*

tzaqualōni. something shuttable. passive agentive from *tzaqua.*

tzahtzaqua, nic. to shut in, jail. Class 2: *ōnictzahtzauc.* reduplicated form of *tzaqua.*

tzahtzi, ni. to shout, yell, scream. Class 1: *ōnitzahtzic.*

tzāuhqui. spinner, weaver. pret. agentive of *tzāhua.*

tzayāna, nic. to rip, tear. Class 2: *ōnictzayān.*

tzicalhuia, nic. applicative of *tzicoa.*

tzicoa, nic. to seize, hold, detain, stick something to something else. Class 3: *ōnictzicoh.*

tzilīni. for a bell or bells, or the like, to ring. with time, o'clock. Class 2: *ōtzilīn.*

tzilīnia, nic. to ring a bell or bells. Class 3: *ōnictzilīn.* based on *tzilīni.*

-tzīn-. reverential of nouns, also sometimes diminutive, or implying pity or tenderness. pl. *-tzitzīn(tin).*

-tzīnco. reverential of relational words.

tzīnquīxtia, nic. to reduce something. Class 3: *ōnictzīnquīxtih. tzīntli, quīxtia.*

tzīnyauh. for an animal to get a pain in its flank. pret. *ōtzīnyah.* functions differently in a text in Lesson 19 here than in Molina. *tzīntli, yauh.*

-tzīnoa. Class 3 reverential suffix of verbs, used sometimes over and above the normal reverential, but especially when the reflexive prefix has already been used in a semantically meaningful fashion. pret. *-tzīnoh.*

-tzīntlan, complex relational word. below, beneath. *tzīntli, -tlan.*

tzīn-tli. bottom, base, anus.

tzōltic. something narrow, thin. abs. pl. can be *tzōtzōltiqueh.* root *tzōl-* something narrow, pret. agentive form of *-ti.*

tzoniztaya, ni. for one's hair to be or turn white. Class 1 or 2: *ōnitzoniztayac* or *ōnitzoniztaz.*

tzonquīxtia, nic. to finish, end something. Class 3: *ōnictzonquīxtih. tzontli, quīxtia.*

tzonquīzqui. something that is final, at the end. pret. agentive of *tzonquīça,* to end, be finished.

tzontecom-atl. skull, head. *tzontli, tecomatl.*

tzonteconēhua, nic. to give someone a headache through excessive importunity. Class 2:

ōnictzoneconēuh. tzontecomatl, ēhua.

tzontequi, nic. to judge, sentence something. Class 2: *ōnictzontec.*

tzontequilia, nictla. to sentence someone. Class 3: *ōnictlatzontequilih.* applicative of *tzontequi.*

tzon-tli. hair, head. preceded by a number, four hundred.

tzopīlō-tl. buzzard, vulture. abs. pl. sometimes *tzōtzopīlōmeh.* seems to contain *tzotl,* offal.

tzohtzomah-tli. rag, rags, tattered clothing. related to *ihtzoma.*

tzotzona, nic. to pound; to beat a drum or play other more or less percussive musical instruments. Class 2: *ōnictzotzon.*

vācas, huācax. a cow. Sp.

vārah. a Spanish yard, a little less than three feet. Sp.

viĕrnes. Friday. Sp.

vīllah. town, a rank between pueblo and city granted to some indigenous municipalities. Sp.

vīrrĕy. viceroy. Sp.

vīsorrĕy. viceroy. Sp.

vīsperah. eve (of a saint's day, etc.). Sp.

xahcalli. hut (made of thatch). seems to contain *calli.*

xāl-li. sand.

xelhuia, nic. applicative of *xeloa.*

xeloa, nic. to divide something. Class 3: *ōnicxeloh.*

x(i)-. replaces the 2nd person subject prefixes of verbs in the optative/imperative.

xiccāhua, nic. to neglect, abandon. Class 2: *ōnicxiccāuh.* contains *cāhua.*

xīcoh-tli. a type of large bee.

xihu-itl. year; also certain greenish things, grass, herbs, greenstone, turquoise. possibly two words of different origin and same shape.

xīma, nic. to shave wood, stone, hair. Class 2: *ōnicxīn.*

xināch-tli. seed.

xīni, ni. to collapse, crumble, fall in, fall apart. Class 2: *ōnixīn.* related to *xitīni?*

xīnia, nic. to destroy, tear apart, knock down. Class 3: *ōnicxīnih.* based on *xīni.*

xinōlah. same as *señōrah.*

xiquipilli. bag. preceded by a number, eight thousand.

xitīni, ni. to collapse, come apart. Class 2: *ōnixitīn.* related to *xīni?*

xiuhtlapōhual-li. year count, calendar. *xihuitl, tlapōhualli.*

xihxicuin. glutton.

xihxicuinyō-tl. gluttony. *xihxicuin, -yōtl.*

xihxīnia, nic. to destroy, take apart, scatter. Class 3: *ōnicxihxīn.* distributive of a lost verb *xīnia,* transitive counterpart of *xīni.*

Xōchimīlco. an altepetl, "place of flower fields."

xōch-itl. flower. combining form sometimes *xōchi-,* sometimes *xōch-.*

xōcoa, nic. to push someone brusquely aside. Class 3: *ōnicxōcoh.*

xocon-. equal to *xicon-.*

xoco-tl. fruit.

xōcoyō-tl. youngest child; with dynastic names, the Younger. in the possessed form and vocative, a polite or affectionate form of address. *xōcoh* youngest child, -*yōtl.*

xocoquahu-itl. fruit tree. *xocotl, quahuitl.*

xolāl. lot (laid out and assigned in connection with streets). Sp. *solar.*

xolopih-tli. idiot, simpleton.

xolopihyō-tl. idiocy, stupidity, an act of stupidity. *xolopihtli, -yōtl.*

ya. older form of *ye,* already, seen in certain negative forms like *ayamō,* and also instead of free-standing *ye,* especially in peripheral regions.

-ya. imperfect ending of verbs. also incorporated into verb stems as a durative, as in *pi(y)a* to hold, keep, *chi(y)a* to await, -*ti(y)a* to be in the process of becoming.

yacāna, nic. to lead, go in front of someone. Class 2: *ōnicyacān. yacatl, āna.*

yac-atl. nose, point, something in the lead. combining form *yaca-.*

yacatzacuilia, nic. to intercept, block, cut off. Class 3: *ōnicyacatzacuilih. yacatl, tzacuilia.*

yahualoa (1), nic. to go around something, to surround it. Class 3: *ōnicyahualoh.*

yahualoa (2), nitla. to go around, to go in procession. Class 3: *ōnitlayahualoh.*

yālhua, particle. yesterday.

yaloa, yalohua. impersonal of *yauh.*

yamānia, yamānilia, nic. to soften something. Class 3: *ōnicyamānih, ōnicyamānilih.*

-yān. place where an action occurs.

yahqui. archaic singular of pret. of *yauh,* often seen in records of Tlaxcalan region.

yāōchīhua, nic. to make war on. Class 2: *ōnicyāōchīuh. yāōtl, chīhua.*

yancuicān, particle. newly, for the first time. related to *yancui(y)a,* to be renewed; contains -*cān.*

yāōquīça, ni. to go to war. Class 2: *ōniyāōquīz. yāōtl, quīça.*

yāōquīxīhua, impersonal of *yāōquīça.*

yāōtequihuah. war leader. *yāōtl, tequitl, -huah.*

yāō-tl. enemy; in compounds, war.

yāōyō-tl. war, fighting. *yāōtl, -yōtl.*

yauh (1), *ni.* to go, leave. present pl. *huih.* irregular verb with roots *ya/yā* and *hui.* pret. *ōniyah.* imperfect *nihui(y)a.* future *niyāz.*

yauh (2), *non.* to go along (well or badly). mainly in 3rd person.

ye. already, much used with anything past, also with imminent events. *in ye iuhqui,* when things are ready.

ye. suppletive stem of the verb *cah* in various tenses.

yēcahui. to get finished. Class 2: *ōyēcauh.*

yēceh, particle. but, however, nevertheless.

yēcchihchīhua, nic. to fix something up, get it into good condition. Class 2: *ōnicyēcchihchīuh. yēctli, chihchīhua* (itself to fix up, arrange).

yēctēnēhua, nic. to praise. Class 2: *ōnicyēctēnēuh. yēctli, tēnēhua.*

yēctia, ni. to become good. Class 2: *ōniyēctix. yēctli, -ti(y)a.*

yēc-tli. something good, pure, fine.

yēcyō-tl. goodness. *yēctli, -yōtl.*

yēguah, yēhuah. mare. Sp.

yehhuāntin, independent pronoun. they. short form *yehhuān,* reverential *yehhuāntzitzin.*

yehhuā-tl. he, she, it, that. independent pronoun. shortened forms *yehhua, yeh.* reverential *yehhuātzin. yehhuātl īn,* this. *yehhuātl ōn,* that. abs. pl. *yehhuāntin.*

yēi. three. see *ēi.*

yēīntin. three persons or animals.

yeliz-tli. being, essence. *cah* (alternate root *ye*), *-liz-tli.*

yēppa, particle. formerly, before, always before; in Laso de la Vega, soon, expectedly, of negative occurrences. *yēuh* before, *-pa.*

yēqueneh, particle. finally, additionally.

yetzticah, nino. reverential of *cah.* in fact virtually never in first person. *yetz-* irregular reflexive combining form of *cah* plus *cah* as auxiliary.

-yeyān, locative noun. the place where one is or usually is; one's quarters. *ye* alternate root of *cah, -yān.*

yeyēca-tl. see *ehēca-tl.*

yez. future of *cah.*

-yoh. forms a noun meaning someone or something covered with what is named by the noun stem to the left. abs. pl. *-yohqueh.* combining form *-yohcā-.*

yōcoxcā, pret. agentive as adverbial particle.

calmly, peacefully. often follows *pāccā* or *i-huiān* in a pair. apparently from a verb *yōcoya,* but semantic relationship to the known verb of that shape not clear.

yōcoya, nic. to create, invent. Class 2: *ōnicyōcox.*

yohua. to be or grow dark. Class 1: *ōyohuac.* see also *tlayohua.*

yohuac, particle. at night. from *yohua?*

yohual-li. night. patientive noun from *yohua.*

yohuatzīnco. very early in the morning. *yohuac, -tzīn* diminutive?

yōlcuītia (1), *nic.* to confess someone, hear his/her confession. Class 3: *ōnicyōlcuītih. yōlli* heart, *cuītia* to declare.

yōlcuītia (2), *nino.* to confess (one's sins).

yōli, ni. to live. Class 2: *ōniyōl.*

-yōlia. one's means of living, one's spirit or life principle, used as synonym of Sp. *ánima,* soul. *yōli, -ya* (instrumental construction).

-yōlīc. slowly, gently. possessive prefix most often but by no means always in 3rd person sing. combining form *-yōlīcah,* thus may be by origin a pret. agentive noun used adverbially. source not clear. length of the *i* not entirely certain.

yōlihtlacalhuia, nic. to offend, grieve. Class 3: *ōnicyōlihtlacalhuih. yōlli* heart, *ihtlacalhuia.*

yōlizmatiliz-tli. prudence, ingenuity. *yōliz-* shortened from *yōliliztli* life, *mati, -liz-tli.*

yōllālia, nic. to make content, console. Class 3: *ōnicyōllālih. yōlli,* heart; *tlālia* in the meaning to settle.

-yōllohcopa, also *yōllohcacopa,* complex relational word. willingly, voluntarily, gladly, from one's heart. *yōllohtli, -copa.*

yōlloh-tia, nic. to inspire someone to do something. Class 3: *ōnicyōllohtih. yōllohtli, -tia²*.

yōlloh-tli. heart. most often seen in the possessed form, *-yōllo. -īx, -yōllo,* spirits, mood, etc. *iuh cah noyōllo,* such is my intention or conviction, or I am easy in my mind.

yōlqui. a live being, an animal, often a beast of burden. pret. agentive of *yōli.*

-yohmah, possessed form behaving much like a relational word. in person; also spontaneously. especially in 3rd person. probably related to *iyoh* alone. The grammars speak of *-nohmah* with identical structure and meaning, but *-yohmah* is seen more in actual texts.

-yō-tl. abstract or collective nominal suffix; when possessed can express inalienable or organic possession.

yūntah. a yoke (of oxen), or the amount of land they could plow. Sp.

-z. ending of the future tense. pl. *-zqueh.* related to the *-z* in the *-liz-tli* gerund formation.

zapato, see *çapātox.*

-zquia. ending of the tense called conditional, which more often expresses that something was going to happen but didn't. pl. *-zquiah.*

Index

Abbreviations: in writing Nahuatl words, 108; in writing Spanish loanwords, 118

Absolutive: main treatment, 1–3; indefinite possession equivalent of, 27; plural suffixes, 51–53 [mentioned many other times]

Adjectives: 90, 156, 169, 180

Admonitive statements in testaments: 43, 46, 47

Adverbial phrases: tend to precede verb, 182

Adverbs: 103. *See also* Anticipation, Particles

Agent: never expressed with passive, 76

Agentive nouns: *See* Present agentives, Preterit agentives

"a la" loan nouns: 122

alphabetization: in Molina, 157; in Siméon, 158; in Karttunen, 160; in vocabulary of this volume, 207

altepetl (*āltepētl*): 45, 167

aço (*ahço*), perhaps, whether, if: 37

Amecameca, Amaquemecan: 201

Amith, Jonathan: 162

ana (*āna*), to take: defined, 25

Annals: selections from, 86–87, 201–03

Anderson, Arthur J. O.: *The Tlaxcalan Actas* described, 141; *Florentine Codex* described, 142–43; *Codex Chimalpahin* described, 144; *Beyond the Codices* described, 144–45; *Psalmodia Christiana* described, 147; *Coloquios* described, 147; remark on grammars, 148; *Rules of the Aztec Language* described, 150; mentioned, 158; selection from *Tlaxcalan Actas*, 192–93; selection from *Florentine Codex*, 197–97

Andrews, J. Richard: Alarcón *Treatise* described, 147; *Introduction to Classical Nahuatl* described, 149; and Karttunen's orthography, 160; Vocabulary of grammar described, 161–62; terminology for relational words, 164

Animates: 2, 9

Antecessive: 85; *See also o-* (*ō-*), sign of the preterit

Anticipation: 83–85; with *-ic,* 94; with *iuh,* 97; effect on Molina's manner of citation, 156; with quantifiers, 172; general precedes specific, 185; example of with *ompa,* 186

Applicative: 14–15; in reverential formation, 15–16; applicative verbs are Class 3, 34; and passive, 77; frozen, 185 [many other mentions]

"Article" in Nahuatl: 11 n4, 17 n3, 60; repeated discussion of in relation to use in an actual text, 164–86 passim

Assimilation: of *tl* to *l,* 2, 5 n3, 47, 73, 133, 169; with *nocon-* and *tocon-,* 14, 178; of *y* to preceding consonants, 17, 18, 57 n1, 65, 69, 174, 183, 208; with numbers, 45, 50; of fricatives and affricates in general, 106; of *a* to preceding *y,* 111; occurs within a phonological phrase, 113

auh, and/but: 82, 110

Auxiliary verbs. *See nequi,* Purposive motion forms, *-ti-* "ligature"

axcan (*āxcān*), now, today: 173

Azcapotzalco: section of a 1738 text from, 124–25

Bancroft Dialogues: edition of described, 142; selection from, 197–99

Bautista, fray Juan: *Huehuehtlahtolli* described, 146–47

Berdan, Frances: *The Tlaxcalan Actas* described, 141; *Beyond the Codices* described, 144–45; mentioned, 157; selection from *Beyond the Codices* analyzed, 163–89; selection from *Tlaxcalan Actas,* 192–93

Beyond the Codices, introduction to older Nahuatl texts: described, 141 n1, 144–45; detailed analysis of a selection from, 163–89

Bierhorst, John: *Codex Chimalpopoca* described, 143; *Cantares Mexicanos* described, 148 n1; *Nahuatl-English Dictionary and Concordance to the Cantares Mexicanos* described, 162 n1

Body, concept of: 70

Breve: 197

Brewer, Forrest and Jean, Tetelcingo dictionary of: 162

Bulking up short words: use of *on-* for, 32 n2, 39, 178

-c-, third person singular object prefix of verbs. *See* Object prefixes

-c, form of locative *-co. See -co*

-c, preterit suffix of Class 1 verbs: 31, 38

-c(a)-, negative "ligature": 41, 42 n1

ca, introductory particle: with nominal equative statements, 8 n2; in disambiguation, 11 n3; in answering questions, 37; example, 48; brief discussion of, 55; as marker of main clause or nuclear complex, 58, 81; and anticipation, 84

ca (*cah*), stative verb to be: as auxiliary, 38, 173; how to recognize, 55; as irregular verb, 64–65; *onca* to express existence and possession, 66–67; place in order, 83 n1

-ca, instrumental relational word: 22–23; confusion with *-tica* verbal auxiliary, 38, 55; use in testament formula, 45; possible relation to *ic/inic,* 93

-ca, Class 1 verbs ending in: 33

-ca, pluperfect ending, 64–65

-ca- (-cā-), as ancient preterit suffix, 31; in history of future tense, 35; as combining form of preterit agentives and also for present agentives, 54–55; importance of for ability to deal with texts, 55; compared with similar-looking elements, 55; in formation of adverbs, 56; relation to pluperfect, 63; used as combining form with possessor suffixes, 70–71; possibly in *-can* locative ending, 78

ça (*çā*), only: 101 n1, 102 n1; in Molina, 156; in an idiomatic phrase, 165

cabecera, head town: 133

cactimani, to be quiet, deserted: 66

callalli, house-land: 46, 70

244

ments, 127, 131; in conjunction with exhaustive analysis of a text, 163–89 passim
Directional prefixes: 14; orthography of *on-*, 16 n2; place in prefix order, 26; with *onoc on-* sometimes considered part of root, 65; temporal meaning, 75 n4
Directions, solar and nonsolar: 46, 48
Distributive reduplication: 51, 67, 73; reduplication of prefix, 87; main treatment, 91–92; how cited in Molina, 156; example of analyzed, 182–83

-e (*-eh*), possessor suffix. *See* Possessor suffixes
-e, masculine vocative ending: 71
ehua (*ēhua*), to depart: 40
Elision: 1–2, 11 n2; with *itta*, 16; in Molina, 154 n1; none after long vowels, 182
Emphasis: and *in*, 60. *See also* Focus, Independent pronouns, Preposing
Equative statements (verbless): 1, 41; extended example of, 45; general discussion of, in relation to *in*, 60–61; and quantifiers, 83; nature of in Nahuatl nearly grasped by Garibay, 151; brief discussions of, 166–67, 174
Equivalence relationships: 124

Factitive verbs: 81 n2, 84; with *inic*, 94
fiscal, church steward: 79
Florentine Codex: *See* Sahagún
Focus: 4. *See also* Emphasis
Future of verbs: 35–37; of some irregular verbs, 65; as component of "conditional," 67; and *inic*, 93; brief discussion of, 176

Garibay K., Angel María: effect of a passage in, 1; work on Nahuatl song of, 148 n1; *Llave del náhuatl* described, 150–51
Gender: 1
Gentile nouns: 51, 73
Glides: 113–14, 183
Glottal stop: not represented in examples of this volume, x; practice of representation of, 2 n4; deducing presence of in nouns in absolute singular, 2; as a plural, 2–3, 31, 51–52, 63; effect of not writing on understanding verbs, 3, 9; effects of in *-itic*, 23; role in consonant weakening, 34; role in Class 3 and 4 verbs, 34; distinguishing *mah* from *mā*, 41; at end of Spanish words in vowel, 46, 112, 122, 207; in reduplication, 51, 91–92; as nominal absolutive plural, 51–52; effect of at end of stem on plurals, 51; with the possessor suffixes, 70, 72; sometimes written as *h*, which intervocallically can become *y*, 71; orthography of, 104–05, 197, 203; and the Bancroft Dialogues, 142; in Molina, 153; Karttunen's dictionary primary reference for, 159; how represented in Karttunen and effect on alphabetization, 160; in Andrews' Vocabulary, 161–62; how represented in vocabulary of this volume, 207
Grammars, Nahuatl: description of several: 148–51
Grave accent: 105, 197, 203
Güemes, Lina Odena: *Historia tolteca-chichimeca*

described, 143
Guzmán, don Juan de, indigenous nobleman of Coyoacan, lived 16th–17th centuries: section of will of exhaustively analyzed, 163–189; testimony of, 199–201
Guzmán, doña Juana, late 16th-century indigenous noblewoman of Coyoacan married in Xochimilco: 189, 199–201

(*-h*), absolutive plural ending, 2–3, 51–52; *See also* Plural
-h, as representation of glottal stop, 104–05, 207
Hassig, Ross: Alarcón *Treatise* described, 147
Hierarchy of vowels: 2, 31, 111
Hinz, Eike: *Aztekischer Zensus* described, 144 n1
Historia tolteca-chichimeca: described, 143
Horcasitas, Fernando: *Teatro náhuatl* described, 146
House layout: 46, 48
-hua, impersonal verb ending, 33
-hua (*-huah*), possessor suffix: *See* Possessor suffixes
hual- (*huāl*). *See* Directional prefixes
huallauh (*huāllauh*), to come: reverential of, 17; as irregular verb, 64–66
-huan (*-huān*), possessive plural ending, 3–4; confusion with *-hua* possessor suffix, 71
-huan (*-huān*), with: 22; with numbers, 50; example discussed, 184
huel, intensifying and modal particle, 102–03
hui, second root of *yauh*: *See yauh*
-hui, possessive ending, 3
-huic (*-huīc*), toward, from: 24–25
huica (*huīca*), to take etc.: reverential of *yauh*, 17; defined, 25
huiquilia (*huīquilia*), applicative of *huica*: meaning "to owe money," 17 n2, 25, 26, 48, 123; not in Molina in this meaning, 152
huitz (*huītz*), to come: 39
Hypercorrection in letter substitutions: 120; in native words, 132

[i], orthography of, 62, 164
ic (*īc*), quasi-relational word, 94–95. *See also inic*
icac (*ihcac*), to stand: 38–39, 64–65
-icampa (*-īcampa*), behind: 23
ichpochtli (*ichpōchtli*): maiden, daughter: 180
-icpac, on top of: 23
Idioms: importance of relational words in, 21; how cited in Molina, 156; how cited in Siméon, 158
-im-, rare element marking direct in addition to indirect object: p. 56
ihui, thus, like: 96, 98
Images of saints: 47
Imperative. *See* Optative
Imperfect: of some irregular verbs, 38–40; general, 63; rapprochement of preterit and imperfect with irregulars, 64–65; as component of the "conditional," 67; relation of ending to durative, 89; imperfect instrumental construction, 178
Impersonal verbs: 33, 76–78; and locative nouns in

Martínez Baracs, Andrea: edition of Tlaxcalan annalist Zapata described, 145
Mass (the holy): 79
mati, to know: 34, 64
-me (-meh), absolute plural ending: *See* Plural
Measurements: 94
Medial consonants: 113
Merging of sounds and letters: 112
Metathesis, 15
Method for approaching Nahuatl texts: 187–88
Mexico City: 1565 punctuated passage from, 109; selection from annals concerning, 201–03
micca- (miccā), with kinship terms, 130
Molina, fray Alonso de: citation of nouns in possessed form in dictionary of, 2 n5, 8 n3; orthography of [s] in, 33; citation of reduplicated plurals in, 53 n3; citation of *-ca (-cā)* adverbs, 56; treatment of *in* in citations, 60; manner of writing *teuctli* compared with others, 105–06; grammar by described, 150; full-scale analysis of dictionary of, 152–58; and Campbell's *Morphological Dictionary*, 160–61; orthography of [w] in, 169
Monjarás-Ruiz, Jesús: *Colección de documentos sobre Coyoacán* described, 147
Monosyllabic verbs: 32; in Tlaxcala, 35 n1

-nahuac (nāhuac), close to: 23
Names, personal: 166
namictia (nāmictia), to marry: 88, 89
Nasal omission and intrusion: 112–13, 127, 174, 179
ne-, indefinite reflexive prefix: 28–29
nemi, to live: 40
nequi, to want, modal verb: with verb in future as object, 36–37; contrasted with *-ti-* auxiliaries, 40–41
-ni, agentive ending. *See* Present agentives
niman, then: 82–83; in negative expressions, 101–02
niman ic (niman īc), thereupon: 83
nocon-: 14, 42
Nonactive agentives: 90–91
Nouns: major sections on, 1–8, 11–12, 27–30, 51–56, 69–72; *in* with, 60–61; noun pairs, 61, 69, 70; in Molina, 155–56; in Siméon, 158; in Karttunen, 159; how represented in vocabulary of this volume, 208
Nuclear word or complex: mentioned, 2; adverbs precede, 56, 82; at core of sentence, 81; and anticipation, 85; and *in*, 85; reason for the nature of Nahuatl particles, 103; and orthography of the glottal stop, 105; and phonological phrase, 164, 174
Numbers: 49–50; plurals of, as quantifiers, 53; and *ic/inic*, 94; with *oc*, 99

o (ō), sign of the preterit, 31, 32, 34–35, 54 n1; with imperfect, 63; with *iuh*, 97
-o (-ō), passive verb ending: *See* Passive
-oa verbs: applicative of, 15; reverential of, 16; *-oa* loan verbs, 123–24
Object prefixes: main treatment, 9–10; indefinite and general order, 26–27; retained in deverbal nouns, 27–28; in relation to *o-*, 34–35; direct and indirect,

56; lack of specific in passive, 76; as anticipation, 83
oc, still: 35, 98–99; *oc cenca (oc cencah)*, especially, 99
Olmos, fray Andrés de: orthography of, 105; *Arte* described, 150
om-, plus with numbers: 49–50
Omission of one of two final vowels in Spanish loanwords: 120
Omission of two segments at morpheme boundary by way of reduction: 15 n1; with *-liztli* nouns, 28; with passives, 76 n1; with verbal prefixes, 136 n
ompa (ōmpa), there: 83, 186
on-: *See* Directional prefixes, Bulking up
on (ōn), that: 61–62
oncan (oncān), there: 59, 83
onoc, to lie: 39, 64–65
Optative: 41; of the purposive motion forms, 74 n2
oquichtli, male, man: 3, 61 n5
Oral admonitions in testaments: 43, 46
Organic possession: 69–70
Orthography: in this volume, x; of [ia-iya], 34, 38, 63, 106–07; full chapter on, 104–15; of [oa-owa], 106–07; of Molina, 152–53, 167; of Siméon, 158; of Karttunen, 160; of Campbell, 161
otli (ohtli), road: 3
overbars: 107, 179

-pa, toward, from: 24–25; as times, 50
-pampa, because, etc.: 22; and *-pa*, 25
-pan, in, on, etc.: 20–21; in *-pampa*, 22; in *-ixpan*, 23; with numbers, 50
pano, to cross, as equivalent of Spanish *pasar*: 124
Particles: place in word order, 81, 173; functions as adverbs and as conjunctions intermixed, 81, 179; as syntactic guideposts, 82–83; discussion of several important, 93–103; general discussion, 103; on occasion can be separate complexes with own emphasis, 110; spacing of in writing, 110; loan particles, 124; in Molina, 156; and phonological phrase, 174; brief general discussion of, 179
Parts of speech, importance in analysis: 20–21, 187; difficulty of telling verbs from nouns, 28
Passive: active reflexive as equivalent of, 11; relation to patientive nouns, 29; all passives Class 1, 32; main treatment, 76–78; how to recognize, 172
Patientive nouns: 29–30
Phonological phrase: adverbs protected by coming in first part of, 56; and Carochi's orthography, 106; writing of *y/i* in relation to, 107, 164; in relation to punctuation, also syntactic, 110; orthographic and other assimilation occurs only within, 113, 174
pia, to guard, hold, have: 33–34; as to have, 47, 67, 117, especially 123; not in Molina as to have, 152
pialia as to owe: 123
pilli, nobleman, in other forms child: list of different forms of, 57 n1; examples of use, 70, 71; another discussion of forms, 169; never overtly reverential in meaning noble, 180
Place names: 21. *See also* Sociopolitical units
Pluperfect: as preterit with irregular verbs, 38, 39, 40;

o tuh as equivalent, 58–59, 97; imperfect as, 63; main discussion, 63–64

Plural: conditions of use, 2; detection in written form, early forms of, 31, 63; of preterit verbs, 31–32; of various kinds of nouns and nominal elements, 51–54; *t* protected in some verbal plurals, 64; of *yauh* distinguished from singular in present, 65; of purposive motion forms, 74; of Spanish loanwords, 122–23; of native words influenced by Spanish, 124; when distinguished from singular in verbs, 171; and body parts, 178

Poole, Stafford, C. M.: *The Story of Guadalupe* described, 142; selection from, 203–05

Possessive prefixes: compared to subject prefixes, 1; presence and absence with locative nouns, 78

Possessive suffixes: discussed, compared to absolutive suffixes, 3–4; *-yo* as, 69–70

Possessive state of nouns: 3–4; and constituent order, 11; possession with *-yo*, 69–70; use of possessed form in Molina, 155; *-tzin* a symptom of, 164; and human constituent parts, 178

Possessor suffixes, 70–71, 166

Prefixes: *See* under the various kinds

Preposing: 81

Prepositions: Relational words Nahuatl equivalent of, 20, 164, 179; Spanish borrowed in Stage 3, 117, 124; effect of lack of on borrowing nouns, 122

Present agentives: 53, 54; accept the masculine vocative ending, 71; cannot be combined, 71; nonactive present agentives, 90–91

Preterit (of verbs): general analysis, 31–35; apparent preterit stem with *-ti-* auxiliaries, 38; preterit as present, 38, 64; *in* with the preterit, 58–59; *ye* with, 100

Preterit agentives: *qui-* suffix of, 31; main treatment, 53–55; preterit agentive origin and characteristics of possessor suffixes, 70; accept the masculine vocative ending, 71; provide "adjectives," 90; and particles, 103

Progressives: *See -ti-* "ligature"

Pronunciation: x, 96, 104; and writing by Nahuas, 111. *See also* Orthography

Puebla, annals of: 205–06

Punctuation: *in* as, 61; in writing, 109–11

Purposive motion forms: 74–76

q, calligraphic marks over: 107–08; extended example of use of, 192–93

Quauhtinchan: *See* Cuauhtinchan

Quauhtitlan: *See Codex Chimalpopoca*

Quantifiers: 53; and *in/on*, 62; in apposition to crossreferent, 67; and anticipation, 83–84; with *oc* and in comparative structures, 98–99

-que (*-queh*), verbal suffix: as preterit plural ending, 31–32, 171; as future plural ending, 35–36; as plural ending of agentives, 54; as plural ending of possessor suffixes, 70, 72

-qui suffix: archaic preterit ending and suffix of preterit agentive verbs, 31–32; role in history of

future tense, 35; with agentives, 54; with verb *ca*, 64; *-qui-* third person singular object prefix: *See* object prefixes

quiça (*quiça*), to emerge, etc.: 40

-quiuh (*quiuh*), verbal auxiliary form. *See* Purposive motion forms

Reciprocal: reciprocal meaning of reflexives, 10

Reduction, processes of: 31–32; of double *c*'s, 165. *See also* Omission of two segments . . ., Orthography

Reduplication. *See* Distributive reduplication, Long vowel reduplication

Reflexive prefixes: 10–11; possible confusion with possessive prefixes, 28; indefinite reflexive prefix *ne-*, 28–29; and reduction, 179

Reflexive verbs (verbs in the reflexive): in derived forms, 28–29; as passives, 76. *See also* Reflexive prefixes

Relational words: chapter on, 20–25; and *in/on*, 62; and anticipation, 84; relation of *ic/inic* to, 93; and particles, 103; in Molina, 156; in Siméon, 158; in Karttunen, 156, 159; brief general discussion, 164; use of *-ti-* with, 171; *-tzinco* as reverential of, 177–78

Relative clauses: *in* creates, 45, 46, 48, 59, 170; placed before the noun, 48; example of two consecutive, 60 n1; placing of *in* relative clauses, 85, 170

Restall, Matthew: anthology of pieces on testaments described, 147

Reverential: of nouns, 5–6, 53; of verbs, 15–17, 28, 168; inversion of, 49; use of, 171; and first person, 177; not used with some inherently reverential words, 180

Reyes García, Luis: *Historia tolteca-chichimeca* described, 143; edition of Tlaxcalan annalist Zapata described, 145; *Documentos sobre . . . Cuauhtinchan* described, 145

Rojas Rabiela, Teresa: *Testamentos indígenas novohispanos* described, 146

Root changes: shortening, 2 n3, 24, 207, 208; with applicative and causative, 14–15, 168, 184; with *-liz*, 28; with passive and impersonal, 77; in various contexts and reason for, 175

Ruiz de Alarcón, Hernando: *Treatise* described, 147

[s], orthography of: 114–15

Sahagún, fray Bernardino de: orthography of, 108; punctuation in, 110; editions of Florentine Codex described, 142–43; Book 6 of Florentine Codex and fray Juan Bautista's work, 146; *Psalmodia Christiana* described, 147; *Coloquios* described, 147; selections from Florentine Codex, 193–97

Saltillo: 2 n4. *See also* Glottal stop

Schroeder, Susan: *Codex Chimalpahin* described, 144

Semantic differences between loanwords and their originals: 123

Series: 22

Siméon, Remi: dictionary of described, 158–59

Sociopolitical units, names of: with *-tzinco*, 21; locative nature of names, 24; hard to distinguish from ad hoc descriptions, 47; often double, 167

Song, Nahuatl: 148 n1

Sousa, Lisa: *The Story of Guadalupe* described, 142; selection from, 203–05

Space. *See* Spacing.

Spacing, between strings of letters in writing: 110–11, 126; in Molina, 153

Spanish influence: on Nahuatl orthography, 104; on Nahuatl texts in general, whole chapter on, 117–24

Spanish loanwords: plurals of, 52; those in vowel have glottal stop at end, 112; orthography of, 118–21. *See also* Spanish influence

Stage 1: briefly described, 114; less briefly described, 117; contact phenomena of, 121

Stage 2: briefly described, 114; standard orthography product of, 114; less briefly described, 117; some substitutions of carried on into Stage 3, 121; retention of Stage 1 traits, 121; general contact phenomena of, 121–23; two full texts from, 126–32

Stage 3: briefly described, 114; orthographic developments in, 114–15; less briefly described, 117–18; letter substitutions in, 121; general contact phenomena of, 123–24; selection of a text from, 124–25; a full text from, 133–39; developments with kinship terms in, 136

Stages, of adjustment of Nahuatl to Spanish: briefly described, 114; described in more detail, 117–18. *See also* Stage 1, Stage 2, Stage 3

Subject prefixes: 1; compared to object prefixes, 9; ways of distinguishing singular and plural, 33; exceptions to standard use, 45, 49; omission in vocative, 71, 72; as anticipation, 83; apparent change of use in Stage 3, 136 n

Subjunctive: *See* Optative

Substitutions of letters in Spanish loanwords: 119–21

Sullivan, Thelma: *Documentos tlaxcaltecas* described, 146; *Compendio de la gramática náhuatl* described, 151

Suppletive verbs: 38, 39, 64, 65

Syntactic phrase: *See* Nuclear complex, Phonological phrase

Syntax: 11–12; *ca* (*cah*) tends to come last, 55; role of *in*, 58–61; chapter on word order, 81–85; brief statement of constituent order, 174

te- (tē): indefinite personal object prefix, 26–27; as indefinite possessor, 27; provides absolute forms of kinship terms, 45

Teatro náhuatl: described, 146

-tecatl (-tēcatl), ending of gentile nouns: 73

-tech, next to, etc.: 21–22, 41

temi (tēmi), to fill up: with chinampas, 47

Temporal meaning of locative expessions: 78–79

Tena, Rafael: edition of work of Chimalpahin described, 144

teopan (teōpan), church, at the church: 186–87

teopantlaca (teōpantlacah), church attendants: 79

-tepotzco, behind: 23

Testaments: sample testament fully analyzed, 43–49; a Stage 3 transcribed, translated, and analyzed, 133–39; one from Culhuacan, ca. 1580, 190–92

Tetelcingo: 162

Texts in Nahuatl: published described, 140–48; full in original orthography, 126–39; portion of one exhaustively analyzed, 163–189; ten selections in original orthography, 190–206

-t(i)- ligature: with relational words, 22–23, 171; with verbal auxiliaries, 38–40; brief discussion of the two types, 173

-ti, denominal verbs in: 89–90

-tia, various forms of that look confusingly similar, 90

-tia, causative ending: 15, 39

-tia, creates deverbal nouns meaning to provide: 88–89

-tia (-tiah), preterit of *yauh* auxiliary, 39, 90

-tic, ending of preterit agentives with adjectival tendencies, 90

Tilde: 107

-timo- auxiliary: 40

-tin, absolute plural suffix. *See* Plural

-tiuh, present of *yauh* auxiliary. *See* yauh

-tiuh (-tīuh), verbal auxiliary form. *See* Purposive motion forms

-tl, absolutive singular ending, 2

tl [tl], the sound: 2, 5 n3, 32, 47

-tla, verbs in: 32

tla-: indefinite object prefix, 26–27; as indefinite possessor, 27; in patientive nouns, 29–30; with passive and impersonal, 77; with intransitives to form impersonal, 78, 87; reduplicated, 87; creates intransitives, 95, 181; can refer to a whole human group, 155

-tlan, next to: 23

-tlan (-tlān), place of: 73

tlatoani (tlahtoāni), ruler: 55, 69

Tlaxcala: use of *-ti-* ligature in, 22 n1; use of archaic *-qui* suffix with finite verbs in, 35 n1; *ixquichime* in, 53 n3; orthography of Olmos in, 105; *The Tlaxcalan Actas* described, 141; edition of work of Tlaxcalan annalist described, 145; editions of documents from described, 146; *Actas de cabildo de Tlaxcala* described, 147; selection from municipal council records, 192–93

-tli, absolutive singular ending, 2; patientive nouns in, 29–30; and *-e* vocative, 71; loanwords in, 122

-to, verbal auxiliary form: *See* Purposive motion forms

-toc, verbal auxiliary. *See* onoc

tocon-: 14, 42

Toluca region: part of 1731 text from, 115–16

Toponyms. *See* Place names

Transcription: types of discussed and compared, 126; discussion of in relation to specific works, 140–48

Transitive verbs: 9–10; endings and reverential of, 16; with indefinite object prefixes in effect can become intransitive, 27; Class 2 transitive verbs with intransitive variant in Class 1, 32–33; tend to end in *a*, 33; and locative nouns, 78

Transitivity: in relation to word analysis and dictionary search, 176–77

Translation: general discussion, 140; example of double, 142; specific translations discussed, 141–48

tz, not present in earliest orthography: 108

-tze vocative form: 132

-tzinco (*-tzīnco*), reverential of relational words: 20–21; used with *-chan*, 25; brief general discussion, 177–78

-tzinoa (*-tzīnoa*), reverential of verbs: 177

-tzintlan (*-tzīntlan*), below: 24

-tzin(tli) (*tzīn-tli*): *See* reverential of nouns.

-uh, possessive ending, 3–4

Verbs: in idiom formation, 21; indicating direction of movement, 24; order of verbal prefixes, 26; the four classes of verbs, 31–32; role of *o-* and *ye* in the verbal complex, 34–35; adverbs precede, 56; *in* with verbal clauses, 58–60; loan verbs, 123–24; manner of citing in Molina, 153–55; manner of citing in vocabulary of this volume, 207–08. Consult Table of Contents of this volume for major sections on

Vetitive: 132

Vocative: 71–72, 203

Vowel quantity: not represented in examples of this volume, x; all final *o* in verbs long, 32; ignored in orthography, 104; indicated by Carochi, 142; Karttunen's dictionary primary reference for, 159; in Andrews' Vocabulary, 161–62; and elision, 182; in the Bancroft Dialogues, 197; how represented in the vocabulary of this volume, 207; stressed vowels in Spanish are long in Nahuatl, 207

Vowels of Nahuatl: 106

Weakening of syllable-final consonants: 106, 112, 115, 127

Weak vowels: 111, 207. *See also* Elision, Hierarchy of

vowels

Wills: *See* Testaments

Witnesses in testaments: 48

Word complex: 109. *See also* Phonological phrase

Word division. *See* Spacing

Word order. *See* Syntax

Words: like phrases and clauses in other languages, 81

xocon-: 42

Xochimilco: Nahuatl testimony given in, 199–201

[y], orthography of: in [iya], 34, 38, 63, 106–07; in Stage 3, 115

-ya, imperfect ending of verbs. *See* Imperfect

-ya durative, 89

-yan (*-yān*), locatives in: 78

yauh, to go: reverential of, 17; as auxiliary, 39; as irregular verb, 64–66; *-ti-* auxiliary form compared with purposive motion forms, 75; place in order, 83 n1; auxiliary form *-tia* compared with other forms, 90

ye, already: 35, 99–100

ye, second root of *ca*. *See ca* (*cah*), stative verb to be

yetz-, irregular combining form of *ca*: 66–67

-yo, nominal suffix of inalienable or organic possession: 69–70, 174; *See also* -yo(tl)

-yo (*-yoh*), suffix meaning "covered with": *See* possessor suffixes

-yo(tl) (*-yōtl*), abstract and collective nominal suffix: 69–70; compared with *-yo* "covered with," 72; with denominal *-tia* verbs, 89

-z future verb ending: 35–36

Zacapoaxtla: 162

Zapata y Mendoza, don Juan Buenaventura: edition of work described, 145

Zimmermann, Günter: work on Chimalpahin of, 144, 145 n2

-zquia "conditional" verb ending, 67